319 Samuel — Pres. Rutherford
B. Hays

Smith 302 (Lewis cheek)
Pg. 229

Hayes — P. 319

Cheek — P. 302

WM. E. RAILEY

Author of sketches of Woodford County Pioneers and "The Raileys
and Their Kin."

He is a Presbyterian who doesn't believe that any sect can save souls;
a Mason without duplicity; a Thomas Jefferson Democrat who believes in
liberty of speech, of press, of assembly, and of religion, with Jefferson's
interpretation—vote against no man on account of his religious views,
and vote for no man on account of his religious proclivities.

HISTORY

OF

WOODFORD COUNTY,

KENTUCKY

By

WILLIAM E. RAILEY

Baltimore
REGIONAL PUBLISHING COMPANY
1975

Reprint of 1938 edition
Frankfort, Kentucky

Reprinted
Regional Publishing Company
Baltimore, 1975

Library of Congress Catalogue Card Number 74-21773
International Standard Book Number 0-8063-7999-5

The publisher gratefully acknowledges
the loan of the original volume from
The Filson Club
Louisville, Kentucky

Made in the United States of America

WOODFORD COUNTY, KY.

By W. E. Railey.

PART ONE.

Reprinted from the Register of the Kentucky State Historical Society, 1920-29.

In consenting to write a brief account of Woodford county and its citizenship from the pioneer days, I did so with a full sense of the difficulties that would confront me, as well as my inability to do justice to such an interesting subject, even under more favorable conditions.

In the first place, I find that so many years have elapsed since the county was established that there are now living very few of the grandchildren of the settlers, and they seem unable to relate anything concerning their ancestors or the events of that period, and the great-grandchildren are, as a rule, and have been, so absorbed in the present and the prospects of the future as to know but little of the remote past. Horses, cattle, hogs, sheep and all of those things that enter into and represent dollars have absorbed so much of their time, and attracted so completely their attention as to preclude nearly all recollection of the men and women who toiled so faithfully and cheerfully that this generation might reap so abundantly. Now, while imputing to this generation forgetfulness and a degree of indifference as to the past, I do not want to be understood as attempting to underrate their main characteristics, for like their forbears, they are a hospitable, lawabiding, intelligent and refined class who have contracted the habit, so general at this period of living in the present, with the vision cast forward. That affliction seems to be confined to no particular section or class as far as I have been able to observe, the world over.

However, I have consented to garner the facts so far as I am able to do so, from descendants, both in and out of the county, and I will print them in the manner in which they come to me, trusting that some county man in the near future will have pride enough to assemble them in a more orderly manner. This should have been done at a much earlier period, for much of an interesting character could have been recalled, indeed, was recalled within my recollection, say fifty years ago, in social and political gatherings in the county. Many of the hardships that the pioneers encountered, endured and overcame were related then, but not recalled now with a distinct clearness.

Woodford county was first surveyed and shaped in 1788, before the district of Kentucky was admitted to statehood, and was then a part of the county of Fayette, created some years before, by an act of the Virginia Legislature. In fact it was the last of the nine counties established before statehood was conferred. At that time a large area was embraced in its formation, extending along both the Kentucky and Licking rivers to the Ohio river. (However, some years later the counties of Scott and Franklin were formed and they deprived Woodford of much of its original territory, making it one of the smallest counties in the state.)

When the county was named it was paid a very high compliment, as General Woodford was a very distinguished Virginian. He served Virginia in the Revolution as a gallant officer, and distinguished himself in many hard fought engagements with the British and Indians, becoming a prisoner during the siege at Charleston, South Carolina, in 1780. While a prisoner in New York he died in a hospital, in the prime of his life, and the zenith of his glory, faithful to his country and loyal to American ideals and institutions.

In 1784 the tide of immigration set in and it continued to flow until 1800, regardless of the dangers and hardships that daily confronted these sturdy pioneers, men and women. Many of them were fresh from the bloody conflicts of the Revolution, and they were generously equipped with arms that helped win our independence.

Franklin and Scott had at that time been formed, and not only absorbed much of Woodford's territory, but, as many of their population had settled in and near Frankfort,* which, prior to that time, was a part of us, our population was also much depleted. The remaining population in the county lost no time in arranging for the protection of their several interests from marauding bands of savages that infested the surrounding country at that time, for many stockades were erected in the several parts of the county, and they also took precaution to forestall disorders within their own citizenship by establishing iron-clad rules for the maintenance of order. It became necessary for them to form neighborhoods, easily accessible to each other, in order that help might be concentrated in clearing the canebreaks and thickets that formed ambush for the Indians, and which had to be cleared before pasturage could be secured or cultivation undertaken.

The greater portion of the settlers of the county migrated from Virginia, but many came from Maryland, North Carolina and Pennsylvania, while small groups came from other states, northeast of us. There were also a few foreigners, principally Irish and German, and these proved themselves not only good citizens, but very useful, as they were workmen in wood and stone, so necessary at that time in constructing houses for both man and beast.

Fully seventy per cent of the settlers brought slaves with them to Kentucky, who were utilized in clearing the forests and building fences, but afterward proved serviceable in any department of farm work, in hemp factories and workshops, when they became necessary later on.

Those who preferred rural life soon located the land they afterward entered for settlement, and tradition informs us that they were a very happy people, notwithstanding the danger that so

---

*Frankfort, when established, was in Fayette County, but was transferred to Woodford County when that county was established in 1788 and remained until it became the State Capitol, 1793.

often threatened them. Those who were prepared for professional or commercial life sought with as little delay as possible a suitable site for an urban society, a county seat, so that they might have a community center for trade and barter, as well as better protection in case of an uprising of either Indians or slaves, hence the town of Versailles was established in 1792. It was customary in those days to seek an elevation for a fort or a town, in as close proximity as possible to a good flow of spring water, so in selecting the site for the town of Versailles both desires were satisfied. With as little delay as possible they began the organization of a town government and a county court of justice where all disputes might be adjusted and a record made of all land transactions, with boundaries, titles, etc.

Versailles was the only incorporated town in the county from 1792 to 1835, when the village of Mortonsville was established, therefore the settlers in the meantime were compelled to go either to Lexington, Frankfort or Versailles to lay in their supplies, or sell the products of their farms. The village of Midway was not established until February, 1846, and like Mortonsville, it soon became a thriving little town.

The soil of Woodford has ever been very fertile and productive, as the succeeding generations would often fertilize with deep rooted grass to prevent degeneration. The depth of the soil ranged from eighteen to thirty-six inches, varying according to the lay of the land, and it covers a clay subsoil that usually rests upon limestone for a base. This subsoil has always been of

great protection to crops as it holds the moisture during a serious drouth. Strictly speaking, there is but little flat or table land in the county, that is, land incapable of self-drainage. On the contrary the undulating slopes are so gradual as to give perfect drainage without doing violence to the surface during the wet periods, hence the settlers often repeated crops on the same land without detriment, and on account of this fertility of the soil, visitors to the county early in its history often referred to it as the "Asparagus Bed" in the "Garden of the Blue Grass," and its superior qualities, from any angle, are as apparent today as in the days of our forefathers. Certainly no county in the state produces more per acre or a greater variety of crops, corn, wheat, barley, hemp and tobacco being the staple crops, the two latter being the most profitable.

The farms were originally very large, many of them containing thousands of acres, but frequent subdivisions to heirs through inheritance (that so frequently occurred) the farms grew smaller until now one hundred and fifty acres is perhaps a fair average to each property holder.

The Kentucky river bounds the county on the south and west, and separates it from the counties of Mercer, Anderson and a part of Franklin. Franklin county constitutes the northwest, Scott the northeast and Fayette and Jessamine the eastern boundaries. The land is drained by a number of small streams, and as the county seat has a great elevation, the sources of the greater number of these creeks and branches are in that locality, where there are many gushing springs of crystal water. They meander through the county in various circuitous routes, some of them emptying into the Kentucky river, while others pursue a more northerly course and drain into classic Elkhorn, a stream that separates Woodford county from Scott. As springs are quite numerous over the county, many of these smaller streams furnish stock water throughout the year, which has made Woodford so popular for stock raising. Formerly these streams would become so swollen by freshets as to be a menace to settlers, especially in traveling, but our modern system has overcome this disadvantage by spanning all streams with concrete and steel bridges. These streams were usually known by the name of the first man who settled upon them; for instance Woodford county has Steele's branch, Grier's creek, Glen's creek, Cedar creek and Clear creek.

Tradition informs us, and there are a few evidences today of the truthfulness of the story, that the forests of the county during the latter part of the eighteenth, and the early part of the nineteenth century were unsurpassed in their beauty and picturesquesness, as well as in the great variety of the timber that adorn the surface, such as hickory, ash, walnut, sugar, beech and other varieties too numerous to mention, and each species valuable beyond any knowledge of the pioneer, and they have proven a great asset to succeeding generations. Besides affording delightful retreats for man and beast during the heated term, they gave great protection to both during storms and the severe cold of the winter. In fact these giants of the forests were utilized in many ways by the settlers for their comfort, convenience and profit. Very little coal was available at that time, and they supplied the fuel for fires for more than fifty years before coal was received in sufficient quantities to be appreciated as a substitute. They were also split into rails that entered into the construction of the worm fence which was almost exclusively used in the county for division fencing for a hundred years. It was built V-shape, and when staked and ridered was quite strong and durable.

With the exception of occasional stone and brick, all houses of the pioneer days were constructed of logs, with rock and mortar chinking and they were decidedly comfortable dwellings.

In a few years there was a great demand for sawed timber, and this necessity produced crude upright saws which were installed in several parts of the county and much timber was converted into boards.

To each gable of the homes built by the pioneers a stone chimney was attached and every room contained a large fire-place, equipped with andirons, some of the irons very stately in appearance, with brass molding, making them quite as ornamental as useful. These irons supported the seasoned logs that burned so brightly and cheerfully, and heated so thoroughly every part of the room as to make one loath to leave the glow. Such were the happy surroundings of the settlers, and they prevailed largely with succeeding generations down to the Civil War, after which so many conditions changed, and interest in the past and its traditions began to wane.

Beginning with the period immediately succeeding the war of the rebellion the spirit of money making seemed to take possession of the citizenry. The woodman's axe was laid at the root of the tree, and those beautiful old forests began to disappear. Now we find only a woodland here and there is left to revive the memories of the past, and it seems like "an echo in a deadening"—"an oasis in a desert"—to one who recalls their former beauty. However, this will remind the visitor of the beauty and grandeur that once adorned our broad acres. May we forget, and the good Lord forgive the ruthlessness of the past if the generation of the present and those of the future will only hold these relics more sacred.

By the year 1820 quite a number of brick residences were constructed over the county, some of them quite imposing and historic and it is my purpose to mention those in a later chapter.

For many years after the county was settled the means of transportation were crude and most of the travel was afoot and horseback, both sexes using that method, even for long journeys across the neighborhoods or state. In fact there were but few vehicles in the county before 1800, and the increase was very limited until about 1830, when the roads were sufficiently improved to invite investment in wheeled conveyances. After some of the main thoroughfares were macadamized between 1835 and 1840, buggies and carriages, some of them quite pretentious, were more numerous. "The family carriage" possessed much ornamenta-

tion, and for that reason was very heavy, but they were quite as comfortable as they were imposing in looks. The colored driver sat pompously upon an elevated seat in front and pulled the reins upon two spirited horses, and took delight in calling members of his own race, not so fortunate as he, "Niggers," and white persons who couldn't afford a carriage "poor white trash." Such a vehicle was a luxury that but few afforded, as the people of that period were cautious and would not consider for a moment the question of mortgaging the home for a pleasure conveyance. But after the Civil War road construction had so far advanced that all character of vehicles were in common use.

The census of 1810 shows that the colored population of Woodford, slaves and free, almost equaled in number the whites at that time, and would have been a menacing factor to the settlers had they embraced the suggestions of the red men so frequently offered for an uprising, but the negro was loyal to the master, and he not only warned him of danger, but stood ready at all times, and under all circumstances, to help protect his interests at any sacrifice. That spirit of loyalty characterized the slaves until a few itinerant Baptist preachers from Ohio sowed tares in the settlers' field and made some of them restless, others a little reckless, but the average remained quiescent and faithful until Mr. Lincoln issued the emancipation proclamation. In short, the ante-bellum negro in Woodford was a happy, well-fed, well treated slave, and at no time since the Civil War has any county in the state had a better behaved colored citizenship than has this one. Much of this is due to the training they received from their several God-fearing masters.

The first surveyors in Kentucky were Hancock Taylor and James Douglass, under the directions of Col. William Preston, and they passed through in 1773. Among the first explorers and hunters to invade this part of Kentucky some years later were Col. Robert Patterson, Andrew Steele, Patrick Jordan, Joseph Lindsey, John Lowry, Hugh Shannon, John Lee, Col. John Floyd and David Perry.

We cannot, must not, forget their unselfish sacrifices and heroic deeds. Upon their return to Virginia their friends were filled with the spirit of adventure by their flattering accounts of the fertility of the soil and the abundance of game the forests of Kentucky afforded. But the real curtain of history making in Woodford was not lifted until Captain Elijah Craig blazed the way and pitched his tent, about 1782, with a view of residence, settling five miles from what afterwards became the town of Versailles, and in the direction of Lexington. Following close upon his heels came Col. Thomas Marshall, who settled at "Buck Pond;" General Marquis Calmes, whose home, "Caneland," adjoined "Buck Pond;" General Charles Scott, who settled on Kentucky river, and built his cabin at Scotts Landing; Major John Crittenden, whose farm was on the Lexington pike and recently owned by the late Hawkins Cleveland; General James McConnell, who, I think, owned a farm on the McCowan's pike;

Major Herman Bowmar, who was the first deputy sheriff of the county; Col. William Steele, whose farm bordered on the Kentucky river just above lock No. 5; Dr. Louis Marshall, who was the owner of "Buck Pond" after his father moved with his family to Mason county; Charles Buck, III; Rev. William Buck, who was an eminent Baptist preacher; Col. George Muter,* a Revolutionary veteran; Rev. John Taylor, a pioneer Baptist preacher, Judge Caleb Wallace, an eminent jurist; Col. Richard Young, one of the founders of Versailles; John Mosby, who settled in that part of Fayette county that was transferred to Woodford in 1788; Capt. Virgil McCracken, who was wounded at the River Raisin; Nicholas Lafon, who was one of the founders of Frankfort; Col. John Francisco, of the war of 1812; William B. Blackburn, a legislator for many years; George Blackburn, the founder of the prominent family of that name; Robt. Alexander, who established the "Woodburn" stock farm; Robert Johnston, member of the convention that declared Kentucky a sovereign state; Joseph Lindsey, the first nurseryman in the state; Benjamin Berry, Lewis Sublette, Edmund Woolridge, Edward Trabue and others that I purpose to write brief sketches of later on.

Many of the present generation will find the names of their ancestors in the census of 1810 that follows. The first national census was taken in 1790, before statehood was declared; the second in 1800, but both were destroyed when the city of Washington was cap-

*See pages 59 and 390 for Muters.

turned by the British and the torch applied during the war of 1812.

The census of 1810 was taken by George Railey, who was deputy marshal of the United States under Col. George Crocket, and a copy of that paper was preserved, and it shows the following resident heads of families, the slave holders appearing first, and those without slaves following in turn:

Slave holders in Versailles in 1810

Head of Family	Number in Family	Slaves
Richard B. Bohannon	2	4
William Bohannon	15	23
Preston W. Brown	7	44
Charles Buck	23	31
David Campbell	7	1
Thomas Cooper	7	2
Nathan Dedman	7	1
William Dickerman	2	1
George Fritzlin	2	2
Joel Henry	4	2
Nathan Hitt	5	3
Absalom C. Hunter	3	1
John Jackson	14	44
Archibald Kinkead	9	6
John Kinkead	2	5
Joseph Kinkead	12	5
Joseph Lindsey	3	6
Alexander Loughborough	8	4
John Long, Jr.	6	2
Reuben Long	3	1
Edward Meredith	3	1
William P. Meredith	10	1
Moses Paine	2	3
William Peacock	2	1
William Phillips	11	5
Vincent Ross, Jr.	6	1
Rhodham Routt	11	4
Daniel Spangler	10	1
Benjamin Vance	5	1

	Number in Family	Slaves
William Vawter	9	14
Henry Watkins	6	15
Without slaves		
German Brittingham	3	
Hannah Brown	1	
Elizabeth Day	3	
James Seatson	1	
Edmund Vawter	3	
Jesse Vawter	4	
Free colored	9	

In county outside of Versailles:

Heads of Family	Number in Family	Slaves
James Ashley	3	4
James Arnold	7	5
James Ayers	3	5
Peter Alexander	11	11
Alexander Andrews	7	1
Joel Ashley	9	2
Thomas Alsop	9	2
William Alwood	4	4
John Allen	7	7
John Andrews	9	1
Andrew Anderson	12	3
William Adams	8	18
John Allen	4	3
John Armstrong	3	1
Hugh Allen	9	10
John Allen	11	12
John Allen	10	11
John Ashford, Sr.	10	3
Thomas Ashford	8	6
Robert Alexander	1	20
Robert Abbett	8	1
Nancy Arnold	2	2
Lewis Arnold	6	4
Walter Ayers	7	5
John Boze	6	3
Samuel Brooking	12	5
John Barnett	5	3
Samuel Berry, Jr.	5	10

Allen Berry	4	1	John Blackmore	8	10
Robert Bowmar, Sr.	3	1	William Christopher, Jr.	6	4
Elijah Burbridge	9	6	William H. Cosby	3	1
James Blanton	10	2	Allen Caldwell	6	3
John W. Brooking	3	2	Andrew Combs	6	6
Wilson Brown	3	7	Isaac Crutcher	7	5
Richard Bridgeford	4	1	George T. Cotton	6	14
John Brown	12	12	William Campbell	4	2
John Bohannon	6	1	Thomas Clygett	8	5
Henry Brown	6	5	Thomas Coleman	4	3
Jeremiah Buckley	12	5	James Caldwell	5	3
George Bain	5	6	John Collins	7	12
Thomas Bell	4	9	Benjamin Cloak	4	1
Nancy Blanton	8	23	Samuel Campbell	8	3
George Blackburn	3	20	John Cook	5	14
Jonathan Blackburn	3	1	Richard Cole, Jr.	10	3
William Buford	5	11	Richard Cole, Sr.	2	5
Abigail Blackford	3	1	Jacob Caplinger	2	1
Samuel Berry, Sr.	6	9	Joseph Christman	13	1
Benjamin Berry	12	27	George Carlisle	12	14
John Buck, Sr.	5	22	George Caplinger	4	6
James B. Brown	3	1	Agness Clarke	1	5
Catherine Beasley	1	2	Benjamine Clarke	9	3
Charles Bradley	7	1	Marquis Calmes	7	33
Richard Bastin	5	1	George Crosby	7	5
James Bell	6	17	William Clarke	3	10
John Buford	5	11	Henry Cassell	4	1
Benjamine Bondurat	5	4	James Cox	6	2
Abraham Beard	1	13	John Cotton	7	2
Elliott Bohannon	4	20	Spencer Cooper	4	16
German Bohannon	3	4	Johnathan Carpenter	4	2
Susanna Byers	4	1	Joanna Campbell	2	4
Thomas Blanton	9	3	William Campbell	9	1
George J. Brown	6	12	Jacob Creath	6	11
Simeon Buford	4	6	John Calhoun	2	7
Herman Bowmar	7	22	Rowland Chambers	9	8
Letitia Bowderly	3	6	Leforce Cawthorn	4	1
Lewis Bowderly	7	4	Lewis Castleman	10	14
Charles Beasley	9	11	Richard Cave	7	16
Edmond Beasley	9	11	Reuben Cave	9	9
William B. Blackburn	4	6	Joseph Collins	10	9
Margaret Burnett	4	2	Elijah Creed, Sr.	9	15
Thomas Bullock	9	15	John Carter	8	2

James Coleman	6	20	Joseph Edwards	6	6
Judith Crittenden	5	14	Simeon Edwards	3	3
John Carpenter	9	2	John Elliott	9	1
Major Cheatham	5	8	James Edwards	7	1
Samuel Campbell	8	3	Daniel T. Elliston	4	4
John Duvall	4	14	Joseph Edrington	11	1
Aaron Darnell	5	6	Jesse Ellis, Sr.	4	2
William Barr	8	5	William Florence	2	1
James Dupuey	3	15	William Finch	9	4
Joel Dupuey	4	12	John Finnie	11	9
George Dale	8	2	James Finnie	8	7
Nat Dale	8	5	John Francisco	3	2
William Dale, Sr.	10	1	James Ford	6	4
Thomas Davis	5	7	Andrew Francisco	6	6
William Davis	8	10	John Ford	2	9
John Davis	2	2	George Freeman	8	9
Jacob Dunkle	7	2	Jacob Froman	6	1
James Dickie	2	7	William Florence, Sr.	7	2
Hezekiah Douglas	2	6	Absalom Ford	12	5
Alexander Douglas	4	13	Leonard J. Fleming	9	24
Joseph Darnell	5	9	Richard J. Fox	10	9
George Duvall	4	2	Samuel Gwinn	4	1
John Dale	3	1	Jesse Graddy	9	6
Thomas Duvall	10	2	John Graves	9	9
John Doyle	7	7	Ann Garnett	5	5
Thomas Davis	11	4	Spencer Gill	3	5
William S. Dunham	2	15	William Gaines	6	6
Fortunatus Davenport	5	4	John Green	5	4
Abraham Dale	9	3	Abraham Gregory	4	17
Mitcheal Dickie	1	3	Benjamine Guthrie	7	2
Raleigh Dale	5	3	William George	9	7
John Dawson, Jr.	6	5	Johnson Gwinn	9	2
Henry Davis	5	7	Margaret Griffin	1	4
Delaney Egbert	5	3	William Garnett	10	5
Cornelius Edwards	2	2	William Glenn	5	1
James Edwards	6	2	Joseph Gwinn	7	1
Moses Edwards	8	1	William Guthrie	4	1
John Edwards, Sr.	9	11	James Gough	2	3
John Edwards, Jr.	6	1	Vivian Goodloe	11	4
Joseph Endicott	8	11	John Glanton	8	1
Isaiah Atkins	12	12	John Gay	8	6
Frederick Elgin	12	3	John Gibson	7	2
William Elliott	7	2	William Garrett	8	1

Burwell Glanton	5	1	James Howard	4	6
James Garner	9	2	John Hudson	4	2
John Hamilton	4	5	Mary Hunter	3	4
Thomas Helm	10	10	Hugh Holmes	5	1
William Hedger	9	1	John Harris	9	16
Edward Howe	7	42	James Hackett	2	1
Nathaniel Hart	13	19	David Harris	2	11
Lewis Hieatt	4	19	John M. C. Irwin	4	2
William Henderson	3	1	Francis Jackson	4	3
Moses Hawkins	8	7	Isaac Johnston	9	1
Willis Hawkins	6	1	John D. Johnston	3	1
Charles S. Hunter	4	1	Rebecca Kirtley	2	5
William Strother Hawkins	4	10	Guy Kinkead	10	8
John Hazzard	7	10	William Kinkead	2	8
Edward Holman	4	1	John Kinkead	3	4
Obediah Hancock	12	7	James Kinkead	4	3
Smith Hale	10	31	Sarah Livingston	4	1
George Holloway	8	19	Garrard Long	1	4
Zachariah Henry	7	11	James Long	7	3
Daniel Holman	3	11	Gabriel Lilley	9	11
William Hancock	5	11	Mary Long	6	5
Henry Harrison	5	5	Nicholas Lafon	6	9
Michael Harper	9	7	Robert Lankford	4	2
Lewis Hampton	4	2	Robert Lockridge	6	7
Henry Harper	6	2	Elizabeth Lee	8	26
Adam Harper	7	8	Adam Lynn	7	1
John Hamilton	2	3	John B. Lambkin	4	1
Andrew Hamilton	8	14	Thomas Lyne	5	2
Robert Hopkins	12	10	Francis Lee	5	9
Thomas Hicklin	3	2	John Lewis	7	4
William Hicks	9	21	John Long, Sr.	5	15
Nathaniel Harris	11	11	George McDaniel	9	11
William Hopkins	6	4	John McQuiddy	10	6
Leroy Howard	5	9	Alexander McClure	8	8
Isaac Howard	6	7	Elizabeth McCracken	8	7
Charles Hiter	8	6	James McCormack	4	13
James Hawkins	4	4	Robt. McKee	8	8
Arthur Haydon	3	2	Elizabeth McClary	6	5
Charles Hammond	13	5	Patrick McFern	9	1
Mary Hammond	3	5	Andrew McKnight	10	1
John Hammond	9	9	Margaret McDowell	4	7
George Hanks	5	3	Isaac McCuddy	5	3
Vincent Howard	3	5	William McCuddy	5	3

William McIlvain	5	6	John Obannon	2	17
Virgil McCracken	3	7	William Obannon	4	5
John Minter	4	2	James Owen	4	1
Samuel P. Menzies	16	28	John Peters	9	7
Samuel Morrow	5	10	William Powell	4	3
Col. William Mayo	4	3	Moody J. Pulliam	4	1
Frederick Mitchell	8	1	Matthew Pleasants	6	8
James Mann	2	1	John Pace	5	1
George Muter	1	7	Charles Palmer	7	4
Robert Mosby	6	8	Francis Peart	3	11
Elizabeth Moss	5	10	Alexander Patrick	2	13
Giles Mitchell	4	1	Philemon Price	8	9
Jane Minter	7	12	Lewis Peters	6	3
Robert Moss	4	1	William Peters	5	9
Lewis Martin	8	1	Nimrod Peters	10	1
Robert Moffitt	4	2	James Peters	9	7
Robert Moffitt, Jr.	5	1	Nathaniel Peters	2	10
Thomas Mattox	7	1	Charles F. Paine	11	6
James Meek	2	10	Thomas Poore	10	5
James Matthews	9	1	Lewis Perry	5	10
John Matthews	3	3	Robert Perry	10	3
Thomas Munday	8	1	Larkin Price	2	2
James Marshall	5	3	Ambrose Pittman	5	4
James Mitcham	3	5	James Parrish	5	12
Dudley Mitcham	10	21	John Paul	6	2
Sarah Morton	1	8	Roderick Perry	16	6
Anne Morgan	8	1	Tandy K. Perry	4	4
Jeremiah Morton	2	7	Tunstall Quarles	5	15
William Morris	11	1	James Quarles	2	6
William Morton	12	1	Thomas Reynolds	7	4
Samuel Martin	10	1	Charles Railey	10	12
Thomas Morton	10	3	John Read	6	3
Solomon Mitchell	3	1	Handkerson Read, Jr.	2	2
John Mosby	13	3	John Rucker, Sr.	7	2
William Moss	6	3	Thomas M. Redd	6	6
Nicholas Mosby	5	15	Thomas Railey	8	15
Louis Marshall (5 free)	11	5	Isham Railey	10	6
Samuel B. Mills	4	1	William Railey	5	10
William Moore	6	1	Cornelius Robinson	5	5
Charles L. Nall	7	6	Handkerson Read, Sr.	6	16
William H. Nall	4	2	Dennis Rearden	2	2
George H. Offutt	13	28	Seth Ramsey	10	1
John Oliver	8	2	Cornelius Ruddle	10	1

William Rowland	9	8	Thomas Steele	2	3
James Rennick	8	2	John Steele	5	4
Elizabeth Rice	8	1	Richard Shipp, Jr.	10	2
Randolph Railey	3	13	Labon Sebree	5	1
Richard Rice	8	8	Samuel Stephenson, Sr.	7	7
King Redmond	9	2	Henry Steele	6	6
Thomas Redd	5	18	Lewis Sullivan	10	11
Abner Rucker	7	1	Jechonias Singleton	11	9
James Rucker	6	2	James Scarce	3	9
Ahmed Rucker	8	1	John Stevenson	6	1
Joseph Roper	7	2	Margaret Stevenson	5	1
George Robinson	6	12	James Stephenson, Jr.	5	9
Thomas Ratliffe	9	6	Clayton Skirvin	3	1
William Rucker	5	1	John Steger	12	5
Henry Rowland	9	3	Richard Saunders	6	3
Robert Scearce	10	2	George Shelton	9	9
James Sullivan	9	6	Benjamine Steward	7	1
Benjamine Stevenson	7	8	Henry Smith	7	4
Henry Stone	4	6	Henry Shouse	8	3
William Scott	3	3	Daniel Shouse	3	1
William Smith	9	3	Thomas Stephenson	7	7
Edward Searcy	3	12	Lewis Sublett, Jr.	4	6
Pluright Sisk	4	1	William W. Sutton	2	1
David Scearce	4	6	John Short	5	1
Isaac Stevenson	9	3	Richard Searcy	3	4
James Stevenson, Sr.	6	2	James Thornton	9	1
William Scarce	7	10	Archibald Terrill	10	5
Col. William Steele	9	14	Joseph P. Taylor	11	2
John Smith	3	2	John A. Torbitt	6	3
William Summers	6	1	James Torbitt, Sr.	7	11
Lucy Samuel	7	7	Edward Trabue	11	10
Joel Smith	9	1	William Todd	7	10
Leonard Searcy	6	2	John Taylor	7	1
Lewis Sublett, Sr.	7	3	Nathaniel Thompson	9	6
Samuel Shouse	3	1	Thomas Todd	13	21
Benjamine Smither	5	5	Richard Taylor	9	19
Samuel Smither	3	1	Lewis Y. Tutt	5	3
James Stapp	10	7	Chapman Taylor	7	16
William Suter	8	4	William Thompson	6	8
Thomas H. Starling	11	1	Hansford Tutt	9	4
George Stringfellow	8	3	Robert Taylor	4	1
Ebenezer Sprague	5	3	Davis Thompson	12	8
Mary Sullinger	4	6	George Turpin	8	7

Reuben Twyman	7	29	Susanna Weaver	13	8
Richard M. Thomas	7	9	John Willis	11	12
Griffin Turngile	6	4	William Walker	4	2
Alexander Turner	3	3	William Warren	3	11
Tapley Thomas	2	6	Travis Walker	4	3
John True, Jr.	7	1	James Wilson	5	1
Anthony Thompson	7	8	Edmond Walker	7	2
Thomas Turnham	3	4	Col. Richard Young, Sr.	4	20
Argyle Taylor	7	6	Richard M. Young	2	3
William Tillery	12	3	Robert Yancey	8	5
Jacob Utterback	6	1	Burket G. Yancey	5	2
Benjamine Utterback	5	1	Lewis Young	11	15
Lewis Utterback	3	4	Free negroes in county in 1810		71
John Uselton	6	3			
John Vaughan	7	11			
Hanley Vance	4	1			
Henson Violett	8	3			
Edward Violett	4	1			
John Williams	7	12			
Samuel Ware	6	3			
Littleton Whittington	12	6			
William Whittington	13	8			
Thomas Withers	6	1			
Joseph White	3	5			
Josiah Williams	8	4			
Daniel Wilcoxson	8	2			
Benjamine Watkins	7	1			
Steward Wilkins	6	2			
Josiah Wooldridge	10	12			
Elisha Wooldridge	7	10			
John Williams	2	9			
William Williams	7	1			
Phoebe White	4	1			
Nicholas Whitalow	4	3			
John Wilmin	3	1			
Joseph Wallace	7	4			
Susan White	3	2			
Caleb Wallace	7	24			
Benjamin Wilson	10	21			
Edward B. Wood	3	8			
Loyel Woolfork*	5	22			
Joshua Whittington	9	6			

Those who possessed no slaves in 1810:

Heads of Families	No. in Family.
Francis Allen	10
Henry Atkinson	9
William Akin	3
John Akin	4
James Akin	7
James Atwood	3
John Armstrong	4
James Armstrong	5
John Atkins	6
Robert Black	6
John Boze	3
Juliana Beavis	5
Johnson Ballard	7
Elliott Brown	9
Josiah Boone	4
Bennet Bevin	4
Edmund Ball	7
Patrick Burk	6
Levi Buchanan	5
Salomon Boone	12
Simeon Buchanan	3
Hezekiah Boone	6
John Beckham	3
James Burk	5
George Bennett	10

*This name should be Sowel Woolfork, the Sowels were related to the Woolforks.

Jane Bishop	3
James Black	5
James C. Butler	10
James Burton	5
Charles Barnes	7
Richard Bryant	3
Dawson Brown	8
Joseph Buchanan	9
John Cunningham	5
William Cunningham	5
Gasper Collins	4
Elijah Creed, Jr.	3
Jacob Carrel	7
Jeremiah Collins	16
Edward Carr	5
Reuben Carr	4
Joseph Corn	3
Josiah Cash	3
Ralph Cowgill	4
William Culley	3
Henry Caldwell	2
John Cloke	7
Jonathan Cloud	6
William Coleson	5
Thomas Carrill	6
Basil Carlisle	13
Goodloe Carter	6
John Dorsey	6
Nancy Duncan	3
John Dunnagan	6
Alexander Dale	4
Jesse Dennis	7
John Durham	8
Phillip Daugherty	9
Richard Davis	3
Daniel Daugherty	5
William Dale	8
James Daugherty	9
John Bevins	3
Thomas Dean	5
Joseph Deringer	5
Martin Deringer	4
Mary C. Deringer	3

Jacob Deringer	11
John Dick	7
Michael Deringer	5
William Dawson	4
Robert Dale	5
William Dawson	2
Richard Davenport	10
Solomon Dunnagan	9
Margaret Dredden	5
Leonard Ellis	10
Henry Evans	5
Uriah Edwards	4
Benjamine Edwards	3
William Endicott	4
Jesse Ellis, Jr.	3
Mary Edmiston	2
Benjamine Ealum	11
Samuel Evans	6
Isham Everitt	3
David Erick	4
Joseph Eaton	12
John Eaton	11
Daniel Fitzgerald	9
Lenuel Ford	3
John Florea	4
Levi Floyd	12
John B. Floyd	1
John Finnie, Jr.	3
Elijah Finnie	3
John Frauner	9
John Finn	5
Ellis Fitzgarrel	5
Stephen Furr	8
Charles Forston	10
Spencer Gill, Jr.	10
Andrew Gudshall	8
Abraham Gudshall	3
Robert Gaines	6
Robert F. Gale	10
Samuel Gillett	1
Morgan Gibbons	3
Edward Green	5
Larkin Garrett	4

Paul Green	6	John Hackney	4
James Green, Sr.	7	Jacob Hendrix	6
James Green, Jr.	3	Luke Hilton	9
John Guthrie	5	James Hambleton	6
John Gregory	10	Ezra Hammond	9
Thomas Guthrie, Sr.	5	Clayborn Hall	6
Thomas Guthrie, Jr.	7	Judith Harber	3
William Green	3	George Hubbard	5
Sarah Green	5	John Hanks	2
John Gruwell	10	Henry Hoover	4
Hugh Garrett	7	Rawley Hudson	7
John Garrett	9	Thomas Johnston	7
John Gudshall	8	Henry Johnston	7
William Gilpin	9	Thomas Jenkins	5
Robert Gwinn, Sr.	5	Robert Jackson	7
Robert Gwinn, Jr.	10	Elizabeth Johnston	6
George Grymes	3	David Johnston	3
Henry Green	7	David Jackson	7
Jonathin Gray	7	Ebenezer Jackson	4
Joseph George	7	Fielding Jeter	7
Benjamine Graves	8	Philip Kennedy	8
John Holmes	5	Joseph Kenady	8
James Holbert	4	Joseph Kinney	5
Samuel Hunter	4	John Kenady	2
Thomas Hinton	11	John Kerby	7
Isaac Holeman	6	Charles Kenady	5
George Hoover	13	Abraham Louderback	5
Thomas Herendon	2	William B. Long	2
Henry H. Hazard	7	John Lea	5
Elijah Hanks	3	James Leavel	4
Elijah Hughes	8	William Laforce	6
William Herenden	1	Lawson Lyon	4
Elizabeth Harper	6	Matthew Latta	10
John Harper	5	Elijah Lacy	7
Margaret Harper	10	James Lansby	8
Jonathin Hicklin	8	James Lambkin	6
Edward Holland	8	James Lewis	5
Conrad Hendrix	9	Fielding Lewis	9
John Hubbard	11	William Lizenby	9
Luke Harrison	4	John Levinsher	5
Robert Humble	5	Abraham McManis	6
Catharine Hendrix	6	Samuel McLain	7
Nicholas Hensley	10	John McQuire	5

Basil McDevit	6
James McClanahan	3
General James McConnell	10
Samuel McGeorge	4
John McManis	5
Samuel McGee	6
John McManama	9
John McFatridge	5
Richard McGrow	6
John Merchant	12
John D. Mitchell	11
Robert Mitchell	12
George Mitchell	10
William Mitchell	4
Michael Mitchell	10
Enas Mix	5
Isaac Miles	10
John Maddox	5
William Minter	7
Nelson Maddox	8
John Masters	7
Edward Mosby	8
William Moffitt	5
Jane Meek	3
James Malone	5
John Malone	7
John Malone, Jr.	4
Samuel Martin	10
James Moffitt	11
Jacob Miller	7
William Martin	10
John Murphy	2
William Mahan	9
William Monroe	9
Aaron Moore	5
John Miller	5
Casper Moretz	2
Jacob Middleton	6
Edmond Mitchell	8
Nathaniel Mattox	10
John Moss	4
William Mitchell	3
James Martin	8

Robert Nevil	5
James O. B. Nelson	2
George W. New	6
Henry Newman	10
Jeremiah Nash	8
William Nicholson, Jr.	5
William Nicholson, Sr.	5
Charles Norwood	6
Sarah O'Briant	4
Kean O'Hara	7
Henry Overstreet	5
Abraham Owens	5
William Palmerck	1
Joel Pace	10
Franklin Perry	7
William Pulliam	7
John Paine	11
Elizabeth Pry	4
Allen Perry	5
James Petty	7
John Prall	3
Robert Pilkerson	8
Benjamine Peyton	7
Thomas Peyton	9
Ephriam Porter	11
Robert Pearce	5
William Pullen	9
George Peyton	9
Mary Parker	4
Nehimiah Redding	5
Alexander Rennick	5
Richard Robinson	5
Thomas Ritchie	7
Richard Rowland	11
Thomas Robinson	6
Turner Rodgers	8
Nancy Rearden	8
Mary Rankin	5
Vincent Ross, Sr.	6
James Ratcliffe	7
James Redmond	4
William Roach	13
Agatha Redd	3

William Raney	13	Jesse Snelling	3
Vincent Reynolds	8	Samuel Smith	2
Jeremiah Rankin	5	Joseph Smith	6
Joseph Redmond	11	Humphrey Smith	11
Andrew Ross	3	Robert Sanderson	1
Samuel Stephenson, **Jr.**	2	George Smith	4
William Spaulding	8	William Scanlon	4
James Spaulding	6	Gideon Scanlon	6
Michael Stucker	11	John Stapleton	6
Jacob Stucker	12	Richard Sampson	7
William Sample	6	Hugh Scott	5
Andrew Sample	4	William Smither	6
Jacob Sample	4	Thomas Scurlock	4
Susannah Smith	2	Jacob Stewart	8
John Smith	12	Elizabeth Stone	4
James Standford	10	Catherine Stone	6
James Steele	6	John Singleton	2
John Story	7	William Sheets	10
William Sargeant	10	William Smithey	2
Adam Snyder	5	Robert Shelton	7
Thomas C. Scroggins	3	James Scarce	1
Benjamine Sheets	13	Joseph Sellars	7
John Stuart	3	William Stevenson, **Jr.**	8
Joseph Styne	5	Arthur Turner	7
James Sanford	3	Elijah Tinder	12
Alexander Smith	4	Priestley Terrell	4
Robert Seward	4	James Tinder	10
John Smith	3	George H. Tutt	2
Merriman Stephens	6	John Topass	7
Joseph Shannon	8	John Thorn	6
John Suter	11	Zachariah Taylor	6
William Shipton	4	Robert Torbitt	10
John Sheppard	9	Joseph Taylor	4
Richard Shipp, Sr.	5	Bartlett Turner	5
James Spillman	10	John True, Sr.	6
Christopher Shotten	5	William Taylor, Sr.	5
Elizabeth Scott	9	William Taylor, Jr.	6
John Sellars	4	Henry Taylor	5
Robinson Spaulding	11	Nimrod Utterback	11
Nancy Scott	4	Henry Varble	7
John Scarce	9	Charity Veatch	5
John Stevenson, Sr.	4	Osby Veatch	2
John Snelling	6	Daniel Vaughan	8

Thomas Violett	4
Augusta Violett	5
Asa C. Veach	4
Benjamine Veatch	1
John Williams	10
John Warren	2
Daniel White	10
Abednego Walden	3
Wilton Warwick	8
Jesse Wilhoit	5
Levi Williams	9
William Woodson	1
James Wright	9
Michael Wilhoit	4
William Webb	5
Elijah Walden	5
Joshua Wilson	7
William Wilson	2
Alexander Wilson	6
John Wilson	5
Henry Walker	5
Absalom Wilson	11
Thomas Whiting	10
William Weaver	2
William L. Williams	10
Jeremiah Wilson	10
Joseph Walden	9
Richard Young, Jr.	8
William Young	5

John Young	8
William Young	6

White population of Versailles:

Slaveholders	216	
Non-slaveholders	15	
		231

White population outside of Versailles:

Slaveholders	3,229	
Non-slaveholders	2,497	
		5,726

Total whites	5,957

Colored population in Versailles:

Slaves	195	
Free	9	
		204

Colored population outside of Versailles:

Slaves	3,179	
Free	71	
		3,250

Total colored	3,454

Total population of county	9,411

WOODFORD COUNTY

By W. E. Railey

PART TWO.

Pensions from Revolution.*

The following names represent citizens of Woodford County who, in 1810, drew pensions for service rendered in the Revolution:

Preston W. Brown, Charles Buck, David Campbell, Thomas Cooper, John Jackson, John Kinkead, Joseph Kinkead, Joseph Lindsey, Reuben Long, William P. Meredith, William Phillips, Benjamin Vance, William Vawter, James Ashley, James Arnold, Peter Alexander, Thomas Alsop, John Akin, John Allen, John Andrews, John Armstrong, James Armstrong, John Armstrong, Hugh Allen, John Allen, John Allen, John Adkins, Robert Alexander, Robert Abbett, Lewis Arnold, Walter Ayres, John Boze, Sr., Samuel Brooking, Samuel Berry, Jr., Robert Bowmar, Sr., Robert Black, John Brown, John Boze, Jr., Thomas Bell, William Buford, John Barnett, Samuel Berry, Sr., Benjamine Berry, John Buck, Sr., Josiah Boone, James Bell, John Buford, Edmond Ball, Levi Buchanan, Thomas Blanton, James Burk, James Black, James Burton, Charles Barnes, Lewis Bowdery, Dawson Brown, Margaret Burnett, John Blackmore, John Cunningham, William Cunningham, Gasper Collins, Isaac Crutcher, George T. Cotton, William Campbell, Ralph Cowgill, Thomas Coleman, William Culley, James Caldwell, John Collins, Samuel Campbell, John Cooke, Richard Cole, Sr., Thomas Carril, Goodloe Carter, Benjamin Clarke, Marquis Calmes, Joseph Crass, William Clarke, James Cox, John Cotton, Dominicus Cownover, John Clarke, Spencer Cooper, William Campbell, Reuben Cave, John Collins, Joseph Collins, John B. Carter, John Carter, James Coleman, John Carpenter, Hugh Cunningham, James Cunningham, Thomas Cunningham, Samuel Campbell, John Duvali, Solomon Davis, John Dawson, Aaron Darnell, John Dorsey, William Dale, Sr., John Durham, Thomas Davis, William Davis, John Davis, Richard Davis, James Dougherty, John Dale, Thomas Davis, William Dawson, William Dawson, Henry Davis, Solomon Dunnagan, James Edwards, Leonard Ellis, Henry Evans, Moses Edwards, John Edwards, Sr., Benjamin Edwards, Jesse Ellis, Sr., Samuel Evans, William Elliott, Joseph Edwards,

*This list was arranged by A. C. Quisenberry, while he was a citizen of Washington City, and although he was a painstaking researcher, there are errors in the table. I used this with the permission of Mrs. Jennie C. Morton.

Joseph Eaton, John Elliott, James Edwards, John Eaton, Jesse Ellis, Sr., Daniel Fitzgerald, William Florence, William Finch, John Finnie, James Finnie, James Ford, John Ford, John Finn, William Florence, Sr., Samuel Guyn, John Graves, William Gaines, John Green, William George, Paul Green, James Green, Sr., John Guthrie, John Gregory, William Guthrie, William Green, John Garrett, William Garrett, Henry Green, George Grymes, John Hamilton, Thomas Helm, Edward Howe, Nathaniel Hart, William Henderson, Moses Hawkins, Willis Hawkins, William Strother Hawkins, John Hazzard, George Halloway, Daniel Holeman, William Hancock, Henry Harrison, Lewis Hampton, William Herendon, Henry Harper, William Harper, John Harper, John Hamilton, Andrew Hamilton, William Hicks, Nathaniel Harris, John Hubbard, William Hopkins, Robert Humble, James Hawkins, James Hambleton, Clayborn Hall, Charles Hammond, John Hammond, James Howard, John Hanks, John Hudson, John Harris, Henry Hoover, James Hackett, David Harris, Francis Jackson, Thomas Jenkins, Robert Jackson, James Jackson, Fielding Jeter, William Kinkead, Joseph Kenady, John Kenady, Charles Kenady, James Long, John Lea, James Leavel, William Laforce, Elijah Lacey, Adam Lynn, James Lewis, Fielding Lewis, John Lewis, John Long, Sr., George McDaniel, John McQuaddy, Alexander McClure, James McCormick, John McQuire, James McConnell, Samuel McGee, John Minter, Samuel P. Menzies, Robert Mitchell, George Mitchell, William Mitchell, Enos Mix,

William Mayo, Frederick Mitchell, John Maddox, George Muter, John Masters, Robert Mosby, William Moffitt, Thomas Mattox, John Matthews, James Malone, Samuel Martin, Thomas Munday, Jacob Miller, James Marshall, William Martin, John Murphy, William Monroe, John Miller, William Morris, Edmond Mitchell, William Morton, Samuel Martin, Thomas Morton, Nathaniel Mattox, John Mosby, William Moss, John Moss, William Mitchell, Louis Marshall, James Martin, William Moore, William Nicholson, Sr., Charles Norwood, John Oliver, John O'Bannon, Henry Overstreet, James Owens, John Peters, William Palmere, Joel Pace, William Powell, John Paine, John Pace, Charles Palmer, William Peters, James Peters, Thomas Poore, Robert Perry, John Paul, Thomas Peyton, William Pullen, George Peyton, James Quarles, Thos. Reynolds, Richard Robinson, John Rucker, Sr., Cornelius Robinson, Thomas Robinson, Dennis Rearden, William Roach, Cornelius Ruddle, Richard Rice, Thomas Redd, George Robinson, Henry Rowland, James Sullivan, Henry Stone, William Scott, William Smith, Michael Stucker, Jacob Stucker, John Smith, James Steele, William Steele, John Smith, John Story, Adam Snyder, John Stuart, James Sanford, Lewis Sublett, Sr., Samuel Shouse, Benjamin Smither, Alexander Smith, James Stepp, John Smith, William Suter, John Sheppard, Thomas Steele, John Steele, James Spilman, Samuel Stephenson, Sr., John Sellers, John Stevenson, Sr., John Snelling, Samuel Smith, Joseph Smiths, George Smith, John

Stapleton, Richard Saunders, George Shelton, Hugh Scott, Henry Smith, William Smither, John Singleton, William Smithey, John Short, James Thornton, William Todd, Edward Trabue, ———— Trabue, John Taylor, Nathaniel Thompson, Thomas Todd, Richard Taylor, Prestley Terrill, James Tinder, William Thompson, Robert Taylor, George Turpin, Reuben Twyman, John Thorn, Zachariah Taylor, Joseph Taylor, Alexander Turner, John True, Sr., Thomas Turnham, William Taylor, Sr., Henry Taylor, William Tillory, Benjamin Utterback, Hanley Vance, John Williams, John Williams, Samuel Ware, John Warren, Daniel White, Joseph White, Daniel Wilcoxson, Josiah Wooldridge, Jesse Wilhoit, John Williams, William Williams, Levi Williams, William Woodson, James Wright, William Webb, Elijah Walden, Benjamin Wilson, William Wilson, Alexander Wilson, John Wilson, Henry Walker, Thomas Whiting, William Weaver, John Willis, Jeremiah Wilson, William Walker, William Warren, James Wilson, Edmond Waller, Robert Yancey, William Young, John Young, William Young, Lewis Young.

The Revolutionary soldiers who came to Woodford County after 1810 and drew pensions were: John Allison, Daniel Barnet, Nicholas Baker, Stephen Chelton, John Cox, Dennis Dailey, Jane Ellis (widow), Robert Gaines, Henry Goodloe, Michael Kirkham, William McCoy, John McKinney, John McQuiddy, Elijah Milton, John Mitchell, Leonard Moseby, George W. New, George Peyton, John Pollet, Reuben Smithey, and Enoch Wingfield.

Public Officials.

Woodford County has been greatly honored by the election of the following of her citizens to distinguished positions of trust:

To the Governorship, General Charles Scott, John J. Crittenden, and Luke P. Blackburn.*

To the Lieutenant Governorship, William B. Blackburn, Thomas P. Porter, and Charles M. Harriss.

The following countymen have represented the district in the State Senate:

Robert W. Johnson, 1792-95.
Robert Alexander, 1795-1802.
William Vawter, 1806-10.
Herman Bowmar, 1814-17, 1820-22.
William B. Blackburn, 1818-20, 1822-24, 1834-38.
Andrew Muldrow, 1824-29.
David Thornton, 1846-50.
R. C. Graves, 1850-53.
Thos. P. Porter, 1857-61.
J. Kemp Goodloe, 1861-65.
James Blackburn, 1874-79.
Samuel T. Leavy, 1887-88.
Henry L. Martin, 1893-96.
J. W. Newman, 1906-9.
Charles M. Harriss, 1917-20.

These citizens have represented the county in the House of Representatives:

John Watkins, 1792.
Col. William Steele, 1792.
John Grant, 1792.
Col. Richard Young, 1792-95, 1803.
Humphrey Marshall, 1793.
Bennett Pemberton, 1793.

To this list should be added the name of Gov. Albert Benjamin Chandler, who was elected in 1935.

General Marquis Calmes, 1795.
John Jouett, 1795-1796-1797.
Tunstall Quarles, 1796.
William Vawter, 1797-1799-1800.
Lewis Young, 1799-1800.
James Liggett, 1801-2.
Thomas   Bullock,   1801-1803-1805-
1806-1808-1809.
Preston Brown, 1802.
William B. Blackburn, 1804-5-6-7-
1811-12-13-14-15-16-25-26-27-28.
Charles Railey, 1807-1831.
Charles Buck, 1808-9.
Peter Buck, 1810.
Virgil McCracken, 1810-11.
William S. Hunter, 1812-13-14-15-17-
18-1820.
Thomas Stevenson, 1816-1819-1820.
Willis Field, 1817-18-1829.
William B. Long, 1819.
Percival Butler, 1821-2.
Andrew Muldrow, 1822.
James McConnell, 1824.
John Buford, 1824-1827.
Alex. Dunlap, 1825-26.
Southey Whittington, 1830.
Thomas   F.   Marshall,   1832-38-39-
1851-53.
John Watkins, 1833.
William Agun, 1834.
Samuel H. Wallace, 1835.
Francis Kirtley Buford, 1836.
William Buford, Jr., 1837.
Zachariah White, 1840.
William B. Kinkead, 1841.
Medley Shelton, 1842.
Luke P. Blackburn, 1843.
David Thornton, 1844.
Richard Gilbert Jackson, 1845.
John Steele, 1846.
Lewis A. Berry, 1847.
Jesse Hayden, 1848.
Ezekiel H. Field, 1849.

Robert H. Campbell, 1850.
Thomas P. Porter, 1853-54.
John Kemp Goodloe, 1855-1860.
Zeb Ward, 1861-2.
Henry C. McLeod, 1863-64.
James P. Ford, 1865-6-1869-70.
Hart Gibson, 1867-8.
Jo. C. S. Blackburn, 1871-2-1873-4.
John Andrew Steele, 1875-6.
Gen. Abe Buford, 1877-78.
John Andrew Steele, 1879-80.
Swift Darneal, 1881-82.
John H. Jesse, 1883-84.
David L. Thornton, 1885-86.
Richard H. Gray, 1887-88.
Samuel H. Shouse, 1889-90-91-92.
Thomas M. Fields, 1893-94.
John Andrew Steele, 1895-96.
German Bohannon Stout, 1897-8-99-
1900.
Lewis A. Nuckols, 1901-2.
J. W. Newman, 1903-4.
Ed. Mulcahy, 1905-6.
Harry A. Schoberth, 1907-8-1909-10-
1911-12.
George T. Davis, 1913-14.
David J. Howard, 1915-16-1917-18-
1919-20.
Dr. Alford Blackburn, 1921-22.
Clinton W. Hawkins, 1925-28.

SECRET ORDERS.

Masonic Fraternity.

Land Mark Lodge No. 41, F. A. M.,
was chartered August 27, 1817, and
soon thereafter it was organized by
the appointment of three of its charter
members to fill the chairs. John Y.
Hiter was appointed Master, John H.
Smith, Senior Warden, and John Mc-
Kinney, Jr., was appointed Junior
Warden, hence the first meetings of

Although the citizenry of Woodford County was noticeably divided on the issues of the Civil War and many warm arguments were indulged in wherever there was a group or gathering, as this writer well remembers the situation was not hopeless, as I can truthfully say that when the shadows of that sad conflict rolled by the scars at once entered a healing process through the brotherly offices of the Masonic fraternity.

There were both Union and Confederate sympathizers in the membership of that order, but they were real men. I think it was in the summer of 1866 that Versailles Commandry gave a picnic in one of the beautiful woodlands, which was repeated for several years, and on these occasions men who wore the blue and the gray mingled socially and danced merrily to the tune of "Dixie."

I recall the personnel of the Versailles Commandry at that time and its membership constituted as fine a body of men as ever wore the uniform of a Sir Knight and the inspiration took possession of me as a mere boy and I resolved to be a Mason. It is now nearly forty years since I embraced the noble teachings of Masonry, and I was soon thereafter a member of Versailles Commandry.

It gives me great pleasure to say that my name is on the roster there now and will be upon its tablets long long after this body has been consigned to the tomb in which it will rest until called forth some time, some where, in response to the Grand Master's call.

I was born in Woodford County and was baptized into Masonry in her borders, therefore I love the old county, and I love Masonry because its teachings has made of me a man without the slightest hate for any human being, with the greatest reverence for my God, love for my country and respect for myself. May the light on the altar of Versailles Commandry never grow dim. May its usefulness ever expand and its membership ever grow in numbers and grace.   Very truly,

                                                            WM. E. RAILEY.

the lodge were presided over by three Johns who were good men and true, but neither pretended to be as holy as the two Johns of blessed memory, St. John and John the Baptist whom all Masons revere, and whose lives and works constitute, next to duty, our guiding star.

Land Mark Lodge has had smooth sailing for more than a century and today is one of the best lodges in the State, the very best type of the citizenship of the vicinity of Versailles at all times constituting its membership.

The following were some of the charter members and officers:

John Y. Hiter, Worshipful Master.

John H. Smith, Senior Warden.

John McKinney, Jr., Junior Warden.

Webb Chapter No. 6, Royal Arch Masons, was organized at Versailles, December 4th, 1821, nearly a century ago. The charter members were: Thomas P. Hart, William B. Blackburn, John McKinney, Jr., William H. Cosby, Churchill J. Blackburn, John H. Smith, James S. Berryman, Phillip Swigert, John Buford, James D. Caldwell, Virgil McKnight, Thomas W. Sellars, George McDaniel, Jr., Leonard Searcy, William W. Hawkins, Daniel C. Paxton, Lewis W. Lampkin, Innis T. Harris, John T. Parker, Percival Butler, John Y. Hiter, and Robert Poor.

Thomas P. Hart was chosen the first Most Excellent High Priest; William B. Blackburn, first King, and John McKinney, Jr., Scribe.

This chapter has passed down the years without loss of interest or numbers and is today in a healthy condition.

Versailles Commandery No. 3 was the third organized in the State. Several Masons of the Blue Lodge at Versailles, also the Chapter, having been initiated into Webb Commandery No. 1, at Lexington about 1840, made application in 1842 for a dispensation to organize a Commandery in Versailles, which was granted during that year and a charter issued September 10, 1844.

When the Grand Commandery of Kentucky was organized at Frankfort in 1847, Sir Knight William Brown of Versailles Commandery presided over that assemblage, and the following year was Captain General of the Versailles Commandery. Other Sir Knights of the Versailles Commandery who participated in the organization of the Grand Commandery at Frankfort were: Joseph Peters, Samuel F. Patterson and Thomas U. Kinkead. Sir Knight Joseph Peters was Grand Generalissimo for the first two conclaves held in the State and was elected Grand Commander in 1849. He was prominently associated with both the grand and local commanderies until his death in 1856.

In 1847 Boone Railey was Commander of Versailles Commandery and was selected to represent Kentucky Templars at the grand encampment of the United States at Columbus, Ohio, that year.

For several years before and for several years after the Civil War the Masons of Woodford County united in giving annual picnics or barbecues in the beautiful woodlands of the county, and occasionally in the village of Clifton, so picturesquely nestled beneath the hills of the Kentucky river, and they were most enjoyable affairs. The men of that period were noble specimens, the Sir Knights being of that type of the southern gentleman mostly gone, but not forgotten, and their bearing in their uniforms was a model for any artist. Some of them that may yet be recalled by the living witnesses were Capt. Harry Brown, Judge Cave Graves, Jo. Taylor, John Amsden, Sr., Boone Railey, Jesse Haskins, H. H. Culberson, David P. Robb, Lon Peters, Berrywick Craig, Lewis Sublett, Jr., Warren Viley, Rev. John W. Venable, T. U. Kinkead and a host of others who left their impress upon those who followed them in the fraternity who are now carrying the beautiful and sublime tenets of the order worthily.

The Grand Commandery met in Versailles in 1850, and in 1866, and again in 1902. Not one of the men who were members of the Commandery in 1866 is living today.

I. O. O. F.

McKee Lodge No. 35, I. O. O. F. of Versailles was organized May 5, 1847. It owned no building at that time in which to hold its stated meetings, so they assembled for quite a few years in the building then used for public school purposes.

It was named in honor of Col. William R. McKee, whose life was sacrificed upon his country's altar at Buena Vista in 1847, the very year of the organization of the lodge.

Its charter members were Col. George T. Cotton, H. C. Bradford, John W.

Stevenson, Thomas S. Foushee, F. Hartye and John Thompson.

Woodford Encampment No. 16, I. O. O. F. was organized the following year at Versailles.

The Rev. John W. Venable, the popular Pastor of the Episcopal Church for many years, united with McKee Lodge in 1857 and retained his membership there until his death in 19—. He was Grand Chaplain of the Sovereign Grand Lodge of the United States for more than forty years, an exceedingly fine gentleman, as well as a popular pastor.

John S. Minary was also an honored member of McKee Lodge for more than fifty years, filling from time to time all of the chairs in the encampment as well as in the local lodge.

In 1871 the members of McKee Lodge built a home of their own on Main street, near the court house, that is not only a credit to them, but an ornament to the town, and the order is in a most prosperous and promising condition.

K. of P.

Another secret order of patriotic citizens that has moved along by leaps and bounds, with every prospect of a bright future is the Knights of Pythias. It is known as Gray Lodge No. 27. In naming this lodge they paid tribute to one of Woodford's worthy sons, Richard H. Gray, who opens his hand and his heart to all laudable undertakings. He has served the people of the county in various capacities for nearly a half century and was a charter member of this lodge.

The lodge was organized in 1889,

and the following year a Uniform Rank of K. P. No. 23 was organized.

This organization has had a long struggle for life—yea, it has literally passed through fire—but it was composed of men who were undaunted and knew not failure, so with persistent perseverance they have made it a force in the community and have long ago overcome a severe loss by fire.

Red Men.

The Improved Order of Red Men is another secret order that was organized at Versailles. Huron Tribe No. 56 was organized in 1900 and was composed almost exclusively of young men, full of enthusiasm and push, and they have always been public spirited citizens. In all things they are actuated by brotherly love, friendship and charity. Its membership includes a lengthy list of splendid, progressive business men. I am told that the lodge is in a flourishing condition.

Some Celebrated Stock Farms and Their Owners.

The character of cattle, horses and other stock brought into Kentucky by the pioneers was said to be of an inferior quality, and for many years the stock that grazed in the pastures were but little improved, but dating from 1820, when the spirit of improving the grades took possession of the stockmen, every decade showed marked improvement. The herds and stables of the east were visited and well bred stock imported into Kentucky at reasonable intervals with the view of crossing them upon our stock, thereby producing a grade that would stim-

ulate values and trade. Finally Robert Alexander and Richard Gilbert Jackson became so impressed with the advances made by, or before 1850, that they, or their agents, imported into Woodford County some pure bred stock from Europe, some of them costing as much as $5,000.00, and the people thought them unbalanced, but they were only wise in their day. By 1855 all grades were so improved that Woodford County took first rank as a producer of high grade stock, and she is still unsurpassed.

Robert Alexander purchased his "Woodburn" stock farm from the heirs of General Hugh Mercer, March 2, 1790, the original tract containing "2,000 acres, more or less, situated in the county of Kentucky, on the waters of Elkhorn Creek." He was born in Scotland in 1767, and when three years old, his mother died, and his father, William Alexander, took his family to France where they were residents for quite awhile. In 1787 William Alexander came to Virginia to purchase tobacco for his brother, A. J. Alexander, who was a prominent merchant of Scotland. At that time his son Robert was preparing himself for the law at Lincoln Inn, London. A year later, however, the son joined the father in Virginia and in the course of time, as stated, "Woodburn" farm was purchased.

Dr. A. J. A. Alexander is now in possession of the original land grant signed by Thomas Jefferson as Governor of Virginia. It is not known by any descendant just when Robert Alexander first resided at "Woodburn," for he had a residence at

Frankfort, and his time was divided for some years between Frankfort and the farm, but certainly not later than 1795, as he represented Woodford in the State Legislature from that year to 1802. In 1801 he was a charter member of the Kentucky River Navigation Co., and in 1807 was a member of the board of directors of the First Bank of Kentucky. He was elected by that board president of the bank, but retired in 1820 because of the excitement created by the decision of Judge Clark on the nullification act of that year. After his retirement from the presidency of the bank he spent the most of his time on his farm in Woodford. The census of 1810 reported he owned twenty slaves.

In 1814 he married Eliza Richardson, a daughter of Daniel Weiseger of of Frankfort. They had two sons, Robert Aitcheson and A. J. Alexander, and two daughters, Lucy and Mary Belle. Mrs. Alexander died in 1839 and her husband only survived her two years. Robert Aitcheson Alexander was then in England where he had gone to complete his education, so after the death of their father and mother, A. J. Alexander and his two sisters went to England to complete an educational course, and they did not return until about 1847, when they took charge of "Woodburn." Robert A. Alexander in the meantime had declared his allegiance to Great Britain in order to inherit a large estate from an uncle in Scotland, and he remained a subject of England until his death in 1867.

Robert Alexander, the original purchaser of "Woodburn," sold a part of the tract, that upon which Dr. Alexander now resides, to Col. William Buford in 18—, but Robert A. Alexander repurchased it after his return from Europe about 1850, and at his death in 1867, A. J. Alexander inherited the entire estate.

In 1851 A. J. Alexander married Lucy Humphreys, daughter of David Humphreys, of Woodford County. She died shortly thereafter and later A. J. Alexander married Lucy Fullerton. Dr. A. J. A. Alexander, the present owner of "Woodburn," is a son of the last marriage.

In 1850 Robert A. Alexander's herds were regarded as very fine, but during that year he imported from England some pure bred shorthorn cattle and Southdown sheep that soon gave his herds and flocks a nation wide reputation. He was also fond of the racer and liked the race course, owning some fine speciments of racers, such as the great Lexington. However, when his brother, A. J. Alexander, took charge in 1867 he continued breeding thoroughbreds, but discontinued the racing feature. He also established annual sales on the premises, advertising extensively in the public prints and a multitude of people attended these sales every June. I recall the sale of 1890, and that was perhaps an average. Thirty-four head of thoroughbred colts were auctioned to the highest bidders and the average price was $4,000.00.

More recently Dr. A. J. A. Alexander, who now owns "Woodburn," has turned his attention almost exclusively to pure bred cattle and sheep. The greater part of this splendid estate is in bluegrass and its pastures and woodlands are conceded to be the most beautiful in central Kentucky, and the occasional glens that wind serpentine like through them add an additional charm that pleases the numerous visitors to this attractive estate.

It is situated on the L. & N. Railroad, three miles from Midway. In fact, the stop known as Spring Station is located on one corner of the tract.

The Harpers were also pioneers in stock raising. Their farm joined the "Woodburn" estate and was within two miles of Midway. This noted farm was called "Nantura," and the land was also purchased from the heirs of Gen. Mercer about 1795, and it contained about fifteen hundred acres. This property at that day was bought for a small consideration and is a splendid body of land.

Jacob Harper, the original purchaser, and the head of the Harper family in Woodford County erected his residence by an ever-flowing spring on the Midway and Spring Station road, where he raised a large family. *His father was a Hollander, and his wife was of the same extract. He was a fancier of horses and cattle but was not of the turfman type, but his grandson, John Harper, who inherited, with his brothers and sister, the greater part of the estate, built the house on the old Lexington and Frankfort road that he occupied so long, and indulged his inclination to breed and run from "eend to eend" his thoroughbreds, and when he died, the estate went to his nephew, Frank B. Harper, who con-

tinued the business until his death about 1905, and he in turn left it to his nephew, Frank Harper Hawkins, who abandoned the breeding of thoroughbreds and has turned his attention to diversified farming.

Such noted racers as Longfellow, Ten Broeck, Jills Johnston and other noted animals were raised here and by their speed, and the plethoric purses they won for the Harpers, gave "Nantura" a wide reputation.

"Nantura" was also widely known for the manifest cordiality and hospitality dispensed, and many prominent men were entertained within the gates of "Nantura," especially during the occupancy of Col. Frank B. Harper.

The original log house still stands and is owned by Gertrude Hawkins of Midway. Frank Harper Hawkins is of the fifth generation and the present owner of "Nantura."

"Silver Pool" stock farm has never passed out of the possession of descendants of the Williams name. Soon after the Revolution, Daniel Williams, who was captain of a company under the command of General Green, came to Kentucky with his wife, Mary Jackson, who was a near relative of President Andrew Jackson, and settled upon the above farm. His children were Mary, who married Robert Forsythe; Katherine, who married James Orr; Daniel Jackson, and John who married Elizabeth Pringle of Lexington. Daniel Jackson Williams inherited the farm, but soon thereafter sold it to his brother John, who engaged extensively in the manufacture

*The Harpers were Hollanders, but lived in Germany for some years before coming to U. S.

of hemp into bagging and twine, as well as the live stock industry. He was born in Woodford in 1789. His wife's mother was captured by the Indians when a child and held for three months before she was rescued. When John Williams died his estate passed to his son, Thomas Smith Williams, who married Martha Francis Beauchamp. After his death, his son, Claude S. Williams, was the owner, and is a successful farmer and stockman.

"Silver Pool" stock farm is on the Mount Vernon and Pisgah road, several miles from Versailles. Four rooms of the present house were built by Daniel Williams, the addition by his great grandson, Claude S. Williams. Daniel Williams and his wife were among the first members of the Mt. Vernon Baptist Church and both were buried in the family burying ground near the church.

Daniel Williams was descended from Sir William Williams, a Welsh Baron; also from Sir Roger Williams the founder of the State of Rhode Island. Each generation has displayed those characteristics so necessary to good citizenship. "Silver Pool," as a country seat, has been changed to "Haltura."

"Glen Lake" stock farm is another of the farms in Woodford from the early days that has been noted for the character of stock it produced, especially harness gaited animals. The Stouts were always deeply interested in speedy trotters. The first of the name in Woodford County was Amos Stout, a native of New Jersey,* who settled in Mason County soon after the

Revolution. He removed to Woodford County during the war of 1812, or about that time, and located a farm within a mile of Mt. Vernon Church. He married Olivia Hicks, a daughter of William Hicks, and his wife Bettie Harris of the county. Of this union three sons were born as follows: John in 1821, William in 1824, and Robert Hicks in 1828. John inherited the estate of his father and lived and died there, honored and respected by every one who knew him. In 1884 he married Susan Bohannon, daughter of German Bohannon and his wife Sallie Hamilton, she the daughter of Alexander Hamilton of Virginia. For many years John Stout was moderator of the Elkhorn Baptist Association, and served as chairman of the board of trustees of the Cleveland Orphans' Home at Versailles until his death in 1883. He had nine children, one of whom, German, inherited the home of his father, and his grandfather, and died there in 1900. The home is still in possession of descendants.

William Stout, second son of Amos Stout and Olivia Hicks, was a farmer until the last years of his life when he resided with his daughter in Midway. He married Judith Jameson in 1848, and four of their children were born and reared in the county. They were Rev. Amos, Rachel, Newton and Olivia.

Robert Hicks Stout was the third son, who, after several years under the tutorage of B. B. Sayre of Frankfort, engaged in general merchandising, and later entered the general commission business at Midway. He was elected sheriff in 1883 and re-elected.

*See page 303.

In 1853 he married Fannie Gillespie. They have two sons, Professor Edward G. and Judge Robert Lee Stout, who is the present Circuit Judge.

"Sunny Slope Farm" lies off the Versailles and Midway road, one mile west of the road, and about four miles from each of those towns. It was settled by Richard Shipp soon after the county was established and it has never been out of possession of descendants of the family name. From the first, stock raising was combined with the ordinary duties of farm life, but it was not known extensively for its most successful results in breeding and training until the present owner, J. V. Shipp, took charge about 1885, and brought it into public notice by producing some marvelous runners, some of the racers trained under his supervision selling for as much as $10,000.00.

"Buck Run" stock farm was settled by Charles Railey in 1796 when he arrived in Woodford County from Chesterfield County, Virginia. This farm also has remained all of these years in possession of descendants of the Railey name. Charles Railey married Mary Mayo, daughter of Col. William Mayo, of Richmond, Va., and Catharine Swann, and they raised a large family of children on this farm, which is in full view of the Grier's Creek Church, three miles out of Versailles. He had a fancy for fine stock, inherited from his father, Col. John Railey, who maintained a race track on his Virginia estate for many years. Logan Railey was the youngest of thir-

teen children and inherited the "Buck Run" estate at the death of his father, and he was for fifty years one of the most successful breeders and handlers of saddle horses in or out of Kentucky. His sons, under the style and name of Railey Brothers, were no less successful as proprietors of the estate for many years. Their training of fancy saddle gaited horses was so thorough that their reputation became national, and any horse bred and trained under their management and direction, commanded a fancy price in any part of the country.

After the death of the late Russell Railey, at the Frankfort Fair a few years ago, his brother Irvin assumed the management, and he is no less successful.

Nearly all of Charles Railey's children settled in Louisiana and Mississippi as they reached their age of responsibility, others settled in Missouri. The only descendants now residing in the county besides Irvin Railey, are the grandchildren of David Thornton, who for forty years was president of the Bank of Woodford. Fannie Turner and the wife of W. O. Davis are granddaughters of David Thornton, and great-granddaughters of Charles Railey.

The Raileys were never office seekers, but Charles Railey twice represented the county in the State Legislature, first in 1807, and again in 1831. David Thornton, his son-in-law, served in both branches of the Legislature.

The house that Charles Railey built about 1797 still stands with a few modern improvements. In 1810 Charles

Railey had ten members in his family and twelve slaves according to census.

Within a week after this sketch was writen Irvin Railey was a corpse. Returning from Lexington on the night of November 9th, 1919, he retired, but the angel of death smote him in the small hours of the morning and his busy life was ended. His life was honorable and clean, and duty and application ever actuated him.

The family of Charles L. Railey, who married Ada Pepper, reside at Lexington.

———

"The Highland Place" was established by William Garrett about 1784, and four generations have domiciled themselves on this splendid estate six miles from Versailles on Shannon's road. I think the last of the name to own this fine estate was **Joseph M.** Garrett.

William Garrett, the original owner, was a Scotchman, with an Irish tinge, and like his people, he was a fancier of fine stock, and none of his descendants departed from that pride in fancy steeds that gave to "Highland Place" an extended reputation for well bred and well trained horses.*

———

"Maple Hill" is one of the lovely old homes, and one of the most noted stock farms in the county. The Ball Brothers have taken premiums all over the West as well as at home. So their string attracts attention wherever they go, and their reputation for fair and square dealing is universally acknowledged. They have been so thorough in their methods, and management, that their saddle gaited horses command the highest price in any market.

The farm is situated four miles from Versailles on the road to Nicholasville and is a splendid body of rolling bluegrass land, with numerous springs of excellent stock water.

This fine body of land was purchased †by Dudley Mitchum about 1784. His wife was Susan Allen, both natives of Virginia, and Woodford County was sparsely settled when they erected their home on this estate soon after its purchase. They had several children, but the farm was inherited by the youngest daughter, Susan. In 1810 Dudley Mitchum was not only owner of this farm but owned twenty-two likely slaves, and his family was composed of ten members.

Susan, the youngest daughter, married John Ball, of Boyle County. He was born in 1802 and she in 1803. They took charge of the farm immediately upon the death of her father, and both lived and died there. At their death, their son, Dudley Mitchum Ball, inherited the home and in 1840 laid the foundation for one of the best stock farms in the State, and its reputation has never waned. He was born in 1824 and married Joana Chrisman. The following children resulted from this union: John, who married Elizabeth McConnell; Josie, who married Worth Harris; Dudley Mitchum Ball; Minnie, who married Col. Dan L. Moore; Howard D. Ball, Ernest C. Ball, and Susan Mitchum, who married Charlton Alexander.

———

*See page 82.
†See pages 77, 129-30, 317, 396, 398.

About twenty-five years ago the last of the buildings erected by Dudley Mitchum was torn down and modern structures have taken their places.

Besides the children of Dudley M. Ball, the other descendants of Dudley Mitchum in the county are: Mrs. Bettie Hurst Nuckols, Mrs. Lucy Bailey Thornton, Lena, John and Charlton Graves, Mrs. Minary and Hadley and Cornelia Stone.

"Greenwood" is another stock farm that has meant much to Woodford County as well as the Graddy family. Jesse Graddy, the head of the Woodford County family of that name, was both a landowner and a slaveholder in 1810. "Greenwood" is one of the county's most beautiful homes, built upon a plateau that gives you a pleasing view of the country for miles around. It is situated between the Clifton pike and the Glenn's Creek pike about five miles from Versailles, and three miles from Clifton.

For more than forty years Henry Graddy owned this estate, and he amassed a fortune out of the droves of mules and herds of Shorthorns that he bred and raised on the premises. The farm is splendidly adapted to the use of either pasturage or cultivation. The residence is of the spacious Southern type that is inviting, and the several Graddy families who have presided over the estate have dispensed a liberal hospitality.

At the death of Henry Graddy the estate passed to his son, Joseph C., who is the present owner. He turned his attention to the breeding of Hereford cattle, a species that is both desirable and profitable and has made a wonderful success of it.

———

*The home of George Blackburn was located a mile below Spring Station on the Louisville and Nashville Railroad. He located there about 1792 and erected his home soon thereafter. He also built a stockade around the spring that was in the yard, and in easy reach in case of emergency. This stockade was built not only for the safety of the family, but for the better protection of the community as well. Whenever an uprising of the Indians was imminent, or even suspected, all persons living in the vicinity took refuge in "Blackburn's Fort."

He lived there for many years and reared a large family of children. The farm is now owned by James Withrow.

His son, "Ned" Blackburn, was a great lover of the horse and bred many racers on his farm which cornered at Spring Station, just one mile distant from his father's home. Here was born quite a family of children, several of whom distinguished themselves in the political arena. Dr. Luke P. Blackburn was in the Legislature in 1843, Governor of the State 1879-83, member of the committee of doctors who successfully combatted, and finally stamped out yellow fever in the South, that dreaded disease that had so scourged that section for years. Jo. C. S. Blackburn was another son who represented Woodford in the Legislature during the sessions of 1871-2, and 1873-4; was in Congress 1875-85; in U. S. Senate 1885-95, and again in 1901-7; Governor of Panama 1907, and

*See pages 61, 176, 209, 212, 388, 320, 399.

chairman of Lincoln Memorial Commission at Washington 1914-18. James Blackburn was still another son who was in the State Senate 1875-79; Secretary of State 1879-83, and member of the Constitutional Convention in 1890.

The "Ned" Blackburn farm has been the property of the Blackburns for more than one hundred years, the present owner being Dr. Alford Blackburn who saw service in the World War. Captain Joe and Captain James Blackburn both served the Confederacy 1861-65.

The Blackburns and Bufords, during the early days, were gentlemen sportsmen and often indulged in racing on their local tracks that gave entertainment and delight to their neighbors and friends in Woodford and adjacent counties.

Many are yet living in the Ashland district who will recall with pleasure the memorable contest waged by Ed. C. Marshall and Jo. C. S. Blackburn for Congress during the early seventies. They both were residents of Woodford, and they were termed the "oratorical gladiators." Sparkling scintillations from the forum characterized every joint meeting and drew greater crowds than ever gathered in the old district before or since.

Capt. Joe, as he was affectionately known by his friends, was a knightly gentleman who held his friends as if by hooks of steel. To know him was but to love him.

I have made strenuous efforts to locate some one who could tell much of Wm. B. Blackburn,* who was in the county in 1810, owned a farm and six

slaves and had four members in his family. That he was popular and able goes without further proof than to say he was in the Kentucky House of Representatives during the following years, 1804, 1805-6-7-11-12-13-14-15-16-25-26-27 and 28. Was in State Senate 1818-20-1822-24 and 1834-38. He was also Lieutenant Governor in 1818-20. Pretty good record. He was a brother of George and Jonathan Blackburn, but I can learn nothing further of him.

Edward M. Blackburn was known as "Uncle Ned."

Huguenots and Other Prominent Families

Some of the most prominent people of the State and Nation, socially, politically, religiously and professionally have Huguenot blood coursing through their veins, and Woodford County is indeed to be congratulated that so many of these people were among our early settlers. Many of their descendants migrated to other parts of the State in after years and the great southwest and they are the leading spirits in every community. During the Revolution and the war of 1812-14, almost to a man they were in the front ranks fighting for that liberty that they were denied in their native France. No foreigners that ever came to our shores have been more patriotic, never flouting that contemptible prefix, Franco-American, in the faces of loyal Americans, and that is the main reason for their being such patriots, and against all foreign potentates who would dare to meddle in our domestic affairs, especially the

*See pages 62 and 175-6.

subversion of our institutions that have been built up under our democratic constitution.

France incurred a serious loss when she forced these people to flee from that wrath that refused to be either subdued or suppressed, and America has never had to regret her action of shelter and protection from their persecutions.

Col. John Buck, Rev. William Buck and Charles Buck, III., were Virginians who came to Kentucky and settled in Woodford County the latter part of the eighteenth century. They were sons of Charles Buck, II*., and Anne Richardson of Virginia, she a granddaughter of Marquis De La Calmes, the Huguenot.

The above Charles Buck, III., enlisted in the war of 1812 from the county of Woodford, serving in the company of Capt. Jack Bayliss who, through his dare-devil courage during his service in the Revolution and war of 1812, acquired the soubriquet of "Fighting Jack Bayliss." After the war Charles Buck, III., married a sister of Capt. Bayliss and settled upon his Woodford County farm.

Charles Buck, III., and Lucy Bayliss were the parents of Col. John W. Buck who owned a farm on the Georgetown pike that adjoined the Leavy estate, near Midway. Chas. William Buck, son of Col. John W. Buck, lived there also with his interesting family and was a member of the county magisterial court. While a resident of that vicinity, in 1885, he was appointed Envoy Extraordinary

and Minister Plenipotentiary to the Government of Peru by President Cleveland. Since his service in Peru, Charles William Buck has been interested in politics and literary work, and in both fields he has succeeded. His historical novel, "Under the Sun, or the Passing of the Incas," published in 1902, has been widely read and favorably mentioned.

Charles Neville Buck, a son of Charles William, was also a citizen of the county and is an author and novelist of much merit. Both now live in Louisville, Ky.

The Rev. William Buck was in Woodford before his brother Charles, III., arrived, and settled near Versailles. He was one of the most noted Baptist preachers of that day. After a lengthy residence in Woodford he removed to Louisville where he founded a religious paper known as "The Western Recorder," said to be the first Baptist paper published west of the Allegheny mountains, and its influence has grown until now it is considered the leading paper of that denomination in the United States. After thoroughly establishing this paper he moved to Waco, Texas, where he lived the remainder of his life.

Col. John Buck, Thomas Buck and Charles Buck, II., were Virginians. They married three of the granddaughters of Marquis De La Calmes, Miriam, Anne and Mary Richardson. The two former Bucks were in the Revolution, and the latter was the father of the three brothers who settled in Woodford County.

"Lawyers and Lawmakers of Ken-

---

*See pages 181, 318.

tucky," a publication issued from a Chicago press in 1879, by H. Levin, of the Illinois Bar, says: "The Colonial records of London narrate that the first House of Burgesses in Virginia was opened with prayer by the Rev. Richard Buck, who was chaplain to Sir Thomas Gates, the first Governor of the Coloney, in 1610."

"Genesis of the United States," by Alexander Brown, says: "Richard Buck united in marriage John Rolfe and Pocahontas." In 1611 Rolfe writes of him as "a verie goode preacher." He was the origin of the Bucks in Virginia, Charles Buck, I., being the first in a direct line, and his three sons, as before stated, married the three Richardson girls, granddaughters of the Huguenot Marquis De La Calmes. Chas. Buck, III., was in Legislature in 1808-9, and Peter Buck in 1810.

———

Captain Nicholas Lafon was a Virginian who came to Kentucky as early as 1786 and made his first residence in Frankfort, where he engaged in real estate business extensively and amassed a nice fortune. Before leaving Virginia he married Maria Upshaw, daughter of John Upshaw and Mary Lafon. John Upshaw was a prominent and wealthy Virginian, and his sons held many important positions in the army, navy and state. His youngest son, Dr. William Upshaw, was a surgeon on the staff of General Wilkerson and fought a duel with General Winfield Scott.

Col. Nicholas Lafon retired from business in Frankfort, and about 1808,

moved to Woodford County, where he had a fine estate and owned a splendid brick mansion. This estate was on the Frankfort and Versailles road seven miles from either town. He called his country seat "Spring Garden." Captain Lafon not only engaged in practical farming, but took great pride in the stock that he bred and raised on the premises. He was one of Woodford's prosperous farmers until his death during the year 1836.

At the time of Captain Lafon's death, Richard Gilbert Jackson, who married Mary Virginia Lafon in 1825, *was living on a farm near Versailles, but he purchased the interests of the other heirs and moved his family to the Lafon estate. He was no less partial to fine stock than was Capt. Lafon and was quite as successful. He owned the famous race horse "Monmouth Eclipse" that attracted so much attention in the forty's, and his herd of Durhams was unsurpassed for that time.

Richard Gilbert Jackson died in 1852, and soon thereafter this home was purchased by Captain Elijah Fogg who died there about 1881, after which the splendid old mansion was razed, more than a decade ago.

The descendants of Richard Gilbert Jackson will appear under the sketch of the Youngs and allied families.

———

General Marquis Calmes was a distinguished Virginian who came to Woodford County about the same time that Col. Thomas Marshall came. 1 knew his kinsmen, George Calmes, of Lee County, and Marque Calmes, of Frankfort, but when I sought to inter-

———

*Afterward known as the Douglass Young farm, but later known as the Wade Hampton farm.

view them I learned that both were dead, and when I had despaired at getting in touch with any one who could give me satisfactory information, I ran across the sketch of the General written by Capt. John Andrew Steele some years ago, and by permission, I am appropriating it. General Calmes was a brother of Isabella Calmes who married William Richardson, Jr., the mother and father of the three Richardson girls who married the Buck brothers, spoken of in a previous sketch, hence the Buck brothers were nephews of General Calmes and were his neighbors as well in the county of Woodford. Captain Steele's sketch follows:

"One of the earliest settlers of Woodford County was General Marquis †Calmes, a noted Revolutionary soldier and Indian fighter whose name deserves honorable mention in the history of our State and county. He was born in Shenandoah County, Virginia, in the year 17—. He was of Huguenot ancestry, his father, the Marquis De La Calmez (Anglicised into Calmes) was a nobleman of wealth and culture who fled to America to avoid religious persecution and to find a home where he could worship God according to his belief and the dictates of his conscience. With many others of the same sect he landed first in Carolina, but finally located permanently in the valley of Virginia. There he married Lucy ‡Neville, said to be a lineal descendant of the Earl of Warwick, "the King Maker" of England, and reared a large family, the oldest of which was Marquis.

†For wife see pages 227-229.
‡See pages 21, 318, 363.

When young Calmes arrived at the proper age he was sent abroad to be educated, as was the custom of the wealthy persons of that period. During that time the war of the Revolution broke out and being deeply imbued with a love of freedom and liberty he hastened home, raised and equipped a company at his own expense, and as its Captain joined the third regiment of the Virginia line commanded by Col. Thomas Marshall, father of the great chief justice, himself an officer in the same command. As the battle of the Brandywine Col. Marshall was badly wounded, and Calmes, who had risen to the rank of Lieutenant Colonel, afterwards led the regiment with distinguished bravery. He crossed the Delaware with Washington, fought at Monmouth and other engagements and was at Yorktown when the combined forces of Washington and Rochambeau, assisted by the French fleet under Count De Grasse compelled the surrender of Lord Cornwallis, the result of which was the Independence of the Colonies.

It is related that upon one occasion he, single-handed and alone, captured three British soldiers. He had gone to a spring for water, and seeing them approach from the opposite direction concealed himself in the bushes. Upon reaching the spring and suspecting no danger they laid their guns aside when Calmes sprang forward like a tiger from his lair, seized their arms and marched them into the American camp amid the plaudits of the army. After the termination of the war, having heard of the great fertility and boundless resources of the country west of the Alleghenies, and filled with the spirit of adventure, he determined to seek a home in Kentucky, then the frontier county of Virginia. With a company of men he came down the Ohio river in keel boats to the mouth of Cabin Creek near Maysville, thence across to "Indian Fields" in what is now Clark County where he located a large body of land and raised a crop of corn. He soon after removed to Woodford, then a part of Fayette County, and located at "Caneland," adjoining "Buck Pond," the home of his old friend and comrade, Col. Thomas Marshall, where each built a brick house, among the first of the kind in the county (both of which are in a good state of preservation today).* Here for some years he was busily engaged in clearing land and improving his property.

When war was declared against England in 1812, he was again ready to meet his old enemy and promptly offered his services to his country. He was made a Brigadier-General and placed in command of the first brigade of Kentucky riflemen composed of the regiments of Colonels Trotter and Donaldson. He served with great credit during the arduous campaign at the northwest under Harrison and Shelby. He was with the army upon the invasion of Canada, and was present at the battle of the Thames which resulted in the death of Tecumseh and the defeat of Proctor, but on account of sickness, the result of hardship and exposure, he was not able to take an active part, but

his brigade was ably commanded by Col. George Trotter. After the conclusion of the war he returned to his fine estate, where, surrounded by a retinue of servants, he lived with his family in ease and comfort until his death, which occurred February 27, 1834.

His remains now repose by the side of those of his wife in a stone mausoleum, built with great care by his direction, and under his supervision before his death, about three miles east of Versailles and near the railroad from that place to Lexington. General Calmes was a man of striking and unique personality, nearly six feet in height and weighing over two hundred pounds, with blue eyes and fair complexion. His bearing was soldierly, his step lithe and active and his manner was courteous and elegant. He never abandoned the colonial customs of style of dress. He wore his hair in a queue and neatly tied with a black ribbon, a broad cocked hat, sweeping blue cloth coat with metal buttons, velvet knee pants, and stockings, and shoes with large silver buckles. Thus equipped he would ride to Versailles to attend county court, of which honorable body he was for many years a valued member. He owned a number of slaves and had them taught the various trades so necessary to the farmers of the earlier times. He owned his sawyer, carpenter, blacksmith and shoemaker and brewed his own whiskey and brandy, which he dispensed with a generous hospitality to his many friends and guests.

When Lafayette visited America in†

---

*Both were log, afterward weatherboarded.
†See page 362.

Home and Mausaleum of Genl. Mark Calmes

HOME OF BARTHOLOMEW DUPUY

1800

Son of John James Dupuy of Virginia, and brother of Olympia Dupuy, mother of Col. Ed. Trabue. The Wooldridges lived there many years, and John R. Darnell lived there at the close of the Civil War.

1825, he stopped in Versailles. He and Calmes had been warm friends during the Revolution, and the meeting between the two old soldiers was touching and pathetic as they embraced each other and wept like children. Sarah Calmes, a daughter of the General, headed a committee of young ladies to strew flowers in the path of the old hero, but Lafayette displayed his gallantry and greatness by walking around them instead of over them.

In early life General Calmes was happily married to Priscilla Hale, a lady of culture and refinement, to whom he was devotedly attached and whose death preceded his own some years.

As a disguise to his sorrow, nearly every year he built a boat at the mouth of Cedar Creek on the Kentucky river, and accompanied by a few of his friends and servants he sought the wilds of Arkansas to enjoy hunting, his favorite amusement, returning overland horseback. He was one of the projectors of the town of Versailles, assisted in laying it out and named it after the city of Versailles in France. He never sought political honor or preferment except in 1795 he represented Woodford County in the Legislature. He was essentially a soldier, and when the duties of that calling were performed he preferred the quietude of his home rather than the applause and heraldry often sought by others less deserving. Possessed of an ample fortune he was kind to the poor, respected and beloved by the neighbors. He was the father of nine children, five sons and four daughters, none of whom are now living. Not one of his de-

scendants is living in Woodford County today, but are scattered over different parts of this and other states. George W. Calmes, of Lee County, Kentucky, to whom the writer is indebted for valuable information, is a grandson.

"Caneland" was afterward the home of Col. Ezekiel Field and is now owned by the Dunlap heirs. The grand old forests of the Calmes manor have gradually disappeared before the relentless stroke of the woodsman's axe, and in their stead an expanse of cultivated fields is now to be seen, and few persons today, as they pass and repass, are conscious that beneath that venerable pile hard-by rests the remains of one whose life was guided by that spirit of patriotism which proclaimed to the world the Independence of America and which, as a citizen and soldier, he preserved untarnished to the day of his death.

———

The Rev. John Dupuy of Pocahontas County, Virginia, a Baptist minister, came to Woodford County about 1786, but some years later removed to Shelby County, Kentucky, where he died in 1831. His brother, Bartholomew Dupuy, Jr., married Mary Motley in Virginia, and came to Woodford County at the time the Rev. John came, but he only lived a few years after taking residence in the county, dying in 1790. His will, giving the names of his children and devising his estate, bearing date June 5th, 1790, is recorded in the office of the county court. His children who married in the county were, Joel, who married Lucy Craig; Nancy, who married Alexander McClure; Martha, who married Col. Abraham Owen, who lost his life at Tippecanoe, and Elizabeth, who married Mr. Fogg. There were eleven children in all. Joel Dupuy, son of Bartholomew, built a mill three miles from the old Grier's Creek Church and operated it for many years. The walls of the mill are standing, but I am under the impression that the roof has fallen in. I am told that Joel and his wife, Lucy Craig, afterwards lived on a farm that adjoins the Hart estate on Frankfort pike two miles out of Versailles, and that they died there. Elizabeth and Mr. Fogg also lived and died in the county, and I think he was a relative of Captain Elijah Fogg, the father of Mrs. Oakley Thompson of the county.

Mary Motley Samuels, a granddaughter of Bartholomew Dupuy and Mary Motley, married David Castleman Suggett of Scott County and the late Mrs. Sophronia Offutt, of Midway. Ky., was a daughter. Manly Offutt, of the Citizens Bank of Midway, is a son of Mrs. Sophronia Offutt.

The Dupuys were Huguenots and closely related to the Sublett, Trabue and Wooldridge families who came to Woodford County about the same time.

Daniel Trabue was born in Chesterfield County, Va., in 1760. At an early date he came to Woodford County, Ky., and settled on Grier's Creek, where he built his residence, and a mill, just across the creek from the home of Lewis Sublett. Before coming to Kentucky he had borne a conspicuous part in the Revolution, as had all of his kinsmen. His wife, whom he married in Virginia, was Mary Haskins, daughter of Col. Robert Haskins. He served as sheriff and justice of the peace and died in

1840. Some of his children settled in Louisville and have been, and are now prominently identified with the social, business and religious interests of that city. Others went South and West, and all have been prosperous and leading citizens wherever located.

Daniel was a Captain in the Revolution, was at Yorktown, served with General George Rogers Clark, under Lafayette and Muhlenberg. He died in 1840.

Col. Edward Trabue was a brother of Daniel and an officer in the Revolution. He, too, came from Chesterfield County, Va., where he was reared, and located in Woodford County about the same time that Col. Thomas Marshall and General Marquis Calmes came. He was born in 1762 and was just sixteen years old when he enlisted for service in the Revolution. When he reached Woodford County he decided to locate on a tract of land near Sublett's Ferry, about two miles from where Daniel had located, on a prominence that overlooks the village of Tyrone in Anderson County, and he built a spacious brick house that is standing today in fine condition. From the house you have a splendid view of the bridge of the Southern Railroad that spans the Kentucky river at Tyrone.

The Trabue home belonged to Sallie Neal during the Civil War, and for some years thereafter, but it is now the property of Willis Field, son of Col. Tom. The elevation at this point is very great and the view from the towering cliff is very pleasing, as the country that lies in the distance, in both Anderson and Woodford, is de-

HOME OF JOEL DUPUY

1800

Built on road from Shryocks Ferry to Munday's Landing road. It is in
fine condition today and nestles in romantic surroundings. He sold it,
however, and built another adjoining Hartland Farm, that was later the
home of Clairburn Nuckols.

After selling his home near Shryocks Ferry, Joel Dupuy built this on his
farm adjoining Hartland. It was the property of Clairborn Nuckols
about 1830 or 1840. The walls in both homes over three feet thick.
About 125 years old.

Home of Edward Trabue that overlooks Tyrone and a beautiful stretch of country in Anderson County. 150 years old. Present owner Willis Field.

cidedly romantic. On this farm Edward Trabue established and maintained a deer park, similar to the one that was maintained on the Hart farm, and remained there until a short period preceding the Civil War. Many of those ranges existed over the county early in the nineteenth century.

Edward Trabue was twice married, first to Martha Haskins in 1786; second to Jane Clay, a cousin of Henry Clay, in 1797.

Nancy Trabue, a daughter of the first marriage, married Asa Pitman, son of Ambrose Pitman, a Baptist preacher, who also came from Chesterfield County, Va. Asa Pitman was with General Harrison in the war of 1812, and as a prisoner was sent to Canada. After the war he returned to Woodford and engaged in business in Versailles. One of his daughters married Jesse Graddy Crutcher, who has a son, Richard Crutcher, now a resident of Frankfort. Another daughter married Rev. Zach Smith, who at one time was the State Superintendent of Education, and later wrote a history of Kentucky.

Charles Clay Trabue, born 1798, was of the second marriage. He served with General Jackson in the U. S. Army, and in 1820 married Agness Wood and lived in Woodford quite a number of years but finally moved to Missouri, where he served in the Legislature, and later removed to Nashville, Tenn., where he was elected mayor of that city. His grandson, Chas. Clay Trabue, is a lawyer of standing at the bar of that city today.

One of the daughters of Edward

Trabue made an oil painting of the lovely old home in Woodford, and I am told by one of his descendants that it is reverently preserved.

In 1810 Edward Trabue was the owner of ten slaves and had eleven members in his family. Several of these, however, were sisters. His mother, Olympie Dupuy Trabue, who lived to be 93 years old, was also a member of the family. She had fifteen children.

Edward Trabue died in 1814, and his mother in 1822. He and his two wives and his mother are buried in the family graveyard on the premises, and a monument erected in memoriam. He and his kindred, the Dupuys and Watkins families, were staunch believers in the Baptist faith, and many preachers were developed from these families.

Elijah Pepper, accompanied by his *wife, Sarah Neville O'Bannon, and his brother-in-law, John O'Bannon, came to Kentucky about 1790. In 1795 John O'Bannon, John Crittenden, William Whittington and John Jimms were appointed trustees of Versailles and in 1810 he, John O'Bannon, and. his wife were living in Woodford where he owned a farm and seventeen slaves. He was in the war of the Revolution.

Elijah Pepper and John O'Bannon built a distillery just below the big spring that gushes from a cave back of the court house in which they distilled whiskey in a limited way. This partnership continued for several years, or until Elijah Pepper bought a large tract of land seven miles below the spring on

---

*See pages 72, 248, 276, 305, 362, 387 for O'Bannons.

Glenn's Creek, when the partnership was dissolved. John O'Bannon continued the distillation of whiskey at Versailles. Elijah Pepper erected on his farm on Glenn's Creek a comfortable log house on an elevated slope above the creek that faces the Versailles and Millville road, and in the creek below he erected a distillery plant where he continued to manufacture "Old Pepper." The residence is still standing but in recent years has been weatherboarded. From its design you would understand it was built at a very early date to guard against attacks from the roving bands of Indians that infested the country for some years after they were driven westward from Virginia.

The distillery was small and only a few evidences remain of its existence, and they are within a short distance of the Labrot and Graham distillery, that succeeded the Pepper plant some years after the Civil War. On his farm he raised the grain that entered into the manufacture of his liquid product.

After the death of Elijah Pepper, his son Oscar took charge and continued the business of his father until about 1865. In the meantime the brands of "Old Pepper" and "Old Crow" had grown very popular, due largely to the fact that the elder Pepper had kept in his employ a highly educated Scotchman—a trained chemist—who was the distiller. The name of this Scotchman was James Crow, and* the famous brands that he distilled made a fortune for the Peppers.

Col. James Pepper, a son of Oscar

who was reared there, operated a distillery at Lexington, Ky., for many years very profitably, and Col. Robert Pepper, a nephew of Oscar, moved to Frankfort after the Civil War and engaged in the manufacture of whiskey there. Mrs. Charles Logan Railey of Lexington is a daughter of Oscar Pepper.

James Crow, who was an expert chemist, after years of experimenting, insisted that no more than two and one-half gallons of unadulterated whiskey could be produced from a bushel of grain, and I am persuaded that he was right. The departure from his rule was the beginning of the end of the whiskey business, culminating in the death of John Barleycorn in the year of our Lord, 1920.

Sarah Neville O'Bannon, wife of ‡Elijah Pepper, was a sister of Lieutenant Presley Neville O'Bannon of the United States Marine Corps who, in the war of Tripoli, led a detachment of marines on a six hundred mile march from Alexandria, Egypt, to Derne, arriving April 26, 1805. After the fortification had been shelled by the Hornet, Nautilus and Argus on April 27th, they were stormed by marines under Lieutenant O'Bannon, the Tripolitan ensign was hauled down, and for the first time the U. S. flag was hoisted over a fortress of the old world. In honor of this brave Lieutenant, Secretary Daniels named a destroyer, "The O'Bannon," during the recent world war.

John O'Bannon, 4th born; Presley Neville O'Bannon, of Tripoli fame, 5th

*See pages 42, 113, 181 and Supplement.
‡See page 387.

born, and Sarah Neville O'Bannon who married Elijah Pepper, 13th born of William O'Bannon and Ann Neville, the latter thirteen years of age when she married William O'Bannon.

John was a prominent citizen of Woodford County, coming to the county as early as 1790.

Elijah Pepper and his wife had a large family they raised in Woodford County. The following were four of their children: Elizabeth, who married Dr. John Sullinger; Samuel Pepper, who married Mahala Perry; Oscar Pepper, who married Nannie Edwards.

Samuel Pepper and Mahala Perry had: Susan Matilda, who married William Patterson; Sarah Elizabeth, who married Aaron Darnell; Robert P., who married, first Ann Kinkead, second Elizabeth Starling; Lena, who married Clay Hatchett, was a daughter by first wife. Louisa, daughter of Samuel and Mahala, married Joseph McCoun, and they lived in a large brick residence on Glenn's Creek opposite Elijah Pepper's residence.†

Oscar Pepper and Nannie Edwards had: Ada, who married Charles Logan Railey; Jas. E., who married Ella Keene (nee Offutt); Oscar, Jr., Thomas Edward, Mary Belle, and Dixie.

Col. William Steele was another of Woodford's pioneer citizens, loved and honored by all who knew him.* He was a soldier of the Revolution and came from Virginia to Kentucky not later than 1783 and settled in that part of Fayette County that afterward became Woodford. His name appears on the census of 1810 with a family consisting of nine persons, a possessor of much real estate and fourteen slaves. He located his land on the Kentucky river and built his residence half mile above lock No. 5. His line ran upstream from the lock to Edward Trabue's line opposite Tyrone, thence away from the river to Major Herman Bowmar's line near the† "Narrows," thence to the lock, which constituted a large body of land. His residence was erected of logs, afterwards weatherboarded, and was located at what was known for more than a half century as "Steele's Landing" just above lock No. 5.

From the very first of his citizenship he was thoroughly interested in every movement of any merit that stood for the county's advancement, and was usually found in the van of such movements. He was a member of the convention held in Danville in 1793 to frame the first Constitution of Kentucky, and also a member of the convention of 1799 held in Frankfort which shaped the second Constitution of the State. He represented the county in the Legislature in 1792, and he and Robert Alexander and a few other public spirited citizens were charter members of the Kentucky River Improvement Company, a corporation organized in 1801 to bring about improvements that would admit of better navigation, and it was mainly due to their efforts that the river was locked and dammed to a point that rendered the coal fields accessible.

Besides being a thorough-going busi-

†This was the farm upon which Sam'l Pepper and Mahala Perry lived and died.
*He married Sarah Bullock.
†A ridge between Buck Run and the Kentucky River below Lock No. 5.

ness man he was also a very charitable man, and it was said of him that no deserving person ever applied to him for assistance without being comforted.

He and his neighbors, the Raileys, had interests in salt works in Virginia, and Thomas Railey made annual visits to the old state on horseback for many years looking after those interests.

Col. Steele's daughter, Agnes, married Col. Zach White. He built a modern residence of large dimensions on an eminence some distance back of the old Steele residence, and for thirty years before, and several years after the Civil War, this interesting family embarked on a Kentucky river steamer each succeeding fall for a winter's sojourn on their Louisiana plantation, the boat docking at Steele's Landing in order that they might take passage. By the same means of transportation they returned each spring when campfires would burn for several nights at "Steele's Landing" in anticipation of the arrival of the steamer with Col. White and family, which was uncertain owing to the long route and the varying conditions of the weather.

Col. Zach White was a prominent citizen of Woodford County and at all times interested in the county's welfare. He was a member of the Legislature in 1840. His son, Zach White, Jr., was one of Morgan's dashing band of soldiers in the Civil War. No man in Woodford County ever claimed a wider circle of friends than he. He was sheriff of the county, but his health was so impaired during the war that he only lived a few years after becoming sheriff. He married Dolly Carter, one

of the lovely daughters of Dr. Jo. Carter. Dr. Thomas White, another son of Col. Zach, married Judith Walhn, a granddaughter of William Railey and Judith Woodson. They had a son, Dr. Phillip White, who died in Cincinnati in 1902.

Elizabeth White, daughter of Col. Zach and Agnes Steele White, married Dr. F. E. Morancey and they were the parents of Agnes Morancey who married Dr. John R. McKee; H. P. Morancey who married Nannie Morancey, and Emelius and Frank Morancey.

Jane Steele was a daughter of Col. William Steele and Sarah Bullock, his wife. She married Samuel Wilson and their residence was a large stone building on an eminence on the opposite side of Steele's branch that overlooked lock No. 5. There they lived unostentatiously to a ripe old age. Their children were: Anne Mary, who was the first wife of Charles Craig; Barbara, who was the second wife of Charles Craig, and Sallie who married William Woolridge. Charles Craig bought the old Herman Bowmar farm and lived there many years. It joined the Samuel Wilson farm and extended to "the Narrows." Will Wooldridge bought the old Sam Railey farm near Grier's Creek Church.

John Steele, son of Col. William Steele and Sarah Bullock, married Catharine Swann Railey in 1816. He was a member of the Legislature* in 1846. Their daughter, Agnes Wingfield Steele, married Thomas F. Thornton of Versailles in 1835, whose daughter, Susan Catherine Thornton, married Sandy Brown in 1856. He was

*See correction, page 62. And see page 251 for war record.

of a pioneer family and a popular citizen of the county for many years, but some years after the Civil War he and his family migrated to St. Louis. His children are now residents of St. Louis and Joplin, Mo.

About 1817 Col. William Steele turned his log house over to his son-in-law, Col. Zach White, and built a residence of stone on the elevation on the opposite side of Steele's Branch where he lived until his death in 1826. His family continued to reside in the stone dwelling, which he willed to his youngest daughter, Jane, who married Samuel Wilson. Col. William Steele and his wife, Sarah Bullock, were buried in the burial lot near the stone house, as were the remains of Samuel Wilson and his wife, Jane Steele. I think that several of Col. Steele's family were buried in the lot in the old orchard near the log house on the river, as were also members of Col. Zach White's family.

Lewis Sublett, the first of the name in Woodford County, was a son of Lewis Sublett and his wife, Frances Mc-Gruder of Chesterfield County, Va.† They descended from the Subletts and Dupuys, both of whom were Huguenots, and escaped from France during the period of religious persecution.

Lewis Sublett was born in Virginia in 1759 and died in Woodford County during the year 1830. When a boy he enlisted in the Revolution, acquitting himself with credit as soldier and a gentleman, and at the conclusion of his military service he returned to his home in Chesterfield County where he engaged in business. On March 5th, 1779, he married Mary Trabue, a sister of Edward, of whom I have already written, one of the fifteen children of John James Trabue and Olympie Dupuy. They arrived in Woodford County in 1783 in the company of many relatives and friends and settled on Grier's Creek in the neighborhood of Edward and Daniel Trabue. Here he built a two-story log house that is standing today in good condition, the logs joined together with wooden pins and the shingles were tacked on with wooden pegs. Several holes around the walls of the house were sawed into the logs for rifle use in case of attack from Indians.

At the mouth of Grier's Creek opposite Tyrone is where he established and maintained a ferry over the Kentucky river that was known for more than fifty years as Sublett's Ferry, but after the Civil War the ferry passed into possession of the Shryock family, and has been known as Shryock Ferry since. His wife, Mary Trabue, had several children before she died in 1792. Their names were William, born in Chesterfield County, Virginia, in 1780; James, born in Woodford County in 1783; Lewis Sublett, Jr., born in Woodford in 1787, and John, born in Woodford in 1790. Each of these boys enlisted in the war of 1812, and all returned except John, who lost his life at the battle of the Thames.

Some years after the death of his wife, Lewis Sublett, Sr., married Sarah Samuel, by whom there were several children, Samuel being the youngest,

† Many early settlers of Woodford County came from Chesterfield County, Va., as you will notice in this book.

and he was born in 1800. He inherited the home of his father and lived there during his entire life, dying about 1870, after which the property passed into possession of Dunlap Cotton, a kinsman, but it is now owned by ———— Wade.

Lewis Sublett, Jr., the third son of the first wife, married Susan Coleman in 1808, and they had several children, two of whom were Lewis III, and Thomas, both of whom lived and died in the county. Lewis the III. died about 1870. For forty years he was one of the best known and best liked men in the county, recognized as a leader in all of Woodford's worthy enterprises; also a leader in Masonic and fraternal circles, and he numbered his friends by the number of his acquaintances. His brother Thomas, who died a few years earlier, was also popular and well known, especially by the patrons of the postoffice where he was employed for many years preceding and after the Civil War.

Samuel Sublett, who was the youngest of the second marriage to Sarah Samuel, married Fannie Aynes, and both died in the home where he was born. They were the parents of: First, Elizabeth Sublett, who married Wm. Strother Hawkins, Jr. She died in 1919, 93 years old. Robert Hawkins, the present sheriff, is her son, and Mrs. Thomas Edwards, and Mrs. John Ed. Hawkins of the county are daughters. Second, Mary Sublett, who married Moses Hawkins, Jr. whose children are Mrs. John Trumbo, Mrs. Ephriam Lil-

lard, and Mrs. David Castleman. Third, Ann Sublett, who married James Keith Hawkins, whose sons were Thomas and Samuel Hawkins. Fourth, Belle Sublett, who married Wm. Strother McGinness, whose children are Woodford, Keen, James, and Matt Strother, who reside at Frankfort. Fifth, Arthur Sublett, who married Ruby McClure and they have several children who are residents of the county, among whom are Dr. Samuel O. and Frank. Sixth, James Sublett, who married Matt Cotton. Seventh, John Sublett, who married Catherine McGinness and have Lewis and several other children in Scott County. Eighth, Bettie, who married Thomas McGinness.

————

When Woodford County was separated from Fayette in 1788, it included in its boundaries much territory that afterwards became a part of Franklin when that county was established some years later. This body of land lay between Glenn's Creek and Elkhorn and included Frankfort and Leestown. Three prominent families who were residents of Woodford at that time owned at least half of this broad stretch of country up to, and including what is Jetts Station on the L. & N. railroad. They were John Major, Sr., ‡Nathaniel Sanders, and Senator Humphrey Marshall, all of whom had seen service in the Revolution.

————

*John Major, Sr., owned the tract of land that lay between the Georgetown and Versailles roads beginning at the

‡See page 223.
*See Supplement.

intersection two miles out of Frankfort and running to the county road intersection at Jetts. His commodious residence, which was destroyed by fire about 1840, was rebuilt by S. F. J. Trabue, who purchased the estate about that time. It was ever known as the "Weehawkin" estate.

†John Major, Sr., had a large family, some of whom settled upon portions of his estate, while others settled nearer Versailles, where they were residents for many years. Three of his daughters were: Frances, who married Nathaniel Thomson; Susanna, who married Robert Wooldridge, and Mildred, who married Powhattan Wooldridge, all of whom, at one time, were residents of Woodford. The eldest son, John Major, Jr., built an elegant brick residence in 1793 just back of the "Weehawkin" mansion, with only a garden separating the two homes, and soon thereafter he led to the altar Judith Trabue, sister of Edward Trabue, of whom I have written, and she was the youngest of the fifteen children born of the union of John James Trabue and Olympie Dupuy of Chesterfield County, Va. Thomas Major was another son of John Major, Sr., and he too, built a residence on a part of his father's estate at the intersection of the Versailles road and the L. & N. railroad, and he was soon thereafter wedded to Susanna Trabue, the fourteenth of the above mentioned family. James Major was still another son of John Major, Sr., and he built a splendid brick house on a part of his father's estate that is opposite the station at

Jetts, and adjoining the farm of his brother, Thomas. Within a hundred yards of the residence he built a brick cotton factory, the odd design of which attracts the attention of every one who passes, and he wonders what was the object of its construction. These buildings are in excellent condition today. These homes are now owned by the following citizens of Franklin County: S. French Hoge owns the home of John Major, Sr.; Judge E. C. O'Rear owns the home of John Major, Jr.; Col. Charles E. Hoge owns the home of Thomas Major, and Thomas Jett owned the James Major home until a decade ago.

*The first gathering of Baptists in this part of the State assembled at "Weehawkin," the home of John Major, Sr., in 1788, the year that Woodford County was organized, and at that meeting ways and means were arranged for the building of "The Forks Church," one of the most popular assembling places for that denomination in the State for one hundred years. They engaged the Rev. William Hickman, and as the congregation gave him a home close to the old church he served the congregation zealously during his entire life, and he kept a church record that has been the admiration of every one who has seen it. It was both unique and interesting, inasmuch as it not only was a roster of membership, and record of church business, but all passing events were noted. It was deemed so valuable that it was sent to Louisville for preservation.

Some of the Major family drifted to

---

†See pages 218, 223.
*See Supplement.

the West, others to the South, leaving but few of the name in Kentucky. The first wife of the late Isham Keith Hawkins was of that name and family and they have a grandson, Judge Isham R. Darnell, now a resident of Benkelman, Nebraska.

---

†Nathaniel Sanders was another of these early settlers of Woodford County, as before stated. He was a neighbor of John Major, Sr., and also one of the founders of the "Forks Church," and these two men were intimately associated in promoting civil and religious welfare in church and community.

His son, Lewis Sanders, was a lawyer of ability and Secretary of State during the administration of Gov. John Breathitt in 1832. He married Margaret Price and they were blessed with five handsome daughters, whose names were Jean, Susan, Edith, Laura and Ezza. Jean was the first wife of James B. Haggin; Susan married Loyd Tevis; Edith married Absalom C. Hunter; Laura married first, George Vorries, second James P. Amsden, and Ezza married Isham Railey, Jr. All of these men, except Mr. Tevis were citizens of Woodford County, some of them for a lifetime, others for a limited term of years, and many of their children and grandchildren are present residents of the county. Both Mr. Tevis and Mr. Haggin became multimillionaires through mining investments in states of the Pacific.

Senator Humphrey Marshall was the

third of these three neighbors who possessed such a vast body of land in Woodford in 1788, and who participated in the organization. His home was located near Leestown, one mile north of Frankfort, and his estate, I think, was bounded on the north by the Georgetown road, on the east by the Versailles road and on the south by the Kentucky river. I was informed that he disposed of much of this land in small tracts to settlers at prices that made him a rich man for that period.

He was a brilliant speaker and a man of rare ability, but was haughty to the extent of superciliousness. His character was always positive, and whatever he planned to execute was pressed with tenacity to the end whether victory perched upon his banner or not. He was indeed of such an irascible temperament that he was frequently involved in political and personal controversies that could only be settled upon the so-called "Field of Honor," and as a result, he very likely fought more duels than any other citizen of Kentucky. He hailed from Virginia, was an officer in the Revolution, married his cousin, Mary Ann Marshall, one of the daughters of Col. Thomas Marshall and his wife, Mary Randolph Keith.* In 1793, he represented Woodford County, including Frankfort and Leestown, in the State Legislature, and was a member of both branches of the Congress. He died July 1, 1841.

General James McConnell was a Revolutionary soldier who came to

Kentucky as early as 1781, during which year he was a lot owner in Lexington. Through the medium of a lottery company in 1789, he drew lots in the town of Cincinnati, at that time a budding town on the Ohio river. I am not sure as to the year he located in Woodford, but it was not later than 1788. The farm upon which he settled was located on the Munday's landing road, five miles out of Versailles, and one and a half miles from Mortonsville. The house that he built was a two-story brick that is standing today in good condition. Early in the 19th century a roving artist traveled through Woodford who possessed much merit in the way of artistic design and painted the walls of many residences in landscape and other gay, but attractive pictures. I recall particularly the homes of General McConnell, Charles Hiter and the old Jackson Williams dwelling back of "Bosque Bonita."

These walls were painted in many designs. Besides landscapes, there were quaint cottages, vehicles with horses attached, brooklet and river scenes with row-boats, sail boats and steamboats, and a score of lads and lassies in coquettish attire and attitudes and others too numerous to mention. The two front rooms of the McConnell home were especially attractive in design as well as execution and the expense bill was not a light one. I am told that these old paintings still retain much of their original charm and attractiveness.

General McConnell donated a corner of his farm to the Baptists of the vicinity upon which they erected a church, which still retains the name of "Hillsboro Church," given it more than a century ago, and much good and effective work for the Master has marked its course to the present time.

General McConnell, for a period of years, commanded the State militia when it was customary to go into camp for practice and discipline annually. These encampments were usually held on the farm of Col. William Hart in the woodland opposite what is now the Camden residence. In the room over the parlor in the McConnell home hung the uniform and sword of the General for several generations.

General McConnell married two sisters. His first wife was Elizabeth Viley, and after her death he married Maria Viley. Both of these girls were born and reared in Scott County and were sisters of Warren Viley who lived and died on the "Stonewall" farm now owned by J. Breckenridge Viley near Midway. By the first marriage was George McConnell, who married Margaret Hord; Robert, who married Mary Thompson, and Mary, who married Jerry Wilson. By the second marriage was James McConnell, who married Katharine Payne; Henry, who married Bettie Moss, and Mary, who married her cousin, George Burch.

George and Margaret Hord McConnell had Kate McConnell, who is now a resident of Versailes. Robert and Mary Thompson McConnell had: 1st, Eliza McConnell, who married W. Hawkins Cleveland, who had* Emma, William T., Kirtley, and Robert Cleve-

*James, who married Leonora Winn, and have Gertrude Farris, and Emily Cleveland.

†land; 2nd, Martha McConnell, who married William Hunter Railey, who had Randolph, James, William Hunter, Jr., Emma, Mary and Martha; 3rd, William Thompson McConnell, who married Mamie Carpenter; 4th, Robert McConnell, who married ———— Glore; 5th, James McConnell, who married Elizabeth Hunter.

Mary McConnell and George Burch lived in the old home of General McConnell after his death, and when they died it was owned by their son, Marion Burch, who resided there until his death in 1907, when the property passed from the possession of descendants and is now owned by J. S. Williams.

———

Major John Crittenden was born in Virginia in 1754 and was in the service of the Revolution from 1778 to 1780. Soon after the expiration of his military service he came to Kentucky and located on a farm within two miles of Versailles in 1782. In 1783 he represented the district of Kentucky in the Virginia Legislature, and in 1775 married Judith Harris, daughter of John Harris and Obedience Turpin, and granddaughter of Thomas Turpin and Mary Jefferson, a relative of Thomas Jefferson's father, Peter. It is not known whether he was married in Kentucky or Virginia, but his wife was born and reared in Virginia.

Major Crittenden was killed, I am told, by a falling tree on his farm about 1809, but the commission to make a division of his personalty among his several children did not act until 1813. This commission was composed of

Charles Railey, Joseph Kinkead and James Stevenson. In 1810 Judith Crittenden, the widow, was living on the estate and Absalom Ford lived on the premises and acted as overseer for many years. At the death of Judith Crittenden, it is of record that the admirers of John J. ‡Crittenden in the county purchased the estate and made that gentleman a present of it. About 1850 William Cleveland purchased it and lived there until his death when it was inherited by his son, W. Hawkins Cleveland, afterwards the property of William Cleveland, Jr., remaining in possession of this family for nearly three-quarters of a century. The elder Cleveland moved the log house of the Crittendens to another part of the yard and replaced it with a splendid brick residence. Both buildings are still standing and serviceable. Randolph Fishback has owned the place for several years. The farm is on the Lexington pike about two miles from Versailles.

But little has been written about, or in fact, known of Major John Crittenden or his antecedents owing to the fact, I am told, that the early records of New Kent County, Va., were destroyed by fire, and there it is said he was born.

A friend writing of John J. Crittenden in the Kentucky Register of 1905, Vol. 3, says: "His father was an officer in the Revolution and lived on a magnificent body of land in Woodford, famed for its richness and for its bluegrass. He came of gentle blood of

‡See pages 244-7 and 388.
†And James Cleveland.

Home of Gov. John J. Crittenden

ancestral distinction on both paternal and maternal lines."

Collins, in his history of Kentucky, is equally brief in his statements of Major John Crittenden. Speaking of John J. Crittenden, he says: "He was a son of John Crittenden, a Revolutionary officer who emigrated to Kentucky soon after the conclusion of the war. The character of the father may be judged of by the virtues of the children." Again Collins says: "By an act passed December 15, 1795, John O'Bannon, John Crittenden, William Whittington and John Jimms were appointed trustees to fill vacancies in the board of trustees for Versailles." That is all I find written of him.

All of the children of John Crittenden and Judith Harris were reared upon this Woodford County estate and educated upon what accrued from its resources. In 1810 the widow was reported as having five members in her family, the first four children being married or away from the county at the time, and she listed fourteen slaves. Their children, all born in the county, were: Harriet, born in 1786, married John H. Smith; John Jordan, born in 1787, died in 1863, married, first Sarah† Lee, second, Mrs. Maria Innes Todd, third, the widow of General Ashley, of Missouri; Thomas T., born in 1789; Margaret, born in 1790, married John McKinney; Henry, born in 1792, married Ann Maria Allen; Robert, born in 1793, married Anne Morris; Caroline, born 1794, married Randolph Railey, Jr., in 1822; and Lucy, born in 1795.

John J. Crittenden was with Gov. Isaac Shelby in the war of 1812, served in the Kentucky Legislature, in Congress, repeatedly in the U. S. Senate, Attorney General of the U. S. under both Harrison and Fillmore, and Governor of Kentucky. His son, George, by the first wife, was a General in the Confederacy; and Thomas, a General in the Union Army; Eugene, a son by the second wife, was a Major in the Union army. No issue by last wife.

Thomas T. Crittenden was at one time Secretary of State and for many years Judge of the Federal District Court of Kentucky.

*Robert Crittenden and his wife, Anne Morris, moved to Arkansas, where he became Territorial Governor, a leading light in the legal profession, and served the state in Congress.

Henry L. Crittenden and Ann Maria Allen, his wife, a daughter of Col. John Allen, of Shelby County, maintained a residence in that county from the time of their marriage and he died there a highly esteemed citizen. He was the father of William L. Crittenden, the martyr, who sacrificed his life on Cuban soil endeavoring to liberate those people from the Spanish yoke and establish a Republic in 1851. When requested to turn his back and kneel before the firing squad for execution, he replied: "A Kentuckian never turns his back to the enemy, and I kneel to none but my God," and died standing erect facing his accusers. His brother, Tom T. Crittenden, studied law in Shelbyville, moved to Kansas

†See Lees, Pages 53, 60, 195, 271.
*Also a son of second wife. See Supplement.
Note—The Crittenden home is now (1937) owned by the Methodist Church and used for an Orphans' Home.—J. T. C.

City, Mo., where he practiced in the courts until elected Governor of that state. Still another brother was Col. John Allen Crittenden who married Virginia Jackson of Woodford County.

Margaret Crittenden and her husband, John McKinney, resided in Versailles during the period of their married life. Their home was in the suburbs on the Lexington pike, after the Civil War known as the Childers' Home. I think John McKinney was clerk of the county court for many years. Both lived to be quite old and left no issue.

Caroline Crittenden and Randolph Railey, Jr., owned the farm that joined the Hart estate now owned by J. N. Camden, and they lived in the brick residence opposite the old tollgate, that is now owned by his daughter, Catharine Fishback, a daughter by a second marriage. By the first marriage were several children, but only one lived to years of maturity, John Crittenden Railey, who enlisted in the Mexican War, contracted a fever at its close from which he died en route home.

Caroline Crittenden and Randolph Railey, Jr., are buried in the Railey lot just beyond Boone's monument in the Frankfort cemetery. He was not only a brother-in-law of John J. Crittenden, but a second cousin of his (John J. Crittenden's) last wife who was a granddaughter of Major Josiah Woodson of the Revolution, an uncle of Randolph Railey, Jr.

Since writing the above I received the following clipping from the Wood-

ford Sun of January issue 1920: "The old Crittenden place that changed hands last week for the third time in three years, and which is to be cut into small tracts and sold again is one of Woodford's noted historic estates. It is a part of a tract of land acquired under a Revolutionary land grant* by Major John Crittenden of Virginia, an officer in the Continental Army, and settled by him in 1783, the same year that 'Buck Pond' was settled by Col. Thomas Marshall, the great-grandfather of Louis Marshall, its present owner. On this farm were born Major John Crittenden's brilliant and distinguished sons, John J., Thomas T., Robert, and Henry."

After the removal of the Crittendens from the county the farm became the property of Dr. John Watson, the grandfather of Commodore John Crittenden Watson of the U. S. Navy. It was owned by the Clevelands for about 65 years when Randolph Fishback purchased it several years ago.

———

Captain Virgil McCracken was a resident of Woodford County in 1810, the owner of a farm and seven slaves, his family small, consisting of three members. He represented the county in the Legislature in 1810, and again in 1811. Cyrus McCracken was his father who, with Hancock Lee, built cabins one mile north of Frankfort in 1782, and called the site Leestown, which village still retains the name and is now in the suburbs of Frankfort. Cyrus McCracken lost his life in No-

*Major John Crittenden's land was a grant under the Virginia Land Commission of 1779-1780, not a Revolutionary Grant.—J. L. C.
See Register 1923—Index.

HOME OF ALEXANDER McCLURE

1800

Great Grandfather of Dr. S. O. Sublett, who owns it today.

vember, 1782, while serving with General George Rogers Clark in an expedition against the Piqua Indians. His widow, Elizabeth McCracken, was living in Woodford County in 1810, her family at that time consisting of eight members, and her possessions were a splendid farm and seven likely slaves. The farm was on the McCracken's Mill road on Glenn's Creek about three miles from Versailles and afterwards became the property of Wiley Edwards, then his son Thomas S. Edwards, and later Thomas E. Henton owned it.

Captain Virgil McCracken, like all of his name, was an intelligent, patriotic and courageous citizen who was ever ready to fight for his country, in defense or offense, so in 1812, with the spirit and daring of his father raised a company of cavalry in Woodford and joined the regiment of Col. John Allen, of Shelby County, who led them to Detroit, Michigan, near where the battle of the "River Raisin" was fought, in which this regiment took a conspicuous part. His military career was brief, but brilliant, as he received a mortal wound in the fierce and tragic engagement at that point.

*Major John Lee was a Virginian who rendered service as an officer in the Revolution before coming to Kentucky. He was a kinsman of the family of Virginians by that name who have written their names high on the scroll of fame, and was an early settler in the county of Woodford. He was one of the several men who founded the town of Versailles, and always felt a keen interest in the progress of both

town and county, being a member of the first board of trustees, upon which he served for many years. He owned a home near Versailles, which I am unable to locate, but upon that estate he died just prior to 1810, at which time his widow, Elizabeth Lee, was in charge of the estate. There were eight members in her family at that time, and she owned twenty-six slaves that they kept busy on their large farm. Sallie Lee, one of their daughters, was the first wife of John J. Crittenden.

———

Alexander McClure came to Kentucky about the same time that the Trabues, Dupuys, and Subletts came in 1783, and with them cast his lot in Woodford County. He purchased a farm between Grier's Creek and Mortonsville, near the Sublett farm, and built upon it a large two-story brick house in which he and his wife lived and died. He married Nancy Dupuy, a daughter of Bartholomew Dupuy, Jr., and Mary Motley, she a kinswoman of the Trabues, a niece of Olympia Dupuy Trabue.

Alexander McClure was in the Revolution and his name appears on the 1810 census, where he reports eight members in his family and lists eight slaves.

His son, Abraham McClure, married Ann Christopher and they dwelt for a lifetime in the ancestral home. They were blessed with a daughter whom they christened Ruth, who married Arthur Sublett, a farmer of the county and for four years sheriff of Woodford. The children of the latter couple

are: Dr. Sam O. Sublett, Frank Sublett, and others who reside in the
county. Frank is domiciled in his
great-grandfather's old home, built in
1796, and it is in good condition today.
Hard by is the home of Bartholomew
Dupuy, and Lewis Sublett's home is
also close, all neighbors and friends, all
built about the same time and on the
McCowan's Ferry road not far from
Mortonsville.

Another interesting and historic old
home in the county is that settled by
Charles Wilkins in the vicinity of
Clover Bottom prior to 1790. The
original residence passed from view
years ago and was replaced by a more
modern dwelling. The property was
sold by Charles Wilkins, or his heirs,
to Francis Lea in 1839. Ten years
later Lea sold the estate to James P.
Ford, who built a residence of the
colonial type in 1856, but lived in the
original house for seven or eight years
before building.

The most interesting feature, and
historic too, is the old stone mill on
the premises that was erected during
the years 1796-7, the first grist mill,
perhaps, built in the county and many
of its patrons lived at a great distance.
This old mill is standing today and in
fair condition, I am told. Here I beg
pardon for digressing just a little in
order to mention briefly the career of
the builders. Thomas Metcalfe was the
architect and builder, one of the best
of his generation, being especially
skilled in stone masonry. Many stone
buildings and bridge supports are to

be seen today in central and northern
Kentucky that are monuments to his
skill. Though a citizen of Nicholas
County, the broad scope of his usefulness made him first of all a Kentuckian. In after years he gallantly served
his State and country in the war of
1812, was elected to the Legislature
from the county of Nicholas, where his
knowledge of the various qualities of
stone, and the purpose to which each
was best adapted, made him a useful
and valued member, as the State at
that time was seriously in need of, and
the several communities earnestly agi-
tating the question of better roads,
and as they had been moving without
compass or rudder—so to speak—
Thomas Metcalfe became the man of
the hour and was urged to formulate
plans whereby the State highways
might be improved. The result was
that he evolved a system that included
several varieties of stone that marked
an epoch in road building in the State,
that was afterward known as the
Macadam system. As a result, Thomas
Metcalfe was elected to Congress, then
to the United States Senate, and was
elected Governor of the State to serve
from 1828 to 1832.

This was a wonderful record for a
man who entered business life a stone
mason, crowning his career as Governor of his State, and lived four years
in the building whose foundation was
built under his supervision, a mansion
he did not dream he would occupy for
four years as the State's Executive.*
His life should be an inspiration to
young Kentuckians, and I especially

---

*He also built the old Watkins Tavern at Versailles owned by Henry Watkins, stepfather of
Henry Clay. See pages 183, 184.

commend him to the boys of Woodford.

Joseph McDonald is the present owner of this estate, and I trust the old mill will be to "him and hisn" a sacred trust.

The old Hart estate is also, for several reasons, both interesting and historic. It lies on the Frankfort and Versailles road one mile from the latter town, and has been for more than a century known as 'Spring Hill' farm. This tract was originally a land grant to Col. William Preston of Virginia, and contained about twelve hundred acres. When Col. Preston's daughter, Susanna, married Nathaniel Hart, Jr., in 1760, her father gave this splendid tract of land to her as a bridal gift, but it was many years before they attempted to settle upon it owing to the conditions that existed at that time, and prevailed for many years in Kentucky. However, Col. Henderson and Captain Nathaniel Hart, father of Nathaniel, Jr., headed a company of Virginians and North Carolinians to negotiate the purchase of Kentucky from the Indians, and after a long siege and frequent parleys with the chiefs, the purchase of Transylvania was consummated about 1775, the deeds executed, and the purchasers secured by an act of the Virginia Legislature in 1778. Soon after this transaction Daniel Boone, with thirty men, was sent into Kentucky and landed at Boonesborough, where they erected a fort, and the following April he was reenforced by Col. Henderson, Captain Nathaniel Hart and others. Captain Hart was the fifth son of Thomas Hart and Susanna Rice of Hanover, Va., and was born in 1734. He came to Madison County with Col. Henderson in 1779 and built a fort one mile above Boone's Fort at a point known as "White Oak Spring," where he located his family for safety. His wife was Sarah Simpson, and their children were as follows: Nathaniel Hart, Jr., who married Susanna Preston, daughter of Col. William Preston; Susanna Hart, who married Gov. Isaac Shelby while she was residing with the family in the fort; Chinoe, who was the youngest child and born in the fort, and several others. In 1782, while Capt. Nathaniel Hart, Sr., was riding in the vicinity of the fort a band of Indians surprised and murdered him. They were pursued by Boone and his comrades and captured. The camp was abandoned soon after this episode. Gov. Shelby and his wife went to Lincoln County, and Nathaniel Hart, Jr., and his wife, Susanna Preston, moved to their estate near Versailles. He built temporary quarters of logs for his family, where they were domiciled until 1805, when he built a commodious brick, and this splendid old colonial home, in due time, became quite historic, some of the leading men of both America and Europe being entertained there at different times. The beautiful woodland opposite the residence became noted as a camping ground where the militia of the State assembled for drill and discipline. The high stake and ridered fence that enclosed the woodlands before the Civil War attracted much attention and wonder. They were built to keep within bounds the several herds of deer that scampered over the bluegrass to the delight of visitors and those who passed by.

This home was always noted for its hospitality, and within its walls such men as General Lafayette, Thomas Jefferson, President Madison, Aaron Burr, General Winfield Scott, Henry Clay, John J. Crittenden, General Calmes, Thomas Hart Benton and General John Cabell Breckenridge were entertained.

This historic old home was destroyed by fire in 1899, and many heirlooms, relics and valuable paintings were consumed in the flames. However, Senator Camden, who married a daughter of Col. William Hart, and granddaughter of Nathaniel Hart, Jr., and Susanna Preston, was the owner at the time of the fire and he erected upon the same site a large residence equipped with modern conveniences, and of modern design, and his hospitality has been no less cordial and lavish than that displayed by former occupants.

The children of Nathaniel Hart and Susanna Preston were in part as follows: Letitia Hart, who married Arthur H. Wallace of Louisville, Ky.; Louisiana Hart, who married Tobias Gibson of Louisiana, and they were the parents of Col. Hart Gibson, who represented Woodford in the Legislature in 1867, and of Sarah Gibson who married Joseph A. Humphries of the county; William Preston Hart, who married Rebecca Tevis and had Susan P. Hart, who married Senator Johnson Camden, and they are the present owners of "Spring Hill."

Mrs. C. D. Chenault and Mrs. Lewis Johnstone are daughters of Joseph A.

Humphries and Sarah Gibson. They reside upon the Humphries estate on the Lexington pike not far from the Fayette line.

———

Captain Reuben Twyman, son of William Twyman and Winifred Cowherd, was born in 1758 in Madison County, Virginia, and died in Woodford County, Ky., in 1839. He married Margaret Griffin, born in 1763, died in 1835. He and his father and brother, William, served in the Revolution, and his father was a large land owner in Virginia.

Captain Reuben Twyman migrated to Kentucky in 1781, making his first lengthy stop at Fort Lexington. By inclination, as well as by habit, he was a prototype of Nimrod, and delighted in hunting and fishing and for several years after reaching Lexington he circled the country for miles to discover a locality best adapted to the indulgence of his inclinations, so about 1783 he located his home in Woodford County on the Midway road almost opposite Buford's "Bosque Bonita" and there he built his residence, a log house, and in a short time he had his family under its welcome roof. The house that is standing today, and at present owned by George McLeod, was built by his son, Joel Twyman very early in the nineteenth century and no trace of the log house remains. In selecting this site Captain Twyman was impressed by a large lake on the premises that tempted the feathered tribes as they passed to and fro in search of suitable climatic conditions for food supply, etc.; it was also a favorite resort for the roving deer that came to slake their thirst and refresh their bodies in the splendid body of water, and these surroundings furnished sufficient attraction for this Nimrod.

In the Revolution, Capt. Twyman was in General Lafayette's command and whenever that distinguished patriot honored America with a visit he never forgot Kentucky, whose citizens were proud to do him honor, nor did he forget Woodford County which contained so many of his old command as well as countrymen, and while remembering old friends and comrades like Calmes, the Trabues, Hart and others he did not forget his old friend Captain Reuben Twyman.

Captain Twyman came into possession of other large bodies of land in Woodford County and as his children married he would deed each several hundred acres, as is attested by the records of the county court.

The Twymans intermarried with the Bufords, Redds, Carters and other prominent families of the county. The children of Reuben Twyman and Margaret Griffin follow: Elizabeth, born in 1789, married Simeon Buford, Jr., in 1806, she died in 1877; Mildred, born in 1792, married Buford Twyman in 1811 (he a son of George and Ann Twyman of Virginia, born in 1791, died in 1835); Simeon Twyman, born in 1794, died in 1846, married Mary Walker Yancey, daughter of Capt. Robert Yancey and Elizabeth Holloway of the county; Joel, born in 1797, died in 1880, in Howard County, Mo., married Margaret Kirtley Buford in 1825; George, born in 1798, married Eliza Crutcher, granddaughter of Simeon

Buford and Margaret Kirtley; Colby Cowherd, born in 1800, died in 1863, married in 1829, Ellen Eliza Stone, daughter of Jacob Stone and Betsy Atwood.

For the children of Simeon Buford and Elizabeth Twyman see Buford sketch; same as to Joel Twyman and Margaret Buford who reared all of their children in Woodford County, but both families moved to Missouri before the Civil War and located near Glasgow. Their great-granddaughter, Mary Twyman, who married Paul A. Klayder, is compiling a history of the Bufords, Twymans, Yanceys and others at her home in Armstrong, Mo. I am indebted to her for generous favors.

Mildred Twyman and Buford Twyman had these children: George Ann, born in 1813, died in 1892, married Dr. John W. Redd; they had no children; Dr. Thornell Warwick, born in 1815, died in 1885, married Margaret Carter, daughter of Goodloe Carter; they had no children; Wilford Wirt, born in 1817, died in 1875; Joel Wayne, born 1818, died 1886, married Ellen Virginia Carter, daughter of Goodloe Carter and Mary Crenshaw; Broadus W., born in 1820, died 1894, married first, Elizabeth Craig, sister of Judge Ed. Craig, second Sallie Johnson, third, a widow, Lucy Blunt.

Joel Wayne Twyman and Ellen Carter had these children: Rudolph, born in 1843, entered the Confederate service and was killed in 1862; Mary Emma, born 1846, died 1897, married Capt. Ben C. Stevenson, who served in the Confederacy; Goodloe Carter, born in 1848; George, born in 1850, died in 1888; Abbie Virginia, born in 1852, married William H. Hiter; William Wirt, born in 1855, died 1891; Margaret, born in 1857, married Hubbard K. Ward; Buford, born in 1864, married Margaret Sanders Railey in 1888, and Mary, who married Thomas F. Baughman.

Broadus W. Twyman had several children by each of his three wives. By the first wife, Elizabeth Craig, was Buford Twyman, born in 1841, died in 1901, married Bettie Pieatt and moved to Louisville, where he practiced law until his death; W. Redd Twyman, who never married. He was reared by Dr. J. W. Redd and his wife, George Ann Twyman. He and Capt. Jo. Blackburn were law partners for many years in Versailles. Buford Twyman and Bettie Pieatt had two sons, Wilford and Allen Pieatt. The former was a Colonel in regular army and served in world war. The latter a lawyer, volunteered his services in recent war and was a Captain of volunteers.

B. W. Twyman, Jr., the millionaire automobile manufacturer, was a son of Broadus W. Twyman and his second wife, Sallie Johnson.

In 1810 Captain Reuben Twyman was reported to have five members in his family, a farm, and twenty-nine slaves. His brother, George, who come to Kentucky with Captain Reuben never married and lived with the family.

Simeon Twyman, son of Reuben Twyman and Margaret Griffin, had issue, all born and reared in Woodford County, as follows: William Henry, born in 1824, married Sarah Elizabeth Hale; Margaret, born 1825, died 1918,

married J. W. Bryant; Simeon Walker, married Mariah Fogel; Clifton, married Margaret Wallace; Mary; and Martha, who married Robt. Nowland; Venecia, born 1838, married Napoleon Wallace, and Robert Yancey Twyman.

———

Another Virginian who came with the early settlers to Kentucky and located in Woodford County was Lewis Hieatt who bought a farm on the Mortonsville road three miles from Versailles. Soon after the Revolution he married Barbara Allen and she accompanied her husband to Kentucky. In 1810 he possessed fourteen hundred acres of land, owned nineteen slaves, and had a small family for that period, consisting of four members. He built for his residence a comfortable log house which is standing today and doing service as a tenant house. While it hasn't the fresh appearance it possessed a century ago, there are no signs of early decay. They had but two children, Allen, who married Hannah* Moore, and Susan, who married Captain Samuel Berry.

At the death of Lewis Hieatt the home place fell to Allen Hieatt, and early in the nineteenth century he built a two-story brick residence near the log house in which he and his family resided. At the death of Allen his son, Harbin L. Hieatt became the owner of the ancestral estate and he married Annie Fox and reared a family of children there. Harbin died in 1898 and the property soon passed out of the possession of descendants, John McDonald's wife being the present owner. Benjamin Moore Hieatt of Midway,

Kentucky, is one of the sons of Harbin L. and Annie Fox Hieatt, and he is a prosperous farmer and successful business man. He married Jesse Belle Martin, daughter of Jesse Martin and Margaret Thornton.

That delightful old song "Barbara Allen," so popular in the long ago, was written in honor of, and dedicated to the wife of pioneer Lewis Hieatt. He and his wife were buried in the family graveyard on the premises, as were also those of all of his children, and many of his grandchildren. This burial ground is well protected by a strong stone wall or fence that surrounds it and it will stand the ravages of time.

Besides Ben M. Hieatt, the following great-grandchildren are residents of the county: Mrs. Susan Scearce Route, Mrs. Anna Belle Turner, and Miss Jennie Scearce.

———

*Col. George Muter was an early settler in Woodford County and like Judge Caleb Wallace, was both a farmer and a lawyer. Before coming to Kentucky he had served in the Revolution as an officer, and upon the expiration of his military service was complimented by his superior officers for his courage and demeanor as a soldier.

He was no less ambitious as a soldier than he seems to have been as a politician and lawyer. He held more offices in a limited period of years than any other citizen of that era. There were two conventions held at Danville in 1785 and he was a member of both. Also a member of the convention held

*See page 390.

there in 1787, each of these conventions having in view the bringing of Kentucky into Statehood, and their splendid efforts had such telling effect that statehood resulted five years later, several delegates representing Woodford in each of these conventions.

In 1785 Col. Muter was appointed one of the three judges of the first district court held in Kentucky. He was an elector and State Senator in 1792 and during that year was appointed Chief Justice of the Appellate Court, serving until 1806 when he retired. Soon after his retirement the Legislature passed an act granting him a pension in consideration of his long and faithful service, but the succeeding Legislature regarded such legislation a grave departure from usage, as well as a very bad precedent to establish, and repealed the act of the previous Legislature. The Governor vetoed the bill, but the Legislature, still viewing that character of legislation as dangerous, if not vicious, repassed the repeal bill over the Governor's veto by a constitutional majority.

In 1812 Judge Muter seems to have again donned the ermine as he was one of the several judges of the State Court. In rendering a decision in a land suit that was not popular he was bitterly condemned by the populace, and the Legislature that followed attempted to remove him and Judge Sebastian, who joined with him in the decision, from the bench, but was unsuccessful.

Judge Muter was in Woodford as early as 1783, and in 1810 he was entered on the county records as the owner of seven slaves and a farm, but as there was only one member credited to his household it is presumed that he died a bachelor or a widower.* I have not been able to locate the farm upon which Col. Muter settled, and of course can't say whether any building he erected is standing or not.

Judge Caleb Wallace was born in Virginia in 1742 and graduated from Princeton college. He came to Kentucky not later than 1785 and settled in Woodford County. In 1792, he was appointed Judge of the Appellate Court by Virginia officials, vested with that authority. He held this office until 1813.

The estate upon which he settled in Woodford County was within two miles of Midway on the road leading to Lexington, and he had his residence erected soon after the selection of the property. He also had erected in the yard, not far from his dwelling, a commodious room that was used as a law office, file room and library. It is said, and I do not doubt it, that the first court held in the county was held in this room, which, I am told, is still standing, as is also the residence, but the old law office is now used for housing servants. Col. John Withrow purchased this estate soon after the Civil War and resided there until his death in May, 1900.

†Judge Caleb Wallace, in 1810, owned this large estate and used twenty-four slaves in looking after the various lines of work. There were seven members in his family at that time. He was

prominent in the early affairs of the State and county, and he and his wife, Rosanna Christian, were always cordial in greeting and entertaining their guests. He died in 1814, after holding many positions of public trust, with the entire confidence and respect of the citizenship of the State and county. In addition to the public trusts heretofore mentioned he was a member of the conventions held at Danville, two in 1785, and one each 1787, 1788 and 1792, and of the convention at Frankfort in 1799. He was in Virginia Legislature in 1783 and presidential elector in 1797.

Samuel McDowell Wallace was one of the sons of Judge Caleb Wallace. He was reared in Woodford County and was the executor of his father's estate, but before his father's death Samuel's health became somewhat impaired and he moved to South Carolina in 1804 where he met and married Anne Maner, during that year. During the time of his residence in that State as a planter two sons were born, the first, Caleb, in 1806, and Samuel Baker in 1811. During the year 1814 his wife died and he returned to Woodford County, where in 1817 he married Matilda Lee, who was related‡ to the first wife of John J. Crittenden. He erected on the farm at Wallace Station, which was a part of his father's estate, an elegant brick residence where he and his family resided for many years. The farm is now owned by Henry L. Martin and is one of the most desirable homes in the county.

Samuel Baker Wallace was the sec-

*See sketch of Thos. Todd and family 390.
†See pages 248 and 249.
‡A sister. See page 197.

ond son of Samuel McDowell Wallace and Anne Maner. He was educated at Transylvania University, and after graduating, he returned to Beaufort, S. C., where he was born. He was a planter there for fifteen years and during that period he married Anna Taylor in 1831. In 1847 he returned to Woodford, bought‡ the old home of Thomas Bullock on the Versailles and Midway road that adjoins the farm of J. Breckenridge Viley. Here he spent the remainder of his life. Clinton Hawkins is the present owner of the farm. The wife of Samuel B. Wallace died there in 1874 and he died in 1894. They were the parents of the following children: Florence, who married the Rev. William H. Whitsitt; Edward, who married Lucy Graddy; Robert, who married Maggie Alford; Andrew, who married Jennie Layton; Annie, who married John B. Swope, and Eugene, who has never married. All of the children above named are now residents of the county except Mrs. Whitsitt, who is dead.

Judge Caleb Wallace descended from the Clan Wallace that had its origin in the "Highlands of Scotland." The emigrant was Peter Wallace, and his wife was Elizabeth Woods, also

‡See page 119

from the heights of Scotland. Peter settled in what was known as the "Back Parts of Virginia" in 1734. They had several sons, one of whom was Samuel Wallace, who married Esther Baker of Prince Edward County about 1739, and the eldest child of this union was Caleb Wallace, who was born in Virginia in 1742, and entered Princeton College in 1768. While a student of this institution he offered himself for the Presbyterian Ministry in 1772 and remained in the ministry for ten years in Virginia and New Jersey, then came to Kentucky in 1782, when he abandoned the ministry, adopted the law, which profession he practiced, when not on the bench, until his death in 1814. He was a firm believer in education and helped establish the following educational institutions: Washington and Lee, Hampden-Sidney and Transylvania.

I should have said earlier that Judge Caleb Wallace was three times married (data having come to me in scraps), first to Sarah McDowell in 1774; second to Rosanna Christian, the youngest daughter of Captain Israel Christian of Stanton, Va., and third to Mrs. Mary Brown of Frankfort.

Samuel H. Wallace was in the Legislature in 1835.

WOODFORD COUNTY

By W. E. Railey

PART THREE

Corrections of May Register and Inquiries.

In the May Register, page 85, col. 1,* I say that John Steele, the son of Col. William Steele and Sarah Bullock, was a member of the Legislature in 1846. This was an error. It was Col. John Steele, the grandfather of Captain John Andrew Steele of Midway, who served Woodford County in the Legislature of 1846.

In the Blackburn sketch of May I represent William Berry Blackburn as a brother of the pioneer, George Blackburn, when in fact he was a son, as will be shown in the January Register.†

I would be glad to get data relating to the Holloway family of Woodford County. I have written to as many as thirty persons without satisfactory results. This was a fine family and I am sure some one, some where, has had pride enough to record the facts and names. I would regret the failure to mention this family.‡

Leonard Israel Fleming was born in Staunton, Virginia, in 1764, and died in Woodford County in 1845. He came to the county and settled not later than 1790, locating his farm one mile out of Midway on the Georgetown road, and built his abode a half mile from the road at a point that overlooked beautiful Elkhorn and its picturesque surroundings. His estate was a large one, extending across the stream into what afterwards became the county of Scott. After his death that part of the estate that included the residence was purchased by the Leavy family, one of whom was Captain Samuel Leavy, that whole-souled gentleman of blessed memory who lived there for nearly a lifetime. The old house, built more than a century and a quarter ago, is still habitable and was splendidly arranged for protection against intruders of that period.

In 1810 Leonard Israel Fleming owned twenty-four slaves who looked after the various departments of farm work and his family was composed of nine members. Of this large family of children, all married and settled either in the vicinity or in neighboring counties. One of his sons, William

*See page 44.
†Pages 34 and 175.
‡See pages 176, 211, 214.

Bowyer Fleming, who married Agnetta Van de Graff, of Scott County, inherited the farm, owned for years by John Cooper, and lived there and reared a family on the estate. Their children were Leonard Fleming, Abraham and Judge William Bowyer †Fleming, Jr. Abraham Fleming was at college preparing himself for the Presbyterian ministry when he became ill and died unmarried; Leonard Fleming married Katherine Lewis and had three children, Clarence, Adah and Elizabeth. Clarence married Cora Wood and died without issue; Adah married John Graham and they reside upon the old Marvin place on the Lexington pike opposite the orphan school. They continue that proverbial hospitality so characteristic of her ancestors. Elizabeth died unmarried before she reached the full blossom of womanhood.

Judge William Bowyer Fleming, Jr., graduated from one of the best educational institutions in the country, adopted the law as a profession, moved to Louisville where he practiced at that bar for a long period. He represented one of the districts of that city in the Legislature during the sessions of 1879-80 and 1881-2. ‡He was one of the electors at large on the Democratic ticket in 1884, was appointed by President Cleveland a Federal judge of New Mexico in 1885; was State Railroad Commissioner 1888-92; was associated with legal department of the U. S. Treasury 1893-96; was appointed by William Jen-

nings Bryan Foreign Trade Adviser in 1913, and later was "Adviser on Commercial Treaties" in the State Department, in which capacity he was engaged when death overtook him in 1918.

In 1870 he was married to Susan Harris, daughter of Major Arnold Harris of the regular army, who owned a residence on the eminence opposite the orphan school, where his family lived for many years prior to the Civil War. He and his wife died in 1918, only a few days separating the two events. They left several children, most of whom are married and living in Louisville. Major Gen. Adrian S. Fleming, of the regular army, who saw duty in the recent strife between the great countries of the world, is a son.

The first of this branch of the Fleming family in America was Col. William Fleming,* a native of Scotland and a graduate of Edinburgh University. He entered the British army as a surgeon and came to Virginia in 1755 where he immediately attached himself to Washington's regiment as a Lieutenant; was Captain in 1762, promoted to Colonel of the regiment in 1774; was at the battle of Point Pleasant where he was severely wounded.

He was a land commissioner of the district of Kentucky in 1779, acting Governor of Virginia during the year 1781. His home was at Staunton, where he and his wife, Anna Christian, (my recollection is that she was a relative of the second wife of Judge Caleb

†See Supplement.
‡He nominated William E. Railey for Sergeant-at-Arms H. R. 1881-2.
*See page 376.

Wallace) resided. Their son, Leonard S. Fleming, married Mary Bowyer and they were the parents of Leonard Israel Fleming, the pioneer in Woodford County. I endeavored to link kinship between this pioneer and Charles Fleming of New Kent County, Va., who was the ancestor of so many prominent families in Kentucky, Missouri, Arkansas and other states of the South and West, but was unable to do so, yet I am sure they were related.

Agnetta Van de Graff, who married William Bowyer Fleming, Sr., was born in Scott County in 1810. She was one of the daughters of Abraham Sebastian Van de Graff and "pretty Jane" Steele, daughter of Captain Andrew Steele of Fayette County. Abraham S. Van de Graff was born in Ceylon, where his father was Governor in 1762. After serving the government of Ceylon for a number of years as Secretary he emigrated to the United States, landing at Philadelphia in 1798, but removed to Scott County, Kentucky, in 1800.

Lewis Castleman was a native of Hampshire County, Virginia, afterwards changed to Clark County. He came to Woodford County and settled on a farm on Clear creek about 1790, and the residence that he built was within four miles of Versailles. After getting his farm in condition for easy cultivation, and erecting an abode for the comfort of his family, he proceeded to build on the premises a tannery and a distillery. Out of the proceeds from these two interests and what ac-

crued from the farm, he amassed a comfortable fortune for that day and time. He called his country seat "Old Mansion," and it was ever an attractive and hospitable home, a kind of gathering point for neighbors and friends to meet and discuss the conditions that existed, and in that light to forecast the future.

In 1819 Lewis Castleman had, besides his large farm, his tannery and distillery, eighteen slaves to operate all, and they were operated in a business way and at a good profit.

He and his wife, Jemima Pearsall, whom he married in Virginia, lived on this estate to a good old age and their remains were buried on the premises. The old tannery vats could be seen as late as the Civil War, but I am not sure that there is any trace of them now.

He confined the product of his distillery to the manufacture of pure apple brandy, never allowing John Barleycorn to be introduced on the premises.

To them were born eight children, whose names, together with the names of their wives and husbands,* follow: Jemimah Castleman married Silas Douthitt; Elizabeth married William Suggett; John married Fannie Gatewood; Lewis married Ann Dudley; Jacob married Sarah White; Sarah married Moses Hawkins, Jr.; Kesiah married Gabriel Tandy, and David Castleman married, first, Mary Breckinridge, second, Virginia Harrison.

The descendants of Jemimah Castleman and Silas Douthitt are in Henry County, a son having represented that

---

*See pages 220, 252, 266.

county in the State Legislature about 1877-8 whose name was also Silas.

Elizabeth and William Suggett have descendants in Scott County.

John and Fannie Gatewood have descendants in Gallatin County, Eldridge, Lewis and Henry Clay being grandsons. David E. Castleman, a lawyer practicing at Covington, but residing at Erlanger, is also a grandson. He married Lee Hawkins, who was a daughter of Moses Hawkins III. and Mary Sublett, and Moses Hawkins, III., was a nephew of Moses, Jr., who married Sarah Castleman.

Jacob Castleman and Sarah White lived at "Old Mansion" after the death of his father, Lewis, and their son George Clinton Castleman, who married Mary Torbit, bought it at the death of his father and lived there many years. Their son Samuel Castleman, of Louisville, was born and reared there.

Jacob Castleman was a Brigadier General in the War of 1812.

Sarah Castleman, who married Capt. Moses Hawkins, Jr.,* of Woodford County, son of Capt. Moses Hawkins and Susanna Strother, lived in Woodford county, owning a farm and a gristmill about five miles from Versailles. In 1810 he reported a family of eight members and possessed seven slaves. I think McDaniels owned the farm and mill after the death of Moses Hawkins, which occurred in 1817. In 1832 his widow sold the farm and with five of her seven children moved to Palmyra, Mo. The other two children, I think,

had already gone to Georgia to live. Their descendants are numerous and prominent in northeast Missouri, Mrs. Lela G. Wright, of LaBelle, being one of them.

I feel quite sure there are in Carroll County descendants of Kesiah Castleman and Gabriel Tandy.

David Castleman, as stated, married Mary Breckenridge, then Virginia Harrison. Two of his sons, Major Lewis Castleman and General John B. Castleman, were brave Confederates. Major Lewis Castleman lived at Frankfort for many years and married Susan Mary Herndon. General John B. Castleman lived at Louisville for many years and married Alice Barbee. Their daughter, Elise, married Elmer Railey, son of Charles Logan Railey and Adah Pepper.†

The wife of Judge George B. Easton, of Louisville, was a sister of General John B. and Major Lewis Castleman.

The old home that has sheltered the Waits family for more than fifty years has rather an interesting history. It is situated on the old Frankfort and Lexington road, better known for more than a half century after the organization of the county as "Cole's road." It is three miles from Midway and about the same distance from Old Harmony Presbyterian Church, that is now, and has been for years, the property of the Baptist denomination.

In 1782 Richard Cole, Sr., came from Pennsylvania and located upon this farm. He was a prosperous, painstak-

---

*Captain Moses Hawkins, Jr., was in War of 1812 and served as Captain in 9th regiment. (See "Commissioned Officers" in Ky. Hist. Society, page 227.)
†And their son, David Castleman, married Adah Railey See page 262.

ing farmer and soon erected a large building on the premises that was only a short distance from the road that not only housed his family, but was also used as a tavern to accommodate the traveling public, that road, at that early day, being the main thoroughfare from Maysville and Lexington to Frankfort and Louisville. Such men as Henry Clay and John J. Crittenden often stopped there for rest and refreshments on travels through central Kentucky in the behalf of clients and the promotion of their political interests. The vicinity was known as "Sodom," the reason for which I cannot give unless I should say that it was a rendezvous for the assembling of the politicians of Franklin, Scott and Fayette counties in order that they might "hob-nob and prognosticate" with their Woodford County friends on the state of the union. At that time Midway was not on the map and all gatherings of the clans in that end of the county was either held at Cole's tavern or Offutt's crossroads.

Richard Cole, Sr., was born in Pennsylvania in 1729 and died in Woodford County in 1814. His wife, Ann Hubbard, was also born in that state in 1730 and died in Woodford in 1795.

In 1810 Richard Cole was reported to have two members in his family and to be the owner of five slaves. At the same time Richard Cole, Jr., his son, reported ten in his family and had three slaves to his credit. He too was born in Pennsylvania in the year 1763, and died in Woodford County in 1839, regarded as one of the county's wealthy men. His wife, whose first

name was Sallie, last name not known,* was born in Pennsylvania in 1765, and died in Woodford County in 1836.

When the county was first organized Richard Cole, Jr., was made a constable but was never in any sense an office seeker. His sale bill is on file in the county court records at Versailles and it is said to be a most interesting document.

Richard Cole, Jr., had three daughters, among other children, that I will mention. Pollie married Elijah Finnie; Elizabeth married Thomas Martin, and Sallie married Henry Lewis. Henry Lewis and Sallie Cole were grandparents of the wife of Howard Gratz of Lexington, and Henry Lewis was an uncle of the late Mrs. Leonard Fleming of Midway.

Thomas Martin, who married Elizabeth Cole, was born in Stafford County, Virginia, in 1792, and came to Kentucky with his father, Lewis Martin, in 1808. He was a member of the Presbyterian Church at Harmony in 1836, made a ruling elder in 1845, moved his membership to Midway when the Harmony Church was purchased by the Baptists and was an elder at Midway until his death in 1884. He was the father of the late Jesse Martin of Midway who was born in 1823, and for more than fifty years was one of the best known farmers and stock traders in the county. He lived for many years on the old George Carlisle farm that lay between Wallace Station and Midway, an equal distance from each point, on the Versailles pike. He married Margaret Thornton in 1847, who was a daughter of John Thornton, a native of Ireland, who resided in

*Sallie Yates, see page 253.

Pennsylvania before coming to Kentucky. Jesse Martin and Margaret Thornton had these children: Henry L., Matt, Mary, Thomas, Margaret, and Jesse Belle.

Henry L. Martin was born in 1848.† He has always maintained a residence in Woodford, but has spent much of his time since the Civil War in New Orleans, where he had an interest in a corporation dealing in live stock, especially mules; also had a plantation there and was interested in the sugar industry. He owns one of the most desirable farms in the county and the splendid residence upon it was built by Samuel McDowell Wallace in 1817 and is one of the best in the county, standing upon an eminence on the Lexington pike that is in plain view of Wallace Station. His wife is a daughter of the late Col. John J. Stephenson of Tennessee. They live in style, yet not ostentatiously. He is a wealthy and useful citizen, ready at all times to help promote any worthy undertaking. He served his district in the State Senate from 1893 to 1896, received the support of the sound money men for U. S. Senator during the session of 1896, is a director of the Citizens Bank of Midway and has been its president since its organization nearly forty years ago. He entered the service of the Confederacy when only fourteen years of age and for eighteen months was a scout, a position that puts brave men to the test as it not only requires courage, but good sense and quick judgment as well. The company with which he fought so gallantly and so long was almost annihilated during the four years of strife, only six of them returning to their homes and their families. He was captured at the bloody engagement at Cynthiana, Ky., where so many of our brave boys were either maimed for life or killed outright. He remained a prisoner until exchanged in March, 1865, and was paroled in June. His children are: Jesse Vick, Margaret, Mary, and Henry L., Jr. They are, however, children of a former marriage to Kate Brooks.

Jesse Martin, the father of Henry L., Sr., was also in the service of the Confederacy for three years, returned to his home after the conflict and farmed until his death in 1904. He attained to the rank of Captain. His daughter, Mary, married H. Clay Poynter; Jesse Belle married Ben M. Hieatt; Mat and Margaret are residents of Midway.

Thomas Martin and Elizabeth Cole had another son whose name was James W. Martin, who married Eliza McCoy, daughter of Daniel McCoy and Jennie, his wife, who came to Woodford County after the War of 1812 from Virginia and settled on a farm on the Georgetown road about three miles out of Midway adjoining the Buck farm, and has always been known as the Cable farm. James W. Martin and Eliza McCoy had a son, Thomas Martin, who married Mary Esther Myles. His daughter Sallie resides with him in Midway, and though he has reached an advanced age, his mind is clear and his physical condition only slightly impaired.*

An interesting and quaint old place

†See page 376.
*See page 253 for additional history.

in the county is now in the suburbs of Versailles, just beyond the cemetery on the Nicholasville pike. Its approach is through a long and narrow avenue, the residence being quite a distance back from the street. For many years the family of Hubbard Ward made this charming old home their abiding place, but it was the pioneer home of William Hunter and his wife, Mary Stewart, who came from Virginia at an early date with a company of emigrants. The dwelling is of the early type and the surroundings delightfully pleasing at that time. William Hunter was dead before 1810 and his widow was conducting the farm at that time. Several children blessed the union and they were in the home with the mother when the census of that year was taken, and four slaves attended to the various duties of the farm. At that time Versailles was but a village, and this home was nearly or quite a mile from the court place.

William and Mary Stewart Hunter had a son, William Stewart Hunter, who owned a farm one mile out of Versailles on the McCracken's Mill, or Glenn's Creek road, opposite the George T. Cotton place. It adjoined the Randolph Railey, Jr., farm on the Frankfort road opposite the old toll gate. He married Catherine Canfield, and of this union the following children were born: Mary, who was the second wife of Randolph Railey, Jr., William Stewart, Jr., who married Mary Brown; Elizabeth, who married John Brown; James, who married Harriet Peters; Catherine, who married Swift Darneal; Ab. C., who married Edith Sanders, and Belle, who never married.

Ab. C. Hunter and Edith Sanders were married in 1857. He was born in 1826, educated at the Kentucky Military Institute near Frankfort, served in the Mexican War in the company of Captain Thomas F. Marshall. He always took an active part in politics and the business affairs of the county and was a prominent member of the Masonic fraternity. He spent his entire life upon the estate of his father, whose country seat was known as "Dupont." He died there in 1883. His widow lived there for years after his death and it is now in possession of one of his sons. The following were born to Ab. C. Hunter and Edith Sanders: Margaret, Catherine, Lewis. Gennie H., Ab. C., Jr., Loyd Tevis, Swift Darneal, William S. and Hugh.

Swift Darneal and Catherine Hunter had no children. He was for more than twenty years clerk of the Woodford circuit court; represented the county in the legislature in 1881-2, after which he retired from active business. His home was upon the site now occupied by Margaret College.

Randolph Railey, Jr., and Mary Hunter had the following children: Randolph married Sallie Thornton; Emma married the Rev. Alexander Henry; Catherine married George M. Fishback; Isham married Ezza Sanders, and William Hunter Railey married Martha McConnell. The children and grandchildren of Catherine Fishback, Isham and William H. Railey are residents of Woodford County. George M. Fishback and Catherine Railey had these children: Emma Woodson married Rev. M. V. P. Yeaman; Jane Lyle married LeGrand Atwood; Ezza Railey;

George Taylor married Elizabeth Bowmar; Catherine Mary married J. F. Stone; Randolph Railey married Cyrene Hunter.

Rev. Alexander Henry and Emma Railey had Mary, Randolph, Rev. Alexander, James, Margaret and William.

Isham Railey and Ezza Sanders had, Margaret Sanders married Buford Twyman; Morton S. married Ida O'Bannon; Mary Stuart married Ben W. Williams; Louise Sharon married John McConnell; Sue Tevis; Edith Hunter; and Lawrence Amsden Railey married Josephine Marshall.

William Hunter Railey and Margaret McConnell had Randolph Woodson; Robert McConnell; William Hunter, Jr., married Mary Lane; James married Gladys Blair; Mary married R. F. Given; Martha married P. Railey Macey; and Emma.

William Stewart Hunter represented the county in the legislature during the following years: 1812, 1813, 1814, 1815, 1817, 1818 and 1820.

There was an Absalom Hunter living in Versailles in 1810 who had a family of three and one slave, but I have been unable to find out the relationship, if he bore any to the first Wm. Hunter of the county.

---

*The Kinkeads (originally spelled Kincaid) were from Scotland, the family seat being in Stirlingshire, as was also the origin of the name, and is one of the oldest in Scotland, as shown by the following taken from Nisbit's Heraldry: "The Kincaids were in possession of Kincaid in 1280 as is proven by a charter still in existence. Kincaid, Laird of Kincaid, of Stirlingshire, for his gallant service in rescuing the castle of Edinburgh from the English in the time of Edward I., was made constable of said castle, and his posterity enjoyed that office for a long period, carrying the castle in their armorial bearings in memory thereof to this day." "Kincaid, according to good English authority, means Head of a Hundred."

The first of the Kincaids in America was the father of Thomas Kincaid who settled at Carlisle, Penn., in 1707. Tradition says that the grandfather of Thomas renounced the Lairdship during the Revolution of 1688 on account of religious convictions and went to the north of Ireland. I have not been able to ascertain the first name of either the father or grandfather of Thomas Kincaid of Carlisle, Penn. Thomas drifted to Augusta County, Va., in 1747, and died there in 1752. This fact is established in a bill in chancery for William Kincaid, a minor, by his next friend, James Lockhart, to recover some land left by Thomas to William, his oldest son.

The above William Kinkead (the method of spelling adopted by him and continued by his descendants) was born at Carlisle, Penn., in 1736 and lived in Augusta County, Va., from 1747 until after the Revolution. He married Eleanor Guy of Virginia in 1756, who was of Scotch-Irish extract. He was a volunteer in the expedition commanded by Col. Bouquet against the Ohio Indians in 1764. In 1765 he

*See page 341.

bought a tract of land from Samuel Hodge on the Great Calf Pasture River, in Augusta County, where he resided until he removed to Kentucky. He served in the Revolution as a Captain of Virginia militia in 1777, and again in 1781. In 1789 he sold his country place in Virginia to William Alexander, father of Sir William Alexander of England, and removed to Woodford County, Ky., where he purchased the beautiful estate known as "Cave Spring." There he lived until his death in 1820. The property is now owned by the widow of John B. Swope, and adjoins "Loto Wano," the beautiful home of Lister Witherspoon on the Midway pike, three miles from Midway, and four from Versailles.

Captain William Kinkead, and his wife Eleanor Guy, had twelve children, all of whom were born in Virginia. Not naming two who died in infancy, the children were: Margaret, Andrew, Isabella, Agnes, William, Eleanor, Susanna, Guy, Rebecca and John. John, who was the youngest of the children, was given the home place. He married Margaret Trotter Blackburn, daughter of George Blackburn and Prudence Berry, of Blackburn's Fort, Spring Station. To this union were born William Berry, George Blackburn, Francis, Prudence and Eleanor Kinkead. Judge William Berry Kinkead moved to Lexington where he married Elizabeth Fontaine Shelby, daughter of Thomas Hart Shelby, and great-granddaughter of Gov. Isaac Shelby. Miss Elizabeth Shelby Kinkead and Judge George Blackburn Kinkead, of Lexington, were born of this union.

Judge William Berry Kinkead was an eminent scholar and jurist, and was active in behalf of Lexington's public affairs for many years before his death, and was a man of lofty traits of character.

Nearly all of the Kinkeads were out of the county at the conclusion of, if not prior to the Civil War, and I am inclined to the opinion that none are in the county now.

George Blackburn Kinkead, Sr., married Elizabeth Pearce, daughter of James Pearce, of Louisville, whose wife was a niece of Gen. George Rogers Clark.

———

In writing of the Youngs and allied families of Woodford County, I will first take up Col. Richard Young who was a native of Farquhar County, Va. During the year 1783 he moved to Kentucky and settled in what was then Fayette County. His wife, Mary Moore, was also a Virginian and accompanied her husband on the long and perilous journey to this State.

When Woodford County was formed in 1788 out of Fayette, his farm, which was near Versailles, was in the new county and he was ever active with friends in placing the county upon a high plane of development.

He was a member of the Danville convention of 1792 that framed the first Constitution of Kentucky, was a member of the first legislature that assembled in 1792 under that Constitution, and was consecutively elected to that body until 1803, which continuous service was a recognition of his ability, and a distinct acknowledgment of his popularity.

The town of Versailles was founded

by General Marquis Calmes, Col. Young, Major John Lee, Cave Johnson and John Watkins in 1792, and they constituted the first board of trustees of the town. General Calmes, whose father was a French Huguenot, had the pleasure of naming the town after the French town of that name.

Col. Young actively supported every movement that had in view the success of the Revolution, and also the War of 1812, and his name should be upon the honor roll. In 1810 his family consisted of four members and he owned twenty slaves that he used on his large estate. His death occurred in his home near Versailles in 1815. His sons were Richard M., Merritt and A. G. Young. His daughters were the wives of Henry Lee, Benjamin Vance, Francis Johnson and John Jackson. His daughter Alice married John Jackson in 1792. He (John Jackson) was a prominent merchant of Versailles from its organization until his death. He was a native of Scotland, and Judge Cave Graves, of blessed memory, speaking of him, said: "He was a man of education and rare business capacity."

John Jackson and his wife, Alice Young, had several sons and daughters who grew to man and woman's estate. One of their daughters, Maria Jackson, was the first wife of Douglas Young,‡ who, for fifty years or more, lived on the farm afterward owned by Samuel Hampton on Griers Creek or Shryocks Ferry pike, two miles out of Versailles, and it was the home of John Jackson before his death. Douglas Young's second marriage was to Elizabeth Randolph Pleasants, daughter of Mathew Pleasants and Anna Railey. Their daughter, Susan Railey Young, *married Dr. T. K. Layton, whose eldest daughter, Jennie Layton, married Andrew Wallace of Versailles.†

Alice was another daughter of John Jackson and Alice Young. She was the first wife of the late Judge William E. Ashmore, for many years connected with the county court. Judge Ashmore's second marriage was to Lettie Lafon, a cousin of his first wife, and two of their daughters, Mary and Lucy Ashmore, now reside in the old Ashmore home near the Southern depot.* Judge Ashmore was a grandson of the Rev. James Keith and Mary Isham Randolph, and hence he was a second cousin of Dr. Louis Marshall who lived so long at "Buck Pond," and also of Chief Justice John Marshall.

Richard Gilbert Jackson was a son of John Jackson and Alice Young. He married Mary Virginia Lafon and lived for a long time in a large stone building not far from the limits of Versailles until the death of Col. Nicholas Lafon, his father-in-law, in 1836, when he purchased that estate and moved there. He and his wife and family were devoted members of the Versailles Presbyterian Church, and he served the congregation as an elder until his death in 1852. He served the county as a member of the legislature in 1845. Three of their daughters were: Maria, who married Col. Geo. T. Cotton, killed at Shiloh; Virginia married Col. John Allen Crittenden of Frankfort (it was a double wedding in 1846), and Miss

‡See Laytons, on page 365 for children of first marriage.
*Now the home of Dr. Alford Blackburn.
†See page 365 for Laytons.

Sally Jackson, who is now a resident of Frankfort, and the only survivor.

Admiral Lucian Young of the navy, and Dr. Frank O. Young, of Lexington, were related to Col. Richard Young.

John Jackson, the son-in-law of Col. Young, though a merchant, was also a farmer, and in 1810 his family consisted of fourteen members and he was the owner of forty-four slaves, one of the largest slave owners in the county. Douglas Young owned the Jackson place for many years, afterward owned by Samuel Hampton. It is on the Tyrone pike opposite the Utterback farm.

———

John Gay was born in Scotland in 1740, and his wife, Sarah Loughridge, was born there in 1754. They came to America soon after their marriage and first settled in Virginia, but only remained there for a few years as the spirit of migration to Kentucky was in a feverish state with their neighbors and friends, so in 1779 they joined the Stevensons, Dunlaps and others in a caravan across the mountains in search of homes on the frontier. At that early day Kentucky was infested with marauding bands of Indians, and when they reached Lexington, all took refuge in the "Old Fort," which constituted Lexington at that time. It was too dangerous to venture out for settlement upon lands, so they remained in this fort for several years, and not until 1782 did they feel it safe to build a home more than a few miles out. During that year John Gay purchased a tract of land near the spot where Mt. Vernon Church was built and as soon as

he could arrange accommodations and comforts for his family he moved them from the old fort and settled them upon the estate he had purchased. He and his wife lived and died there, and his estate has never been out of possession of descendants of the Gay name, the second owner being James Gay, a son of John Gay and Sarah Loughridge, who inherited the property at his father's death. He was born in 1781 while his father and mother were in the old fort at Lexington, and he came to Woodford an infant in 1782. He was reared upon this farm and in 1817 married Catharine Claggett. With other patriotic young men of Woodford County he enlisted for service in the War of 1812, and returned to his home safe and sound when the war was concluded.

Of the children of James Gay and Catharine Claggett, Margaret married ——————— Wasson; J. T. married Sarah Brown, in 1849, and James R. married Kate Lamme in 1852. All have descendants in Woodford and adjacent counties.

The children of John R. Gay and Kate Lamme were, James L., Maggie, Wasson, William, Mary, Horace, Carry and Kate.

The children of John T. Gay and Sarah Brown were, Mary, James, Lelia, John, Sallie, Anna, Mattie, Minnie and Robert.

At the death of James Gay, his son, John R. Gay, took charge and managed the estate, and his sons, James L. and Horace, who lived on adjoining farms, were in charge of the old home place for many years and established a reputation for breeding and raising fine saddle and harness horses that was hardly excelled in the county. They have enjoyed a liberal patronage from foreign buyers, and as they have been very extensively engaged in the business, they have succeeded admirably.

The Gays have been worthy citizens of the county and are universally liked.*

The Cottons and Crutchers were among the very earliest settlers in Kentucky, coming before Woodford County was established.

William Cotton was born in Loudoun County, Va., about 1745, and served in the Revolution. He married Frances Taylor of the same county in which he resided, and in 1787 moved to Fayette County, Woodford then being a part of that county. They were blessed with nine children, many of whom, with their descendants, have been identified with the county's progressive interests. George Taylor Cotton was the second of the nine children, and though a farmer who owned fourteen slaves, I think he and his family of six members resided in Versailles during his entire life, his death occurring in 1823. He married, first, Elizabeth O'Bannon, daughter of Major John O'Bannon, his second marriage to ———— Neville. However, his ten children were of the first marriage. Of these ten children I will mention George Taylor Cotton, Jr., who was the sixth, and was born in 1816. He lost his life in the service of the Union army at Stone River in 1862, holding the rank of Colonel. He was

twice married, first to Maria Jackson, daughter of Richard Gilbert Jackson and Mary Virginia Lafon, second to Emma E. Frazer. He had seven children, one of whom, Maria Jackson Cotton, is the wife of James Gay of the county. They have two daughters, Ruth Parrish Gay, who married Robert Berryman of Versailles, and Georgie Cotton Gay, who married James McFerran.

Charles Cotton, fourth of William Cotton and Frances Taylor, was born in 1781 in the old Virginia home and came with them to Kentucky. When of age he went to Louisville where he lived for several years, then returned to his Woodford County farm near McKee's crossroads, now owned by Pruett Graham of Frankfort, but it has always been known as the "Old Cotton Place." He was twice married, first to Sarah Richardson Buck, daughter of Col. John Buck of the county, second to Sarah Blackburn Puryear of Louisville in 1837. The children of Sarah Buck and Charles Cotton were: William Cotton married Virginia Bonnie† and was for quite a while engaged in the manufacture of rope, twine and bagging at Clifton, in the county. Frances Marian Cotton, who married George Jesse Graddy; Charles Buck Cotton married Jennie Gallagher. By the second marriage to Sarah Blackburn Puryear, daughter of Wm. Puryear and Mildred Bohannon, were: George Taylor Cotton born in 1838, and lived on the "Old Cotton Place" until sold about a decade ago and moved to Versailles where he died. He married Florence Crutcher,

---

*See page 159 for additional data.
†See page 273.

daughter of Richard Crutcher and Elizabeth McKnight, and they had the following children: Elizabeth Cotton married William H. Edwards; Emma Logan Cotton married Richard Redd Crutcher; George Taylor Cotton married Agnes Wish Darrow, and Frances Blackburn Cotton who is not married.

Emma Puryear Cotton was a daughter of Charles and Sarah B. P. Cotton. She married Dr. John Sublett Logan, of St. Joseph, Mo. He was a descendant of the Woodford County Subletts and the Kentucky Logans. Their descendants live at St. Joseph.

Frank Puryear Cotton was one of Morgan's fearless riders and was also a son of Charles and Sarah B. P. Cotton. He married Elizabeth Nooe.

Florence Cotton, the wife of George Taylor Cotton, was a granddaughter of Rev. Isaac Crutcher and Nancy Blanton, and daughter of Richard Crutcher and Elizabeth McKnight. The farm of the Rev. Isaac Crutcher was in Woodford County, an inheritance from his father Henry Crutcher, of Virginia, who received it as a land grant for services in the Revolution. When the county of Franklin was formed, the dividing line ran through the center of the farm, but left the residence of Rev. Isaac Crutcher in Woodford. This farm is in that part of the county between Millville and Jetts Station. The residence of the Rev. Isaac Crutcher is still standing and in good condition. He lived and died there, and at his death his son, Jesse Graddy Crutcher, inherited the estate that lay in Woodford County, and another son, Richard Crutcher,

built on that part that was in Franklin County. These two farms were in the family until recently sold. The Rev. Isaac Crutcher was a prominent Baptist minister and was twice married. First to Nancy Blanton, second to Nancy Graddy. Richard Crutcher was by the first marriage and he married, first, Permelia Berry, second, Elizabeth McKnight. America Crutcher was a daughter of the first wife, Permelia Berry. She married Benjamine Franklin Starks. Another daughter by the first marriage was Susan Crutcher who married James Madison Starks of Midway, and they had Richard Starks, who was one of the businessmen of Midway during his entire life. He married Lucy Proctor. John Price Starks, who was a merchant in Midway, afterwards a member of the firm of Crutcher and Starks of Frankfort, and later at Louisville under the same firm name. He married Sallie Cannon; Isaac F. Starks, now of Louisville, where he is in business under the style of Starks Realty Company. He married Eleanor Cannon of Midway; Bettie Starks, who married Joseph Birch Rhodes, and Eugenia Starks, who married William Preston Burgin. James Madison Starks was a farmer for many years at Midway where he has descendants.

Lafayette Crutcher was one of the sons of Richard Crutcher and Permelia Berry. He married Anna Graves and lived and died on a farm near Grassy Spring Church. They had the following children: Robert, Lafayette, Florence, Percy, Clarence, Anne, Hardin, Eudora, Margaret and

Arthur, all of whom were reared in the county, and some of whom are still residents there.*

Dr. William L. Crutcher and Jesse Graddy Crutcher were sons of Rev. Isaac Crutcher and his second wife, Graddy Crutcher were sons of Rev. Isaac Crutcher and his second wife, Nancy Graddy. Dr. William L. Crutcher married Susan Scearce and they had Dr. William L. Crutcher, Jr., Henry, Walter and Luther, all of whom were living in Franklin County after the Civil War. Jesse Graddy Crutcher was born in 1815, married Martha Pittman and inherited his father's estate, which he sold some years ago and moved to Texas. They had Asa P., Isaac H., Richard L., Edward P., Pittman, Anna, Trabue, Mary, Mattie, Jesse and Flora. All are now residents of Texas except Richard L., who lives in Frankfort, where he married Emma Stevens.

———

Lewis Utterback was born in Virginia in 1776, and died in Woodford County in 1824. He came to Kentucky when it was yet a county of Virginia and was among the early settlers in Woodford. He possessed a fair education, and besides looking after his farming interests, devoted much of his time to teaching, opening a school on his farm where he instructed the young men in the vicinity. His farm was just two miles from Versailles on the Tyrone road and all of the buildings he erected were constructed of logs, and I am told the house in which he resided is now standing and habitable. In 1810 he owned this farm and four

slaves, and had a family of three members. In 1805 he married Frances Berry, born in 1787, daughter of Captain Samuel Berry and his wife Susannah Hieatt, and they were blessed with a large family of children whose names follow: Bettie, who married Lewis Harper; William; Charles; Polly, who married Claigett Stout; John Benjamin; Samuel Berry, and Susan Utterback. William inherited the estate of his father and lived to a ripe old age. He never married, and at his death he left the estate to his namesake, the son of John Benjamine Utterback.

John Benjamine purchased a farm near Mt. Vernon Church and married Elizabeth Ware, daughter of Samuel Ware and Elizabeth Redd, and to them were born the following children: Lewis; Charles; William; Allie, who married William Smith; Lelia, who married J. Cal. Hopkins; Fannie, who married Hardin Fields; Elizabeth, who married David Redd, and John B., Jr., who possessed the estate after the death of his father in 1886. Charles William inherited the estate of his uncle William, which was the ancestral home and lived there many years, but finally sold and moved to Frankfort where he married ——— Taylor.

———

Captain Elijah Fogg was born in Woodford County in 1803 and was the only son of Obadiah Fogg and Elizabeth Shipp, who were early settlers in the county. Elijah Fogg learned the carpenter's trade, at which he was employed until 1840 when he turned his attention to farming, which engaged

———

*See page 166 for Washington Crutcher and Jennie Redd.

his time and thought the remainder of his life. At the death of Richard Gilbert Jackson in 1852 or soon thereafter, he purchased the "Spring Garden" estate seven miles down on the Frankfort road, established by Captain Nicholas Lafon, and died there in 1881. He married Ann Ware in 1833, daughter of Samuel Ware and Elizabeth Redd of the county. They had the following children: Elizabeth married Anderson Chenault; Samuel W. married Fannie Gaines; Agnes married Captain Thomas Steele; Anna married Captain William Gibson Welch; Virginia married Oakley Thompson, and Richard J. married Susie Hawkins. Of the above children, only the wife of Oakley Thompson is now a resident of the county, and she and her interesting family live in the vicinity of Grassy Spring Church. Capt. Sam Fogg, Capt. Welch and Capt. Tom Steele were all in the Confederate Army.

Captain Samuel Fogg's widow and daughters are residents of Frankfort.

For many years Warren Viley was the owner of "Stonewall" stock farm which he purchased from the Colemans in 1852. He was the first of the name in the county, and from the day he located in Woodford in 1838, to the time of his death in 1902, he was regarded as one of the county's most dependable and upright citizens. In fact, his promise was as good as a bond and no one ever doubted that he would meet every obligation.

He was loyal to his friends, devoted to his family and his home, and in the highest sense of the term a gentleman. Like all of the name, he was a typical southern gentleman with a fondness for all high bred quadrupeds, including his collie, but more especially for the fleet-footed runner and trotter.

No home in the county ever dispensed a more genuine and unaffected hospitality than that displayed by the head of the family at "Stonewall," and the simplicity and cordiality of his wife always gave him pleasure, and caused the guests to discard that feeling of restraint that usually attends mere formal functions. It was a delightful home.

Warren Viley spent his life, with the exception of a few latter years, on his farm, and was always in the forefront in progressive methods, and usually obtained the best results. His superior judgment in the breeding and care of stock was very noticeable. He developed the rapid "Capitola," and also her offspring, "King Alfonso." He also developed "Black Bess," the famous mare that he gave to Gen. John Morgan, and upon which that dashing cavalier made so many daring raids, duly recorded in the annals of the Confederacy.

On the "Stonewall" farm many notable events were forecast in gatherings of distinguished men, particularly during that period that preceded, and immediately followed the Civil War, and at several barbecues in the woodland hard-by has occurred the successful launching of more than one political career, notably those of John Cabell Breckinridge, James B. Beck and Jo. C. S. Blackburn. Each of these men, who were staunch friends of Mr. Viley, cast his hat into the political arena at a barbecue given in his honor in this beautiful and historic woodland.

During the Civil War the master of this estate had a stone wall built the full length of the frontage of his farm that has received more favorable comment than any masonry constructed in the county. Although nearly sixty years have elapsed since it was built, little, if any repair work has been required.

After the death of Mr. Viley his son, J. Breckinridge Viley, inherited Stonewall farm and his management has been along lines similar to those pursued by his father, and he too has been eminently successful. His (Warren Viley's) daughter Martinette Viley, married Lister Witherspoon, of the prominent family of that name of Lawrenceburg, and they live on the "Loto Wano" estate that is immediately opposite, and it too is noted for the fine stock produced; besides, it is one of the most attractive homes in the county.

Warren Viley married Catherine Jane Martin, who was descended from the families of Martian, Martin, Pierra, Rapine, Trabue and Bernard, all Huguenots, and since the Vileys have Huguenot ancestors, Warren Viley's children have many prominent strains of French blood of which they may be proud.

The founder of the Viley name in Kentucky was George Viley, a native of Maryland, who settled near Stamping Ground in 1796, when that section belonged to Woodford County. He and his wife, Martha Ann Jones, lived and died in that old home, which is still in possession of Viley descendants.

I find that I have overlooked one of the children of Warren Viley and Catherine Jane Martin, his wife, whose name was Lydia May. She was one of the most beautiful women raised in the county. She was three times married, first to J. Lawrence Jones, second to James C. McFerran, then to Paul Lansing. She has two sons, James C. McFerran, Jr., who married Georgia Gay, and Viley McFerran. John Moore Viley was another son of Warren Viley and Catherine Jane Martin. He lost his life in the "Orphan Brigade" during the Civil War.

John Graves was a native of Culpepper, Va., born in 1768, died 1824. His father was a Revolutionary soldier, and John came to Kentucky soon after the Revolution and settled in Woodford County. In 1810 he had a family of nine members and besides a farm he owned nine slaves. In 1791 he married Hannah Cave, she a daughter of Richard Cave, a prominent Baptist minister, and Elizabeth Craig, his wife. Richard Cave was also one of the early settlers, and in addition to his duties as a preacher, he owned a large farm upon which he found employment for seventeen likely slaves, and his family included seven members in 1810.

John Graves and Hannah Cave had the following children: Absalom, Mary, Reuben, Richard Cave, Benjamine and Joseph C.

Of the above, Judge Richard Cave Graves was born in 1803, lived on a farm several miles from Versailles on the Nicholasville pike upon which he was born. He manufactured rope, twine and bagging in the county for more than a quarter of a century, giving that industry up in 1858. In 1850 he represented the county in the Kentucky Legislature, upper branch; was county judge 1852-56, police judge of Versailles 1856-62. In 1824 he married Lucy Mitchum† daughter of James Mitchum of the vicinity. To them were born two children, James and Laura, the latter of whom married Bartow W. Wasson. His first wife died in 1849, and in 1851 he married a widow, Helen Scott, and to them were born four children, Richard Cave, Clifford, Frank and Alice. His father-in-law, James Mitchum, was an early settler in Woodford, coming at the same time that Dudley Mitchum* came, and he owned a farm near by. In 1810 he owned a farm, three slaves, and had a family of three.

Judge Richard Cave Graves lived to be quite an old man, running far beyond the four score of years, and he enjoyed a wide circle of friends who esteemed him highly. He was a strong union man during the Civil War, but was always fair to his countymen as well as his immediate neighbors and friends. He and Lewis Sublett, Jo Taylor, Herman Bowmar, Jr., Captain Harry Brown and many others that I could recall, were intensely interested in secret order work, and were also great fishermen, delighted during the low water period to feed the finny tribe at Lock No. 5. They were all Knight Templars, and at that time no county in the State had a finer body of Masons than those who composed the Versailles Commandery, just prior to the Civil War, and immediately following.

Reuben Graves was born in 1799 and was an older brother of Judge R. Cave Graves. He married Elizabeth Cox in 1842 and they had the following children: William H., John, Thomas, Hannah, James C. and Hattie. Of these children James C. Graves was born in 1847, was a farmer and breeder of saddle and harness horses, and was quite successful. He married Mollie Huggins in 1868, and of this union the following children were born: Ollie, Laura, Reuben, Ernest and James. They lived in the vicinity of Troy.

———

"Sumners Forest" is one of the noted farms of Woodford County and is situated seven miles from Versailles on the Lexington road. It was a land grant of two thousand acres to Jethro Sumners, of North Carolina, and in receiving its name he was honored. The estate was purchased in 1795 by Senator John Brown, of Frankfort, after which he brought his father and mother, the Rev. John Brown and Margaret Preston, his wife, to Kentucky from Virginia, and domiciled them on this estate. Margaret Preston was a daughter of John Preston and Elizabeth Patton. "Parson" John Brown was the first pastor of the historic Pisgah Church and remained in its service until his death in 1803, but not as its regular pastor. He and his wife were buried in the church yard and a suitable monument erected to their memory, but many years later their remains were removed to Frankfort where they were re-interred in the cemetery of that city. Dr. Preston

———

*His father came.
†See page 317, 391, 399.

Brown came into possession of "Sumners Forest" at the death of his parents and lived there until 1826, when he sold it to his kinsman, David Carlyle Humphries, the son of Dr. Alexander Humphries and Mary Brown, of Virginia, she a daughter of the "Parson." David C. Humphries lived here several years with his wife Sarah Scott, and they were blessed with four children. Before his children were grown, probably before they had reached their teens, he bought three thousand acres of land on the old Cole or Frankfort road near Spring Station, that extended from Alexander's line to Elkhorn. He built in full view of the road a mansion something similar to "Spring Hill," the home of the Harts, and he called this country site "Waverly." The names of their four children follow: Joseph Alexander, Mary, Samuel, and Lucy. The two girls were very much admired for their personal charms.

Joseph Alexander Humphries was born in Woodford County in 1826, was educated at Center College, Danville, then attended Yale, finishing his studies in medicine in Europe. When he returned to Kentucky he was given the "Sumners Forest" home as he preferred the vocation of a farmer to the profession of a physician—his practice ever afterward being incidental. He married his cousin, Sarah Gibson, of Louisiana, daughter of Tobias Gibson and Louisiana Breckenridge Hart, of "Spring Hill," and a sister of Hon. Hart Gibson, who represented Woodford County in Legislature in 1867-68. The original house built at "Sumners Forest" was of stone, and the walls were three feet thick, the chimneys fully ten feet wide, and was likely built before the Browns bought in 1796. The building still stands, but Dr. Joseph Humphries made several additions and other improvements. The farm is still in possession of his daughters, Mrs. Lewis Johnstone and Mrs. C. D. Chenault.

The wife of Dr. Joseph A. Humphries was a lady of fine literary attainments and very popular. Their children were: Lucy, who married Lewis Johnstone; Sallie, who married C. D. Chenault, and Joseph A., Jr., who spends most of his time in the South. He married Mary Taylor, and of this union was a son Joseph A., III., who married Ezza Railey Twyman, daughter of Buford Twyman and Margaret Sanders Railey of Versailles.

Mary Humphreys, daughter of David C. Humphreys and Sarah Scott, was a beautiful woman and a great belle. She married Anthony Dey, of New Brunswick, N. J. They had no children and the wife died in 1880. Many of the citizens of the county will recall the name and face of Anthony Dey as he made many visits to the county, even after the death of his wife. He was a tall, handsome man of the Bismarck type.

Samuel Humphries married Margaret ———— and she too was esteemed for her beauty and many graces. He died a few years after his marriage leaving a widow and two children, David and Thomas, both of whom moved to Illinois where both lived and died, the former a bachelor; the latter married but had no issue.

Lucy Humphries, the last of the four

children, married A. J. Alexander of Spring Station in 1851. They had three children, David, Mary and Robert. The mother died in 1858, and the three children died within eighteen months after the death of the mother.

The "Waverly" home was destroyed by fire soon after the burning of "Spring Hill" and the loss in books, art, tapestry and relics that were precious would be difficult to estimate.

When a boy, the Indians captured Captain James Trimble in Virginia, but in due course of time an opportunity presented itself for a quick getaway and the bright, courageous boy took advantage of the opportunity and made his escape. He came to Woodford County with a company of friends soon after the Revolution, and he had many trials that required courage and daring along the frontier country, but he was never found wanting in either. After reaching Woodford he gave loyal service to the cause of the pioneers until his death in 1804. It was said of him that he never shirked a duty or deserted a post. Some years after his death, but prior to 1810, his family removed to the state of Ohio where several of his sons became prominent in the business and political affairs of that state, his son, Allen Trimble, being honored by election to the governorship. See page 152.

The Guyn family of Troy, and Clover Bottom, is of pioneer stock. The head of the family in Woodford County was Robert Guyn who came early from Virginia and settled near Green's Mill and assisted in the building of Black's

Station, or Fort, not far from Troy. He was a son of Robert Guyn of Virginia, but the maiden name of his mother and wife are not known by the present generation. He raised quite a family of children, the most of whom were girls. His three sons were Samuel, Moses and Robert. Robert was born in Virginia, in 1774, and died in Woodford in 1844. He married Jane Black, a daughter of Robert Black, and they were the parents of the following children: Robert, James, John, Hugh, Andrew, Moses, William, Thomas, Harvey, Rankin, Samuel R., Jane and Hannah Guyn. Jane married ———— Irvin, son of John M. C. Irvin; Hannah married David Black, and Samuel R., born in 1803, married Georgeann Yeagle and they had these children: Martha, who married Samuel McCauley; Robert J., John W., and Edwin N. The latter was a farmer and lived near Troy. In 1845, he was elected an elder in the Troy Presbyterian Church, which office he retained until his death in 1884. His son, Edwin N., Jr., was born in 1840. In 1862 he enlisted with General Morgan's command, serving until the close of the war. He took part in every engagement of his brigade.

Moses Guyn, born in 1805, was another of the sons of Robert Guyn and Jane Black. He was educated in the schools of the county and settled upon a farm in Clover Bottom. In 1833 he married Ann Black, daughter of John Black and Martha McGill, and to them the following children were born: John C., who married Elizabeth Young; William R., who married Sarah Guyn; Charles C. and Angus G., all of whom were members of the Troy Presbyterian Church.

William was also a son of Robert and Jane Black Guyn. He married Elizabeth Long and owned a farm near Troy. Their son, William Rankin Guyn, was born in 1839, educated in the county schools and was a farmer. He married ———— Guyn in 1867, she a daughter of T. R. Guyn and Margaret Rennick. She died within a year after her marriage, and William R. Guyn married second, Ida Baxter in 1883, and of this union were the following children: Wilgus H. and Elmer G. For many years they looked after a grist mill and a general store in Clover Bottom.

Hugh Guyn was still another son of Robert and Jane Black Guyn. As a youth he attended the schools of the neighborhood and turned his attention to farming after reaching years of maturity. He married Jane Long and died in 1869. Their son, William L. Guyn, was born in 1847, educated in the neighborhood schools, became a prosperous farmer and married Henrietta Yeagle, daughter of James Yeagle and Eliza Black, in 1871. To them one child was born, Charles H. In 1875 the first wife died and William L. Guyn's second marriage was to Mary Thompson in 1881, she a daughter of Robt. A. Thompson and Elizabeth Fleming, and to them were born Elizabeth and Hugh T. Guyn.

The Guyns were entered upon the census of 1810 as Gwinns, error in spelling.

———

Simeon Hifner was born in Virginia near Culpepper court house and came to Kentucky some time after the war of 1812. He bought a farm near Troy in Woodford County. His son Thomas Hifner was born in that vicinity in 1832, and after receiving the benefits of a fair education, divided his time between teaching school and farming. His son, Melvin B. Hifner, was under his tutorage until prepared for a collegiate course when he entered Valparaiso Institute, in the state of Indiana, where he took a course in civil engineering.

In 1881 he was elected superintendent of county schools, which position he has filled very creditably to himself and to the entire satisfaction of the patrons for many years, and at various intervals did much surveying in the county.

———

Isaac Johnson and his wife ———— were both native Virginians and migrated to Kentucky late in the eighteenth century, settling not far from Millville in Woodford County and near the river so that he might make good use of his gun and rod when the requirements of his farm permitted his absence therefrom. The census of 1810 reports his household as consisting of nine members and that he was the owner of one slave. His son, Jacob Johnson, was born on the homestead in 1805, and died there in 1855. Jacob married Elizabeth Mitchell of the neighborhood, a lady of German extract, and their son, James Clelland Johnson, was born in the ancestral home in 1844. He was a farmer, but as a mere youth entered the Confederate service in which he served four years. He returned to his home and resumed his duties on the farm when the "Cruel War was over," and conducted his farm successfully until his death in 1915. In 1872 he married Mary Willis of the county, sister of Len Willis, the banker. They reared six children, who live in the vicinity; they are: Ethelyn, who married Frank Watts in 1901; Anna married B. E. Chramme in 1902; George Francis married Margaret Pyles in 1907; James Clelland, Jr., married Virginia Thompson, 1906; Marion married Nellie Grey Lindsey in 1912; Cantrill married, first, Lena Butcher, second, Grace Bishop. Hettie and Yela are not married.

Price Johnson, brother of James Clelland, Sr., married Mildred Taylor, granddaughter of Burket Yancey.

James Black, of Tennessee, came to Woodford with other pioneer settlers and located in the Clover Bottom section of the county. His father was a Revolutionary soldier, and his son, David Black, was born in 1807 in Woodford County, educated in the neighborhood schools and reared on the farm, which calling he pursued during his entire life. He married Pauline Guyn, daughter of Robert Guyn and Jane Black, and of this union the following children were born: Robert W., who married Susan Oliver; Mary Ann; Eliza Jane; David C.; and Sarah, who married W. H. Blake. Many of the descendants are still in that vicinity.

Wm. Garrett was of Scotch-Irish extract, his father being a native of Ireland who came to Virginia in time to take part in the Revolution. William was born in Virginia but came to Woodford County, Ky., soon after the Revolution. In 1810 he owned a farm, had a family of eight members, and owned one slave. John Garrett was one of his several children born in Woodford and raised upon the farm. He enjoyed such benefits in the way of an education as the country schools afforded, married Elizabeth Allen of the county, enlisted in the War of 1812 and was promoted to the rank of a Captain. To them was born a son whose name was Robert Garrett and he too was limited to a common school education.

He spent his entire life on the ancestral farm that had passed down to each succeeding generation, and he accumulated much property. In 1858 he married Margaret Wilmore, of Jessamine County, and their son, John W. Garrett, was born in 1859. His first wife died in 1862 and in 1865 he married Catherine McDonald, and of this union one son, Joseph McDonald Garrett, was born in 1866.

Robert Garrett died in 1872, and his widow conducted the farm until the son was old enough to take charge.*

John McQuiddy was a native of Virginia who served in the Revolution and came with the early settlers to Kentucky and settled in Woodford County. He lived in the vicinity of Mortonsville where he located his farm, and in 1810 he had a family of ten and owned six slaves. His daughter Elizabeth married Jeremiah Nash, who was born in Virginia in 1789 and died

*See "Highland Place," page 32.

in Woodford County in 1852. David Nash was one of the sons and was born in 1822, on the farm that was owned by his grandfather. He married Alpha Barnes in 1869. He lived and died near Mortonsville and was one of Woodford County's substantial citizens.

John Edwards was a native of Wales who came to Virginia at an early period in the history of that state. His son, John Edwards, moved his family to Woodford County, Kentucky, about 1798, and was a farmer. His father had served in the Revolution and the son is listed in the census of 1810 as John Edwards, Sr., who had a family of ten persons and owned eleven slaves. Of this large family of children he had a son, Fielding, who was born in Virginia in 1782. He married Jane Wright of the county, and though a mechanic by trade, he was also a farmer and stock trader. In 1855 he died leaving a widow and a number of children. Five years later she succumbed to the grim monster death. They had a son, Davis Edwards, who was born in 1826, became a farmer and devoted his entire life to the duties of that vocation. In 1854 he married Amanda Latta, who lived but a few years, and his second marriage was to Ann Mastin in 1863. Of this union the following children were born: William H., John G., James Y., Jane, Alexander W., Davis W., and Boyette, several of whom are now residents of the county.

Another son of the pioneer John Edwards was Wiley Edwards. He was born in Virginia in 1787 and came with the family to Woodford in 1798.

He was a wagon maker by trade but owned and operated a distillery in the county from 1828 to 1847, the date of his death. This distillery was on Glenns Creek, not far from the residence of John Edwards, the pioneer, whose home lay between the farm of the late Harry Brown and that of Mason Henry. Wiley Edwards married Nancy Sullinger in 1812 and she died at the residence of her son, Thomas S. Edwards, in 1872. Of this union there were born Thomas S., George, William and Waller Edwards, all of whom are now dead. Thomas S. married Susan Strother Hawkins, daughter of William Strother Hawkins and Katherine Keith, and they died without issue. George Edwards married Elizabeth Jett in 1843 and had these children: Thos. W., Mary, Anna, G. Hiram, Jennie and Jettie. Mary and Jennie are residents of Versailles. William Edwards married Mary Ferguson, daughter of Henry. They lived many years upon a farm that borders upon the town of Versailles and the cemetery. Their children were: Henry W., Margaret, Van H., James H., Nannie and Jo. All of them are residents of Woodford and Jessamine counties.

Thomas S. Edwards and his wife lived the greater part of their lives upon the farm that his grandfather bought from the heirs of Cyrus McCracken on the Glenns Creek or McCracken's Mill road. His father built the brick house that stands there today, the frame of the McCracken's home standing in one corner of the yard and used as a servants' house. Thomas Henton's family have owned it and lived there for more than thirty years. Wiley Edwards built a distillery just below the house on the creek which he operated until his death, after which it was operated by Thomas S. until about 1870, when it was abandoned and afterward dismantled and razed.

Waller Edwards was in the Confederate army during the Civil War and died either during that service or soon thereafter.*

John Sellers was born in Pennsylvania, but was in Mercer County, Ky., soon after the Revolution. He died in 1812 and soon thereafter his son, Thomas W. Sellers, who was born in Harrods Station, now Harrodsburg, in 1788, and his wife, Sarah Ashford, came to Woodford County and settled in the vicinity of Clover Bottom, where he engaged in farming, which he continued during the remainder of his life. He served in the War of 1812, was sheriff of the county for eight years, judge of the county court one term, and for more than a quarter of a century was a member of the county court from the Clover Bottom magisterial district.

Henry M. Sellers, second son of Thomas W. and Sarah Ashford Sellers, was born in Woodford County on his father's estate in 1814, and he too was a farmer, also learned the carpenter's trade at which he worked at odd intervals. He was twice married, first to Henrietta Stevenson, and second to Alethia Rowland, both of the county.

*See page 233.

By the second marriage was Marion, who married O. Kennard.

___

James Hawkins, who settled near Troy in Woodford County, soon after the Revolution, was a native of Virginia and his father saw service in the Revolution. In 1810 James Hawkins owned a farm, four slaves and listed five persons in his family. His son, Senat Hawkins, born in Woodford County in 1810, was a farmer in Clover Bottom where he was born, and he married Mary Dodd. Besides conducting his farm he was a prosperous merchant and was at different times magistrate of his district, and county constable. His wife died in 1842; he survived until 1855 when he too was claimed by death. Their son, James S. Hawkins, born in 1840 in the ancestral home, was educated in the neighborhood schools and started life as a farmer. In 1862 he enlisted in the service of the Confederacy, was in Morgan's command and received a severe wound at Cynthiana in 1863, and other wounds at Bulls Gap. He surrendered with General Taylor in Mississippi in 1865.

In 1866 he opened a general store in Clover Bottom. In 1882 he formed a partnership at Wilmore where he handled coal and grain by wholesale and retail, in addition to his general store, but he retained his large farm in Woodford where he was interested both in farming and stock breeding.

In 1879 he married Dollie Reed. He never moved his membership in the

I. O. O. F. from Troy lodge, where he had filled all of the chairs at various times. He was at one time grand treasurer of the order, and was also a member of the Versailles encampment, and the family retained their membership in the Troy Presbyterian Church. For many years he was active and influential in politics, as well as business, in both Woodford and Jessamine counties and had a host of friends and admirers.

James Sullivan, Jr., was of Revolutionary stock and born in Virginia. His father, James Sullivan, Sr., was born in North Ireland but came to Virginia at an early day and served in the Revolution. His son, James, Jr., came early to Woodford County and was reported in 1810 as having a family of nine and the owner of a farm and six slaves.

James Sullivan married in the county, Jane (Jincy) Collins, daughter of Joseph Collins, who was also of Revolutionary stock, and lived on a farm in Woodford, his family consisting of ten members and he owned a farm and nine slaves. James Sullivan, Jr., and Jincy Collins had a son, Theoderick N. Sullivan, who was born in 1824. Some years later he accompanied his parents to Peak's Mill, in Franklin County, where they became permanent residents.*

Jacob Harper and his wife Mary came from Germany,‡ where they were born and reared, to Virginia where they resided for quite awhile. In 1797 they came to Kentucky and bought fifteen hundred acres of land that adjoined the estate of Robert Alexander near Midway. They had a large family of children as follows: George, Jacob, Adam, Nicholas, John, William Ist., Henry, Barbara, Elizabeth and Mary. After the death of Jacob Harper and his wife Mary, their land was allotted to their ten children, but all of them, with the exception of Adam, William and Barbara, sold their interests, married and moved to Indiana, Illinois and Missouri.

Adam married and had the following children: William, II., Jacob, Adam, John and Elizabeth. William, II., married Ann Whitley, daughter of Col. William C. Whitley and Esther Fuller, and they were the parents of Adam, Frank, Mary and Barbara Ann. Barbara Ann married Capt. Henry E. Owsley and their children were: Gertrude, Alice, Elizabeth, Annie, Henry, Mary and William. Gertrude married Thos. W. Hawkins; Alice married Alfred Stanhope; Elizabeth married Clinton B. Hawkins; Annie married William E. Railey; Henry married Bourne Saunders; Mary married Owen Cooper, and William married Elvie Rickets.†

William Harper the Ist., married Rebecca Wallace, a lady of Scotch-Irish extract. He settled upon a part of the estate settled by his father which, at his death in 18—, was inherited by his son, J. Wallace Harper, who married, first, his cousin, Elizabeth Harper,

*See page 88 for Lewis Sullivan.
†Whose daughter, Agnes, wed Hardin Walcutt. They have an only child, Owsley.
‡Originally Hollanders.

daughter of William Harper, Jr., and Ann Whitley; second, Adelia Bailey. By the last marriage was Walter B. Harper who owns the old home. He married the widow Nellie (Rodman) Walcutt and they had an only child, Wallace Harper.

Barbara Harper, daughter of Jacob and Mary Harper, married ———— Christman, and their daughter, Christena married James McKee, of "McKee's Crossroads," on the Versailles pike. They had two children, Catherine and Dr. John R. McKee. Catherine married Col. John Withrow and they had James, William, John.

Dr. John R. McKee married Agnes Morancy and they have James, Frank, Emelius, Bettie and Agnes McKee. Agnes Morancy was a granddaughter of Col. Zach White and Agnes Steele. (See sketch of Col. William Steele.)

————

The Bowmar family arrived in Kentucky one hundred and forty years ago and have been in Woodford County more than one hundred and thirty years. They were Virginians of the hardy, resolute, courageous type.

In 1779 Robert Bowmar, with his wife, Chloe Collins (related to Judge R. H. Collins, author of Collins' History of Kentucky) and his son, Herman Bowmar, emigrated to Bowmar's Station, or Fort, in Mercer County. In 1789 they removed to Woodford County. Robert Bowmar participated in the bloody battle of the Blue Licks and was one of the fortunate survivors.

The son, Major Herman Bowmar, Sr., served in three campaigns against the Indians and fought under General Anthony Wayne at the battle of Fallen Timbers, near Toledo, Ohio, in 1794, where General Wayne crushed the Indians and stayed their incursions upon Kentucky. In that campaign Major Bowmar, then twenty-five years old, was Brigade Major of General Robert Todd's brigade. He became a leading citizen of Woodford County. The census of 1810 showed him to be one of the largest slaveholders in the county. He was deputy sheriff at twenty-two years of age, Woodford, then including portions of Franklin and Scott; became sheriff; served two terms in the State Senate and was Democratic nominee for Congress in the Ashland district to succeed Henry Clay in 1827, but as the Whigs were overwhelmingly in the majority he was defeated by Judge James Clark of Bourbon County, a Whig.

At the age of eighty-six years he died in 1855 full of honors, and with the "Well done, thou good and faithful servant." He married Frances Adams, of near Richmond, Va., of whom Thomas F. Marshall said: "She was one of the most beautiful women of her times."

One of Major Herman Bowmar's brothers, James Hervey Bowmar, was killed in the War of 1812, and another brother, Joseph Bowmar, was a Captain in the United States regular army for years after the War of 1812.

Of the three sons of Major Herman Bowmar, Sr., only one remained in Woodford, Herman Bowmar, Jr. Dr. Joseph Hamilton Daviess Bowmar removed to Louisiana, and afterwards to Mississippi; Robert Bowmar migrated to another part of the State. He also had several attractive daughters, Cynthia married Judge Daniel Mayes, one of the greatest jurists in the South in his day; Jane married William Barr, father of the late Judge John Watson Barr, of Louisville, by a previous marriage; Lucy married John L. Barclay, member of the firm of Barclay and Tilford, Lexington bankers before the Civil War, and Frances married Dr. Reuben Berry of the county, who owned the home where Hardin Fields now resides.

Herman Bowmar is said to have been the most brilliant man Woodford ever produced. When he graduated from Transylvania University, he carried off the honors, being valedictorian of his class, which included Richard H. Menifee and other distinguished men. He was an able lawyer, but the death of his beautiful and charming wife, who was Eleline Tunis, in his early prime seemed to have deprived him of ambition. He held for thirty consecutive years the office of clerk of the Woodford County Court, which he filled most admirably, but he made no special use of his great talents save in occasional speeches and a brilliant and long remembered display of wit and humor.

As an evidence of his popularity, it is said that for twenty years he was regularly elected as a Democrat, although Woodford County was, during that time, a strong Whig county. Major Herman Bowmar, Jr., was a prominent Mason and was elected Grand High Priest of the Grand Chapter of Kentucky, R. A. M. He was in

great demand as a speaker at important gatherings of the fraternity throughout the State, and was the orator of the day when the cornerstone of the Masonic Temple at Lexington was laid in 1842. His death occurred in 1863.

He was the father of Captain Joseph Marshall Bowmar, a brave officer in General John H. Morgan's cavalry; of Daniel M. Bowmar,* a very brilliant and notable man who was the father of the present editors of the Woodford Sun; and of Robert Bowmar, who was also a soldier in General Morgan's cavalry, commanded by Col. William C. P. Breckinridge, and was killed at the age of sixteen years.

The Bowmars who are at present residents of Woodford County are Aitchison Alexander Bowmar, and Daniel Mayes Bowmar, and their respective families, and the family of George T. Fishback, his wife being Elizabeth Bowmar, and her sister Katherine Bowmar, both daughters of Joseph M. Bowmar. A younger brother of Aitchison A., and Daniel M. Bowmar is Herman Bowmar, III., who resides at St. Louis, Mo., and is general secretary of the Missouri State Sunday School Association. He was born and reared in Woodford and married his cousin, Frances Adams Bowmar, daughter of Capt. Joseph M. Bowmar, also born and reared in the county.

The present editors and publishers of the Woodford Sun, Aitchison A. and Daniel M. Bowmar, Jr., like their father, represent all that is noble and pure in the Christian gentleman, and

---

*Whose wife was Marie Elizabeth Smith. See page 365.

their spirit has animated the several generations from Robert the pioneer to the present generation.

Robert Bowmar, the pioneer, located his farm on the Kentucky River, and the river line ran from Lock No. 5 to the "Narrows" and joined the farm of Col. William Steele. (Samuel Craig, who came from Scott County in 1835, purchased the farm and his son Charlie lived there until about 1890.) His son, Herman Bowmar, owned a farm on the McCracken or Glenns Creek road where Ben Gray lived for many years, and about two miles from town. Herman Bowmar, Jr., lived in Versailles in a brick cottage that I think Theodore Harris has owned for many years.

Lewis Sullivan was a native of Virginia and came to Woodford County just after the Revolution. His father, Wyatt Sullivan, was born in Ireland, came to Virginia and fought for the independence of America, as did his brother, James Sullivan, who was also born in Ireland. Lewis located his farm near Mortonsville, upon which he settled and remained during his entire life. In 1810 he had a family of ten, a farm and eleven slaves.

Dr. R. S. Sullivan was one of his sons, born in Woodford County in 1810, studied medicine at the University of Lexington where he graduated, practiced in the county for more than a quarter of a century in the Mortonsville and Troy sections. He married Elizabeth Arnold of the county and died during the year 1885.

J. H. Sullivan, born in 1849, was a son of this couple. He studied medicine under the direction of his father,

then took a course of lectures in the Louisville School of Medicine for three years, graduating in 1873. Prior to 1890 he moved to Frankfort, Ky., and was a successful practitioner in West Frankfort for many years.

In 1810 Lewis Sullivan, the pioneer, owned a farm and eleven slaves and there were ten members of his family.

———

The Miles family descended from a native of Wales. When they came to America they first settled in Maryland, then migrated to Virginia, finally decided to cast their lot with friends and neighbors who had determined to face all of the dangers that lurked in the pathway that Boone and other pioneers had marked out at an earlier date, so they defied the "Red Men" and made Boone's path plainer for those who came later to Kentucky.

Isaac Miles, who was born in Virginia, was the head of the clan by that name who came some time preceding the year 1800. They found the journey long and tedious, but the caravan lost no time en route, except as necessity required, and in due course of time landed in Woodford County. His wife, Mary Curtis, to whom he was married in Virginia, accompanied her husband and was as courageous and self-sacrificing as the splendid women who preceded her. Before leaving Virginia Isaac Miles had operated a gristmill, and when they located at Millville in the county—which seemed to them a dense wilderness—he immediately began the construction of a residence, after which he erected one of the two gristmills at Millville, his being one of the first built in the county, which he located on the opposite side of Glenn's Creek from his residence, and both the mill and residence were standing but a few short years ago. (The other mill was built by Randolph R. Darnell.) His wife lived to be quite old, and after her death, though quite an old man, he married the widow Guthrie. By the first marriage were the following children: Thomas, John Evans, Jesse, Racheal and Samuel. Several of his children moved to Indiana where they married, lived and died. His son, Samuel, however, remained in the vicinity and succeeded his father in the milling industry. He and an Englishman named Gorbett added a cotton and woolen factory to the other interests in the vicinity, in which they made cotton jeans, and other fabrics that supplied the wants of a vast territory that needed the cloth. They also added a wagon factory, with blacksmith shop attached, that supplied other wants in that territory, and these various enterprises, together with a store filled with general merchandise that they established, put the village on the map and it remained a thriving little town until the Civil War. It is still a wideawake village, but its hey-day was prior to the cruel days of 1861-5.

As a compliment to Samuel Miles, the citizens sought to name it Milestown, but as two gristmills were operating at the time, one at the upper and the other at the lower end of the village, he urged Millville as a more suitable name and it was adopted.

Samuel Miles married in 1825, Elizabeth Hawkins, of Franklin Coun-

ty, and the names of their children follow: John E. Miles, who married, first, Emily Payne of Marietta, Ohio, in 1850, second, Annie Hawkins, daughter of Isham Keith Hawkins and Sarah Hall; William J. Miles, who married Susan Brassfield; Sarah Adelia Miles, who married Thaddeus Smith; Mary Hanna Miles, who married John Taylor, and Samuel I. Miles, who enlisted with General John Morgan's command and was sacrificed at Green River bridge in 1863.

John E. Miles succeeded his father in the milling business which he conducted very successfully for many years, but finally moved to Frankfort where he built a large mill and elevator where he could get the benefit of better transportation facilities. His "J. E. M." brand of flour was very popular for thirty or more years and is now used by a Lexington Milling Company and retains its popularity. By his first marriage to Emily Payne were: James M., Effie, Alma, Iva, and Samuel, most of them now residents of Frankfort. By the second marriage to Annie Hawkins, was Mary Keith Miles, who married Professor Alexander M. Wilson, of Cincinnati. One son, Alexander M., Jr., blessed this union.

Thaddeus Smith and Sarah Adelia Miles moved to Pelee Island, off Put-in-Bay, some years after the Civil War, where they remained and died. He owned a large grape vineyard on this island that was profitable. They had two daughters, Bertha and Minnie, who were beautiful and accomplished girls.

John Taylor and Hannah Miles

lived at Midway, Ky., for many years. No issue.

Walter Ayres was in Woodford County prior to 1810, coming from Virginia at an early date. During that year, and for some years previous, he was living on a farm one mile from Harmony Church on the old Frankfort and Lexington road in the direction of Lexington. He built a brick house for a residence which is still standing, but with a front extension built by Captain Henry E. Owsley, who bought the property at the close of the Civil War and owned it until his death about 1890.

In 1810, Walter Ayres (erroneously spelled in census of that year Ayers) had a family of seven members, and listed five slaves. He married Mary Agnes Maxey (of French Huguenot extract) and raised a large family of children on this Woodford County estate, all of whom, with the exception of his son, Walter N. Ayres, moved to Missouri, where they lived and died.

Walter N. Ayres heired and was the owner of his father's estate until 1854, when he sold it to Robert Alexander and purchased what was then known as the Smith farm on the same road, about one mile from Harmony Church in the direction of Frankfort. It was one of the most attractive sites in that part of the county. His wife was Frances Elizabeth Foster and they had the following children: Mrs. Thos. W. Scott, Mrs. G. P. McCredie, Edward W. Ayres, the horseman and turfman, Mrs. R. J. Thompson, whose husband was a doctor reared at Versailles, Mrs. Thos. L. Gibson, John W.

Ayres, Mrs. A. D. Brown, Mrs. W. T. Runyon, Nathan Ayres and Mrs. J. T. Stribling, all well and pleasantly remembered by the older citizens of Harmony and Duckers. All left Kentucky a score or more years ago, only four of whom are now living, Mrs. Thos. L. Gibson and Nathan Ayres of Fort Worth, Texas, and Mrs. Runyon and Mrs. Stribling at Norborne, Mo. No more popular family ever lived in Woodford County than that of the Ayres.

Walter Ayres was born in Buckingham County, Virginia, in 1779, and married in that state, Agnes Maxey, in 1800. She was a daughter of the French Huguenot, Dr. Boudinot. They came to Woodford County in 1801. His father, Nathan Ayres, came from England in 1720 and settled in Virginia, and he too was of Huguenot descent, his father having emigrated from France to England after the Massacre of St. Bartholomew. Nathan Ayres married Mary Leake, and he served in the Revolution.

Simeon Buford was a son of John and Judith Buford of Culpeper County, Virginia, born in 1756. He was a Captain in the Continental Line during the Revolution. He married Margaret Kirtley in 1777, a daughter of Capt. William Kirtley, and they migrated to Barren County, Ky., in 1789. He soon became identified with the best people, and in touch with the best interests of the county and in 1801, and again in 1803, represented that county in the Legislature. They were blessed with ten children, three of whom settled in Woodford County. They were John, William and Simeon.

John was the oldest of the ten children, born in 1778, was twice married, first to Nancy Hickman, second to Mrs. Ann Banister Watson, widow of Dr. John Watson, of Frankfort, Ky. I am not advised as to the year he became a resident of Woodford, likely about the time of his father's service in the Legislature, but he was in the county when the census of 1810 was taken, his family at that time comprising five persons and he was the owner of eleven slaves. He was regarded as one of the county's solid citizens and a splendid farmer. He represented the county in the Legislature in 1824, and again in 1827.

By the first marriage was Helen Buford, who was born in 1800, and married at Versailles, Ky., General William Johnson in 1817; Napoleon B. Buford, born in 1807, was twice married, first to Sarah Childs, second to Mary Ann Pierce, a widow. He was a Major General in the Federal army 1861-65. By the second marriage was John Buford, Jr., born in 1826, married Martha McDowell Duke. He was also a General in the Federal army 1861-65, and not only selected the site for the battle, but fired the first shot at Gettysburg; Thomas Jefferson, born in 1828, married Grace Bowers and their daughter Sarah Buford, born in 1857, married General James Franklin Bell, of the Regular army, who engaged in the conflict with Spain, serving in the Philippines as a Brig.-General; James Monroe Buford, born in 1832, and married Felicia Clarke.

William Buford, the second of the three brothers who settled in Woodford, was born in 1781, married Frances Walker Kirtley, daughter of Francis Kirtley and Elizabeth Walker, in 1801. She was born in Rockingham County, Va., in 1787, but they were married in Barren County, Ky., from whence they came to Woodford County in 1805. My authority states that his beautiful home was near Versailles and known as "Free Hill," but it is certain that he bought a part of the Robert Alexander tract near Spring Station and built a fine residence there which Dr. Alexander now occupies and it is likely that that was the "Free Hill" farm spoken of by my correspondent. He was familiarly known by his neighbors and friends as Col. "Billey Buford." He and his wife were very industrious and reasonably economical in their early married life and rapidly accumulated a fine estate out of which they contributed liberally towards the educational and social advantages of their children. He spent his entire life in agricultural pursuits, which included the breeding, rearing and training of fine stock. All of the name loved a horse that could "get up and go."

William Buford died in 1848, but his wife survived until 1866. He owned a farm and eleven slaves in 1810, and his family at that time was composed of five individuals. Their children were: Francis Kirtley Buford, who married Mary Walker Mills. He was born in 1803 and represented Woodford County in the legislature of 1836 and died soon thereafter at Versailles, Ky.; Margaret Kirtley Buford, born in 1806, married Joel Twyman, son of Capt. Reuben Twyman and Margaret Griffin, in 1825. He died in 1881; Ann Mary Buford, born in 1808, married Caleb Wallace, Jr., in 1833, and died in 1884; William Buford, Jr., born in 1811, died unmarried in 1848; John Buford, Jr., born in 1813, married Elizabeth Holmes Singleton and died in 1885; Elizabeth Walker Buford, born in 1815, married John W. Allen, of Shelby County, in 1832; Sinclair James Buford, born in 1817, died unmarried in 1851; Abraham Buford, born in 1820 and married Amanda Harris. He graduated from West Point, served in the Mexican War and was a Brig.-General in the service of the Confederacy. After the Civil War he returned to his farm near Versailles, known as "Bosque-Bonita," now owned by John Morris, where he resumed the duties of a farmer and producer of famous racers such as the noted Enquirer and Goodnight, the latter named for Isaac Herschal Goodnight, a colleague in the legislature, from Simpson County, session 1877-78. His only child, Capt. William Buford, an exceedingly handsome and cultured gentleman, and the idol of his parents, died soon after the Civil War and it was a blow to the General and his good wife from which they never recovered. He, General Abe, represented Woodford in the legislature in 1877-8, and died in 1884. Martha and Mary Buford were twins, born in 1821, both of whom died spinisters; Thomas Buford, born in 1824, died in 1885 unmarried. He was a handsome man, and at times affable and entertaining, but, like Humphrey

Marshall, too often irascible and uncontrolled, which led him into trouble; and George Henry Buford, born in 1827, married Sarah Fulton and died in 1887 in Fayette County. They had no children.

Simeon Buford was the last of the three brothers who settled in Woodford County. In 1810 he owned a farm and six slaves and had a family of four members. He married Elizabeth Twyman, daughter of Capt. Reuben and Margaret Griffin Twyman, and they had the following children: Manville Buford, born in 1807, married Elizabeth Shelby; Legrand Griffin Buford, born in 1808 and married Eusibia Mallory; Adeline Buford, born in 1809 and married John S. Nowland; Almira Margaretta Buford, born in 1813, married John V. Webb, and Elizabeth Gabriella Buford, born in 1815, married Judge John S. Ryland.

About 1835 William McDowell Buford, of Scott County, moved to Woodford and bought a large farm within one mile of Midway on Georgetown road, which is now owned by Wm. L. Cannon and known as "Elkwood." He built a commodious residence on the estate and spent the remainder of his life there. He married Margaret Elizabeth Robertson in 1828 and their issue follows: Martha McDowell Buford, who married Col. Willis Jones in 1846 and resided on Lexington pike near Versailles. It was in his woods that the barbecue was given in 1861 when John C. Breckenridge and others of Woodford and surrounding counties delivered farewell addresses, and casting their fortunes with the

Confederacy, left immediately for the South. Many of Woodford's young men, the very flower of the community, were there in their gray uniforms, and they were soon within the Confederate lines. It would be impossible for one who witnessed the scenes of that day to forget them.

Eleanor McIntosh Buford was the second of Wm. McDowell and Margaret Robertson Buford, and she married George Troutman, in 1853; Charles Alexander married Ellen Matthews in 1861; Mary Catherine married Dr. Marcus Evans Poynter in 1869; Wm. Robertson married Sallie Dobyns in 1868; Marcus Bainbridge married Mary Reed Hunter in 1870; Margaret Elizabeth married Milton P. Craig in 1873, and Mary Duke Buford married Lee Miller in 1880.

In order to distinguish this William Buford from Col. William who came from Barren County and settled at "Free Hill," a part of the Alexander estate, the former was called "Scott Billey" Buford, while the latter was designated as "Col. Billey" Buford. They were first cousins, as Col. Abraham Buford who settled in the part of Woodford County near Georgetown in 1792, that afterwards became a part of Scott County, and Simeon, Sr., who settled in Barren County were brothers. Abraham Buford, Sr., married Martha McDowell, and "Scott Billey" was one of their sons. The wife of William McDowell Buford, of Scott County, was Margaret Elizabeth Robertson, and she was a daughter of George Robertson and Eleanor Bainbridge, of Lancaster, Ky. The name Buford evolved from

French Beaufort, which appears in a list of French nobility. It also appears among the Huguenot emigrants to America. It is, in other words, a French word denoting a beautiful fort or castle. The castle of Beaufort was in the Province of Anjou, France.

The French, English and American Beauforts—Bufords—are members of the same family. The American Bufords descended from Richard Beauford who emigrated from Gravesend, England, in 1635, in the good ship Elizabeth, at the age of eighteen years, when he took oath of allegiance to the King. He married Miss Vance and the Buford descent in America is traced through their son, John of Christ Church Parrish, Middlesex County, Virginia.

Abraham Buford, of Scott County, and his nephew, John, son of James, were both in the Revolution and both settled near Georgetown in 1792, which was a part of Woodford from 1788 to about 1800, hence they were both pioneers of Woodford.

———

Three Whittington brothers came to Woodford at an early day from Virginia and located on farms in the county. They were William, Littleton and Joshua, and no citizens of the county were more respected or enjoyed a wider circle of acquaintances and loyal friends. You could always depend upon them to do the right thing at the right time, and their hospitality was open-hearted; nothing they had was too good for a neighbor, or a friend, and no one seeking alms, either for themselves or others in need, were turned from their doors empty handed.

William Whittington was born in Virginia in 1759, died in Woodford County in 1824. He married Lucy Long in 1791, daughter of John Long, Sr., and Mary Haynes. She was born in 1775 and died in 1861. His home was in "Germany," a vicinity midway between Clifton and Millville. His residence was built of logs, but his son, Isaac, who succeeded to the ownership, built a large two-story brick with an ell, which contained ten or twelve rooms.

William Whittington and Lucy Long had fifteen children. The census of 1810 reported thirteen in family, and credited him with eight slaves. The names of his children were: Littleton, born in 1792, died in 1833; Southey, born in 1793, died in 1835. He served in the legislature in 1830; Mary, born in 1795, died in 1876. She was the wife of James McCaslin and for many years a patient invalid; Elizabeth, born in 1797, died in 1852, married ―――― Owens; Anna, born in 1799, died in 1830, married ―――― Davis, and moved to Indiana; John Long, born in 1801, died in 1844; James, born in 1802, died in 1833; William Handy, born in 1804, died in 1855. He was twice married, first to Adelia, and second to Ann Kavanaugh, sisters, of Anderson County. He was a minister of the Christian Church, and a daughter, Mary, was Lady Principal at Daughters College, Harrodsburg, until her death; Atalanta, born in 1806, died in 1878. She was born while her mother was on a visit to Maryland relatives, making

the long trip on horseback, as was the custom in those days. Atalanta married Randolph Railey Darnell, son of Aaron Darnell and Jane Railey; Isaac Stevenson, born in 1808, died in 1882. It was he who abandoned the log house built by his father, and substituted a brick in its stead. The old time hospitality of this home was appreciated by every one in that part of the county and even beyond its border, the latch-string always without. Of the nine children of Isaac Whittington only one is now living. She the wife of N. L. Curry of Harrodsburg. Four of his sons were in the service of the Confederacy. Two of them, Hubbard and Thomas returned to their homes after the Civil War, while James Southey sleeps at Murfreesboro, Tenn., and John Black sleeps at Camp Douglas, Ill., where so many other brave Confederates sleep the sleep of death; Hannah, born in 1810, died in 1838, married Anderson Brown; Samuel, born in 1812, died in 1840; Hervey, born in 1814, married and moved to Missouri; Jemima, born in 1816, married Richard Taylor of the county, but they moved to Missouri after the Civil War, and Henry, the fifteenth, born in 1820, died in 1845.

Randolph Railey Darnell and Atalanta Whittington lived and died in "Germany" not far from her ancestral home, and they reared the following children: Aaron Darnell, born 1828, married first, Katherine Hawkins in 1850, second, Sarah E. Pepper in 1857; Wm. W. Darnell, born 1830, married, first, Sarah Jane Taylor, second, Eleanor Taylor; John R. Dar-

nell, born 1832, married Susan Cotton;
Southey W. Darnell, born 1839, married Sarah Webb; Virginia Darnell,*
born 1841, married Thos. J. Jett; Atalanta Darnell, born in 1843, married
Thos. W. Edwards; Charles Randolph Darnell, born 1845, married Bertha H.
Railey.

Littleton Whittington, the second of the three pioneer brothers mentioned
in the beginning, also lived in "Germany," his residence being in full view
of his brother William's home. This home was still standing twenty years
ago and I presume is yet. He married Sarah Hearn and they had ten children, but I am only able to mention
three of them; Dr. William Wishart Whittington, who was not only a very
popular physician, but one of the best known and most popular citizens of the
county prior to the Civil War. After that period he was so enfeebled and
bent with age that he seldom left his residence, his farm adjoining the old
Cotton and Henton farms near McKee's crossroads; Milcah Whittington,
who married James Smith, and Edward, who married Cordelia Hawkins,
were the three.

Dr. William W. Whittington married Ann Handy and they had the following children: Maria, who married
Robert Berryman; Hannah, Robert, Charlotte, who married John Whittington (the son of James); Mollie
and Jennie. The last named is the only one living. She has passed her
eightieth birthday and is residing at Versailles. John Whittington, who
married Charlotte, was many years associated with the sheriff's office, a part
of which time he was the sheriff.

Milcah Whittington, sister of Dr. Whittington, married James Smith
and they lived and died in the home settled by her father Littleton. Their
children were: James and Cordie Smith. The later is living in Versailles and is a patient Christian invalid who is on the shady side of life.
James Smith, her brother, died in Versailles some years ago. He was
an exceedingly affable gentleman who was popular with every one. He, I
think, served with Morgan, and also with the famous Orphans' Brigade.
He married ——— McCorkle and had the following children: William
Walker Smith, married Charlotte Davis; Bessie Milcah Smith, married
Stanley Hale; David Drake Smith; James W. Smith; Jennie Louise Smith,
married Harrington C. Field; Cordelia Smith, married Dorcey C. Rutherford, and Viola Smith, who married
Burton French.

After the Civil War James Smith was sheriff of the county, then entered
the service of the Woodford Bank as a clerk, and for many years cashier of
the Sellers Bank.

Edward Whittington was one of, if not the youngest of the children of
Littleton and Sarah Hearn Whittington. He married Cordelia Hawkins
and their son, William Littleton Whittington, married Mary Elizabeth
Gaines, who is now a widow living at Versailles. Their children follow:
Cordelia, who married Robert Soper; Florence and Lelia, twins; Ruth;
Miles married Lena Redden; Annie

*See page 253.

Hawkins married Claude A. Witt, and Edward Whittington, who married Kate Hearn.

James Smith, who married Milcah Whittington, was a son of William Smith who settled in Woodford prior to 1810, and was a farmer with a family of nine at that time and the possessor of three slaves. His father was a Virginian who fought in the Revolution. William Smith married Deborah Hearn, sister of the wife of Littleton Whittington. Besides James Smith, who married Milcah Whittington, they had the following children: Jacob Smith, who married Amanda Todd; Josephine Smith, and Jane Smith, who married Warren Hearn. Jacob Smith and Amanda Todd had: Paschal, Elizabeth, Mary and Amanda.

In 1810 Littleton Whittington reported a family of twelve and possessed six slaves.

Joshua, the other pioneer brother, lived in the county in 1810, was a farmer with a family of nine and he also had six slaves. I have not been able to get a line on his descendants and think they went West at an early date.

Lucy Long, the wife of William Whittington the pioneer, was in the fort at Bryan's Station and was one of the brave maidens who volunteered to carry water for a thirsty garrison. At the age of about 85 years she related her experience to me and as a mere boy it thrilled me. However, she was only about seven years old and could not have rendered much service "toting water" for a garrison of several hundred persons, but she always felt aggrieved that her name was not included in the list of heroines who braved the dangers and ventured to go to the Bryant's Station spring for water.

_____

*Robert Edward Coleman lived in Orange County, Virginia, and his estate joined that of James Madison. He served in the Revolution, married Sallie Lightfoot and they were the parents of four sons. They likely had daughters too, but I am not informed. Tradition says that one of their sons, whose name I have not learned, came to Kentucky and settled on a farm in Woodford County near Midway, on the Versailles and Midway road, that many years later became the home of Warren Viley, and has since been known as "Stonewall." This son of Robert Edward Coleman soon grew tired of the undeveloped west and returned to his Virginia home, where he traded his Woodford County possessions to his brother, James Coleman, for the consideration of a pony and a shotgun. James then came to Kentucky with his wife, Sarah Taylor, and took possession of the farm, said originally to have been a large one on which, in 1810, he used his twenty slaves. At that time his family numbered six. He served in the Revolution and was present at the surrender of Cornwallis. He had three sons that I am able to name, and partially account for, and likely had other children. Chapman Coleman, who married Ann Mary Crittenden, daughter of John J. Crittenden; James, who married and moved to

_____

*See Supplement.

Oldham County, and Edward Spillsby Coleman, who married Margaret Vaughan Blanton, daughter of Carter Blanton and Susan Sneed.

Chapman Coleman was appointed U. S. Marshal during the first quarter of the nineteenth century and he and his wife, Ann Mary Crittenden, lived in Frankfort for many years, then moved to Louisville where both lived the remainder of their lives. They had the following children: Florence who married Patric Joyes; Cornelia, married Marriott; Eugenia; Judith, married Charles Adams; Sallie married ———; Gazaway, John Crittenden and Chapman, Jr., who married Jane Hendrick.

James Coleman was three times married but I have not been able to learn the names of his wives. He moved to Oldham County where he died.

Edward Spillsbee Coleman, born in 1786, died in 1860, married Margaret Blanton, born in 1788, died in 1860. They moved to Frankfort where he bought a farm that covered a large portion of South Frankfort, built his residence near Coleman's Spring that is now owned by John Griffin, on the corner of Campbell and Steele streets. His son, James Carter Coleman, was a deputy U. S. Marshal under his uncle Chapman Coleman about 1827, and married Ann Eliza Mills. They have a son, Dr. J. S. Coleman, and a daughter, Mrs. Emma Jameson, at Frankfort. Other children were Edward J. Coleman, married Laura Perkins; Landon Coleman, John M. Coleman, married Emily Woodson, and Sallie Coleman married William Jett, whose daughter is the wife of Dr. Matthew Darnell, of Ducker Station. Chapman Coleman, Sr., was with Jackson at the battle of New Orleans, and his son, Chapman, Jr., served as Secretary of the American Legation at Berlin and later as Consul at Rome.

———

The Carlyles were representative of good old Virginia stock. They came to Kentucky early and located in Woodford County, settling upon a farm near Midway on the Versailles and Midway road. Jesse Martin lived there for many years, and it is now the property of Henry L. Martin adjoining his present site, but nearer Midway.

George Carlyle and his wife Margaret Crockett, and his children, numbering in all twelve persons in 1810, lived here and reared their family. He had fourteen slaves that he used in the cultivation of his large estate. In the census of 1810 his name is erroneously spelled Carlisle. He was an only son of John Carlyle and Sarah Fairfax, of Alexandria, Virginia, and his wife, Margaret Crockett, was a daughter of Alexander Crockett and Margaret Campbell.

George Carlyle and his wife Margaret Crockett had, in part, the following children: Crockett Carlyle, born in Woodford County in 1798, married Lucinda Graddy; Martha Carlyle married William Lee Graddy; Margaret Carlyle married Dr. Jo Coleman Carter of Versailles, and Mary Carlyle married Samuel Nuckols.

William Lee Graddy and Martha Carlyle had the following children: W. Henry Graddy, George Jesse

Graddy, Sallie Graddy, and Margaret Graddy and their descendants appear under Jesse Graddy and Viola Dale.

Dr. Joseph Coleman Carter and Margaret Carlyle had the following children: Dr. D. Drake Carter, Dorothy Carter, and Josephine Carter whose children appear under Goodloe Carter and Mary Crenshaw.

Samuel Nuckols and Mary Carlyle had the following children: George Clairborne, Robert, John and Louisa. Clairborne married Jane Dedman; John married Anne Jackson, and Louisa married Dr. Thomas Iles, of Midway.

Clairborne Nuckols and Jane Dedman had the following children: George, Sam, Lewis Henry, James, Charles and Margaret.

George was with Morgan in the Civil War and died at Camp Butler; and Samuel, 74 years of age, is the only one living in Woodford County at present, and he is living on the farm owned by his grandfather, Samuel Nuckols, two miles from Versailles on the Tyrone pike. I can't say who originally owned this farm but there is an old springhouse built of stone within two hundred feet of the pike that was used as a district clerk's office before Woodford County was established.

Goodloe Carter was born in Albermarle County, Virginia, in 1786. He married Mary Crenshaw and came to Woodford County, Ky., prior to 1810, his name appearing on the census of that year with a family of six persons. He was a son of George Carter and Francis Diana Goodloe, of Spottsyl-

vania, Virginia, but they moved to "Red Lands" near Charlottsville in 1758.

The children of Goodloe Carter and Mary Crenshaw were: Joseph Coleman Carter, who married Margaret Carlyle of Woodford County; Ellen Virginia, who married Joel W. Twyman; Sarah Francis, who married Thomas Graddy; Miriam married Joshua Tevis, and Margaret who married Dr. T. Warwick Twyman.

Dr. Joseph Coleman Carter was born in Albemarle County, Va., in 1808, and was brought to Woodford County during his infancy by his parents and he was a lifetime resident of the county. He was a successful practitioner of medicine and a very popular citizen. He married Margaret Carlyle, born in 1810, a daughter of George Carlyle and Margaret Crockett. The children of Dr. Carter and Margaret Carlyle follow: Dr. D. Drake Carter, born in 1837, married, first, Louisiana Hart Gibson in 1876, and second, Sarah Fullerton in 1882. His son, Joe Coleman Carter, born in 1884, of the second marriage, married in 1909, Carolyne Steele, daughter of Captain John Andrew Steele and his wife Fannie Breckenridge.

Dorothy Carter, daughter of Dr. Joseph, married, first, Zachary White, second, Constance Holt, of Texas; no issue.

Josephine Carlyle Carter, daughter of Dr. Joseph, has never married.

Sarah Francis Carter and Thomas Graddy had children. See under Graddy.

Ellen Virginia Carter and Joel W.

Twyman had children. See under Twyman.*

Miriam Carter married Joshua Tevis and moved to California where they have children.

Margaret Carter and Dr. T. Warwick Twyman lived and died in Woodford County. No issue.

Born in North Carolina in 1767, family history relates that Jesse Graddy, though but a boy of fourteen years, took an active part in the "Battle of the Cow Pens" and that an older brother was killed by the Tories. Jesse Graddy came to Kentucky in 1787 and at once became a pioneer farmer in Woodford County, purchasing a tract of land upon which he built his home on Glenns Creek. His farm adjoined that of Thomas Railey whose residence overlooked the village of Clifton. Jesse Graddy built his residence of Glenns Creek stone and it was standing many years after the Civil War, and may be habitable yet, but I think he or one of his sons built a brick of more imposing dimensions, either on the same estate or the one adjoining at an early day, and it is likely that Jesse Graddy spent his declining years there. The property was never out of possession of descendants until 1919. It is approached from the McCracken's Mill pike and situated five and one-half miles from Versailles, extending to what is known as the "Germany" line.

In 1810 his family consisted of nine members and his possessions were listed as six slaves, besides his real estate. His wife was Viola Dale, but I am unable to state whether she was a native of North Carolina, or a member of the numerous families by that name in the county in 1810, and prior to that time. At any rate, Jesse Graddy and Viola Dale reared a large family of children whose names are here given: Nancy, who was the second wife of the Rev. Isaac Crutcher; Mary who married Richard Robertson; Elizabeth, who married N. E. Martin; Elsie, who married Thomas Ford; Lucinda, who married Crockett Carlyle; William Lee, who married Martha Carlyle, and Thomas, who married Sarah Carter.

Jesse Graddy called his country site "Homestead," and as his children married he gave each a farm adjacent to, or in the vicinity of "Homestead," and finally he and his children owned a block of land extending from the Clifton road to the McCrackens Mill road, and from the home called "Welcome," owned by his oldest son, William, to the line of Thomas Railey at Clifton and "Germany," an immense body of land.

Elizabeth Graddy and N. E. Martin had a daughter Eudora Martin whose birth was in 1836. She married Dr. Joseph P. Woolfolk, of Scott County, a kinsman of Sowel Woolfolk, a wealthy citizen of Woodford. †Dr. Joseph Woolfolk practiced medicine in Woodford for several years, then moved to Mississippi where he was successful both as a physician and a planter, but he returned to Woodford after the Civil War, where he re-

*Page 56.
†See pages 142, 174, 254, 269, 316, 396.

mained on his farm near Clifton until his death in 1883. His wife conducted the farm for many years after his death. At the age of eighty-four she still lives and is an interesting old lady. She divides her time between New York where she has a son, and Woodford County with a daughter who is the wife of Samuel D. Pinkerton. Her children were: Elizabeth, who married Samuel D. Pinkerton, now residing in the suburbs of Versailles and have several married children; Sallie Woolfolk, who married Oscar Blakemore, of Franklin County, and Dr. Joseph P. Woolfolk, Jr., who graduated from Bellevue Medical School in New York and practiced for many years in Bellevue Hospital. He is married and a resident of New York.

Mary Graddy, who married Richard Robertson, lived and died in the county. Her husband was a farmer and stockman and was very successful. If they had other children besides Sidney and Jane Robertson, I have no line on them, but they had relatives in Missouri, and James Miller, former mayor of Versailles, married in Missouri a kinswoman of Sidney Robertson. Sidney Robertson and his sister Jane lived in Versailles on "Rose Hill" and are remembered well.

Nancy Graddy and Isaac Crutcher lived and died in Woodford County near Millville. In 1810 he had a family of seven and owned a large body of land and six slaves. He was a Baptist minister, preaching on Sunday and looking after his farming interests during the week. His father was a Quartermaster under Washing-

ton. Their children were Dr. William Crutcher, who married Susan Scearce, and Jesse Graddy Crutcher who married Martha Pittman. For the children of Dr. William and Jesse Graddy Crutcher see sketches of Cottons and Crutchers.

If Elsie Graddy, who married Thomas Ford, had issue, I am not advised. In fact I have no line on them further than to state that they were married in the county.

Lucinda Graddy and Crockett Carlyle I think moved to Mason County and reared a family there.

William Lee Graddy was one of the two sons of Jesse Graddy and Viola Dale. His country seat was called "Welcome Hall" which I think, was originally settled by Mathew Pleasants. He and his wife, Martha Carlyle, were the parents of William Henry Graddy who married Sallie Belt; George Jesse Graddy, who married, first, Fanny Cotton, second, Mollie Blackburn; Sallie Graddy, who married Henry Johnson, and Margaret Graddy, who married Col. Ben W. Williams.

William Henry Graddy and Sallie Belt had the following children: Lucy, who married Ed. M. Wallace; William Lee Graddy, Jr., who married Mamie Fields; George C. Graddy, who married Catherine Davis, and Joe Carter Graddy, who married Elizabeth Turner. The home of William Henry Graddy was called "Greenwood" and is located on Steele's pike that intersects with Clifton and McCracken's Mill pikes.

George Jesse Graddy and Fanny Cotton had a daughter, Fanny Graddy, who married Arthur Cary, grandson of Thomas Railey and Martha Woodson, and they have a son, Graddy Cary, who is practicing law at Louisville.

Margaret Graddy and Col. Ben Williams had the following children: Pattie, who married James Lisle; Luttrell, now in Idaho; William Graddy, who married Florence Sinclair; Graddy Carlyle, who married Lee Cassedy; Mary, married A. M. Robbins; Deweese, married Mrs. Ford; Ben, Jr., married Mary Railey, and Fannie, who has not married.

Thomas Graddy and Sarah Francis Carter, his wife, lived at "Oakland," a farm that adjoined "Homestead" the farm of his father Jesse Graddy. At the death of his father he became the owner of "Homestead." The following children were born to them: Joseph Carter, George Thomas, Jesse, Jr., and Florence Graddy. The sons alternated in conducting a Bachelor's Hall at "Homestead," Jesse's turn coming last and he was always delighted to see his friends, and they were equally delighted to be his guests and enjoy his liberal hospitality. Late in life, say forty-five, he married Mary Scott and moved to Versailles where he lived the remainder of his life. He sold the estate of his father and his grandfather, to his sister, Florence Graddy Kennedy, who resided there for many years, but sold it in 1919 to a party outside of the relationship. All of these homes, "Homestead," "Welcome Hall," "Oakland" and "Greenwood," have been centers that were noted for the

hospitality and sociability of the several members of each household.

Fannie Ferguson Berry and Blanch Hunter, of the county, are granddaughters of George Jesse Graddy.

———

David Thompson, Sr., enlisted in the Revolution from Louisa County, Virginia, when the clash came between the colonies and England. When the strife terminated he returned to his home where he remained until 1790 when he and a party of friends decided to locate in Kentucky. Some time during that year they reached their destination in Woodford County, and he located a farm on Glenns Creek not far from Millville, known as Alex Wright farm. He remained upon this farm for many years, and his son, David Thompson, was one of his children whose birth occurred in this home in 1795, and he also raised a family there. He married Elizabeth *Beatty and they had several sons, one of whom was Robert Alexander Thompson, who studied medicine in the office of Dr. Joseph Carter in Versailles, and afterwards studied law in the office of and under the advice of Lt. Gov. Thos. P. Porter. A few years later he graduated from the Louisville School of Medicine. In 1861 he enlisted in the service of the Confederacy, following the colors to the end of the war and at its conclusion returned to his home as Captain Thompson.

About 1870 Captain R. A. Thompson moved to Franklin County where he divided his time between politics and farming. Held offices in the legislature for several years and was

———

*See page 281.

elected county Judge of Franklin, which position he held for a number of years.

Joseph F. Taylor was a captain in the War of 1812, enlisting from Woodford County. He came from Culpeper County, Virginia, and settled at an early date in Woodford. I have not been able to learn the maiden name of his wife, but in 1810 his family consisted of ten members, and he owned a farm and two slaves. His farm was in the Clover Bottom section of the county. One of his daughters, Nancy Taylor, married Samuel S. Mitchell, and their son, Charles P. Mitchell, born in 1838, was for a lifetime one of the county's most respected citizens, and for a long period one of the members of Woodford's fiscal court. During that time he was ever watchful of the county's best interests. In 1869 he married Elizabeth Black, who was of the prominent family of that name who came to the county at an early date and assisted in establishing Black's fort. The following children were of this union: Ida, Eudora, Guy, Nannie, Samuel and Lucy. These children were all born and reared in Clover Bottom, and many of them are residents there now.

The Dearings were Virginians of long standing. When they came to Kentucky they settled in that part of Woodford County that about 1796, or soon thereafter, became a part of Franklin County.

Walker Dearing, the progenitor of the Kentucky branch of that family, invented the Dearing plow which he manufactured for many years in Frankfort. It was one of the most popular plows used in Kentucky prior to the Civil War and was extensively used upon the farms, and many of our citizens will recall the splendid service it gave.

When Walker Dearing began the manufacture of these plows in his establishment where the gas house stands, just back of the old Capitol; there were no transportation lines, either rail or water, and he was compelled to transport the output to Louisville and other points in wagons over dirt roads, there being no macadam roads at that early day.

Finally the plant was moved to Louisville, where the business was increased at once and continued successfully for many years. Soon after the war of 1812 Walker Dearing once more became a resident of Woodford County by purchasing seven hundred acres of land from John Blanton and others, his line beginning at a point on the Frankfort and Versailles road six miles from Frankfort and continued on that road to the Grassy Spring road, thence beyond the church to the entrance avenue of the Wood's farm (afterward Gaines'), thence southwest to a point not far from Glenns Creek.

Walker Dearing at first had a temporary frame house, but afterward, about 1822, built a two story brick in full view of the Frankfort road that he was pleased to call "Mansion House," but ever since the Civil War known as "Morris Place." The building is standing today in excellent condition and is occupied.

He gave to each of his four children

one hundred and fifty acres of land as they married; also three or four likely slaves. His son, John Granville, was allotted that part of the estate that bordered on the Versailles and Grassy Spring roads that contained the John Blanton residence, which was purchased from the widow, —— Blanton, about 1820. Squire George Edwards bought the place from Granville Dearing and lived there many years. It is now the property of Wm. E. Bradley, Jr., who has replaced the old residence with a splendid modern brick residence.

Walker Dearing married Sallie McClelland and their children's names follow: Isyphena, who married John Morris; Margaret, who married Henry Hardie; Narcissa, who married Louis Crutcher, and John Granville, who married Susan Brassfield.

Isyphena and John Morris lived and died in the ancestral home and reared three sons there: John, the eldest, married Cordelia Sargent and they had several children, one of whom married Lewis Utterback of the county; James was in the Confederacy, Morgan's division, Duke's brigade, and was a gallant soldier. He married his cousin Louella Dearing; Edward married Edmonia Stevens and reared four sons at the old home, but sold it several years ago and moved to Frankfort where his son, Leslie Morris, is a promising attorney, and served a term as State Senator in 1918.

Lewis Crutcher and Narcissa Dearing had no children. He was a son of the Rev. Isaac Crutcher and Elizabeth Blanton.

John Granville Dearing and Susan Brassfield had the following children: Susie, Emma, Sallie, Narcissus, Cassie, John and Price. I am told that this family went to Missouri prior to the Civil War.

———

Alexander Turner was a native of Culpeper, Va., who joined the Revolutionary forces at the breaking out of the war and served to its conclusion. About 1795 he came to Kentucky and located a farm between Troy and Mortonsville in the county of Woodford.

His son, William Turner, was born in Virginia in 1787 and came to Kentucky with the family when a mere boy. Upon reaching man's estate he engaged in farming and was soon thereafter married to Rebecca Dean, the granddaughter of James Dean, a Revolutionary soldier, and his wife, Patience Holman, both of whom remained in Craig's fort* for quite awhile after arriving in Woodford County from Virginia, but finally drifted to Jessamine County where they spent the remainder of their lives on a farm.

William J. Turner, a son of William Turner and Rebecca Dean, was born in the county in 1821 and married Bettie Carpenter of the county. He was also a farmer, who was highly respected by all friends and acquaintances, and was quite successful. They raised a family of children whose names follow: Albert H., Mattie, John D., William T., James C. and Elizabeth, some of them now

---

*Mrs. Christopher Chenault says that their home, "Summer's Forest," bears unmistakable evidence of the location of Craig's fort. See page 78 and 269.

residents of the county, while others reside in adjacent counties. All are highly respected in their several communities.

---

†Benjamin Berry was born in Virginia in 1757, and died in Woodford County in 1838. His first wife was Mary Allen, whom he married in Virginia in 1780; his second wife was Nancy Blanton, whom he married in Woodford in 1804, she a daughter of Thomas Blanton and Jane .... Thomas Blanton was a Revolutionary veteran who came to the county early, and in 1810 had a family of nine and owned a farm and three slaves.

By the two marriages Benjamin Berry became the proud father of eighteen children, eleven by the first wife and seven by the second. This large family of children were raised in Woodford County, though several of them were born in Virginia. He settled in the county soon after the war of the Revolution, in which he creditably played a part, as a private soldier, and his eighteenth child was married five years before his death. His farm was on the Clifton pike, several miles from Versailles, and extended to the old Railey neighborhood near lock number five on the Kentucky River, and the vicinity in which he lived was ever known as the Berry neighborhood. The homestead at his death passed by inheritance to Col. Lewis A. Berry, his son, then to John T. Berry, son of Lewis A., and I think is still the property of that gentleman or a member of his family. John T. Berry is now approaching the four

†See page 254.

score years, which is not often allotted to men, and is unusually spry for one of his age. The residence of the pioneer still stands, and is in fair condition. He, Benjamin, was a prosperous farmer and accumulated much property, owning a large farm and twenty-seven slaves as early as 1810, at which time he reported twelve members in his family, several of his children having married and left the parental roof prior to that time. The will of Benjamin Berry was quite lengthy and very cleverly drawn. It is of date of March 5, 1835, with a codicil dated April 26, 1838, the year in which he died, all recorded in will book L, pages 24 to 39, and was witnessed by the following neighbors: E. Ducker, Charles Norwood, Jacob Darnell, A. G. Chew, Randolph Railey, Sr., and his brother, Isham Railey, Sr.

The children of Benjamin Berry and his two wives follow: By Mary Allen, the first wife, was: Samuel, Jr., born in 1781 in Virginia, died in Woodford County in 1853, married Susannah Hieatt, daughter of Lewis Hieatt and Barbara Allen, in 1803. She was born in 1783, and died in 1852; Zachariah, born in 1784, died in 1806, unmarried; Polly, born in 1786, died in 1863, married George F. Brown in 1809; Frances, born in 1787, died in 1859, married Lewis Utterback in 1805 (See Utterback sketch for descendants); Lucy, born in 1789, died in 1850, married William Campbell in 1808, whose father was a soldier of the Revolution; Sallie, born in 1791, married John Ford in 1813, whose father was in the Revolution; Benjamin, Jr., born in

1793, died unmarried in 1843; Betsy, born in 1795, died in 1858, married in ——, —— Young; John, born in 1797, died in 1854, married Rebecca Morrison in 1821; Col. Lewis A., born in 1800, died in 1881; married in 1827, Martha Ann Redd, born in 1809, died in 1863; Younger, born in 1802, died in 1868, married, first, Catherine Stone in 1837, second, Mary Ann Sallee in 1855. Children by Nancy Blanton follow: Thomas Blanton, born in 1805, died in 1834, married Agatha Redd, daughter of Thomas and Betsy Redd; Jane, born in 1807, died in 1808, Lucinda, born in 1808, married Lewis Harris in 1826; Patsy, born in 1810, died in 1863, married James W. Redd in 1827; Harriett, born in 1812, married M. W. Redd in 1834; Harrison P., born in 1814, died in 1816; Matilda, born in 1815, died in 1839, married Archibald Redd in 1833.

This is the largest family recorded in Woodford County since its history began to unfold, and all of the descendants, like their forbears, have been men and women highly respected by their neighbors and friends in whatever community they have chosen a residence.

Samuel Berry (the eldest of the children of Benjamin Berry and Mary Allen) and his wife Susannah Hieatt had the following children: America, born in 1804, died in 1839, married Henry Scearce of the county in 1822; Permelia Berry, born in 1806, died in 1839, married Richard Crutcher, son of Rev. Isaac and Nancy Blanton Crutcher in 1823; Jefferson Berry, born in 1807, died in 1827, married

Elizabeth Crutcher; Ann Berry, born in ——, married —— Withers.

Col. Lewis A. Berry (tenth born of Benjamin Berry and Mary Allen) and his wife, Martha Ann Redd, had the following children: Bettie Berry, born in 1831, died in 1893, married in 1852, Alexander Higbee, a long time merchant of Versailles, no issue; John T. Berry, born in 1837, married, first, Anna Gaines in 1860, no issue; second marriage to Lizzie Wheatley in 1870; *Sallie Berry, born in 1842; married in 1865, Joseph C. Bailey who was a Confederate soldier, and circuit clerk until his death; Robert Y. Berry, born in 1844, died in 1885, married Sallie Ware in 1868; Lewis A. Berry, Jr., born in 1847, died in 1894, married Annie Stevenson in 1872, who died in 1879; Fannie Berry, born in 1849, died in 1909, married James M. Saffell in 1869.

John T. Berry and Lizzie Wheatley had issue as follows: Mattie Larue, born in 1871; Frank Wheatley, born in 1872, married Della McFadden; Bettie, born in 1877, married Robert Yancey in 1912; Richard Clifton, born in 1878; Fannie, born in 1881, married William C. Bates in 1911, and Lydia, born in 1886.

Robert Younger Berry and Sallie Ware, had issue as follows: Lewis A. III., born in 1869, married Fannie Branham in 1898; James Ware, born in 1872, died in 1890; John T., Jr., born in 1877, married Grace Talbot in 1905; Robert Younger, Jr., born in 1879, married Jean Briggs in 1915. Robert Y. Berry, Sr., was sheriff and a grain and coal merchant until his death.

Lewis A. Berry, Jr., and Annie

*See page 371.

Stevenson had the following children: William S., born in 1874, married Fanny Graddy Ferguson in 1896; Joe Bailey, born in 1876, died in 1912.

Fannie Berry and James M. Saffell had issue as follows: Pythian Saffell, born in 1871, died 1899, married Francis Taylor in 1891, and they had: Francis Taylor Saffell, born in 1892, married Floyd Ayres Thomasson in 1919; Agnes Saffell, born in 1895, married James O'Rear in 1914, and James M. Saffell, Jr., born in 1897.

Col. Lewis A. Berry, Sr., was a member of the Kentucky Legislature in 1847. In 1829 Gov. Metcalfe appointed him Captain of calvary in the 107th regiment, 3rd brigade. In 1833 Gov. Jas. T. Morehead commissioned him Major in the 106th regiment of the 3rd brigade, State militia.

———

Samuel Berry was another Revolutionary soldier who came to Kentucky about the same time and settled in Woodford County. Some of his descendants think it more than likely that he was the father of Benjamin, but I feel quite sure that he was a brother of Benjamin. Their names appear together in the census of 1810. It it not positively known to whom he was married, but I feel quite sure that his wife was an Allen. He was the executor of Joseph Allen's estate in Spottsylvania County, Virginia, and named his first son Allen Berry. This Allen Berry and his brother, Samuel, Jr., appear upon the census of 1810 taken for Woodford County. Beside the Hieatts and Berrys intermarried, and Lewis Hieatt married Barbara Allen, a daughter of Joseph Allen, and

Benjamin Berry married Mary Allen for his first wife, who was evidently a kinswoman of Barbara. Joseph Allen had two other daughters, Rachel and Susanna, but I am unable to say to whom they were married, if married at all. Samuel Berry, Sr., had these children, in part: Allen, Samuel, Jr., Elizabeth, who married in 1801, John Hughes; Nancy Berry, born 1783, died 1859, married 1802, James C. Long; Susanna; Rachael, who married a Smith, and Polly (Mary), who also married a Smith. You note the similarity of the names of the children of Joseph Allen and Samuel Berry, Sr.

Nancy Berry and James C. Long had these children: John W. Long, married in 1824, Jane Stevenson, second, Winifred Davidson in 1833; Eliza Berry Long, married Alex. Cunningham Scott in 1825; Kitty Long, married Augustus Bower in 1832; James I. Long, married Louisa Jane Jesse in 1834; Cydney H. Long, married Fielding A. Evans in 1836; Henrietta Long, married Albert Bohannon in 1836; Mary Haynes Long, married John Hall, Shelby County, in 1843; William T. B. Long, married Lucy Jane Barkley in 1847; Ambrose Dudley Long, married Mildred Bullock in 1846; Thomas Parker Long, married Nancy Jackson, and Ryland D. Long, married Mary Portwood in 1856.

Mary Haynes Long and John Hall have a granddaughter, Katherine Bryant, who married Dr. Edward Byrnes Smith, living at Shelbyville, Ky.

———

Captain Robert Yancey, born in Virginia in 1750, was a captain in the first regiment of Light Dragoons, Continental Troops in the war of the Revolution. He and his wife were among the early arrivals in Kentucky and they located on a Woodford County farm near Versailles, it being a land grant by the government for services rendered in the war. In 1810 the Federal census reported him as owning, besides his farm, five slaves, and there were eight members in his family. He and his wife, in their old age, died upon the estate, he in 1824, and his wife preceded him several years. A daughter, with three children, was in the home with them in their declining years and gave them great comfort and pleasure.

Robert Yancey and his wife had the following issue: Katherine, who married John Snyder; Martha, who married Robert Campbell and located in Mississippi; George, whose pursuit in life is not indicated; Nancy, who married Captain Settles; Mary Walker, who married Simeon Twyman; Mildred, who died at Louisville, was a guest at the Galt House while a school girl; Charles and Robert, Jr.

Mrs. Veneta Wallace, of Colorado, is the only living grandchild of Capt. Robert Yancey known by the present generation. She is a daughter of Simeon Twyman and Mary Walker Yancey. The children of Captain Robert Yancey, as a rule, emigrated to other states after their marriage, and there are few, if any, descendants in the county today. The wife of Price Johnson, of Millville, was a granddaughter of Burket Yancey,* who resided not far from the Clifton heights in "Germany" on a farm that adjoin-

ed that of William Whittington, and while Burket was related to Captain Robert, I am not able to say whether he was a brother or a cousin. In 1810 there were five members in the family of Burket Yancey and besides his farm he owned two slaves.

From the pension office at Washington the following information was obtained concerning the war record of Captain Robert Yancey:

"He was a quartermaster, first Continental line in 1776; Cornet in 1777; Lieutenant of Dragoons in 1778, and Captain in 1779. Prisoner at Petersburg, Virginia, in 1781, being exchanged at close of war.

"He entered the Revolution from Culpeper County, Virginia, applied for pension in 1818 from Woodford County, Ky., when he was 68 years old. In 1820 his widowed daughter, with three children, was living with him."

———

Samuel Hampton came to Woodford from the county of Jessamine in 1849. His father was Andrew Hampton, a close kinsman of General Wade Hampton of North Carolina. Andrew was one of the early settlers of Jessamine County. Samuel Hampton engaged in the manufacture of rope, twine and bagging in the county soon after his arrival, and continued in that industry —so profitable at that time as to have a factory in many parts of the county —until the internecine struggle between the states from 1861 to '65 rendered that enterprise unprofitable. His parents, Andrew Hampton and Mary Hayden, lived and died in Jessamine. Samuel married Belle Dixon in

*See page 110.

1851, and about 1870 bought the old Jackson estate, better known at that time as the Douglas Young farm, situated on the Tyrone pike opposite the Utterback farm. Here he and his wife spent the remainder of their lives upon the estate. They had issue as follows: Wade, Maggie, Mary and Bettie. Wade married Annie Miller; Maggie married John B. George, son of Judge William George; Mary married Jerry E. Field, and Bettie married James Henton.

Samuel Nuckols was the pioneer of that name who settled in Woodford County some years after the War of 1812. I have not been able to learn anything of his forbears in Virginia, from whence he came to Kentucky, but judging by the splendid type of citizenship of the Woodford County descendants, the Virginia branch was all right. Samuel Nuckols married Mary Carlyle, daughter of George Carlyle and Margaret Crockett, whose home was near Midway on the Versailles and Midway road. He purchased a farm on the Tyrone road two miles from Versailles and he lived in the house that he built on this farm until his death in 1871. The farm is now owned by his grandson, Samuel Clairborne Nuckols.

Evidently there was a house on this farm before Samuel Nuckols bought it, built by an early pioneer, and I am sure that I have heard the older citizens say, during my boyhood, that the original structure was of stone. At any rate, there is an old stone spring house standing not far from the residence and within a few hundred feet of the pike that was one of, if not the

first rock structures in the county, and according to tradition, current when I was a boy, this historic building was used as a district court clerk's office, where business affecting the district of Kentucky was transacted before Woodford County was established in 1788, and this story will be told you by the older citizens of that community today.

This building, and the one on the premises of Judge Caleb Wallace at Midway, in which the first court was held after Woodford was established, should be kept in fair condition by the county court in order that future generations may look upon them as simple monuments of pioneer days. Later I hope to get to Versailles and look up the first owner of this property. Samuel Nuckols and his wife, Mary Carlyle, lived there contented and happy for many years.

They had the following children: George, Clairborne, Robert, John and Louisa.

George married an Iowa girl; Clairborne married Jane Dedman; John married Anne Jackson, and Louisa married Dr. Thomas Iles of Midway.

Clairborne Nuckols and Jane Dedman had issue as follows: George, Samuel Clairborne, Lewis, Henry, James, Charles and Margaret. George was a member of Morgan's command during the Civil War, was captured and sent to Camp Butler, where he died. Samuel Clairborne is the only one of that family now living in the county and he has passed his three score and ten years. He is the present owner of his grandfather's estate and was married to Lewella Wasson of Versailles. They had the following children: Lewis A., Eva, Claude Carlyle, and Lida.

Charles Nuckols married Bettie Hurst, daughter of Dr. Alfred Hurst, and they had the following children: Ada, Minnie, Jane, Charles, Jr., Francis, Sam, Alfred and Horace.

Thomas Henton was born in Virginia, but he and his brother, Evan, came to Kentucky early and were stationed at the stockade in Jefferson County near the falls, about where Seventh and Main streets cross. They were privates in Captain William Harrod's company, it being stationed there to protect the interests of the settlers in that section from the roving bands of Indians who were constantly molesting the several settlements in that vicinity, destroying without mercy or justice both people and property, the Indians being united with Bird's British troops who had also invaded that territory and were largely responsible for the brutality manifested toward the settlers. In consideration of the services of the Hentons they were granted lands in Shelby and Woodford. Thomas settled in Woodford on a fine body of land that included the property on which Grassy Springs Church was built, and his grandson, James Henton, owns that part of the tract upon which Thomas Henton's log house was built and still stands. The residence of James Henton, which his father erected, is approached from the Versailles and Frankfort road, and the driveway passes through a beautiful woodland. It is in full view of the church, a deep ravine separating the two buildings. What is now known as the Harris farm, just back of James Henton, was a part of the original grant, and one of the Hentons lived in an old brick house there many years ago.

Thomas and Evan Henton were sons of William Henton, who likely was never in Kentucky, as he died in Virginia in 1779 or '80. Thomas Henton's wife was Christine Brennen. He was in Woodford County residing upon this property in 1810, and died on the premises in 1829, his remains interred in the burial ground at Grassy Springs.

Thomas Henton and Christine Brennen had the following issue: Cassius, Guy, George, John, Chris, Katherine, Elizabeth, Persis and Thomas, Jr., eleven in the family as reported in 1810 census. Guy was killed in the War of 1812. Thomas, Jr., was twice married, first to Mildred Darnaby, and afterward to her sister, Nancy Darnaby. He lived and died on the ancestral estate, but all of his brothers and sisters, as they were married, moved from the county, some going to other parts of the State while others crossed the Ohio river for homes in the west.

Thomas Henton, Jr., and Mildred Darnaby had these children: Ann, Mildred and Thomas E. By Nancy Darnaby were: Ambrose, Mary and James. The Darnaby sisters were daughters of Edward Darnaby, born in 1765, and Mildred Ellis, born in 1767, and Thomas Henton, Jr., was born in 1797, died 1869.

Mildred Henton married Thomas Thompson and they were the parents of Eliza, who married Thomas Lewis; Elizabeth, who married Thomas R. Shaw; Ella married Virgil Lewis;

Thomas married Mary Quarles; Cynthia married S. Josh Gibson; James married Martha Scott, and Lucy and John who never married.

Ann Henton married Alex. Wright. Thomas E. Henton married Sarah Hammon and had: Thomas E., Jr., married Ethel Mastin; Nellie, who married A. L. Edwards, and Mary.

Mary Henton married Rev. R. M. Dudley and had: Anne married the Rev. W. O. Shewmaker; Mary married W. H. Pittman; June married R. Emmett Harvey; Rose married Ralph Scearce, and Louise never married.

James Henton married Bettie Hampton and they had: Dudley, who married Elizabeth Culter; Sam, who married Mary Kinkead Worthington and died in France in 1918; Jessie married Hiram Wilhoit; Wade married Natalie Brother, and Mary, who served with the Red Cross in France, is not married.

Collins' history says William Henton, son of Evan, the pioneer, was the first white child born in the territory of Kentucky.

———

Burket Yancey was born in Virginia and came with his wife, Ellen Nall, and the early settlers to Kentucky. He settled in that part of Woodford County known as "Germany," his farm being midway between Clifton and Millville, joining Thomas Railey on one side and William Whittington on the other. His wife was a relative of Charles L. and William H. Nall, both wealthy farmers of the county in 1810. At that time Burket Yancey had a family composed of five persons and owned two slaves, but at his death

many years later he owned thirty slaves. I have not been able to learn the names of Burket Yancey's parents, or what relation he sustained to Captain Robert Yancey, but he had a brother, William, and the names of his sisters were: Judith, Millie, and Jennie.

Burket Yancey and Ellen Nall had only two children, Mildred who married Dr. James Botts, a practicing physician at Millville until he died about 1885, quite an old man; and Eleanor, who married, first, Frank Taylor, of the county, and second, William W. Darnell.* By the first marriage was Burket Yancey Taylor, and Mittie Taylor, who married Price Johnson and resides with her husband near Millville. By the second marriage was William Darnell.

———

Charles Scott was born in Cumberland County, Virginia. He was a corporal in the memorable campaign of 1755 which resulted in Braddock's defeat, and when the Revolutionary struggle came on he entered the service as a Captain and rose rapidly in line of promotion until he reached the rank of a General. He was conspicuous for bravery and daring, and was a thorough disciplinarian, which made him a popular idol with the regulars. He was with General Wayne at Stony Point, was at Charleston and other hard fought engagements. In 1785 he came to Kentucky and settled in Woodford County at what was afterward known as Scott's Landing, on the Kentucky River, where he built his log cabin and a fort not far from the town of Mortonsville. Soon after he built

———

*Whose mother was a Whittington.

his cabin and fort he established a trail to Lexington that is yet traveled and known as Scott's road.

Although claiming his citizenship in Woodford until he was elevated to the governorship in 1808, he spent much of his time from 1785 to '95 in intermittent Indian warfare that was so prevalent in this State and Ohio during that period.

During the winter of 1789-90 he built a block house at the confluence of the Kentucky and Ohio rivers, where Carrollton now stands, and bivouacked there again in 1792 when in pursuit of the Eel river Indians.

He was with General St. Clair who sustained such a disastrous defeat in his Ohio campaign in 1791, losing six hundred men, who were killed within an hour's time. During the same year he and General Wilkerson led a cavalry troop in a successful raid against the Indians on the Wabash, and in 1794 he commanded a section of General Wayne's army in the defeat of the Indians at the "Fallen Timbers," which was a crushing blow to the Indians of Ohio. So you will see that General Scott was a very busy warrior, but he found intervals when he could retire to his Woodford County cabin for rest and refreshment.

General Scott was said to be a man of fine natural sense, but had many peculiarities of manner, and many amusing incidents are related concerning him. He had a son who was killed by the Indians while fishing at the mouth of a creek on the opposite side of the river from the cabin, in Mercer County.

Gov. Charles Scott was the fourth executive head of the State, and surrounded himself with a strong cabinet that gave him a successful administration. He was much provoked because the Federal government did not assign Gen. Wm. Henry Harrison in charge of the forces in 1812, so he commissioned him to lead the Kentucky forces. The government later ratified this appointment.*

The first Academy instituted at Versailles was opened in 1806 by Edward Mann Butler of Maryland, who came to Woodford County during the year 1805 or 1806. He graduated in both medicine and law before coming to this State with the intention of practicing one or the other of the professions; but finally decided that his duty was to train young men and boys in the rules of health, morals, civil law, and all that pertains to the breadth and elevation of the mind, rather than endeavoring to rescue those who had disobeyed the laws of nature, and the degenerates who had not been taught to respect the laws that govern society. In the scholastic field he said he could render a better service to both God and man by moulding the minds and characters of the young men who would take part in shaping the policies of government and the destinies of the people, which was the most important duty of a good citizen who was well equipped for such a task.

It is said that he was successful in establishing a first class academy, but early in 1810 he yielded to a flattering offer from Louisville, where his ability

*See page 276 for additional details of this soldier and statesman.

became known, and he was there for many years, but finally drifted to St. Louis, Mo., where he was also eminently successful in the scholastic field.

Soon after he came to Woodford he married Martha Dedman of the county. If they had descendants I have not been able to locate them.

Ezekiel Field was a native of Culpeper County, Virginia, and a son of Col. John Field and his wife Anna Rogers Clark, who, I think, was a sister of Col. George Rogers Clark of the Revolution and the War of 1812; at any rate, she was very closely related. Ezekiel Field married his cousin, Elizabeth, daughter of Henry Field, Jr., also of Culpeper County, a member of Burgesses before the Revolution and vestryman in St. Mark's Church in 1763. Col. John Field was killed in the battle at "Point Pleasant" in October, 1774.

About 1781 Ezekiel Field and his wife, Elizabeth, came to Kentucky with their children and located temporarily at Harrods Fort, now Harrodsburg. In 1782 he was with the heroic band that marched to the relief of the Bryan Station garrison that had been surrounded by the Indians until food was almost exhausted. They routed the Indians and pursued them in their flight to Blue Lick, where the Indians made a stand, and a fierce engagement took place in which many of our boys were slaughtered. In that desperate engagement Ezekiel Field lost his life on the 19th of August, 1782. He left a widow and three small boys who were far away from their old Virginia home and friends, yet they were not

strangers in the fort. In 1785 the widow married Capt. Thomas McClanahan of Bourbon County (then Fayette). One of the three sons by the first marriage was Willis Field, who was reared in Bourbon, where he married his cousin, Elizabeth Field, in 1800, she a daughter of John Field. She died without issue, and in 1805 Willis Field married Isabella Miriam Buck, daughter of Col. John Buck, a pioneer of Woodford County and the first postmaster to serve the patrons of the Versailles post office. Isabella was a great-niece of Gen. Marquis Calmes, a pioneer of Woodford, and a great-great-granddaughter of Marquis De La Calmes, the Huguenot.

In 1813 Willis Field bought the farm on Griers Creek known as "Airy Mount," the large spring not far from the residence being the main source of that creek, a stream that ran a mill and a distillery a short distance below. I presume that Willis Field built the distillery, but my impression is that Captain Daniel Trabue built and operated the mill. At any rate, he owned the farm that ran from the mill to Griers Creek Church on the Tyrone road, the residence but a short distance from the mill. I think Dr. Bohannon owned this farm after Trabue's death, then Major Humphrey Jones owned it and lived there for quite a while before the Civil War, and for many years afterward.

Willis Field lived at "Airy Mount" until his death in 1839. The farm is three miles from Versailles, and the fine old brick residence is approached from the Mortonsville pike. It joins the

Home of Samuel Wooldridge built by Willis Field 1st, is 135 years old. The wing at the left was a schoolroom during and after the Civil War, and this scribe was a pupil 1865-6. Miss Mollie Stockton the teacher.

Isham Railey farm, now owned by Samuel Wooldridge, Jr., and approached from the Tyrone road. "Airy Mount" was owned by Matt Hayden, during, and for many years after the Civil War, and was recently owned by Buford Twyman, Jr. I am not sure who was the first owner of "Airy Mount," but likely one of the Bucks.

Willis Field was an active business man who possessed excellent judgment and he accumulated a vast estate, but besides looking after his varied business interests, he gave much of his time and attention to politics and was a staunch supporter of Henry Clay. His business interests embraced, besides his farm, a gristmill, a distillery, and a hemp factory, all located on the farm. The celebrated distiller, James Crow,* was in his employ about 1826, or at least before he engaged with Elijah Pepper on Glenns Creek.

Willis Field was also a member of the county court for many years, and by virtue of his long service in that capacity being the oldest magistrate in point of service, he automatically, as it were, became the sheriff of the county. He also represented the county in the legislature in 1817 and '18, and again in 1829.

The children of Willis Field and Isabella Miriam Buck follow: Elizabeth, born in 1806, married Major William Jones; John Buck, born in 1808, died unmarried in 1833; Miriam, born in 1809, married William Buck in 1829; Emiline, born in 1811, married Major Humphrey Jones in 1830; Ezekiel H., born in 1813, died unmarried in 1852; Ann Helm, born in 1815,

married Dr. Ben Craig, son of Lewis Craig and Kitty Cox; Willis Field, Jr., born in 1818, married Ellen Craig, daughter of Samuel Craig, in 1842; Sarah Field, born in 1819, died unmarried in 1835; Martha Amelia, born in 1824, married Richard White, who was of the Clay County family of that name, in 1843; Thomas M. Field, born in 1825, married Susan Higbee in 1850, and Charles William, born in 1828, married Monemia Mason in 1855.

Major William Jones, who married Elizabeth, had a residence at Richmond where he was a prominent merchant. He died soon after their marriage and left an only son, Willis Field Jones, who came to Woodford County after attaining his manhood and purchased a farm on the Lexington pike near Versailles. He married Martha Buford, daughter of Col. William Buford (Scott Billey). It was in his beautiful woodland that the noted barbecue was given in 1861 when Gen. John Cabell Breckenridge and others delivered their farewell address and departed that night for the Confederate lines. Stout hearted men and fair women wept that day as they had never wept before.

The wives of Captain Sam Leavy and R. Handy Berryman were daughters, and Willis and Bland Jones were sons of Col. Willis F. Jones and Martha Buford. Col. Jones was born in 1825 and lost his life in the service of the Confederacy.

Major Humphrey Jones, who married Emmeline, was a brother of Major William Jones who married her sister, Elizabeth. He lived on the estate orig-

*See Supplement. Also see pages 42.

inally owned by Capt. Daniel Trabue that was near the old mill. They had William Jones and several daughters whose names I do not now recall.

Ezekiel H. Field was a Lieutenant Colonel in Gen. Humphrey Marshall's command in Mexico, and like many other Kentuckians in that war, he contracted a fever from the effects of which he died soon after his return to the county.

Dr. Ben Craig and Ann Helm Field had: William, Lewis and Thomas Craig, the two former in the service of the Confederacy. William had a daughter who married Dr. Green, son of the venerable pastor of the First Presbyterian Church, Danville, Ky.

Willis Field, Jr., and Ellen Craig had: Alice, Samuel and Willis W. The former married Capt. Henry McLeod, and they were the parents of the able and popular attorney, Field McLeod, and his sister, Susan. Samuel Field was a lawyer and for a time the able editor of the Woodford Sun.

Willis W. Field, the idol of my childhood and a dear friend during all of the intervening years, departed this life July 18, 1920, only a few months after he had supplied the data upon which this sketch was erected. His was a well-rounded life of duty faithfully performed.

To know him was but to love him, and it is doubtful if he had an enemy in the wide world. He was manly and frank, gentle and courteous, loyal and just, and in the highest sense one of nature's noblemen.

When youth has passed the meridian of life, and is yielding to the frost of age, we well know it is only a brief span to the sunset, and we wonder how meritoriously we have lived; not so with Willis W. Field. His life had been so closely measured by the decalogue that he could only approach the evening of life with a pleasing smile.

Peace to his ashes and joy to his soul is my prayer.

Col. Thomas M. Field and Susan Higbee had: Belle, who married Alexander Dunlap; Lena, who married Andrew T. Harris; Willis III., who married Elizabeth Shyrock, and is at present residing on the old Ed. Trabue farm that was owned for many years by Christopher and Sally Neal; John H. Field, who married Lelia Gay and is a resident of the county; Bessie, who married P. Leslie Sloan, and Thos. M., Jr., who has not married.

Charles William Field who married Monemia Mason was educated at West Point and served a number of years in the regular army, but when the Civil War came on he resigned his commission in the regular service and entered the service of the Confederacy in which he rose to the rank of a Major General.

The children of Major Humphrey Jones were by a second marriage to Ophelia Bohannon, daughter of Dr. Bohannon.

The home of Willis Field and Ellen Craig joined Col. William Steele's farm on one side, and Charles Railey on the other and was not far from lock No. 5. It was originally the Cornelius Holman farm that was sold to James Dupuy in 1826, and owned by Logan Railey in 1840. The house was built of logs, but Willis Field added to it and made an elegant colonial residence of it.

Adam Hammon, born in 1688, was a native of Wales. He came to America early in his career and settled in Virginia. It is not known to whom he was married, but his children's names are preserved, and follow: Abraham, Thomas, John, Esther, Nancy, and Scott. Abraham was born in 1720 in Virginia and married Martha Bateman in 1756; their issue was as follows: Ezra, Adam, Joel, Thomas, John, Allen, Enos, Abraham, Mary and Magdaline.

Ezra was born August, 1774, in Virginia and married Hanna Farra, whose birth was in 1782, and whose death occurred in Woodford County in 1844. He came to Kentucky prior to 1810 and settled in Woodford, as the census of that year will verify. The names of John Hammon, Charles Hammon and Mary Hammon all appear on the census of that year too, and they were evidently relatives. Ezra purchased a thousand acres of land on Clear Creek, a part of which afterward became the property of the Holloway heirs, and now owned by John Montgomery, a son-in-law of Wm. B. Holloway. The house in which John Montgomery now lives was built by John Farra, brother-in-law of Ezra Hammon, the stone used in its construction coming from a quarry on Clear Creek. The house was built in the 18th century and is in a splendid state of preservation today.

Ezra Hammon and Hanna Farra had these children: Amos, Dudley, Charles, Abraham, Nelson, John, Eliad, Martha, Margaret and Italy.

Abraham was born in the house described above in February, 1812, and was reared upon the farm. Later he married Penelope Reardin, daughter of Dennis Reardin and Nancy Slaughter. Penelope was born in 1815 and died in 1898. Abraham bought of the Williams heirs a farm on the Frankfort and Versailles road three miles from Versailles in 1844, and lived there until his death in 1899, a period of fifty-five years. The children of Abraham Hammon and Penelope Reardin were these: John Robert, William, Annie Slaughter, Martha, Clara, and Sarah.

John Robert married Lula Hughes. He was a prominent and popular educator during his entire life and many of the young men of the county were trained under his discipline, and had their minds shaped under his instruction. He taught perhaps longer at Midway than any other point and he was popular there with both patrons and students. The writer remembers him with pleasure as his tutor during the Civil War and ever afterward good friend.

William Hammon married his cousin, Mary Reardin. He practiced at the Versailles bar for many years and was at one time county attorney. He afterward moved to Rich Hill, Mo., where he, and Hiter Crockett, of Frankfort, Ky., practiced law, but both eventually returned to their native towns where they practiced law until death closed each career a few short years ago. Will Hammon died in 1901. They have three children: Helen, Nell and W. Henry Hammon.

Sarah Hammon married Thomas E. Henton. He bought the old McCracken or Thomas Edwards farm on Glenns Creek road about 1890, and I think the place is still in possession of a member of that family. Their children were: Thomas Edward Henton, Jr., Nell, and Mary.

Martha Hammon married Robert G. Mastin and they have these children: Nell, Robert, Jennie, Howard and Vernon C.

Clara Hammon married J. R. Sanders and they have: Robert, Edward, Clement, Nellie and Carrie.

Dennis Reardin, the father of Penelope, who married Abraham Hammon, was a Revolutionary soldier and of a splendid old Virginia family. Nancy Slaughter, the wife of Dennis Reardin, was also of a fine old Virginia family, being a first cousin of Gov. Gabriel Slaughter, who was the 7th Governor of Kentucky, succeeding Gov. George Madison in 1816. Gov. Slaughter also fought with Jackson at New Orleans. Dennis Reardin bought a tract of land from the Searcy heirs about 1793, that was on the Clifton road and, I think, joined the farm owned by Col. Lewis A. Berry. Nancy Slaughter came from Culpeper County. Besides Penelope Reardin they had these children: Sarah, John, William, Robert, and Alvie. I don't recall any descendants of Dennis Reardin in the county now who bear the Reardin name. William Reardin, a descendant, was living on Glenns Creek road two miles from Versailles about 1880. The farm upon which he lived adjoined the farm of Captain Harry Brown, likely the old home of Herman Bowmar, Jr.

———

Captain James Meade, while a youth, volunteered his services to his country and rendered valuable aid in many engagements with the British and Indians. He was with Col. Joseph H. Daviess in the Wabash campaign, engaged in the battle at Tippecanoe, where he was promoted from a volunteer in the ranks to the captaincy of a company in the regular army for the bravery and daring exhibited in that engagement.

At the battle of the "River Raisin" in 1813, where Col, Allen, of Shelby County, Capt. Virgil McCracken, of Woodford County, and many others of our Kentucky troops sacrificed their lives upon their country's altar, Captain Meade was conspicuously in the forefront, occupied a very exposed position, and was mortally wounded while gallantly leading his company in a charge.

Richard Collins, in his history of Kentucky, says that Captain James Meade was a native of Woodford County. I am doubtful about that, though I am sure that he was a citizen of the county for a time, probably coming just after the census of 1810 was taken, as many did who have descendants in the county today. If a native of the county when that census was taken, he was certainly absent from the county at that time, as no one by the name of Meade appears on that census. Woodford County is proud to know that he is numbered among her sons, and would be doubly proud to know that he was a native son.

———

The data of this branch of the Steele family would have followed that of Col. William Steele but for the absence from the State of the wife of Theodore Harris (nee Mamie Buford Steele), who furnished the data, and much of her communication is incorporated into this sketch just as it came from her pen.

Thomas Steele was born in Ireland, in Newton-Limavady, and was educated along with his brothers, Richard and Andrew, at the University of Dublin. His wife, Eleanor Moore, was a native of the same community. Thomas, Richard and Andrew were sons of William Steele, and grandsons of Sir Richard Steele, who was secretary to Lord Lieutenant of Ireland, and inspector of Royal Seals of King George I., by whom he was knighted. He resided in the Castle of Ballymund, near Rathdowney, and was the most eminent man of letters and affairs in his day in Ireland.

Driven by oppression and tyranny, the grandsons of Sir Richard Steele emigrated from Ireland in 1745, and landed on the eastern shore of Maryland.

The elder brother, Richard, received a grant of 1,000 acres of land which he located near Mercersburg, Pennsylvania. There he reared a family of eight children, some of whom are mentioned as among the most prominent and useful of the early settlers of that state, West Virginia and Kentucky.

The boys received their earliest lessons in patriotism at their father's knee and hurried to join the contingents which were forming in their neighborhood to aid the patriot army.

General John Steele, who, according to the American Historical Register of February, 1896, was a member of Washington's family, and field officer of the day at Yorktown, was a son of Richard Steele. His brother Richard also saw service in the Revolutionary army.

The brothers, Richard, Andrew and Thomas, inherited much of the talent of their grandfather, Sir Richard Steele, whose life was brilliant, brave and open as before the world, and the family was one of the first in learning and wealth in Ireland. They settled first among their kindred near Mercersburg, Pennsylvania.

It was in this community that Andrew met and married his cousin, Jane Lindsay, great-great-granddaughter of Lord Alexander Lindsay, of Edzell Castle, Scotland, and their daughter, Anne, married her cousin, Col. John Steele of Woodford County. He was the only son of Thomas Steele and was born at Newton-Limavady, Londonderry, Ireland, on June 15th, 1784.

Col. John Steele and Anne Steele had these children: Thomas, William J., Theophilus, and Andrew Steele, all of whom were highly respected citizens of Woodford County.

William J. was born in 1809 and was prepared for the practice of law. He went to Gainesville, Alabama, where he practiced his profession for twenty years, but returned to Versailles in 1853 where he practiced until his death in 1884. In 1855 he was elected county judge, and was consecutively elected to that office for sixteen years. He was a strong union man during the Civil War and retired in 1870 from office and politics, to his farm on the Frankfort road, four miles from Versailles. He married in 1833, Mary Winston, of Tuscumbia, Alabama. The following were their children: John A., Thomas, Jane, Mary, Davis, Andrew F., William

G., Frank, and Theophilus. Thomas was a captain in the Confederacy, as was also his brother, John A.

Theophilus Steele was born in 1811, died in 1895. He studied medicine, and though a prominent farmer, he devoted much of his time to his profession. His farm was on the McCracken's Mill or Glenns Creek pike, almost opposite the McCracken farm, owned for many years by Thomas S. Edwards, later by Thomas E. Henton. E. H. Taylor, Jr., now owns the Dr. Steele and Alex Wright farms, his property now extending from the Glenns Creek to the old Versailles and Frankfort pike.

Dr. Theophilus Steele married Caroline Worthy, of Georgia, and Captain John Andrew Steele, of Midway, is an only child. He served four years in the Confederate service and after the war married, first, Lucy Duke, daughter of James Keith Duke, and Mary Buford, and great-granddaughter of Col. Thomas Marshall; second, Fanny Breckinridge, daughter of General John C. Breckinridge. By the first marriage was Mamie Buford Steele, who married Theodore Harris. By the second marriage was Anne, who married E. Waring Wilson; Francis, who married J. Horton, and Caroline, who married Joseph Coleman Carter.

"The Lost Cause," a publication interested in the Confederate veterans, has this compliment to Mrs. Caroline Worthy Steele, who had done so much to commemorate the valorous deeds of the soldiers of the Confederacy: "While very much have done well, none have surpassed Mrs. Caroline Worthy Steele, of Woodford County,

Ky. We have tested her generosity severely, and never found it to fail in any instance. She came of a noble Georgia family and is a woman of more than usual literary accomplishment, being an extensive reader, and her fine memory makes her a charming companion. Her elder sister was the first wife of General Mirabeau B. Lamar, of Texas.''

Col. John Steele was a man of strong and virile force and marked ability. Born to wealth in the old country, he acquired it here by industry and intelligence, and he quietly enjoyed his independence and prosperity. The turnpike which cuts through from the Clifton to the Frankfort road at McKee's bears his name. He served in the Kentucky Legislature in 1846.

The Steeles were Scotch-Irish Presbyterians. The list of the descendants of the Londonderry Scotch-Irish is an honorable one. They were never appealed to in vain by colonist or pioneer. Their help, with purse or rifle, was always at command.

As a soldier in the War of 1812 Col. John Steele won distinction as an officer. He commanded the regiment which met Lafayette on the road from Louisville to Frankfort and escorted him to Versailles in 1825.

The distinguished Frenchman was housed in the old stone tavern which occupied the site where the bank of J. Amsden and Company now stands.

Much of the land originally owned by their ancestors is still in possession of the Steele family, both in Woodford and Fayette.

Captain John Andrew Steele, son of Dr. Theophilus, was four years in the

Confederate service and has never re-covered from an injury to one of his lower limbs in that service. He twice served in the county in the legislature and has been cashier of the Citizens Bank at Midway for about forty years. He is an elder in the Presbyterian Church and resides, with his wife, in the surburbs of Midway on the George-town pike, both highly esteemed by their neighbors and friends.

The farm owned by Col..John Steele, and settled by him in pioneer days was the farm now owned by Kenneth Alex-ander, in sight of the old Woodford Presbyterian Church. His father, Thomas Steele, owned in the pioneer days the farm known for many years as the Aiken place on the Midway road. About the year the War of 1812 was launched, Col. John Steele sold his farm that adjoined his father's estate near Woodford Church and purchased three farms on the Versailles and Frankfort road, three miles from Ver-sailles; one from Turpin, and one ad-joining from Latta, and one on the op-posite side of the road from Ruddle, all pioneers of Woodford as indicated by the census of 1810. Judge William J. Steele inherited a part of this large farm with the fine old colonial resi-dence. I neglected to say that John A. Steele, son of Judge William J. Steele, was in the service of the Con-federacy as a captain, and his cousin, Dr. Theophilus Steele, Jr., was a Major in Gano's cavalry, Morgan's division.

James Bullock, Sr., wife unknown by authorities I have consulted, was a na-tive of England who came to America before the Revolution and located in Spottsylvania County, Virginia. Though he is said to have had a large family, only two of the names of his children, Edmund and James, Jr., are recalled by the Kentucky branch of the family, and they came to the State and settled in Fayette County, before Woodford was separated from that county. Both married in Virginia and brought their families to Kentucky with them.

Edmund married Agnes Wingfield, and James, Jr., married, first, Rebecca Wingfield, and second, Agnes Waller, daughter of John Waller and Agnes Carr, of Virginia. Many of the de-scendants of these two families are now residents of Woodford and Fay-ette counties, but very many more are residents of other parts of central Kentucky, while Illinois and Missouri are fortunate in claiming a liberal share of them. They are prominent in business and social circles wherever you find them. The Bullocks and Shelbys, of Lexington, are descendants.

The children of Edmund Bullock and Agnes Wingfield were: Edmund, Jr., John, Garland, Sarah, who married Col. William Steele, and Polly, who married William Davenport in 1787.

Col. William Steele and Sarah Bul-lock lived for many years in the home he built just above lock No. 5 on Ken-tucky River, but later he built a large stone house on an elevation on the op-posite side of Steeles Branch where he and his wife spent their declining years. Their children were: Agnes, who married Col. Zach White; Polly, who married Harvie Lamb; Jane, who married her cousin, Samuel Wilson, and John, who married Catharine

Railey, daughter of Charles Railey and Mary Mayo.

Col. Zach White and Agnes Steele had these children: Dr. William Steele White, who married Judith Wahln, granddaughter of William Railey and Judith Woodson, and an only child of this couple was Dr. Phillip White, who married Eugene Dillman, in Paris, France. He died without issue; Bettie White married Dr. F. E. Morancey (and had Agnes, who married Dr. John R. McKee; H. P. Morancey, who married Nannie Morancey; Frank and Emelius Morancey); Agnes White, who married Major William Messick; and Zach White, Jr., who married Dolly Carter. They had no children. Zach, Jr., served four years in the Confederacy and was sheriff of the county after the Civil War.

Harvie Lamb and Polly Steele had several children whose names appear in the various sketches I have written, and will yet write.

Samuel Wilson and Jane Steele inherited the farm with the stone residence and lived and died upon that estate: Their children were: Ann Mary, who was the first wife of Charles Craig; Barbara was the second wife of Charles Craig, and Sally, who married William Wooldridge, who lived on the old Samuel Railey estate that was likely a part of the original Edward Trabue farm.

John Steele and Catherine Railey had: Agnes Steele, who married Thomas Thornton. They had an only daughter, Susan Catherine Thornton, who married popular Sandy Brown, of the county, and they had several chil-

dren. He moved with his family to St. Louis, Mo., several years after the Civil War.

Polly Bullock and William Davenport had these children: Eliza, Edward, America, Rice B., Agnes, William, James Bullock, Mary Ann, Martha and Richard H. Davenport.†

Martha Davenport married Peter M. Smith whose daughter, Laura, married Thomas J. Steele, of Fayette, and they had Brice, Ollie and Wallace Steele; America Davenport married William Smith and had Bird, who married Anne Brice, and Mary, who married William Bullock, son of Thomas Bullock and his second wife, Ellen Dale; Rice B. Davenport, who married, first, Letitia Musick, second, Rebecca Clay; Mary Anne Davenport married John D. Brown, and their children's names follow: Mattie Wingfield, Jeptha and James, both of whom were in the army of the Confederacy; William D., who married Allie Utterback; Sallie T. and Jennie, who married A. T. Parker.

Richard H. Davenport married Sallie Porter, a sister of Lt.-Gov. Thomas P. Porter, of Versailles, and they had these children: Annie, married Ellison Arnett of Midway; Priscilla, who is unmarried; Mary, who married Thomas S. Forman, of Midway, and Charles, who married, first, Mary Eliza Wood, second Mary Davis.

This concludes the descendants of Edmund Bullock insofar as they relate to Woodford County.

James Bullock, Jr., and his first wife, Rebecca Wingfield, had the following children: Thomas, Sr., James, Jr., Mildred, Barbara and Wingfield. Thomas

---

†I knew "Uncle Dick." He lived to be nearly 100 years old.

Bullock, Sr., married first, Lucy Redd, a sister of John and Thomas Redd. He and his wife were living at the Bullock homestead on the Versailles and Midway road in 1810 when he had a family of nine, and owned fifteen slaves. The estate was afterward owned by Samuel B. Wallace, and is now the property of Clinton Hawkins, Jr. Thomas Bullock and both of his wives, Lucy Redd and Ellen Dale, were buried there. The children of Thomas Bullock and Lucy Redd were: James, Melissa, Thomas, Jr., Mordecai,* Wingfield, Anne and Lucy. By the second wife, Ellen Dale, were: William, Mildred, Waller and Bettie.

Thomas Bullock, Jr., married first, Agnes Ware, daughter of Samuel Ware, and his second wife, Betsy (Bullock) Redd, who was a daughter of James Bullock, Jr., and Anne Waller. Thomas Bullock, Jr., and Agnes Ware had several children, but before they were grown the family moved to Eureka, Ill., where Thomas, Jr., had the pleasure of naming the county in which he and his family lived and died, after his native Kentucky county, and it is Woodford County, Ill. They have descendants living in that county today.

Wingfield Bullock married ———— Fleming; Anne married ———— Berry, and Lucy married Jeremiah Vardeman, a Baptist minister. Thomas Bullock, Sr., was a first cousin of Sarah Bullock, who married Col. William Steele, and he and Col. Steele and Robert Alexander were close friends and co-operated in several enterprises of considerable proportions, one of which was the promotion of boat navigation of the Kentucky river.

Barbara Bullock, daughter of James Bullock, Jr., and Rebecca Wingfield, married Benjamin Wilson, of the county, and had these children: Anne, who married Benjamin Moore; Benjamin, Jr., who married Virginia Shouse, and Barbara, who married Dr. Robert J. Thompson, of Versailles.

Benjamin Wilson, Jr., and Virginia Shouse had these children: Lou and Anna, who never married; Inez married Albert Thompson, who was a farmer and extensive cattle dealer, but had his residence in Versailles for many years; and Albert Wilson, who married Fannie Hawkins and resided in Versailles during his entire life.

Barbara Wilson and Dr. Robert J. Thompson had these children: William, who married Virginia Campbell, daughter of Rev. Alexander Campbell, of Virginia, the celebrated preacher; Dr. Benjamin Wilson, who married Fannie Goodwin; Rebecca, who is unmarried; Dr. Robert J., Jr., who married Maxy Ayres, daughter of Walter Ayres, of the county; Katherine, who married J. Tilford Brown; Anna, who has not married, and Oakley Thompson, who married Jennie Fogg, daughter of Captain Elijah Fogg and Anne Richardson Ware.

James Bullock, Jr., and his second wife, Anne Waller, have many descendants at Lexington and throughout Central Kentucky, and a great number in Missouri. Their daughter, Anne Waller Bullock, married John Redd, of the county, and they had: Minor W. Redd, who married Harriet

*See page 302 for this line.

Berry, Agatha Redd, who married Samuel Wilson; Bettie Redd married Elijah Yeager; Nancy married Joseph McPheeters; James B. married Agatha Berry; Caroline married James Mc-† Pheeters, brother of Joseph; Maria married William Boardman, and John T. married Elizabeth Frances. For the descendants of the above Redds and Berrys see sketches of Berrys and Redds.

Betsy Bullock, half-sister of the above Anne Waller Bullock, married first Thomas Redd, brother of the above John Redd, who married her sister Anne Waller; second Samuel Ware. Betsy Bullock and Thomas Redd had these children: James W. Redd, who married first Patsy Berry, second Matilda‡ Starks; Archie O. Redd, who married first Matilda Berry, second Julia Lamb, his cousin. By the first marriage ·were: Harriet, who married William Gray; Bettie, who married Thomas Wallace, and Jennie, who married Washington Crutcher. No children by the second marriage.

Martha Anne Redd, another daughter of Thomas Redd and Betsy Bullock, married Col. Lewis A. Berry; Mordecai Redd married Mary Williams; Agatha Redd married first Thomas Berry, second James B. Redd, son of John Redd and Anne Waller Bullock.

Dorothy Bullock, daughter of James Bullock, Jr., and Anne Waller, married Samuel Redd, a cousin of John and Thomas Redd, and they had: Wal-ler, Oliver and Catherine, who married Charles McDowell.

*Captain John Bullock, who married Elizabeth Railey in Virginia and came to Woodford County about 1800 where he remained for several years, then removed to Bowling Green, Ky., where they lived for a time before migrating to Palmyra, Mo., in which vicinity many of their descendants reside today, is presumed to be a brother of Edmund and James, Jr., who came to Kentucky some years earlier. Many of the descendants of Edmund and James, Jr., moved to Palmyra at a later period than did the family of Captain John Bullock, and the two families intermarried there as they did in Kentucky. For instance above you will notice that Caroline Redd, a daughter of John Redd and Anne Waller Bullock, married James McPheeters, of Palmyra, Mo., and that their only child, Anne McPheeters, married William Russell Anderson. This William Russell Anderson was a great-grandson of Capt. John Bullock and Elizabeth Railey. William Russell Anderson was born March 15, 1835. Married Anne McPheeters May 31, 1860. Their children were: James, Thomas Lilburn, Rev. William, Anne, Russella, and Mary Alby Anderson. The latter was a lawyer and author, and was city attorney of Palmyra, Mo., 1899-1900 and 1901, and was just twenty-one when elected. She married Otho F. Matthew, a lawyer of Macon, Mo., Dec., 1902. Her brother, the Rev. William Russell Anderson, has been pastor of the Shelbyville Presbyterian church for more than a decade. The Andersons were Scotch-Irish and a family of lawyers from the time they struck Virginia soon after the revolution.

George Woodson Railey, who was Deputy Marshal of U. S., and took the census of 1810, married one of the daughters of Capt. John Bullock and Elizabeth Railey, and so did Joseph Crockett, Jr., son of Col. Joseph Crockett, U. S. Marshal in 1810, living at Lexington.

WOODFORD COUNTY

By W. E. Railey.

PART FOUR

Peter Hurst married Ann Rust in Virginia and came to Kentucky about 1812. I have not been able to learn what part of Virginia they came from, but it is well known that they were both of English extract. *Ann Rust was a niece of Chancellor Kent, a distinguished barrister of Virginia and the author of "Kent's Commentaries." Soon after they arrived in Woodford County Peter Hurst was drafted for service in the War of 1812, but his eldest son George, realizing what an important factor his father was, in relation to the maintenance of a family that contained seven or eight children, notwithstanding his youth, volunteered his services as a substitute, was accepted and rendered creditable service. Peter Hurst also had a brother whose name was Harry, who was in the service of the War of 1812, and he was an aide on the staff of General William Henry Harrison. General Harrison was commissioned by Gov. Charles Scott as commandant of Kentucky troops in that war.

Peter Hurst and Ann Rust had the following children: George, Marshall, James, Alfred, Margaret, Kent, Ann, Bettie and Kittie. All married but Kittie. There was no effort to arrange

these names according to birth, as I was not in possession of dates.

Marshall Hurst married Julia Darneal, and they had Shrewsberry and Frank Hurst, who are well remembered business men, in the commission business for many years in Versailles, and farmers as well as commission merchants.

James Hurst, who married Teny Norwood, had no children, but they reared Lewis and Nora Harrison, niece and nephew of his wife.

Margaret Kent Hurst married Henry Ferguson and had these children: Mary Hurst, who married Will Edwards; Lewis, James, Peter, Kate and Millie, who married Hack Skillman. Henry Ferguson and Margaret Kent Hurst lived for many years on a farm near Spring Station that adjoined the farm of David C. Humphries and followed the old Cole road to Harmony Church. This farm was formerly owned by —— Lee, who built a splendid brick residence there early in the nineteenth century.

Ann Hurst married Thomas D. Urmston. She inherited that part of the Peter Hurst estate that lay back of the Versailles cemetery and at her death she bequeathed it to her niece, Mary

*See page 302 for further notes.

Ferguson Edwards, who owns it to this time.

Bettie Hurst married James Alexander, of Woodford County, and they had one son, Charles Alexander, who was for many years a prominent farmer of the county. Charles Alexander was an intense Union man during the Civil War, and ever afterward a strong Republican in politics, a man of Christian character, and well liked by his friends and neighbors. For one term since the Civil War he was Collector of Internal Revenue for the Lexington District, but I fail to recall the years of service or the administration under which he served. His grandfather, David Alexander, was a native of North Carolina, who came to Kentucky just before the war of 1812, in which he took part. Returning to Woodford County after the war he resumed the duties incident to his farm. I am not advised as to whether he had children other than James or not, but James, I think, only had Charles. Charles married Mollie Daniel and they took much pleasure in the old homestead, and were life long members of the Presbyterian church.

Alfred Hurst was born in Woodford County in 1818, reared on the farm of his father, in the "Dry Ridge" vicinity, three miles from Versailles, and his elementary education was obtained in the schools at Versailles. When twenty years of age he entered the office of Doctors Carter and Blackburn where, under their direction and advice, he laid the foundation for a course in medicine. Afterwards he entered the school of medicine in Cincinnati, and later attended the Louisville University of Medicine, where he graduated in 1845. He then formed a partnership with Dr. Jo. Carter, of Versailles, but the firm was dissolved a few years later and he maintained an office alone for many years. He died at Midway during the year 1888.

Dr. Alfred Hurst married in 1840 Adela Craig, daughter of James Craig, and granddaughter of the Rev. Joseph Craig, a noted minister. She died in 1879. Of the nine children resulting from this union, all died at an early age, and unmarried, except their daughter, Bettie, who married Charles Nuckols, of the county, and of this union the following children were born: Ada, Minnie, Jane, Charles, Francis, Samuel, Alfred and Horace.

Sallie Hurst was another daughter of Peter Hurst and Ann Rust whose name I did not get until this sketch was written. She married Hezekiah Ellis and they had Sallie Ellis, who has not married, and Sue Ellis, who married John A. Higgins, now employed in Good Roads Bureau at Frankfort, and they have a daughter, Julia Hume Higgins, who is employed in the Automobile Department of the state government.

———

Benjamine Wilson, Sr., was another Virginian who turned his face westward, hit the Boone trail and landed in Kentucky with the early settlers. He drew a pension for service in the Revolution. Upon reaching Kentucky he decided to locate in that part of Fayette County that afterward became Woodford. The farm upon which he settled was on the Midway and Versailles road, almost directly opposite the old Hibler farm, for many years the home of the family of Lister Witherspoon, and joined the farm of James Coleman, that is now owned by J. Breckinridge Viley. He built his residence of stone and it is still standing and habitable, or was a few short years ago. After he had concluded all arrangements for a comfortable future he married Barbara Bullock, daughter of James Bullock, Jr., and Rebecca Wingfield, who came to Kentucky and settled about 1785, in Fayette County, but I think his residence was in Woodford when the county was formed, and likely owned the farm that afterward was the home of his son, Thomas Bullock, Sr., and later the home of Samuel B. Wallace. He also owned much land at Mortonsville, where his grandson, Thomas Bullock, Jr., lived before going to Illinois.

Benjamine Wilson was living on his farm in the stone residence he built, as early as 1810, and his family consisted of ten members at that time, and he owned twenty slaves to do service on his large estate. Benjamine Wilson and Barbara Bullock had the following children: Benjamine Wilson, Jr., married Virginia Shouse, sister of Rev. John Shouse; Samuel Wilson married Jane Steele, daughter of Col. William Steele and Sarah Bullock; Barbara married Dr. R. J. Thompson; Rebecca married Stith Edgar Burton, and Elizabeth married Beverly H. Miller. The descendants of these sons and daughters of Benjamine Wilson and Barbara Bullock will be found under the Bullock sketches.*

Jane Steele, who married Samuel Wilson, was the youngest child of Col.

*See pages 119, 251, and 294.

William Steele and Sarah Bullock. She was born and partially reared in the log house of Col. Steele near his landing, but before her father died he turned the log house over to his son-in-law, Col. Zach White, and built, in 1817, the stone house on the eminence on the opposite side of Steele's branch, where he was living when his death occurred in 1826. Jane Steele inherited this property. Col. Zach White and family occupied the log house until during the '40's he built quite a mansion on the eminence immediately in the rear of the log house.

———

Toliver Craig was a citizen of Botetourt County, Virginia. While a resident there he married Mary Hawkins, and I am told that they were parents of eleven children, who were born and reared in that state, and, in fact, most of them, if not all, married in that state, and came to Kentucky, many of them accompanying their parents, while others came at intervals not far apart, and some years before Woodford County was established. These twelve families distributed themselves over several parts of Fayette County in such a way that some of them were located in Woodford, some in Scott and others in Jessamine when those counties were separated from Fayette, while others remained in Fayette. The father, Toliver Craig, and his wife, were in Scott I think. Of the heads of these twelve families, some were with the garrison at Bryan's Station during the time that the garrison there was surrounded by Indians, with the prospect for escape unfavorable, as the number of Indians was in proportion of at least five to one, and the garrison, though scantly supplied with food, were brave men and true. A messenger, however, managed to get through the enemy lines with a dispatch to Harrod's Fort, in Mercer County, for reinforcements, and soon a detachment arrived and rescued the beleaguered garrison.

Toliver Craig, the head of the family, died in 1796, but his widow survived him many years. Their children were in part as follows: Elijah, John, Toliver, Jr., Rev. Joseph, Jane and Elizabeth. These members, I think, were all in Bryan's Station during the perils of that garrison in 1782.

John Craig, one of the above sons of Toliver the 1st, married Sallie Page. They had a son, Lewis Craig, who married Kittie Cox. This couple had their farm and residence on Buck Run, a stream that has its source on the farm of Charles Railey, near Grier's Creek Church, and empties into the Kentucky river one mile above Clifton. The residence was one mile from Clifton, on an eminence surrounded by romantic scenery and was approached from the Versailles and Clifton road. Lewis Craig and Kitty Cox lived and died in this home. They had these children: Dr. Ben C. Craig, who married Anne Field, daughter of Willis Field and Isabella Miriam Buck; Henry Harrison, who married Emily Hancock; John P., who married Harriet Johnson, a kinswoman of Col. Dick Johnson, Vice President, U. S.; Herman, Catherine, Betsy, Randolph, Louis and Jefferson. Either Catherine or Betsy

married Samuel Hughes, but I can't say which.

Dr. Ben C. Craig had his residence in Versailles and practiced medicine in that community until his death about 1870. He and Anne Field had these children: William, Lewis and Thomas. The two former served in the Confederate army. Thomas moved to Louisville before the death of his father, and married there. I think he had children. William Craig had a daughter, Anne, who married Dr. Green, a son of the venerable pastor of the Danville Presbyterian Church, and he practiced dentistry at Versailles some years ago.

Henry Harrison Craig and Emily Hancock also lived on Buck Run, just across the creek from the "Narrows" and within two miles of lock No. 5, his farm joining that of Joel W. Twyman on one side and that of his father, Lewis Craig, on the other, and within a mile of Versailles and Clifton road. They had these children: William, Milton, Mary, Wiles, Henry H., Jr., and Dodd. To say that this was one of the happiest, brightest and most charming families I ever knew is not only a childhood memory, but a fact recognized by all who knew them. Though but ten years of age at the breaking out of the Civil War, I recall many of the thrilling incidents, and none clearer than when H. H. Craig, Sr., would send my father word to "skee-daddle," and both would skip by the light of the moon, and within a few hours the home guards would surround the houses, but the two men, with any rebel soldiers that might be on either premises, would be in the hills.

When the rebels had crossed the river

into Anderson County, at Tyrone, and the Federals slipped up on the Woodford side and fired their cannon across the river, there were four rebels who had taken supper in my father's home, and of the five immediate mounts, I was one of them, and I led them across the ford at lock No. 5, and across the hill at Redmons to Lawrenceburg.

William, Milton and Wiles were in the Confederacy, the former forfeiting his life at the fierce engagement at Cynthiana. Milton married Margaret Elizabeth Buford, daughter of Col. William McDowell Buford, of Midway, and his family reside at Corpus Christi, Texas; Mary married John Hickman, of Lawrenceburg, and their children live in Colorado and Texas; H. H., Jr., married Nellie Morgan, and though he resided at Corpus Christi, he owned the old home until his death several years ago; Dodd Craig and his family reside in Missouri.

John P. Craig, another son of Lewis Craig and Kitty Cox, inherited the home of his father near Clifton, on Buck Run, and he and his wife, Harriet Johnson, died there. They had the following children: Jefferson, John, Will, Catherine, Margaret, Mary Ann and Lizzie. Catherine, the last survivor of this large family, died in Lexington in April, 1920. Margaret was the only member who married. It was a devoted band of brothers and sisters who, though not forgetting their neighbors, lived largely in the home sphere. Margaret married George Hunt and lived in Lexington, and I think their descendants own the old home at this time. John Craig was a man of fine character and, though as gentle and

kindly as a woman, was as brave as a lion, a characteristic of the Craigs I have known. John was four years in the service of the Confederacy.

Toliver Craig, Jr., son of the first Toliver, married Elizabeth Johnston, and they resided in Scott County, near the "Great Crossing." Both were within the fort at Bryant Station during the siege of 1782, and she was one of the heroic women who braved the dangers that lay between the fort and the spring in order to relieve the thirst of the large garrison that was surrounded by the Indians in ambush.

Toliver Craig, Jr., and Elizabeth Johnston had, among other children, a son John, who married Alice Todd, daughter of Samuel Todd, of Botetourt County, Va., and John and Alice had a son, Samuel Craig, who married Margaret Craig, a cousin. Samuel and Margaret moved to Woodford County about 1835 and purchased the old Robert Bowmar property that extends from a point near lock No. 5 to the "Narrows," and Borders on Buck Run. They had Ellen, who married Willis Field, Jr., Charles, who married first Mary Ann Wilson, second Barbara Wilson; Berrywick, who married Nannie Thornton, and Eliza, who married first Dr. John W. Craig, second William McCampbell.

The Rev. Joseph Craig was a son of the 1st Toliver. He married Sally Wisdom, and came to Kentucky about the period that his father and other members of the family came. He was a noted Baptist minister, and it is a matter of record that a large proportion of his Virginia congregation came with him, and they held religious services all along the route. This statement is borne out by a book written by an Episcopal clergyman some years ago that was called "The Traveling Church." Another interesting bit of history was related by Richard Blanton, who died at the home of his son-in-law, the Rev. Isaac Crutcher, near Grassy Springs Church, himself a prominent Baptist minister. Richard Blanton lived to be nearly one hundred years old. His revelation was as follows: "Before the Revolution it was not lawful for preachers or teachers of denominations other than the Church of England to speak in public about Gospel truths. The Baptists were rebellious, and the Rev. Joseph Craig was a leader of those who protested. He was apprehended and convicted. I was sheriff of Frederick County at the time and one of my first duties was to arrest and incarcerate the Rev. Joseph, a very unpleasant duty. While he was in the county bastile it was no determent, as he continued to preach and teach through the bars at the jail. As it became evident that he was accomplishing more in jail than was possible before his incarceration, he was released by order of the ecclesiastical authorities."

Both Rev. Jo. Craig and Richard Blanton later in life lived in Woodford County, and were friends, and the Rev. Craig was just as active in Kentucky building churches and congregations, and organizing religious societies as he was in Virginia. He died in 1819 and Richard Blanton about that time, the former 77 years old and the latter over 90.

The children of Rev. Jo. Craig and Sallie Wisdom were the following: Reuben, who married Fannie Twyman, daughter of William Twyman; James, who married Sallie Mitchum, sister of Dudley Mitchum, and they had a daughter, Adelia Craig, who married Dr. Alfred Hurst; Samuel H., who married Patsy Singleton; Thomas, who married Polly Wisdom; Sally, who married —— Allen; Polly, who married Dudley Mitchum, Jr. All of these names are familiar to those acquainted with the citizenship of the county before the Civil War.

Samuel H. Craig and Patsy Singleton had a number of children, two of whom were John W. Craig and Mary Craig. John W. Craig married Mary Twyman, daughter of —— Twyman, and they had a daughter, Mary Craig, who married her cousin, Broadus Twyman; a son, John W., Jr., who married his cousin, Eliza Craig, and Judge Edwin Craig, who married first Eliza P. Mason, second Hontas Thornton, daughter of David Thornton and Charlotte Railey. Judge Craig has a daughter, Mason Craig, by the first marriage, who lives in Versailles; (no issue by second marriage.) She occupies the old Thornton home.

Mary Craig, daughter of Samuel H. Craig and Patsy Singleton, married —— Hughes, and had Samuel, William, James and John. Samuel married a daughter of Lewis Craig and Kitty Cox, and they had a son, Merritt Hughes.

Polly Craig, daughter of the Rev. Joseph, married James Mitchum and they had these children: Lucy, who married Judge R. Cave Graves, and Sallie, who married —— Drake.

Judge R. Cave Graves, who married Lucy Mitchum, had Laura, who married B. W. Wasson; Florida, who married Joseph Graddy; James, who married Kittie Chrisman, and John Graves.

Elijah Craig, who was one of the sons of the 1st Toliver, married Fannie Smith, and I think it was he who Richard Collins said ventured into Woodford County in 1782 and built the first fort, erected near what was afterward Versailles. The fort was located five miles from Versailles and ten from Lexington, likely in the Dry Ridge *section. He was in Bryan Station when that station was beleaguered, and when the rescue took place and the Indians driven north, he slipped over into the Clear Creek section and built his fort. There was an Elijah Craig at Harrod's Station at the same time, who married a McAfee, but I am quite sure that it was the son of pioneer Toliver Craig who built the fort near Versailles. Elijah Craig and Fanny Smith had these children: Joel, Simeon, Lydia, John, Polly and Lucy. I have learned little or nothing of their descendants.

June Craig was one of the two daughters of the first Toliver Craig mentioned in the beginning of this sketch. She married John Sanders, and their names are among the names of those in Bryan Station in 1782. They lived near the Forks of Elkhorn about 1790, which section was then in Woodford County. They had these children: John, Lewis and Nathaniel. Nathaniel married —— —— and was a neighbor of John Major, Sr., whose descendants were sketched in the May Register.

*See page 269, column 2, paragraph 4.

Elizabeth Craig, the other daughter of the 1st Toliver, mentioned in the beginning of this sketch, married Richard Cave, a pioneer of Woodford and a minister of the Baptist Church, who was a resident in 1810, and their daughter, Hannah, married John Graves. They were the parents of Judge R. Cave Graves, who married Lucy Mitchum, daughter of James Mitchum. For descendants see sketch of the Graves family.

———

James Ware was a citizen of Gloucester County, Virginia, and Agnes, his wife, was born and reared in the same county. His birth was in November, 1714, and she was born in December, 1714.

He rendered service in the Revolution, as did several of his sons, and he and his wife, accompanied by the families of their several sons and daughters came to Kentucky soon after hostilities incident to the Revolution had subsided. They settled in what was then Fayette County, but that section became a part of Woodford when the county was established in 1788. However, when they surveyed the line that separated the county of Franklin from Woodford, eight or ten years later, the line passed through the farm of James Ware, and within a short distance of his log residence, and separated his farm into two almost equal parts, one in Franklin and the other in Woodford, but the residence went into Franklin.

His residence, which in recent years has been modernized and enlarged, sets back in an avenue some distance from but in full view of the Frankfort and Versailles road, at the intersection of the Duckers Station pike. It is five and one-half miles from Frankfort, and the farm originally extended to Duckers Station, and included a part of the farm that was afterwards owned by Capt. Elijah Fogg, and all of the farm that was later owned by Robert Scott, and now owned by the Mason heirs. James Ware died about 1795 or 1796, as his will was probated April 19, 1796.

They had the following children, all grown, and many, if not all, married before leaving Virginia: John, born December, 1736; Nicholas, born August, 1739; James, Jr., born March, 1741; Richard, born May, 1745; Clara, born December, 1747; William, born March, 1750, and Edmund, born April, 1753.

†James Ware, Jr., was a physician, and married in Virginia Catharine Todd, in 1764, she a daughter of Dr. James Todd, of Gloucester County. They located in Fayette County, and his will, dated in 1820, is of record in the county court of that county.

‡William Ware married Sarah Samuels, in Virginia, and came to Kentucky with other members of the family and settled in Woodford County on a part of his father's estate, but after the death of his father he took charge of the old home and died there. He and Sarah Samuel had these children: Elizabeth, who married John Bacon in 1799, and lived in Frankfort; Agnes, who married first Philemon Rowzee, second William Porter; Rebecca, who married Willis Blanton in 1812; Sarah,*

who married William Porter, and Samuel, who married first Anne Read, second Betsy (Bullock) Redd, widow of Thomas M. Redd.

William Porter and Sarah Ware had a daughter, Elizabeth, who married J. D. C. Atkins, who was a United States Senator.

Willis Blanton, who married Rebecca Ware, was a son of John Blanton and Nancy Roberson, who lived near Grassy Springs church. He and his wife, Rebecca, lived on the farm now owned by the widow of Lafayette Crutcher, on the Versailles and Frankfort road, in full view of the church. Their children in part were: Dr. John William Blanton, who married first Elizabeth Anne Samuel, second Lucy Buck, both Woodford County girls; Horace T., who married first Martha Lamb, second Eliza Thompson. John William Blanton, of Paris, Tenn., is a son by the second marriage. See Blanton sketch.

Samuel Ware and his first wife, Anne Read, who was a daughter of Hankerson Read, a pioneer, lived on a farm not far from Duckers Station, a part of his father's estate. They had the following children: William, Jr., James, Jr., Hankerson, Agnes and Ann Read. By the second marriage to Betsy Bullock Redd was Elizabeth. Samuel Ware served in the Revolution—at least he drew a pension for services rendered.

Agnes Ware married Major Thomas Bullock, Jr., who resided on the farm now known as the Walker farm, beyond Mortonsville, but moved to Illinois. (See Bullock sketch.)

†See page 319 for heirs.
‡See page 319 for James Ware, born May 12, 1780.
*See page 309 for Sarah Ware, who married William Porter, Jr.

Ann Read Ware married Capt. Elijah Fogg, and their descendants appeared under the sketch of the Foggs.

Elizabeth Ware married John Benjamine Utterback. For descendants see Utterback sketch.

The Bradleys, of Woodford County, originally spelled the name Bradlee. They came from England to Virginia before the Revolutionary War and settled in Culpeper County. My data only carries me back to three brothers who were born in that county in Virginia. One of them, Abraham, remained in Virginia; Thomas moved to Tennessee, and Charles came to Kentucky about 1800, and settled in Woodford County, where he reared a large family of children. In 1810 the federal census of Woodford gave him a family of seven members and credited him with one slave.

Charles Bradley was born in 1777; married in Culpeper, Virginia, in 1799, Elizabeth Walton, born in 1783. When he came to Woodford he located on Glenns creek, and in the vicinity of Glenns Creek church, of which he was one of the founders. He served in the war of 1812 in the command of General Green Clay, and was in the battle of the "River Raisin." Squire Davis Edwards is quoted as saying that "Charles Bradley was as honest and just as any man that ever lived in the county."

Charles and Elizabeth Walton Bradley had thirteen children, whose names follow: Judith Bradley, born in 1800, married William A. Pierce Sept., 1820; Ann Bradley, born in 1802, never married; Polly Bradley, born in January,

1804, married William N. Pettit, May, 1825; Thomas W. Bradley, born in March, 1806, married Harriet Phillips in 1828; Virginia, born in January, 1808, and died unmarried; James D. Bradley, born October, 1809, married Minerva Gardner in Nov., 1834; Harriet Bradley, born Nov., 1811, and never married; Isham, born in 1813, and never married; Benjamine C. Bradley, born February, 1816, married Susan Mary Jones in January, 1840; William D. Bradley, born January, 1818, and never married; Mariah Bradley, born in 1820, married James H. Hackney Dec., 1843; Elizabeth Bradley, born Sept., 1823, married Richard M. Jones Dec., 1843, and Samuel Herman Bradley, born in 1825, married Joretta Smith Dec., 1848.

The Bradleys were a genial, friendly people, and everyone liked them. I recall two of the above children of Charles and Elizabeth Walton Bradley whom I knew very well in my boyhood days. Miss Harriet was a spinster when I first knew her and was one of the best liked ladies in the county, and she in turn was everybody's friend. She generously devoted her entire life to her family and her neighbors. In the days preceding, during and immediately following the Civil War there were no telephones, and in case of sickness or suffering of any kind it was difficult to get a physician in the country districts, so in the vicinity between Glenn's Creek and Grier's Creek churches, a broad scope of territory, Miss Harriet Bradley was regarded as an angel in disguise by those who suffered. Her womanly gentleness and beautiful patience linked with her observations and experience in divers sick rooms rendered her presence in every emergency a necessity, and her services were always in demand. Her spirit of self-sacrifice was beautiful.

She never made a charge, and was even reluctant to accept gifts. She was an authority on household affairs and was often sent for in the family carriage or the best family vehicle, to come. She was also an expert on canning, preserving, weaving, cutting, fitting and sewing, so there was a rivalry among the neighbors for her companionship and neighborly offices. So it goes without saying, that every wish of "Miss Harriet" was anticipated and gratified by her neighbors and friends. An old citizen of Woodford, long since dead, once said of her: "Her life work was indeed a fine example of the practical Christian spirit."

On July 4, 1868, at the home of her friend, Mrs. Mary C. White, where she died, there assembled one of the largest crowds ever gathered in the county to pay their last tribute to a loving friend.

She was buried on the farm of Col. Lewis A. Berry, where her father and mother were buried.

Samuel Herman Bradley was the other member of the family that I remember so well. He served in the Mexican War, and after returning to his home he resumed farming until 1870, when he moved to Franklin County among relatives, where he remained until 1882, when he removed, with his large family, to Texas, since which time I had lost trace of them until recently, under pleasing circumstances I received a letter from a son, Alex. Kemp Good-

loe Bradley. Samuel Herman Bradley —the middle name for Major Herman Bowman, Sr.—died in Texas in 1895, and his wife, Joretta, died in that state in 1906.

The Bradley family never craved riches, and always endeavored to act upon the golden rule in every transaction, and they were liked and respected by all who knew them.

Samuel Herman Bradley and his wife, Joretta, had these children: Mary P., born in April, 1851; Charles Bruce, born in Nov., 1854; Alex Kemp Goodloe Bradley, born Feb., 1858; Younger Berry, born Aug., 1860; Elizabeth, born Dec., 1862; William Mathew, born Dec., 1866; Harriett, born Feb., 1868; Jo. Robinson, born Nov., 1870; Urban, born Dec., 1872, and Pearl Louise, born Oct., 1875.

The data from which this sketch was written came from Alex Kemp Goodloe Bradley, of Tioga, Texas, whom I knew very well as a child. His brother, Charles, and sister Mary, were my childhood school mates. In his letter he exhibits a recollection of the past that is not universal among Woodford County boys of his generation. He says: "I left the county when a boy of twelve years of age, but I knew, as a boy knows, all of the old families. Of the Raileys, I knew Boone, Logan, Irvine and his brother whose first name I do not recall, yet I can see him in my mind riding one of the finest saddle horses in the county. I also remember Peter I. Railey, Hubbard and Will White, the Maceys, Gus and Robert, Ed Marshall and sons, Louis and Fred, Col. Lewis A. Berry, and his sons, Lewis and Bob; Dr. Craig, Doctors Jo. and Drake Carter and Miss Joe Carter. Well, I suppose I knew nearly everybody, though few noticed or knew me as a boy. It has been forty-five years since I was there, but I am sure I would know all of the pikes, if nothing else.''

"I would be glad to assist you in any way that I can, and if you haven't gotten the Hensley family, who lived at Midway, I will look up J. L. Hensley, who lives in these parts, and have him tell you all he knows.''

Benjamine C. Bradley and Susan Mary Jones, his wife, had these children: Susan, born April, 1841; Sidney, January, 1843; Frances, January, 1845; Mary, March, 1847; Annie, March, 1849; Henrietta, February, 1851; John, March, 1853; Lewis, Sept., 1855; and Quinn, Sept., 1856. Susan Mary Jones was a sister of the mother of Hon. Thos. W. Scott, of Franklin County, and for many, many years Susan Bradley, the eldest of the children of Ben C. Bradley, made her home with the Scotts, and she was as popular in the vicinity of Harmony church as her Aunt Harriet was in the Grier's Creek neighborhood, loved and respected for her splendid qualities by all who knew her.

In 1840 Ben C. Bradley was a housekeeper in Versailles and clerked in the store of Judge George. Later he owned a grocery and drug store in Versailles which he sold in order to enter a partnership with George Carter and Judge Cave Graves to manufacture hemp, but about 1856 he sold his interest in the rope walk (quite a number of them in Woodford at that time) and moved his

*See page 296.

family to Champaign, Ill., where many of them are today. Miss Susan is living at an advanced age, but a letter from her that I have just received shows her to be just as bright and jolly as she was twenty or more years ago, but she longs for old Kentucky that, she says, is like an oasis in a broad desert in her memory.

————

Richard Blanton and his wife, Elizabeth, were of English extract, and were living in Spottsylvania County, Virginia, in 1734. They had these children: Richard, Thomas, Sr., Priscilla, Elizabeth and Mary.

Thomas Blanton was born about 1724 and spent a greater portion of his life in the county of Spottsylvania. He served in the Revolution, married Jane ——, and came to Kentucky after he had reached his three score years and ten, but before the state had been admitted into the union. He disposed of all of his real estate in Spottsylvania County as early as 1786 and came to Kentucky and settled on a farm in Woodford County on the Frankfort and Versailles road. It was quite an extensive tract of land, extending from a point near the Franklin County line to the road that leads to Grassy Springs church, and running back to Glenns Creek, near the Franklin line. I think he also owned the tract on the opposite side of the road, now the home of the widow of Lafayette Crutcher.*

Thomas Blanton, Sr., and his wife, Jane, had these children: John, James, Phoebe, Betsy, Mary, Lindsey, Sallie Blanton and Richard, Jr. Like a sensible old man with a large estate, he deeded it to his several children while yet living. In deed book "C," Woodford County Court, page 154, he deeds the property in this manner: "For love and affection" to John Blanton, who married Nancy Roberson; James, who married —— ——; Phoebe, who married Rodenham Route; Betsy, who married George Bone; Richard, who married Maria Snead, &c.

To John I think he deeded the property of Mrs. Lafayette Crutcher. He died before 1810, at which time his widow, Nancy (Roberson) Blanton was living on the estate and was the owner of twenty-three slaves. John and Nancy had these children; Sallie, who married Richard Taylor; Thompson, who married Elizabeth Thompson in 1812; Benjamin, who married —— Roberson, and had John Blanton, of Hannibal, Mo.; Willis, who married Rebecca Ware in 1812, daughter of William Ware and Sarah Samuel; Richard, III., who married —— ——; Elizabeth, who married Anderson Shipp in 1816; James, who married Hester ——, and moved to Warsaw, Ky.; Ann, who married William Wood in 1812, and Dorothy, who married John M. Hopkins in 1820.

Willis Blanton and Rebecca Ware were on the farm with his mother, Nancy, in 1812, and inherited the home at her death. They had these children: John William, who married first Elizabeth Samuel, second Lucy Buck, both Woodford County girls; Horace, who married first Martha Lamb, second Eliza Thompson; Elizabeth married John Y. Mills, and Maria Louise married Nathaniel Currier.* Horace and

Martha Lamb had Martha, who married James Cooper, and by the second wife, Eliza Thompson, were John, William, Edward H., Horace, Nettie and Mary. John William Blanton, son of Horace and Elizabeth, is a resident of Paris, Tenn., and is in possession of the chain and surveying outfit with which his grandfather, Willis Blanton, surveyed the line that separates Franklin and Woodford counties.

James Blanton, son of the first Thomas Blanton and his wife, Jane, lived on the farm now owned by William E. Bradley, Jr., but sold it as early as 1820 to Walker Dearing, and left the county. (See Dearing.)

Richard Blanton, Jr., son of the first Thomas and his wife, Jane, came to Kentucky with other members of the family, perhaps a little later. His brother John was drafted for service in the Revolution, but as he had married Nancy Roberson and was rearing a family of children, Richard, though but sixteen years of age, offered himself as a substitute for his brother and was accepted. After the Revolution Richard married Sarah Snead and they had these children: John, Jr., Charles, Richard, Carter, William, James, Mrs. Vaughan, Mrs. Daniel, and Nancy, who married Rev. Isaac Crutcher. Dr. James F. Blanton, son of the above John Blanton, Jr., moved to Owen County and was for many years one of the leading Democratic politicians of that county. He frequently represented the county in the Legislature before the Civil War, when that body was overwhelmingly Whig, and it is said that he never cast a vote that

---

*Another daughter was Sarah Ann Blanton, who married John Porter. See page 309.

pleased the Whigs. He left his impress upon the body politic of that county and it is noticeable even now. The Blantons have uniformly had Jeffersonian tendencies.

Richard Blanton, Jr., the hero who offered his services in lieu of his brother in the Revolution, tradition says, became homesick at the defeat of General Gates and ran to his home sixty miles away without a stop or a look around. It was his own story, but likely in jest. Just after the Revolution he was living in Frederick County, Virginia, and was elected sheriff of that county. One of his first, as well as one of the most unpleasant duties was the arrest and incarceration of the Rev. Jo. Craig for violating a statute prohibiting any preacher or teacher other than an Episcopalian clergyman from preaching or teaching Gospel truths in public. Behind the bars the Rev. Jo. preached with such convincing force and inspiration as to double the number of his converts, so he was soon released.

Richard Blanton died under the weight of many years, at the home of his son-in-law, Rev. Isaac Crutcher, near Grassy Springs church. He had a son Richard who married an aunt of Gen. Leslie Combs, of Lexington, remembered by the old citizens as provost marshal during the Civil War. Some of the Blantons sold out their interests in Woodford as early as 1820 to Walker Dearing, and I do not recall any one by the name living in the county after the Civil War,* though there may be descendants there now.

They were intermarried with some of the best families in Virginia and Kentucky.

———

Harrison Harris, a Revolutionary soldier of Virginia, emigrated from Goochland County about 1786, and settled on 1,500 acres of land adjoining and partially surrounding Mt. Vernon church, in Woodford County, Ken-† tucky. This land was on both sides of Elkhorn creek, and his home was located where Monette Wiglesworth‡ now lives, known as the Utterback place. He and his wife, with several of their family descendants, are buried in the family graveyard at that place. His will was recorded in the county clerk's office at Versailles in August, 1795. Caleb Wallace, Sam'l Deweese and Thos. Marshall were witnesses. The will specifies the following children, and leaves each land as follows: land left David is now the home of Monette Wiglesworth; land left Randolph is now owned by Wade Hampton; land left Nathaniel is now the home of Thomas F. Dunlap; the land left Susanna is now owned by Wade Hampton; land left Mary Elizabeth is now owned by Thomas F. Dunlap, and the land left Mourning is now owned by John W. Stout.

The surname Harris is of Welsh origin and means literally "son of Harry." The postmaster of Merthyr-Tydvil in Wales writes that the Harris family in that country is legion.

The Harris papers include several other pioneer families with whom they were intermarried, and are prepared in

———
*But there are.
†See page 305.
‡Supplement.

such a way as to be easily comprehended. As the papers cover many generations of large families I have decided to enter them just as prepared by John H. Field, son of Col. Thomas M. Field and Susan Mary Higbee. All of the descendants of Harrison Harris are represented by numerals running consecutively from 1 to 153, the first generation running from 1 to 6, the second from 7 to 26, the third from 27 to 76, and the fourth from 77 to 153. The consecutive numbers are on a line to the right, while the numerals representing the heads of each of the generations are to the left.

1. David Harris, married 1st Jane Mims, 2nd, Ellen Hart.

2. Randolph Harris, married Hester White.

3. Nathaniel, married Mary Howard.

4. Susanna, married George Calhoun Caldwell, of South Carolina, a cousin of John Caldwell Calhoun, the statesman.

5. Mary Elizabeth, married William Randolph Hicks.

*6. Mourning, married William Adams.

1. David Harris and Jane Mims had

7. David Oliver Harris, who married Mary Hanna McKinney.

By Ellen Hart, second wife, was

8. Duke Harris, who married ―――― Wallace.

2. Randolph Harris and Hester White had

9. David Harris, who died without issue.

10. Samuel Harris, who died without issue.

3. Nathaniel Harris and Mary Howard had

11. Jackson Harris, who was adopted by Missouri.

12. Richard, who married Frances Redmond. Went to Missouri.

13. Lewis, who married Lucinda Berry.

14. William Smith, born 1811, died 1883, married Pamelia Palmer Anderson, who died in 1879.

4. Susanna Harris and George Calhoun Caldwell had

15. Mary Caldwell, who married Alexander Dunlap.

16. Betsy Caldwell, who married John Curd.

17. Paulina, who married 1st John Higbee, 2nd Joseph Chrisman.

5. Mary Elizabeth Harris and William Randolph Hicks had

18. Kittie Hicks, who married Spencer Anderson.

19. Olivia Hicks, who married 1st Amos Stout, 2nd Newton Alexander.

20. Elizabeth Hicks, who married Henry Downs.

21. Sarah Hicks, who married Daniel Williams.

22. Robert Hicks, who married Mary Hagar.

23. Anne Hicks, who married 1st Tavner Branham, 2nd Micajah Stone.

24. Susan Hicks, who married Isaac Williams.

25. Mary Hicks, who married Philemon Price.

6. Mourning Harris and William Adams had

26. Sarah Adams, married Lewis Brassfield.

*See page 393.

7. David Oliver Harris and Mary Hanna McKinney had

27. Fannie Harris, who married Ben Meek.

28. Nellie Harris, who married James Bohannon.

29. Mollie Harris, who married Henry Berryman.

12. Richard Harris and Frances Redmond had

30. Nathaniel W. Harris, who migrated to Missouri, where he married.

31. Edward H. Harris, who migrated to Missouri, where he married.

14. William Smith Harris and Pamelia Palmer Anderson had

32. David S. Harris, who married Dora Brown.

33. Mary Ellen Harris, who married Jonathan R. Briggs.

34. William Henry Harris, who married Mary Aiken.

35. Annie Tompkins Harris, who married Robt. Hagar Hicks.

36. Andrew Thomas Harris, married 1st Susan Ella Dunlap, 2nd Lena C. Field.

37. Dora B. Harris, not married and resides in Danville.

38. Clarence C. Harris, who married Anna Crockett.

15. Mary Caldwell and Alexander Dunlap had

39. George Caldwell Dunlap, who married 1st —— Legrand, 2nd ——.

40. Agnes Dunlap died without marrying.

41. Susan Dunlap, who married Col. Ezekiel Field.

42. William Alexander Dunlap married Amanda Branham.

16. Betsy Caldwell and John Curd had

43. John Curd, married 1st Lydia Downing, 2nd —— Downing.

17. Paulina Caldwell and John Higbee had

44. Alexander C. Higbee, who married Betty Berry.

45. Henry Higbee, who married Emma Davidson.

46. Susan Mary Higbee, who married Col. Thomas M. Field.

47. Charlton H. Higbee, married Belle ——.

17. Pauline Caldwell and Joseph Chrisman had

48. Kittie Chrisman, who married James M. Graves.

19. Olivia Hicks and Amos Stout had

49. John Stout, who married Susan Bohannon, daughter of German.

50. Robert Hicks Stout, who married Fannie Gillespie.

51. William Stout, who married Judith Jameson.

52. Amos Stout, Jr., killed in battle at Wilson Creek, Mo., in the service of the Confederacy.

21. Sarah Hicks and Daniel Williams had

53. Jackson Williams, married 1st Amanda Weathers, 2nd Susan McClure.

54. John Hicks Williams, married Jane Eichelberger.

22. Robert Hicks and Mary Hagar had

55. Robert Hagar Hicks, married Annie T. Harris.

56. Harris Hicks married Hattie Murrain.

23. Anne Hicks and Tavner Branham and

57. Amanda Branham, who married William A. Dunlap.

58. Martha Branham, who married B. Frank Starks.

59. Sarah Branham, who married John Gay.

60. Susan Branham, who married 1st Robt. H. Davis, 2nd James W. Parrish.

24. Susan Hicks and Isaac Williams had

61. Isaac Williams, married —— ——.

62. Joseph Williams, married —— ——.

62. Anne Williams, married James Starks.

25. Mary Hicks and Philemon Price had

63. Martha Price, who married James Ware Parrish.

63. Mary Phil Price, who married James Ware Parrish.

64. Elvira Price, married Bird Smith.

26. Sarah Adams and Lewis Brassfield had

65. Anne Brassfield, who married Dr. Douglas Price.

66. —— Brassfield, married William Cotton.

30. Dr. Nathaniel W. Harris and —— —— had

67. Henry W. Harris, president Third National Bank, Sedalia, Mo.

68. Nathaniel W., Jr., died without issue.

69. Charles Harris is married and living at St. Louis, Mo.

70. Lula Harris, who married —— ——.

31. Edward H. Harris and —— —— had

71. Richard Harris.

72. Sallie Harris, who married —— Johnson.

73. Fred Harris.

74. Edward Harris.

75. William Harris.

76. Mary Harris.

32. David S. Harris and Dora Brown had

77. Pauline Harris, married —— Weber.

78. Eugenia Harris, who married Conduit Hayden.

79. Dr. David S. Harris, Jr., is married and living at Dallas, Texas.

80. Dr. Morris Harris is married and living in Texas.

33. Mary Ellen Harris and Jonathan R. Briggs had

81. William H. Briggs, who died without issue.

82. Harry Lee Briggs, who is with the Citizens National Bank, at Danville, Ky.

36. Andrew T. Harris and Susan Ella Dunlap had

83. Palmer Harris, who married Bernice Bradford.

84. Lottie Lee, who has not married.

36. Andrew T. Harris and Lena C. Field had

85. Field Harris, who married Katherine Chism.

86. Andrew Earl Harris, who is not married.

39. George C. Dunlap and —— Legrand had

42. William A. Dunlap and Amanda Branham had

87. Martha Dunlap, who married W. Clark Arnett.

88. Alexander Dunlap, who married Belle Field.

89. Ella Dunlap, who married Andrew T. Harris.

90. George W. Dunlap, who married Kate Childers.

91. Thomas F. Dunlap, who married 1st Minnie Crouch, 2nd Mattie Crutcher.

92. Branham Dunlap, who married Tabbie Whitley.

93. Ernest Dunlap, who married Margaret Farra.

45. Henry Higbee and Emma Davidson had

94. John Higbee, who died unmarried.

46. Susan Mary Higbee and Col. Thomas M. Field had

95. Belle Field, who married Alexander Dunlap.

96. John H. Field, who married Lelia Gay.

97. Willis Field, who married Elizabeth Shryock.

98. Lena C. Field, who married Andrew T. Harris.

99. Thomas M. Field, who is not married.

100. Bessie C. Field, who married P. Leslie Sloan.

47. Charlton Higbee and Belle —— had

101. Annie Higbee, who married Robert Maddox.

102. Bird Higbee, who married Valney Hildreth.

103. Sue Higbee, who married Tarlton Embry.

48. Kittie Chrisman and James M. Graves had

104. Lula Graves, who married George Minary.

105. Lena Graves, who never married.

106. John Graves, who married Pattie Bird.

107. Charlton Graves, who has not married.

108. Belle Graves, who married —— ——.

49. John Stout and Susan Bohannan had

109. Addisonia Parker Stout, who married James A. Slaughter.

110. Sarah Louisa Stout, who married Louis Dedmond.

111. Olivia Stout, who married Sim D. Slaughter.

112. Mary Isabel Stout, who married Prof. John N. Bradley.

113. German Bohannon Stout, who married Eugenia Jackson.

114. Eva Southworth Stout, who married George Branham.

115. Henrietta Bohannon Stout, who married Ben A. Thomas.

116. John Woolfork Stout, who married Tillie Cox.

50. Robert Hicks Stout and Fannie Gillespie had

117. Rev. George Edwin Stout, who married Nellie Beard.

118. Judge Robert Lee Stout, who married Florence Offutt.

51. William Stout and Judith Jameson had

119. Mary Ann Stout, who never married.

120. Rev. Amos Stout, who married 1st Nannie B. Crouch, 2nd Margaret Wright.

121. Rachael Stout, who married Ben Sid Branham.

122. Nellie Stout, never married.

123. Newton Stout, who has never married.

124. Ollie J. Stout, who married J. W. Taylor.

53. Jackson Williams and Amanda Weathers had

125. Laura Williams, who married the Rev. —— Baker.

126. Bettie Williams, who married John O. Rogers.

53. Jackson Williams and Susan Mc-Clure had

54. John Hicks Williams and his wife, Jane Eichelberger, had

127. Preston Williams, who married 1st, Maggie Miller, 2nd Louise Price.

56. Harris Hicks and Hattie Murrian had

128. Dr. Robert Hicks, who married Edna Starks.

129. May Hicks, who is not married.

58. Martha Branham and B. Frank Starks had

130. Price Starks, who married Georgia Maddox.

131. Martha Starks, who married John Taylor.

59. Sarah Branham and John Gay had

132. Bettie Gay, who married John Hanna.

133. Annie T. Gay, who married David H. James.

134. James Gay, who married Maria Cotton.

135. Martha Gay, who married William Swope.

136. Lelia Gay, who married John H. Field.

137. Minnie Gay, who married Garrett Watts.

138. John Gay, Jr., who married Mattie Bridgeforth.

139. Robert H. Gay, who married 1st Florence Bowman, 2nd Eva Nuckols.

60. Susan Branham and Robt. H. Davis had

140. Annie Davis, who married 1st Taylor Wallace, 2nd Dr. T. H. Hudson.

141. Robert H. Davis, who married Nolie Trimble.

60. Susan Branham and James Ware Parrish had

142. Ruth Parrish, who never married.

62. Joseph Williams and —— —— had

143. George Williams, who married Mary Adelaide Holt.

144. Joseph Williams, who married Ora Lee Letton.

145. Annie Williams, who married —— LeCompt.

146. Stella Williams, who married William Davis.

62. Annie Williams and James Starks had

147. Isaac Starks, who married 1st Minnie Ferguson, 2nd Eleanor Cannon.

148. Eugenia Starks, who married Preston Burgen.

63. Martha Price and James Ware Parrish had

149. Thompson Parrish, who married Kate E. Rogers.

150. Philemon Parrish, who married Emma Magoffin.

63. Mary Phil Price and James Ware Parrish had

151. Mary Phil Parrish, who married Rev. R. C. Ricketts.

64. Elvira Price and Bird Smith had

152. Thaddeus Smith, who married Adelia Miles.

153. Mary Moss Smith, who married Thos. V. Sanford.

The old Virginia families were noted for their inclination to intermarry with blood relatives, and many of them followed the example for years after they came to Kentucky, and the four or five families who located in the Mt. Vernon vicinity, who are recorded above, were not exceptions to the custom so popular in Virginia. For instance, the grandmothers of William A. Dunlap and his wife, Amanda Branham, were sisters, and both were sisters of Nathaniel Harris. Again, David Sanders Harris was a cousin of his wife, Dora Brown. Nathaniel Harris, the grandfather of Annie Tompkins Harris, who married Robert Hagar Hicks, was a brother of Robert Hagar Hicks' grandmother, Elizabeth Hicks. Alex Dunlap married Belle Field, and their grandmothers were sisters. Andrew T. Harris married Susan Ella Dunlap, and their grandmothers were sisters of Nathaniel Harris; and the grandmother of his second wife, Lena C. Field was a sister of Nathaniel Harris. And Dr. Ben Parrish and his wife, Hallie Gay, were grandson and granddaughter of two sisters, and sisters to Nathaniel Harris. And the grandmothers of John H. Field and his wife, Lelia Gay, were sisters, and sisters to Nathaniel Harris.

Harrison Harris left a codicil to his will that was witnessed by Caleb Wallace, Rosanna Wallace and Don D. Holmes.

Zachary Taylor, Jr., was a son of Zachary Taylor, Sr., and his wife, Elizabeth Lee. He was a brother of Col. Richard Taylor, who married Sarah Strother, and also a brother of Hancock Taylor, who is mentioned in Collins' history as having done much surveying in Kentucky county for the Virginia authorities, and who, on one of his return trips, with surveying data to file with the authorities in Virginia, was shot by a band of Indians, in 1774, from the effects of which he expired after reaching a point within two miles of Richmond, Madison County, Ky. The spot where he was buried has been marked by the daughters of the American Revolution. He was shot near the mouth of the Kentucky river.

Zachary Taylor, Jr., married his cousin, Alice Chew, daughter of Thomas Chew and Martha Taylor, and came to Woodford County, Kentucky, soon after the Revolution, in which war he served as a captain. He settled upon a large estate on South Elkhorn that I think extended into what afterwards became Jessamine County. His wife, Alice Chew, was a cousin of President Madison and a schoolmate, and she made the crimson cloth clothes that that distinguished statesman wore when he first entered Congress.

Zachary Taylor and Alice Chew had these children, who were born in Virginia: Samuel, Sarah and John. Sarah married Richard Woolfolk and moved to Jefferson County, where they located on a farm between Harrods creek and the Ohio river, not far from the home of her uncle, Col. Richard Taylor, where they raised a family of children; John Taylor married Parthenia Dawson and had Richard, Mary Ann, Parthenia and Catherine.

Zachary Taylor, Jr., served Virginia for a long time in the military branch of the government. He was a member of Washington's Rangers, who were conspicuously successful at Braddock's defeat. Both he and his brother, Col. Richard, were men of extraordinary physique, each measuring six feet two inches and weighing about two hundred and fifty pounds, neither having an ounce of surplus flesh, carrying a frame of bone and muscle. Whenever in a reminiscing mood he would relate the fact that he and Gen. Washington were the only members of the Rangers who could stand at the foot of the Natural Bridge in Virginia and cast a stone to the top of the bridge. After the death of his wife he went to Jefferson County to live with Richard Woolfolk, who married his daughter, Sarah. Before he left Woodford his brother, Col. Richard, often visited the county, dividing his visits between his brother Zachariah and his father-in-in-law, William Strother, who lived on farms not far apart. Tradition says that Col. Richard Taylor always wore knee pants and long stockings, but that the queue and silver buckles were conspicuously absent.

Zachary Taylor was living in Woodford in 1810, and there was a John Taylor living there at the same time, but whether it was his son John or not I can't say.

The Taylors hailed from Orange County, Virginia. Col. Richard Taylor and his brother, Hancock, who died early, surveying in Fayette, Woodford and Franklin, were the first Americans who descended the Ohio river on a trading voyage, going to New Orleans in 1769. They returned by sea, disembarked at Charleston, S. C., and walked to their home at Orange Court House, Va.

Richard Taylor, son of Commodore Dick Taylor, and a cousin of Zachary, Jr., Col. Richard and Hancock Taylor, occasionally visited Woodford County in pioneer days. He was at Scott's Landing when Gov. Scott's son was shot, on the Mercer County side of the Kentucky river by the Indians. Young Scott's body was laid on the river bank by the Indians as a decoy for white men. Richard Taylor discovered the body, undertook to rescue it and was wounded in such a way as to affect the use of his limbs, and he was ever afterwards known as "Hopping Dick" Taylor.

———

Four brothers by the name of Wilhoit came from Germany to America during the year 1787, and settled in Culpeper County, Virginia. One of the brothers bore the name of Adam, and he took unto himself a wife before leaving his native Germany, but the maiden name of his frau is not known by any of the descendants with whom I have communicated. Adam and his wife had, among other children, a son whom they named John, who married Elizabeth Blankenbaker, and this couple reared a son they named Elijah. Elijah married at Madison Court House, Madison County, Virginia, Nancy Vawter, a daughter of Richard Vawter. Elijah Wilhoit and Nancy Vawter came to Kentucky in 1814 and located in Woodford County. He bought a farm at Mortonsville from Col. Richard Taylor that was inherited by Col. Taylor's wife from her father, William Strother. This farm adjoined the farm of Thomas Coleman, whose wife was a sister of

Col. Taylor's wife, she having inherited her estate from the same source.

Elijah Wilhoit and Nancy Vawter had a son, Hiram, who married Sophia Thornton, granddaughter of Thomas Coleman and Susanna Strother Hawkins (widow of Captain Moses Hawkins) and they had several children, of whom Judge James T. Wilhoit, the present postmaster at Versailles, is the only survivor. He married Alice Bohon and they have a son, Hiram, who married Jessie Henton, daughter of James Henton. Hiram Wilhoit, Jr., is connected with the Woodford Bank in some capacity; Martha B. married W. W. Johnson; J. C. married Lora Holloway; Sophia T. married Victor Bradley; George B. and John.

Elijah Wilhoit and Nancy Vawter also had a daughter, Malinda, who married Medley Shelton, the popular proprietor of the old Tavern in Versailles that was supplanted by the present hotel. Medley Shelton was a very popular citizen as well as host, and quite a clever politician. Within his tavern such men as Henry Clay, the Crittendens, the Breckinridges and other luminaries of that period were entertained and it ranked as one of the most popular hostelries in Central Kentucky. Medley Shelton represented the county in the Kentucky Legislature in 1842. It is my impression that the mother-in-law of Col. Medley Shelton, Nancy Vawter, was closely related to William Vawter, who represented Woodford County in the Kentucky House of Representatives in 1797, 1799 and 1800, and was a member of the State Senate, 1806-10, but I am not

able to establish how closely they were related, as I have not been able to get in touch with descendants, if he had any. But Col. Medley Shelton and William Vawter were close friends, although the former was many years the junior of the latter.

Richard Vawter, the father of Nancy, was at home at Madison Court House, Va., and there are evidences in Versailles of business transactions between Richard Vawter and Henry Field, Jr., in Virginia, ancestor of Willis and John H. Field, of the county.

———

William Strother of "Orange." was born about 1720, in Orange County, Virginia, and lived in that county until he came to Kentucky. He was twice married, both events occurring in Virginia. His first marriage was to Sarah (Bailey) Pannill, in 1751. She the widow of William Pannill; second to Anna Kavanaugh, widow of Philemon Kavanaugh.* There was no issue from the second marriage. By the first marriage was Susanna Strother, who married first Captain Moses Hawkins, second Thomas Coleman; William Dabney Strother, who was killed at the battle at Guilford Court House while an officer of a company in the regiment of Col. Richard Taylor, his brother-in-law; and he and Sarah Strother, who became the wife of Col. Richard Taylor, were the parents of General Zachary Taylor, who was commander of our armies in the Mexican War, and afterwards elected President.

William Strother was a large land holder in both Orange and Culpeper counties, Va., as various documents of

*Philemon Kavanaugh and his wife Anna had a son, Philemon.

record in these counties disclose, and copies of these records are in possession of Henry Strother, of Ft. Smith, Ark., who has made many trips to Virginia in research work. In Culpeper County one deed, among others, reveals property deeded by William Strother in 1758 to his daughter Susanna, and his son William Dabney Strother. On August 1st, 1727, Margaret (Thornton) Strother conveyed to her son, Francis Strother, certain slaves, by name, with reversion at his death to his son, William Strother, of "Orange," and these slaves were delivered to William, at the death of his father, Francis, in 1752. When William Strother arrived at the age of maturity he had an uncle in Stafford County whose name was confused with his in business affairs, so the one was ever afterward known as William of "Orange," and the other as William of 'Stafford,'' in business and social affairs.

†Captain Moses Hawkins and his wife, Susanna Strother, were married March 3rd, 1770, and they had the following issue: 1st Sarah Bailey Hawkins, 2nd William Strother Hawkins, 3rd Lucy Hawkins, and 4th Moses Hawkins, Jr. Captain Moses Hawkins entered the service of the Revolution early in that conflict and was killed at the battle of Germantown, Oct. 4, 1777. After the war his widow married Thomas Coleman, who was a neighbor, and friend of Captain Hawkins before the war, and a corporal in his company during the war.

Within a few years after the Revolution William Strother of "Orange"

and his wife, Anna Kavanaugh, accompanied by Thomas Coleman, his wife, Susanna Strother Hawkins, and her four Hawkins children, came to Kentucky and settled not far from Mortonsville in Woodford County, and very near the home of Jeremiah Morton, whose wife, Judith Coleman,* was a sister of Thomas Coleman, and it is likely they all came to Kentucky at the same time, but just what year I am unable to state, but it is a matter of record that William Strother bought land in the county from Col. Richard Young as early as 1789, and from James Bullock, Jr., in 1794. In his will (see will book C, page 105 county court) he devised the homestead to Susanna Hawkins Coleman, his daughter, and the adjoining farm to his daughter Sarah, who married Col. Richard Taylor. I am informed that the old homestead is now the property of J. A. Eaton. I am quite sure that the remains of William Strother, his wife, Anna Kavanaugh, Thomas Coleman and his wife, Susanna, and perhaps a number of descendants were buried on the Eaton farm. By his will his son-in-law, Col. Richard Taylor, and grandson, Hancock Taylor, were executors of the estate.

Col. Richard Taylor and Sarah Strother settled in Jefferson County, where they raised a large family, most of whom were born in Virginia. Gen. Zachary Taylor also had a large family, of whom General Dick was the most distinguished. He served in the Confederacy, and after the war wrote a history of the "Civil War;" Sarah Knox Tay-

---

†See Supplement for his will.
*This is an error. See page 374.

lor married Captain Jefferson Davis, of the regular army, afterwards became President of the Confederacy; and Anna Mackall Taylor, who married Gen. Robert C. Wood, of the Confederacy. They have a son, Trist Wood, who now resides at New Orleans. General Zachary Taylor, through his grandmother, Elizabeth Lee, the wife of Zachary of Orange County, Va., is descended from Col. Richard Lee, who was also the ancestor of General Robt. E. Lee, and progenitor of that family in America. Although the census of 1810 discloses a large citizenship of Taylors in Woodford, and Col. Richard Taylor's wife owned a farm there, near Montonsville, I don't think that any of his children ever lived in the county, yet he, his wife and his children were frequent visitors to their relatives. Besides his father-in-law, William Strother, his brother, Captain Zachary Taylor, who married Alice Chew, lived in Woodford County and died there.

Sarah Bailey Hawkins, 1st of Captain Moses Hawkins and Susanna Strother, married James Thornton. She was named for her grandmother, the first wife of William Strother, and for the reason of the namesake she was the only one of the four grandchildren mentioned in her will (Sarah Bailey Pannill) on record in Orange County, Va., and she was handsomely remembered. James Thornton and his wife, Sarah Bailey Hawkins, had these children: Damascus Thornton, who, as a very young man, went to Louisiana and managed the plantation of General Zachary Taylor. The climate was against him and he died within a few

years; William, who married and went west at an early age; Willis, who married a southern girl and left two daughters, one of whom married Bishop Key, of the Methodist church, whose daughter, Sarah Versel, is in charge of the North Texas College, at Sherman, Texas; James, Jr., who went south at an early age to take charge of General Taylor's plantation after the death of his elder brother. He did not return to Woodford County until he reached his fiftieth birthday, and soon afterward married Elizabeth Kidd; Richard Taylor Thornton, who enlisted in the regiment of Col. Whittaker in 1861 and was killed at the battle of Shiloh; Susan Strother Thornton who, upon the death of her mother, took charge of the home and the care of the younger children and died a spinster; Sarah, who married John P. Cammack, who has a son living in Dallas, Texas; Emma, who married Thomas J. Waller; Lucy Ann, who married —— Busby and died without issue; Sophia, who married Hiram Wilhoit, and had James T. and John.

Sue Thornton, who married Zach T. Walker, had Mabel and Les Walker; and Lutie Thornton, who married Joel Chiles, were daughters of James Thornton, Jr., and Elizabeth Kidd. She, the latter, and her children live in Missouri.

William Strother Hawkins 2nd of Captain Moses Hawkins and Susanna Strother was born June 1, 1772, and died October 26, 1858. He married Katherine Keith Oct. 14, 1802, she a daughter of Captain Isham Keith and Charlotte Ashmore, and a granddaughter of the Rev. James Keith and

Mary Isham Randolph. William Strother Hawkins and Katherine Keith had these children; Isham Keith, who married first Lucy Major, second Sarah Hall; Charlotte Ashmore, who married† James Vaughan; Benjamine Dabney, who married Jane Watts; Lucy, who married Thomas McGinnis; Moses, III, who married Mary Sublett; Susan Strother, who married Thomas S. Edwards; William Strother, Jr., who married Elizabeth Gough; Katherine Keith, who married Richard Henry Railey, Feb. 25, 1852; and James Keith Hawkins, who married first Ann Sublett, second Amanda Joiner.

Isham Keith Hawkins and Lucy Major had James and Elizabeth, who died young, and Katherine, who married Aaron Darnell and had Isham Randolph Darnell.

Isham Keith Hawkins and Sarah Hall had Mary Frances, who died single; Annie who married John E. Miles and had Mary Keith; William T., who served with Morgan during the Civil War, and married Gertrude Owsley, and had William Hall and Lena; Callie, who married George Byrnes; Clinton B., who married Elizabeth Owsley and had Frank H. and Clinton; and Susie, who married Richard J. Fogg and had William Clinton, Sadie and Richard J., Jr.

Charlotte Ashmore Hawkins and James Vaughan had Edmond Vaughan, and William Vaughan.

‡Benjamine Dabney Hawkins and Jane Watts had Cliff Hawkins, who married ——— ———, and had Susie; and Lucy Hawkins, who married Capt.

Bush Allin, who was elected circuit clerk of Mercer County soon after his return from the Civil War, and was re-elected consecutively until his death, about 1909. They have a son, Ben Casey Allin, who is propreitor of the old Graham Springs, at Harrodsburg, and another son, Bush, Jr., who is President of the Mercer County National Bank; and other children.

Lucy Hawkins and Thomas McGinnis had William Strother, who married Belle Sublett and had Lucy, Woodford, Keene, James, and Matt Strother McGinnis.

Moses Hawkins, III, and Mary Sublett had Ballard, who married John Trumbo; Sallie, who married Christopher Lillard, and Lee, who married David Castleman.

Wm. Strother Hawkins and Elizabeth Gough had Katherine, who married John Ed Hawkins; Robert, who married Mamie Lindsey; Francis, Eliza, Mary Belle, Matt, Charlotte and Bessie.

Katherine Keith Hawkins and Richard Henry Railey had Wm. E. Railey, born Dec. 25, 1852, who married Annie H. Owsley, May 26, 1886, and had Jennie Farris, born June 28, 1887, who married Douglass Wheeler King, June, 1918; Bertha Hontas Railey and P. Woodson Railey.

Lucy Hawkins, third child of Captain Moses Hawkins and Susanna Strother, and William George, her husband, had Katherine, Joseph and Sallie.

Moses Hawkins, Jr., and Sarah Castleman, daughter of Lewis Castleman and Jemima Pearsoll, lived on Glenns creek, on a farm, and he owned a grist mill that he operated for many years, known as Hawkins' Mill. My impression is that McDaniel afterward bought the property and operated the mill. Moses Hawkins, Jr., died in 1817, and in 1832 his widow moved with five of her seven children to Palmyra, Mo. Their descendants are numerous and prominent in Missouri. Mrs. Lela G. Wright, of LaBelle is a great granddaughter and has done much towards preserving this branch of the family history. (See Castleman sketch, page 62.)

The Strother line: William Strother (1) and his wife, Dorothy. William Strother (2) and his wife, Margaret Thornton. Francis Strother (3) and his wife, Susanna Dabney. William Strother (4) of "Orange," and his wives, Sarah Bailey Pannill and Anna Kavanaugh.

———

John Long was one of Woodford County's early settlers, arriving soon after the Revolution, he having played a gallant part in that struggle as a soldier. He married Mary Haynes in 1772 in Bedford County, Va., and she accompanied him on his long western journey. He was born in 1749 in Virginia, and died in Woodford County in 1832. His wife was born in Virginia in 1751 and died in Woodford in 1825.

In 1810, according to the census of that year, John Long, Sr., possessed a fine farm, was the owner of fifteen slaves and had a family consisting of five members within his domicile at that time, which fact is borne out by the family Bible. He was the proud father of twelve children, but all except three

were married and housekeeping in 1810.

The children of John Long, Sr., and Mary Haynes follow: Garrard Long, born in 1773, married ———; Lucy, born 1775, married William Whittington in 1791 (see sketch of Whittingtons); James C., born 1776, died 1859, married in 1802 Nancy Berry, daughter of Samuel Berry, Sr., and his wife, Mary Allen; John Long, Jr., born 1778, married Polly Stevenson in 1805; Reuben Long, born 1780, married ——— Macey; Frances, born 1783, married James Marshall (?); William B. Long, born 1786, died 1825, married Susan Holeman in 1816; Betsy Long, born 1787, married George McDaniel (?); Polly Long, born 1789, married John W. Brooking in 1809; Sally Long, born 1790, married Robert Clark in 1811; Willis Long, born 1792, married first Harriet Thomas, in 1817, second Eliza Agun in 1829, and Anderson Long, born in 1795, died in 1810. Both parents were living in 1810 and only three of the twelve children were single and living at that time in the home, which bears out the census report of that year.

James C. Long and Nancy Berry had these children: John W. Long, born 1803, died in 1870, married first Jane Stevenson in 1824, second Winifred Davidson in 1841; Eliza Berry, born in 1805, married Alexander Cunningham Scott in 1825; Kitty B., born 1807, married Augustus Bower in 1832; James L. Long, born in 1811, died 1859, married Louisa Jane Jesse in 1834; Cydney H. Long, born in 1814, married Fielding Evans in 1836; Henrietta Clay Long, born 1817, married

Albert H. Bohannon in 1836; Mary Haynes Long, born 1819, married John Hall, of Shelby County in 1843, and they have a granddaughter, Katharine Bryant, who married Edward Byrnes Smith, a physician of Shelbyville. She deserves much credit for the service she has rendered her kindred in collecting and assisting in preserving the interesting story of her people; William B. Long, born in 1821, married Lucy Jane Barkley in 1857; Ambrose Dudley Long, born in 1823, died in 1864, married Mildred Bullock; Thomas Parker Long, born 1826, died 1857, married Nancy Jackson (?); and Ryland D. Long, born 1828, married Mary Portwood in 1856.

The descendants of Henrietta Clay Long and Albert H. Bohannon will appear under the sketch of the Bohannons. Frank Bohannon, the popular deputy sheriff, is the only one that I recall now living in the county.

Of the descendants of Eliza Berry Long and Alex Cunningham Scott I recall Benjamin and Al Scott, both of whom enlisted in the Confederate service with many of their associates in the county, and no braver soldier than Ben and Al served the Confederacy. Al is dead and Ben is growing old. I think there are other descendants in the county but I failed to get their names.

Reuben Long and his wife, ———— Macey, were the grandparents of Arthur, John, Burt and Lulie Long, who were living at Midway about 1910, but now residents of Georgetown.

Jane Stevenson, the wife of John W. Long, was a daughter of one of the numerous families in the Pisgah neighborhood of that name. I can't recall any descendants of theirs now living in the county, but that there are is most likely.

Mildred Bullock, who married Ambrose Dudley Long, was a descendant of James Bullock, Jr., of Woodford County.

For the children of Lucy Long and William Whittington see sketch of the Whittingtons. Their descendants were always grieved that the name of Lucy Long was absent from the published list of the heroines in Bryan Station when that fort was beseiged in 1782, but from her birth date, she was only about seven years of age at that time, and owing to her tiny person could not have rendered much service in relieving the thirst of that large garrison, and was liable to have been overlooked, as many children no doubt were, but she never tired of telling of the dire distress that hovered over the fortress.

The will of John Long, Sr., was dated February 15, 1831, and was witnessed by John Fitzlen and William M. Craig. The executors were Samuel Berry and James C. and Willis Long, the two latter sons of deceased.

The Dunlaps of Virginia and Kentucky constituted an interesting family of people in the early period of the history of both Commonwealths, and the same attractive qualities of head and heart that were manifest about the Revolutionary period, continue to characterize the generation of today, and I am indebted to the Hon Boutwell*

Dunlap of Auburn, Cal., for the data from which this sketch is written. He is a noted writer and has assembled a mass of facts concerning early Virginians and Kentuckians, which facts are worth preserving, each generation of the Dunlap family having left their impress upon the social, military and civic fabric in each of the several communities in which they have lived.

In Woodford County they were intermarried with the families of many of our pioneer settlers, and it was a tradition that the Dunlaps, the Gays and the Stevensons were the first settlers of the county. At any rate, Draper and Shane, who did so much to preserve all that was worth while of the past, were of that impression I believe, but Collins, who did so much to collect and preserve a record of the past, thought that Captain Elijah Craig was the first good faith settler. Be that as it may, it is certain that all were in the county by, or before 1784, about which time Captain Craig built *his fort or hut near Dry Ridge. It is recorded that the Craigs came from Orange County, Va., to Kentucky in 1781, and it is said that James Gay, the elder, explored in the region of Woodford County as early as 1776, when there were so many exploring parties in Kentucky. His son-in-law, Major Samuel Stevenson, who was at Lexington, in 1779, is said to have slipped down into Woodford County from McConnells Station, where he and his wife and kindred were located, and did some planting in the vicinity of Pisgah.

*See page 269.

McConnells Station is now a part of Lexington.

Another son-in-law of James Gay was Col. Alexander Dunlap, who bought land in Woodford County as early as 1784 (see Fayette County records), settling on it near Pisgah in February of that year.

A son of the first James Gay, mentioned above, was Captain James Gay, later on "Mound Hill," Clark County, as a young man of twenty-two years, in Woodford County with Captain Haggin in 1780, but returned to Augusta County, Va., where he was an ensign during the Revolution. Later he returned to Kentucky with his brothers-in-law, Patton and Harrison, and they are said to have brought the first improved cattle into the state. His second wife was a Dunlap, his third a Kirtley, a relative of the Bufords.

As previously stated, James Gay, Sr., came from Orange County, Va., as far west as Woodford County in 1776, and besides his son-in-law Samuel Stevenson, Benjamin Blackburn and William Elliott accompanied him. Some of the Elliotts later settled in Woodford. James Gay, Sr., returned to his Virginia home where he died in 1779. Soon thereafter the Dunlaps, Gays and Stevensons brought to the attention of their neighbors the attractive qualities and seductive advantages of Kentucky County, Va., so in a short time those people living in the vicinity of the "Pastures Region," the Kinkeads, Armstrongs, Elliotts, Clarks, Hamiltons, Carlyles, Hicklins, Lockridges, McIlvains, and Meeks came to Kentucky and many of their descendants are in the county today. The Kinkeads and Carlyles settled near Midway, the Hicklins near the old Harmony church, the Meeks near Frankfort and a large proportion of the others, if not all of them, settled near Pisgah.

Captain Alexander Dunlap, who led the settlers into that part of Augusta County, Va., known as the "Pastures," was related to the Preston family, according to tradition, and contemporary records seem to confirm it, but Hon. Boutwell Dunlap has not been able to find positive proof of it.

In 1743 Captain Dunlap was the farthermost settler on the Virginia frontier. In that year he was appointed captain of horse and died in 1744. He was a son of a soldier who was at the siege of Londonderry, and a cadet of the Dunlaps of Dunlap, Ayrshire. His wife was Ann McFarland, a descendant of Calan McFarland, and they the parents of these children: 1st John Dunlap, 2nd Robert Dunlap, and 3rd Col. Alexander Dunlap.

John Dunlap the first lived in Rockbridge County, Va., and was an extensive land holder in Virginia, Kentucky, and Ohio. His Kentucky holdings were very valuable, and descendants are still in possession of some of them. His daughter, Elizabeth, born in 1762, was the second wife of Captain James Gay, of "Mound Hill," Clark County, Ky. John Dunlap made a trip to Ohio in 1776. His wife was a daughter of James Clark, of Augusta County, Va., a relative of General George Rogers Clark, and some of her Clark relatives came early to Woodford County.

Among the distinguished contempo-

rary descendants of John Dunlap and —— Clark, his wife, are Professor Robert E. Young, a Kentuckian, who is associated with Vanderbilt University, and a leader in Southern educational work; Renick W. Dunlap, Agricultural Scientist, member of Ohio State Senate, and State and Food Commissioner of that state; Anna Dunlap, a daughter born January, 1768, married Robert Bratton, of "Lockwood," Montgomery County, Ky.; another daughter, Mary, married first Samuel Hodge, second Robert Crockett, of Bath County, Ky., where there are descendants.

Robert Dunlap the 2nd, of "Aspen Grove," Rockbridge County, Va., married Mary Gay and was an ensign at Guilford Court House, where he was killed. He furnished money to the McConnells, then living on the "Pastures Region," to found McConnells Station, near Lexington, Ky., now within the corporate limits of that city, for which he was to receive five hundred acres of the present site of Lexington, but this was lost to grandchildren by a decision of the Court of Appeals in 1805. Case of McConnell's heirs vs. Dunlap Devisees. His daughter, Ann Dunlap, born Dec., 1765, married David McKee, of Jessamine County, Ky. He was a son of John McKee, and brother of Miriam, who married Col. John McKee, and sister of that John McKee who married an aunt of Sam Houston, President of the Texas Republic, and was father of John McKee, Congressman from Alabama. David McKee, who married Ann Dunlap, of Jessamine County, was one of the founders, and an elder in the old Cedar Creek Pres-

byterian church. Some of his descendants lived in Woodford County.

Among the noted contemporary descendants of Robert Dunlap and Mary
Gay are James W. Bashford, Methodist
Episcopal Bishop of China, author and
President of Ohio Wesleyan University; James W. McMurtry, American
Archaeologist; Robert W. Bashford,
dean of the law school of the University of Wisconsin; Boutwell Dunlap.
historian and eugenist, of San Francisco; Rev. O. E. Brown, church historian of Vanderbilt University; Rev. W.
M. Morrison, D.D., African missionary, who stirred foreign governments
to action against the Congo atrocities.

Col. Alexander Dunlap was the 3rd
and last of Captain Alexander Dunlap
and Ann McFarland. He was born in
Augusta County, Va., Oct., 1743, and
built his home on the Greenbrier river,
in what is now Pocahontas County,
West Va., and was known as Clover
Lick Fort, an outpost used during the
Revolution against the Indians. This
estate had been sold to his cousin,
Major Jacob Warwick, when he removed to Kentucky, and settled in
Woodford County, near Pisgah church,
where many of his descendants now reside, and some of them entertain the
belief that he settled in that vicinity
as early as 1779, but no contemporary
record bears it out. In fact, records
extant are proof that he came to Kentucky with his brother-in-law, John
Gay, in September, 1783. En route
they were overtaken by the Rev. Adam
Rankin, the pioneer Presbyterian minister who was, I think, the first pastor
of Pisgah church, and also by Col. Russell. Col. Alex. Dunlap and John Gay

remained the first winter at Todds
Station, and February, 1784, moved
out into what is Woodford County, and
opened and operated a sugar camp.
Soon thereafter they erected living
quarters suited to the times and comfort of their respective families.

Although his brother-in-law, Major
Samuel Stevenson, gave the land, Col.
Alexander Dunlap was the founder of
Pisgah church, and also the academy.
In 1804 he removed to Brown County,
Ohio, where he founded another church
that was known as Dunlap's church.
He was an elder in Pisgah church, but
in after years was so much impressed
with Alexander Campbell's interpretation of Gospel truths that he united
with that faith, making the church he
built in Ohio one of, if not the first, edi-
fices used by the Disciples of Christ in
that state, as was the church at Pisgah the leader in Presbyterianism in
Kentucky.

In 1795 Col. Alexander Dunlap and
Major Samuel Stevenson explored
southern Ohio for desirable lands. On
one of these trips he accompanied Allen
Trimble, a pioneer of Woodford County, whose adventurous career I have already briefly written in the Woodford
County notes. As stated in that sketch
Allen Trimble removed to Ohio and
became Governor of that Commonwealth.

As a result of that trip, Col. Dunlap
bought tracts of land in Brown County,
Ohio, and also near Chillicothe, on the
Sciota. Major Samuel Stevenson also
bought large tracts near the Indian
village of Old Town, near the present
city of Xenia, to which section three
of his sons emigrated. Several of the

Dunlap children also took residence upon estates purchased by their father, Col. Alexander Dunlap, in Ohio, and much of that land is yet in possession of Stevenson and Dunlap descendants.

Col. Alexander Dunlap was an Indian fighter in the Greenbrier,. and on the Weaw campaign in Kentucky. His title of Colonel was received through service in the Virginia state militia.

When Agnes Gay, his wife, died in Woodford County, in 1804, he made his home with his Ohio children. One of his daughters, Polly Dunlap, married James Stevenson, Jr., and a son, Col. Alexander Dunlap, III., married Mary Caldwell, and inherited the Dunlap estate in Woodford County, upon which he and his wife lived and died, and the property is still in possession of descendants.

Col. Alexander Dunlap, Jr., married Agnes Gay, in Virginia, January, 1768. She was born September, 1745. The family joined the husband and father in Woodford County soon after he settled there in 1784. All of the children spent their youth, or at least a part of it, in the county, and all of them were educated at Pisgah Academy. They were: 1st, Col. James Dunlap, born April, 1769; 2nd, Anna Dunlap, born Nov., 1770, and married William Kinkead, of the county; 3rd, William Dunlap, born Nov., 1772; 4th, Polly Dunlap, born January, 1775, married James Stevenson, Jr., clerk of Woodford County; 5th, Agnes (Nancy), born September, 1777, married at Pisgah. summer of 1801, Dr. Alexander Campbell; 6th, Sarah (Sally), born Nov., 1779, married Thomas Dickings, of Brown County, Ohio; 7th, Robt., born April,

1781, and died young; 8th, Margaret Dunlap, born July, 1783, married at Pisgah the Rev. Samuel Thornton Scott, D.D.; 9th, Col. Alexander Dunlap, III, born Dec., 1785, and married Mary Caldwell, of the county.

Col. James Dunlap the 1st, while yet a boy, during one of the Indian forays in Virginia, was mounted on a black stallion, whose back had been tarred so as to enable him the better to stick to his steed, was sent with a message through the Indian lines, from the "Clover Lick" fort of the Dunlaps, to Warwick's fort, to bring assistance in an effort to repel the Indians. He was also out in the Weaw Indian campaign in Kentucky. He left Woodford County for Chillicothe, Ohio, in 1796, to take charge of his father's estate near there, but returned the following year to marry Elizabeth Stevenson, June, 1797. She a daughter of James Stevenson, Sr., a distant relative of Major Samuel Stevenson, who settled at Pisgah also. He was a justice of the court of quarter sessions, of Ross County, Ohio, in 1799; member of the first Legislature of Ohio in 1803, and also of later sessions; member State Senate; Presidential elector in 1812, and also a Colonel in the war of that year; Whig candidate for Governor of Ohio in 1816 and again in 1818.

Anna Dunlap 2nd and William Kinkead moved to Ohio about 1800. He owned large estates in Brown County at Chillicothe and at Columbus. He was a son of Captain William Kinkead, who moved from Augusta County, Va., to Woodford County in 1789; was adjutant of the 12th Va. regiment during the Revolution. (See Kinkead sketch.)

The mother of William Kinkead (the wife of Captain William Kinkead) was Eleanor Gay, who was captured by the Indians in 1764 on the Ohio and rescued by the Bouquet expedition. She died in Woodford County, and Dr. William Smith's account of the expedition, published in Europe a few years later, and which has been reprinted in America, has made the wife of Captain Kinkead quite famous.

William Dunlap 3rd and Mary Shephard, his wife, moved to Brown County, Ohio, about 1797. He became an anti-slavery leader in that state. He was the father of Dr. Alexander Dunlap, vice president of the American Medical Association, who shares honors with Dr. Ephriam McDowell, of Kentucky, as the two first physicians of the modern world to successfully perform ovariotomy, neither knowing at the time of the other's line of work. (See Appleton's Cyclopedia under Alexander Dunlap.) He was the grandfather of Charles Kephart Dunlap, a leading railroad man in America (see "Who's Who"); also great grandfather of the Rev. Samuel McChord Crothers, D.D., American essayist, the second "Oliver Wendell Holmes," now preaching at Harvard University (see "Who's Who.")

Polly Dunlap, the 4th, and James Stevenson, Jr., her husband, remained in Woodford County. He was for a long time clerk of the county court. They were the parents of these children: Dr. Alexander Dunlap Stevenson, who died with cholera in 1853, soon after entering upon the practice of his profession; James R. Stevenson, who married Caroline Elliott, daughter

of James Elliott and Sallie Johnson, and they had a daughter, Sallie Elliott Stevenson who married Hon. John H. Jesse, and a son, popular James Stevenson, who was sheriff of Woodford County during the 80's. Will Jesse, the present county attorney, is a son of John H. Jesse; Margaret Stevenson, born in 1812, married Dr. Robert Hervey Wasson, a son of William Wasson and Mary Orr, who were of pioneer stock, and settled in the vicinity of Pisgah. They had Mary Elizabeth Wasson, born in 1836, married Harney W. Worley, son of Joshua Worley and Jane Caldwell; James Stevenson Wasson, born in 1842, practiced law at Lexington and died in 1891; William Wasson, born in 1846, was a member of Morgan's cavalry and died in 1863 at Camp Chase, and Anna Wasson, who married Col. John D. Anderson, of Denver, Col.

Mary Elizabeth Wasson and Harney W. Worley had Mary Elizabeth, who married Dr. Samuel Maddox Steadman, and Anna Margaret, who married George L. Douglas, son of Rev. Rutherford Douglas.

Elizabeth Stevenson, daughter of Polly Dunlap the 4th, and James Stevenson, Jr., married William Cooper.

Agnes (Nancy) Dunlap the 5th and Dr. Alexander Campbell were very prominent socially and politically. He was born near Winchester, Va., in 1779, the son of Alexander Campbell and Joanna Nelson. His parents moved to East Tennessee, and thence to Morrison Station. The father died on a return trip to East Tennessee, and the widow bought land in Woodford County, where she reared her son, Dr.

Alexander Campbell, near Pisgah, where he was given a classical education under William Steele. He afterwards studied medicine under Drs. Ridgely and Brown, at Lexington. In 1800 he went to Cynthiana and was elected to the State Legislature from Harrison County. In 1804 he moved to Brown County, Ohio, and was elected to the Legislature of that state in 1807, and repeatedly elected to that body, being elected Speaker in 1808-9; was defeated for the United States Senate by Senator Meigs; was afterward Postmaster General; United States Senator 1810-13; Presidential elector in 1820, and again in 1836; was defeated as an anti-canal party for Governor of Ohio by Col. Allen Trimble, a pioneer of Woodford County, whose sketch appeared in earlier issue of the Register, page 78.

Sarah (Sally) Dunlap the 6th, born March, 1779, joined her brother, Col. James Dunlap, in Ohio in 1798 and married Thomas Dickings, of Brown County, that state. He was a member of the Lake expedition in the war of 1812, and was a son of Thomas Dickings, Sr., of Princess Ann County, Va. They had a daughter, Albertine Dickings, who married Jeptha Beasley, nephew of Gen. Nathaniel Beasley, the pioneer of Ohio, and they had a daughter, Albertine Beasley, who married Samuel D. Ingham, of Pensacola, Fla. Agnes Gay Dickings was another daughter of Thomas Dickings, and she married William H. McCogne, manufacturer, of Ripley, Ohio, and grandnephew of Thomas Kirker, second Governor of Ohio.

Margaret Dunlap the 8th, and Rev.

Samuel Thornton Scott, D.D., moved to Indiana, where they spent an interesting life. He was born in 1777, came to Woodford County as a lad and was educated at Pisgah under the tutorage of William Steele. In 1806 he founded Indiana Presbyterian church, at Vincennes, the first Protestant church established in that state. In 1807 he became the first president of Vincennes University, the first college established in Indiana. A daughter of this couple married the Rev. Samuel Rannels Alexander, D.D. (uncle of General William DeWitt Alexander, historian of Hawaii).

Rev. William Thornton Scott's son, Alexander Dunlap Scott, was clerk of Knox County, Indiana, and the father was a son of William Scott, an early settler in Woodford County, and one of the first elders of Pisgah church.

Col. Alexander Dunlap, the 9th (of Col. Alexander Dunlap and Agnes Gay), and his wife, Mary Caldwell, lived and died on the estate owned by his father near Pisgah. He was born in Woodford County soon after the arrival of the family from Lexington. He served as a Colonel of state militia and was in the Kentucky Legislature in 1825. His wife came from South Carolina, but was reared in Woodford County. She was a relative of John Caldwell Calhoun, the lawyer and statesman of South Carolina.

Col. Alexander Dunlap, III, and Mary Caldwell had these children: George Caldwell Dunlap, Sr., born June, 1812, married first Martha Crockett, in 1834, who died the following year; second, Sarah LeGrande, of Lexington. He moved with his family from Woodford County to Marion County, Mo., to take charge of the Dunlap estates there in 1848. His son, Edward L. Dunlap, is a wealthy citizen of Victoria, Texas, who has served in the Legislature of that state; another son, E. Field Dunlap, died unmarried, in Clay County, Mo., and still another son, the youngest, is George Caldwell Dunlap, who is a resident of Louisville.

Susan A. Dunlap, a daughter of Col. Alexander Dunlap, III, and Mary Caldwell, was born January, 1816, married Col. Ezekiel H. Field (see page 110), who was with General Humphrey Marshall in Mexico, and arose to the rank of a General in the Confederacy. No children.

William A. Dunlap, son of Col. Alexander Dunlap, III, and Mary Caldwell was born March, 1819, and married Amanda Branham. He was educated for a surveyor, and while engaged in the survey of a highway from Owingsville to the mouth of the Big Sandy river, in Northeastern Kentucky, was stricken with a malady, and he never recovered from the indisposition. He resided on the ancestral estate, never sought political honors, preferring to devote his time to his business and his church. The original homestead is now owned by Ernest Dunlap, the youngest son of William A. and Amanda Branham Dunlap, and he and his wife, Margaret Lewis Farra Dunlap, reside there, making the fourth generation in 136 years to possess the estate.

The other children of William A. Dunlap and Amanda Branham are the late Alexander Dunlap, who married Belle Field, daughter of Col. Thomas Field and Susan Mary Higbee; George

Dunlap, who married Kate Childers, and Thomas F. Dunlap, who married Mattie Crutcher, daughter of Washington Crutcher and Jennie Redd. Thomas Dunlap's first wife was Minnie Crouch; Martha Dunlap married W. Clark Arnett; Ella Dunlap married Andrew T. Harris and Branham Dunlap married Tabbie Whitley.

The Dunlap family is one of the oldest and most distinguished of the Scotch-Irish Presbyterian families of the south. Several kinsmen of the name, born in Ireland, settled in Augusta County, Va., about the middle of the 18th century, and from them have sprung many prominent descendants. Among them I will mention Major William Dunlap, of Fayette County, who was born in 1743. His wife was Rebecca Robertson, aunt of Chief Justice George Robertson. They were the ancestors of the Rev. James Dunlap, General James Dunlap of the Union army; Millard F. Dunlap, banker and treasurer of the National Democratic Committee; Brig. Gen. Edward McClernand, of the Union army; Congressman George W. Dunlap; Eugenia Dunlap Potts, writer; Col. William Watkins Dunlap, who left West Point to join the Confederacy; Major Alexander Dunlap, captured at Dudley's defeat, aid to Jackson at New Orleans, and Major in Mexican War; Col. George Robertson Dunlap, of Fayette, member of the Kentucky Legislature, in the battle of the Thames, Colonel of Kentucky militia and father of Gen. Henry C. Dunlap, of the Union army.

———

Moses McIlvain was born in Ireland, came to Virginia, and in 1763 bought land on the "Calf Pasture" river, in Augusta County, of Capt. James Lockridge, a justice of the county, who had relatives to migrate to the county of Woodford with the early pioneers. He was in Clark County, Ky., as early as 1779 with Cartwright, the early Kentucky surveyor, and was captured by the Indians, but through the influence of one McCormick, an Indian trader who had known him in Ireland when a boy, he was released. Soon after this incident Moses McIlvain joined the colony from the "Pastures," who had settled in Woodford County, and was one of the first to claim membership in the old Pisgah church. He married in Augusta County, Va., Margaret Hodge, daughter of Samuel Hodge, of the "Calf Pasture," who died in 1773.

Moses McIlvain was the father of Capt. William McIlvain, of Woodford County, who married Sarah Gay, daughter of John Gay and Sarah Lockridge. He died and Sarah Gay McIlvain became the second wife of James Stevenson, Jr., county clerk of Woodford County, whose first wife was Polly Dunlap, daughter of Col. Alexander Dunlap and Agnes Gay.

Captain William McIlvain and Sarah Gay had a son, William McIlvain, Jr., who died in Lexington while preparing himself for the profession of medicine, and another, John Watson McIlvain, born in 1811 at "Shannondale," in Woodford County. He married first Rebecca Wright, daughter of Col. Wright and Annie Jackson, of Bourbon County; second, Mary Anderson Gay, daughter of Benj. Patterson Gay.

It is my impression that there are McIlvain descendants in Woodford now.

Major John Stevenson, whose father was in the siege of Londonderry, was born in Ireland, emigrated to Warwick County, Va., thence to "Calf Pasture" river in Augusta County. He received a grant of 5,332 acres of land for services as Major in the Revolution, and married Martha Warwick, who was killed by the Indians in Augusta County, Va., upon a return from church services. All of his sons were famous Indian fighters.

The eldest son, John, Jr., came to Lexington in 1779, when there were only four cabins and a blockhouse there.

The Stevensons, the Gays and the Dunlaps are credited with bringing the first thoroughbred race horses into Kentucky. It is known positively that Captain James Gay, of "Mound Hill," Clark County, assisted by his brothers-in-law, brought to Kentucky the first improved cattle. It is also a matter of record that John Stevenson, as early as 1779, brought out to Kentucky an "English filly," the name then given a thoroughbred filly or racer.

Illustrative of land and equine values at that time, Captain (Buck) William McConnell offered to trade 500 acres of land adjoining McConnells Station, now a part of Lexington, for this fine filly. At another time, according to the account left by his son, John Stevenson arranged to trade one of his horses with one of the Bryants, at Bryants Station, for 1,000 acres of land between the station and Lexington, but Col. John Morrison, believing the pioneers could not hold the country, prevailed upon John Stevenson not to make the trade.

This John Stevenson was a sergeant in Captain Robert Patterson's company in the expedition against the Shawnees in 1781, and was in some of George Rogers Clark's campaigns. He and his family lived at McConnells Station and Lexington from 1779 to 1784, when he planted a crop in Woodford County and they moved down to the vicinity of Pisgah, March 5, 1784.

"The night after we moved down a snow fell and Sam tracked and caught sixty raccoons," says the account of James Stevenson, a son of John Stevenson.

Major John Stevenson's son, William, came to Lexington also in 1779. He was in the pioneer Indian fighting, and while in an effort to get into Bryants Station at the time that garrison was attacked in 1782, had his horse shot from under him while in the saddle. He turned about face and killed an Indian, but being cut off from the station, he endeavored to make his escape, and in so doing ran twelve miles in the direction of Georgetown. So closely was he pursued by the enemy he could not change his course, and the strain was so great that he never fully recovered from it. In 1787 he bought land from Major John Crittenden at forty pounds per 100 acres.

Other children of Major John Stevenson were Thomas, who came to Lexington in 1779 and was killed at the battle of "Blue Licks" soon after the attack on Bryants Station; and James Stevenson, who came in 1787; and Robert Stevenson, who moved first to Nolo-

Chucky, in the state of Tennessee in 1779, but at the urgent request of his brothers came to Kentucky in 1787; the youngest son, Major Samuel Stevenson, born March, 1744, and married Jane Gay in May, 1771, who lived on the "Calf Pasture," in Augusta County, Va., she born 1750. In 1775 Major Samuel Stevenson and his wife, Jane Gay, moved to the Greenbrier river, in Virginia, being the third English family to settle there. He was elected captain of an unofficial military company of settlers organized for defense against the Indians, this point constituting the extreme frontier of Virginia.

In 1776, in company with James Gay, his brother-in-law, Benjamine Blackburn, and William Elliott, he made an expedition to Kentucky, as before stated, and was through Woodford County at that time. In 1779 he and his wife moved to Lexington, Ky., where she was said to be the second white woman in that section, the wife of Col. John Morrison being the first.

Major Samuel Stevenson brought out with him also "Wild Cat" John McKinney, famous as Lexington's first school master, who came near losing his life at the battle of Point Pleasant during the Revolution.

In the account of her life given to Rev. John Shane by the wife of Major Stevenson, and preserved in the Draper collection in the Wisconsin Historical Society, she says she arrived in Lexington in October. "There was every sort of people there, and that was what took us away. We had no notion of raising our children among the sort of people."

On April 2, 1780, they moved to Mc-

Connells Station. From then until March 1st, 1784, they planted crops in Woodford County, on which date they moved down near Pisgah.

Major Samuel Stevenson was an officer of the state militia of Kentucky, was in the Illinois expedition of General George Rogers Clark, and in the expedition of Captain Robert Patterson against the Shawnees in 1781. He generously donated the land upon which Pisgah church was erected. About 1795 he purchased large tracts of land near Xenia, Ohio, to which property three of his sons removed about 1799, and their descendants have been, and the present generation are now very prominent in civic, social and military affairs. Samuel Stevenson, Jr., one of his sons, remained in Woodford County and served in the war of 1812, being captured at Dudley's defeat in May, 1813.

James Stevenson, Sr., father of James, Jr., an early clerk of the county court, was a distant relative of Major Samuel Stevenson.

Tradition says that the Gays were citizens of Warwick County, England, but removed to the north of Ireland, where they were located when the first of the name came to Virginia.

William Gay was a soldier in the siege of Londenderry, and he was the father of William Gay, Jr., John Gay, James Gay, Robert Gay, Samuel Gay, Henry Gay and Eleanor Gay; the latter married Capt. William Kinkead, one of Woodford's prominent pioneers. The Gays, like the Dunlaps and Stevensons, settled in the "Pasture" section of Augusta County, Va., by or prior to 1750, but first settled in Pennsylvania.

John Gay, born January, 1740; Sarah Lockridge, born March, 1754.

Robert Gay, born June, 1776; Rebecca Worley.

John R. Gay, born November 3, 1804; Catherine Hall.

Sallie Frazer Gay; T. J. Ward Macey.

Fannie Macey; John Shockency.

Birdie Shockency; Robert S. Strader.

Mona Strader; Harrison Williams.

The above John Gay was in the Revolution and served in the 6th Virginia Regiment, commanded by Col. John Gibson, enlisting for one year. Was transferred October, 1778, to Capt. Ben Taliaferros Comp. 2nd Va. Regiment commanded by Col. Christian Febiger. Was transferred in November, 1778, to Capt. Stokes Company same regiment, and was discharged February 17, 1779. See National No. C. A. R. 23211. Line of descent pages 157-9, "Woodford County Pioneers."

Henry Gay was the ancestor of John Henderson Gay, born in 1787, and was a pioneer of St. Louis, where he became the head of the family who attained great riches in the sugar industry and are very prominent in the south.

William Gay, Jr., married Margaret Walkup, whose brothers covered themselves with glory in the service of the Revolution. They had Mary Gay, who married Robert Dunlap, of "Aspen Grove," and Agnes, who married Robert Clark, kinsman of George Rogers Clark.

John Gay married Jean Ramsey. They were the parents of three girls and one son. The son was Major John

Gay, who married Agnes (Nancy) Mc-Kee. She was a first cousin of General Sam Houston, of Texas. Major John Gay came to Woodford County and remained a citizen for some years, but finally drifted into Indiana. Gov. James Brown, of that state, married his daughter.

James Gay, as before stated, explored Woodford County as early as 1776. He married Jean Warwick, who was killed by the Indians. He died in Virginia in 1779. They had John, Jr., Agnes, Jane, James, Martha, Samuel and Robert Gay. John Gay, Jr., settled in Woodford County in 1784, and his descendants have held estates there ever since. He was born January, 1740, and married Sarah Lockridge, born March, 1754, daughter of Captain James Lockridge,* of Augusta County, Va.

The children of John Gay, Jr., and Sarah Lockridge follow: 1st Margaret, born Sept., 1771; 2nd Mary, born January, 1774; 3rd Robert, born June, 1776; 4th Agnes, born February, 1779; 5th James Gay, born Nov., 1781; 6th Sarah Gay, born April, 1784; 7th John, born Nov., 1786; 8th Rebekah Gay, born May, 1790; 9th William Dunlap Gay, born May, 1793; 10th Samuel Gay, born March, 1796 and 11th Kinkead Gay, born Oct., 1799. Of this large family of children reared in Woodford County, only three raised families in the county, viz.: Robert, Sarah and John Gay.

John Gay, the 7th, married Catherine Claggett. The Claggetts were prominent Marylanders, and related to Bishop Claggett (first Episcopal Bishop

in the United States). They had Mary D. Gay, born in 1818, married Guy Hamilton Kinkead, born in Woodford but moved to Brown County, Ohio; Sarah Gay, born in 1819, married Edwin Wright, son of Col. William and Annie Jackson Wright, of Bourbon County; Margaret Gay, born in 1821, married Dr. Robert Henry Wasson, of Pisgah (whose parents came from Greencastle, Pa.). She was his second wife, and they had Rebecca Wright Wasson, born in 1851, married Dr. Robt. Singleton Hart; Kate Claggett Wasson, born 1856, married Peter G. Powell, Sr.; Caroline Douglas Wasson, born in 1858, married J. Wilmore Garrett; Robert Herbert Wasson, Jr., born in 1861, married Mary Talbott Farra; and John T. Wasson, born in 1864, married Alma Brooks.

John Thomas Gay, son of John Gay, 7th, and Catherine Claggett, born in 1823, married Sallie Branham and had: Elizabeth, who married John S. Hanna, son of Wm. Chenoworth Hanna and Margaret Smith; Anna S. Gay, who married David Hunt James, of Lexington; James Gay, married Maria Cotton and had Ruth Parish Gay, married Robert S. Berryman, and Georgia Cotton Gay, married James Viley McFerran; Mattie B. Gay, married William Swope; Lelia Gay, married John H. Field, son of Col. Thomas Field and Susan Higbee; Minnie B. Gay, married Garrett Watts; John Thomas Gay, Jr., married Mattie Bridgeforth; Robert Hicks Gay, married first Florence Bowman, second Eva Owens Nuckols, daughter of Samuel Nuckols and —— Wasson; Hallie Gay, married Dr. Ben-

*Daughter of Robert Lockridge, see page 315.

jamine Parrish, son of Thomas Ware Parrish and Kate Rogers.

Elizabeth Gay, born in 1825, daughter of John Gay 7th and Catherine Claggett, married Elijah A. Hopkins and lived in Brown County, Ohio.

James Robert Gay, born in 1828, son of John and Catherine Gay, married Catherine Lamme and they had: Milton W. Gay, James Lamme Gay, Margaret Gay, who married George C. Bird, William D. Gay, who married Virginia Farra, Thos. J. Gay, Mary Lee Gay, who married Newton B. Mitchell, John Horace Gay, who married Florence Powell, Carrie Rutherford Gay, who married J. Wilmore Garrett, and Katherine, who married John W. Redding.

William Douglas Gay, born in 1830, son of John and Catherine Claggett Gay, married Elizabeth Hume Graves, and they had Benj. Patton Gay, who married Elva Gatewood, Jacob Douglas Gay, who married Lucy Field Graddy, Agnes Gay, born in 1833, married Horace Ardenger, of Lexington, Mo.

Watson Gay, born in 1835, died about 1855.

Catharine C. Gay, daughter of John and Catherine, was born in 1837, but never married.

Rebecca C. Gay, born in 1839, daughter of John and Catherine, married first Lee Bird, of Shelby County, second Samuel Wentworth, of Lexington, Mo.

Sarah Gay, the 6th of John Gay and Sarah Lockridge, married first Captain William McIlvain, second James Stevenson, clerk of Woodford County in the early days. (See Stevenson sketch.)

Robert Gay, the 3rd of John Gay and Sarah Lockridge, was born in June,

1776, married Rebecca Worley, daughter of Joshua Worley and Rebecca Caldwell. He remained in Woodford County and was the father of John R. Gay, who married Catherine Hall. John R. and Catherine Hall Gay had a daughter, Sallie Gay, who married Capt. T. J. Ward Macey, and their children were Robt. Ward Macey, who married Josie Railey and had Robt. Ward 11, W. Railey, Pattie and Sadie Macey; Fannie, who married John Shockency; Kate, who married James Neet; Gus, who married Lena Portwood, and Wilyou Breckinridge, who married D. Thornton Edwards.

Jane Gay, daughter of James Gay and Jane Warwick, born Nov., 1750, married Major Samuel Stevenson in May, 1771. (For descendants see Stevenson sketch.)

Agnes Gay, daughter of James and Jane, was born in 1745, and married Col. Alexander Dunlap. (See Dunlap.)

But few families in Kentucky have held more tenaciously to ancestral domains than have the Gays. What we find in Woodford County relative to them is duplicated in Clark, Bourbon, Fayette and in other counties where they domiciled themselves.

Mary Gay, who married Tyler Nash, of Pisgah, was the daughter of L. W. H. Gay and Elizabeth Boyle; and L. W. H. Gay was one of the sons of Benjamine Patton Gay, who married —— Anderson; and he was one of the sons of Capt. James Gay and Sarah Patton, and he was one of the sons of James Gay and Jane Warwick.

———

I have a sketch of the Pisgah church that I prepared during the summer of

1920, but it will not appear until all of the family sketches that I have completed, and others in course of construction, have appeared in print. However, a brief statement here of facts relative to the old church and academy at Pisgah that are not included in that sketch will not be inappropriate. I am persuaded that they will be more appreciated and interesting if inserted now.

While the land upon which the church and academy were erected was generously donated by Major Samuel Stevenson, Col. Alexander Dunlap, the first, was the dynamo, so to speak, back of the project to build these institutions. But so great was the religious zeal in the community, especially among the half dozen families who early settled there, they didn't wait for the erection of a building, but dedicated their respective homes to the service of God, and the Rev. Adam Rankin, then stationed at Lexington, was engaged to preach in the vicinity every alternate Sabbath, the services to be held in the private homes until a church was erected and dedicated, and these services began in the fall of 1784. There is a record extant of the Rev. Rankin having preached in the homes of Major Samuel Stevenson, Capt. William McConnell, Moses McIlvain and Samuel Kelley. The meeting house was built at Mt. Pisgah in the spring of 1785, and the first elders were Capt. William McConnell, Samuel Kelley, Hugh Campbell and, I think, Col. Alexander Dunlap. Is it any wonder that these people have succeeded so admirably?

One of the very interesting events

in connection with the old church was the assembling of the picked men of the Lewis and Clark expedition there for the purpose of listening to a sermon calling for God's blessings before starting on their perilous pilgrimage over the great undeveloped western country. One of these heroes who offered his services, and his life if need be, to open a path for the purpose of expanding the currents that lead to civilization and development, was William Bratton, who was a son of Major James Bratton, of Bath County, Va., a half brother of Col. Alex Dunlap, of Pisgah.

Various historians have exploited this school and that school, especially existing in the early periods of America, as having surpassed all others in point of results, considering the means, but I am doubtful if any of the country schools or academies can show a better record for achievement than the little academy established at Pisgah the latter part of the 18th century, and very successfully conducted for at least a half century.

From its roster has sprung three cabinet officers, and an extended list of other celebrities who took advantage of the curriculum of that institution. In its early period, during the principalship of that thorough student, Wm. Steele, and later Dr. Louis Marshall, the enrollment of the students included the names of Robert Trimble, Justice of the U. S. Supreme Court; William T. Barry, Postmaster General and member of Congress; Alexander Campbell, U. S. Senator from Ohio; James Clark, Governor of Kentucky; Allen Trimble, Governor of Ohio; John J.

Crittenden, Attorney General, U. S. Senator, and Governor of Kentucky; John C. Breckinridge, Vice President of U. S., Secretary of War C. S. A., and Major General. Besides these, the Marshalls, Bufords, Gays, Dunlaps, Castlemans and scores of Congressmen and military chieftians were students there; also such distinguished divines as Thomas Clelland, Samuel Thornton Scott and John L. Wilson.*

In his notes on Pisgah Senator Alexander Campbell says: "Many lawyers, doctors and non-professionals who passed through this institution have become eminent in their professions and citizenship in the several states of the union." Such facts are worth preserving as a halo to radiate and reflect for future generations the glorious achievements of our illustrious ancestors. Let us not allow the record of the past to be obscured in favor of the pedigree of animals.

The Mortons were of French extract, descending from Robert de Mortaine, a French Huguenot who fled from his native land to escape the cruelties to which they were subjected during the 17th century. They were intense lovers of liberty, both in thought and action.

Robert de Mortaine first took refuge in England, but finally decided to join those of his countrymen who had ventured across the ocean and found solace in America. Here he found freedom of speech and liberty of conscience and action to the limit of that decency that respects the rights and welfare of others, hence they were good Americans who spurned the prefix Franco-Americans.

Jeremiah Morton was a descendant of the above refugee, but how many generations removed I am unable to say, but several at least. He came to Kentucky about 1792 and settled in Woodford County, where he died in 1823. He was from Orange County, Va., and his wife, Judith Coleman,† lived in that county also and they were married there. After reaching Woodford County they decided to settle in that part of it five miles above lock No. 5, and chose a site for building on an elevation that sloped to that part of the farm where he, a few years later, started the village of Mortonsville. This village was not incorporated, however, until 1835. Jeremiah Morton built his log residence near the top of this incline in full view of the village, but a part of this residence was destroyed by fire many years ago, though rebuilt by descendants who were living there at the time.

In 1810 Jeremiah Morton was living on this estate, at which time he owned seven slaves and was in very comfortable circumstances. His wife was a sister of Thomas Coleman,* a Revolutionary veteran who married the widow of Captain Moses Hawkins, in Orange County, and came to Kentucky with William Strother, his father-in-law, about the same time that Jeremiah Morton came.

The home of Jeremiah Morton remained in possession of heirs to the sixth generation, as the following clip-

---

*This name is Joshua L. Wilson.
*See page 381 for correcion, Judith Moore.

ping from the Woodford Sun of January, 1920, discloses. It follows: "The Hudson farm, on the McQuowns Ferry pike, which has just been sold by W. H. Hudson, has been in the family for six generations, the title going back to his maternal ancestor, Jeremiah Morton, for whom the village of Mortonsville was named. Part of the dwelling on the place was built of logs and is more than one hundred years old. In one of the rooms Bishop Kavanaugh, Methodist Bishop of Kentucky, preached many years ago."

Bishop Kavanaugh is well remembered as one of the ablest preachers of his day. He married Mary Railey, daughter of Charles Railey and Mary Mayo, and he often visited Versailles before, during and after the Civil War, and held successful revivals in the county.

Jeremiah Morton and Judith Coleman† had two daughters, Lucy and Nancy. Lucy married Isaac Wilson, but I have not been able to get a line on their descendants.‡ Nancy married Abner Rucker, who was a citizen of the county in 1810. They had these children: Betsy, Agnes, Anthony, Jeremiah, Julian and Jonathan. Agnes married her cousin, Isaac Rucker, and they had these children: Jane, Edward, Susan, Martha and Nancy. Martha married Charles A. Ware, and Nancy married James Hudson. To the last couple was born a son, whose name is W. H. Hudson, who recently sold the ancestral estate. He married Emma Bond and they have a daughter, Leva Ware Hudson, who is a member of the

faculty of Margaret College at Versailles, Ky.

In the will of Jeremiah Morton I learn that he purchased a large tract of land in that section, 250 acres of which was a part of the military claim or survey of James Bullock, Jr. (another part purchased by William Strother). He also had a large tract that he called "Mount Airy," that he bequeathed to his daughter Lucy, who married Isaac Wilson. Willis Fields' home in the same vicinity was called "Mount Airy," but whether they were one and the same I am unable to say. Thomas Bullock (son of James, Jr.), Isaac Wilson and William Morton were named as executors, and Noah Haydon, Isaiah Boone and Dawson Brown were witnesses.

In his will devising his home property he mentions a line between his farm and William Morton's on Tanners creek, with a spring on the line that was used by both. He also mentions a line that was a dividing line between his farm and the farm of Thomas Morton. I am sure that these three Mortons whose farms adjoined were related, but how closely I am unable to say. When a boy I often heard my mother's family speak of "Uncle and Aunt Morton," referring to Jeremiah and his wife, but don't recall ever having heard anything about William and Thomas, but a friend of mine recently told me that it was his impression that one of them was the ancestor of Judge Jere Morton, of Lexington, who was long a circuit judge in this district.

†Judith Coleman 381, Judith Moore.
‡See Morton and Wilson families 382.

A codicil to the will of Jeremiah Morton was witnessed by William Christopher and William Dale.

Mordecai Redd came to Woodford County soon after the Revolution and settled on a farm near Mortonsville that is now, and has been for many years, the home of Judge James T. Wilhoit. The splendid old colonial brick residence was built about 1804, according to tradition, and as Mordecai did not die until 1807, it is presumed that he built the house. My information is that his son, Thomas M., lived there with his mother, Agatha, after the death of his father, but a descendant at Versailles more than three score and ten thinks that Thomas M. lived in Versailles, but the census of 1810 challenges that view and classes him as a farmer. Thomas M. died in 1820. Agatha Redd, the wife of Mordecai, was executrix, and Thomas Bullock, Sr., and John Redd, son of Mordecai, were executors of the estate. Benjamine Wilson, Sr., Austin Williams and Samuel Martin were witnesses. Will was probated in 1807.

Mordecai was a Revolutionary soldier and came from Virginia, but what part I am unable to say, as descendants failed to keep a record, and what I write of this interesting old family I have gathered from the various records of other families I have written up, but I visited the county clerk's office, where I spent a day verifying the main points. I tried in vain for six months to get in touch with some descendant in Missouri, Oklahoma, Illinois or Kentucky, who could furnish me with data.

Mordecai Redd and Agatha Minor, his wife, had these children: Elizabeth, who married Austin Williams, Lucy, who married Thomas Bullock, Sr., Alice, who married —— Yeiser; Nancy, who married Isaac Hows; John, who married Anne Waller Bullock; Mordecai, Jr., who married —— ——, and Thomas M. Redd, who married Betsy Bullock. Thomas Bullock, Sr., who married Lucy Redd, a sister of John and Thomas M. Redd, was a son of James Bullock, Jr., and his first wife, Agnes Wingfield; and Anne Waller Bullock, who married John Redd, and her sister Betsy, who married Thomas M. Redd were daughters of James Bullock, Jr., and his second wife, Anne Waller.

Lucy Redd and Thomas Bullock, Sr., had these children: James, who married —— Sullivan; Melissa, who married —— McClanahan; Thomas, Jr., who married Agnes Ware, daughter of Samuel Ware, and his first wife, Anne Read; Mordecai, who died without issue;* Wingfield, who married —— Fleming. For further details of this line see Bullocks and Wares.

John Redd and Anne Waller Bullock had these children: Minor W., who married Harriet Berry; Agatha, who married Samuel Wilson; Bettie, who married Elijah Yeager; Nancy, who married Joseph McPheeters; James B., who married the widow Agatha (Redd) Berry, daughter of Thomas M. Redd, and Betsy Bullock; Caroline, who married James Mc-Pheeters; Maria, who married William

---

*See page 302 Bullocks.

Boardman, and John T., who married Elizabeth Francis.

Thomas M. Redd and Betsy Bullock had these children: James W., who married first Patsy Berry, second Matilda Starks; Archie O., who married first Matilda Berry, second Julia Lamb; Martha Anne married Col. Lewis A. Berry; Mordecai married Mary Williams; Agatha married first Thomas Berry, second James B. Redd.

Minor W. Redd, (son of John Redd and Anne Bullock) and his wife, Harriet Berry, had these children: Matilda, Laura, Mary, Martha, Lewis and Thomas.

Agatha Redd, daughter of John Redd and Anne Bullock, and her husband, Samuel Wilson, had these children: Francis, who married A. B. Lansing; Bettie, who married first Thos. L. Tillery, then Joseph Bryan, Sr.

Betsy Redd, daughter of John and Anne Bullock Redd, and her husband, Elijah Yeager, had John, who married Emily Anderson, Minor and Edward; Robert, who married Nolie Forbes, and Susan, who married Edward Wesley.

Nancy Redd, daughter of John and Anne Bullock Redd, and her husband, Joseph McPheeters, had only one child, James R. McPheeters, and he died at Little Rock, Ark., serving the Confederacy.

James B. Redd, son of John and Anne Bullock Redd, and his wife, Agatha (Redd) Bullock, daughter of Thomas M. and Betsy (Bullock) Redd, had these children; Theodore, John James, Archie, David, Lou, Belle and Carrie, all married and had issue.

Caroline C. Redd, daughter of John

and Anne Bullock Redd, and her husband, James McPheeters, like his brother Joseph mentioned above, had only one child, Anne, who married William Russell Anderson, a great grandson of Capt. John Bullock and Elizabeth Railey, and they had these children: James, Thomas Lilburn, Rev. William, Anne. Russella and Mary Alby Anderson. The latter was educated in the law and when barely 21 years old was city attorney of Palmyra, Mo., for three consecutive years, 1899, 1900 and 1901. She married Otho F. Mathews, a lawyer of Macon, Mo., December, 1902. Her brother, the Rev. William Anderson, was pastor of the Shelbyville, Ky., Presbyterian church for many years, and only recently severed his connection with that congregation to accept a flattering call from a church at Little Rock, Ark. The Andersons are a family of Scotch-Irish Presbyterians and an unusually large number of them lawyers.*

J. T. Redd, son of John and Anne Bullock Redd, and his wife, Elizabeth Francis, had issue: Anne, Jennie, Emma, Walter, Kate, Minnie, Lucy, Fannie, John and James.

Maria Redd, daughter of John and Anne Bullock Redd, and her husband, William Boardman, had the following children: Waller, John, Bettie and Martha.

James W. Redd, son of Thos. M. and Betsy Bullock Redd, and his first wife, Patsy Berry, had these children: Anne, who married John H. Williams; Dr. Thomas, who married first a Bowman, then a Taylor; Irene, who married Jesse Glass.

*See page 255.

James W. Redd and his second wife, Matilda Starks,† had issue: Mordecai, Lou, Robert, Bettie and Archie.

Archie O. Redd, son of Thomas M. and Betsy Bullock Redd, and his wife, Matilda Berry, had: Harriet, who married William Gray; Bettie, who married Thomas Wallace and had a son, Archie; Jennie, who married Washington Crutcher and had Mattie, Overton, Olynthus, James, Redd, Berry, Allie, Maria.

Archie O. Redd and his second wife, Julia Lamb, had these children: Allie, Agatha and Maria.

Martha Ann Redd, daughter of Thomas M. and Betsy Bullock Redd, and her husband, Col. Lewis A. Berry, had these children: Bettie, John T., Sallie, Robt. Y., Lewis A., Jr., and Fannie Berry. For their descendants see Berry sketch.

Agatha Redd, daughter of Thos. M. and Betsy Bullock Redd, and her husband, Thomas Berry, had no children. By her second marriage to James B. Redd, son of John and Anne Bullock Redd, were Theodore, John, James Archie, David, Lou, Belle and Carrie. For other children of Betsy Bullock Redd see notes of the Wares, as her second marriage was to Samuel Ware. Thomas M. Redd died before his children were grown, and Waller Bullock, only son of James Bullock, Jr., and his second wife, Anne Waller, and a brother of Betsy Bullock Redd, was appointed guardian of the minor children, they becoming wards of Samuel Ware (who married their mother, Betsy Bullock Redd) from 1821 to 1830, when all had reached their ma-

jority years, I think. The appraisers of the estate of Thomas M. Redd were Rodham Routt, Archibald Terrell and Samuel Martin. In 1829 the court appointed N. Hayden, David Thornton and William Barr commissioners, to settle accounts of Walter Bullock, guardian.

According to the census taken of Woodford County in 1810 Thomas M. Redd was both a land and slave owner. Thomas Redd, Sr., a brother of the first Mordecai, and also a Revolutionary veteran, was also living in Woodford in 1810 and owned a farm, and eighteen slaves. His family consisted of five members, including himself, his wife, Jemime, and these children: Samuel, John and Patsy. Samuel married Dorothy Bullock, daughter of James Bullock, Jr., and Anne Waller, hence she was a sister of Betsy and Ann Waller Bullock, who married respectively Thomas M. and John Redd, his cousins. Thomas Redd, Sr., died in 1812, and his will was witnessed by Thomas Bullock, Jonathan Gray and Thomas Coleman.

Agatha Redd, wife of the first Mordecai, survived her husband many years. I think she was closely related to Benjamine Berry, between whose families there was so much intermarrying.

I recall Dr. J. W. Redd, who lived in the county both before and after the Civil War, but have been unable to place him. It is likely that he was a grandson of Thomas Redd, Sr., and Jemime, but I was unable to establish his line. There are those in the county who can recall that he was not only a clever physician, but also one of the best auctioneers that ever cried a sale in the county. He married George Ann Twyman, sister of Joel W. and Dr. Warwick Twyman. He was a jolly, whole-souled fellow and everybody liked him. He and his wife raised Redd Twyman, who became one of Woodford's leading lawyers after his return from service in the Confederacy.

Since writing this sketch I have learned that Mordecai Redd was from Spottsylvania County, Va., and that his wife was Agatha Minor, daughter of Alice Thomas and Thomas Minor, of "Locust Hill," Spottsylvania County, Va. Elizabeth Redd, daughter of Mordecai and Agatha, married Austin Williams, and their son, Minor Williams married Cyrene Viley. Minor Williams and Cyrene Viley (aunt of Warren Viley) had these children: Dr. James Williams, who married Annie Glover; Elizabeth Williams, married James McHatton; Maria Williams married George Viley Ward; Martha Williams married Charles Musick; Merritt Williams married the widow Irene (Smith) Bullitt, and Charles Williams married Annie Brumleigh.

Bernard Gaines was born in Amherst County, Virginia, in June, 1767, and in March, 1791, was appointed ensign in the United States First Infantry, which rank is equivalent to second lieutenant in our present army; promoted to first lieutenant March, 1792; assigned to 1st sub-legion, into which the 1st infantry was merged September, 1792; promoted to Captain

April, 1794; organization again designated 1st infantry November, 1796, from which regiment he resigned January, 1797.

He also served in the campaigns of Generals St. Clair and Wayne against the Indians in the northwest.

He came to Kentucky and was married in Woodford County to Sarah Force Cook in 1812. She was born in Berkley County, Virginia, in March, 1781, and died in Versailles, October, 1867. He died on his farm in 1839.

The home in which they lived was in full view of Grassy Springs church, the road that goes to Glenn's creek by the church passing the entrance to his avenue at that time, but since the Civil War the entrance has been on the Versailles and Frankfort pike. I am not sure whether one of the Blantons or Bernard Gaines built the residence on this farm, but it is standing today in fair condition after more than a century's service.

His widow conducted the affairs of the farm for years after her husband's death, but finally sold and moved to Versailles. John Mastin owned this farm after the Civil War, and it now belongs to the King heirs of Frankfort, and is managed by J. J. King.

*Bernard Gaines and Sarah Cook had three children: Elizabeth Ward, born January, 1814, died April, 1849, married first her cousin, Charles Foree Nourse, second Sylvanus W. Johnson; Catharine Mary, born in 1816, died June, 1839, married Oscar Pepper, of the county. No issue; and Gustavus Cook, born in November, 1818, died February, 1867.

---

*See page 301.

Gustavus Cook Gaines married first Ann Gibson, in Woodford County, August, 1843. She died in June, 1855; second marriage to Catharine Mary Cromwell, in February, 1856. She was born in Jefferson County, Va., in 1831, died in March, 1881. Children by the first marriage were: Bernard Gaines, born March, 1847, died April, 1918. He was a ready speaker, fluent both on the rostrum and in social circles, but lacked practical application of his endowments; Fannie Gibson, born December, 1849, married February, 1871, Samuel Ware Fogg; Lucy Belle, born in 1852, and Sarah Cook, born in 1855. By the second marriage were John B. Gaines, born in March, 1857; Ann Elizabeth, born April, 1860. Since 1888 she has been principal of the girls school at Hiroshima, Japan, conducted under the auspices of the Southern Methodist Church; Gustavus Nathan, born November, 1862, died July, 1892, and Rachael Cromwell, born November, 1865. She is now, and has been for several years, a teacher of English in the Government Normal School, at Hiroshima, Japan.

The children of Fannie Gibson Gaines and Samuel Ware Fogg are: Anne Belle, Jennie, Fannie, who married John Church; Lucy, who married Curtis Lawson, and Mary Breckinridge.

John B. Gaines married Mary Kendall Davidson November, 1886, and is now a resident of Leeburg, Fla. Has just been appointed Attorney General of that state.

Bernard Gaines, the pioneer, was a son of Daniel Gaines of Amherst County, Va., who was a justice before the Revolution; a major of minute

men in 1775; colonel of Amherst militia in 1781; vestryman of Lexington Parish in 1782; twice sheriff of Amherst County; by a special act of the Assembly he was appointed a commissioner to sell "Glebe" lands in Amherst County; was granted and received patents for 6,000 acres land in "Kentucky District of Virginia;" owned lands in Georgia, where he lived from 1791 to 1794. Court records in Kentucky furnish evidence of his death prior to 1810. Now this Daniel Gaines, father of the Woodford County pioneer, Bernard Gaines, was of the 5th generation in America. The generations run as follows: 5, Daniel; 4, Bernard; 3, George; 2, Bernard; 1, Daniel. Captain Daniel, of the 1st generation, lived in Rappahannock County, Va., and was the first of the name we have any record of in America, and he is supposed to be the immigrant. He received grants of land in 1653, and again in 1663. He was a justice of the peace in 1670, and military and civil officer in 1680.

In his will he left his silver hilted sword and the attached belt to his son Bernard, of the 2nd generation. This Bernard Gaines married Martha Taylor, daughter of Col. George Taylor, and he was the father of George Gaines, of the 3rd generation, and this George was the father of Bernard of the 4th generation, who married Elizabeth Ward, daughter of Seth Ward; and Bernard of the 4th generation was the father of Daniel Gaines, of the 5th generation, who died in Kentucky prior to 1810.

———

Col. John Francisco came to Wood-

ford County at an early date and settled upon land that included the present town of Midway. His residence,
no doubt built of logs, was erected
within one hundred yards of the present residence of Capt. John A.
Steele, on the Georgetown road, in the suburbs of Midway, and while the building has disappeared, there remain evidences, plainly visible, of this old birthplace of several Francisco children,
who romped upon the hillside and
made merriment around the homestead.

*Just when Col. Francisco came to
Woodford County I am not advised,
but he was in the county and on this
farm in 1810, his family was composed of three persons, and he owned
two slaves at that time. I think he
had a son named Andrew. I heard
much of this family from two of the
great grandsons, who lived at Rich Hill,
Missouri in the '80's, but as I was not
contemplating this service then, much
that was definite has passed out of my
recollection. Col. Francisco married
Priscilla Steele, daughter of Capt.
Andrew Steele, of Fayette County. She
was a maternal aunt of Dr. Theoph
Steele, the father of Capt. John Andrew Steele.

Col. John Francisco commanded a
regiment of Kentucky troops in the
war of 1812, was a brave officer and a
man of commanding presence, who
not only had the respect and love of
his regiment, but also the respect of all
of his neighbors and friends.

Andrew, the son of Col. John and
Priscilla (Steele) Francisco, married
—— ——, and had a son, Andrew, who
was born after the death of his father,

in Woodford County, January 3, 1809.
He married Joan Christy, in Winchester, September 23, 1835, who was
born in Fleming County, March 2,
1817. They went overland with an ox
team October, 1839, and settled at
Marshall, Saline County, Mo., and he
died on his farm there February 2,
1868. His remains now repose in the
Presbyterian Church yard that adjoined his farm. His widow removed
to Warrensburg, Mo., in 1876, in order
to have the benefit of better educational
facilities for her children, and afterward moved to Butler, Mo., where she
died September 30, 1895. They had
a large family of children, several of
whom were born in Kentucky. Their
names were Andrew, Charles, Elizabeth, Henry Clay, Joseph, Priscilla
Jane and John Steele Francisco. Andrew and Henry Clay were in the service of the Confederacy for four years.
In my visits to Missouri and Oklahoma
I met Andrew and Priscilla and they
bore a striking resemblance, both in
person and manners, to their Steele
relatives in Woodford County. Two
others that I failed to name were Simeon Payne and Albert B. Francisco.
John Steele and Simeon Payne were
prominent lawyers at Butler, Mo., and
Albert B. was a preacher. The former
married Bertha Henry, who, I think,
was a descendant of Mason Henry, a
former resident of Woodford County.
In fact I am quite sure that she was a
granddaughter of Mason Henry.

Zachariah Henry, Sr., was born and
reared in Orange County, Va. In
1803 he married Lucy Kirtley, of Cul-

---

*See Supplement for other interesting history, and corrections of this family.

Home of Col. John Francisco, Midway, Ky.

peper, Va., who, I think, was a kinswoman of the wife of Simeon Buford,
Sr. They came to Woodford County
in 1805 and settled on a farm that lay
between the Clifton and Glenn's creek
roads, three miles from Versailles, I
think the farm owned by his son,
Mason Henry, or at least upon one of
the several farms in that vicinity occupied by his children. In 1810 he
had a family consisting of seven members, and owned eleven slaves. He
died in 1830, but his widow lived until
1862. This family was not only popular, but were also splendid citizens.
The children were: Newton K., Sr.,
Helen, Mason, Salinda, Thompson and
Martha.

Newton, the first of these children,
was born in 1803, and was just two
years old when the family came to
Kentucky. He married in 1828 Lavinia Brown, who was also born in
1803. They had these children: Lucy,
Affiah, Helen, William and Thomas.

Lucy was born in 1830, died in 1901,
married Joseph A. Payne in 1846, who
was born in 1818, and died in 1850.
Kate Payne, born in 1848, was their
only child. She now resides in Lexington.

Affiah, born in 1832, married
Reuben Munday. Both of them died
at the home of Capt. Harry Brown, on
Glenns creek, three miles from Versailles, in 1909.

Helen was born in 1835, and married
Scott Green in 1855. Their daughter,
Ina Green Miller, is now living with
her son, Scott Miller, in Versailles.

Captain William Henry, born in
1840, was prepared for college at

Sayre's select school, at Frankfort,
graduated from Centre College, Danville, with high honors in 1859. He
taught school in Woodford while preparing himself for the law, but before
he was fully equipped for practice the
tocsin of war rang out at Charleston
harbor and turned loose the pent-up
fury that existed between the two sections of our country. He responded
immediately to the clarion call to arms
of his loved southland, enlisted with
General Simon Bolivar Buckner and
fought with gallantry until General
Lee surrendered his sword to Gen. U.
S. Grant. After the war Capt. Henry
returned to Woodford and opened a
select school for boys in Versailles,
which he conducted very successfully
until his death in 1906. He married
Josephine Williamson in 1868, and she
resides in Versailles.* She has long
been a member of the woman's rights
club, and an advocate of suffrage for
her sex. They had an only child,
Frederick W., who was a promising
youth but met a tragic death on a railroad train in 1891.

Thomas Newton Henry, born in
1843; married Elizabeth Newton in
1871, and died in Versailles in 1910.
They had a daughter, Mary, who married Joseph Trabue, who, with his wife,
is a resident of Versailles. Other descendants in Versailles are Lavinia
Crockett and Nell Henry.

Helen Henry, second of Zach Henry,
Sr., and Lucy Kirtley, was born in
1808, and married Powhatan Dorr.
They moved to Missouri, where they
left posterity.

Mason Henry, third of Zach and

Lucy Henry, was born in 1810, married Eliza McGuffin in 1835. He lived on a farm on the Clifton pike on the opposite side from Col. Lewis A. Berry and adjoining the farm so long owned by Thos. S. Edwards that fronted the Glenn's creek pike. Mason Henry reared a large family on this farm, whose names follow: Rebecca, married William Edwards in 1867, and they have a daughter, Wilmon, who lives in Versailles. William Edwards was a brother of the late Davis Edwards, and was a member of Morgan's command during the Civil War.

Capt. Zach B. Henry, son of Mason Henry, born in 1838, married Josephine Patterson. They have two children, one of whom is Dr. Buford Henry, a wealthy mine owner of Missouri. Capt. Zach Henry was an exceedingly handsome man and a courtly gentleman. He served in the Confederacy for four years, and during that time met Frank and Jesse James before they engaged in guerilla warfare, and he always maintained that they were fine fellows who had been goaded into that life.

Laura and Lucy, daughters of Mason Henry, were twins. The former married her cousin, James McGuffin, Jr., of Illinois, and the latter married Dr. Oscar Rennick, of Butler, Mo. Both are widows, residing with their children in Kansas City, Mo.

Martha, daughter of Mason Henry, married James Keith, of Missouri, and they have children in that state.

Newton Henry, son of Mason, born in Woodford in 1850, was a fine fellow

and one of my boyhood companions. He died in Missouri.

Josephine, youngest daughter of Mason Henry, married Joseph McLaughlin.

John C. Henry, youngest son of Mason, married Annie Ellett, and they reside in Missouri.

Mason Henry, with his interesting family, moved to Missouri in 1867, and he engaged extensively in raising fine cattle and horses. The town of Odessa, quite a nice town, was laid off and built upon a corner of his farm, and he gave it the name that it bears. One of the main streets was named Henry in his honor.

Salinda Henry, the fourth of Zach, Sr., and his wife, Lucy Kirtley, married Scott Brown in 1828. They were the parents of Sallie, Zach, William, Lucy, Helen and Sam. They lived on a farm that was adjacent to the farms of Thomas S. Edwards and Mason Henry. Sam and Zach both joined the Confederacy. Sam never returned; Zach came back and taught school in the county, this scribe being one of his pupils. He married Fannie Winn, daughter of Hezikiah Winn,[*] several years after the war, moved to Nashville, Tenn., soon thereafter, where he established a splendid school, with which he was associated until his death, a decade or more ago.

Martha J. Henry, born in 1821, the youngest of Zach, Sr., and Lucy Kirtley Henry, married Capt. Harry Brown in 1840. He was a brother of Gen. Scott Brown and Judge Reuben Brown, of Franklin County. His farm adjoined the farms of his brother-in-law,

*And his first wife ——— McKnight. See page 282 for second wife of Hezekiah Winn.

Scott Brown, the avenue running down to the Glenn's creek pike, three miles from Versailles. They had no children, but some of the relatives were always with them. Capt. Harry Brown was a strong union man during the Civil War, while his two brothers in Franklin sympathized with the Confederacy, as did all of his kinspeople in Woodford, but he was never offensively partisan, and was a courtly gentleman of the old school. He was active and popular in Masonic circles, and was a prominent Knight Templar.

In 1844 there came to Woodford County a man destined to become the leader in educational and religious work, the originator and founder of an enterprise of which the citizens of the county, more particularly of Midway, might ever point to with pride, viz.: The Female Orphan School. This gentleman was conspicuous in any company for his personal charms, as well as his intellectual and spiritual endowments. He was no less a personage than Dr. L. L. Pinkerton, who was born and reared in Baltimore County, Maryland, but went as a young man to Carthage, Ohio, where he engaged in training the minds of the youth of that locality.

While thus engaged he prepared himself for the profession of medicine, which profession he practiced successfully in that vicinity until Alexander Campbell, the great leader of Christian thought, dropped into the community and persuaded him to abandon his profession and enter the field of soul-saving through the medium of the ministry. After a few years spent in Jefferson County in the interest of Christian work, Dr. Pinkerton moved to Fayette County, where, with Lexington as his basis, he was engaged in religious work when the Christian Church was erected on the spot where the Union station now stands. From Lexington he moved to Midway, where he was the leader in organizing the Christian Church at that point, and became its first pastor. He erected the large brick residence on Winter street, now owned by the Rumleys, and opened a female school there, which he called Baconian Institute, where the wives of Robert Hicks Stout, E. Y. Pinkerton, Dr. J. P. Woolfolk and others that I might name, received their training.

Through an incident that occurred while conducting a meeting in Madison County, when a poor blind girl was led into the church he conceived the idea of building an orphan school at Midway, and he strained every nerve for several years thereafter to turn this thought into a reality. In a letter to a friend in 1846 he said: "the project shall succeed;" and ultimately it did succeed, and the institute has remained in a flourishing condition, and stands today as a monument to his indefatigable work.*

While Dr. Pinkerton was residing yet in Fayette County he conducted a meeting during the summer of 1840 at New Union Church, in Woodford County, on the old Lexington and Frankfort pike. At that meeting

*John P. Starks has recently contributed much money to the beautifying of the school and premises, as did his father before him. He built Starks Hall.

James Ware Parrish, whose residence was between that church and Midway, made a profession of his faith and was received into the membership of the church. Dr. Pinkerton, through his wonderful personality, exercised great influence over young Parrish, and time opened the bud of friendship into full blossom, and it lasted until the sickle of death cut the cord.

It was soon after the conversion of young Parrish that Dr. Pinkerton began organization work of the orphan school, so he took the young man into his confidence, whereupon he agreed whole-heartedly to render any assistance possible, and his support was invaluable. Then followed the support of such men as William F. Patterson, James Starks, Isaac Williams, Bird Smith, Richard Davenport, and many other good men and women of the congregation, who gave hearty support to the enterprise.

Outside of the Midway congregation, such men as Dr. John T. Johnson, of Georgetown, Dr. Philip Fall, of Frankfort, and other pastors on behalf of their congregations, rendered great service.

In 1852 Dr. Pinkerton sold his "Baconian Institute" to James Fall, of Frankfort, and purchased the home of Richard Davenport, for many years the home of the Stanhope family, and devoted all of his time and energies to the welfare and progress of the orphan school that he loved so much.

During the years 1857 and 1858 two events occurred that distressed Dr. Pinkerton very much, viz.: the death of James Ware Parrish during the former, and the destruction of the or-

phan school during the latter year. Dr. Pinkerton had just accepted a call to the church at Paris, which had been tendered him, when the school was reduced to ashes, but he at once canceled the call and immediately undertook the work of restoring the splendid edifice and rehabilitating its working power. In the meantime, however, he repurchased and moved back into the home he built some years before and used as a female academy, in which he opened a school for both boys and girls, in 1859. The Rev. John Shouse, the Rev. William Moore, the Rev. Sidney Moore, Richard Starks and his brother, John P. Starks, the prominent Louisville business man, were among his students.

In 1860 Dr. Pinkerton was elected to and accepted the chair of English Literature in Kentucky University, then located at Harrodsburg. Quite a number of his students followed him there, and several of them, already mentioned, adopted the ministry.

During the sixteen years of residence at Midway it was said of him that he was preacher, teacher, physician and friend of the whole community. He was the head and front in building and establishing, on a firm basis, the orphan school, and the foundation he so carefully laid will not be shaken. The institution, though a monument to past achievements, points the way to still greater achievements to be attained.

Since the above sketch was turned over to the printer I have received the following interesting data relative to the Pinkertons: Dr. Pinkerton's father, William Pinkerton, was reared in southwest Pennsylvania, his father, John Pinkerton, having emigrated from Ulster, Ireland, in 1735. The Pinkertons were Scotch Presbyterians and fled from Scotland to north Ireland to escape religious persecution at home.

In 1833, at Carthage, Ohio, Dr. Pinkerton was married to Sarah Ann Ball, a descendant of one of the six Ball brothers who, in 1636, emigrated from Wiltshire, England, five of them settling in New York and New Jersey, and the sixth, whose name was William, settled in Virginia, and was the progenitor of the family of that name in that state, the most famous of whom was Mary Ball, the mother of President Washington.

Dr. Pinkerton and Sarah Ball had these children: William White, who joined the Confederacy, and after the Civil War married Ella Chew, daughter of Dr. William Chew, of Midway; Virginia L., who graduated under the direction of Prof. John Augustus Williams, and married the Rev. Samuel W. Crutcher, of the Christian church; Rev. Burnet J., graduate of Transylvania, who married Sallie Walker, of Richmond; Rev. James Parrish. who married Kate Patterson, of Lexington; Samuel D., graduate of Transylvania, married Lizzie M. Woolfolk and resides in the suburbs of Versailles; Dr. Lewis, Jr., who married Massie Quisenberry, of Clark County, and Mary Belle, who married J. Downing Price, of Covington, Ky., but now a resident of Ormond, Fla.

In writing a sketch of the descend-

ants of George Blackburn in the May issue of the Register,* I found that there were three Blackburns who registered for the census taken in 1810. They were George, William B. and Jonathan. I soon obtained the data I used relative to George, but no one approached in Woodford, Franklin, or Fayette could tell me anything about William B. or Jonathan, so I concluded they were brothers of George, and so stated that impression in concluding the sketch, but resolved to continue my investigations, as William B. was too prominent in the early political history of the county to merely receive a casual mention. So, while in a meditative mood one pleasant day in the summer of 1920, my mind reverted to incidents of the long ago, and I recalled the face of William Bartlett, of Versailles, a man I never passed during my boyhood without a mutual exchange of greeting and pleasantry. He was totally blind from birth, as was his sister, but he was a remarkably bright fellow, possessing one of the most beautiful Christian characters I have ever known, and it was the delight of every one to greet him cordially in passing. He was gifted in many ways, and if he ever heard your voice, and it was associated with your name, he never forgot either.

The moment he flashed into my mind I remembered that he had told me that his grandfather had served in the Kentucky Legislature for nearly forty years; therefore, as I had in the former sketch mentioned the long service of William B. in the halls of legislation, I knew that he was Bart-

*See page 33 and 175.

lett's grandfather. I immediately took the matter up with a lady in Versailles who knew quite well the Bartlett family and the rest was easy.

I found that William B. and Jonathan, instead of being brothers of George, of Spring Station fort, were the first and second sons. This instance impressed me with the importance of the work I am doing, and I see more clearly the need of it as I proceed, and it encourages me to go forward with the work, although I declined for several years to undertake it.

George Blackburn, I have learned through the Kentucky Library, married Prudence Berry, in Virginia, in 1771, and I will here give a brief mention of some of their descendants not mentioned in the former sketch, which will include William B. This is at least a partial list of the children of George Blackburn and Prudence Berry: William B., who married Martha Watkins, a half-sister of Henry Clay; Jonathan,* who married Prudence Buford; Mary, who married Captain George Holloway; George, Jr., who married first Julia Flournoy, second Anna Branham; Luke, who likely never married; Edward M. (Uncle Ned), who married Lavinia Berry; Elizabeth, who married Samuel Lewis; Mildred, who married William White; Margaret, who married John Kinkead; Ann (Nancy), who married Anthony Bartlett, and Dr. Churchill, who married first Elleanor Arnold, second Lydia Paxton.

†William B. Blackburn and Martha Watkins had these children: Henrietta, Henry C., Prudence and Jonathan.

Henrietta was three times married, each of her husbands being her cousin, and each a cousin of the other. The first marriage was to Dr. David Flournoy, and by this marriage was David Flournoy, Jr. By the second marriage to Thomas Bartlett were William and Prudence Bartlett, both blind from birth. The third marriage was to Francis P. Holloway, with no issue.

Henry C. Blackburn was, by the will of his father, executor of his estate, and named without bond. He married Susan Chiles and had William, an only son, and likely an only child. He moved with his family to Rock Island, Ill., before the Civil War.

Jonathan Blackburn, the second of George and Prudence Berry Blackburn, and his wife, Prudence Buford, had Major William Blackburn, who married Mary Bohannon and moved to St. Louis, Mo. Their descendants in that locality are quite prominent. Jonathan Blackburn, I am told, was a Baptist minister, but never had a regular assignment, preaching where it suited him.*

Mary Blackburn and George Holloway lived on a farm on the opposite side of the railroad from Spring Station, and the house in which they lived was, I think, built in full view of the station, and is likely standing now. He and his wife and some of their children are buried in the graveyard there. Their children were: Mary Ann, George, Jr., Mildred, Frank P., Georgia Ann and Martha.

Frank P. married first Mary Blanton, second Henrietta Bartlett, widow of Thomas Bartlett. By the first marriage was Betsy Blanton Holloway, who married W. F. Sherlock; Georgia Ann Holloway, who married first William T. Willis, Jr., whose father was killed at Buena Vista; second —— Johnson; George Holloway, Jr., married Mary Hodges; Martha Holloway, who married —— Monroe; Mildred, who married Judge —— Hewitt, and Mary Ann married Dr. Leonard Young Hodges. The descendants of Capt. George Holloway and Mary Mitchell Blackburn will appear under the Holloways, to be published later.

George Blackburn, the pioneer, his wife, Prudence Berry; the Rev. Gideon Blackburn, and a sister, Elizabeth Blackburn, who married Richard Bohannon, other relatives and a number of friends, came to Woodford County about 1784. George Blackburn was born in Virginia about 1746, and his wife, Prudence, was born in Virginia November, 1754. The father and mother of George Blackburn were Edward and Anne Blackburn, of Middlesex County, Va., and the grandfather and mother were William and Elizabeth Blackburn, of that county and state.

Elizabeth Blackburn and her husband, Richard Bohannon, first located in Woodford County, but before 1810 were living in Jefferson County.

†The Rev. Gideon Blackburn was a resident of Versailles, and about 1800 was active in the Presbyterian ministry in Woodford County. He was a brother of George and Elizabeth, but very much younger, his birth occurring in August, 1772, and he died at Car-

†See page 319.

linville, Ill., in May, 1837. He married in Virginia in October, 1793, his cousin, Grizzell Blackburn, and followed his brother George, about 1794, to Kentucky. His wife was born October, 1774. They had these children: The Rev. John Newton Blackburn, born in January, 1795, died in July, 1838. He was twice married, first to Isabella Berryhill, second to Catherine Edwards, who, I think, was a widow, residing in Oldham County, Ky.; Betsy Henderson, born January, 1797; James Harvie, born May, 1799, died in 1818, at Maryville, Tenn.; Samuel Emmons, born Jan., 1803, died at Shawneetown in 1835; Jane Mathews, born Sept., 1805, died Oct., 1827, at Middletown, where she married —— King; Gloriana, born Nov., 1807, died Oct., 1825, at Louisville; Grundy Henderson, born May, 1812; William Whitfield, born Feb., 1814; Gideon Hervis, born Dec., 1816, died May, 1837, and Anderson M. Blackburn, born in March, 1818.

I am not advised as to the time that the Rev. Gideon Blackburn left Woodford County and moved to Illinois; likely not until all of his children were grown and married, but I do know that he established a college in Carlinville, that state, at an early day that is still doing service in enlightening the world.

Of these children I will only run out the line of the Rev. John Newton Blackburn, the oldest child, who married Isabella Berryhill. They had two daughters, Mary Anderson, and Elizabeth. The latter died quite young; Mary Anderson Blackburn married Thomas F. Thornton, of Versailles, and was his second wife. They had these

children: Mary Belle, who married
James A. Edwards in May, 1860;
Agnes, who married William W.
George; David Laws Thornton, who
fought through the Civil War, came
home and studied law, and has continuously practiced at the Versailles
bar to this good day; and Elizabeth,
who married Henry George in 1869.
David L. Thornton married Lucy
Matthews, of Missouri, in 1892. These
four lines will be extended under the
sketch of the Thorntons.

By the second marriage to Catherine
Edwards were Margaret Isabella and
Eugenia Blackburn. The latter never
married; Margaret Isabella married
—— Head.

The Rev. John Newton Blackburn
was, as was his father, a Presbyterian
minister, and preached often at the
old Griers Creek church, the old Woodford church, at Alexanders, and the old
Macedonia church that, if my memory
serves me aright, was built on a corner of the farm of Thomas Railey, on
the road that separated the farms of
the Whittingtons from that of William
Strother Hawkins, and near "Clifton
Heights." I have been told that the
Rev. John Newton Blackburn was the
pastor at the old Woodford church
when he departed this life during the
summer of 1838.

Eugenia Blackburn, second daughter
of the second marriage, went with her
mother to Carlinville, Ill., after the
death of her father, the Rev. John
Newton, remained a spinster and lived
to quite an old age. She was born in

July, 1837, an infant when her father
died, and died in May, 1912.

The Rev. John Newton Blackburn
combined teaching with preaching.
Away back in the early '30's he taught
school at Griers Creek church—the old
*school house still standing near the
spot where it was originally built—
and also near the Macedonia church,
in the vicinity of Clifton. He was then
a widower and while teaching at the
former place he and his daughter Mary
abided with the family of P. I. Railey,
Sr., and at the latter point they were
domiciled with John Berryman and his
wife, Jane Railey. The Raileys and
Berrymans were his pupils and constituted his choir at both Griers Creek
and Macedonia, and often rode horseback with him to old Woodford church
near Midway, where they assisted in
the singing. It was not until after the
Civil War that interest in old Griers
Creek and Macedonia churches began
to wane in favor of the church at Versailles.

————

Col. Thomas Marshall was one of the
sons of John Marshall, "of the Forest," and Elizabeth Markham, both of
Westmoreland County, Virginia. John
"of the Forest" was born in 1700 and
died in 1752. His wife was a great-
aunt of William Fleming Markham,
who was engaged in business in Versailles in 1825, and married Susanna
Railey, daughter of Thomas Railey and
Martha Woodson.

In 1754 Col. Thomas Marshall married Mary Randolph Keith who was

born in 1738. She was one of the daughters of Rev. James Keith and his wife Mary Isham Randolph who was born in 1718, and married in 1733. Col. Thomas Marshall and his wife, Mary Randolph Keith, came to Kentucky and located in Woodford County in or about 1782, locating his estate, which he called "Buck Pond," within a few miles of Versailles.

Col. Marshall served in the Revolution, at first commanding the Third Virginia regiment, continental line, but afterward commanded a regiment of Virginia artillery. In his native Virginia he was both a neighbor and a close friend of General George Washington.

After the war had practically subsided he was appointed surveyor-general of the lands in Kentucky appropriated by Virginia to the officers and soldiers of the Virginia state line.

Col. Thomas Marshall and Mary Randolph Keith had fifteen children, all of whom were born in Virginia, and, without an exception, all were brilliant men and women, a characteristic that has been, and is today, reflected in the lives of the descendants.

Unlike most of the pioneers, who chose the "wilderness road" to Kentucky, Col. Marshall and his family came to Kentucky by way of the Ohio river to Limestone, afterward Maysville, thence across the country to Woodford County. Several of his elder children, including Chief Justice John Marshall, were married and remained in Virginia. Six of his seven sons, Captain Thomas, James M., Charles, William, Alexander, Keith and Dr.

Louis, accompanied their father and mother to Kentucky, the former becoming the first clerk of the county court of Mason County. Alexander Keith was associated with the Kentucky Court of Appeals as court reporter for many years, while Dr. Louis was a widely known educator, a man of letters, but found time to look after "Buck Pond" which was his inheritance at the death of his father. In 1855 he became president of Washington and Lee University, at Lexington, Va. However, he had successfully taught a large class of young men, both at Pisgah and Versailles, before accepting the presidency of Washington and Lee.

Of the eight daughters of Col. Marshall and Mary Randolph Keith, Elizabeth married Rawleigh Colston; Mary Ann married her cousin, Humphrey Marshall, who did so much to make the name illustrious; Judith married George Brooks; Lucy married Col. John Ambler; Susanna married Col. William McClung; Charlotte Ashmore married Dr. Basil Duke; Jane married George Keith Taylor, and Nancy married Col. Joseph Hamilton Daviess.

I think it was about 1800 that Col. Marshall removed from Woodford to Mason County, where his daughter, Charlotte, and her husband, Dr. Duke, and other members of his family, were then living, leaving "Buck Pond" in the care of Dr. Louis Marshall, but he soon returned to Woodford County and died at Buck Pond during the summer of 1803.*

Humphrey Marshall, who married his cousin, Mary Ann Marshall, daugh-

---

*Mistake. He died at Washington, Mason County 1802.

ter of Col. Thomas, represented Woodford County in the Legislature in 1793, when North Frankfort was a part of Woodford County. He also served in both branches of Congress, and fought a duel with Henry Clay, but a reconciliation was effected between the two families, after which his son, John J. Marshall married a niece of Henry Clay's wife.

Humphrey Marshall was a son of John Marshall and Jane Quisenberry, of Virginia. His last work was to write a history of Kentucky. The only daughter was killed by lightning in the county of Woodford before she reached mature years. Of his two sons, born in Woodford County, I believe, John J. and Thomas A., the former was Judge of the Louisville Circuit Court for many years, was on the Supreme Court bench for more than twenty years, serving as Chief Justice for quite a period. He was also a member of Congress.

Thomas Alexander Marshall, the other son, possessed to a high degree intellectual and legal attainment. The late Judge James P. Harbison, an eminent jurist, said of him: "He was a Christian gentleman, a classical scholar, an erudite jurist, and altogether the greatest and best man I ever knew."

In the second chapter I erroneously wrote of Humphrey Marshall as General Humphrey when, I think, he had never attained to a higher military rank than captain. General Humphrey Marshall was a son and lived in the period of the Mexican War.

Col. Joseph Hamilton Daviess, who married Nancy Marshall, was a lawyer

of note. It was he who had Aaron Burr apprehended and tried, he being the prosecutor, but he was unable to convict owing to lack of incriminating evidence. He served gallantly under General Harrison in the western campaign and lost his life at Tippecanoe.

Dr. Louis Marshall, born in 1773, died in 1866, married in 1800, Agatha Smith, of Frankfort, daughter of Major Francis Smith and his wife, —— Preston. Their two sons, Thos. Francis and Edward C., were distinguished citizens of Woodford County, and their daughter, Agatha, a talented lady, married Caleb Logan, of Shelby County. Thomas F. Marshall, able lawyer and statesman, was one of the most distinguished orators in the nation. His birth was in 1801, and he died in 1864. He married Elizabeth Yost, but had no children.* Many of the present citizens remember his last speech, delivered in the old court house during the Civil War, and not long before his death. I now see his tall, gaunt figure and long black beard as he delivered his "farewell."

Edward C. was no less distinguished as a lawyer, statesman and orator, but was perhaps not quite so scholarly. His birth was in 1821, and he died in 1893. His wife was Josephine Chalfant, to whom he was married in 1852. Their son, Louis Marshall, is the present cashier of the Woodford Bank of Versailles, and the present owner of "Buck Pond," which has never been out of possession of the Marshall name since it was established about 1782.

Thomas F. and Edward C. Marshall cast great lustre upon their county.

---

*An only child died in infancy.

Both served in Congress and in other distinguished capacities, and their reputation as orators was country wide.

Dr. Basil Duke and Charlotte Ashmore Marshall lived at Maysville after the year 1794, and they reared a family there. A granddaughter, Lucy Duke, married Captain John Andrew Steele (his first wife), of the county, and they have a daughter, Mamie Buford Steele, now living at Versailles. She married Theodore Harris, of the Sellers, Harris Banking Co. She and Louis Marshall and his children are the only descendants of Col. Thomas Marshall and Mary Randolph Keith, now residents of the county that I recall.

The Marshall family has produced as many prominent lawyers, doctors and ministers doubtless as any other of the distinguished families that came out of Virginia. Many have been bright stars in the army and navy. They were largely represented in the Civil War, chiefly in the cause of the Confederacy.

Caleb Logan and Agatha Marshall, daughter of Dr. Louis Marshall, were the grandparents of Scott, William Marshall and Keith Bullitt, three prominent attorneys now practicing at the Louisville bar.

———

Thomas Helm came from Frederick† County, Virginia, to Woodford County, Kentucky, about, or before 1800.

In 1797 he married Elizabeth Buck,‡ daughter of Col. John Buck, of the county, and they had these children: 1st John Newton, who went to Mississippi before he reached his majority

and married in that state Helen Marie Timberlake, in 1824, who was related to the Kentucky family of that name; 2nd James Hervie, who also went to Natchez quite young, contracted the yellow fever and died in 1822; 3rd Amanda, who married James Bates Walker and lived in Richmond, Ky.; 4th Isabella, who married Thomas Washington Catlett; 5th Miriam, who married —— Crowe; 6th William Meredith, who went to Mississippi and married Ann Gipson; 7th Sarah Ann, who married George Pinkard; 8th Thomas Erskin, who went to Mississippi and married Mary Biggs, a half sister of John Newton's wife; 9th Huldah, who married Frederick Stanton and moved to Natchez, Miss., where they have grandchildren, and 10th Dodd Helm, who married Mary Logan and lived in the ancestral home on the Nicholasville pike not far from the present limits of Versailles. This country seat of the Helms was known as "Helmsly," and is, or was a few years ago, the property of J. W. Newman.

Many of the citizens of Woodford County during the Civil War, who are now living, will recall the face of Dodd Helm with pleasure, as his was a pleasing personality. He was a lovable and most estimable gentleman. He spent his winters in Mississippi on his plantation, and his summers in Woodford County on the ancestral estate. He was small of stature, always neatly and faultlessly dressed, a perfect Chesterfield in deportment, and altogether one of the most elegant and

†See page 249, John Upshaw Warring.
‡See page 35.

popular gentlemen raised in the county. His intimates were such men as Joe Taylor, Lewis Sublett, Judge Cave Graves, Ambrose Young, Col. Willis and Col. Thomas M. Fields, Captain Harry Brown, Warren Viley, John Amsden, Sr., the Raileys, the Marshalls and others too numerous to mention. All delighted in the company of Dodd Helm.

Dodd Helm and Mary Logan had two children, Logan and Maggie. The former died in early manhood, a bright, popular young gentleman. His aunt, Maggie Logan, established a circulating library in Versailles in memory of her nephew, and many of the present generation will recall that library, and the benefits derived from its select volumes. I rather think it is yet in existence and doing duty, but am not quite sure, but I do know that it did a great and appreciated service for a great number of years. Maggie Helm, the daughter, was living in Lexington, and I presume is there yet. She possessed many of the rare qualities of her father and mother.

John Newton Helm, the 1st, and his wife, Helen Maria Timberlake, had several children. Their daughter, Ann Elizabeth, married Charles Randolph Railey, of New Orleans, a grandson of Charles Railey and Mary Mayo, of "Buck Run" stock farm. They have two daughters, Annie Maria, who married Dr. W. W. Black, and Jennie Railey, who married Andrew A. Woods; and a son, William Mayo Railey, who married Lina Howell, all residing in New Orleans.

Amanda, the 3rd, who married James Bates Walker, has two grand-daughters living in Lexington, one of them Laura Stone, who married George Blackburn Kinkead, and another, Anne Stone, who married Arthur Fithsdale Maxwell.

Issabella, the 4th, and Thomas Washington Catlett, moved to southwest Kentucky, and their descendants are living at Hopkinsville and Eddyville.

Miriam, 5th, and —— Crowe moved to St. Louis, Mo. Know nothing of issue.

William Meredith, the 6th, and Ann Gipson have descendants in Mississippi, in Rapids Parrish.

Thomas Erskin, 8th, and Mary Biggs have descendants living at Jackson, Miss.

Huldah, the 9th, and Frederick Stanton, have grandchildren at Natchez, Miss.

Thomas Helm was a man of wealth. The census of 1810 credited him with a farm, ten slaves and a family consisting of ten members. Tradition says that he possessed much cash and tided many hard-luck souls over the breakers in the early days, who always esteemed him for his readiness to oblige his neighbors.

Elizabeth Buck, the wife of Thomas Helm, died at her home near Versailles in 1851, her husband having preceded her many years. The remains of both, together with those of Col. John Buck, repose in the Lexington cemetery not far from the Clay monument.

The Rev. Thomas Railey Markham, son of William Fleming Markham and Susanna Railey, pastor of a Presbyterian church at New Orleans for forty years, was with John Newton Helm, son of Thomas Helm and Elizabeth Buck, during his last hours in 1871, and he said that he was one of the truest Christians he had ever known.

In this character of work we meet with many discouragements, and often when we have despaired in our efforts to get a line on people or events our efforts are suddenly rewarded by stumbling upon a bed of rich lore. When a boy I was told that the old stone tavern that occupied the spot where Amsden's bank now stands, and known as Watkins' Tavern was owned and operated at an early day by the mother of Henry Clay. I wrote a brief sketch of this old hostelry, with the mother of the great commoner associated with its management, with a few incidents that I recalled as having heard, but as it has been my purpose to have everything I write about verified by some one in position to know, I sought verification through an elderly gentleman, Capt. John Andrew Steele, who was born near Versailles about eighty years ago, and who, by contact with the social circles of Woodford County all of his life, ought to have known all about this old edifice, but he wrote me disclaiming any knowledge of Clay's mother ever having had anything to do with the old inn, so I cast the sketch aside. However, a friend was looking over some old clippings in possession of the Kentucky Historical Society and found one taken from the Courier-Journal forty or more years ago that contained a fine picture of the old inn, and just the data I had written, but vastly more that bristled with interesting accounts. I am attaching the clipping in whole and only hope I will be able to secure a cut of the engraving of the old building. To me this bit of history is precious, and as the name of Mrs. Samuel Woolridge appears in ink on the margin, I presume the county is indebted to her for for her thoughtfulness in removing and preserving this clipping. I had already written a brief sketch of the Watkins family, but this sketch covers the family so much better than I had done that I will let it take the place of my sketch.

Many of the older citizens would view the old landmark with refreshened memories of by-gone days. The structure was destroyed by fire during the late '70's or early '80's. It is certainly interesting to know that this splendid piece of masonry was built under the supervision of Thomas Metcalfe, who was Governor of Kentucky from 1828 to 1832, the same who built the stone mill on the Wilkins or James P. Ford farm, in the Clover Bottom section.

My impression is that the old inn was built of stone taken from the Kentucky river, not far from lock No. 5, the same that was used in the construction of the columns in the old Capitol at Frankfort, and likely in the old Capitol building too.

The clipping follows:

Versailles, Ky., March 29.—On page fifty-four of Order Book "B," in the county clerk's office here there appears the following:

"Woodford County Court—Agreeable to an order of said county to us directed, we have settled the accounts of Henry Watkins, guardian of Henry Clay, orphan of John Clay, deceased, for the years 1794, 1795 and 1796, and find that there is due said Watkins from the estate of Clay the sum of twenty shillings. Given under our hands this 27th day of October, 1797.''

"RICHARD YOUNG,
"CHARLES RAILEY.''

"Henry Watkins, guardian, was *Henry Clay's stepfather. He and Mrs. Watkins kept the first tavern that was established in Versailles—quite a celebrated hostelry a century ago, and the rendezvous of great lawyers, pedagogues and statesmen of the day. Around the crackling logs in the great fireplace in its spacious hallway such men as Maj. John Crittenden, the father of John J. Crittenden; John Breckinridge, Senator John Brown, Col. Thos. Marshall, Judge Caleb Wallace, John Watkins, Prof. Kean O'Hara, the father of the great poet-journalist, gathered in the candlelight to discuss the news of the nation, when news traveled only by stage coach. Gen. Lafayette, on his tour of the country in 1825, was banqueted at the Watkins tavern and addressed the assembled citizens from the upper story of the building.''

"Even the young people of today clearly recollect the quaint old stone building, which occupied the present site of Amsden's Bank, at the corner of Main and Court streets, for it remained standing until a few years ago.''

"Henry Watkins was the brother of John Watkins, founder of the town of Versailles and who was a delegate in the Constitutional Convention at Danville in 1792 as well as a Representative in the first Legislature. The Watkinses

married sisters. John was married to Mary Hudson and Henry married Mrs. Elizabeth Hudson Clay, who had been left a widow, with several children, by the death of the Rev. John Clay, of Virginia. Henry Watkins and family came to Versailles in 1792, soon after the founding of the town making the journey from Virginia in wagons and bringing with them quite a retinue of slaves.''

"Henry Clay, as is well known, remained in Richmond, as deputy in the clerk's office. During every summer, however, he made visits to his mother, in Versailles, and entered freely into the quiet social life of the village. Of a frank, generous, chivalric nature, he had here as a young man many friends who looked forward to his periodical visits. Mr. Clay moved from Richmond to Lexington in 1797. In the words of Chief Justice Robertson, "he came leaning alone on Providence, a widowed mother's prayers and the untutored talents with which God had been pleased to bless him.'' His visits to this community thenceforth were more frequent than before. And even after his mother's death, in 1829, he came at intervals to spend a few days with his step-sister, Mrs. Blackburn.''

"Mrs. Clay-Watkins was a remarkably attractive woman, of striking individuality. Great is the pity that no portrait of her has been handed down to the present day. While not a beauty, she had a sweet face, full of character. Her eyes and hair were dark. Her manners were gracious and she was an animated and very entertaining conversationalist. Her natural qualities

*See page 363.

Watkins Inn, at Versailles, Ky.

fitted her to develop in her son the high-minded frankness and sincerity of character which marked his entire life.''

"The last person in Versailles who personally remembered Mrs. Clay-Watkins was Mrs. Mary E. Scott (the mother of Mrs. J. C. Bethel, of Louisville), who died three or four years ago at the age of eighty-eight. Mrs. Scott, as a child, lived next door neighbor to Mrs. Watkins for several years and was warmly attached to her. She said that Mrs. Watkins was a most hospitable and sympathetic neighbor and kind to everybody.''

"The Watkinses quit their tavern at some time between 1815 and 1820 and settled upon a farm which they owned three miles south of Versailles, where Mrs. Watkins died in 1829, at the age of eighty years. Her body was buried in a country graveyard nearby, and there rested until 1851, when her son Henry had the remains reinterred in the Lexington cemetery.''

"Four children born of the union of Henry Watkins and Mrs. Elizabeth Clay-Watkins lived to maturity. The one daughter married Col. William B. Blackburn, of Versailles, whose eminence as a lawyer and in politics made his name historic. He was an uncle of Senator Joe C. S. Blackburn. Of the three sons, Frank, a clergyman of the Baptist church, and Nathaniel, a lawyer, removed to Missouri, in which state many of their descendants now live. John Watkins, the eldest son, remained in Woodford County and died here. He is said to have borne a strong resemblance to his mother. John Watkins married Miss Caroline T. Milton,

daughter of Elijah Milton. Two of his sons, Elijah and Ebenezer Watkins, both of them bachelors, past seventy-five years of age, live together at the old Milton homestead, five miles east of Versailles. Another son, Thomas B. Watkins, resides in Lexington, and they have a sister, Miss Eliza Watkins, in Arkansas.''

"Elijah Watkins, Esq., is said by Mr. Thomas M. Field, an old resident of Woodford County, who was well acquainted with Henry Clay, to more closely resemble his illustrious half-uncle than either of Clay's own sons.''

"The historic Watkins tavern was destroyed a few years ago in a fire which burned the block of business buildings between Main, Court and Morgan streets. There was an old tradition that Stonemason Thomas Metcalfe (afterward Governor of Kentucky), who built the tavern, had placed a carefully sealed jug of whiskey under the cornerstone of the building. For months after the fire, connoisseurs of liquor and relic hunters made laborious and careful excavations beneath the foundation, but the jug was never found.''

The "Menzies Clan," of the highlands of Scotland, was composed of a small but brave and honorable band of kinspeople. One of this clan was the Rev. Adam Menzies, who was a clergyman in the Scotch branch of the English Episcopal church. Tradition says that he favored the cause of the young pretender, Charles Edward, and in consequence had to flee the country. Accordingly, in 1745, he landed on the shores of Virginia a fugitive from the wrath of those who were of the ruling dynasty.

After he had gotten his bearings, he settled in Richmond County, not far from the home of George Washington, in the adjacent county of Westmoreland, and it ever afterward pleased him to be cognizant of the fact that he and the Washingtons had exchanged neighborly courtesies and greetings.

After he was thoroughly settled he took charge of the old Farnham church, one of the "Glebe Churches" of Virginia, and soon thereafter married Phoebe Peachy, who, I think, was a daughter of Samuel Peachy, who is mentioned in a list of the vestry of the South Farnham church, spoken of by Bishop Meade in "Old Churches and Families of Virginia."

The Rev. Adam Menzies and Phoebe Peachy had two children, both boys, whose names were George and Samuel Peachy Menzies. Both were born and reared in Richmond County, and after reaching man's estate both became imbued with the revolutionary spirit which had overwhelmed all of their neighbors with a consuming desire to throw off the yoke of Great Britain, and like their neighbors and friends, they too volunteered their services in behalf of liberty and justice. The former entered the Revolution as an ensign, which is the present rank of a second lieutenant, while the latter entered the service as a lieutenant.

At the battle at Yorktown, owing to the absence of the captain, for reasons not stated, Samuel Peachy Menzes (or Minnis), as Virginians pronounced it, gallantly led the company, and he was

ever afterward known as Captain Menzies.

Soon after the Revolution Captain Menzies was married to Frances Miskel, of Richmond County, the daughter of a neighbor, and they had these children: Elizabeth Phoebe, William Adam, born in 1785, Fannie and Thomas, all born in Richmond County, Va., and were all grown before coming to Kentucky, about 1805. Samuel P. Menzies' name appears on the Federal census of Woodford County in 1810, when he listed his family as sixteen in number, an unusually large family, which must have included some relatives or friends, perhaps both. He also owned a large farm and twenty-eight slaves. His farm was on Clear creek, three miles from Versailles, in the "Dry Ridge" vicinity. I think the farm he owned was the farm James Bright owned so long and sold when he moved to Shelby County. At least it was in that vicinity. Samuel P. Menzies died there in 1833, and he and his wife were buried in the Versailles cemetery. His surroundings made him quite a well-to-do and influential citizen, and he always appeared in public dressed in the colonial style of knee pants, stockings, pigeon-tail coat, slippers with silver buckles, and cocked hat. I have the names of his four children who, with him and his wife, made only six members of the family, so of course others abided under his hospitable roof besides his immediate family to account for the sixteen.

His first wife died in 1820, and in 1823 he married Hannah Hunt, a widow of the county, but no issue came of this marriage, and she survived him many years. Fannie Menzies, one of the daughters, had a friend, Catherine Canfield, who came with the family from Virginia; she may have been a relative. A few years later she married William Stewart Hunter. (See Hunter sketch, 66 page.)

Elizabeth Phoebe Menzies, the eldest child, married Dr. George Timberlake, of Cynthiana; William Adam married Martha Elizabeth Garber, of Staunton, Va.; Fannie married Dr. Richard Banks Bohannon, of Versailles, and Thomas married first Polly Singleton, second Martha Taylor, both of Woodford County.

The families of Dr. Timberlake and Thomas Menzies are long since extinct. William Adams Menzies was born in Virginia in 1785. When the family came to Kentucky he remained in Virginia to complete his education at Washington College, then went to Staunton to study law with Chapman Johnson, and there he met and married Martha Elizabeth Garber, then came to Kentucky on the honeymoon, where they remained. He formed a partnership with Lt. Gov. William Berry Blackburn, eldest son of George Blackburn, and practiced law at the Versailles bar for some time, but finally abandoned the law, bought a farm near Versailles which he managed very successfully until 1819, when he sold it and purchased one in Bourbon County, wither he moved. Their children, born in Woodford, were Dr. Samuel Garber Menzies, who married Sallie Ann Winston; Marguerite, who married George Nicholson Johnson (son of Chapman Johnson, of Staunton, Va.); Caroline F., who married Dr. E. S. Clarkson;

Sarah, who married the Rev. Thornton Mills; John W., who married first Eliza Jane Butler, second Samuella Lewis, and Katherine, who departed this life February, 1920, in her 83rd year, unmarried.

George Nicholson Johnson and Marguerite have a daughter, Rosa M. Johnson, living at Covington with other family relations. I am much indebted to her for assistance in gathering data relating to this interesting pioneer family of Woodford County. John W. Menzies served in the Legislature, in Congress and was associated with the judiciary at Covington for many years.

Fannie Menzies, daughter of the pioneer, Captain Samuel P. Menzies, and Dr. Richard Banks Bohannon had these children: Francis, who married —— Potts; Bettie, who married Capt. William W. George, who so long and so well presided over the Woodford county court; Ophelia, who married first Virgil McCracken, second —— Wood, and third Major Humphrey Jones; and Henry Buford Bohannon, who married Mary Todd.

Francis and —— Potts had two children, Dick who had a drug store during and after the Civil War on the corner where Breck Smith's drug store is now located, opposite courthouse; and Ellen, who married John Brown, a brother of Sandy, and uncle of Preston Brown, now a resident of Versailles.

Bettie Bohannon and Capt. W. W. George had William, Jr., who married Agnes Thornton; Frank, who never married; Richard, who married —— ——; Henry, who married Elizabeth Thornton, and John, who married Maggie Hampton, daughter of Samuel Hampton.

Ophelia Bohannon and Major Humphrey Jones had: William, who married —— ——; Fannie Bohannon, who married William L. Taylor, and Elizabeth Blackburn, who married George Copeland. William L. Taylor and Fannie Bohannon Jones had Harry Clay Taylor and Ophelia Bohannon Taylor, both now residents of the county.

Henry Buford Bohannon and his wife, Mary Todd, had a large family of children. They lived on the old Twyman farm, on the Midway pike, where the McLeods now live, and, though the owner of this large farm, the yearly expense of his large family was in excess of his income, so about 1870 he sold his farm and moved with his family to Missouri. I think there was only one girl, Fannie Bohannon, and she married Noah Griffith.

Henry Buford Bohannon is well remembered by many of our citizens. His buggy and carriage were always drawn by a good looking span of horses, and he was always well dressed, and a hospitable and popular gentleman.

Of the numerous descendants of Capt. Samuel P. Menzies, the pioneer, I can only name four who are now residents of the county. They are Harry Clay Taylor and his sister, Ophelia Bohannon Hoppins, and Isola and Wade George, children of John George and Maggie Hampton.

John W. Menzies, Jr., son of Hon. John W. Menzies, is clerk of the Federal District Court at Covington.

Dr. Richard Banks Bohannon, while yet a young man, rode horseback from his home in Culpeper, Va., to Philadel-phia, where he graduated in medicine under the celebrated Dr. Rush, who founded the University of Pennsylvania and was one of the signers of the declaration of independence. With preparation, and such favorable surroundings, Dr. Bohannon was splendidly equipped for a successful prosecution of his profession, and for forty years he was a very successful practitioner in the county, as well as one of the leading physicians of the state, being widely known and patronized. For many years he resided in Versailles, but some years after the war of 1812 he purchased the old Daniel Trabue farm that lay across the road from Griers Creek church, and separated from the Lewis Sublett farm by a creek. He died there in 1858 at the ripe age of 72 years, much honored as a neighbor and friend, and all of his children were reared there.

His wife, Fannie Menzies, was a beautiful woman and a talented musician. Upon her wedding day he presented her with an upright piano, said to have been the first of the kind in the county, if not in the state. She died in 1831, only forty-five years of age. When he died in 1858 the farm was transferred to his daughter, Ophelia, who was then the wife of Major Humphrey Jones. Major Jones was an uncle of Col. Willis Jones, of the county, who lost his life in the service of the Confederacy. (See Field and Buford sketches.) Major Humphrey Jones and his wife died on the Griers creek farm during the '70's, and a part, if not all, of the old home is now in possession of Ophelia Bohannon Hoppins, a granddaughter.

I am told that Dr. R. B. Bohannon was not related to William or German Bohannon, unless very remotely. They were also pioneers of Woodford County. But it is certain that Dr. Richard Bohannon was a close relative of Richard Bohannon, who married Elizabeth *Blackburn, sister of George and the Rev. Gideon Blackburn, who, after a residence in Woodford County, moved to Jefferson County in 1798. Both families were of the highest type of citizenship, and that characteristic has been reflected in the lives of each generation to the present.

I have heard Henry Buford Bohannon relate on several occasions that his father, Dr. Richard Bohannon, and Henry Clay were friends in their youth and made a trip together on horseback to Philadelphia in search of knowledge that served each so well in after years. Dr. Bohannon came to Kentucky some years before Henry Clay came, but when the latter did come the friendship was renewed and continued unabated until death closed the scene. I also heard him say more than once that when his father came to Woodford County the "Big Spring" was surrounded by a canebrake that covered the present site of Versailles, and extended quite a distance down the creek. These cane thickets covered much of the surface of the county at that time, and much of it remained until after the Civil War.

There is an interesting old relic here in the rooms of the Kentucky Historical Society, within ten feet of me as I write this sketch, that should interest citizens of Woodford County. It was

manufactured in London, England, in 1800, by Murzio Clementi, an Italian composer and manufacturer, and is known as a "Spinet." It was imported to Staunton, Va., the year it was manufactured, by the father of Martha Elizabeth Garber, who married William Adam Menzies, and was given to her as a bridal present, and they brought it to Woodford County in 1810, across the mountains, I believe. It was one of the first pianos to arrive in this country, so it created much interest in Woodford at that early day. It was donated to this society in 1882 by the wife of George Nicholson Johnson, mentioned earlier in this sketch as a daughter of William A. Menzies and his wife, Martha Elizabeth Garber.

This quaint old musical instrument has an oval tablet of ivory in front with the name of the manufacturer and date manufactured (1800) inscribed on it, but owing to age and service, the inscription can scarcely be traced.

Since writing this sketch, in tracing the families of Elliott and German Bohannon I learn that Elliott was a brother of Richard, who married Elizabeth Blackburn, and closely related to Dr. Richard Banks Bohannon. I had to go out of the county, and largely out of the state, to get the data relative to the Bohannons, but it is authentic. A sketch of the other Bohannons who were in Woodford County in 1810 will appear in the May Register, 1921, with a number of other interesting sketches.

Two Thornton families came to Kentucky and settled in Woodford County at an early date, one of them arriving about 1790, the other about 1810. I am not able to state positively that they bore relationship, but I incline to the belief that they were related, though the degree may have been a little remote, for there is a most striking resemblance in looks and actions between all of the members of each family that I have known, their chief characteristics being modesty, honesty and the purity of their Christian lives. I bear marriage relationship to both of these pioneers, the one on my mother's side and the other on my father's, but I give their characteristics without bias. James Thornton, the first to arrive (both bore this name) was a bachelor who had served in the Revolution, and as he was born in 1752, he was past the meridian of life when he arrived in Woodford County. The family record, now in Sherman, Texas, takes the name back to William Thornton, Lord of East Newton, Yorkshire, England, in 1313. This William Thornton married Isabella, daughter of William de Newton, and for ten generations thereafter the family lived in England, but William Thornton, of the eleventh generation, came to America in 1646 and settled in York (now Gloucester) County, in Pebsworth Parish, Va.

In the fourth generation of the American branch the above James Thornton, son of William and twin of Sarah, first saw the light in 1752. Soon after the Revolution, in which he had participated, he came to Woodford County, say about 1790, and settled near Mortonsville where he met and married Sarah Bailey Hawkins, daughter of Captain Moses Hawkins and Susanna Strother, the latter the only

sister of the wife of Col. Richard Taylor.

James Thornton and Sarah Bailey Hawkins had these children: Willis, Damascus, Susanna, William, James Jr., Elizabeth, Sarah, Richard Taylor, and Sophia Strother Thornton. I am not sure that these names are arranged chronologically, but as most of their lines were extended under the Strother sketch, I will only mention here the descendants of Willis, who were neglected under that sketch, owing to a lack of data that I have since received. He was born in 1795 and married Esther Stephens, of the county. Their daughter, Sarah, was born in 1836, and Lucy was born in 1839. The former married Dr. W. Y. Gadberry, and the latter married first Dr. Henry Byrd Kidd, second Bishop James S. Key, one of the most distinguished divines in the service of the Methodist church in the south. After the marriage of these two girls the families moved to Yazoo City, Miss., before the Civil War. Bishop Key and his wife, Lucy, afterward removed to Sherman, Texas, where his wife took charge of and re-established north Texas Girls' College, and made it the celebrated Kidd-Key College, which had wonderful prosperity under her management. Its conservatory of music ranks today with the highest in the United States, and it continues to progress under the charge of Sarah Versal, daughter of Dr. H. B. Kidd and Lucy Thornton, and step-daughter of Bishop Key, who is at present managing its affairs. See Strothers for other descendants of James Thornton and his wife, Sarah Bailey Hawkins. Page 142.

The other branch of the Thornton family came to Woodford County about 1810 or very soon thereafter. The earliest information I have concerning this branch of the family is that three Thorntons, brothers, sailed from England for America, one of them locating in Virginia, one in North Carolina and another in Delaware. The name of the latter was David Thornton, who married in that state Sarah Knox. This couple had a son whose name was also James Thornton, born in 1772, died in 1840. He married first Eleanor Davis, in the state of Delaware, in 1795; second the widow Susanna McCuddy, daughter of John Fisher and Vilator Laws, of Woodford County. The family notes indicate that this James Thornton came to Woodford County and married the widow McCuddy in 1809, but as his name doesn't appear on the census of 1810, I think it must have been as late as autumn, 1810, unless, perhaps, he came to the county from Louisville, where he first settled, entered the second matrimonial venture in 1809 and returned to that village to settle up his affairs, then later returned to Woodford.

By the first marriage to Eleanor Davis came David and James Thornton. David married first, Nancy Railey, in 1820, daughter of Isham Railey and Susanna Woodson. She died in 1821 leaving no issue. The second marriage was to Charlotte Railey, in June, 1823, daughter of Charles Railey and Mary Mayo. James Thornton, Jr., married Mary Elliott Nov., 1830.

By the second marriage of James Thornton, Sr., to Susan McCuddy were Thomas Fisher Thornton, who married

Agnes Steele in 1835, daughter of John Steele and Catharine Swann Railey; John Wesley Thornton, who married Matilda Jones in 1834; Alexander Laws Thornton, who married Janette Markham in 1840, and Cassandra Thornton, who married John West.

David Thornton and Charlotte Railey have these children: Mary Eleanor, who married David I. Porter in 1841; James III, who married Mary Simpson, in 1855; Bettie, who married Ulyssus Turner in 1849; Hontas, who married Judge Edwin S. Craig; Edwin K., who married Lucretia Hobbs; Woodford Railey, who married Lucy Dupuy Bailey in 1866, and Charles Randolph, born in 1847, died young.

David I. Porter and Eleanor Thornton had these children: Alice, born Sept., 1842, married James M. Preston, Aug., 1864; Thornton, born July, 1845, lost his life at the battle of Vicksburg in 1863 in the service of the Confederacy; Edward Lacey, born Nov., 1847, married Sallie Boulden Sept., 1870; Mary, born Nov., 1849, married Daniel Cooper, May, 1867; Charles Randolph, born Oct., 1852, married Elizabeth Bennett, Jan., 1875; Elfreda Oak, born Dec., 1854, married Frederick Madeira, Dec., 1880, and Pauline, born Aug., 1861, married James Montgomery, Oct., 1886.

James Thornton, III, and Mary Simpson had Bettie, born Aug., 1856, married James Stevens, of San Antonio, Texas, in Dec., 1879. She was a leading club woman of that city, doing much charity work, and respected by all. She died in that city Oct. 30, 1920; James Simpson, born April, 1861, married Catharine Foster Dec., 1882; Charlotte, Mary and Eleanor.

Ulyssus Turner and Bettie Thornton had Charlotte, born Oct., 1851, married Joseph Marshall Bowmar June, 1876; Lester, born July, 1853, married Annie Roe in June, 1876; Ella Steele, born May, 1845; Hontas Virginia, born Feb., 1857; Edwin Thornton, born Dec., 1858; Fannie, born Oct., 1860; Mary Logan, born Oct., 1863, married William O. Davis Feb., 1887, and Ulyssus. Jr., born April, 1866, married first Genevieve McDougal, second Anabel Scearce.

Judge Edwin S. Craig and Hontas Thornton had no children, but reared Mason Craig, a daughter of Judge Ed Craig by a former marriage. She is the present occupant of the old Thornton home in Versailles.

Edward Kavanaugh Thornton and Lucrecia Hobbs had Wilbur Hobbs, born March, 1862, married Laura Hiter in 1884; David, born 1864, married Catharine Haley Jan., 1885; Stanley, born Sept., 1867, married Virginia Woodson, Oct., 1888; James, born July, 1870, and Edward Thornton, born Feb., 1876. These boys live in Kansas City and are associated with banking institutions there.

Woodford Railey Thornton and Lucy Dupuy Bailey had no children, and Charles Randolph Thornton died unmarried.

David I. Porter and Eleanor Thornton moved to Independence, Mo., to reside in 1857. During the Civil War, owing to their strong southern sympathies, their home was burned over their heads by Kansas Jayhawkers, who confiscated their personalty

and sent their negroes across the Kansas line. They returned to Kentucky and remained until 1879, when they moved to Sedalia, Mo.

David Thornton, Sr., learned the saddler's trade in his youth, and operated a shop for a limited time, but early in his business career engaged in the banking business, and was for thirty years or more president of the Woodford Bank. He represented the county in both branches of the Legislature, and was an honored member of the Methodist church from its organization until his death. He was a modest, dignified and unassuming citizen, respected by every one who knew him, and was altogether a man of great influence in the community. He died in 1873 in his 78th year.

James Thornton, Jr., and Mary Elliott had Theodore, who married Margaret Smarr; Nannie, who married Judge Berrywick Craig and lived in Versailles. ·Theodore and Margaret Smarr Thornton resided at Midway and they had Ann T., who married Lee P. Thompson, and Thomas and Walter Thornton. Berrywick Craig and Nannie Thornton had Nettie, Alma and several sons.

Thomas Fisher Thornton, born in 1812, died July, 1849, and his first wife, Agnes Wingfield Steele, daughter of John and Catherine Railey Steele, born Sept., 1816, had an only daughter, Susan Catherine Thornton, born Sept., 1836, married Sandy Brown in 1856, and they had Charles Rowland, who married first Mamie Edwards, who was a niece of President Lincoln's wife; second Grace Hatch; Agnes Steele,

George Adams, Robert Alexander, and Thornton Lee Brown.

Thomas Fisher Thornton and his second wife, Mary Blackburn, had these children: Mary Belle, who married James A. Edwards May, 1860; Agnes who married William W. George, Jr., Oct., 1860; David Laws, who served in Morgan's command throughout the Civil War and married Lucy Mathews Nov., 1892, and Elizabeth, who married Henry George in 1869.

The above Mary Anderson Blackburn, the second wife of Thomas Fisher Thornton, was a daughter of the Rev. *John Newton Blackburn, and a granddaughter of the Rev. Gideon Blackburn. Both of these men were of the Presbyterian faith, but neither confined himself to the pulpit, each devoting much time to teaching. The Rev. John Newton Blackburn taught at Griers Creek church and also at old Macedonia church, that was, I think, built on one corner of the farm of Thos. Railey, who lived upon the heights overlooking Clifton. While at Griers creek teaching he and his daughter, Mary Anderson, lived in the home of P. I. and Judith Woodson Railey. At Macedonia they lived in the home of John Berryman and Jane Railey, and the Raileys and Berrymans were among his pupils.

James A. Edwards and Mary Belle Thornton had David Thornton Edwards, who married Wilyou B. Macey; Elizabeth, James A., Jr., and Thomas T.

William W. George, Jr., and Agnes Thornton had Abner Hunter, Ernest T. and Alexander L. George.

David Laws Thornton and Lucy Mathews had Janette, Marion and David L., Jr.

Alexander Laws Thornton and Janette Markham had these children: Sallie, who married Randolph Railey, III; Charles, who was four years in the Confederate service, and died unmarried; Catharine, who married Joseph B. Lewis, and they have a son, Thornton Lewis; Mamie, who married Richard Lyle, who have several children.

Alexander L. Thornton was many years the owner of a livery business on Main street, and was a live stock commission merchant. He died in 1877, and his wife died in 1902. She was a niece of William Fleming Markham, a merchant at Versailles in 1830, and a sister of John Markham, who also was a merchant of Versailles before the Civil War.

When James Thornton, the pioneer of this line of the family came to Kentucky, about 1810, he gave freedom to his slaves before leaving Delaware. His sons, David and James, by the first marriage, were mere boys, the former about ten and the latter about five years of age. They crossed the mountains in a private conveyance, and at Pittsburg embarked on a flatboat for Louisville, but finding only a village there that was surrounded by a flat malarial country, which was not regarded as conducive to health, they drifted up into Woodford county, where he entered his second matrimonial venture within a short period of time. Here he reared his two sons by a former marriage, and a large family

*See page 294, 319.

of children by the second marriage, but in after years, accompanied by a part of his family, he moved to Springfield, Ohio. The two older sons, David and James, Jr., remained in Woodford, as did several of the children by the second marriage.

In 1807 three brothers, William, Oliver and George Douglas Brown, were residents in county Derry, in "Ould Ireland," but during that year they set sail for America; the youngest of the brothers, George Douglas, had not yet attained his majority. Soon after their arrival in this country they came to Kentucky, William and George Douglas settling at Georgetown, while Oliver chose Frankfort as his abiding place for a short time, where he was employed in erecting one of the early buildings that housed the Legislature and state officials, but not the present old capital, that was erected in 1827-28.

Oliver was born in 1767 and died in 1837; William was born in 1769, and died in 1845, and George Douglas Brown was born in 1787, and died in 1862. William married Jane Adams, of Georgetown, a widow, who was the mother of three daughters by a former marriage to Alexander Adams. Their son, William Brown, Jr., married Sallie Ferguson, and a son of this couple was William Reynolds Brown, a Presbyterian minister, who married Mary Barkley, of Danville.

Oliver Brown married Nancy Garrett, and their son, Douglas Brown, married his cousin, Martha Brown, daughter of George Douglas Brown and Mary Adams. For his services in connection with the building of the "Old Mansion House" and state capitol, at Frankfort, Oliver Brown was given 300 acres of land in the outskirts of Versailles, and in 1814 came to Woodford County to reside. I understand that Douglas Stevenson, a descendant, owns a part of the original tract at this time.

George Douglas Brown, the youngest of the three brothers, married Mary Adams, step-daughter of his brother William, which made her a sister-in-law of her step-father. They had nine children, as follows: Jane, who married Henry Mount and moved to Elkhart, Ill.; Mary, who married William Stewart Hunter, Jr., of Woodford County (see Hunter sketch); John McKinney Brown, who married Ellen Potts, of Versailles (see Menzies sketch); Robert Ward Brown, who married Mary Hart; Sandy Brown, who married Susan Catharine Thornton (see Thornton, Steele and Railey), and Martha M. Brown, who married first her cousin, Douglas Brown and lived and died in the original Brown home in the suburbs of Versailles on Lexington pike; second, Captain Robert Willis, who was for many years after returning from service in the Confederacy, a popular merchant of Versailles.

Mary Brown and William Stewart Hunter, Jr., had Mollie and John B. Hunter.

John McKinney Brown and Ellen Potts had Jennie, who married ——— Harner.

Robert Ward Brown and Mary Hart had a daughter, who married Jerry McMeekin, a son, Hart Brown, and several daughters, who live in Richmond, Va.

Sandy Brown and Susan Catharine Thornton had Charles Railey, who married Mary Edwards, a niece of the wife of President Lincoln; Robert A., who married Kate Eberhart; Thornton L., Agnes Steele, and George.

Martha Brown and her first husband, Douglas Brown, had Preston, who married Ruth (Bell) Wilson, widow of Charles Wilson, and they reside on the old homestead; Sandy, Ollie and Normie, who married William Stevenson.

After his marriage to Susan Catharine Thornton Sandy Brown moved with his family to Booneville, Mo., but later removed to St. Louis, where he was engaged in business until his death in 1893. He and all of his brothers possessed rare musical talents, each playing on some musical instrument, hence their presence was an added charm to any company or gathering in and near Versailles for many years prior to the Civil War.

While the west was still in its infancy Sandy Brown made two trips overland to California. The first venture across the plains occurred in 1849, during the gold fever, and this trip was repeated in 1852. He had the pleasure of introducing to the citizens of the Pacific slope the first thoroughbred horses seen in that part of the country.

In the May Register I gave a brief sketch of the Lee family, who came among the earliest emigrants from Virginia to Kentucky, and settled in Woodford County. Major John Lee*

*See page 271.

was one of the founders of Versailles, and I determined to continue my investigations, as I was certain that he and General Robert E. Lee had a common ancestor in America. He has had no descendants in Woodford County for more than a half century, and it was difficult to locate any one who could tell me more than what Collins said of him, hence I had but little to write of him, either on a rising or descending scale. However, I recently got in touch with some of the kinship from without the state, who gave me some additional data which enables me to write more fully of this distinguished family. None of the families who came to Virginia produced a sturdier or more honorable class of citizens than did the Lees.

These are the additional facts to supplement what appeared in the May issue:

Col. Richard Lee, wife unknown to any of my correspondents, was the first of the name in America. He came from England, where the name was prominent among the cavaliers and other leading spirits for generations. His children were: 1st Henry, 2nd John Francis, 3rd Richard, Jr., 4th William, 5th Thomas, 6th Hancock, 7th Elizabeth, and 8th Charles. General Robert E. Lee descended from Col. Richard Lee, as follows: His son, Henry Lee and Mary Bland, she a granddaughter of Col. William Randolph and Mary Isham; then Henry Lee, Jr., and Lucy Grimes; then "Light Horse" Harry Lee and Anne Carter; then Robert E. Lee, who married Mary Randolph Custis, a granddaughter of the widow Martha Custis, who married President Washington.

General Zachary Taylor also descended from Col. Richard Lee through his son, Hancock Lee and Sarah Elizabeth Allerton; then Elizabeth Lee and Zachary Taylor, Sr., of Orange County, Va.; then Col. Richard Taylor and Sarah Dabney Strother, daughter of William Strother of "Orange," who settled in Woodford County, and Sarah (Bailey) Pannill (see Strothers); then President Zachary Taylor, who married Margaret Smith.

Major John Lee, of Woodford County, a pioneer, came from Col. Richard Lee also, through Hancock Lee and Sarah Elizabeth Allerton; then Hancock Lee, Jr., and Mary Willis; then Major John Lee, who married first Letitia Atwell, second Elizabeth Bell, of Virginia.

Major John Lee was not only one of the founders of Versailles, but was also one of the leading spirits in all improvements in the county until his death during the winter of 1801-2. Before coming to Kentucky he was a major in the Second Virginia troops. His first wife was a Virginian; his second wife was a daughter of Captain Thomas Bell of Virginia, whose wife, Elizabeth Taylor, was a daughter of Zachary Taylor, Sr., of Orange County, Va., and Elizabeth Lee, his wife; so they were cousins. Major John Lee married Elizabeth Bell in Dec., 1781, likely just before he came to Woodford County.

Hancock Lee, Jr., the father of Major John Lee, of Woodford County, came to Kentucky with Cyrus McCracken (see McCracken sketch), as early as 1776, and they were the founders of Leestown, which they located one mile northwest of Frankfort. Each of them built a cabin at that point, at that time, where they made their headquarters, and where they purposed to locate their families when they made their contemplated trip to Virginia and back. Mary Willis, the wife of Hancock Lee, was a daughter of Col. Henry Willis, of "Willis Hill," Va., and Mildred Washington, his wife, a kinswoman of the President. Cyrus McCracken's wife was Elizabeth ——.

Unfortunately circumstances of a serious nature intervened that interfered with the consummation of the plans of these two men. After building their cabins Cyrus McCracken decided to join the command of Gen. George Rogers Clark, who had planned an expedition against the Piqua Indians, and he was killed in one of the engagements. Some years later Captain Virgil McCracken, son of Cyrus, accompanied his mother and the family to Kentucky and settled on Glenns creek, in Woodford County, about three miles from Versailles, and it was either he, or one of the name, who was the first husband of Opelia Bohannon, daughter of Dr. Richard Bohannon and Fannie Menzies. (See McCracken and Menzies sketches.)

Captain Virgil McCracken raised a company of troops, joined the regiment of Col. Allen, of Shelby County, and was mortally wounded at the battle of the "River Raisin."

Although I find no record of Hancock Lee, Jr., returning to Kentucky, his kinsmen, Willis Lee and Willis Atwell Lee both came to Kentucky and settled at Leestown prior to 1800. The former was killed by Indians, and the latter was an office holder at Frankfort during his entire life.

In the county of Northumberland, Parish of Great Wycomico, and within sight of Chesapeake Bay is an estate and mansion called "Ditchley." It was built by Hancock Lee, Sr., son of Col. Richard, about 1720. He married first Mary Kendall, daughter of Col. William Kendall, of "Newport House," Virginia, who was for many years a Burgess; second Sarah Elizabeth Allerton, daughter of Col. Isaac Allerton, whose grandfather, Isaac Allerton, Sr., came over in the Mayflower in 1620.

Major John Lee had only one child by the first marriage to Letitia Atwell, whose name was Willis Lee, and he married Mary McAfee. By the second marriage, to Elizabeth Bell, were John Hancock Lee, who married his cousin, Anne Lee, daughter of Henry; Thos. Bell Lee, who, if married, I find no evidence of it; Mary Belle Lee about 1805 married Dr. Andrew F. Price; **Sarah Allerton Lee, who married about 1806 John J. Crittenden; Elizabeth Taylor Lee, who married about 1812 Dr. Lyddall Wilkerson; Lucinda Lee‡ who married about 1818 Senator Call; Matilda Lee, who married about 1817† Samuel McDowell Wallace, son of Judge Caleb Wallace, of Midway, and Lewis Lee, who married Sarah Temple.

*Capt. Thomas Bell, the father of Elizabeth, who married Major John Lee, came with his wife, Elizabeth Taylor, to Woodford with the earliest settlers and owned a farm in the county, but I am not able to locate it, I am sorry to say. In 1810 his family consisted of four members and he owned nine slaves. He was a kinsman of James Bell, who was also a pioneer, with a family of six members and owned seventeen slaves that he gave employment on his farm. Both drew pensions.

I am under the impression that one of the sons of Major John Lee once owned the farm that was so long owned by Squire Henry Ferguson, that corners at Harmony church.

———

An interesting man in Woodford County in 1810 was Col. Tunstall Quarles. At that time he owned a farm in the Pisgah neighborhood, owned fifteen slaves, and had a family consisting of five persons. In 1816 he was a member of the Pisgah church, and I am quite sure he served in the war of 1812. He was a member of the Kentucky Legislature during the session of 1796; was in Congress 1817-20, and was a Presidential elector in 1829.

James Quarles was also a resident of Woodford County in 1810, and likely a brother of Tunstall Quarles. He also owned a farm and six slaves, but only had two in his family, perhaps him and his wife. He drew a pension, but I think it came as the eldest son of a father who rendered service in the Revolution, rather than any personal

---

*I think this Thomas Bell did not come to Kentucky. See pages 281 and 358. The wife of Thomas Bell, who came to Woodford County, was Elizabeth Weir. If he did come, he was not there in 1810.
**See Crittendens, page 50.
†Page 60.
‡See page 271.

service that he had rendered. At that time the eldest son, according to the laws of Virginia, was the beneficiary in a war service claim. I have sought in and out of the state to get a line on descendants of these two men, but was unable to find a descendant. What I present here I have scrapped from several books and papers.

There was a Tunstall Quarles, Jr., who represented Pulaski County in the House of Representatives in 1811-12, and again in 1828; was a Senator from that district in 1840; in Congress later, but I have not learned his relationship to Col. Tunstall Quarles, of Woodford. The Quarles family of Frankfort came originally from Union County and know nothing of the Woodford County family of that name.

Since writing the above I learn that Tunstall Quarles, Jr., organized, Sept. 1, 1812, a company No. 3, which was with regiment 2 in the war.*

Captain John Christopher was in Woodford County at an early date. In 1810 he owned a farm, four likely slaves and his family consisted of six members. He enlisted in the war of 1812, commanding a company of troops under General Marquis Calmes in the battle of the Thames.

Lewis Perry was of Revolutionary stock, and was born in Culpeper County, Va., about 1754. He and his wife, Jane Bourne, came to Kentucky in 1784 and settled on a farm in Woodford County. In 1810 he owned the farm upon which he lived, and ten slaves, and there were five members in his

family. He and his wife lived to a ripe old age and they were buried in a private graveyard on the farm. When their children married they moved to Jessamine, Bath and Rowan counties, but Catharine married Samuel H. Shouse, Sr., and they were the parents of Samuel H. Shouse, Jr., who twice represented the county in the Legislature during the '80's.

Samuel H. Shouse, Jr., married Mary Orr in 1857, who was a descendant of pioneer settlers of Woodford County. They had Eunice, Fannie, James, Albert, Henry and Mamie Shouse.

I know of no other descendants of Lewis Perry and Jane Bourne who have been recent residents of the county.

Samuel Pepper married Mahala Perry, but I am not sure that she was a daughter of Lewis Perry. They were the parents of Col. R. P. Pepper, the distiller, of Frankfort, Ky.

The Samuel family—several brothers and sisters—came to Woodford County during the latter part of the 18th century, where they located. They came from Virginia about the same time that the Wares, Reads and others came, and were prominent citizens. I shall refer to them from the standpoint mainly of court records, as I have not been able to get much from descendants.

In 1794 Giles Samuel was in Woodford County and according to will book "A," page 108, he was guardian of Larkin Samuel and Peter Samuel, orphans of Jesse Samuel. The account was examined by William Ware.

Oct. 14, 1798, the estate of John Samuel, deceased, was appraised by An-

*See page 341 for Quarles history. More complete.

thony Bartlett, John Scott and Richard Taylor, will book "B," page 71.

Will book "C," page 40, Lucy Samuel was appointed administratrix of John Samuel, deceased.

Dec. 24, 1795, a marriage license was issued to William Samuel to wed Judith Dupuy.

Dec. 22, 1794, the will of Peter Samuel was dated, and the Franklin County records show that the will of Peter Samuel, of Woodford County, was probated. It names wife, Susanna; sons, John and Reuben and daughter Anne Samuel.

Will book "C," page 107, estate of John Samuel, deceased, appraised by Richard Taylor, Thomas Todd and Edmund Ware; heirs, Lucy Samuel, the widow, Spillsby, Betsy, married a Loughborough, John, Fanny, Larkin, married a Graham, Kitty, married an Anderson, Lucinda, married a Welch, and Richard Samuel.

I think the most of the Samuel family who came to Woodford County had sold their interests and moved away before the Mexican War, some of them locating in Frankfort, but many of them left the state.

Lucy Samuel, widow of John, was living on a farm in Woodford County in 1810 with seven members in her family. She owned seven slaves. I think the late Ed Samuel, cashier of the Bank of Kentucky, at Frankfort, and Miss Annie Samuel, who is employed in one of the state departments, are descendants.

Reuben Samuel, who married a sister of Gov. Letcher, was a brother of Sarah Samuel, who married William Ware, of Woodford County (see Ware

sketch), and Catharine Samuel, who married Richard Coleman, formerly of Woodford County, but lived in the greater port of his life in Frankfort, and they had a brother, William Samuel, whose daughter, Elizabeth Anne Samuel, married John William Blanton, of Woodford County (see Blanton sketch).

Sarah Samuel and William Ware had a daughter, Elizabeth Ware, who married John Bacon, of Franklin County. John Bacon and Elizabeth Ware had Ann Apperson Bacon, born in March, 1800, died October, 1888, married the Rev. Philip Fall, and they had Elizabeth Sarah Fall, who married Edmund Haynes Taylor, many years cashier of the old Kentucky Bank of Frankfort. Edmund H. Taylor and Elizabeth Fall were the parents of Mrs. Jouett Taylor Cannon, secretary-treasurer of the Kentucky Historical Society; the late Philip Fall Taylor and Edmund Haynes Taylor, Jr., (married Mary Arnett, of Woodford County) who resides at Tampa, Florida. William R. Fall, son of the Rev. Philip Fall, married Edmonia Taylor and they were the parents of the present U. S. Senator, A. B. Fall, of New Mexico.

John and Lucy Woolfolk Samuel were married in 1798 and the following are some of their children, if not all. Betsy, married Thomas V. Loughborough; Lucinda, married William Welch; Frances, married William Gibson.

Thos. V. Loughborough and Betsy Samuel had Isabella, who married her cousin, William Gibson, Jr., son of William Gibson and Frances Samuel. William and Isabella had Thomas L. Gibson, who married Elizabeth Ayres; Preston L., who married Mary Miller Wilson; S. J., who married Cynthia Thompson, and Lula.

William Welch and Lucinda Samuel had Capt. Gibson Welch, who married Annie Fogg, daughter of Captain Elijah Fogg and Ann Ware.

John Samuel was one of Woodford's pioneer citizens and he settled on a farm at Ducker Station, known for many years as the Gibson farm, and it only recently passed out of possession of descendants, Preston L. Gibson being the last to own it. Three or four generations of the relationship are buried there in a private burial ground.

WOODFORD COUNTY

By W. E. Railey.

PART FIVE

Previous to the Revolution the Holemans were residents of Kent County, Maryland. It is more than probable that the name was originally spelled Wholeman, meaning a man of sterling worth, but now, and for many years, the various families as a rule have dropped the letter "e" and the prevailing custom is to spell it Holman.

In 1774 Henry and Edward Holeman accompanied by their nephew, George Holeman, and his friend, Richard La-Rue (the two latter taken by the two former as orphans to rear), left their home in Kent County, Md., and moved to Pennsylvania, but in the early spring of 1776 they descended the Ohio river and pitched tents at the mouth of the Kentucky river when that country was a dense wilderness (so stated by George Holeman in his military history). Here they planted a small clearing in corn, that had been prepared by another, at no distant date, but abandoned for good and sufficient reasons that soon dawned upon these new adventurers who likewise departed without waiting, even for the crop to mature, their surroundings becoming more threatening as the days rolled by, the war clouds looming up rather than rolling by. They moved cautiously up the Kentucky river until

reaching Clemens Station, near the present site of Georgetown, where they remained for a short period, then removed to the station at Harrodstown (now Harrodsburg), where they were in the spring of 1777 when a party of Indians attacked a sugar camp at Shawnee Springs, four miles from Harrods Station, killing William Ray and capturing Thomas Shores. Gen. James Ray escaped and appraised the Garrison at once of their danger. The fort was besieged the following day and an intense battle was staged which lasted for some hours. The garrison hastily banded a company in readiness under the command of Genl. George Rogers Clark, with Captain Harrod, Lieutenant Levi Todd, Ensign Francis McConnell and First Sergeant Edward Holeman filling the other stations, and they defended the fort with great credit and skill. Quite a number were wounded, among them Col. Hugh McGary, who owned the camp at Shawnee Springs, and John Guess (see George Holeman's Military History). During that summer another engagement took place in which George Holeman rendered service and Ensign Francis McConnell was killed. Quite a number were wounded. Though Major George Rogers Clark commanded the troops, the organization was known as "Harrod's company." About the spring of 1779 the Indians ceased their hostilities, and on Feb. 11, 1781, a wagoner by the name of Evan Hinton was sent from the Block House at Louisville to Boone's old station for provisions, who also had a lot of empty barrels to be used for salting down meat for the troops. George Holeman, then sixteen years of age, and Richard LaRue, nineteen years of age, were sent as guards to protect the wagon from depredations of the Indians who were suspected of lurking along the route through which they were to pass. Evan Hinton drove the wagon, while LaRue walked a few paces ahead and Holeman about the same distance behind. As they ascended a hill about eight miles from Louisville, Hinton heard some one say: "Whoa." He stopped the horses and immediately the notorious Simon Girty emerged from his concealment, accompanied by thirteen Indians who demanded surrender or an immediate forfeit of life. Of course the little party, so greatly outnumbered, made a virtue of necessity and surrendered. The wagon and its contents were left by the roadside but the horses and the prisoners made a hasty dash for the Ohio river, under direction of their captors, where they crossed and continued the journey to Camp Waupacanatta, Ohio. Here each of the prisoners had to "run the gauntlet," and each made a hairbreadth escape. At night the three prisoners were tied together for safety. Hinton, who was desperate to see his wife and children, loosed himself and made his escape, only to be recaptured

and meet death by means of the stake. The scalp of Hinton was threateningly exhibited to Holeman and LaRue with assurances that they would meet the fate of their "red-headed friend" if they attempted to escape.

One of the Indians adopted Holeman as a son, another adopted LaRue as a brother, the former having lost a son and the latter a brother. For quite a time they were confined to that part of the country that bordered along the Wabash river and around Detroit, Mich. Finally George Holeman learned that the Indians at Waupacanatta were destitute of food, and diplomatically suggested that he had a rich uncle at the falls of the Ohio (referring to his uncle Henry) whom he could influence in their behalf if they would furnish him a guide to direct his course. He was at once dispatched upon the mission that he assured them would relieve their condition. After reaching his destination he was ransomed by Genl. George R. Clark. LaRue made his escape about the same time after a captivity of three years and a half.

Afterwards George Holeman served with General Clark up the Wabash river relieving many garrisons before their return. In 1786 or 87 he married Elizabeth Fisher, of Louisville, and moved to Woodford County, where his two sons, Joseph and William, were born. Joseph in Oct., 1788, and William later. William was a Methodist minister who was known in early days as "Father Holeman." He served in the War of 1812 and was captain of a company.

George Holeman was a citizen of Woodford County from 1787 until he moved to Wayne County, Indiana, in 1804. His signature is on the old will of his uncle Henry (who had also moved to Woodford County), in the county clerk's office at Versailles. Richard La-Rue, who was a resident of Woodford County, also moved to Wayne County, Ind. I am not able to say when Henry Holeman and his family moved to Woodford, but it is certain that he entered land at an early day, but owing to title troubles that resulted in the forfeiture of their claims by Boone, Kenton and other contemporaries, he was caught in the same net and all of the Holemans lost their claims too.

Henry Holeman had a son, Edward, born in Kent County, Md., in 1760, who married Abigail Williams, and this couple had a son, Henry Holeman, Jr., who married first Eliza Jones, by whom he had two sons and five daughters. His second marriage was to Nancy Nash, of Calloway County, Mo., about 1825. He had another son, Jesse L., who was born in Danville, Ky., in 1784.

David Darst, son-in-law of Henry Holeman, Sr., was one of the executors of the estate and it was he who filed the suit against Col. Thomas Marshall to recover five hundred acres of land that Col. Marshall had surveyed in interference with the one thousand acres Henry Holeman had entered. The suit was filed in Frankfort and was in the courts for quite a length of time but Col. Marshall finally won.

The will of Henry Holeman was dated March 6, 1789, in Woodford County, and witnessed by James Fisher, Edward Holeman, Sarah Williams and George Holeman. He was killed by Indians about August, 1789. In his will

he named Edward Holeman, David Darst, and Richard LaRue as executors. This will, filed and probated in the old stone building, the first district court room, which is yet standing on the Sam Nuchols farm, on the Shryocks Ferry pike, one and a half miles from Versailles, which was then called "Big Spring on the Frankfort trail." (See Nuckols sketch.) Cave Johnson was the clerk of the Kentucky District Court. The personal estate of Henry Holeman was then estimated at 218 pounds and nine shillings. The maiden name of Henry Holeman's wife is not known, but she is called Jane in his will. Their children were Nicholas, Edward, Rozetta, Elizabeth, Mary, Cornelius, William, Isaac, Jesse, Jane, Martha, Sallie and Nancy. Sallie married John Turner, Nancy married John Scearce, Isaac married Susanna ———, Rozetta married David Darst, who was born in Shenandoah County, Va., Dec., 1757, and Rozetta was born in Maryland January, 1763, and died in Calloway County, Mo., Nov., 1848. David Darst came to Woodford County in 1784 and in 1798 removed with his wife and seven children to Charles County, Mo., settling in a river valley that is yet known as "Darst's Bottom." It was in the vicinity of Daniel Boone's home, who also lost out in Kentucky on the question of land titles. These two men and their families went to Missouri about the same time, and when that territory was yet under Spanish dominion. Some of the leading men of this state gave David Darst complimentary letters of introduction to the Spanish authorities at St. Louis, which enabled him to obtain several grants of land for himself and his children. The following were the names of his children: Mary, Elizabeth, Absalom, Isaac, Sarah, Jacob, Samuel, Nancy and David H.

Jacob later went to Texas and was killed at the side of Col. Crockett, at the battle of the Alamo.

Henry Holman's son Isaac, remained in Woodford and died in the county, but his (Henry's) sons Cornelius, William and Jesse Lynch, finally moved to Indiana. Judge Jesse L. was only about four years old when his father was killed in an effort to relieve a beleaguered blockhouse in Woodford County which was surrounded by hostile Indians in the summer of 1789, but Jesse L. was plucky and persevering. He obtained the benefit of a common school education, and later took a course in higher mathematics and general literature, after which he studied law under Henry Clay. When he moved to Indiana in 1820 he was regarded as a successful lawyer and was appointed Judge of the Territorial Court. Aurora, Indiana, was of his making and he abided there. He and his son, William Steele Holeman, each made quite a reputation in the Congress of the U. S. William Steele being a co-laborer with our own Jo Blackburn for many years, and through the public prints was known as the "Watch Dog of the U. S. Treasury." He was in the National House during the times of Tilden and Cleveland and I often heard Capt. Jo Blackburn say he would be President.

The home of Jesse Lynch Holeman, at Aurora, Ind., was, and is yet I am told, known as "Holeman's Hill." William Holeman, his brother, moved from Woodford to Ripley, Ind., where he died. Isaac lived and died in Woodford County. Cornelius owned the farm purchased of him by Willis Field, who lived and died there, and it is now the property of the heirs of the late Willis W. Field. It is situated on the road from Griers Creek church to lock No. 5, and bounded by the farms of Edward Trabue, Col. William Steele, Major Herman Bowmar, Sr., Randolph Railey, Sr., Charles Railey and William Railey, Sr. In 1826 Cornelius sold the property to James Dupuy and moved to Indiana; in 1840 James Dupuy sold to Logan Railey, who sold it in 1845 to Willis Field. Cornelius Holeman was supposed to have been killed by an Indian while surveying in Indiana. It is my impression that Isaac Holeman lived on the same road as Cornelius, but on the opposite side and not far from Griers Creek church.

Daniel Holeman was also a citizen of Woodford and a cousin of the sons of Henry and Jane Holeman. In 1810 he had a family of three and owned a farm and eleven slaves. He was a veteran of the Revolution and a good citizen. His son, John Holeman, married Betsy Duvall, of Huguenot extract, and this couple had a son, James Duvall Holeman, who was the father of Frederick V. Holeman, of Portland, Oregon, a man very prominent in the affairs of that city at present.

The above Daniel Holeman was a son of Thomas Holeman, of Surrey County, N. C. Daniel's son, John, left Woodford County for Oregon about 1843.

———

James Finnie and John Finnie, Sr., were early settlers in Woodford County, arriving some years after the Revolution, in which war their father, who was an Englishman, took an active part. James owned a farm, had eight members in his family, and was the owner of seven slaves in 1810; and John, Sr., had a farm, eleven members in his family, and owned nine slaves.

One of these men had a son, Elijah, who married Pollie Cole, daughter of *Richard Cole. Elijah Finnie and Pollie Cole had a son, George Washington Finnie, who married Martha Ann Donovan; and this couple had a daughter, Mary Finnie, who married Henry Shipp, of Midway. George Washington Finnie died when his daughter was a child and left no data relating to his ancestors.

Henry Shipp and his wife, Mary Finnie, have a son, Henry, who has been L. & N. agent at Midway for several years. This brief sketch will have to suffice as a testimony to the early Finnies of Woodford County, who were well-to-do men.

Daniel Jackson Williams, Sr., came to Woodford County about the time of the War of 1812, or soon thereafter. He was one of the sons of Daniel Williams, who came from Virginia soon after the Revolution and settled in Pendleton County, Ky. He married Sallie Hicks and though many children were born of this union, only two, Daniel Jackson, Jr., and John Hicks, lived to years of maturity.

For many years Daniel Jackson Williams, Sr., was one of the leading citizens of Woodford County. He owned a large farm to which he gave a liberal

share of his attention, but he also taught school and devoted a part of his time to surveying. He was regarded as a man of high character and rare intellectual force, possessing a wonderful mathematical mind. He was profoundly imbued with the Christian faith, and was a consistent member of the Baptist church.

Just at a time when he was at the zenith of his usefulness he received a fall in an attempt to mount his horse, from which he never recovered.

Daniel Jackson Williams, Jr., received his early training under the tutorage of his father, who for many years taught the high school in Woodford County. Daniel, Jr., entered Georgetown College, from which he was graduated at sixteen years of age. Subsequently he entered Transylvania University, where he took a course in both law and medicine, graduating from that institution. On return to his home he engaged with his father in farming, but found time, as did his father before him, to teach and survey, possessing as he did, in a large measure, the mental and other qualities of the parent. Prior to and during the Civil War he was very successful, and acquired quite a fortune in real estate, stock and money. Before the war he affiliated with the Whigs, but during the conflict his sympathies were with the South, and after the conflict of arms he espoused the cause of Democracy until his death.

He too was noted for his executive ability and fine business judgment. When he died, I think in 1881, he owned 2,000 acres of land in the county and owned much real estate in other

*See pages 65, 253.

states. Like his father, he was a believer in the doctrines of the Baptist church, and was a member of Glenns Creek church. He was one of the founders of the old Woodford Bank and one of its directors from its organization until his death. In him the Cleveland Orphan School had a good friend, and he donated $15,000 toward its maintenance.

He was born in 1821, and was twice married, first to Amanda Weathers, in 1851; second to Elizabeth McClure. By the first marriage was a daughter, Laura, and by the second was a daughter Elizabeth. Laura married the Rev. Frank Baker, a Baptist minister who resided on the Frankfort pike just outside the limits of Versailles, and Elizabeth married John O. Rogers, whose farm adjoined that of the Rev. Frank Baker, and near the old toll gate.

James Arnett came to Woodford County from Virginia about 1812 and was classed as one of our early settlers. He located his home in the Clover Bottom section, but I have not been able to ascertain the maiden name of his wife. They had a son, William L. Arnett, who married Sallie White and lived near the Jessamine County line, where John Arnett, their son, was born in 1835. This son engaged in farming until 1862, at which time he enlisted in the Confederacy, was a member of Company A, the famous Second Kentucky Cavalry, under command of General John H. Morgan. He was captured in 1863 at Buffington Island, and remained a prisoner for fifteen months when he was exchanged and immediately rejoined his

regiment and served with gallantry until July, 1865.

After the war he resumed the duties pertaining to his farm, which he conducted successfully until his death. He was a brave soldier, a good friend and an honest citizen who possessed a supreme contempt for people of small calibre, and for that reason many people classed him as among the eccentric type of citizenship.

John Amsden was born in Sheffield, Mass., in 1809. He came to Woodford County during the year 1839 and was for many years one of the most popular merchant-tailors ever engaged in that business in Versailles. He continued in this business until 1872, but in 1867 he established the Bank of Amsden and George, the partner being Henry George, son of Judge William W. George and Bettie Bohannon. In 1878 this bank was chartered and increased its capital stock, which largely extended the scope of its business, commanding today a liberal share of the business of the community, and enjoying the entire confidence of the public.

John Amsden was the only son of John Amsden, Sr., and Lydia Kearney, of Massachusetts. He married in 1843 Lucrecia Lewis, of New York, and they had two sons, John, born in 1844, and James P., born in 1847, both of whom were popular business men, and both interested in the bank after the retirement of Henry George, in 1868.

John Amsden was prominent in Masonic circles, being a Knight Templar, was an Odd Fellow and a member of the Episcopal church.

Both of his sons were in the service

of the Confederacy, and popular in business and fraternal circles, prominent Masons.

William Edward Ashmore was an only son of Walter Ewell Ashmore and Behethland Ford, of Virginia. He was born in Prince William County, Va., April, 1794. His father was of English extract and was born in Fairfax County, Va.

In 1816 William Edward Ashmore moved to Woodford County from the county of Mason, from which county he entered the service of the war of 1812. His grandmother was a daughter of the Rev. James Keith and Mary Isham Randolph, of Tuckahoe, Va., hence he was a second cousin of Chief Justice John Marshall. As a young man he served in the office of county clerk under John McKinney, Jr., who was clerk of the county court, but after reaching mature years he became a farmer, owning a large tract of land through which both railroads now run, the brick residence standing today midway between the two depots. Two of his daughters, Mary and Lucy, reside there now, and own a part of the original tract of land.* He also engaged extensively in the manufacture of hemp.

He was twice married, first to Alice Jackson, daughter of Hon. John Jackson and Alice Young; second to Letitia Lafon. By the first marriage was Alice, who married M. J. Newman. By the second marriage was Letitia, who married L. M. Nutt; Florence, who married William J. Cowles; James Keith, Mary and Lucy. James Keith entered the Confederate service, and his father

being such an uncompromising southern sympathizer, took residence in Louisiana for the duration of the war, but returned to the county at its conclusion and resumed farming. For a number of years he was Master Commissioner of the Circuit Court, and died at quite an advanced age, in 187—. His daughter Mary owned the old Capt. Nicholas Lafon place at Frankfort, opposite the Feeble-Minded School until 1919. Capt. Lafon was her grandfather.

William Alexander, father of Robert Alexander, the first owner of Woodburn Stock Farm, remained in Virginia for several years after Robert came to Woodford County. In fact he did not arrive in the county until 1816, coming from Richmond. He at first stopped with Robert, but during that year four of his children by a second marriage, one girl and three boys, came to the county also. The three sons settled on farms that were in the vicinity of "Woodburn." The names of these four children were: Andrew Jonathan, who married a daughter of Gov. Madison; Charles, who married —— ——; John Regis, who married —— ——, and Appoline, who married Thomas Hankey, director of the Bank of England.

Andrew Jonathan Alexander settled upon the estate that was for a long period of time the home of Daniel Swigert, and now owned by James Williams, the turfman, immediately back of Spring Station. He owned a sawmill on the branch that ran through the premises, which was standing after the Civil War, the ruins of which may yet

---

*Both have since died, and Dr. Alford Blackburn owns the farm.

be seen. In this saw-mill Andrew Jonathan lost his life while the machinery was in motion, his clothing becoming entangled in the fly-wheel, resulting in a badly mangled body. He and his wife, —— Madison, had these children: George, who married —— ——, and moved to Paducah, where he practiced law; Appoline, who married General Frank Blair and moved to St. Louis, Mo., where he and his family were prominent in social and business circles, and Andrew, who married —— ——, and was in the U. S. Army with the rank of a Major.

Charles Alexander owned the farm at the junction of the Spring Station and Leestown pikes, opposite the Humphrey place. I think Anthony Dey owned this tract for many years.

John Regis Alexander bought from his half-brother, Robert, the farm that was for several generations known as the Gratz farm, a very fine body of land that Regis Alexander called "Roslins." It lies at the intersection of the Lexington and Frankfort and McKee's crossroads pikes. He built the residence on this estate in 1820, a typical southern home surrounded by a variety of beautiful forest trees, and the quaint old designs in flower beds that were constructed under the direction of Regis Alexander are yet to be seen as designed by him—one hundred years after their creation. The house is in perfect condition now and speaks well for the Shipp brothers, who were the designers and builders.

Two years later, or in 1822, John Regis Alexander built a hemp factory at the intersection of these two roads, in which he gave employment to about twenty-five slaves. Primitive methods were then used, hand looms being used in weaving bagging, and a pulley with horse power was used in twisting or spinning the rope. There were quite a number of factories similar to this scattered over the county at that time, but they died with slavery. Many wrecks of these old institutions may yet be seen over the county, while the building here is in perfect condition today, but has been used for a half century for housing hay and tobacco, and sheds for cattle.

In 1840 Regis Alexander built on the old Cole or Leestown road the Presbyterian church known as "Harmony church." Many of the old families of that community—principally Presbyterians—attended services there, among them the Steeles, Blackburns, Fergusons, Lees, Humphries, Scotts, Freemans and Bedfords, but about 1852 this church building was sold to the Baptists and the Presbyterian membership transferred to Midway.

Regis Alexander was married to —— ——, and to them five sons were born, whose names follow: General William Alexander, who moved to Texas and served that state as its Attorney General; Dr. James Alexander, who moved to Paducah; Thomas Biddle Alexander, who moved to Brookport, Ill.; Robert Alexander, who was also prepared for the law and moved to Austin, Texas, where he practiced law; and Charles Alexander, who also moved to Paducah, Ky.

After the death of his first wife John Regis Alexander married Elizabeth Brooks Van de Graffe, sold his fine farm to the Gratz family of Lexington and moved to Paducah, to which point two of his sons had preceded him.

By his second marriage was John Campbell Alexander, who returned to Woodford County about 1890 and bought the old Parrish farm, just across the road from his father's old hemp factory, and he has reared an interesting family of children there. Benjamine Crosby is the present owner of "Roslins," and he has substituted the name "Canewood" for "Roslins."

The Bohannons of Woodford County descended from Duncan Bohannon, of Weymouth, Dorset County, England, and his wife, Sarah ——, was also a native of that country. They emigrated to America, landing at Jamestown, Virginia, in 1690, but finally settled in Kings Parish, King and Queen County.

As a result of the above union the following children were born: [1]Sarah, [2]Judith, [3]William, [4]Duncan, Jr., [5]Robert, [6]Markus, [7]Elliott and [8]Phillis. This data is authentic, being taken from the Register of Kings Parish June 12, 1722, and signed by Henry Bolton, keeper of the records. The original copy is nearly two hundred years old, and in possession of Mrs. John Willis, nee Margaret Bohannon, daughter of James Bohannon and Nellie Harris (see Harris sketch). She was reared at Versailles but is now a resident of Nowater, Oklahoma, and she has, like so many of the former residents of Woodford County, who are now residents of the south and west, shown her pride in keeping alive the past of her ancestry and the worthwhile incidents of the past.

Of the children above named, Robert Bohannon was born in March, 1707, and moved to Bloomfield Parish, Madison County, Va., in 1730. He married Basheba ——, and an only son, Elliott, resulted from that union, in 1729. He married Ann Walker and had these children: Richard, born Dec., 1748; Mildred, born in 1750, married Robert Gaines; Ambrose born in 1752, married —— Gibbs; Elliott, Jr., born in 1753; Anne, born in 1754, married —— Kirtley; John, born in 1756, married —— Lewis; and Mary, born in 1757, married —— Herndon. Of these children, Richard and Elliott, Jr., moved to Kentucky, where, in 1789, they settled in Woodford County.

Richard married in Virginia, Elizabeth Blackburn, sister of George Blackburn, who lived at Spring Station, and the Rev. Gideon Blackburn, of Versailles. Richard and Elizabeth Black-[*]burn Bohannon, after a residence of ten years in Woodford County, removed to Jefferson County, in 1798, where they settled on "Floyd's Fork" of Salt river. This incident was disclosed in a letter written by Elliott, Jr., to a brother in Virginia, said letter sacredly preserved by the Virginia relationship to this day.

Elliott Bohannon, Jr., was also married in Virginia, but I have not been able to learn his wife's maiden name. She died in Virginia, and he married a second wife in Kentucky, but I have not been able to ascertain her maiden name. By the second marriage were: Mary, who married Jeremiah Burton; German, who married Sallie Hamilton, and Albert H. Bohannon, who married Henrietta Clay Long, in 1836, she

*See Blackburn sketch 33rd page.

a daughter of James C. Long and Nancy Berry.

Mary and Jeremiah Burton moved to Jefferson County, where they settled upon a farm in the vicinity of her uncle, Richard Bohannon. German Bohannon and Sallie Hamilton remained in Woodford, where they reared a family of children, one of whom, Susan, married John Stout, Sr., and they had German and John Stout, Jr., Nettie, who married Ben A. Thomas, Jr., of Shelbyville, and others.

Albert H. Bohannon and Henrietta Clay Long also remained in Woodford County on a farm, and they had these children: John Neet, born in 1837; Sarah Ann, born in 1839; Willett, born in 1841; Albert H., Jr., born in 1843; James Long, born in 1850, married Nellie Harris; Richard G., born in 1852; Claude; Frank, who married Lelia Reid, and Mamie. Frank has been deputy sheriff so long that he is a kind of fixture in that office.

Notwithstanding the present generation tell me there was no relationship between Richard and Elliott Bohannon who came to Woodford County in 1789, and Dr. Richard Banks and William Bohannon, of Versailles, who came about the same time, I can safely say they were not further apart than second cousins, and I think they were first cousins.

Elliott, Jr., lived and died on his farm in Woodford County, his brother Richard died in Jefferson County. Dr. Richard Banks Bohannon married Fannie Menzies and lived in Versailles for some years, then bought the Daniel Trabue farm, at Griers Creek and lived and died there (see sketch of Menzies).

Mrs. Ophelia Hoppins, a great granddaughter, owns the farm now. William Bohannon lived in Versailles and I think he was a brother of Dr. Richard Banks. I have not been able to learn the name of his wife, or anything in regard to his children, but the census of 1810 credited him with a family of fifteen members, and with the ownership of twenty-three slaves, and classes him as a citizen of Versailles. In 1810 Elliott had a family of four and owned twenty slaves and a farm. Dr. Richard Banks had two in his family in 1810 and owned four slaves. In such circumstances there could be no doubt of the social or financial standing of the Bohannons.

The descendants of Dr. Richard Banks Bohannon were extended under the sketch of the Menzies.

———

Aaron Darnell, when a mere boy, entered the Revolution and served in the drum corps. In 1793 he joined a large company who purposed locating in Kentucky, the leader of which was William Railey, who was returning to the state with his bride, Judith Woodson. Charles Railey and Randolph Railey, Sr., were also of the party, as was their sister, Jane Railey, and it was under these circumstances that she became acquainted with the drummer boy. I think all of the company located in Woodford County. The acquaintanceship of Aaron Darnell and Jane Railey developed into a love affair and on January 21, 1797, just three years after arriving in the county, they were married. For several years they lived in the vicinity of Griers Creek church, but later they moved to the "Germany" neighborhood, near Millville, where they spent the remainder of their lives. He lived on a farm, but being an "herb doctor," he did most of the "physicing" in that vicinity for many years, and was unhampered by opposition. They had these children: Elizabeth Pope, born April 30, 1798, married Aaron Mershon May 30, 1820; Randolph R. Darnell, born February 12, 1800, died December 29, 1860, married Atalanta Whittington, daughter of Wm. Whittington and Lucy Long; and Virginia Darnell, born August 26, 1805, married John Markley, a merchant of Versailles, in 1837.

Randolph R. Darnell had these children: Aaron Darnell, Jr., married first Katherine Hawkins, second Sarah E. Pepper; William W., born in 1830, married first Sarah Jane Taylor, second Ellenor Yancey Taylor; John R., married Susan Cotton; Southey, married Sarah Webb; Virginia, married Thomas Jett; Atalanta, married Thomas W. Edwards, and Charles R., married Bertha Railey.

Aaron Darnell had by the first marriage Judge Isham R. Darnell.* By the second marriage were Samuel Pepper, Mayme, Sarah E. and John R., Jr.

William W. and Sarah Jane Taylor had James, John and Randolph.

John R. Darnell and Susan Cotton had Ann Elizabeth, John M., William R., Atalanta, Southey, Charles, Susan, Dunlap and Dr. Matthew Cotton Darnell.

Virginia Darnell and Thomas Jett had: Elizabeth, Jennie, William, Thomas, Alvin Duvall and Myrtle.

Atalanta Darnell and Thomas Ed-

wards had: Charles Eugene, Virginia, George R. and Wiley.

Southey Darnell and Sarah Webb had: Henry R., George L. and Varsalina.

John Markley and Virginia Darnell moved to Milton, Ky., where many of their descendants now reside.

John H. Jesse was born in Woodford County in 1842, and was one of the sons of Reubin Jesse and his wife, Jane Steele, also born in Woodford County. His farm and residence were on the Lexington pike, not far from Versailles. He was educated in the neighborhood schools and the high school at Versailles. In 1866 he married Sallie Stevenson, a daughter of James R. Stevenson and Caroline Elliott, both of whom were natives of Woodford County, James R. Stevenson coming from one of the several families of that name at Pisgah, and James Elliott, the father of Caroline, was one of our earliest settlers.

John H. Jesse served in the legislature, session of 1883-4, and was honored with a renomination for the session of 1885-6, but died just before the election of 1885.

He and his wife were blessed with four children, as follows: Carry, Henry, Joseph and William. The latter is the present county attorney.

George Holloway was born, reared and died in Scotland. His wife was a Scotch lassie and also lived and died in the land of her nativity. They had several children, one of whom was George the eldest. The laws of Scotland recog-

*See page 222. Katherine Keith Hawkins.

nized the eldest child as heir-apparent, so George, Jr., was heir to his father's estate in the event that he survived his father.

Tradition says that when George, Jr., arrived at the age of sixteen his father died, and two younger brothers so envied him that they conceived the idea of eliminating him as a recipient of parental favor or endowment, so they arranged a coup by which they would themselves get the estate if the master stroke worked successfully. It was admirably planned and with as much dispatch as possible was executed. For a consideration they made arrangement with the officer of an outgoing ship whereby their brother's person could be landed on the shores of America. In order to carry out their designs George, Jr., was drugged, his body placed in a box sufficiently perforated to render suffocation impossible, the box billed as merchandise and entered with the ship's cargo. When out on the ocean, where a return was impossible, he was to be released from his uncomfortable quarters and in due time landed at an American dock.

Upon reaching the shores of Virginia he found himself without means of transportation for a return, so he made the best of the situation and located at Culpeper Court House, where he ingratiated himself into the esteem of the Blackburn family, so after that he joined the Revolutionary forces and served through the war, coming out a full-fledged Captain, which title he ever afterward bore.

When the Blackburns came to Woodford County, Kentucky, he accompanied them, having married Mary Blackburn, a daughter of George Blackburn, of Spring Station, and his wife, Prudence Berry. Captain George Holloway and his wife, Mary Blackburn, built a home in which they spent their entire lives, that adjoined the home of his father-in-law, at Spring Station, and tombstones mark the spot where rest the remains of him and his wife, not far from the residence.

In this home they reared a large family of children, several of whom are buried in the family graveyard. Several of their children intermarried with their Blackburn relatives. It is likely that the old house still stands, but I am not sure.

The names of the children of Captain George Holloway and Mary Blackburn were: Frank P. Holloway, who married first Mary Blanton, second his cousin, Henrietta Bartlett, widowed daughter of Gov. William Berry Blackburn and Martha Watkins (see second sketch of* Blackburn); 2nd Mary Ann; 3rd George, Jr.; 4th Mildred; 5th Georgianna and 6th Martha.

Frank P. Halloway and Mary Blanton had Betsy Blanton Holloway, who married W. F. Sherlock; Georgianna and Churchill Blackburn Holloway. Betsy Blanton Holloway and W. F. Sherlock had George, Bennie and Charles. Bennie married Grant Willis and they are residents of Versailles.

Georgianna Holloway, the 5th, married first William T. Willis, son of Captain William T. Willis, who lost his life at Buena Vista; second John W. Johnson, of the county. By the first marriage were: Len Hodges Willis, who married Adelia Young; George, who married Margaret Gorbet; Thompson, who married Dora Bixby; Hettie, who married William Tutt, and Mary Bird, who married James Clelland Johnson.

Len Hodges Willis and Adelia Young have children living at Nicholasville, where he died in 1914. He was born in Woodford County in April, 1841. When fifteen years of age he went to Independence, Mo., to reside, but upon the outbreak of the Civil War he volunteered his services to the Confederacy under the command of General Price. He was twice wounded; was captured but made his escape; served with distinguished gallantry at the battles of Springfield, Mo., Vicksburg, Miss., and Mobile, Ala. After the war he returned to Kentucky, and soon thereafter moved to Nicholasville, where he was elected circuit clerk. In that capacity he soon acquired a sufficient knowledge of law to enable him to pass a creditable examination, after which he entered upon the practice of law and prosecuted that profession with eminent success until his death a few years since.

Hettie Willis and William Tutt have children living in the vicinity of Millville, where the widow also resides. William Tutt was a son of William H. Tutt and Cynthia Johnson, and grandson of Thomas Johnson and Betsy Warren, all pioneers of Woodford County.

Mary Bird Willis and James Clelland Johnson lived on Glenns Creek near Millville. Their descendants were named in the sketch of the Johnsons.

Thompson H. Willis and Dora Bixby and Bixby Willis, who is engaged in the brokerage business in Kansas City, Mo.

Mary Ann Holloway, the 2nd of Capt. George Holloway and Mary Blackburn, married Dr. Leonard Hodges. They had George Hodges, who married Cora Macey; Henry Churchill, who married Sallie Milam; Bettie Hodges, who married Ben Durrett; Laura Hodges, who married Ben Hughes. Laura Hodges and Ben Hughes had Lieut.-Col. Leonard Hughes, who married Marguerite Von Fritch; James Hughes, who married Edwina Cochran; Laura, who married George W. Stallings; Ben Hughes, who married Gladys Rodman, and Josephine.

George Holloway, Jr., 3rd of Captain George Holloway and Mary Blackburn married first Mary Hodges, second Mary Snodgrass. By the first marriage was a daughter who married Powhatan Woolridge. By the second marriage was Margaret, Frank, Cecil, Lyman and Jennie. I think this Frank married Mary Blanton and lived and died in Versailles. Their daughter, Betsy Holloway, married Dr. —— Berry.

Captain William T. Willis, of Beuna Vista fame, though himself a citizen of Jessamine County, had several other children besides those mentioned above, who reared families in Woodford County. Dr. James Willis, who married Mary Sublett Hawkins and practiced medicine in the vicinity of Clifton for thirty years, was a son, as was also Capt. Robert Willis, who was four years in the service of the Confederacy, and afterwards was a merchant of Versailles. He married the widow of Douglas M. Brown. Sallie and Theresa Willis were daughters of Capt. William T. Willis. The former married Ed. N.

Berryman, a merchant of Versailles, and had Willis Berryman, who married Elizabeth Scearce; Theresa, who married William Barbour, who was many years county attorney of Woodford, and Robert, who married Belle Portwood.

Theresa Willis, the other daughter, married James T. Berryman, of Woodford County, and had John W., who married Louise Price; Sthreshly, who married Mary Wright; Annie, who married W. Horace Posey, and Mollie.

There was another Holloway family in the county that I always thought was closely related to the family of Capt. George Holloway, but I am informed that they were not related, unless so remotely that the present generation isn't aware of it. The head of this Holloway house was William Barry Holloway. In 1820 he purchased the home of John Farra and Ezra Hammon, on the Nicholasville road (see Hammon sketch), not far from Versailles—several miles out—and lived there until his death in May, 1898. His daughter, Irene, who married John Berryman Montgomery, owns the home and they are residing there now. The residence was built of chipped stone from the Clear creek quarry, by John Farra, about 1800, and has never been altered—interior or exterior—except to the extent of equipping it with modern conveniences such as would supply water, heat and light. This dwelling has always been known as "Stone Castle," and is one of the best built houses in the county, its capacity twelve rooms, and the farm is one of the most productive, being kept in a high state of cultivation.

William Barry Holloway was a son of Spencer Holloway and Sarah Read, of Virginia, who located in Jessamine County in pioneer days, where they lived and died upon the farm on which they settled. They had five sons and two daughters, William Barry being one of the sons.

William Barry Holloway married Alice Chilton and they had William Spencer Holloway, who practiced law at Nicholasville for many years; Dr. W. G. Holloway, who is now a resident of Troy; Dr. Walter Watkins Holloway, who died recently in Fayette County; Mattie, who married ——— Gordon; Ida, who married Judge Charles A. Hardin, of Harrodsburg, and Irene Holloway, who married John Berryman Montgomery of "Stone Castle." The latter couple have three boys and three girls, viz.: Robert Barry Montgomery, who saw several years' service in the U. S. Navy in the recent World War; George, Jack, Francis, Alice Hardin, and Laura Dean Montgomery.

Spencer Holloway, the pioneer of Jessamine County, was one of the sons of Captain James Holloway, of the Revolution, and his wife, Martha Spencer, and Capt. James Holloway was a son of Sir James Holloway and Elizabeth Rowland, who emigrated to Virginia during the early years of the 18th century.

Captain James Holloway died at his home near Keene, and his son, Spencer, died there at the advanced age of 93 years.

Richard H. Gray, in point of years, is one of our oldest citizens, as well as one of our most popular. He was born in Woodford County on the ancestral estate near Mortonsville in 1837. He graduated from Georgetown College about 1860, taught school for a period, entered the ministry of the Baptist Church and preached for a season, then enlisted in the Federal Army, and was assigned to a Chaplaincy during the war between the states. He returned to his native county upon cessation of hostilities and engaged in farming, but soon cultivated a taste for the political game, which has absorbed much of his time and attention for nearly fifty years. At a period of time beyond the memory of the average citizen of the county—not later than 1880—he was elected sheriff, and was re-elected in 1884. Was elected to the legislature, session 1887-8, and when that service ended he was elected county clerk, to which office he has been continuously elected, no one daring to dispute his tenure to this good day.

I think he is a member of all of the secret societies in the county, and has occupied all of the chairs in each of the several orders. I would have given a more extended account of his family if he had not been too modest to tell me anything about them.

He had a brother Samuel who was also born near Mortonsville in 1829, and died in Nelson County in 1882, where he was a resident at that time. He, too, was educated at Georgetown, took a course in law at Transylvania and practiced at the Versailles bar before the Civil War. He was a member of the Confederate Congress, representing the state of Kentucky. During that fratricdal war he was impelled by a sense of duty to offer his services to the cause of the Confederacy as a private in the ranks, but owing to his courage and skill soon rose to the rank of a Colonel.

He was at Shiloh when that memorable engagement was fought with such disastrous results to the south, and at that same battle his brother Richard was a participant under the stars and stripes in that clash of arms, the former clad in gray and the latter in blue.

Samuel moved to Nelson County after the war, where he was soon elected County Judge, and was a candidate for Congress from that district in 1882, with a splendid chance of the Democratic nomination when his political career was suddenly ended by the messenger of death.

———

Thomas Weakly, of Virginia, married Elizabeth Redding in Farquier County, that state. He came to Kentucky in 1786 and settled in Woodford County during that year. They had the following children: Stephen, who married Elizabeth Arnold in 1798; Mary, who married Abraham Dale; Letitia, who married Nathan Scearce in 1797; Rebecca, who married John Shouse; Jinsey, who married Younger Arnold in 1812; a daughter who married George Scroggin in 1801; Sarah, who married George Stevenson, and Thomas, who married Peggy Tyler in 1810. Abraham Dale was in Woodford County in 1810, owned three slaves and had a family of nine persons. Younger Arnold, John Shouse and George Stevenson were also in the county in 1810, but were living with their parents and listed with them in the census of that year.

After the marriage of his children Thomas Weakley removed to Shelby County with his wife, and I think that nearly all of his children moved there too. However, several of his children remained in the county and have descendants there now, particularly the Arnolds and Dales.

Captain William Sargent was born in Pearson County, North Carolina, and came to Woodford County, Ky., about 1806, while yet in his youth. After the war of 1812 he was an officer in the home guards. He was married to Mary Moore, of the county, and both lived to be quite old. They had these children: John, William, Robert, Lucy and Mary.

William married ———— Kyle and moved to Mercer County; Robert married Mildred Gwynn about 1829 and settled on a farm on the road from McKee's Cross Roads to Spring Station, where he raised a large family, the youngest of whom was Samuel, who lived on the estate until his death a decade or more ago. The father and mother also died there, the former about 1872, and the latter at a much later date; Lucy married a Tutt and they lived and died in the "Germany" neighborhood; Mary married a Kyle and moved to Mercer County.

Robert Sargent and Mildred Gwynn had these children: Joseph, who died unmarried; Mary Agnes, who married Silas Kersey about 1850; Lucy Ann, who married the Rev. T. W. Benton, a Methodist minister; Robert Moore, who married the widow Nourse; Cordelia Jane, who married John R. Morris;

Catherine, who married Presley Cole, and Samuel, who never married.

Silas Kersey and Mary Agnes Sargent had ten children, four of whom are now living, viz.: Anna Kersey Payne, Mary Florence Peel, Charles Edward and Samuel Major Kersey.

John R. Morris and Cordelia Jane Sargent had Isaphine, Robert, Clarence, Theodore, Aloise, John, Mildred Gwynn and Arthur, all of whom, I think, are residents of Woodford County, the father and mother in the suburbs of Versailles, on the Nicholasville road.

————

The Wooldridge family is numbered among the earliest of the settlers of Woodford County, being very prominent in the early affairs of the county, and their descendants of today, of whom there is quite a colony, are no less interested, and no less prominent in all that pertains to the welfare and progress of the county.

They intermarried with the families of Major, Trabue, Moss and others. Though I could learn but little of the family record from the branch of the family now residing in the county, I was enough interested in them to search for some one who could tell the story, so the following letter will be appreciated by all who have kept in touch with this generation of the Wooldridge family:

"Responding to your letter of Sept. 11th beg to advise that my Wooldridge ancestors were from Woodford County, Ky., but that I being the younger son of a younger son, have never been in possession of any of the family records or documents.

"My great grandfather was a native of Albemarle County, Va., and made the trip to Kentucky with Daniel Boone on the latter's second expedition. His name was Edmond Wooldridge, and he located in Woodford County some four miles from Versailles, at a point on the Mortonsville pike adjacent to what is known as 'Moss-side.' His wife was Sallie Watkins, a sister of John and Henry Watkins, the latter proprietor of the old Watkins Tavern in Versailles (see Watkins Tavern), and the former was a delegate to the first Constitutional Convention, and a member of the first legislature.*

"Three months after her husband moved to Kentucky she, Sallie Watkins, followed him, bringing with her the children, of which my grandfather, Powhatan, then six weeks old, was the youngest.

"There were a number of boys and several girls in the family. Edmund, Jr., the oldest son, moved to Mississippi in early life and became State Treasurer. Samuel went to Texas after mature years and his descendants are living at Austin, Paris and other parts of that state; Josiah moved to Western Kentucky, in the vicinity of Hopkinsville, and had two sons, Robert and Joseph, possibly others.

"My grandfather, Powhatan Wooldridge, married Mildred Taylor Major (see Major sketch), a daughter of John Major (and Elizabeth Redd) who lived in that part of Woodford County that was afterward a part of Franklin. Their children were: Edmund, Jr., III, Cora (Thomson), Samuel Louis, John Major, Belle (Boulden), William Henry, Powhatan, Jr., and Elvie

(Smith). My father, Powhatan, was the youngest son.

"My great grandfather, Edmund Wooldridge, was buried on the farm which he owned in Woodford County. His widow (Sallie Watkins) married John Moss and became the mother of Henry Moss, who was thus my grandfather Powhatan's half-brother.

"My grandfather, Powhatan, moved with his family to Western Kentucky, and from thence later to Central Missouri. Three of his sons, viz.: Edmund, for whom Wooldridgetown, a suburb of Versailles, was named, Samuel Louis and William Henry, returned to Woodford County and all three died there within the memory of the present generation.

"The family Bible, and possibly some of the papers giving the family history, is in the possession of Samuel L. Wooldridge, Jr., of Versailles (who is still hunting for them), having passed to him from John S. Moss, who inherited it from his father, Henry Moss, of 'Moss-side.' P. M. and H. M. Wooldridge, of Versailles, are sons of my uncle John Major Wooldridge, who died in Missouri. His widow (Bell Moss) and their children moved back to Woodford County after my uncle's death.

"I regret that I am not able to furnish any information relative to my great grandfather's brothers and sisters who followed him to Woodford County.

"Wooldridge, Cooper County, Mo.; Wooldridge, Campbell County, Tenn.; Wooldridge, Botetourt County, Va.; Wooldridge, Russell County, Ala.; Wooldridge, Phillips County, Mont., and Wooldridge, a station on the interurban line in Oldham County, Ky., are all named for descendants of the pioneers of that name who settled in Woodford County.

"The first Wooldridge in America came from South of England. He served as a Captain in the Duke of Monmouth's army, and when the rebellion was suppressed, his punishment was transportation to the colony of Virginia, and his son, William Henry, was a member of the first House of Burgesses of the colony.

"I am without information as to the services of the Wooldridge family in the Revolution, but it is evident they were among those present, and helped to carry on the strife, as my cousin, Mrs. Kate Wooldridge Latham, formerly of Memphis, Tenn., and prominent in D. A. R. and U. D. C., both in the state and nationally, joined the D. A. R. on the record of her ancestors of the Wooldridge line. Both she and her husband are dead and I don't know who has charge of her papers.

"Trusting that the foregoing will be of service to you in the matter you have in hand, and with best wishes for your success in the work you have undertaken.

"Very truly yours,
"James R. Wooldridge.
"Wooldridge, Tenn.,
"Sept. 15, 1920."

James R. Wooldridge has done posterity a great service and I am sure they will appreciate it. The foregoing letter is a very comprehensive one and covers a wide circle of his relationship. In the supplemental sketch of the Major family that follows will be found addi-

*See page 220.

tional mention of the Wooldridge family.*

A brief sketch of the family of John Major, Sr., and his wife, Elizabeth Redd, appeared in the Register of May, 1920, and this supplement is written because of much additional data relating to old Woodford County citizens that was not in my possession at that time.

As stated in that sketch, John Major, Sr., and Elizabeth Redd were residents of Woodford County in 1788, when the county was established, living three miles out of Frankfort on the Versailles pike, and they were citizens until that part of the county was transferred to Franklin, a short time before 1800. Many of their children and grandchildren were in the county as late as 1830, while quite a number of descendants are residents of the county at this time. From the first this family intermarried almost exclusively with prominent families of the county, and many of their children remained in the county until they reared families, when many of them moved west and southwest. The names of their children follow: John, Jr., who married Judith Trabue; Susanna married Robert Wooldridge, who, I think, was a son of Josiah Wooldridge, who moved from Woodford to Christian County and they had a son, Thomas Major Wooldridge, who married Eliza Cates; Frances Major, who married in 1795 Nathaniel Thomson, son of Anthony Thomson, Sr., and Ann Bibb, who came from Virginia to Woodford County in 1785; Thomas Major, born in 1769, married Susanna Trabue in 1793; James Major married

Betsy Minter, daughter of the Rev. Joseph Minter and Jane Trabue, and Jane Trabue was a daughter of John James Trabue and Olymphia Dupuy (See Trabue sketch); Lewis Redd Major, married Mildred Elvira Thompson, daughter of General David Thompson and Betsy Suggett; Martha Major married Charles Sanford in May, 1823, and moved to Henry County; Mildred Taylor Major married in March, 1815, Powhatan Wooldridge, son of Edmund Wooldridge and Sallie Watkins (see Wooldridge letter); Elizabeth was the youngest of John Major, Sr., and Elizabeth Redd. If she married I am not advised.

John Major, Jr., and Judith Trabue (14th of John James Trabue and Olymphia Dupuy) were married in 1789 at the Edward Trabue home that overlooks Tyrone. They had a son, William Trabue Major, born in 1790, who married Margaret Shipp, of the county, but he and his interesting family moved to Illinois where are now many of their descendants. One of their sons, Laban Shipp Major, married Elizabeth Dunlap.

Another son of John Major, Jr., and Judith Trabue was Benjamin, born in 1796, married Lucy Davenport, daughter of Jonas Davenport and Alice Redd, daughter of Mordecai Redd and Agatha Minor (see Redd sketch). They, too, moved to Illinois with their family, where Benjamin established, and maintained for a long time, Eureka College. Eliza Major, sister of William and Benjamin, married the Rev. William Davenport, son of Jonas Davenport and Alice Redd, and they had a son,

John J. Davenport, who married his cousin, Lucy Bullock; another son was William H., who married Mary Willis. William Davenport, who lived with the family of Willis Field and his wife, Ellen Craig, before, during and after the Civil War, was a kinsman.

Chastine Major, another son of John, Jr., and Judith Trabue Major was born in 1800, and married Joanna Hopkins, a kinswoman of William and Robert Hopkins, who were in Woodford in 1810. He also moved his family to Illinois, where they have descendants.

Francis Major and Nathaniel Thomson lived at "Thomson's Manor," the farm inherited from his father, Anthony Thomson, in Woodford County, who died in 1794, and as the eldest son drew his father's pension for services rendered in the Revolution. He and his brother, Anthony, Jr., were living on farms in Woodford County in 1810. Nathaniel and Frances lived at "Thomson's Manor" and reared a large family of children. For descendants see Thomson sketch.

Thomas Major and Susanna Trabue were also married on the heights overlooking Tyrone, in 1793. For a description of their home see Major sketch,* Their daughter, Olivia, married Alex Carlyle, of the county, and a son, Minor Major Carlyle, married his cousin, Sallie Thomson.

James Major and Betsy Minter, daughter of Rev. Joseph Minter and Jane Trabue, lived at what is now Jetts Station (see Major sketch).* They had a son, Joseph Major, who married Jane Boone, kinswoman of Daniel, and they resided in the vicinity

* See page 46.

of Millville some years before the Mexican War. Boone Major, one of the sons† of this couple, was a youthful companion of John E. Miles and William† Strother Hawkins, Jr., and they were volunteer comrades in the Mexican War. Before the Civil War Boone Major moved to Lexington, Mo., where he amassed a comfortable fortune before his death in 1905. There were quite a number of brothers and sisters of Boone Major, all of whom I believe moved to Pettis County, Mo. His sister, Jane, married Albert Branham in 1833, and his brother, Benjamin Randolph Major, married Sallie Leftwick in 1846, whose daughter, Lelia, married Col. Phil. C. Kidd, the celebrated auctioneer, who is well remembered in Woodford, where he was the owner of the "Col. Billy" Buford farm at Midway for some years. This farm is now owned by William L. Cannon. The children of Col. Kidd and his wife, Lelia Major, were: Major P., Samuel Wooldridge, James Franklin and Phil C., Jr.

Lewis Redd Major and Mildred Elvira Thompson moved to Missouri about 1840, perhaps a little earlier, and he was the founder of Georgetown, Mo. The prominent families by the name of Gentry, in Pettis County, Mo., are descendants.

Martha Major and Charles Sanford have many descendants in Henry County and Louisville. Harriet Sanford, who married Judge John D. Carroll, ex-Chief Justice of Kentucky, and Marie Sanford, who married David R.

*Castleman, Jr., of Louisville, are granddaughters. David R. Castleman, Jr,. is a prominent lawyer and politician and a great grandson of General Jacob Castleman and Sarah White, of Woodford County, who inherited "Old Mansion" from his father, Lewis Castleman, whose wife was Jemima Pearsoll, pioneers of Woodford County (see Castleman sketch),‡ David R., Jr., was a son of David R., Sr., and Joanna †Pryor, daughter of Chief Justice William S. Pryor, of Henry County, and David R. Castleman, Sr., was one of the sons of George Clinton Castleman, who inherited "Old Mansion" from his father, General Jacob Castleman, and on this estate David, Sr., was reared. The wife of George Clinton Castleman was Jane Torbett (see Castleman sketch). George Clinton Castleman sold the old ancestral home on Clear creek, in Woodford County, just prior to the Civil War, and moved either to Henry or Carroll County. His father, General Jacob Castleman, was an officer in the war of 1812.

Mildred Taylor Major and Powhatan Wooldridge had these children: Edmund, Jr., who married his cousin, Bettie Moss, of "Moss-Side," daughter of Henry Moss and Belinda Snodgrass (Henry Moss was a son of John Moss and Sallie Watkins Wooldridge, widow of Edmund Wooldridge, Sr.); Cora Wooldridge, who married —— Thomson; Belle Wooldridge, who married Daniel W. Boulden; Elvie, who married —— Smith; Samuel Louis, who married first Anna May Holloway, sec-

†See pages 146, 298.
*See pages 64 and 252.
‡See pages 64, 252, 266.
†See page 311.

ond Mattie Avent; John Major Wooldridge, who married Belle Moss, sister of Bettie; Powhatan, Jr., married Anna Maria Washington.

Edmund Wooldridge, Jr., and Bettie Moss had Mary Wooldridge, who married Major George Emack, who lived and died on his estate on the Midway pike opposite the old fair grounds.

Samuel Louis Wooldridge and his first wife, Anna May Holloway, had Powhatan Wooldridge, who married Chamie Johnson. They originally lived on the farm now owned by Lister Witherspoon. They have Powhatan, Samuel, Mary Tyler and Anna May Wooldridge.

Samuel Louis Wooldridge and his second wife, Mattie Avent, had Samuel L., Jr., who married Mary Russell Wasson, daughter of Edgar Wasson and Mary Russell, and they lived many years on the old Isham Railey farm on Shyrock's Ferry pike, but he now resides on the adjoining farm originally owned by pioneer Willis Field, that fronts on Mortonsville pike.

Samuel Louis Wooldridge, Sr., was for many years director in the Bank of Woodford, and for a time was its President. His home, upon which his widow resided for many years, is in the suburbs of Versailles, between the Tyrone and Mortonsville pikes.

John Major Wooldridge and Belle Moss had Powhatan M. and H. M. Wooldridge, who are at present engaged in the coal business in Versailles. He and his wife and children moved to Missouri many years ago, where he died, and his widow and two sons returned to Woodford County to reside. She died in Versailles more than a decade ago.

Powhatan Wooldridge, Jr., and Anna Maria Washington had Carrie, William Washington (who has a son Powhatan), and James R. Wooldridge, who is a wealthy coal mine operator who resides at Wooldridge, Tenn. The latter married Cora Virginia Thomson, of Sedalia, Mo., who I think was a descendant of General David Thomson and Betsy Suggett, of Scott County, of whom I have written.

Anna Maria Washington, the wife of Powhatan Wooldridge, Jr., was a daughter of W. H. Washington and Caroline Blount, of North Carolina.

John Major, Sr., the pioneer, and his wife, Elizabeth Redd, lived and died in the large frame residence built by him, and burned about 1845. The farm was purchased by S. F. J. Trabue, and the brick building now standing and owned and occupied by S. French Hoge, was built prior to the Civil War by S. F. J. Trabue. Elizabeth Redd was a relative —probably a sister of Mordecai and Thomas Redd, Sr., of the county, and their grandchildren, as was not infrequently the case in those days, intermarried. Pioneer John Major, Sr., was a kinsman, how closely I can't say, yet tradition says a grandson of Richard Major, who was born at "Hursley Manor," Hampshire, England, in 1615. Richard Major came to this country with his wife, Jane Ire Monger, and settled in New Kent County, Va. They had many descendants in Kentucky the early part of the 19th century, especially numerous in Mercer, Shelby and Franklin counties.

Four of his generations were born in Virginia, who were ancestors of the Kentucky Major families. They were:

George, of the first generation, born in 1651; George of the second generation, born in 16—; Samuel of the third generation, born in 1712, and married Elizabeth Jones; John, of the fourth generation, born in 1755, and married first Elizabeth Porter, second Euphrates Sleet.

By the second marriage of John Major and Euphrates Sleet was Lucy Major, born at Farmdale, Franklin County, Ky., who was the first wife of *Isham Keith Hawkins (son of William Strother Hawkins and Katherine Keith, pioneers of Woodford County). They had a daughter, Katherine, who was the first wife of Aaron Darnell, Jr., and this latter couple had a son Judge Isham Randolph Darnell born in Woodford County, about 1850, who married Macie Carter and is now a resident of Benkelman, Neb., where they have reared an interesting family of children. Judge Darnell read law under the advice of Judge Pat Major, of Frankfort.

Another line was Samuel, of the third generation, mentioned above, who was born in Middlesex County, Va., in 1712, and died in 1800. He was married to Eliazbeth Jones in June, 1735; he was a grandson of the first George, and a son of the second George.

Samuel Major and Elizabeth Jones had, besides John Major, who married Euphrates Sleet, another, Francis Major, who married Margaret Porter, and this couple had a daughter, Elizabeth, who married William Pryor Foree; and Samuel I. M. Major, Sr., who married Martha Bohannon.

William Pryor Foree and Elizabeth

*See page 146.

Major moved to Shelby County. They had a son, Joseph Pryor Foree, who married Mary Price Marshall, and they reared these children in Shelby County: Susan B., who married Dandridge Crockett, Jr., son of George Crockett and Elizabeth Ellison; Sallie Foree, who married her cousin, R. M. Foree; Pryor J. Foree, one of the brightest young lawyers trained at the Shelby bar; and Charles Marshall Foree, a young lawyer who entered the United States Treasury at Washington as a legal adviser during Cleveland's second administration, and is yet associated with the Treasury in the capacity of Assistant Comptroller. His brother, Pryor J. Foree, served the county of Shelby in the legislature in the 90s and was regarded as one of the most talented and popular young men in the state. He would have reflected great lustre upon both his name and state had not the sickle of death removed him from the busy scenes of this life soon after his legislative service. On the paternal side he was a close kinsman of Chief Justice William S. Pryor, of Henry County, and on the maternal side he was, I think, a great grandson of Col. Thomas Marshall and Mary Randolph Keith of "Buck Pond," Woodford County, his mother being of that name and family, which makes him a distant kinsman of Louis Marshall, cashier of the Bank of Woodford.

S. I. M. Major, Sr., and Martha Bohannon, mentioned above, settled at Paris, Ky. She was related to the Woodford Bohannons. They had Judge Patrick Upshire Major, born in 1822, and practiced law at Frankfort for a lifetime; Col. S. I. M. Major, Jr., who was owner and publisher of the old Yeoman, a flourishing and popular newspaper published at Frankfort for a half century. He married Mary Scott, daughter of Col. Robert Scott and Elizabeth Watts Brown. Col. Samuel I. M. Major, Jr., and Mary Scott have a son, Samuel I. M. Major, Jr., III, who is an officer in the United States Navy.

In the Register of May, 1920, in sketches of Nathaniel Sanders and* John Major, Sr., both pioneers of Woodford County (and both of whom have quite a number of descendants there now), I mentioned briefly their relation to the "Old Forks church" that was built on the farm of Nathaniel Sanders. Recently I came across a letter written by the Rev. William Hickman, the first pastor of that church, and deeming that its contents would be interesting to these descendants I have decided to include it in my notes. It follows:

"About this time, 1787, the Forks of Elkhorn began to be settled. Mr. Nathaniel Sanders, old brother John Major, brother Daniel James, old William Hayden, old Mr. Lindsey and a few others had moved down. As there was a prospect of a large settlement Mr. Sanders suggested to his neighbor John Major that it would be right to get a minister to come down and live among them. This pleased Mr. Major, he being an old Baptist. They consulted as to whom they should get. Mr. Sanders, who had a slight acquaintance with me, mentioned my name. This seemed strange, as he was a very thoughtless man about his soul. However, they agreed among themselves to make me a present of 100 acres of land. They tendered me the call, and Mr. Sanders tendered me the farm on which I now live, a part of his own estate. He was not a professor, but I found that his wife was a devout Baptist. I said to him one day: 'Sir, you don't care for religion, I want to know why you wish me to come?' He replied: 'If it is never any advantage to me it may be to my family.'

"My son and I built a cabin upon the farm at once, and I moved my family into it about Christmas time, 1787 (just one year or less until all of these people were in Woodford County). About the 17th of the following January I had an appointment to preach at the home of brother Major. Everybody came out. I took the subject: 'Let me die the death of the righteous, and let my last end be like His.' To my great pleasure Mr. Sanders came forward and gave his experience, and soon thereafter he found peace with the Lord, and our meetings continued until brother John Taylor, author of 'The Ten Churches,' came down from Clear creek to preach and help us on. Afterward he came to take charge of 'Buck Run' church and preach for that congregation, and we were neighbors."

Nathaniel Sanders was the grandfather of the wives of Ab Hunter, Isham Railey and James Amsden. The two preachers mentioned above preached for the two churches named for a lifetime, and were buried within a mile of each other, both having preached during their lives from every Baptist pul-

* See pages 46, 47.

pit in Woodford County in the early days.

———

This clipping was taken from a Louisville paper during the fall of 1920, and evidently relates to descendants of early Woodford settlers of those names:

Paris, Mo.—A trunk of curios, owned by the late Squire M. Moss, and which he kept under his bed for years, untouched by other hands, has just been brought to light by his daughter, Mrs.* E. L. Major, who opened it and discovered that it contained many articles more than 100 years old. Among them was an old-time charm string that belonged to Squire Moss' mother when she was a little girl. It was made of old-fashioned buttons and beads strung on a wire and is more than 100 years old.

There also was found a pair of brass-toed baby shoes, worn by the Squire's oldest brother, who died when young, and a little calico dress, worn by a baby sister, who also died when young. Sentimental interest centered about a daguerrotype of his wife when young. In the back of the case were two locks of hair, one very brown, taken from her head when she was young, and another, gray, taken when she was old. Pictures of all his children as babies and the picture of the first railroad train that ran into Paris, were also found in an album the trunk contained.

———

During the year 1784, or about that time, Henry Shouse, a gentleman of German extraction, who first settled in Pennsylvania, came to Woodford County and located on a splendid farm near

*See pages 216-220.

Mortonsville that is still in possession of descendants. He was twice married, but the name of his first wife is not now known by the descendants. His second wife was Elizabeth Jones, of Bath County. One child resulted from the first marriage, but quite a number was the result of the second marriage, all growing up under the influence and guidance of Elizabeth Jones. The names of the children follow: Samuel, born in 1784, and married Catherine Perry, who was born in 1789; Daniel, born in 1786, died in 1866, married Mary Lea in 1807, she born of Welch parents in 1787, daughter of Francis W. Lea and his wife, Mary, who were with the colony at Bryant Station, and pioneers of Woodford County; Thomas Shouse, born in Woodford County, where he died about 1821. He married Mary McQuiddy (kinswoman of pioneer John McQuiddy) and moved to Terre Haute, Ind., about 1810; William Shouse, who married first Lucretia Smith, second Bettie Wells; and Permelia, who married Samuel Jesse, of Shelby County.

Samuel, the first born, and Catherine Perry, had Jane Ann, born in 1810, who married Josiah Felix, of Mortonsville, and died in 1895; Benjamin F., born in 1811, married —— Farrell and moved to Missouri, where he died in 1889; Russell, who never married; Lewis, born in 1817, and married —— Dawson and moved to Missouri, where he died; Nancy, born in 1824, married first James Murrain, second Newton Dale; Samuel Henry, born in 1827, married Mary J. Orr, and Catharine, born in 1829, who married William Garvey.

Daniel, the second born, and Mary Lea, had Francis Henry, who married Mary Conn and moved to Union County about 1844; Jeptha, who married first Jane Dale, daughter of John Dale, a Baptist minister, second Hattie Ragland; William O., who married Harriet Bryant, daughter of Joseph Bryant, of Shelby County, and they moved to Kansas City, Mo., in 1836; Newton, married Mary Dehorney and moved to Louisiana after the Civil War; Benjamin H., married Vassie Dale, a widow, and moved to Shelby County; Daniel Lewis, born in 1827, married Martha Mahon and moved to Kansas City, Mo., in 1855, where he engaged in the banking business until his death in 1873.

Thomas Shouse, the third born, and Mary McQuiddy, settled on Wabash river, in Indiana, in 1810. He helped build Ft. Harrison and fought in the battle of Tippecanoe under General Harrison, in which engagement he was wounded. His wife died soon thereafter and Thomas came back to Woodford County and married Susan Edwards, a widow. His six children by the first wife, and one by the last wife, are here given: James, born in 1800, died unmarried in Woodford County; John went south in 1831; Elizabeth, married Thomas Dehorney, of the county, and had a daughter, Mary, who married her cousin, Newton Shouse, a son of James Shouse, of Shelby County; Sallie, married her cousin, James H. Shouse, who moved to Henry County, where they have descendants; Permelia, married first Woodford Arnold, and second John B. Scearce; and Dudley Jones, who married Mary Combs and moved

to Henry County, where he died in 1903.

William Shouse, the fourth born, and his wife, Lucretia Smith, had these children: James and Albert, both of whom died in Woodford County, as bachelors, I believe; Clark, who married Amanda Haydon, of Louisville; Amanda, who married Ed Hawkins, of Carroll County; Virginia, who married Benjamin Wilson, Jr. (see Wilsons, pages 125 and 378), both of whom lived and died in Versailles and they had Inez, who married Albert Thompson; Anna and Lou, spinsters, and Albert, who married Fannie Hawkins; Mildred Shouse married Dr. Samuel Ayres, of Meade County.

William Shouse, the fourth born, and his second wife, Betsy Wells, had these children: Charles, *Rev. John Samuel (of blessed memory), born in 1840, died May, 1914, in Lexington. He was an able and popular minister of the Christian church, having preached from nearly every pulpit of that denomination in Central Kentucky. He married Anna Armstrong, and their son, Jouett Shouse, is a prominent lawyer of Kinsley, Kansas, but temporarily residing at Washington, D. C., where he was Assistant Secretary of the Treasury under the Wilson regime. He has several times represented the Seventh Kansas District in Congress. He married Marian Edwards in 1911. Other children of Rev. John Shouse and Anna Armstrong were: William Mitchell, who married —— ——, and had a son, Charles; Loulie, who married Prof. Richard Howell Ellett, of Transylvania University, who was educated for the

---

* Father of Jouett Shouse, who is today nationally known.

ministry in the Christian church; they have a son, Lawrence Howell Ellett; Mary Lee Shouse died in 1902; Jean Paul died in 1913, and Angie Armstrong Shouse, who married Sidney W. Smith, of Nebraska, in 1911.

Josiah Felix and his wife, Jane Ann Shouse, daughter of Samuel and Catherine Perry Shouse, were long residents of Mortonsville and they had Samuel who, I am informed, never married; Albert died in the service during the Civil War; Elizabeth married James Hall; Nancy married Christopher Botts; John married Alma Lillard; Rev. William Felix married Hattie Haydon; Sarah married Augustus Clark; Cordelia married first James T. Carpenter, second Charles T. Dale; Mary married Benj. P. Carpenter; Emma married Leslie J. Cleveland, and Rev. Joseph Felix married Maria Louise Doniphan. William and Joseph were both noted Baptist preachers.

James Murrain and Nancy Shouse, daughter of Samuel and Catharine Perry Shouse, had a daughter, Hattie, who married Harris Hicks. They had two children, Dr. Robert and May Hicks. The former married Edna Starks and practiced medicine at Midway. They have a son, Robert, Jr.

Samuel Henry Shouse, son of Samuel and Catharine Perry Shouse, and his wife, Mary Orr, had these children: Eunice, born 1858, married William Yeoman; Francis Bell, born 1860, is a spinster; James Orr, born 1862, married Christine Felix; Albert F., born 1865, married Loulie Shropshire, Rev. Henry M., born 1868, married Edith Feiso; Samuel Edgar, born 1870, and Mary Armstrong born 1875.

Samuel Henry lived on the ancestral estate until his death a score of years ago. He served many years as a member of the magisterial court, and served the county in the General Assembly, sessions of 1889-90 and 1891-2.

Eunice Katherine Shouse and William Yeoman had Samuel S., born 1883, and William Henry, born 1886.

James Orr Shouse and Christine Felix had John F., born in 1898, and James Lillard, born 1901.

Albert Felix Shouse and Loulie Shropshire had Eunice K., born 1894, and Samuel Heady, born 1897.

Rev. Henry M. Shouse and Edith Feiso had Paul Judson, born 1905, Clark Feiso, born 1907, John Henry, born 1909, and Albert Francis, born 1912.

Joshiah Felix and Jane Shouse had a daughter, Cordelia, whose first husband was James Carpenter, and their daughter, Mary, married John A. Davis, who is a resident of Versailles.

The first of the Heale family known in America was Nicholas, who was a planter in York County, Va., in 1654. He was born in England. His son, George Heale, was a justice of the peace 1684-93, in Richmond County, Virginia, burgess in Lancaster in 1694-97. He died in 1698. His wife was Ellen Chinn and they had these children: Hannah, who married William Ball, and had Sarah; Captain George Heale, who married Catherine Chinn and had Nicholas, and William Heale, who married Priscilla Downman and had George Heale, born in 1728, died in 1806. He was a Burgess of Lancaster and Fauquier counties in 1757-59. He married Sarah Smith.

George Heale and Sarah Smith had these children: William Heale, who married Susanna Payne, of Goochland County; Smith Heale, who married Nancy Douglas, daughter of Col. William Douglas, a native of Ayrshire, Scotland, and his wife, Elizabeth (Offutt) Lewis, widow of Stepen Lewis, of Virginia; Joseph, who married first Margaret Bronaugh, second Ann Carter Bronaugh; Phillip, who married Catherine Douglas; Mary, who married —— Love; Priscilla, who married General* Marquis Calmes; Sarah, who married Hugh Wilson; Elizabeth, who married ——Ewell, and Jane Heale, who married William Bronaugh.

Of these children it is known that Smith Heale and his wife, Nancy Douglas, and Priscilla Heale and General Calmes came to Kentucky and settled in Woodford County soon after the Revolution.

Before leaving Virginia Smith Heale's neighbors had the habit of addressing him as Hale, disregarding the second letter, so after coming to Kentucky he was always greeted as Smith Hale, in a social way, so it was decided to have it Hale in business matters as well.

He was regarded as one of the wealthiest, as well as one of the most influential men in the county, as he owned thirty-one slaves who did service on his large estate. His farm was near Spring Station, and adjoined the farm now owned by James Withrow, but settled by pioneer George Blackburn. The farm of Smith Hale has been in possession of a half dozen different owners since his death in 1813, now owned by Benjamin Hieatt. On the premises, in a private burial ground, the remains of him and his wife repose, and likely other members of the family. A marble shaft and several tombstones marked the spot within the memory of the present generation, but some thoughtless person, in possession of the premises removed these marks of respect to the memory of the dead and used them, I am told, in constructing a driveway for the living.

In this home Smith Hale and Nancy Douglas reared a large family of children. Their names follow: Sarah, who first married Hiram Moffett, second —— Patterson. They moved to Missouri; Katherine, who married Nathan Payne; Eliza, who married first William Hamilton, second her cousin, —— Calmes, son of General Marquis Calmes and Priscilla Hale; Margaret married Capt. Morey and moved to Missouri; Maria married Edward Payne; Susanna Smith Hale married William Holman Martin; Louis Douglas Hale married Letitia Flournoy, and Antonette married Dr. Ezra Offutt. Of these, Susanna Smith Hale and William Holman Martin, and Letitia Flournoy and Louis Douglas Hale raised families in the county. Susan Smith Hale and William Holman Martin had these children: Catherine Jane, who married Warren Viley and had Martinette, who married Lister Witherspoon and had Warren Viley Witherspoon, who married Lilly Fuhs, of Virginia; Ellen Douglas Witherspoon, who married M. Allen Buffington, of Falls River, Mass.; Ethel

* See page 36.

Witherspoon, who married O. L. Alexander, of Blue Field, W. Va., but now residing in New York City; and Lister Witherspoon, Jr., who died in young manhood; J. Breckinridge Viley, who married Mary Philamon Parrish (see page 232); and Lydia May (see Viley sketch); Louis Martin, who married Lucy Ann Dedman and had Robert Edward, Pattie, who married Charles Stone; Susan, who married Webb Shropshire, and Antoinette, who married William Stanhope; Antoinette Martin, who married Harvie Tompson and had Sarah Winfred, who married Benjamin Craig and had a daughter who married James Starks, and William James and John; Ann Martin, who married Dudley Peak.

Louis Douglas Hale and Letitia Flournoy had two daughters, Cassandra, who married her cousin, Walter Buck, and Fannie, who married Churchill Blackburn, son of Edward M. Blackburn (uncle Ned).

Walter Buck and Cassandra had several children who were reared on their farm that lay in an oval shape between the railroad and pike, just above Duckers Station, and in full view of her grandfather's farm. For many years after the Civil War this farm was owned by Dr. Robert J. Thompson. The children of Walter Buck and Cassandra married and moved to Missouri.

Churchill Blackburn and Fannie Hale went south before the Civil War and settled in Arkansas, where many of their descendants now reside.

Besides his farm and thirty-one slaves, Smith Hale owned a unique carriage that attracted much attention and

admiration, one of the very limited number in existence at that early day. It had a seat at the rear for the footman, but none in front for the driver, as was the custom, so a rider was substituted for a driver, and he sat astride the horse with glittering stirrups suspended from a flaming red saddle, in order to guide the animal and direct its speed. The family made frequent trips to Lexington, some times in a social way and at others for the purpose of shopping, and usually when they returned the carriage was groaning beneath the weight of jeans, linsey, and other supplies for the family and servants. In those days there were no millinery, mantua or haberdashery establishments or shops and the female members of the Hale family, as was the custom of their neighbors, wore homemade bonnets and gowns.

*Priscilla Hale and General Marquis Calmes had five boys and four girls, and of this large family I am only able to report the name of one, Sarah. She was of the bevy of young ladies, daughters of the Revolutionary veterans, who were selected to carpet the pathway of General LaFayette with flowers upon the occasion of that distinguished gentleman's visit to Versailles while touring Kentucky in May, 1825. On account of the intimate relationship of her father and the eminent Frenchman in the Revolution, she bore a conspicuous part, in a modest way, in all that pertained to the pleasure of the guest and the occasion. The other children of General Calmes and Priscilla Hale who lived to years of maturity married and left the county leaving no marks upon

*See pages 36 and 362.

the tracing board, so to speak, and I regret not being able to preserve their names. For General Marquis Calmes' services in the Revolution see sketch of him in May, 1920, issue.

Smith Hale, as was the custom of all of the pioneers, especially the Revolutionary veterans, always appeared in public with knee pants, stockings, shoes with buckles, sweeping coat of the pigeon-tail variety, colonial hat and hair in queue. General Calmes did likewise.

The ancestral lines of the Hales and their connections were nearly all Huguenot strains and I will here mention a few of them, as the most of them were in Woodford before 1810.

William Holman Martin, who married Susanna Smith Hale, was a son of James Martin and Esther Smith, who came from Powhatan County, Va., to Woodford County, at an early date, and this James Martin was a son of Anthony Martin and Sarah Holeman, of Virginia, and Anthony Martin was a son of Pierre Martine and Mary Anne Rapine, both of whom were Huguenot refugees from France to Virginia.

Sarah Holeman, the wife of the above James Martin, was a daughter of James Holeman, Jr., and his wife, Jane ——, of Cumberland County, Va., and the father of James Holeman, Jr., was James Holeman, burgess from Goochland County, Va.

The above Esther Smith, wife of James Martin, was a daughter of the Rev. George Smith and Judith Guerrant, who migrated to that part of Woodford County that a few years later became Franklin County, and absorbed quite a number of our pioneer settlers; and the Rev. George Smith was a son

of Mary Anne Rapine (widow of the above Pierre Martine) and Thomas Smith, her second husband.

Judith Guerrant, wife of the Rev. George Smith, was a daughter of Peter Guerrant and Magdalen Trabue. The father of Peter Guerrant was Daniel Guerrant, a Huguenot emigrant to Manikintown, Va., in 1700, and Magdalen Trabue was a daughter of Anthony Trabue and Magdalen Verneil, who were also refugees to Manikintown in 1700.

From these several lines come the Hales, Trabues, Dupuys, Subletts, Martins and many others of the settlers of Woodford County. The Vileys were French, and the present generation descend from all of the above lines.

In 1738 a number of Scotch-Irish Presbyterians left their native Ireland because the atmosphere, so to speak, was as little conducive to health, comfort and safety as it is in that unhappy land today, so they crossed the ocean and settled in Pennsylvania, where they found greater freedom, and an entirely different environment that was better suited to their several inclinations.

Among these several families were a number of brothers by the name of McKee, variously estimated at from five to ten in number. They settled near Lancaster, Penn., but two of them, Robert and John, removed to Rockbridge County, Va., in 1757, and settled near Lexington. In 1760 another brother, William, moved down into Augusta County, Va., where he established a home and reared a family. These brothers were all devout Presbyterians and regarded by their neighbors as gentlemen without question and well to do citizens, and the three above named brothers were the progenitors of all of the Kentucky McKees of whom I have knowledge.

Robert was of the sturdy type, so characteristic of the entire name. He was mild mannered and quite devoted to his own affairs, both secular and religious. His wife was Agnes, surname not now known, and they had two sons whose names were John and William. The latter figured quite conspicuously in the Revolution; was at Point Pleasant and engaged in many of the other battles during the war. He was also prominent in state affairs for several years thereafter—for a time Colonel of state militia. He served in the Virginia convention of 1788 and voted for ratification of the Constitution. In that convention his colleagues were such men as Henry Lee, Edmund Pendleton, Gov. Randolph, John Marshall (Chief Justice), James Madison and George Wythe, all for it, and Alexander Robertson, Patrick Henry, William Grayson, James Monroe and George Mason opposing ratification. These names represented a galaxy of talent and ability second to none that ever sat together in a Virginia assembly, and it was quite a compliment to have been associated with such an array of distinguished men.

He married his cousin, Miriam (daughter of John McKee and Jane Logan, of whom I shall speak later) and he and his wife came to Kentucky to live about 1790, locating in that part of Lincoln County that is now Garrard. 1752; Robert, Jr., born in 1754; Wil-

His wife died some years after coming to Kentucky, and Col. William McKee afterward married a widow by the name of Davis.

Besides his farm near Lancaster, he owned five slaves. His son by the first marriage was Samuel McKee, born in Rockbridge County, Va., in Oct., 1774. The son was a prominent lawyer, served in the Kentucky Legislature, was a member of Congress, Circuit Judge and had many other positions of public trust. He married Martha Robertson, of Mercer County, and they had two very distinguished sons in Hon. George *R. McKee, of Lancaster, and Col. William Robertson McKee, who fell mortally wounded at Buena Vista Feb. 23, 1847.

John McKee, the other pilgrim from Pennsylvania to Virginia in 1757 was regarded as a splendid type of man, every inch a gentleman, but likely less mild, and at times perhaps a little easier perturbed than his brother Robert. He was very positive in speech and action, and never sought popularity by cringing and, of course, didn't court or cultivate the namby-pamby class who shake hands freely and often for self-sake.

His first wife was Jane Logan, to whom he was married January, 1744. She was killed by the Shawnee Indians in one of their raids and massacres in Rockbridge County in 1763. His second wife was Rosanna Cunningham, to whom he was married in 1765. According to his will, dated October, 1791, he had these children: Mary Weir, born 1746; Miriam, born 1747; James, born 1759; William, born in 1759; David, born 1760,

---

* He served in Kentucky Legislature as Senator.

and John, born 1771, all children of the first wife except the last named. William's name was often confused with that of his cousin, Col. William McKee, who married his sister Miriam. Like his father, William was a man of positive character, whose dealings were square and open and he had the entire respect and confidence of his neighbors. He died in Virginia, about 1790, in which year his family moved to Kentucky with a company that included Col. William and his wife, Miriam, and they located at Mt. Sterling.

Robert McKee, Jr., married Margaret Hamilton in 1786, and with his brother David moved to Kentucky in 1790 and settled on a farm in Woodford County that is still in possession of descendants. It was about five miles from Versailles on the Frankfort road, at what has been known for many years as McKee's Cross Roads. By this marriage he had two sons, John, born 1787, and Samuel, born in 1789. Margaret Hamilton McKee died after a residence of three or four years in Woodford county, and her husband, Robert McKee, later married Jane Jacque, in 1795, and by this marriage came Robert III, Margaret, Mary and James.

Robert McKee, Jr., and his wife, Jane Jacque were living on their farm in 1810. They owned eight slaves, and the family consisted of eight persons. He died in 1812 in the old log house that was near the present residence, built before the Civil War, and now owned by his grandson, Dr. John R. McKee. John and Samuel, sons of the first marriage, settled on farms near Farmdale, in Franklin County soon after the war of 1812. The former was the grandfather

of Major Lewis, John and Will McKee, of Lawrenceburg, and Samuel was the grandfather of the wife of Jake Bashford, of Farmdale. Robert, III, son of the second marriage, moved to Missouri and James, the youngest son, married Christina Christman, granddaughter of Jacob and Mary Harper, who owned the farm, and lived in the house that stood near the gate of "Nantura," the farm of John, and then Frank Harper, now owned by Frank Hawkins, on the Alexander pike.

Mainly by frugality and energy, but also by inheritance, James McKee and "Tina" Christman, his wife, accumulated a large estate in land and negroes, purchasing much of the land from the executors of the Hon. Thomas Hart Benton, who was an able United States Senator from Missouri with large landed interests in Woodford County, being a relative of Col. William Hart. The large woodlands in the direction of Versailles from the McKee home are still known as the Benton woods. Col. Benton often visited the county in the 40s.

James McKee was reared in the old log house built by Robert McKee, Jr., on the cross-road to Spring Station, but about 1830 he bought the farm of Richard Fox that lay across the road from Dr. John R. McKee's residence and lived there until a few years before the Civil War he built the handsome residence now occupied by the family of his son. The old stone house built by Richard Fox prior to 1810, and occupied by James McKee and his wife for so many years, was burned to the ground more than a decade ago. It, too, was a land-mark, quaint in design and construction. The residence built by James McKee prior to the Civil War is quite an imposing structure and he and his wife "Tina" spent their declining years there. They had two children, Katherine, who married Col. John Withrow, and Dr. John R. McKee, who married Agnes Morancy, granddaughter of Col. Zach White and Agnes Steele (see sketches of Steeles and Bullocks).

Katherine McKee and Col. John Withrow lived for nearly a half century on the farm settled by Judge Caleb Wallace, near Midway. They had these children: Dr. William, who never married; James M., who married Maude Davis, and is at home on the old George Blackburn farm near Spring Station; John, who married Ermie Davis, and Lillie, who married Dr. Joseph C. Hughes.

Dr. John R. McKee inherited his father's estate and he and his wife, Agnes Morancy, are living there. They have these children: Dr. Emelius McKee, a leading physician of Lexington; James and Frank, who live with their parents and manage the large estate; Bettie, who married T. Vernon Foreman, of Lexington, and Agnes, who married Dr. John W. Gilbert, of Lawrenceburg.

David McKee, who came to Kentucky with his brother, Robert, Jr., married Ann Dunlap, daughter of Robert Dunlap and Mary Gay, and finally settled in Jessamine County, near Nicholasville, where he was one of the founders of the old Cedar Creek Presbyterian church, in which he was an elder when he died. They had a large family. One of his sons, David, Jr., came to Wood-

ford County to reside and was a citizen of the county for many years, but I have no line on his descendants.

Hon. H. Clay McKee, of Mt. Sterling, was a descendant of William McKee, the pilgrim from Pennsylvania to Augusta County, Va., in 1760. In 1788 this family came to Kentucky, where they divided, some of them settling in Mason County, others in Montgomery.

Wherever the McKees have been put to the test their gallantry has been conspicuous, especially upon the field of battle, and their integrity and efficiency in the discharge of duty, both private and public, has been no less in evidence. In the Civil War the name bore arms on both sides, and wherever they were mentioned in the annals of that war it was in praise of their valor.

On the 15th day of February, 1921, within a month after the above sketch was prepared for the Register, Dr. John R. McKee's spirit passed from the busy scenes of this life.

He, like his father, lived to a venerable age, nearly four score years, and died surrounded by all of the necessary comforts calculated to make this life worth while.

Dr. McKee was born and reared amid plenty, chose medicine as a profession and went to Europe, where he added the finishing touches to his equipment, during the Civil War, but his large farm, in which he took great delight, occupied the most of his time and attention. It is my impression that he never solicited patrons, but was always ready to serve those who suffered, and was very skillful and successful in his practice.

His demise removes one of a very few

men of his generation in the county, whose social and political relations were welded during the Civil War into unbreakable links by the exciting incidents of that period.

In the Wiley Edwards sketch, Page 81, I stated that Waller Edwards died during the Civil War, or soon thereafter. I knew that he had served the Confederacy, but had overlooked the incidents in connection with his tragic death until Capt. John A. Steele called my attention to them in a letter that I am using here:

"Believing that from your family connection an account of Waller Edwards' death may be of interest to you, I will write it as I remember it. During the greater part of the Civil War the Cumberland river was the dividing line between the Federal and Confederate forces. Early in June, 1863, a strong Federal force under command of Col. R. T. Jacobs crossed the river and attacked our outposts. General John H. Morgan who, with the main body of his troops, was some distance further south, at once moved toward, and after a rapid march attacked and in a spirited engagement forced them back across the river.

"After this our command was spread out to prevent a similar incursion. The Fifth Kentucky Cavalry (of which I was the forage master) was stationed at 'Howard's Bottom,' in Clinton County.

"Forage on our side of the river, which is so essential to the efficiency of cavalry, seeming exhausted I concluded to cross the river to the opposite side and find out what was there. It was

rather a hazardous venture but after finding a fording place near the mouth of Crocus creek I crossed over. I soon learned that there was no considerable body of Federal troops nearer than Glasgow and Columbia, and that only scouting parties occasionally approached the river, I rode up the creek two or three miles and found a good supply of corn, but it was a question how to get it across, as the ford was too deep for the passage of wagons. The only way which appeared feasible was to impress wagons hard to the river and let the men cross on horses with their forage sacks and then convey it to camp. Upon my return I reported the result of my investigation and was furnished a detail of twelve men to execute my plan, and Waller Edwards was one of the party. It was always the delight of 'the boys' to be chosen on such details, as they were free for a while from the restraint and monotony of the camp and could get what they termed a 'square meal' at some farm house. Our trip was without special interest, and after our return to the river, and while we were unloading the wagons, a citizen came and reported that two of our party had been killed about a mile in our rear. I looked over our party and found that Waller Edwards and a young soldier named Bell were missing.

"I at once recrossed the river and reported. In a few minutes two hundred men were in the saddle and in hot pursuit of the marauders. We soon came to a house near the road and found the dead bodies of the two men. Persons living at the place told us that a party of Federal soldiers, lead by a bush-whacker named Keyton, had surrounded the house and that the latter had shot them down in cold blood. This greatly inflamed the minds of the command and the pursuit was rapidly continued.

"We came to a point where the road forked, one leading to Glasgow and the other to Columbia. Numerous horse tracks in either direction were confusing, so it was decided to take the Glasgow road. We soon came upon a body of troops resting under the shade of trees in an orchard, and without halting a charge was made and they scattered in all directions through the woods and bushes. Some were captured, but fortunately for them it was proven they were not of the party that had committed the foul and cowardly deed.

"So Waller Edwards died, not upon the battlefield, as he would have chosen, but his life was given for a cause in which thousands of brave men sacrificed their lives for that which they believed to be just and righteous."

This statement gives the war record in part of two gallant, courageous and knightly young Woodford County Confederates, one returned a corpse, the other a cripple for life, both gentlemen, in war as in peace.

George Epler was born in Bucks County, Penn., Nov., 1764. He was with General Wayne in the Ohio campaign in 1794, but after the treaty of that year he came to Kentucky, and my impression is that he settled first in Fayette County. He married Elizabeth McClain in Dec., 1810, and soon thereafter moved to Woodford County.

where he and his wife took charge of the old log hotel that stood back of the Amsden Bank, and established a popular hostelry there. In 1812 they had the pleasure of dining the company of Captain Virgil McCracken the day they left Woodford County for the battle of the "River Raisin"—becoming a part of the regiment of Col. John Allen, of Shelby County—who immediately crossed the Ohio river and moved forward to Detroit, Mich., where they took part in that lamented battle,* both Col. Allen and Captain McCracken being mortally wounded, and William Railey, son of William Railey and Judith Woodson, succumbed after a stroke from a tomahawk, in the presence of his comrade, Joseph Frazer, who died near Versailles in 1864.

George Epler was one of the early jailers of Woodford County. I think the first jail was also built of logs, and the prisoners received food cooked in the Epler Hotel kitchen, and those who remember this family will guarantee that the prisoners received more than crumbs. About 1816 George Epler gave up the hotel and jail and moved down on the Kentucky river, where he occupied the old residence of Col. William Steele, at Steele's Landing, just above lock No. 5, but about 1823 he bought property at Milners (Raileys Station) where he lived until 1835 when he sold that home, with the old hemp factory, to Jack Shryock, and bought the Finch farm that lay between the Willis Field farm and that of Randolph Railey, Sr., in view of the property he had just disposed of. There he died in 1840. His widow and children then sold this

---

* Of the "River Raisin."

home and purchased the George Hunt farm, on "Buck Run," that lay in the shadow of "The Narrows," just below lock 5. George Hunt built and operated a distillery there for many years, and John and Boone Epler continued to operate and made pure bourbon whiskey there until after the Civil War. This property was originally owned by Thomas Fisher Thornton, father of David L. Thornton, of Versailles.

The Epler family was a very large one and well liked, not only by their neighbors, but by all who knew them, and their friends were only limited by their acquaintances.

The children of George Epler and Elizabeth McClain follow: Thomas M., born Dec., 1811, died Dec., 1865; Sam Steele, born June, 1813, went to New Orleans with a flat boat cargo and never returned; Ann born Aug. 31, 1814; Sarah Ann, born Sept. 1817, died Oct., 1892; William G., born Aug., 1819, died Dec., 1843; John C., born Sept. 1821, died June, 1903; Mira, born Jan., 1824, died Sept., 1855; Boone R., born March, 1828, died Aug., 1883.

Mira Epler married Hugh Shields, a kinsman of Gen. —— Shields, and they had James, born Feb., 1846, died April, 1916; George, born June, 1847, and is a resident of Versailles, and Samuel, born Feb., 1849, died in Versailles Dec., 1920.

John C. and Boone Epler lived and died on the old homestead at "The Narrows," and were bachelors. Their sister Sallie Ann was a spinster, and the housekeeper. She too died at the old home, loved and venerated. The memory of this entire family was te-

nacious; and they never tired of telling amusing incidents of the past, and many of our good citizens availed themselves of every opportunity to exchange greetings with them. They were intensely Union during the Civil War, but fair.

————

Dabney Parrish was a citizen of Spottsylvania County, Va., and was quite an old man when the Revolutionary War was launched.

He was married but there is no known record to indicate the maiden name of his wife, but the names of at least two of his children were preserved. They were Timothy and James. If Timothy was ever married I have no evidence of it, although it is likely that he was, and that he was the ancestor of Judge Leroy Parrish who, for many years, was county judge of Woodford County. I am sure he, Judge Parrish, was of the line of Dabney, but I have not been able to get any of his children now living in the county interested in tracing their line.

James Parrish married Tabitha —— and their descendants are quite numerous in this county and in the south and west. I have good reason for believing that his wife was a Thompson, but am not positive.

Both Timothy and James Parrish left Spottsylvania County, Va., in 1781, at the same time that one of the noted "Traveling Churches"* began its long journey, their destination being Kentucky, and both accompanied that caravan in its meanderings over the mountains and along the river valleys of Virginia and Kentucky. In December of

*See page 238.

that year they landed in that part of Lincoln County that is now Garrard, where they pitched tents and at once set to work to make themselves as comfortable as possible against the inclement weather that was just ahead of them, and rapidly approaching. That meant first of all a comfortable home, which was in due time provided, and the other necessaries followed in due time, and rendered their situation very comfortable and pleasant.

It would be interesting reading if one could run across the minutes of this company of pious pilgrims that moved over the mountains of Virginia and Kentucky so cautiously and deliberately frequently arresting their forward movements for the purpose of religious service, occasionally interrupted by bands of roving Indians or menacing beasts of the forest. But they journeyed under the influence and inspiration of prayer and it reminds us of those who were "led by a pillar of cloud during the day, and by a pillar of fire by night." I dare say, however, that while the distance and length of time put in would not compare with Moses' journey with the children of Israel, the journey was made with far less friction, as tradition says it was harmonious, nothwithstanding the many dangers encountered. So much for prayer. It has always been thus, and always will be.

James Parrish and his wife, Tabitha, reared a large family in Woodford County whose names were: Joanna Thompson, who married James Ware in 1810; Sallie, married Captain William Woods; James, married Margaret Shipp; Jonathan, married Sarah Baty,

and Mathew, who married and has relatives living near Lincoln, Neb.

Joanna Thompson Parrish and James Ware had eight children, most of whom moved to Mississippi and Texas.

Sallie Parrish and Captain Woods had a daughter, Eudora, who married William G. Davis, of Woodford County, and they had Thompson P., who married Lucy Trumbo, at one time deputy sheriff of Woodford and a long time merchant of Midway; William W., who married Stella Williams; John, who married Rosa Gorin; Bonnie, who married Arnett Pritchett; Margaret, who remains single, and E. L. (Bird) Davis, who married Margaret Martin, daughter of Henry L. Martin, and Kate Brooks.

James Parrish and Margaret Shipp lived near Spring Station, in the home now owned and occupied by John C. Alexander. They had Samuel, Richard and Thomas Parrish, all of whom were born and reared in this home, and Richard, I think, now owns and resides upon a portion of the original estate.

Jonathan Parrish and Sarah Baty lived in Woodford County and they had these children: Thompson Margus, born in 1810, and married Mary Blackburn, no issue; Mary B., born in 1812, and married Frank Starks, no issue; James Ware, Sr., born in 1815, and married first Martha Ann Price January, 1836, second Mary Philamon Price in 1841; third Susan (Branham) Davis, widow of Robert Davis. By the first marriage was Thompson Margus born in July, 1837, died June, 1902, married Kate Elizabeth Rodgers; Philamon Price, born in 1840, died in 1916, married Margaret Emily Magoffin Dec., 1870.

By the second marriage was Mary Philamon, born May, 1843, married R. C. Ricketts, Dec., 1862. By the third marriage were James and Ruth Parrish, both of whom died before years of maturity.

James Ware Parish, Sr., lived near Midway, on the Lexington pike, and was ever an influential citizen, being one of the promoters of the Female Orphan School at Midway, and he ably assisted Dr. Pinkerton in every movement that had in view the betterment of conditions and surroundings in that community.

Thomas Margus Parrish and Kate Elizabeth Rodgers had these children: Mamie Elizabeth, born in Sept., 1860, married Judge Ben F. Roach, of Harrodsburg and they had William Hughes, Kate Parrish, Thompson Parrish and Bessie Ware Roach; James Ware Parrish, born in 1862, married Lillie M. Stone. They have no children, but they have a portege in the person of Clara Kenney, who has given them pleasure from childhood; Dr. Benjamin Franklin Parrish, born May, 1866, married Hallie Gay, and they have Thompson and Lillie Parrish; and Isaac W. Parrish, born Aug., 1868, married Desdemona Wingate, and they have Honeywood, Katherine and James Ware Parrish, Jr., III.

Philamon Price Parrish and Margaret Emily Magoffin had Charles Ware, born Nov., 1872, married Catharine Wallace; Margaret Emily, who died young; Mary Philamon, born January, 1877, married Capt. J. Breckinridge Viley, and had Warren, Breckinridge and Philamon Viley, and Ruth Parrish, born Oct., 1879, married the Rev. Humphrey Folk, brother of Gov. Folk, of Missouri, and they have Emily Parrish and Humphrey Folk, Jr.

Mary Philamon Parrish and R. C. Ricketts had Agnes Margaret, born in 1863, and married Hill Thompson, no issue, and Elvira Ricketts, born July, 1866, and married William J. Owsley July, 1892, and they have Agnes Ricketts Owsley.

James Ware Parrish, Jr., owns a very fine farm that borders on the suburbs of Midway, and his splendid residence commands a view not only of the town, but of a wide scope of beautiful country that surrounds it. A stable on his farm shelters the celebrated racer Midway, and others that are being developed.

Captain Edward Parrish, of Yorkshire, England, was the first of the name in America. He was at one time connected with the British Navy, and transported the colonists who accompanied Lord Calvert, first to New Foundland, and later to Maryland, in which state he also cast anchor as a citizen, about 1632. He brought his four younger brothers, Robert, John, Richard and William, at a later date. It was from one of these brothers that Dabney Parrish, of Spottsylvania County, Va., descended, but the record between these five brothers and Dabney, covering at least two generations, was in such shape that I was unable to trace the line of Dabney back with any degree of accuracy, but the descendants of Captain Edward claim relationship with the descendants of Dabney now living in Kentucky.

Mr. Robert A. Parrish, of Maryland, has the original family record (ascending) and it carries the family back to Robert, King of France, and his father, Hugo of the Capet Dynasty, and several other royal families in Russia and Constantinople.

Captain Edward Parrish was born in England in 1600, and died at his home in West River, Maryland, in 1679. He made several voyages before finally determining to settle in America. In 1652 there was a formidable uprising among the Nanticote Indians, which aroused the colony to arms. Captain Parrish organized a company of troops and faced the enemy. By a special act of the Assembly of the province Capt. Parrish and his comrades were reimbursed for expenses they incurred, payment in tobacco, which seemed to be legal tender at that time in Maryland and Virginia, and worth a penny a pound, which was the equivalent of eight or ten cents a pound in our present coin. He was, as nearly all Marylanders were at that time, an extensive grower of tobacco, and that habit has characterized the generations to this good day—especially those in Kentucky.

Captain Edward Parrish left a valuable estate, principally in land and slaves.

You will notice above that I say that Timothy and James Parrish came to Kentucky with one of the "Traveling Churches." This because the party who gave me the data on the Parrish lines said it was not the same "Traveling Church" that the three preachers, Rev. Lewis, Elijah and Joseph Craig came with, but I have since read the book of the "Traveling Church," and of the 130 or more names it presents,

those of the two above named Parrishes appear alongside the Craigs and several other preachers. They left upper Spottsylvania Baptist church Sept., 1781, and the greater portion of them located at Logans Fort, on Dix river, then Lincoln County. Other preachers in the list were Ambrose Dudley, William E. Waller and John Waller, he who was so profane in early life, and was of the grand jury that had the Craigs arrested for preaching that which was contrary to law, but afterwards was himself a Baptist preacher and stirred Central Kentucky in the early days as no other did. His name was revered in Woodford within my recollection. Rev. Joseph Craig was he who laid down in the road in Virginia and refused to go to jail, and it was he who told his niece, who was desperately ill that it would be "the meanest thing you ever did if you die and leave these little children for your husband to rear." She recovered. The Rev. John Clay would have been with this caravan except that his demise occurred shortly before. He was the father of the "Commoner."

The three Craigs who were Baptist preachers were descended from Rev. John Craig, a Dominican Friar, about 1600, who, after reading Calvin's works, was suspected of heresy and condemned to burn at stake, but through connivance of a soldier friend he escaped about the time the reformation triumphed.

The Rev. William Marshall, brother of Col. Thomas Marshall, was with the "Traveling Church" also.

———

Richard Bastin and Joseph Roper

were early arrivals in Woodford County, both listed in the Federal census of 1810, the former having a farm and one slave, and his family consisted of five members. The latter owned a farm and two slaves and his family consisted of seven members.

Richard Bastin was born in Virginia in 1781, married in Woodford County in 1804 Polly Roper, born in Virginia, April, 1784. She was a daughter of Joseph Roper, who was a Virginian by birth. The children of Richard Bastin and Polly Roper were born in Woodford County. He died in 1816, and a few years later his wife and her four small children, in company with her brother, Jesse Mimms Roper and his family, migrated to Howard County, Mo., where very many of our pioneer citizens or their children located. The land upon which they settled in that state is still in possession of descendants, the homestead being the property of Henry C. Thorpe, a grandson of Richard Bastin. Many of the Buford descendants are in that county and state also. I am informed that the Bastin descendants have always been a very industrious, and a very religious class. The children of Richard Bastin and Polly Roper were: Henrietta, born October 12, 1806, died April, 1889, in Howard County, Mo., married August, 1823, Jackson Thorpe, born July, 1799. He was a son of Thomas Thorpe who was a son of the Rev. Wat Thorpe and Eleanor Jackson, of Madison County, Ky.; John Vardin Bastin, born in March, 1808, died Dec., 1851, married Ann Peary; Jesse Roper Bastin, born May, 1810, married Harriet McAdams,

and Mary Ann Bastin, born Sept., 1812, died May, 1901, married Dec., 1839, James Cash.*

———

Elijah Pepper whose family was sketched in the May issue of the Register, was, according to Biographical Cyclopedia of the Commonwealth of Kentucky, published in 1896, by John M. Gresham Company, a native of Virginia, who came to Kentucky in 1780. The county of Culpeper, Va., was named in honor of Sir John Culpeper, the progenitor of the Culpeper family of America, but the family name was changed by Elijah Pepper, the pioneer of Kentucky, after his removal to this state.

———

John Scearce was an early settler of whom I have learned but little. I have not been able to learn the name of his wife, but know that they had seven children. He is reported in the census of 1810 as having a family of nine persons. The names of the children follow: [1]James, born March, 1790; [2]Laban, born Jan., 1793; [3]John, born Sept., 1795; [4]Nancy, born March, 1797; [5]Lucinda, born Jan., 1799; [6]Henry, born April, 1800, died 1852, and [7]Martha, born March, 1802.

Laban, the first born, married and moved to Missouri, Clay County, where many of his relatives are now living.

Martha, seventh born, married —— Watkins, and they have a son, Laban Watkins, living at Liberty, Mo.

Henry, the sixth born, married America Berry, daughter of Samuel Berry, of the county, in 1822, and they had Susan Ann Scearce, who married Dr.

———

* The above notes were sent me by Mrs. Paul A. Klayder. See page 56.

William L. Crutcher (See pages 71 and 279), in 1841; Samuel B., born in 1825, died in 1877, married Lucy† Vaughan in 1840; William H., born in 1827, married Mary Johnston in 1849; John, born in 1832, married Martha Crutcher in 1854, and moved to Missouri before the Civil War, where they left issue; James L., born in 1834, married Ruhanna Ellis and had several sons; Dr. Jefferson B. Scearce, born in 1837, died in 1911, married Louise Vimont in 1860, and Amelia Scearce, the youngest, who was said to be the most beautiful woman in Woodford County, married James R. Barnes and died in 1851.

Susan Ann Scearce and Dr. William L. Crutcher had Henry Scearce Crutcher, Dr. William Lee Crutcher, Jr., Walter, and Martin Luther, (the latter two my school mates).

Samuel B. Scearce and Lucy Vaughan lived on a farm on Glenns creek that adjoined the farm of Dr. Theoph. Steele, which is now owned by E. H. Taylor, Jr. They had these children: Ed. H., who married Martha Reardin and moved to Reeds, Mo., about 1880; Blanton, who went to Clay County, Mo., about 1880, where he died, and Elizabeth, who married Willis Berryman, of Versailles. They have a daughter, Julia, who married the Rev. R. F. Campbell, of Ashville, N. C.

William H. Scearce and Mary Johnston lived many years on the farm that was afterward the home of Davis Edwards until his death. It was near the crossing of the Clifton pike by Steele's pike. William Scearce sold it in 1856 and moved to Shelby County, where he died in 1891.

John Scearce, the third of John Scearce, Sr., married Elizabeth Middleton in 1821 and they lived and died in Shelby County, where they have descendants. William Pratt Dale, a prominent lawyer of Louisville; Julian K. Dale, a government chemist, and Mary S. Dale, who married Prof. C. C. Freeman, of Transylvania College, are grandchildren. Adam Fulton, youngest son of John and Elizabeth Middleton Scearce, married Susan White and they lived and died in Shelby County. Their son, John C., married Anna Henton, daughter of Evan Henton, of Shelby County (see Henton sketch), and Ralph Scearce married Rosa Dudley, daughter of Rev. R. M. Dudley and Mary Henton. Anna Hinton was a cousin, and Mary Henton a sister of James Henton, of Woodford County (see Henton sketch). The Hentons of Woodford and Shelby are descended from two brothers, the one in Shelby spelling it Hinton and the one in Woodford spelling it Henton.*

While I am not able to trace the line back, tradition assures the Scearce family that they are descended from French Huguenots who, after the experiences of Bartholomew, crossed the ocean and settled in North Carolina before coming to Woodford County, Ky.

———

The old Shelton Tavern, at Versailles, run for a lifetime by Col. Medley Shelton, and which had its main rival in the Watkins Inn, the old stone hostelry sketched in the January issue of the

Register, was a very popular lodging house for more than a half century. The present hotel was built on the site of the old Shelton tavern.

From a window in the attic of this building, that looked diagonally across the street at the old court house, that was replaced by the present building in the '70's, the shot was fired that terminated the mortal existence of John Upshaw Warring.

———

A deed from Benjamin Craig to William Ware, Feb. 1, 1794, mentions the bounds of Edmund Ware's line.

———

June 23, 1813, Hankerson Read, a prominent pioneer of Woodford County, father of Ann Read, the second wife of Samuel Ware, mentions the following beneficiaries in his will: Thornton Read, Reuben Long Read, Samuel Ware Read, James Allen Read, Nathaniel Richardson Read and Lucy Read, and is witnessed by John Read and Lucy Read, and by John Read, and grandson, Hankerson Read Ware.

———

Will book G, page 33, notes dower allotted to Elizabeth Ware, whose maiden name was Betsy Bullock. She was a daughter of Col. Thomas Bullock, the first wife of Thomas M. Redd, and the second wife of Samuel Ware (see Bullocks, Wares and Redds).

———

On May the 30, 1799, a marriage license was issued by the Franklin County Court to John Bacon to marry Elizabeth Ware, daughter of William, the father of Samuel Ware, who married Betsy Bullock. The license was witnessed by Ed. Vaughan.

The following marriage licenses were issued in Woodford County to the following members of the Blanton family: Phoebe Blanton to Rodenham Route, Sept. 12, 1794; Betsy Blanton to George Bane, March 11, 1795; Thompson Blanton to Elizabeth Thompson, Jan. 20, 1812; Anne Blanton to William Woods, Nov. 15, 1812; Elizabeth Blanton to Anderson Shipp, Nov. 24, 1816, and Dorothy Blanton to John M. Hopkins, Aug. 6, 1820. The above Blantons were reared on farms in sight of Grassy Spring church.

———

Scott County was named in honor of Gov. Charles Scott, of Woodford County. McCracken County was named for Capt. Virgil McCracken, of Glenns creek, Woodford County. Crittenden County was named for Gov. John J. Crittenden, who was born and reared in Woodford County. Meade County was named for Captain James Meade, of the county, who lost his life at the battle of the River Raisin, as did Captain Virgil McCracken.

———

George Woodson Railey, son of Thomas and Martha Woodson Railey, was a deputy U. S. Marshal under Col. George Crockett, and took the census in 1810.

———

Robert Alexander, Captain Thos. Bullock, Col. William Steele, Captain Nicholas Lafon and others of the earlier settlers, were charter members of the Ky. River Navigation Company, organized in 1801, for the purpose of rendering navigable that stream by erecting locks and dams, so necessary at that time, owing to the lack of rail facilities, and inferior wagon roads.

Major Herman Bowmar, Sr., was the first deputy sheriff of the county, when Franklin and Scott were a part of it.

Robert Johnson, of Woodford County, was a member of the convention held in Danville in 1792 which framed Kentucky's first Constitution, and he represented the county in the State Senate 1792-95. His name does not appear in the census taken in 1810, which fact would seem to indicate that he was either dead or had moved from the county in the meantime.

John Mosby represented Fayette County in the Virginia Legislature in 1782, and again in 1784. He resided in that part of Fayette that became Woodford in 1788, and in 1810 the census reported him the owner of a farm and three slaves, and gave him a family of thirteen members.

John Taylor was a popular and noted Baptist minister who settled in Woodford County prior to 1788. He lived on Clear creek and preached for the Clear Creek Baptist church, likely its first pastor. He wrote one of, if not the first book printed in Kentucky, a book that was very popular with the early Kentuckians, known as "The Ten Churches." It is now rare and much sought for. The only one I know of extant is in the Louisville Baptist Theological Seminary.

He eventually moved to Franklin County, where he took charge of the old Buck Run church, which he retained until his death.

Edmund Waller was upon the pension list in 1810. He came to the county about 1784. There were seven members in his family and he owned a farm and two slaves. I am told that he was the father of the Rev. John L. Waller, who, as a Baptist minister, might be termed a spell-binder. His name was upon every tongue in the county before the Civil War. In 1784, perhaps just before he came to Woodford County, Edmund Waller assisted Simon Kenton to build the blockhouse at Limestone, afterward Maysville.

Marshall County was named for Chief Justice John Marshall, son of Col. Thomas Marshall, of "Buck Pond."

Hart County was named for Captain Nathaniel Hart, the father of Col. William Hart, of Woodford County.

The first newspaper publisher in Woodford County was the "Woodford Pennant," which was published in 1859 and edited by Coppage and Shrum. The next paper of record was edited by E. A. Routhe in 1866, and was called the "Central Kentuckian." In 1869 Clarence Greathouse, one of Woodford's brilliant and distinguished sons, and Capt. Henry McLeod, the father of Field McLeod, established and edited the "Woodford Weekly." This paper was ably edited by Samuel Field, a young lawyer, for some years, but was purchased by the Rev. Ben Deering, who put much pep and punch into the several departments, having a corps of country correspondents (W,m. E. Railey one of them) who were instructed "to shake the bushes" and send in all ripe fruit, and if that quality was scarce, top off with a few turn-ups. He consolidated the Woodford weekly with the Midway Sun and called it the Woodford Sun.

About 1880 Daniel M. Bowmar, Sr., succeeded to the proprietorship and edited the paper until his death, being ably assisted by his two sons, Aitchie and Daniel M., Jr. After the death of their father these two young men, scarcely out of their teens, succeeded to the management and editorship like veterans, and they have by good sense, good judgment, and push, made it one of the best weeklies in the state. It has always been Democratic in tone but clean-cut in advocacy of party principles, viewing everything from a moral standpoint rather than from the point of expediency or party regularity.

In 1875 Benjamin Deering established the Midway Sun at Midway. He was a good newspaper man, a practical printer, and for several years conducted it successfully. In 1877 he purchased the Woodford Weekly and sold the Midway plant to Daniel Lindsey, a practical printer from Lexington, who became its publisher, with the editorial department in charge of Dr. M. E. Poynter and Judge John Gillespie. They gave it the name of the "Blue Grass Clipper," which name it still bears. Several years later the paper was purchased by Chas. W. Buck, who, after a brief experience, sold to Bush J. Newlon. Newlon sold to F. D. Spotswood in 1884, who, shortly thereafter

sold to J. M. Hoge, who ran it for a year and sold to Godson and Williams. In 1897 the plant was purchased by Cooper and Railey. In 1916 Brown and Walters purchased the plant and continue to own and edit it. It has always advocated the principles of the Democratic party.

The population of Woodford County increased rapidly between the advent of Capt. Elijah Craig in 1782 and 1788, when it was bounded and established. Indeed there was such an influx that the population in the latter year was as great as it was in 1847. Of course we lost considerable territory, and suffered heavily in the loss of population when Franklin and Scott were formed, just prior to 1800, which accounts for our set-back in population.

The original corporate limits of Versailles constituted a circle with the point where the court house now stands as the center, the limits extending in every direction 660 feet from the center. The town was established by an act of the Legislature on June 23, 1792, the same year that Kentucky became a state in the union. The land upon which it was built belonged to an infant, and in order to procure one hundred acres thereof, power was vested in John Watkins, Richard Young, Cave Johnson, Marquis Calmes, Richard Fox, John Cook and Parmenos Bristow as trustees to lay off the same into lots and streets, dispose of the lots, execute deeds and adopt rules and regulations. Richard Young and John Watkins were appointed commissioners to sell the lots, receive the money therefor, to pay the money that accrued from that source, with lawful interest, to the infant heir, Hezekiah Bledsoe, "when he shall have attained his lawful age."

By an act of the legislature, Dec. 15, 1795, John O'Bannon, John Crittenden (father of the Governor), William Whittington, and John Jimms were appointed trustees to fill vacancies in the board.

The water that issued from the cave spring, in the rear of the court house, was sufficient in volume to run a distillery and a wool carding factory that were in operation soon after the town was established, besides supplying the citizens with water for all necessary purposes. This spring is the main source of Glenns creek.

The distillery was first operated by Elijah Pepper and his brother-in-law, John O'Bannon, but Elijah Pepper withdrew some years later and erected a distillery seven miles below on Glenns creek, where he manufactured the famous "Old Crow" whiskey. Col. John O'Bannon continued to brew after Elijah Pepper withdrew. I have not been able to learn who operated the "carding mill."

———

Collins' History contains the statement below, but all of the old citizens with whom I have talked concerning it disclaim any knowledge of the existence of such a formation, or any recollection of such a village:

"In 1819 there was a peculiar structure near Lovedale, in Woodford County, that was evidently the work of people of whom we have no record, and evidently erected for religious purposes,

or by a tribe who knew something of ancient secret orders. The structure was octagonal in shape, measuring one hundred and fifty feet on each side, was nearly or quite six feet high, and had three graded ascents or exits, one at each of the northern angles, and one at the middle of the western side, and one point each in the west, south, and east, where there seemed to be raised altars."

———

In 1860 John J. Crittenden delivered a speech at "Edgewood Farm," one mile from Versailles, on the Lexington pike (now owned by Hardin Field), at a barbecue given for the purpose of moulding sentiment against disruption of the union. I have been told that it was the largest attended gathering ever assembled in the county, being estimated at 25,000 people. It was said that for two hours Mr. Crittenden advocated union, and it was claimed that this meeting and speech was the turning point that kept Kentucky from seceding.

Many distinguished men from other states, as well as from all parts of Kentucky, were present to lend their influence either for or against the union of states.

———

One of the first banks established in Woodford County, was located in Versailles, and was organized in 1852. It was a branch of the Commercial Bank of Paducah.

———

*Col. Thomas Marshall died in Woodford County in 1803. Col. William Steele died in 1826. Robert Alexander died in 1841.

———

* He died at Washington, Mason County, 1802.

In 1854 the trial of Matt Ward for the murder of William Butler, in the city of Louisville, was the sensation of the day. The Wards were artistocratic, and the murder was generally regarded as without the slightest justification, if not positively brutal. The ablest attorneys in the state were employed, both Gov. John J. Crittenden and Thomas F. Marshall were retained by the defense, and equally strong talent was employed by the prosecution. But the speeches of both Crittenden and Marshall overcame the invective of the Commonwealth, so full of eloquence and pathos that the jury was completely swayed and rendered a verdict of acquittal, and the jury, verdict and defense counsel were bitterly condemned by the citizens of Louisville.

This case is presented here that the generation of today, and tomorrow, so to speak, may realize the forensic powers of these two distinguished sons of Woodford.

Col. Thomas Hart Benton, U. S. Senator of Missouri, was a close kinsman of Col. William Hart, of "Spring Hill" farm. He owned extensive tracts of land in Woodford County, beginning near the Hart estate and running very near to McKee's Cross Roads, and he made frequent trips to Woodford prior to his death in 1858. One writer says that he lived on his farm in Woodford County between sessions of Congress, but one of the best authorities in the county tells me this is a mistake, but confirms that part of the statement that relates to his extensive possessions and frequent visits.

The following men who distinguished themselves, and reflected great credit upon their native county of Woodford were John J. Crittenden, Judge J. Marshall, of the Louisville District Court in 1840; his brother, Thomas A. Marshall, Chief Justice of the Supreme Court; Thomas F. and his brother Edward C., both of whom served in Congress; Lieut. Governor William Berry Blackburn and his two nephews, Gov. Luke P. and Senator Jo. C. S. Blackburn.

Some of the lively encounters between the early settlers and the Indians occurred on Glenn's creek, near Millville.

An old newspaper says that Versailles had its first chartered bank in 1818, but it gives no name to the institution.

In 1824 there was a stage line from Louisville to Maysville by way of Shelbyville, Frankfort, Versailles and Lexington. This was the route over which LaFayette traveled in 1825, when he was handsomely entertained by the citizens of each of these towns. The good people of Versailles turned the keys of the town over to him with the assurance that there was nothing too good for the distinguished guest.

In 1826 the Ashland District was largely Whig, and so was Woodford County. Major Herman Bowmar, though a Democrat, had never been defeated for a county office, so the Democrats nominated him for Congress against Judge James Clark, of Bourbon, the Whig nominee, hoping that Major

Bowmar would be as popular in the district as he had always been in Woodford County, but the Whig vote was too large to overcome. Judge Clark was afterward elected Governor of the state.

In 1835 an epidemic of cholera swept over the county wiping out fifteen per cent of the population, and the remainder were more or less panic stricken. That was a huge percentage, and it was some time before the people recovered from the shock that the dreadful scourge wrought.

In 1835 Woodford was one of the ten counties to furnish a company of troops to protect the frontier from marauders. They went into camp at Frankfort to await orders, but the disorders soon subsided and the company returned to the county and was in due time disbanded.

In 1835 Daniel Webster and his interesting family were guests of Woodford County, and a number of receptions were tendered them, in which prominent citizens of neighboring counties took part to pay their respects to the distinguished guests.

In 1839 the Southwestern Railway Bank undertook to get a charter from the legislature to organize a branch at Maysville, which the citizens of that town opposed, employing Thos. F. Marshall to represent them before the legislature.

In 1841 the Hon. William Great-* house, of Woodford County, was employed to prosecute the Rev. John Mahan, of the state of Ohio, who was charged with aiding and abetting fugitive slaves, many of our slaves at that time crossing the river into Ohio, where much trouble and expense were incurred in locating and restoring the fugitives. The Rev. Mahan was proven guilty by an Ohio jury, and as a result the number of slaves who crossed the border of Canada was not so great.

During the year 1841 the friends of John J. Crittenden subscribed $17,000 with which they purchased the farm of his father, Major John Crittenden, located on the Lexington pike, and presented it to that gentleman, which was a high tribute to his popularity. He owned it and lived there a portion of the time until just before or during the Civil War it was purchased by the father of J. Hawkins Cleveland.

In 1842 Thomas Francis Marshall fought a duel with Col. James W. Webb without serious results.*

Lieutenant Colonel Ezekiel Field was an officer of the First Cavalry in the Mexican War in 1846 (see Field sketch). Capt. Thomas F. Marshall commanded a company in that war, and it was during that war that he fought a duel with Lieut. J. S. Jackson. Edward C. Marshall fought a duel with a Ward in Missouri.

In 1848 the negroes of Woodford County planned to steal horses from their masters in order to escape into

Ohio from whence they expected to make their way into Canada, but the plot was discovered just before the get-a-way and the arrangement was frustrated.

In 1849 violent and disastrous storms occurred in Kentucky, including Woodford County, and the residents of that day never tired of telling about the storms of '49, especially the colored population, many of whom got their religion for the first time.

In 1854 Robert Alexander, of the Woodburn Stock Farm, imported into the county the highest priced bull that had entered the county up to that time, and his neighbors thought him "beside himself" to pay $3,500 for a bull. But Robt. Alexander's motto was then, as it was ever afterward, it pays to buy high grade stock, regardless of price, and his act was an eye-opener for those interested in stock raising, and it marked an epoch in that' industry. He afterward imported cattle, sheep and horses at a cost that staggered many, but the investments brought handsome returns.

Gov. John J. Crittenden was entertained by the citizens of Woodford County for the last time during the year 1858. The reception was given in Versailles and every detail was well planned and admirably executed. It was through the influence of him and Mr. Clay that Woodford County was held so long in the grip of the Whig party, the pendulum never swinging

†See page 362.

back with force until the slaves were lost without remuneration.

During the late winter of 1862 the State Auditor reported that Woodford County was one of the ten counties that had paid the taxes assessed against it for the year 1861, which was the first year of the Civil War.

The old stone tavern, sketched in the January number of the Register, was one of the noted hostelries the first quarter of the 19th century, as was the old Mansion House at Frankfort. Many distinguished men were on its register, and many notable events took place within its walls. It was the scene of the grand ball given in 1825 in honor of the distinguished Frenchman,† LaFayette, when he was touring the state to pay his respects for the last time in person to his old friends and comrades of the Revolution.

The ball was given by the citizens of the county and each person vied with the other to make the occasion such a success that it would not be forgotten by any one of that generation, and it certainly was not forgotten at the time of the Civil War, being discussed around the fireside frequently at that time. As a boy, more than sixty years ago, I recall the vivid descriptions of that brilliant event by the elderly citizens, descriptions of the grand pageantry headed by Col. John Steele, the grandfather of our venerable Captain John Andrew Steele, of Midway.

Col. Steele, with a company of mounted militia, met the distinguished visitor near Frankfort and escorted him to Versailles. When he reached the town he was driven to the home of the widow of George Taylor Cotton, *Sr., nee Elizabeth O'Bannon, who was a daughter of Major John O'Bannon, one of the founders of Versailles. This home was on Elm street, and is now the home of the McLeods, but the old colonial home of the Cottons is now only a memory. Here LaFayette was tendered a reception that deeply touched the old soldier. Instead of the widow of George T. Cotton waiting on the porch, or within the portals of the home in the formal manner of the period to greet the veteran, she descended the steps and met him cordially with outstretched hands as he approached the house, after alighting from the carriage. I often heard that the scene was graphic. As this beautiful lady extended her hand the patriot grasped it with emotion, bended his body low and pressed his lips to it. Too bad that such a picture was not preserved on canvas.

At the grand ball and pageantry every feature was a success, as every means of enjoyment was unconfined.

LaFayette wept more than once in greeting his old comrades-in-arms, Calmes, Sublett, Dupuys, Trabues and others of French extract.

Judge Caleb Wallace and his wife, Rosanna Christian and Elizabeth Paulding, widow of Col. Henry Paulding, of the Revolution, who was a sister of Judge Wallace, were buried on the farm near Midway. However, their remains were disinterred during

*See pages 305, 387.

the summer of 1920 and now repose in the cemetery at Versailles.

———

Judge Caleb Wallace received his first appointment as judge in 1783 over the District of Kentucky, from Gov. Benjamin Harrison, of Virginia, he the ancestor of President William Henry Harrison, and also of President Benjamin F. Harrison.

———

Although Woodford County became such in name in 1788, it was not until May the 5th, 1789, that the citizens met at the home of Judge Caleb Wallace, near Midway, and organized a county system of government. Out of this assembly came the Court of Quarter Sessions and the selection of county officers, which included clerk, sheriff and constable, and the commissioning of justices of the peace, who had already been appointed by the Governor of Virginia and were sworn in that day. On May the 6th, 1789, the Court of Quarter Sessions met at the same place and proceeded to complete the organization and transact business. Later on several sessions were held in the "old Woodford church," on the farm of Robert Alexander, and still later several sessions were held at the residence of Col. William Moffatt, whose farm adjoined the home of Col. John Steele, and near old Woodford church, but on April 7, 1790, a session was held at "Falling Spring," the headwaters of Glenns creek, the spot where, in 1792, the town of Versailles was laid off. Since that date all courts have been held there, and all business of a judicial nature transacted there. However, the

Judge Caleb Wallace's law office, on Wallace place, where first courts of
Woodford County were held.

Stone building on Nuckols' farm used during decade 1782-92
as a Federal Court room.

Governor Charles Scott's cabin, near Kentucky River,
Woodford County, Ky.

first Federal court business transacted in the county was within the walls of the old stone house that is standing on the Sam Nuckols farm, one mile out on Tyrone pike.

On an adjoining page will be found cuts of the old court room on the Wallace farm, the old court room on the Nuckols farm, and the cabin built and occupied by Gov. Charles Scott from 1781 or 82 until his election to the Governorship in 1808. See sketch of Gov. Scott, page 109.

Judge Caleb Wallace was a presiding elder in the old Woodford church, near Midway, for many years. In writing his will be prefaced the document in this language: "In the first place I commend my soul to the mercy of God, through the merits and mediation of our Lord Jesus Christ, the only and all-sufficient savior of sinners, and my body to the grave, to be buried in a decent and frugal manner in the hope of its joyful resurrection."

He was educated for the ministry and occupied the pulpit for several years before he abandoned that profession and adopted the law.

John Upshaw Warring owned property in both Woodford and Franklin counties, had relatives in both counties, and divided his time between the two counties. Much has been written of him, and much more could be written. He was a lawyer by profession and had been reared in cultured circles, but he developed into one of the most unhappy, if not desperate men that lived in the county. He was as much

dreaded in Franklin as he was in Woodford. His life was never uneventful, and just here I am reminded of an incident related to me when a boy, and again by an old citizen recently in connection with Warring. It might best be termed serio-comic, as it is both sad and laughable, and is a typical exhibition of the man's character. I here relate it.

One of the best men in the county, Thomas Helm, a Christian gentleman, rode horseback to Versailles one day some years after the war of 1812, and purchased some china and glassware which was placed in a basket and handed to him while he was in the saddle. He moved his steed off slowly in the direction of his home. John U. Warring had an imaginary grievance against this elderly citizen, saw him start in the direction of his home with the basket of breakables and immediately conceived the idea of distributing the contents along the highway, so he immediately mounted his steed with whip in hand, and started in pursuit. He overtook the party in the outskirts of town, laid whip to the flanks of the horse and continued to pelt him until fragments of the basket's contents were strewn for more than a mile along the road.

After this episode Warring rode up to the front gate of the gentleman and pinned this card upon the gate-post:
"Here lives old thirty-three and a third per cent;
The more he got the more he lent,
And the more he got the more he craved.
Good Lord, can such a soul be saved?"

He should have added the following lines:

Good Lord, you know my soul's depraved
And from the first towards hell was bent.

When his assassination was announced in 1845, men and women in both counties heaved a sigh of relief.

Another incident in connection with the life of John U. Warring was staged in the old court house, that was replaced by the more imposing one built after the Civil War. The incident occurred in the early '40's, and was related in my presence when a boy. Warring was by no means a coward, but in all of his frays he sought, and usually got the advantage, but in this episode he crossed swords, so to speak, with the wrong man. Col. Zach White was of small stature, but undoubted courage, that had not often been tested, and Warring had cultivated a dislike for him. On a public occasion, when the court house was crowded, Warring took advantage of an opportunity to be offensive to Col. White and when that gentleman defiantly retorted, Warring thrust his sword-cane, which he always carried, into the face of the doughty Colonel, with the expectation that he would grasp it, release the sword which he would immediately thrust into the person of Col. White, but that gentleman anticipated the purpose, and instead of catching the cane he knocked it aside with his left hand, and in the twinkle of an eye swung his good right at Warring's temple, which brought him to his knees, and

then with a few stupifying thrusts he turned him over to his friends. Warring was never offensive to him again.

Another incident in the life of John U. Warring was about 1825, when the old and new court parties were overshadowing both the Whig and Democratic parties. The decision of Judge James Clark (afterward Governor) on the question of the nullification act, in that year, was the occasion of the two old parties merging into old and new court parties. The two contestants entered the political arena full of bitterness, and many friendships were badly strained, some to the breaking point. During that year (1825) Solomon P. Sharp, of Frankfort, was a candidate for the legislature on the new court ticket. The old court party, it is said, used every means to defeat him, both fair and foul. Warring, who had interests in Franklin as well as Woodford, espoused the old court side of the controversy, and wrote several threatening letters to Col. Sharp. Before the conclusion of the campaign Col. Sharp was assassinated upon the threshold of his home. Owing to the threatening letters, the finger of suspicion was at once fixed on Warring and he was arrested and prosecuted by the brilliant Samuel Q. Richardson, a kinsman of the Bucks and Calmes families, of Woodford County.

Before the trial was concluded, certain evidence that was being unfolded pointed unmistakably to one Beauchamp as the culprit, and Warring was dismissed, but he did not forget Richardson and his fearful arraignment that continually rankled in his bosom.

Ten years later he came in contact with Richardson (whose home was in

Lexington), on the stairway of the old *Mansion House at Frankfort and deliberately shot him to death. He was committed to jail without bond, but after three juries in three years wrestled with the case—the former two being tied, the latter acquitted him. Do you wonder that the people made no effort to apprehend the assassin in 1845?

Now these were dark days in Woodford County, but of the period antedating John Upshaw Warring, and the period that has intervened since his assassination, Woodford has been one of the most law-abiding counties in Kentucky. His life was the only one that even in a remote degree, brought discredit upon the fair name of Woodford, and I delight to chronicle the fact. While it may be to some very dull reading, unaccompanied by many tragedies with occasional intervals of peace and quiet, I prefer much sunshine with few shadows, and I am sure that Woodford County's Christian citizenship appreciates the even tenor that has characterized the past and holds the present in its embrace.

Col. William Steele and Sarah Bullock had two sons in the War of 1812. They were John and Samuel Steele, and both served under Captain Virgil McCracken, and in the regiment of Col. John Allen, of Shelby County. Samuel lost his life at the battle of the River Raisin, and John was a good citizen of Woodford County for many years after the war.

I have been told that a pioneer by

the name of Pearl donated land in the county for Seminary purposes, but my effort to locate this property, or ascertain what disposition was made of it has been without success.

The old Commercial Bank was organized in Versailles May 29, 1852. David Thornton was elected its first president, and served continuously until his death in 1873. His successors have been men identified with the best interests of the town and county, as you will observe by casting your eyes on the following names: Col. Lewis A. Berry, J. W. Twyman, Robert McConnell, George W. MacLeod, Lister Witherspoon, James M. Graves, Samuel L. Wooldridge, Sr., and J. N. Camden.

During its more than sixty-eight years of service the bank has had but four cashiers, viz.: Richard Shipp, Jr., who resigned to take charge of a bank at Midway; Edward Kavanaugh Thornton, D. P. Robb and Louis Marshall, the present cashier. For many years they transacted business in the brick building opposite the post office as you approach the cemetery. This building is one of the landmarks of Versailles. During the 70's, I think it was, this bank moved to the opposite side of the street, somewhere near the present site of the Amsden Bank, and the name was changed to the Woodford County Bank, or vice versa; later it moved to the corner of Main and Lexington streets, near the hotel, and still later moved to the opposite corner, where Ed Wasson conducted a drug store for many years,

* Now Peoples Bank Bldg.

and is now doing business as The Woodford Bank and Trust Co.

This advertisement appeared in the old "Frankfort Commonwealth" of May 28, 1833:

"Woodford County Farm For Sale.

"I offer for sale, on liberal terms, my farm in Woodford County, on the road from Versailles to Georgetown, about four miles from Versailles and two and one-half miles from where the road crosses the Lexington and Ohio railroad (this road crossed where the line separates the H. L. Martin farm from the Tom Woods farm, and at that time the L. & N. wasn't built, nor was Midway on the map). As a stock farm, or for cultivation of hemp it is equal to any in that beautiful and desirable part of Kentucky. It contains about 365 acres, and might be divided to great advantage in two parts, to suit purchaser, if desired, each having a comfortable dwelling house and other necessary buildings on it. Near one-half the tract is well timbered, and the farm, fences, etc., in excellent condition, and a good part of it well set in bluegrass, timothy and clover, with two good springs and a very abundant supply of stock water.

"For terms apply to Thomas Bullock, on adjoining premises (the Wallace or Clinton Hawkins farm) or to Major John McKinney, Jr., or Randolph Railey, Jr., Esq., Versailles, or to subscriber in Louisville.

"Chapman Coleman.
"April 9, 1833."

This is the farm upon which Capt. J. Breck Viley now resides, his father having purchased it and moved there about 1838. (See Coleman sketch in Sept., 1920, Register). Chapman Coleman was one of the sons of pioneer James Coleman and Sarah Taylor. He married Ann Mary Crittenden, daughter of John J. Crittenden and niece of the wives of Major John McKinney, Jr., and Randolph Railey, Jr., to whom purchasers were referred.

In the sketch of the Castleman family I said that Lewis Castleman, the pioneer, was a native of Virginia, but I was in error. Lewis, Jacob and David were three brothers of an English family who moved to Holland where they resided for some time, but clung to their English traditions and tongue. About 1740 these three brothers came to America and settled in West Virginia,* at what they called "Castleman's Ferry," which still retains the name, I am told. Jacob later removed to Maryland or Pennsylvania, where his descendants are quite numerous. Lewis came to Woodford County, Ky., and David remained at "Castleman's Ferry," where many of his descendants now reside. The old home they established there is still standing and used as a summer resort or boarding house. It was built about one hundred and eighty years ago, and the only change that has taken place is an addition that was erected about 1845.

The same party who makes this correction informs me that Samuel Castle-† man, of St. Matthews, Ky., has in his possession portraits of pioneer Lewis Castleman and his wife Jemimah Pear-

---

* It was in Virginia at that time.
† See page 64.

sall, of Woodford County. See sketch of Castlemans in September number Register.

The September number Register also contained a sketch of the Cole family.* of whom I have since gotten additional facts, not obtainable through my former correspondence. For instance, I did not give the maiden name of either the wife of Richard Cole, Sr., or Richard Cole, Jr., which I very much regretted, but through a later correspondent I ascertained the names of these two women and gathered some additional data as to descendants. Richard Cole, Sr., married Ann Hubbard, and his son, Richard, Jr., married Sallie Yates.

My former correspondent also stated that the Coles came to Woodford County, Ky., from Pennsylvania, but my later correspondent states that they domiciled for a time in Culpepper County, Va., before coming to Kentucky, which I think is true, as all of the Pennsylvania families that I have sketched moved first to Virginia or Maryland, then to Kentucky.

I was only enabled to give a partial list of the children of Richard Cole, Sr., in the September issue, but from the files of the wife of Dr. Matthew Cotton Darnell I will now give a complete list of his children. They were: John, who married Nancy Hines and lived in Barren County; Richard, Jr., who married Sallie Yates; Jesse, who married Nancy Sparks; Rachael, who married Willa Jett; Betsy, who married —— Snape; Agnes, who likely never married; Sallie, who married Ben Graves; Alice,

who married Anthony Lindsay, and Lucy Cole, who married Jonathan Cropper.

Willa Jett and Rachael Cole had a son, Thomas, who married Elizabeth Swetnam, and they were the parents of William Willa Jett who married Sallie Coleman, a descendant of James Coleman, who settled on the Viley farm. The latter couple were the parents of Ermina Jett, who married Dr. Darnell. Thomas Jett was another son of Thomas Jett and Elizabeth Swetnam, who married Virginia Darnell. (See Darnell for descendants, page 93).

Six miles from Versailles and eight miles from Frankfort stands a two story frame house, with an ell, that was very popular in the early days with both the traveling public and the dwellers in the vicinity. I am told that anything from a tooth-pick to a sprig o' mint could be obtained for the price. This hostelry was known as "Dorsey's Tavern," the house more than one hundred years old but splendidly preserved, and in the period of stage-coach travel, was very popular and well patronized. In those days, that was the main method of transportation, and in use on this highway from Maysville to Louisville, via Lexington, Versailles, Frankfort and Shelbyville, and these taverns were a haven of delight to the weary travelers who could stop in a delightful community for a short period to refresh themselves.

On the opposite side of the road was a store room to supply the wants of the dwellers in the vicinity who were the Blantons, Hentons, Lafons, Whitting-

*Page 65.

tons, McKees, Thomsons and others. The proprietor was Patrick Dorsey, who was universally popular.

Edmond Shipp, who likely built the second house erected at McKees crossroads, served in the war of 1812, and was the father of "Dick" Shipp, who, for twenty years or more had charge of the county bastile, and was such a popular host. Dick Shipp saw service in the Confederacy for about four years.

I think the first house built at McKees was an old stone residence that stood opposite the gate entering Dr. John R. McKee's home, and was built before 1800 by Richard Fox, who was residing there in 1810, having a family of ten persons, and was the owner of nine slaves.

Benjamin Berry's will was likely the longest recorded in Woodford County, and his family, eighteen children, the largest of any of the early families in the county.

Sowel Woolfolk* was a wealthy citizen of the county in 1810, having a large farm and twenty-two slaves to his credit, and a family consisting of five members. I have not been able to get anything definite about this pioneer, either relating to his ancestors or descendants. I hope some day to get in touch with some one of his relationship. It is my impression that Lucy Woolfolk, who married John Samuel in 1798 was a daughter, and that Richard Woolfolk, who married Sarah Taylor and moved to Jefferson County, near the home of

Col. Richard Taylor, was a son. Sarah Taylor was a daughter of Captain Zach Taylor and Alice Chew, of Woodford County. See Taylor and Samuel sketches in January Register.

Woodford County built a jail of stone in 1835, or about that time, and the stone that was used in the structure was taken from the quarry at the mouth of Steele's branch, just above lock No. 5. I was told when a boy that much of the stone used in the old lock walls was taken from that quarry.

Benjamin Berry, Sr., owned a distillery and mill on Buck Run, not far from his residence, and not far above the "Narrows," that he operated for a long period, but some years after his death these two plants were transferred to the Hackneys, who owned and operated them until after the Civil War.

---

†Captain John Bullock and his wife, Elizabeth Railey came to Woodford County about 1800. They were married in Chesterfield County, Va., she being the third daughter of Col. John Railey and Elizabeth Randolph of "Stonehenge." She was born April 26, 1757, and married Capt. Bullock, Sept. 9, 1786.

Captain Bullock served in the Revolution and was a kinsman of James Bullock, Jr., and Edmond Bullock, both of whom came to Woodford County at a much earlier date and were sketched in the September, 1920, Register, but I am unable to state the degree of relationship.

---

*See Woolfolks, pages 316, 396.
†See pages 106, 119, 121, 302.

Captain Bullock and Elizabeth Railey had three daughters, all born in Virginia. They were Jane Railey Bullock, born Aug. 23, 1787, died January, 1833, married David Anderson, December 5, 1805; Elizabeth Randolph, born May 20, 1789, died March 27, 1821, married Dr. Joseph Crockett, Jr., March 25, 1813, he a son of Col. Joseph Crockett and Elizabeth Woodson; and Maria Patterson Bullock, born March 12, 1791, married her cousin, George Woodson Railey December 8, 1818, he a son of Thomas Railey and Martha Woodson. George W. Railey was appointed Deputy U. S. Marshal under Col. Joseph Crockett, and he took the census of 1810 of Woodford County. See pages 9 to 20.

Captain Bullock and Elizabeth Railey removed to some point in the vicinity of Bowling Green prior to 1810, and he died there shortly thereafter. David Anderson and Jane Railey Bullock also moved to that part of the state, where he died in 1827. Soon after this death his wife and her children and mother, accompanied by George Woodson Railey and his wife, removed to Palmyra, Mo., where all of them lived and died, and where many of their descendants now live. The wife of Dr. Joseph Crockett died in Versailles, where he practiced medicine until his death, and her remains, with his, repose in the Crockett burial ground in Jessamine County.

The Andersons were Scotch-Irish Presbyterians, and the Raileys were also of that faith. They were a family of lawyers, and many of the leading lawyers of Missouri, both in the male and female lines, past and present,

sprang from this Anderson family. Thomas L. Anderson, son of David Anderson and Jane Railey Bullock, served the Palmyra, Mo., district in Congress before and during the Civil War, serving with John J. Crittenden and Humphrey Marshall. He was a presidential elector for Harrison, Taylor, Scott and Clay, but was recognized as a Democrat during and after the Civil War. The Rev. William Anderson, the much loved pastor of the Presbyterian church at Shelbyville for a decade or more, is a grandson of David Anderson and Jane Railey Bullock.

John Pleasants, of Norwich, England, born in 1643, married Jane Tucker and came over to "Curles," Henrico County, Va., in 1668. His grandson, John Pleasants, of "Pique-Nique" (Picker Knocker), Va., son of Joseph Pleasants and Martha Cocke, married Susanna Woodson, daughter of Tarleton Woodson and Ursula Fleming. They had several children, two of whom were James Pleasants, of "Contention," and Mathew Pleasants. The former married Anna Randolph, daughter of Col. Isham Randolph and Jane Rogers, of "Dungeness," Va., and had James Pleasants, who was U. S. Senator and Governor of Virginia, and Martha (Pattie), who was the second wife of Randolph Railey, Sr., of Woodford County, whose descendants will appear under sketch of Raileys.

Mathew Pleasants, born at "Pique-Nique," Va., died in Woodford County in 1818, married Anna Railey, February, 1784, daughter of Col. John Railey and Elizabeth Randolph. She was born

September 16, 1757, and died in Woodford County in 1826. Mathew Pleasants and his wife came to Woodford County with Capt. John Bullock and family about 1800, and they settled in the vicinity of the Graddys, on the Clifton road, not far from Glenns creek, I think the place now known as "Welcome Home;" at any rate, it was in that vicinity. He was reported in the 1810 census as having a family of six and owned eight slaves.

Their children were Caroline Fleming Pleasants, born July 27, 1787, died February 21, 1852, married Col. William Mayo in 1808, he the 7th born of Col. William Mayo and Catherine Swann, of Richmond, Va.; George Woodson Pleasants, born July 1, 1789, died in Woodford County in 1812; Peyton Randolph Pleasants, born April 19, 1791, died 1817, married Ann Catharine Humphries, no issue; Pauline Pleasants, born July 16, 1793, died in 1816, married Robert Johnston, of Fayette County; Benjamin F. Pleasants, born Nov. 10, 1795, died June 2, 1879, married Isabella McCalla Adair in 1817, and Elizabeth Randolph Pleasants, born Jan. 9, 1796, died Dec., 1881, married Douglas Young in 1835.

Col. William Mayo was proprietor of a tavern in Versailles that he and Caroline Pleasants gave much attention to. As "Col. Billy" Mayo he was a very popular host, and about 1846 he moved to Shelbyville and engaged in business, but a few years later he, with many others, got the Missouri fever and moved to Cooper County, Mo.

They had a son, Dr. Addison Mayo, born Dec. 6, 1809, who practiced medicine at Versailles until a short time prior to the Civil War he moved to Colorado; Georgiana Mayo, born April 11, 1813, died Oct. 16, 1840, married Dr. William P. Harriman in 1837. He practiced medicine in Versailles, and their son, William P. Harriman, Jr., moved to Missouri, where he became a successful banker at Pilot Grove.

Benjamin F. Pleasants and Isabella Adair, she a daughter of General John Adair, who was Governor of Kentucky 1820-24, located at Harrodsburg and remained there until he was appointed to a responsible position in the U. S. Treasury in 1830 by President Jackson, at which time he moved his family to Washington, where his service was continuous until a short time before his demise in 1879. Three of his sons, George W., John Adair, and Mathew F., Jr., were lawyers of ability, the former a judge upon the Supreme Court bench of Illinois for thirty years, the two latter prominent at the Richmond, Va., bar until they died a decade or more ago.

Douglas Young and Elizabeth Randolph Pleasants resided on the Jackson farm, on the Tyrone pike, where the late Sam Hampton lived for many years, and where they died at an advanced age. They had an only child, Susan Railey Young, who married Dr. T. K. Layton, Dec. 2, 1856. She born March 31, 1836, and now living in Ferguson, a suburb of St. Louis, quite old, but fairly well preserved. Dr. Thos. K. Layton, built a residence and office on the far end of the Douglas Young estate and he enjoyed an enviable practice until his death in the 80s. They had these children: Jennie Layton, who married Andrew Wallace;

David W., Whitney, Douglas Young, Thomas K., Jr., Nannie, Susan, Hugh and Ambrose Young Layton. David is married and living at Hematite, Ky., and the other members live near their mother in the vicinity of St. Louis, Mo. Whitney and Hugh were successful business men at St. Louis.

Manoah Singleton, who was an early settler near Keene, in Jessamine County, had thirteen children. His wife was Sarah Craig, daughter of Talliaferro (Toliver) Craig and Mary Hawkins (see sketch of Craigs). Of this large family of children the following married and lived in Woodford County for ᴛ time, and some of them have descendants in the county now. They were: Jekoniah, born March, 1776, married Jane Taylor, daughter of Rev. John Taylor, pastor of the Clear Creek Baptist Church, and author of the "Ten Churches;" Elizabeth Singleton, who married George O'Neil; Mason, who married Fannie Garnett; Ann, who married James Hiter, and Susan, born in 1793, married Joseph Hughes.

I have not been able to get a line on the descendants though some of them now live in the county. Mrs. Nathaniel Porter, who was the head of a boarding house in Midway for many years, and was said to be one of the characters in "Tempest and Sunshine," was a descendant.

The father of "Tolliver" Craig, the 1st was John Craig, Jr., of Scotland, who died in 1704, and whose wife was Jane Talliaferro. After his death his widow came to America with her two brothers, Robert and John Talliaferro, where her posthumous son "Tolliver" was born, in Spotsylvania County, Va., in 1705. He married Mary Hawkins in 1730, and they were the parents of Lewis, Elijah and Joseph Craig, the three preachers who led the famous "Traveling Church" into Kentucky from Spotsylvania County, Va., in 1781. John Craig, the father of "Tolliver," was either a son or a grandson of John Craig, the Friar, mentioned in the sketch of the Parrishes. Page 232.

John Long, who married Mollie ——, was one of Woodford's very early settlers whose descendants I have not been able to get a line on. He likely died in 1797, as his will is of record in the county court and dated in that year, and was witnessed by Samuel Brooking, Henry Lurton and Sallie Long. The names of his children provided for in the will are: Lucky Long, Jane, William, Willis, Sallie and Richard Long.

There were five Railey brothers who came from Chesterfield County, Va., to the county of Woodford between 1790 and 1796.* When a boy I was told that the first two of these brothers came as early as 1783 or 84, and the other three at intervals between 1786 and 1793, but I had the pleasure recently of seeing a tax book that was used by Col. Richard Young in 1788, and no Railey was listed. I went to Versailles and investigated the records and found that the Raileys made their purchases in the Griers creek neighborhood in the 90s, instead of the 80s, as

---

* The Trabues, Subletts and Dupuys also came from Chesterfield County and all settled in the same neighborhood in Woodford County.

1 had been told, and I am glad that I made this discovery before writing this sketch, as I wish to be accurate.

The names of these brothers were: Thomas, Isham, William, Charles and Randolph, Sr. They were sons of Col. John Railey, of "Stonehenge," Chesterfield County, Va., and his wife, Elizabeth Randolph, and Elizabeth Randolph was a daughter of Col. Isham Randolph and Jane Rogers of "Dungeness," Va.

*Thomas Railey was born in Virginia, Sept. 22, 1754, died in Woodford County in 1822, married Martha Woodson, daughter of Col. John Woodson and Dorothy Randolph, of Goochland County, Va., Dec. 21, 1786. She was born July 6, 1764, and died in Woodford County in 1834. Thomas Railey located his home on the heights that overlook the Kentucky river at Clifton, and a vast expanse of broad fertile acres in Anderson County. Thomas called his country seat "Clifton," and the village in the valley below took its name from the home above. The view from this point over a large area in both Woodford and Anderson counties rivals the scenery that meets the vision from the home of Edward Trabue five miles above. Such a beautiful view as these two points afford may be equaled, but hardly surpassed.

†Isham Railey was born in Virginia in the ancestral home July 15, 1758, and died in Woodford County March 14, 1814. He married Susanna Woodson, daughter of Col. John Woodson and Dorothy Randolph, in Goochland County, Va., Sept. 17, 1784. Her birth oc-

curred June 26, 1760, and her death occurred in Woodford County Dec. 6, 1818. Isham Railey bought the farm on Tyrone pike, recently the dwelling place of Samuel L. Wooldridge, Jr.; three miles from Versailles and a half a mile from Griers Creek church. This farm was known as "Vine Grove," and remained in possession of descendants until about 1900. The Thomas Railey farm passed from the ownership of descendants about 1890, the late George Railey Berryman being the owner until his death. It is now owned by James Miller.

†William Railey, born in Chesterfield County, Va., Feb. 26, 1760, died at his country seat "Liberty Hall" in Woodford County Feb. 8, 1818. His home cornered at Griers Creek church and followed the road to Milners Station. The two and one-half story brick house he built there near the church was one of, if not the first, built in Woodford County of the kind, and all of it, except a wing that was destroyed by a gale after the Civil War, is in good condition. He married Judith Woodson, daughter of Col. John Woodson and Dorothy Randolph in March, 1793. She was born in Goochland County, Va., Feb. 16, 1767, and died at "Liberty Hall" Dec. 26, 1831. Dorothy Randolph was also a daughter of Col. Isham Randolph and Jane Rogers.

†Charles Railey was born at "Stonehenge," Chesterfield County, Va., Oct. 26, 1766, and died on his estate "Buck Run" in Woodford County, Oct. 27, 1837. He purchased a farm that adjoins the estate of his brother William,

---

* Goochland County.
†Cumberland County; so was William and Charles. See Raileys and Kindred families, page 103, for birth place of these brothers.

HOME OF CHARLES RAILEY, "BUCK RUN"

1800

This home is now the property of Louis Morancy passing from Railey
heirs early in the 19th Century.

HOME OF WILLIAM RAILEY

"Liberty Hall," built in 1796. Great grandfather of Wm. E. Railey.
William Railey's children and grandchildren born there.

HOME OF RANDOLPH RAILEY, "CANE BRAKE"

1800

Randolph Railey and his wife, Patsy Pleasants, are buried in a walled in lot near the house. Patsy Pleasants was a sister of Gov. Pleasants of Virginia, and niece of Matthew Pleasants, who married Anna Railey, a sister of Randolph Railey.

the Southern railway running through both farms. He married April 4, 1796, Mary Mayo, daughter of Col. William Mayo, of Richmond, Va., and his wife Catharine Swann. She was born July 12, 1779.

Randolph Railey, Sr., married first his cousin, Mary Elizabeth Keith, while she was visiting Kentucky relatives in 1800. She was a daughter of Capt. Isham Keith and Charlotte Ashmore, of Virginia, and the granddaughter of the Rev. James Keith and Mary Isham Randolph. She was born in Virginia in 1781, and died at her home in Woodford County in 1803. He married second his cousin Martha (Pattie) Pleasants, of Virginia, in 1819, daughter of James Pleasants, of "Contention," and his wife, Anna Randolph, hence she was a sister of Gov. Pleasants. Her birthdate Dec. 2, 1779. Her death occurred at "Canebrake" in Woodford County July 10, 1849. Randolph Railey was born May 14, 1770, in Chesterfield County, Va., died on his estate "Canebrake" in Woodford County, May 28, 1837. His farm adjoined that of his brother Charles and he built a substantial brick house that is in fine condition today. The residence of Charles Railey was built, I think, of logs and weatherboarded, and is in good shape today, though just a little modernized and is still in possession of descendants.

The children of Thomas Railey and Martha Woodson were: Thomas, Jr., born in 1787, died in 1821, married Sarah Railey, his cousin, in 1820; George Woodson Railey, born 1789, died 1846, near Palmyra, Mo., married

Maria Bullock 1818. He was just 21 years old when he took the census of 1810, included in the first chapter of the Woodford County notes; Peter I. Railey, Sr., born March 16, 1793, died July 1, 1832, married Judith Woodson Railey August 21, 1817; Jane, born 1794, died Nov. 28, 1865, married John* Berryman Aug. 9, 1819; Mary Railey, born 1795, died May, 1817, married Philip Woodson; Lucy, born Aug. 5, 1796, died Sept., 1852, married first John D. Kinkead, second Rev. William M. King in 1832, and Susanna Railey, born January 15, 1801, died May 1, 1872, married William Fleming Markham July 19, 1825.

Peter I. Railey and Judith Woodson Railey had Richard Henry, born April 26, 1823, died Oct. 3, 1888, married Feb. 25, 1852, Katherine Keith Hawkins, born Oct. 18, 1825, died June 22, 1902. She was a daughter of William Strother Hawkins and Katherine Keith (see Strothers); Peter I., Jr., born Aug. 25, 1829, died Feb., 1910, and was thrice married, first to Sarah E. Frazer Oct. 22, 1852, second to Rebecca Gough, 1861, third to Seville Church in 1898.

Richard H. Railey and Katherine Keith had William Edward, born Dec. 25, 1852, married Annie Owsley, May 26, 1886, whose daughter, Jennie Farris Railey, born June 28, 1887, married Douglas Wheeler King June, 1917; Bertha Hontas, born April 26, 1854, and P. Woodson Railey, born July 24, 1865.

Peter I. Railey, Jr., and Sarah Frazer had Josephine, born Sept. 22, 1852, died 1919, married Robt. Ward Macey Nov. 21, 1872, whose children are Pattie,

*See pages 361, 372.

Sadie, Robert Ward, Jr., married ——†
——, and P. Railey Macey, who married Martha Railey and have Railey and Martha.

Jane Railey and John Berryman had Mary Elizabeth, born Jan. 5, 1820, died June 4, 1905, married George Hamet Cary Sept. 1, 1840. James, Mary, Mattie and Elizabeth Cary, of Versailles, are grandchildren; other grandchildren are Jennie Cary, Mary Louise, Daniel† B. and Alice Price, and Graddy Cary. Other descendants live in Louisville.

James T. Berryman, born April 22, 1822, died June 4, 1879, married first Theresa Willis, second Sallie Steele Church. By the first marriage was John W., who married Louise Price and had Price Berryman, Theresa Willis, who married Oliver Farra, and Robert S., who married Ruth Gay; J. S. Berryman and Mary Wright have descendants in Louisville; Mollie, spinster, and Annie, who married W. Horace Posey. By the second marriage was Cary M., who married Emma Portwood; Church, Claude, Clifford,* and Hervie Berryman.

Robt. H. Berryman, born April 17, 1824, died April 4, 1878, married Maria Whittington (see Whittington sketch).

Edwin H. Berryman, born March 14, 1826, died Dec. 26, 1896, married Sallie Willis May 27, 1852 (see Holloways).

Mattie Woodson Berryman, born April 24, 1836, married Robt. Fry Montgomery June 10, 1856, and had George Berryman, Jane Railey, Mary, Mattie Woodson, John B. and Robert Montgomery (see Holloway).

George Railey Berryman was born 1838, died 1882. He served in the Confederacy for four years, came home and took charge of "Clifton," the old home of Thomas Railey and maintained a bachelor's palace until his death.

Frank P. Berryman, born 1842, died 1921, married Susan Hassenger, of Palmyra, Mo., in 1866. He was four years with the gallant Morgan, and after his return from the war he engaged in farming. Their children were John, who married Annie Harris; Kate, Newton, Wilhelmina, Sidney Robertson and Frank P., Jr.

Lucy Railey had no children by the first marriage to John D. Kinkead. By the Rev. William King was Rev. Samuel Alexander King, who moved to Texas and preached for the Presbyterian church at Waco for forty years.

Susan Railey and William Fleming Markham moved to New Orleans about 1830. Their son, Thomas Railey Markham, was a chaplain in the Confederate service, and preached for one congregation of Presbyterians in that city for forty years, barring the time he was in the army. He and the Rev. Samuel A. King, afterward visited their relatives in Woodford County and occupied the pulpit in the old Griers Creek church and the old church at Versailles.

Isham Railey, Sr., and his wife, Susanna Woodson, had these children: John, born July 18, 1785, died Aug. 7, 1844, married his cousin Elizabeth Railey, of Virginia; Elizabeth, born in 1792, died in 1866, married J. B. McCormick in 1812; Randolph, Jr., born Dec. 19, 1794, died May, 1873, married first Caroline Crittenden 1822, second

---

† Elizabeth May Love, April 29, 1913, and have Joseph and Elizabeth Love Macey.
† See page 287.
* Who married Kate Durfee.

Mary Hunter, daughter of William Stuart Hunter and Catharine Canfield; Caroline Railey, born Feb. 12, 1796, died March 3, 1859, married Joseph Frazer July 29, 1825; Jordon, born Aug. 14, 1797, died Dec., 1816, while a law student at Frankfort; Martha Woodson Railey, born Aug. 15, 1802, died July 17, 1886; Nancy, born in 1803, died Oct. 29, 1821, was the first wife of David Thornton in 1820, and Dr. Isham Railey, born in 1805, died Sept. 4, 1845, married Sarah Webster in 1835, no issue.

Randolph Railey and Caroline Crittenden (see Crittenden sketch) had these children: John Crittenden Railey, born in 1823, volunteered his services and was with the army throughout the Mexican conflict, contracted a fever toward its close and died en route home. He was one of Woodford's most popular young men, and as handsome as popular, and his untimely death was deplored by a wide circle of friends. A friend in Frankfort recently called my attention to an item in the old Frankfort Commonwealth of July 25, 1848, relating to the death of John C. Railey, and as it bears the names of quite a number of Woodford citizens, and relates to one of her popular sons, I give it in full:

"**Funeral Honors to John Crittenden Railey.**

"At a meeting of the young men of Versailles on Monday, July 17th, J. Kemp Goodloe was called to the chair, and Lon B. Peters appointed secretary.

"Upon motion the following named gentlemen were appointed a committee to draft a preamble and resolutions expressive of the sentiments of the meeting upon the death of John Crittenden Railey: Vince L. Moore, Joseph Coleman Carter, L. Hensley, George T. Cotton, Swift Darneal, A. Woods, Joseph B. Kinkead and John A. McKinney, Jr., who, after retiring, reported the following:

"'Whereas, information has been received that John C. Railey, a citizen of the county, attached to the army of the United States, a late member of the company of cavalry which went from Woodford County to the Rio Grande, died on his passage from Vera Cruz to his home, of yellow fever; therefore,

"'Resolved, that no event has caused us more grief, or made a deeper impression of sorrow upon our hearts than the death of our late amiable and esteemed friend, John C. Railey. Second;

"'Resolved, that the friendship and intimacy commenced in youth, and continued unbroken and unchanged through youth and manhood, has been strengthened by the noble qualities displayed by him under all circumstances, and firmly cemented by his unflinching principles of honor and his unchanging kindness and amiability.

"'Third, that we have seen him when the hearts of men were most tried, when danger threatened us, and when souls of the bravest were not without some fear, but his courage and native chivalry shone all the brighter from the gloom of darkness which encompassed us. Fourth;

"'Resolved, that we have always considered John C. Railey as the soul of honor and the champion of chivalry; that not one ungenerous action, or one unworthy motive stains his character; that those who know him best, love him most; that he is dear to the hearts of his friends, and that his memory will be cherished by us so long as honor, virtue and patriotism animate our bosoms and form the mainspring of our action.

" 'Fifth, that we tender our heartfelt sympathy to his family for the loss they have sustained in the death of their noble, amiable and talented son.

" 'Sixth, that a copy of these resolutions be sent to the father of John C. Railey, and another to the Frankfort Commonwealth with a request to publish them.

" 'J. Kemp Goodloe, Chairm.
" 'Lon B. Peters, Secty.' "

Other children of Randolph Railey, Jr., and Caroline Crittenden were: Margaret, Ann and Caroline C., all of whom died as they were budding into womanhood, and are buried beside their parents in the Frankfort cemetery, just beyond the Boone monument.

By the second marriage to Mary Hunter were: Randolph Railey, Jr., III, who married Sallie Thornton, daughter of Alex Thornton and Janette Markham; Emma, who married Rev. Alexander Henry; Isham, Jr., who married Ezza Sanders (see Sanders page 47); Catharine, who married George M. Fishback (see Hunter sketch, page 67), and William Hunter Railey, (see Hunter sketch, page 67), who married Martha McConnell (see McConnell sketch, page 48).

Caroline Railey and Joseph Frazer* had Sarah E. Frazer, who married

Peter I. Railey, Jr. (under Thomas Railey and Martha Woodson); Nancy had no children; neither did Dr. Isham Railey and Sarah Webster.

William Railey and his wife, Judith Woodson, lived and died at "Liberty Hall." Their home was a popular resort for the "Virginia and Kentucky Kin." They had these children: William Randolph Railey, born Feb. 14, 1794, and lost his life at the "River Raisin." His tragic death at the hands of an Indian after the surrender was often related in my presence while yet a mere lad, by Joseph Frazer, a kinsman by marriage, and a comrade in arms; Sarah Railey, born March, 1796, died 1862, married first Thos. Railey, Jr. in 1820, second Parham Wahln in 1829, while on a visit to relatives near Bowling Green, and Judith Woodson Railey, born March 15, 1799, died Oct. 31, 1842, married her cousin, Peter I. Railey, Sr., Aug. 21, 1817, he a son of Thomas Railey and Martha Woodson.

Sarah Railey and Parham Wahln had Judith Ann Wahln, born June, 1830, died Aug., 1862, married Dr. William White, son of Col. Zach White and Agnes Steele, March 18, 1853, and they had a son, Dr. Philip White, who was reared in the county, completing his course in medicine in Paris, France, where he met and married Eugene Dilman. He died a score of years ago and his widow returned to France.

Peter I. Railey, Sr., and his wife, Judith Woodson Railey, had Richard Henry, who married Katherine Keith Hawkins; Peter I., Jr., who was thrice married (see Thomas Railey and

* Son of William Frazer and Jane Muldrow, and William was son of Patrick Frazier and Nancy Allen. Jane Muldrow was daughter of Hugh Muldrow and Rachel Gray.

Martha Woodson sketch for descendants). They should have been here as these two brothers were reared at "Liberty Hall," which they inherited at the death of their parents, and this writer rolicked over these fertile fields often in his childhood, and the name of the estate always calls up sweet memories of the bygone.

Richard Henry Railey, my father, was a most companionable man, splendidly educated, and prepared to enter the law office of Black Kinkead when his mother died suddenly, which left her two boys orphans, but in comfortable circumstances, so Richard did not carry out the plans of his mother as to a course in law, which he lamented in after years. Daniel M. Bowmar, Sr., knew him all of his life, and the following obituary, written by him upon the death, Oct. 3, 1888, is a true representation of the characteristics of the man.

"Richard H. Railey.
(Woodford Sun.)

"Alas, poor Yorrick, I knew him well."

"The trite quotation is not unmeaning, for we did know him well, and he was, as Yorrick was, 'a fellow of infinite jest.'

"Richard H. Railey was a son of P. I. Railey, Sr., and his wife, Judith Woodson Railey, of whose children P. I. Railey, Jr., is now the only survivor. Richard was born April 26, 1823, on land settled by his maternal grandfather, adjoining the farm now owned by Logan Railey. He died at Rich Hill, Mo., on Oct. 3, 1888, and was buried in Versailles on the 5th inst. His wife and three children, William Edward, Bertha Hontas and P. Woodson Railey, survive him.

"A kinder heart than Dick Railey's never animated a human breast. A sunnier nature never brightened the rugged pathway of life. Gifted with a superb physique, reared amid plenty, if not luxury, a descendant of the Raileys, Randolphs and Woodsons, of Virginia, a kinsman of Jefferson, he was a gentleman by instinct, and his joyous laugh was as natural as the song of a bird. He married one of Kentucky's uncrowned queens, Miss Katherine Keith Hawkins, a lady who would adorn a palace or a thatched cottage with equal grace.

Fortune smiled on him more than once, not with her winsome smile, but rather as if in mockery. At once generous and improvident, money was to him contemptible dross. Judged by the world's standard he was not a successful man, but if to illumine his own home with sunshine, to scatter gladness wherever he went, to inspire his children to noble aims of success, then the beautiful flowers which decorated his grave were laurels fairly won. His closing years were brightened by a steadfast faith in the promise of God.''

WOODFORD COUNTY

By W. E. Railey.

PART SIX

Charles Railey and Mary Mayo lived upon their Woodford County estate from their arrival, about 1796, until death severed the earthly ties, near the middle of the 19th century.

He called his estate "Buck Run," for the reason that the spring in the ravine below the house was a favorite resort for deer, that came daily to satisfy their thirst in the refreshing water that gushed from the slope. He possessed his father's fondness for a spirited horse, and every generation to the present has been imbued with the same spirit. There are now many living who recall that his son Logan, and grandsons, Charles, Russell and Irvin, were very successful horsemen and graceful equestrians who captured so many premiums in Central Kentucky, from the Civil War to a date later than 1900. This clipping, relating to a great-great-grandson of the first Charles, was taken from the Frankfort Journal Sept. 3, 1920, and reminds one of similar accounts in Central Kentucky papers fifty years ago :

Winner of Blue Ribbon.

"Mr. Logan Railey, the young son of Mr. and Mrs. Elmer Railey, won the premium Wednesday morning at the Blue Grass Fair in the ring for the three gaited pony class. He made a gallant and attractive figure in his Boy Scout uniform and riding a pretty little mare called "Topsy." His family and other friends felt quite proud when seeing him with the blue ribbon."

They were reminded that both the young rider's grandfathers, the late General John B. Castleman, of Louisville, and Mr. Charles Logan Railey, were prominent horsemen and skillful riders, never more handsome than when appearing on one of the beautiful mounts, both preferring the gaited saddle horses.

General Castleman mentions this, as one of the incidents of greatest delight to his boyhood days, in his book, "Active Service."

Mr. Henry Cullins, of Philadelphia, was the judge in the ring awarding Mr. Railey the blue ribbon—Lexington Herald.

When General Castleman was a boy. exactly the age of his grandson, Logan Railey, he rode his pony in a ring at the Louisville Fair, his first appearance, and carried off the blue ribbon. After that he was the winner of money premiums in those days when horsemen were enthusiastic in such contests.

Charles Railey, Sr., served in the Kentucky legislature in 1807, and again in 1831, but like his brothers and kindred of the name, he never sought or cared for office.

Charles Railey and Mary Mayo had these children, all born and reared at "Buck Run:" James Railey, born Mar. 11, 1797, died Sept. 2, 1860, married Matilda Green Dec. 14, 1820, both of whom lived and died in Mississippi; Charles Railey, Jr., born Aug. 3, 1798. married Jane Reams July 26, 1819; both lived and died in Louisiana; Catharine Swann Railey, born Jan. 2, 1800, died Jan. 29, 1872, married John Steele, son of Col. William Steele and Sarah Bullock; Nancy Scott Railey, born Sept. 29, 1801, died Sept., 1875, married Allen Rowland Dec. 23. 1828; Samuel Railey, born June 11, 1803, died Oct. 27, 1884, married first Martha Rowland, Feb. 28, 1825, second Sarah Tucker, Dec. 4, 1850; Charlotte Railey, born Mar. 29, 1805, died Jan. 31. 1882, and was the second wife of David Thornton, whom she married June 3, 1823; Margaret Crittenden Railey, born Jan. 5, 1807, died Oct. 7, 1863, married first William Green, Dec. 8, 1825, second Bishop H. H. Kavanaugh, of the Methodist church, July 24, 1828; Lewis Clark Railey, born Dec. 27, 1808, died September 29, 1891, married Susan Mary Hardin, of Harrodsburg, Aug. 16, 1830; Tarleton Railey, born September 1, 1810, died August 21, 1879, married first Sarah McBrayer, of Lawrenceburg, October 27, 1835, second Mary Blackwell, of Lawrenceburg, Aug. 15, 1839; Logan Railey, born Feb. 17, 1813, died Oct. 28, 1891, married Harriet Rowland June 19, 1836; Martin Railey, born Jan. 18, 1815, died Sept. 23, 1837, and Frances Sweeney Railey, born Nov. 7,

1816, died Aug. 19, 1843.

James Railey and Matilda Green had a daughter, Mary Elizabeth, who married the Rev. Frederick Boyd, and their son, Tilghman Boyd, is the publisher of the Milwaukee Journal; Charles Railey, Jr., and Jane Reams had a son, Charles Randolph Railey, who married Elizabeth Helm, granddaughter of Thomas Helm and Elizabeth Buck (See Helms, Jan., 1921 Register, page 96); Catharine Swann Railey and John Steele had a daughter, Agnes Wingfield, who married Thomas F. Thornton (see Bullocks, Browns and Thorntons.) Samuel Railey lived for a number of years on a road that leads to Shryock's Ferry, and near the intersection of that road and the road from Grier's creek to lock No. 5. It was afterward known as the Will Woolridge farm. He and his family moved to St. Joseph, Mo., before the Civil War and his daughter, Margaret Kavanaugh Railey, is a resident of Clarksdale, near St. Joe, and numerous descendants are in the community; Charlotte Railey and David Thornton lived and died at their home in Versailles. See Thorntons for their descendants; Margaret C. Railey and Bishop Kavanaugh had several children who died before years of maturity; Lewis Clark Railey and Susan Mary Hardin have descendants in Colorado, Texas and Virginia; Tarlton Railey has descendants by both wives in St. Louis and Kansas City who are prominent socially and professionally. Judge Robert Tarlton Railey,* of the Missouri Supreme Court, is a son, and he and this scribe were pupils

* Judge Robert T. Railey was one of nature's noblemen. He died Feb. 25, 1928, just after he resigned from the Supreme Court of Missouri.

of Judge Ira Julian, of Frankfort, at the old Grier's creek school house 1864-5. Robert T. Railey was associated with U. S. Senator Geo. W. Vest in the practice of law at Harrisonville, Mo. His son Thomas is at present attorney for the Mo. Pac. Ry., with headquarters at St. Louis; the descendants of Logan Railey and Harriet Rowland were given in the May, 1920, Register under "Buck Run" farm, but I discover that I neglected to say that Charles Logan Railey, their son, married Ada Pepper (see Pepper sketch), and that Charles Elmer Railey and Ada Railey were two of their children. The former married Elise Kane Castleman, and the latter married David Castleman, son and daughter of Gen. John B. Castleman and Alice Barbee (see Castlemans, Sept., 1920, page 63.)

Randolph Railey, Sr., built his residence on the farm that adjoins his brother Charles' farm, the farm was known as "Canebrake," and the house is still doing service. He and his two wives, Mary Elizabeth Keith and Martha (Pattie) Pleasants, his son Boone, and several of the Mayo family are buried there. *Boone Railey was born Oct. 26, 1820, died Mar. 28, 1869. He came of the second marriage to Martha Pleasants, and he married Elizabeth Wheeler June 14, 1853. Of this marriage came Randolph Railey, born in 1854, died in 1860; Samuel Wheeler Railey, born April 29, 1856, practiced law in Louisville and Washington City, was associated with the legal department of the U. S. Treasury for twenty-five years, and only recently

resigned, since which time he died; and Anna Railey, born April, 1860, married John Calhoun Burnett, a lawyer of Louisville, Nov. 16, 1883, and they had Gilbert and Theodore L. Burnett, the former a doctor who died in the service of his country during the World War, the latter a practicing attorney at the Louisville bar. John Calhoun Burnett died several years ago and his widow* is residing in Louisville.

The Randolphs, the Woodsons, the Mayos, the Pleasants, the Keiths and the Raileys of Virginia were intermarried as follows: Thomas Randolph and Col. Isham Randolph were brothers, and two of the seven sons of Col. William Randolph and Mary Isham, of "Turkey Island," Va. The home of the former was at "Tuckahoe," and the latter at "Dungeness," Va. Thomas was married to Judith Fleming, daughter of Charles Fleming, of New Kent County, Va. Thomas and Judith Fleming had a son William, who married Maria Judith Page. Thomas and Judith Fleming also had Mary Isham Randolph, who married the Rev. James Keith, and Judith Randolph, who married her cousin, the Rev. William Stith, son of Capt. William Stith and Mary Randolph, daughter of Col. William Randolph and Mary Isham.

Col. Isham Randolph married Jane Rogers, of "Shadwell" St., London, while a consul at that port. They had these children: Capt. Thos. Isham, who married Jane Carey; William, who married —— Little; Jane, the eldest, who married Peter Jefferson; Mary, second born, who married Capt. Charles

---

* Died in 1926. Her father, Boone Railey, is buried at Winchester I am informed.

Lewis, Jr.; Elizabeth, who married Col. John Railey; Dorothy, who married Col. John Woodson; Anna, who was three times married, first to Daniel Scott, second to John Pleasants, and third to James Pleasants, of "Contention;" and Susanna Randolph, who married Carter H. Harrison, of "Clifton," Va. Jane and Mary, the two oldest, were born in London, the others in Virginia.

Jane Randolph and Peter Jefferson were the parents of Thomas Jefferson, the President; Mary Randolph and Captain Charles Lewis, Jr., were the grandparents of Judge John Lilburn Thomas, who served in the Missouri legislature, was circuit judge of the Springfield, Mo., district, was judge of the Supreme Court of that state and was Assistant Attorney General of the U. S. under the Cleveland regime, 1893-97. They were also the great-grandparents of Virginia Mitchell, who married Hon. Richard Bland, of Missouri ("Silver Dick Bland") who so long and so ably represented tha state in the Congress as a friend and colleague of our own Joe Blackburn; Elizabeth Randolph and Col. John Railey were the parents of the five Railey brothers and three Railey sisters who came to Woodford County in pioneer days; Dorothy Randolph and Col. John Woodson were the parents of Martha, Susanna and Judith, the three sisters who married three of the above brothers, Thomas, Isham and William Railey, and of Major Josiah Woodson, of the Revolution, who married his cousin, Elizabeth Woodson, and settled at Maysville, Ky., and whose grand-daughter, Elizabeth Moss, married General William H. Ashby, a representative in Congress from Missouri prior to the Civil War. He died and she became the third wife of Gov. John J. Crittenden, whose sister, Caroline Crittenden, married Randolph Railey, Jr., a nephew of Major Josiah Woodson; Ann Randolph and her third husband, James Pleasants, of "Contention," were the parents of Gov. James Pleasants, of Virginia, and "Pattie" Pleasants, who was the second wife of Randolph Railey, Sr., of Woodford County; Susanna Randolph and Carter Harrison were the grandparents of the Rev.* Cabell Harrison, a Presbyterian minister who often preached at the old Grier's creek church when visiting relatives in Woodford County, and they were the direct ancestors of the two Harrisons, father and son, each of whom served a number of terms as Mayor of Chicago, the former a great-grandson.

William Randolph, son of Thomas of "Tuckahoe," and his wife Maria Judith Page, had Col. Thomas Mann Randolph, whose son, Thomas Mann Randolph, Jr., married his cousin Martha, daughter of Thomas Jefferson, and served Virginia as Governor; Mary Isham Randolph and Rev. James Keith had Captain Isham Keith, who married Charlotte Ashmore, and Mary Randolph Keith, who married Col. Thomas Marshall.

Captain Isham Keith and Charlotte Ashmore had Katherine Keith, who married William Strother Hawkins, grandparents of the writer. See Strothers, page 144. Mary Randolph

* He was a son of Robert Carter Harrison of Fayette County, Ky., who moved to Kentucky 1806.

Keith and Col. Thomas Marshall were
the parents of Chief Justice John Marshall and ancestors of the Woodford
County Marshalls down to the children
of Louis Marshall, of the Woodford
Bank & Trust Co., and the wife of
Theodore Harris, who was the granddaughter of Dr. Basil Duke and Charlotte Ashmore Marshall.

John Pleasants, of "Pique-Nique,"
*Va., was a son of Joseph Pleasants
and Martha Coke, of Va., and grandson
of John Pleasants and Jane Tucker, who
came from Norwich, Eng., in 1668 and
settled at Curles, Va. He married Susanna Woodson and they were the parents of Mathew Pleasants, who married
Anna Railey, and of James Pleasants,
of "Contention," who married Anna
Randolph and had Gov. James Pleasants and Martha, the wife of Randolph
Railey, Sr.

Col. William Randolph was one of
the sons of Richard Randolph, of "Morton's Hall," Eng., who emigrated to
Virginia about 1669, and his wife,
Mary Isham, was a daughter of Henry
Isham and Katherine Banks, of "Ber-
muda Hundred," their home on the opposite side of the James river from
"Turkey Island."

Col. John Woodson, who married
Dorothy Randolph, was a son of Josiah
Woodson and Mary Royall, of Virginia,
and Josiah was a son of John Woodson
and Judith Tarleton; and John Wood-
son was a son of Robert Woodson and
Elizabeth Ferris, of Virginia, and Rob-
ert Woodson was a son of Dr. John
Woodson and Sarah Winston. Dr.
John Woodson was from Dorsetshire,

and his wife from Devonshire, Eng.
He came over in 1620 with a troop of
soldiers and was the surgeon of the
regiment that was under the command
of Sir John Harvey, of the English
army. They were stationed at "Middle
Settlement," near Richmond, Va. It
was from his great grandson Tarlton
Woodson (brother of the above Josiah)
and his wife, Ursula Fleming, that
sprang the prominent Bates family,
one of whom served in President Lincoln's Cabinet, another was Governor
of Missouri and still another was very
prominent in Arkansas. The prominent Venables came from this line also.

The Rev. James Keith, who married
Mary Isham Randolph, was a native of
Scotland and attended "Aberdeen College" with his cousins, George Keith,
10th and last Earl, and James Francis
Edward Keith, of Prussia. In his
youth he participated in one of the unsuccessful rebellions of that country,
and his activity and zeal so compro-
mised him that he was compelled to
flee the country, and took refuge in
Virginia. Soon thereafter he entered
the ministry of the Episcopal church,
and as soon as he received a charge he
married. He brought with him to this
country a history of his family that was
attached to his Bible, but a kinsman in
Virginia many years ago wrote that his
mother was in possession of this ancestral history, which was destroyed
during the Revolution. She lived to
be 96 years of age and her son, Judge
Isham Keith, of Virginia, who wrote
the above letter, lived to be quite an

* I think this should be John Pleasants.

elderly gentleman, his death occurring in the '80's.

The following brief history of the Arnold family, of Woodford County, was furnished me by Emmet O'Neal, the Louisville attorney, whose father was a citizen of Woodford for many years. This family was one of the earliest in Woodford County, and I am delighted to include it in my notes concerning the pioneers.

John Arnold was born in Virginia on January 10th, 1754, died in Woodford County May 4, 1818. He was the son of Nicholas Arnold and his wife, Margaret ———, and it is believed that his residence was in Culpepper County, Va.

John Arnold married Elizabeth Hitt, a daughter of Peter and Sarah Hitt. She was born in Fauquier County, Va., on the 12th day of Mar., 1751, and they were married Aug. 29, 1775.

John Arnold and his wife emigrated to Kentucky in Aug., 1781, in company with about one hundred and eighty persons. They came with John Craig and made their first stop at Bryant's Station and were there when the siege took place in Aug., 1782. This body constituted the church of Lewis Craig, which came in a body to Kentucky (Draper MSS., 13 c. 110). A full account of the siege is a matter of Kentucky history, and it is not necessary to mention it here.

Lewis Arnold, a son of John, the pioneer, evidently came to the state with his parents, as he was present at the siege of the fort. (Draper MSS., 1 c. c. 245.)

John Arnold was not with the pursuing army at the battle of Blue Licks because of a serious accident which resulted in temporary blindness. He had a double triggered gun which became stubborn, so to speak, and refused to fire. He removed the lock, and when he replaced it, the gun was accidentaly discharged in his hand. Two women narrowly escaped being shot, owing to the premature discharge, and the powder flashed up into his eyes and blinded him for quite a siege. (Draper MSS., 11 c. c. 241-45.)

The interesting experiences of John and Elizabeth Arnold at the fort at Bryant's Station are to be found in the Draper MSS., and they personally describe what is now a matter of established history.

John Arnold's wife speaks of her brother, Nimrod Hitt, who was in Kentucky at one time, and also mentions two brothers-in-law, Lewis and James Arnold. At another place she specifically states that the Arnolds in Franklin County are not in any way related to her husband. The records of the descendants of Lewis and James Arnold pertaining to that generation are very meager.

From Bryant's Station or Fort, John Arnold and his wife moved to what is now Woodford County, and settled at a small fort known as Craig's Fort.* There were eleven in the party, and they reached this fort either the last of January or first of February, 1783. The fort was located at what was known as Woolfolk's farm in later days. It was evidently near the beautiful spring which is on the road to Troy, about

---

* On Troy road near Woolfolk farm. See page 396.

seven miles from Versailles. Elizabeth Hitt Arnold mentions the members of the party in Draper MSS., 11 c. c., 241-45.

Later John Arnold owned a great deal of land in the neighborhood which he divided among his children. He and his wife lived many years, and their home was the congregating point for all religious activities in their vicinity. This was before the church was built (I suppose the Clear creek church is meant) and the accounts of the meetings and the character of Elizabeth Hitt Arnold and members of her family are told in great detail in the history of "Ten Baptist Churches," by the Rev. John Taylor, published in 1827. The children of John Arnold and Elizabeth Hitt were: Lewis, Younger, John, Thomas, Wyeatte, Joel, Sarah, Elizabeth, who married Stephen Weakley, of Shelby County (see page 212); Polly, who married Thomas Dale, of Shelby County; and Nancy, who married William Rice. Nearly all of the children remained in Kentucky except Joel, who left the state but where he located is not positively known, but it is believed that he went to Florida. The other brothers remained in Woodford County, where they died and were buried. Each reared a large family of children.

Sarah married George Churchill and moved to Illinois; Elizabeth and Stephen Weakley moved to Shelby County, where they have many descendants; Mary (Polly) and Thomas Dale moved to Spencer County and left many descendants; Nancy and William Rice lived on the border of Jessamine and Woodford, and their children moved to Missouri; John Arnold had three children who moved to Missouri; Thomas Arnold and his wife, ——— Arnold, moved to Missouri, where they have descendants; Lewis was three times married and reared a large family whose descendants are in different parts of Kentucky, and a few live in Missouri; Younger Arnold and Jane Weakley had a large family, some going to Missouri, several to Illinois and one, Elizabeth, remained in Woodford and married Merrit Singleton O'Neal. They had these children: George Younger, who married Mollie Dean; Silas O'Neal, who married ——— Dale; Jasper T. O'Neal, who married Lydia Wright; Starks O'Neal, who died unmarried; Filmore, who married Annie Johnston, and Elizabeth, who married C. G. Arnold.

George O'Neal and Mollie Dean had William and Mattie O'Neal; Silas O'Neal and ——— Dale had Ruth, Mary Morris, Bettie, Lou and Claude; J. T. O'Neal and Lydia Wright have Merit, J. T., Jr., Godloe and Emmet O'Neal, four brothers who constitute a popular and able law firm in the city of Louisville; Filmore and Annie Johnston, reside in Florida and have Younger, Carrie, Gladys, Rae and Filmore; Elizabeth and C. G. Arnold have Otho, C. G., Jr., Joe Irvin and Lydia, who married James Miller.

Wyeatte Arnold, son of John, the pioneer, and his wife, Sallie Rice, had Cave, who married ——— Peters; Irvine, who married ——— Carter and moved to Missouri; William, who married Sallie Weakley and moved to Shelby County; Mildred, who married ——— Peters; Jeannette, who married Noah Tillery;

Mary, who married first James Garnett, second John Sullivan; Elizabeth married Dr. Robert Sullivan; Louisa married Newton Dale, and John W., who married Catharine Garnett and their daughter married Clifford Graves. (See Graves family Sept., 1920, page 42.) Clifford Graves and his wife live on a part of the land granted to John Arnold in 1782, it never having been out of possession of descendants.

W. Irvin Arnold was a son of John W. Arnold. He married Florida Rowland and they are residents of the county.

———

In the January issue on page 192, I stated that Lucinda Lee, daughter of Major John Lee, of Versailles, Ky., married in 1818 ——— Call. I should have added the statement that their son, Wilkinson Call, born at Russellville, Ky., represented the state of Florida in the United States Senate within my recollection, and his services covered eighteen years.

———

In writing the sketch of the Henton family in the Sept., 1920, Register, page 107, I said that the Woodford County family of that name spelled it Henton while the Shelby County branch spelled it Hinton. In this statement I was in error; both of these branches spell it Henton, while the Bourbon County family of that name spell it Hinton.

———

Ralf de Tirel had his castle near the village of Tirel, on the banks of the Seine, a short distance below Paris, from which he took the surname of Tirel. By the transposition of two letters that village is now called Triel. From that period the family name has had many transformations in the orthography such as de Tirel, Tirell, Tyrell, Tyrrell, Tirrell and Terrell.

They were originally from the district of Vexin, which lay between France and the ducal possessions of the House of Normandy, and was sometimes under the suzerainty of the Norman dukes, and then under the French crown, but finally were absorbed by the latter.

Hugh Tyrrell established the family name in England while yet maintaining a residence in France, and he was known as Hugh Tyrrell, 1st Prince de Poix, about four hundred years ago. The family figured prominently in the Crusades; held high position at the court of the Kings of France in the early days; were Governors of cities, and of high merit in military and civil history of north France. These facts were gathered by the late Edwin Holland Terrell, of San Antonio, Texas, who was American envoy and minister to Brussels, 1889-93. He often did research work upon his frequent visits to London, and he gathered many interesting genealogical notes on the Terrell—Tyrell family, and he said in London they persisted in pronouncing his name as though it were spelled Tirrell.

In the old colonial records at Richmond, Va., where we find the first American ancestors of the name, it appears as both Tirrell and Tyrrell by two brothers, William and Richmond, the former spelling it Tyrrell and the latter Tirrell, and though it soon was spelled Terrell, it has always been pronounced as though it was spelled Tir-rell.

The traditions of the descendants of William and Richmond Tirrell are a little contradictory as to the point in England from whence these two brothers came, but they are in accord as to both being descended from Sir Walter Tyrrell, III, through his great-grandson, Hugh Tyrrell, 1st. These two brothers were large land holders in Virginia, and tradition says that they came over in some official capacity in connection with the Crown lands, like-ly as surveyors.

Of descendants in Georgia, one has a gold watch that was brought from England that has the crest of the Tyr-rells of Heron engraved upon it, and in Virginia another descendant has a ring, a family relic, that carries the same engraving.

The late Edwin Holland Terrell was a resident of San Antonio, Texas, for about forty years. His father was Wil-liamson Terrell, who was born in Clark County, Kentucky, June 12, 1805. His mother was Martha Jarrel, born in Frankfort, Ky., in 1808, and was a daughter of James Jarrel and Rachel Powell, both of whom came to Ken-tucky from Dover, Del. Williamson Terrell was a son of Captain John Ter-rell, who distinguished himself in the early Indian campaigns in the west un-der Harmer, St. Clair and Wayne. He, Capt. John, was born in Spotsylvania County, Va., April 3, 1772, and came to Kentucky with his father in 1787. He was married to Abigail Allen, a daugh-ter of Archibald Allen, of Albemarle County, Va., who was also the father of Chilton Allen, the famous Kentucky

lawyer who, when Henry Clay was elected U. S. Senator succeeded him in the Ashland District as Congressman, where he rendered service for ten years. Captain John Terrell was a son of Henry Terrell, Jr., born in Carolina, Va., March 29, 1735, and married Mary Tyler, born in Virginia in 1743, daugh-ter of Captain William Tyler. Henry Terrell, Jr., was a son of Henry Terrell, a lawyer and planter of Caroline Coun-ty, but born in Hanover County, Va., about 1695, and died there in 1760. The elder Henry was a man of wide in-fluence, was quite wealthy and was twice married, first to Annie Chiles, sec-ond to Sarah Woodson, daughter of Tarleton Woodson. Henry Terrell, Jr., was a son of the first marriage, and his father, Henry Terrell, was one of the younger sons of William Terrell, or Tyrrell, one of the two emigrants. This William Tyrrell married Susannah Waters, and tradition says that Wil-liam had been in the colonies for some time when Susannah came across the "deep blue sea" to become his wife, she sailing in the company of William's brother, presumably Richmond.

About 1807 Archibald B. and Prest-ley Terrell came to Woodford County and it is more than likely that they were actuated by their Clark County kinsman, Capt. John Terrell. I say kinsman, but I am not able to prove the relationship. I am unable to find the name of Archibald anywhere else in the Terrell line, and as Capt. John Terrell married the daughter of Archibald Allen, I am persuaded that Archibald Terrell was closely related. Prestley had served in the Revolution before he came to Woodford County, and while I am unable to state the relationship between him and Archibald B., the other pioneer in Woodford, the evidence is strong enough to conclude that they were closely related, if not brothers, as Archibald B. named his first child born in Woodford County Prestley.

Archibald B. Terrell married in Virginia Sarah Hutchison and they had ten children, five born in Orange County, Va., and five in Woodford County. Those born in Virginia were: Vivian, Sidney, Susan, Martha and Dr. William H. Those born in Woodford County were Prestley, Jr., John, Reuben, Edmond and Agnes. Reuben and Agnes never married; Vivian, the first born, died of an affection that resulted from exposure during the war of 1812, in which he rendered valuable service; Sidney married Robert Scrogin, March, 1817; Susan married Luther Scrogin, brother of Robert, and they moved to Missouri, where they have descendants; Martha married Robert Beadle and they lived and died in Versailles; Dr. William Henry was born in Orange County, Va., July 4, 1806, and died in Versailles July 16, 1864, and was but an infant when he came to our county. He was twice married, first to Lucinda Wilcox, in 1829, second to Susan Jane Ross, a widow, to whom he was married in 1854, she a descendant of the Waller and Rhodes families, of Lexington. She survived her husband many years and died in Louisville in 1903.

Sidney Terrell and Robert Scrogin lived on a farm near Midway, where they died, their remains being interred in the burial ground at Pisgah. They reared a large family, as follows: Frances, married Mattie Switzer; Susan married Judge Henry H. Haveland, of Cynthiana, and they have a daughter, Sidney Haveland; Lewellen lost his life in the Confederacy, and Sidney Alvin, who married Mollie Fonroy.

Susan Terrell and Luther Scrogin have descendants in Missouri, to which state they moved.

Martha Terrell and Robert Beadle had Sarah, who married Dr. —— Dabney, and Dee Wilton, who married Clara Whitman, of Louisville, to which point he moved some years after the Civil War, and they have children who are residents of that city now.

Dr. William Henry Terrell and Lucinda Wilcox had Dr. William Henry, Jr., born in 1840. He was a druggist at Versailles, served the Confederacy for four years, married Virginia Bon-†nie Cotton, daughter of William Cotton and Virginia Bonnie (see page 72), and* moved to Louisville about 1870, where he died in 1889; Luke Wilcox Terrell married Katherine Poole. They have children in Louisville and Chicago. It is my impression that he, too, served the Confederacy; Ella Virginia Terrell married Charles F. Wood and they have Amelia Wood, Lawrence F. and Eugene C. By the second wife, Susan Jane Ross, was Maggie, who married A. V. Paine, of Louisville.

John Terrell, who was born in Woodford County, married —— Magill and moved to Bourbon County, where they have a son, Robert, who is now living on his father's farm.

Edmond Terrell married Margaret

*See Cottons 73.
†See page 363 for correction.

Peters and they had William Terrell, who, I am told, has three children living in Woodford County; Mary, who married Joseph Rogers and has children living in Georgetown, and Bettie. who married Fielder Barnes; they have a son living at Mt. Sterling.

I find that I neglected to mention Amelia Agnes Terrell, the second of Dr. William H. Terrell, Sr., and Lucinda Wilcox. She married first William Parker, of Louisville, second Frank W. Hill, of St. Louis. They have no children.

Archibald B. Terrell owned a farm that bordered on Rose Hill, extended down the Clifton pike about one mile, thence across Glenns Creek to the McCracken Mill road and back to Rose Hill. This farm contained about three hundred acres and remained the property of the family for about one hundred years. I don't know whether the home on Rose Hill was built by Dr. William B. Terrell or by his father, Archibald Terrell. It has been for many years the home of Ed. M. Wallace, the attorney.

In 1810 Archibald Terrell had a family of ten members and owned five negroes.

*Dr. William H. Terrell, Sr., graduated from Transylvania and attended a school of medicine in Philadelphia. He was a devout member of the Methodist church, a prominent Mason, and a high class gentleman, as is remembered by many of my generation. He and his parents are buried in the Versailles cemetery, and a shaft near the center of the grounds marks the spot. The farm did not pass from family possession until 1904, when the widow of Dr. W. H. Terrell, Sr., died.

———

In presenting a few notes relative to the old Kentucky Academy, at Pisgah, in the January, 1921, issue of the Register, I mentioned three prominent Presbyterian ministers who attended that institution, and on page 159 I am made to say that the Rev. John L. Wilson was one of them. It should have been Joshua L. Wilson. He was a student there in 1796, and was married at Pisgah in 1801, at the home of John Stevenson, to Sarah McKay.

When a boy of seven he came to Kentucky from Bedford County, Va. (where he was born Sept. 22, 1774), with his mother, Agnes Lacy (Wilson) Templin, his step-father, John Templin and a half-brother, the Rev. Terah Templin, in October, 1781.

Sarah McKay was born in Baltimore, Md., April 30, 1779, the only child of George and Margaret McKay. She came out to Kentucky at an early day with her father (whose wife was dead), and was a pupil at the Kentucky Academy, at Pisgah, at the time that Joshua L. Wilson was a student, and there the acquaintance began that ripened into love and culminated in marriage a few years later.

Hon. Samuel McKay Wilson, the prominent attorney at Lexington, is a grandson.

———

Benjamin and Charles Hiter were early settlers in Woodford County, and were cousins. They located in the vi-

---

*I also remember with much pleasure Dr. Wm. H. Terrell, Jr., and his brother Luke. They were both very popular.

cinity of Troy, where each owned a farm. Charles was in Woodford County at a time antedating 1810, as his name appears in the census table of that year, but I have not been able to learn the exact date of his arrival. He listed his family as consisting of six members, and his slaves as numbering eight. The name of Benjamin was not included in that census, but he may have been temporarily absent at the time the census was taken. At any rate he was known to be a citizen of the county not later than the period of the war of 1812. He married Elizabeth Combs,† a sister of General Leslie Combs, who was well known in Kentucky and the mother state, Virginia, and they had Porter Hiter, who married Sallie Harlan, of Frankfort, sister of Judge John M. Harlan, who recently died at Washington after a long service as a Justice of the Supreme Court of the U. S.

Porter Hiter and his wife lived and died upon an estate on the Clifton pike,‡ near the cross-roads at Brookies. They had Eloise, who married Alfred Grant; Laura, who married Wilbur Hobbs Thornton (son of Edward Kavanaugh Thornton and Lucrecia Hobbs) (see Thornton sketch, Jan., 1921, Register, page 187); and James Harlan Hiter, who likely never married.

After the death of Benjamin Hiter his widow, Elizabeth Combs Hiter, married Meredith Furr, son of Stephen Furr and Arlimacia Taylor, who were pioneer settlers in that vicinity, and they were the parents of Charles Combs Furr, of Frankfort, who served in the Federal army during the Civil War.

After the war he accepted a position in the Internal Revenue Service that took him from the county to Frankfort, where he has since resided. He married in Frankfort Kate Owens, and their children are Combs Furr, who married Florence Shaw, and Western, who married Mary Hamilton.

Other children of Meredith Furr and Elizabeth Combs Hiter were John Wesley and T. Combs Furr.

Charles Hiter, the other pioneer, married Betsy Oliver and had Christopher, whose wife's name I have not learned, but they had a son, William Hiter, whom I remember quite well. He married Abbey, daughter of Joel W. Twyman and Ellen Virginia Carter (see Twymans, page 55).

Andrew Combs was a pioneer of Woodford County, who also owned a farm near Troy, upon which he used six slaves in 1810, at which time his family consisted of six members. His wife was Eleanor Oliver, a relative of Betsy Oliver, who married Charles Hiter, mentioned above. Both Andrew Combs and his wife, Eleanor Oliver, were from Virginia, but both died in Woodford County and were buried there. Two of their children were Elizabeth Combs, who married first Benjamin Hiter, second Meredith Furr, and John Combs, who was provost marshal during the Civil War and a familiar figure in Woodford and Fayette counties about that time.

It is my impression that Andrew Combs, the pioneer of Woodford, was an uncle of General Leslie Combs, the lawyer and soldier of Fayette County,

†See page 365 for correction. A cousin.
‡See page 365 for correction. He died in Louisville, she in Missouri.

who was a son of Capt. Benjamin Combs and Sarah Richardson, of Clark County, Ky.

———————

In the Sept., 1920, Register, page 109, I gave a brief account of the active life of Gov. Charles Scott, who had his residence in Woodford County from about 1786 until his election as the Chief Executive of the state in 1808. Recently I came into possession of additional data that is interesting inasmuch as it goes a little into detail in reference to his family.

He was born in Cumberland County, Va., in 1740, and I think maintained a residence there until he came to Kentucky, perhaps to a later date, as I am unable to state whether his wife ever came to Kentucky or not. His first wife was Francis Sweeney, to whom he was married in Virginia. They had the following children: Martha Tabb, who married Judge George M. Bibb, a lawyer and jurist who was a resident of Frankfort where he died in 1859; Sarah, who married John Postlewhaite; Ann died unmarried; John Scott, who, I think, was never married; Charles Scott, Jr., who was killed by the Indians on the banks of the Kentucky river in Mercer County opposite his father's Woodford County residence while fishing in 1790 (see pages 109 and 141); Merrit Sweeney, who was an officer in the U. S. navy, serving under Decatur at Tripoli and doubtless a comrade of Lieut. Neville O'Bannon in that far away land.

I cannot say whether Gov. Scott's wife ever lived in the Woodford County

home or not, nor do I know what proportion of his children were there. I only know that his son Charles was there much of the time, if not all of it, until he was murdered by the Indians, he looking after the interests of his father while the General was on occasional expeditions against the Indians. For instance Gov. Scott was with General St. Clair in his disastrous defeat in 1791; he served under Gen. Wilkinson in his successful campaigns on the Wabash. In 1794 he had charge of Gen. Wayne's forces at "Fallen Timber," in Ohio.

After these campaigns he returned to his Woodford County estate, where he was much of the time until his election to the Governorship in 1808. One authority that I have read states that he remained in Woodford County until his death in 1820. Another authority that I do not question states that during his term as Governor, or soon thereafter, he was married to the widow Gist, of *Lexington, and he died in 1820 on her farm, "Canebrake," in Fayette County. Tradition also bears out the latter statement.

General Scott was a soldier at 15 years of age, an officer at 18, and commanded a brigade at Charleston, hence of necessity his educational advantages were limited. As a soldier he was of the rough and ready type, but in statecraft he was well equipped as he surrounded himself with counsellors who were selected through his rare good judgment, hence the ship of state sailed smoothly.

A unique campaign was that of Gen. Scott and Col. John Allen, of Shelby

*See page 364 for correction. "Canebreak" was in Clark County instead of Fayette.

County, for the Governorship. In self-abnegation I doubt if it has a rival in any other election that has taken place in any of the states. Gov. Scott was in the contest at the instance of his friends and admirers, rather than any ambition of his own, as he was aware that he was essentially a soldier, hence he was absolutely indifferent as to the result. In fact from the stump he admitted his inability, and said that his election would be too great a reward for his services, and for that reason he urged his friends to support his brilliant and popular opponent, Col. Allen, but in spite of his insistence that the citizenry vote for his opponent, an appreciative electorate gave him a majority of one vote. I do not recall a similar instance in any state, though history may record such.

Keen O'Hara, the celebrated pedagogue, came from Ireland to America during the year 1798 accompanied by his father and two brothers, Charles and James. Keene finally anchored at Danville, Ky., in 1820, where he was prominently associated with the educational interests of that community for some time, then came to Versailles, where he taught the youth of that vicinity for several years; then removed to Frankfort, where he established O'Hara's famous institute that he maintained for the remainder of his life.

His distinguished son, Theodore, was but an infant when he came to Versailles, and as he grew to manhood his preparatory or fundamental training was under his father's tutorage; the finishing touches were at St. Joseph's College, Bardstown, Ky., where he graduated.

The O'Haras were devout Catholics and fled their native Ireland to escape the persecutions of the Church of England, a spirit that has actuated too many sects at various times in the world's history, as is slightly borne out by data that I have inserted from time to time in my notes on Woodford County. The spirit of intolerance should not be exercised by Christian people. In fact, it will not exist among liberty-loving people, the American spirit.

On page 180 of the Jan., 1921, Register, I had a sketch of the old Watkins Tavern and incidentally mentioned the fact that the mother of Henry Clay was hostess at the old inn. This lady married Henry Watkins in Virginia, and came to Woodford to live and died at an advanced age on their country estate on the Mortonsville road, in 1829. This farm was afterward the Wooldridge, then the Moss, and later the Robert McConnell farm, I believe. At any rate, the McConnell family have owned it for more than a half century.

With Henry Watkins and his wife came Porter Clay, a son by her former marriage to the Rev. John Clay, a brother of the Commoner, and it is of the Clays that I wish to speak briefly. Porter Clay practiced law at Versailles until his appointment by Gov. Gabriel Slaughter as Auditor of State in 1816, I think. In that capacity his official duties claimed practically all of his time, so he moved his residence to Frankfort, where he was living when his long service as Auditor ceased in 1830. His first wife was Sophia Grush, a sister of the wives of Thomas Hart, and John W. Hunt of Lexington; second wife the widow of Martin D. Hardin, who was one of the daughters of General Benjamine Logan. Later in life Porter Clay relinquished the law and followed the example of his father in adopting the Baptist ministry. His daughter Elizabeth, who was by the first marriage, was the first wife of Edmund H. Taylor, Sr., who was for thirty years cashier of the Branch Bank of Kentucky, at Frankfort.

The Kentucky Clays were descended from Sir John Clay, of Wales. He had three sons, Charles, Thomas and Henry. These three brothers came to Virginia and settled near Jamestown. Charles and Thomas had large families, but Henry left no posterity.

General Cassius M. Clay, the unterrified abolitionist, of Madison County, was descended from Charles Clay, and Henry and Porter were from Thomas through the Rev. John Clay, who died in Hanover County, Va., about 1780.

The parents of the wife of Henry Watkins (widow of Rev. John Clay) were George Hudson and Elizabeth Jennings, and her grandparents were John Hudson and Elizabeth Harris. In England they were classed among the "gentry."

There were several families of Hudsons near Mortonsville in 1810, and a descendant was living in the county on the old Jeremiah Morton farm, but whether they were related to the Clay Hudsons or not I can't say, but as they were neighbors I incline to the opinion

they were related (see Morton sketch), Jan. 1921, Register, page 160.

———

*Anthony Thomson, Sr., and his wife, Ann Bibb, came to Woodford County about 1786 from Louisa County, Va., formerly Hanover County.

The Thomsons were originally citizens of New Kent County, Va., but when Hanover County was formed from New Kent they were identified with Hanover.

Ann Bibb's father was Henry Bibb, a son of Benjamin Bibb, of the adjoining county of King William, and from this Benjamin Bibb descended the two prominent Bibbs, the one Governor of Georgia, the other Governor of Alabama. He was also the ancestor of many of the Kentucky Bibbs. Judge George M. Bibb and John Bibb, of Frankfort, Ky., were closely related. The latter lived until after the Civil War and to him I was indebted for much of my data relating to the Strother family. (He was a portly, handsome old gentleman, a lawyer of prominence, who served his state in several distinguished capacities.)

Henry Bibb, the father of the wife of Anthony Thomson, Sr., married a daughter of William Fleming, sheriff of Hanover County, Va.; he the father of Robert Fleming, sheriff of Hanover County, Va. They were of the family of Charles Fleming, of New Kent County, whose daughter Judith was the second wife of Thomas Randolph, of "Tuckahoe," Va.

Anthony Thomson, Sr., was a soldier in the French and Indian wars, preliminary to the Revolutionary struggle,

*See page 360 for Henry Thomson who moved to Ohio County about 1827.

and while there is a tradition that he participated in the Revolution, I incline to the opinion that he did not, doubtless due to his age, and his sons were too young for that service.

He disposed of his Virginia estates between 1780 and 1784, by which time he had acquired property in Kentucky and Ohio for services rendered his country. He entered four hundred acres at Portsmouth, Ohio, at the mouth of Scioto river. This tract was the site of an Indian settlement, and his descendants live there now. Three thousand acres were entered in what was then Nelson County, now Ohio County, Ky., and I am told that descendants are still in possession of much of this tract. A large tract was also entered in what was then Fayette County, but now Greenup County, and there are descendants still in possession of much of this tract. In March, 1784, he acquired five hundred acres in Woodford County, purchasing two years thereafter one hundred and seventy-five acres adjoining the original tract and moved his family, with the exception of his eldest son Robert, who remained in Virginia, to Woodford County, Kentucky. He built his residence of stone, which was erected in 1786, directly opposite the residence of James Henton, on the Versailles pike to Frankfort. This home was built on an elevation that made it quite conspicuous, and could be seen from McKee's cross-roads on the east, and was in plain view from the old Captain Lafon place, on the west, and even beyond that. The writer lived on a part of the Anthony Thomson tract, the farm now owned by Arthur

Crutcher, that is in plain view of Grassy Springs church, until 1884, when it passed out of the Railey possession. I recall the locality as it was immediately following the Civil War, when the dense timber that covered that section had all been removed and the old Thomson castle or fort stood above the skyline so conspicuously that you could not look in that direction without being attracted by this curious structure that invariably recalled some story of a deserted castle.†

Anthony Thomson, Sr., called this home "Thomson's Manor," and it was so known as long as it remained in possession of the relationship, passing from that ownership prior to the Civil War. It was rather a curious structure, according to tradition the house and the servant's quarters forming a quadrangle, which design gave the protection of a fort.

Anthony Thomson, Sr., died in 1794. His children were all born in Virginia, and their names follow: Robert, who married, lived and died in that state; Anthony, Jr., who married first Ann Pemberton, of Franklin County, April 2, 1793, one of the daughters of Richard Pemberton; second Katherine Mason; Nathaniel Thomson, who married Oct., 1795, France Major, daughter of John Major and Elizabeth Redd (see Major sketch, May Register, 1920, page 46, and May, 1921, page 215); Henry Bibb Thomson, born in 1781, died in 1810 at the home of his sister, Susanna, the wife of Edmond Vaughan, whose farm was just in the rear of "Ingleside," formerly the home of Thomas Major (but now the property

---

†Now razed.

of the heirs of the late Col. C. E. Hoge);
Eleanor Thomson, born in 1759, died
in 1827, married her cousin, David
Thompson,* son of Waddy Thompson;
Judith Thomson, who married Thomas
Bell, of Woodford County and moved to
the Green river tract in Ohio County;
Susanna, born in 1768, died in 1823,
married Edmond Vaughan; Sarah, died
in 1800 a spinster; Elizabeth died in
1798, spinster, and Mary, who married
her cousin, Samuel Waddy, of Waddy,
Shelby County. No issue.

Anthony Thomson, Jr., and Ann
Pemberton lived in the home now occupied by the wife of Lafayette
Crutcher, near Grassy Springs church.
After the death of his first wife, his second (Katherine Mason) was the mis-
tress of the home until several years
after the death of Anthony, Jr., in 1827.
They had these children: Richard P.,
born Jan. 1, 1798; Anthony, III, born
March 25, 1800, killed accidentally by
Francis Black, his brother-in-law,
while hunting, Sept. 3, 1827; Ann Bibb,
married Francis Black who, after her
death, married the mother of Richard
Bland ("Silver Dick"), the distinguished Missouri* Congressman; Margaret married Thomas Berryman;
Mary married ——— McDonald, and
Katherine married William Hines.

Henry Bibb Thomson, Jr., who must
have been a son of Anthony, Jr., or of
Henry Bibb Thomson, Sr., was born in
1808, died July 7, 1877, on Green river,
where he was living. He was twice
married and left descendants in that
section of the state. I think this Henry

Bibb Thompson was a son of Anthony,
Jr.

Nathaniel Thomson and Francis
Major lived at the "Thomson Manor"
after the death of his father in 1794.
The children of Nathaniel and Frances
were all born in the ancestral home,
and attended school at Grassy Springs,
their teacher being a Scotchman named
Beck, who interested himself in the educational welfare of that community for
a number of years. The parents and
children held membership in the Grassy
Springs church for years. They had
these children: Elizabeth Redd Thompson, born in 1797, married William
Hicklin, of Franklin County. They
moved to the land grant in Greenup
County, where she died without issue;
Ann Bibb, born in 1799, married James
Dillon, and their three daughters, Elizabeth, Cordelia and Melita, went to
Missouri with their father after the
death of his wife, and they married in
that state, where they have descendants; Martha Major, born in 1801, married James Crutcher and they had Reuben and Elizabeth, neither of whom had
issue; John Major, born in 1803 and
never married; Maria, born in 1805,
married Morris English and settled
upon a part of the Greenup County estate where she was living at an advanced age and had a son, John English, who reared a large family; Zoraida
Thomson, born 1807, June 12th, died
in Frankfort, Feb. 20, 1859, married
Thomas J. Crutcher, her brother-in-law
(the husband of a deceased sister), and
their children were all born at "Thomson Manor." They were Mary Louise

*Anthony Thomson spelled his name without a (p), while the husband of his daughter, Eleanor,
used that letter (p).
*Who served in Congress for many years with Senator Joe Blackburn.

and Elvira Major Crutcher who lived in Lexington; Ann Crutcher, born April 3, 1844, died Sept. 18, 1911, married Jerry V. Downing, of Lexington, and they had George C., Mary, Pat Major, Jerry Jefferson, and Elvina Downing.

Eleanor Thomson and her husband, David Thompson,† had Anthony, born 1782, married Sarah Thomas and they settled upon the Greenup County grant; Anderson, born 1784, died and was buried in the family graveyard in Woodford County. He married in Virginia, but I have no record of issue; Waddy married Cynthia Thomas and they settled upon the Greenup County estate. He was drowned in the Ohio river endeavoring to rescue a young son. Their children were William, David and Robert Thomas Thompson. The latter married Mildred Henton,‡ sister of James Henton, of the county, and they had Thomas, who married Mollie Quarles; William, who is a bachelor; James R., who married Mattie Scott and had Scott Thompson, who married Dorothy Mulcahy, of Versailles, and James R., Jr., who married Lula Scruggs; Lucy, who never married; Ella, who married —— Lewis; Cynthia, who married S. J. Gibson, and Elizabeth, who married Thomas Shaw. Robert Thomas Thompson and Mildred Henton lived and died at the old Smith Hale farm, now owned by Benj. Hieatt. His grandparents, David Thompson and wife, Eleanor, lived and died on the farm for many years the home of Alex Wright, but now the stock farm of E. H. Taylor, Jr.

David Thompson was a Revolutionary soldier. Other children of David and Eleanor Thompson were Elizabeth Thompson, who married Thomas Blanton in 1812 (see Blanton, Jan., 1921, Register, page 132); Louisa, who married Joel Thomasson in 1812; Mary, who married Edmond Shipp in 1813; Ann Bibb, born 1790, married Robert Adams in 1817; William Thompson, born 1797, died in 1869, married Eliza Peters, of Versailles, and had a daughter, Mary, who married Robert McConnell, the parents of the wives of W. Hawkins Cleveland, William Hunter Railey, and John Ball; also Will, Robert and James McConnell, of the county; David Thompson, Jr., who married in 1827 Eliza Beatty (daughter of George and Martha Beatty), and they had an only son, Robert A. Thompson, who married Lavinia Sneed Wingate. (See Thomson sketch); and Sarah, the 11th child of whom I have no account.

Judith Thomson and Thomas Bell, of Woodford County, while living on the Green river estate, had these children: Thomson, John, Samuel, Thomas and Robert Bell. They have descendants in that part of the state now.

The second paragraph in the second column above is in error. Edmond Vaughan and Susanna Thomson, his second wife, were the parents of James Vaughan, who married Charlotte Ashmore *Hawkins; and Mary Ann Vaughan who married Dandridge Crockett named in the third paragraph. The above Edmond Vaughan was twice married, first to Sarah Samuel, and they had a son, Edmond,

---

†Anthony Thomson's name was without the usual p, while his cousin used that letter.
‡See page 109.
*Daughter of William Strother Hawkins, Sr., and Katherine Keith of Woodford County.

Jr., who married Sythy Blanton. It was this couple who were the parents of Elizabeth Sarah Vaughan, who married Hezekiah Winn of Woodford County, and Lucy, who married Samuel B. Scearce, also of Woodford County. (See pages 236 and 294 for Scearce). I regret I was misinformed in the above statement of which I have never ceased to believe, and the sketch of the Vaughan family that I have had in contemplation for several years, and just completed January, 1933, gives me the desired opportunity to correct the misstatement. (See Winns.)

General David Thomson, of Scott County, spelled his name as did the Woodford County family of the name, being a full-blooded Scotchman, and I have been told by those who have seen members of both branches that there was a very striking resemblance between them. Both families married into the Major family, but neither side has been able to trace relationship if any exists. Both came from Louisa County, Virginia, to Kentucky, and settled in neighboring counties. General David was a son of William Thomson, born in Virginia in 1727, died there in 1778, where he married Anna Rodes. David was the eleventh child, born August 21, 1775. He died in 1789 and shortly thereafter his widow, Ann Rodes, came to Scott County,* Ky., with her large family. Her son David proved to be a successful farmer, and as a result the family prospered. He married Betsy Suggett, of Scott County, and when the war of 1812 came on he enlisted and was rapidly promoted

until he was commissioned Brigadier General, assuming command of his regiment at the battle of the Thames when Col. Richard M. Johnson was wounded. Family tradition insists that he killed Tecumseh notwithstanding the claims of the friends of Col. Richard M. Johnson and Col. William C. Whitley. One of his descendants at St. Louis, the wife of Theodore Shelton, a great granddaughter, has an earring worn by the Indian chief and says that her ancestor received all of the trophies on the person of the chief at the time he was killed by a Kentuckian, among them a tomahawk.

General David Thomson was a senator from Scott County 1811-20; was deputy U. S. Marshal in 1820, when he took the census of that county; was also sheriff and a very popular citizen. The children of General David Thomson and Betsey Suggett were: Manlius V., who married Mary Ann Thomson. Both died and were buried in Georgetown; Mildred Elvira, who married Redd Major, son of John Major and Elizabeth Redd. The wife of Theodore Shelton, of St. Louis, is a granddaughter; Melita Ann, married George R. Smith, of Georgetown, Ky. They were the parents of Sarah Elvira Smith, who married Henry Smith Cotton, of Sedalia, Mo. Her nickname was "Sed," and the city of Sedalia, Mo., was named for her; Milton T. Thomson, who married Amelia Ann Scroggin; Morton Thomson married Sarah Ann Powell; Monroe married Charlotte Lester; Marion Wallace married Thomas Allen Gunnell; Melcina Elizabeth married Robert Rush Spedden.

*My impression is that Scott was a part of Woodford at that time.

The first of this branch of the Thomsons of whom I have any record was Samuel Thomson, born in Ayrshire, Scotland. On account of his religious views, being an Anabaptist, he was compelled to leave his home because of persecution in that Presbyterian stronghold. Samuel went to Wales in 1715, where he became a merchant at Richmond. While there he married Mollie McDonald, a Scotch lassie, and soon afterward came to America, where their only son, William, married, as before stated, Ann Rodes, and had twelve children, General David being the eleventh.

In 1831 General Thomson, accompanied by his two sons-in-law, Lewis Redd Major (see Major family) and George R. Smith went to Missouri and bought land in Saline County. In 1833 they repeated the trip, when they purchased large tracts in Petis County, upon which they settled in the fall of that year with their several families. On land that they settled they established the town of Georgetown, in compliment to the town of that name near the old Kentucky home, and it was for some years the county seat of Petis County, but when Sedalia appeared on the map Georgetown surrendered the county seat.

Betsy Suggett was an aunt of Col. Richard M. Johnson, who became Vice President of the United States.

Manlius Thomson, eldest of General David and Betsy Suggett Thomson, remained a resident of Georgetown when the family moved to Missouri and if I am not mistaken was at one time President of Georgetown College; at least he was connected with it in some capacity.

In naming the nine children of Gen. David and Betsy Suggett Thomson an unusual case is presented, viz.: the name of each begins with an M—but whether this was designed or merely incidental I can't say.

Many of these people spell it Thompson, but Thomson is correct.

In writing a sketch of the Crutcher family, that appeared in the Sept., 1920, Register, page 71, I only mentioned the Rev. Isaac Crutcher and his descendants as representing Henry Crutcher, the pioneer. Isaac was by a first marriage to a lady whose name I have not learned. I have since learned that the pioneer was twice married; the second marriage was to Martha Beasley, daughter of William and Ann Beasley, of Caroline County, Va. By this marriage were two sons, half-brothers of the Rev. Isaac, whose names were Henry, Jr., and Reuben, the former born in 1780, died in 1852; the latter born in 1782, died in 1863, both were boys when they came to Kentucky. Henry, Jr., married first Susan Hancock, second Susanna Shipp. Reuben married first Elizabeth Onion, daughter of Charles Onion, a soldier of the Revolution, who once lived in the Crutcher neighborhood; second Sarah Scanland.

Both of these brothers settled upon farms each containing a comfortable log house built about 1800, and both of these dwellings are in fair condition and at present occupied. They were built in full view of the old Leestown road, a little west of Harmony church.

Each of these brothers raised a large

family. The children of Henry and Susanna Hancock Crutcher follow: Eliza, Loetitia, Levi Todd, who married Rebecca Dixon, granddaughter of Cyrus McCracken, of Woodford County; John, who married Mary French; Thomas, Bartlett, and others. Many of the descendants are living in the vicinity of Ducker's Station at this time.

Levi and Rebecca Dixon lived for a lifetime on a farm on the heights east of Frankfort that overlooks the country that surrounds that town. This estate constituted the home of Willis Blanton for many years. It is still in possession of descendants of Levi Crutcher.

Levi and Rebecca had these children: John, Lewellen, N. M., who married Mary Ellen Giltner; W. P. and Wash T., who have never married; Martha; and Susan, who married Will Shryock.

Bartlett Crutcher lived with his family on Elkhorn, near Harmony church.

Reuben Crutcher and his wife, Elizabeth Onion, had Isaac, Jr., born 1802, and married Eliza Ramsey; James, who married Martha Major Thomson, daughter of Nathaniel Thomson and Frances Major; Reuben, Jr., who married —— Craig and moved to Indiana; Lewis, who married —— Craig and moved to Gallatin County, Ky.; Robert, who married Susan Hancock and had several daughters; Thomas J., born in 1819, married first Mary Louise Thomson, second Zoraida Thomson, sister of his first wife. By the last marriage were six children, only one of whom married. Ann Crutcher was born at "Thomson's Manor" April 3, 1844, and married Jerry Downing, of Fayette County, son of Joseph Downing and

Sarah Taylor. For their children see Thomson, page 274.

———

Hon. John Andrew Steele, of Midway, Ky., a charter member of the Kentucky Historical Society, and one of its staunchest friends, departed this life June 11, 1921. He was ever loyal to his friends, true to his convictions, and therefore honored and respected by all who knew him.

His name has been repeatedly mentioned in the notes I have written in these columns concerning Woodford County and its pioneer families, because his people were identified with the county's best interests from the beginning, and no citizen has shown greater love for the county of his birth—the home of his ancestors—than has he.

At a meeting of the officers and stockholders of the Citizens Bank of Midway, of which he was cashier for about forty years, the following modest resolutions were adopted, and the sentiment expressed therein will be indorsed by every citizen who knew Captain Steele. The clipping containing the resolution is from the Lexington Herald, and it follows:

RESOLUTIONS ON DEATH OF CAPT. STEELE

———

Officers of Midway Bank Express Appreciation of Character and Services.

———

Midway, Ky., July 3—In the death of Captain John Andrew Steele, Woodford County lost one of its most respected, useful and distinguished citizens, and the sense of his loss is daily evident to the people of the county that delighted to honor him and relied upon his ability, patriotism and sense of duty. The officers of the bank at Midway, which he organized a generation ago, expressed in resolutions their sense of loss and appreciation of his character and services.

The resolution follows:

"Whereas, on the 11th of June, 1921, the life of our beloved associate, Captain John Andrew Steele, was ended here and his spirit entered the mystic realms of that life beyond;

"Therefore, be it resolved that we by this endeavor to voice our sense of the irreparable loss we have sustained and the feeling that a void has been created which cannot be filled. Born in this county, for more than four score years, he has been among us. For more than 40 years he has been a potent factor and influential force in the life of this bank and community, conservative and wise, in counsel, firm in his convictions of duty, yet ever kindly and filled with love for his fellowman. His loyalty and devotion to the welfare and success of this bank was excelled only by his great desire for the happiness and prosperity of all with whom he came in contact.

"As a soldier of the Lost Cause, he was courageous and true. As a legislator he was thrice sent to represent his county in the General Assembly of Kentucky; an elder in his church; a friend of education, serving as treasurer of the board of education without compensation from the opening of the school until his death.

"As officers of this bank and as citizens of this community, we all love and respect his memory.

"To the youth of our people we would say, here is a career and a character well worth of emulation, and to his posterity, one to which they can ever point with pride as a priceless heritage.

"To his family so bereaved we can only say that it is our privilege to mourn with you.

"Hy L. Martin,
"B. F. Parrish,
"C. B. Patterson,
"Breckinridge Viley,
"Committee."

Thomas Guthrie, Sr., and his wife, Mildred Howell, came from Virginia to Kentucky in 1783, and located near Midway, I am told, in Woodford County. In 1810 the census report of the county gave but five members in his family at that time, but it is known by descendants that they had ten children, six boys and four girls, so the conclusion is that several of them were married and housekeepers, some probably out of the county at that date. Their children follow: Mary, who married John Frauner; Thomas, Jr., who married —— Woods; John, who married —— Tiller; James, who married Elizabeth Gibbs; William, who married —— Yates; Nancy, who married Richard Bridgeford; Betsy, who married James Gibbs; Mildred, who married Adam Montgomery; Robert, who married Sarah Long, and Caleb Guthrie, who married Betsy Smith.

James Guthrie and Elizabeth Gibbs moved to Shelby County prior to 1810, as did so many of our early citizens, and their children were Agnes, Nathan, James, Mildred, Isaac Newton, Julius, Thomas J., Jeptha Dudley, who was twin with Granville C., Elizabeth and William J. John Frauner and Richard Bridgeford were living in Woodford County in 1810. The census of Woodford County in 1810 also discloses the names of Benjamin Guthrie, John, of the Revolution, William, of the Revolution, and Thomas Guthrie, Jr. At least a part of them were sons of Thomas Guthrie, Sr.*

Col. Joseph Crockett married Elizabeth Moore Woodson, widow of Tucker Woodson, in Virginia in 1782, and in 1784 they left Charlottsville with her son, Samuel Woodson, for Kentucky. They located in Jessamine County, but Col. Crockett's figure was familiar, and he was as well known in Woodford as in his home county, his home being just over the Woodford County line, near Keene. He was a civil engineer and Col. Thomas Marshall engaged his services in assisting him to straighten out the errors in the careless surveying that had been done at a much earlier period in Fayette County, from which Woodford had not yet been separated.

His wife was a daughter of John Moore and Mary Jouett, the latter a daughter of Matthew Jouett, Sr., the ancestor of the prominent artist of that name.* Many of the lines that had to be re-surveyed were in that part of Fayette that is now Woodford County, and Col. Crockett was engaged in this work for several years.

Later Col. Crockett became promi-

nent in business and political circles. He served in the first legislature and was appointed U. S. Marshal by Thomas Jefferson June, 1801, and served in that capacity until 1810, when he retired in favor of his eldest son Robert, who succeeded his father. Col. Crockett appointed †George Woodson Railey his deputy marshal, and his services extended over a number of years. It was he who directed the taking of the census of 1810 that was copied into the Register of January, 1920. George Woodson Railey and Dr. Joseph Crockett, son of Col. Joseph Crockett and Elizabeth Woodson, married daughters of Capt. John Bullock and Elizabeth Railey. The former married Maria Bullock, and the latter, after graduating from Transylvania, married first Elizabeth Randolph Bullock in 1813. He practiced his profession in Versailles until his death, about 1823. His first wife died in 1821, in Versailles, and he married second in 1822 Sallie Kenney, and died soon thereafter. Both he and his first wife are buried in the Crockett burying ground in Jessamine County.

John Crockett was another son of Col. Crockett and Elizabeth Woodson. He married Elizabeth Bullock who, I think, was a daughter of either Edmond or James Bullock, pioneers of Woodford and Fayette. He was in the campaign of 1812 when he was severely wounded. He was also at the battle of New Orleans.

I was told upon reliable authority that Col. Joseph Crockett, as U. S. Marshal, served the papers on Aaron Burr,

---

*See supplement for interesting data of Guthries.
*See Jouett family 392.
†George Woodson Railey was a first cousin, once removed, to Thomas Jefferson.

who was arrested for treason. I was also reliably informed that when Lafayette visited Versailles in 1825 Col. Joseph Crockett, his cousin Anthony Crockett and Captain Peter Dudley rode in the carriage with him from Frankfort, and also accompanied him to Lexington upon the conclusion of his visit to Versailles. They were Revolutionary comrades, and it is said that the meeting at Frankfort between the Crocketts and the rugged Frenchman was of such warmth as to be touching. The Crocketts themselves of French extract, coming from Antoine de Perronette de Crocketague, a native of South France, who took refuge in Ireland when heretics were ordered from France. It was in North Ireland that the name was so abbreviated as to be Crockett.

It is said that Col. Crockett always appeared in the colonial style of dress, and according to his wish, was thus prepared for burial.

Samuel Hughes Woodson was for years clerk of both circuit and county court in Jessamine, but in 1811 he turned his attention exclusively to the practice of law, resigned the clerkship in favor of his deputy, Daniel Branch Price, who married a daughter of Col. Crockett. He was the grandfather of *Daniel B. Price, Jr., who was a popular merchant of Versailles for many years.

Samuel Hughes Woodson was a successful lawyer and practiced in all of the courts of Central Kentucky, including Versailles, where he had many rela- †tives. He was repeatedly elected to the legislature, represented the Ashland

district in Congress. In 1803 he was married to Ann Randolph Meade, daughter of Col. David Meade, of "Chaumere," Jessamine County. They had several sons who were distinguished lawyers and jurists.

Tucker Woodson and Elizabeth Moore had another son, Tucker, Jr., who remained in Virginia to complete his education, when the family came to Kentucky. He married in Virginia Martha Epps Hudson, and came to Kentucky about 1800. Later he moved to Hart County, where he established the town of Woodsonville. The late Isaac T. Woodson, who represented Hart County in the legislature about 1880 (when the writer was an officer of the legislature), was a grandson. Afterwards he practiced law in Louisville, and died there several years ago. Isaac Woodson was a lawyer by profession and a gentleman by nature.

———

Patrick Davis was a Virginian by birth, was reared in that state and married there, but I am not able to give his wife's maiden name. He had an only son, whose name was William, and he too was born in Virginia, his birth occurring about the year 1755, and of course he had reached years of maturity long before he came to Kentucky. Patrick and his son William arrived in Woodford County about 1785, and since nothing in the family records says anything about the wife of Patrick it is presumed that she died in Virginia. Patrick died in Woodford County in the vicinity of Midway, in 1790, and I understand his will was recorded in the county court during that year. In his will I am told that his son William was the sole beneficiary. William married Ann Worley in Virginia and they lived near Midway, where both died, he in 1837. They reared a large family of children, consisting of two sons and six daughters, whose names were: William, Jr., who lost his life in an accident; John W., who married America Gaines (daughter of Richard Gaines and Rebecca Gatewood, of Scott County), on Nov. 24, 1825; Rebecca Davis married James Gough, many of whose descendants live near Russellville, Ky. (see Goughs, page 306); Betsy Davis married John Frazer, and their son George Frazer moved to Franklin County, near Leestown, where he and his wife died. They have descendants at Frankfort and Atlanta, Ga.; Mary married —— Gray; Sallie married —— Whittaker; Patsy married —— Letcher, and Amanda died unmarried.

John W. Davis and his wife, America Gaines, raised ten children, whose names follow: Columbia, who married John P. Innes, of Fayette County; William G., who married Eudora Woods, daughter of William Woods and Sallie Parrish (see Parrish; May, 1921, page 232); Rebecca Davis, who married Judge Press Morrow, of Versailles, no issue; John W., who married Elizabeth Innes, of Fayette County; Mollie, who married John H. Payne; James, who married Anna Whitney; Elizabeth, who married William Ross, of Carlisle; Amanda and Sallie, who never married, and Hillary, who married Sammie Cassell.

Columbia Davis and John P. Innes had two children, America and George.

America married George H. Whitney and they have, 1st George, 2nd Estelle, who married Maury Kemper, of Lexington; 3rd Harold, who married Eleanor James; 4th Columbia, the wife of William C. McDowell, and 5th Mary Sayre, wife of Guy Hueglet.

William G. Davis (second of John W. and America Gaines Davis), and his wife, Eudora Woods, had Thompson P. who married Lucy Trumbo; William W. Davis, who married Stella Williams; Margaret, who is a spinster; Bonnie, who is the wife of Arnett Pritchett; John W., who married Rosa Gorin, of Glasgow; Edward Lee, who married Margaret Martin, daughter of Henry L. Martin and Kate Brooks (see Coles, Sept., 1920, page 64). Thompson P. and Lucy Trumbo Davis had Allen W., who married Mary Raines; and Dora, who married William B. Cogar. John W. Davis and Rosa Gorin have John W., Jr., and Rogers Gorin Davis. Edward Lee Davis and Margaret Martin have Louise, who married Edgar Bradford, and Katherine and Dorothy.

John W. Davis, Jr. (son of John W. and America) and his wife, Elizabeth Innis, had a daughter who married David McChord. They have Sarah, who married William McLain; and John McChord.

Elizabeth Davis and William Ross have Columbia Ross, who married Frank Lindsey; Ed., who married Lucy Waller; Mary, who married Ed. Ingles; William, who married Mary Andrews; Innis, who married —— Parker, and Martha, who married Faris Templeman.

Hilary Davis and Sammie Cassell

have Lilley, who married William Lehman and have Elizabeth, Jeanette, William and Joseph; Ermie, who married John Withrow and left a son, John Withrow, Jr.; Maude, who married James M. Withrow, and they have a daughter, Katherine; Columbia, who married Boyd White and they have a daughter Anna; William Percey Davis, who died unmarried, and Bessie, who married Andrew Mitchell and they have Andrew Steele and Marjory Mitchell.

Patrick Davis settled on the farm now owned by the widow of Hilary Davis, opposite the cemetery at Midway, and doubtless built his home of logs. At his death his son William inherited this estate and built the house that is now the home of Hilary Davis' family, in 1789. Patrick's parents were natives of Ireland. I do not know what year he came to Virginia. The census of 1810 reports a William Davis who served in the Revolution and owned ten slaves, possibly the William Davis mentioned above.

I stated above that Eliza Davis, of Midway, married George Frazer. I did this upon data that was furnished me, and thought it a mistake at the time, but had no positive means of disproving it. However, I am informed that Eliza Davis married John Frazer, and that they were the parents of George Frazer, who lived at Frankfort, and Sally Frazer, who married Christopher Neal and lived on the old Ed Trabue farm, now owned by Willis Field. To the best of my recollection the above John Frazer was a brother of Joseph Frazer, who married Caroline Railey, and also of Emma Frazer,

who married Col. George T. Cotton. They were all closely related to Oliver Frazer, the Lexington artist.

In the Davis sketch I also stated that the farm upon which Mrs. Hilary Davis lives is the original Davis home, but G. G. Gough, of Russellville, thinks it the original home of his grandfather Gough, whose sketch also appears in this issue of the Register. The Davis family examined the record in the county court and insist that they are right.

In the pioneer days the various sections of the county were distinguished by neighborhoods, named by the early settlers, hence we had Mt. Pisgah (afterwards Pisgah), Mt. Vernon, Glenns Creek, Grassy Spring, Griers Creek, Harmony, Clear Creek and others, these names indicating in some instances the loyalty of the pioneers to the communities from whence they came, as Mt. Pisgah, Mt. Vernon, Harmony and others were transplanted, as it were, from Virginia, and many of these people were also loyal to the traditions of their ancestors, being characterized by sobriety, purity and piety, and all of those attributes that lead to honor and justice. When the houses of worship were erected they usually bore the names applied to the community, or vice versa.

The Mt. Pisgah neighborhood was settled by a colony of Scotch and Scotch-Irish, from Virginia—pious Presbyterians, who settled there several years before the county was established, and they built the Pisgah church, five miles east of Versailles, on the Shannon's Run road, and one mile from the Versailles and Lexington road, near Ft. Garrett. These people came into the county soon after the advent of Elijah Craig, not later than 1783 or 84. When the old church, which has stood for more than a century and a quarter was built, the only approach was by way of Indian trails that followed "Shannon's Run," dusty in summer and miry in winter. There were no Macadam roads in the county then, and thoughts of railroads, trolleys and river transportation would have been regarded as an iridescent dream, while thoughts of auto spins and air navigation were not within the range of reason at all. How different now; the clang of the engine's bell, the shrill whistle of the trolley, and the honk of the auto reverberate around these sacred walls; yea, the worshippers at this Christian shrine are now upon tiptoe of expectancy as to when the noisy whir of the airship will also enliven the changed condition. But while these marvelous changes have been going on these people have never been in a state of innocuous desuetude, but have been busy promoting and expanding the religious sphere. They have done their duty not only locally, but are deeply interested in mountain work, and even beyond the mountain peak, and across the deep blue sea their influence has been exerted for humanity and Christianity.

Of the one hundred and thirty odd years of existence, two pastors served the congregation for seventy years. The pastorate of Dr. James Blythe covered about forty years, and Dr. Ruth-

erford Douglas, an able and popular minister, occupied the pulpit for about thirty years, and it was only ended when his spirit was at rest and his heart-beats stilled in death.*

The first pastor was the Rev. Adam Rankin, who found a congregation and church edifice awaiting him upon his arrival at Mt. Pisgah, as it was known at that time.

The Stevensons, the Gays, the Dunlaps, the McIlvains and other pioneer families who arrived from Lexington Fort and built their log houses in this vicinity about 1782 or 83, immediately entered upon the construction of a house of worship, and soon thereafter another for educational purposes. These buildings were at first constructed of logs.

The first conference of Presbyterians in this section met at Cane Run church, in Mercer County, on the 30th day of March, 1785, and the Rev. Adam Rankin was present. This conference met again in July of that year with representatives from twelve congregations present. The representatives from Pisgah were William Evans and William Scott. Caleb Wallace at that time represented the Cane Run church. At that time, as stated above, the meeting house as Pisgah was constructed of logs and built in what was then a wilderness of heavily wooded land.

On Oct. 17, 1786, the new Presbytery met in the court house in Danville and the Rev. Adam Rankin represented Pisgah. Soon thereafter he took an unpopular position toward several other denominations and the Pisgah congrega-

---

*I remember with pleasure the eloquence and earnestness of this beloved divine who preached many sermons at Griers Creek Church.

tion suggested that he dissolve his pastoral relations with the church, and the Rev. James Blythe succeeded him and began a pastoral relation that lasted forty years.

In 1802 the Kentucky Synod was separated from Virginia, placing Pisgah in the new Synod, and that church has never been without a representative in that body.

Moses McIlvain was a member of Pisgah whose duty it was to look after the exchequer, and the finances were never at a low stage. At the communion service in those days it was customary to have several ministers present and the services were long and tedious, and it was often near the evening shadows when the congregation was dismissed.

In addition to his pastoral duties, Dr. Blythe was a professor in Transylvania, and his salary as pastor was only $130.00 per annum.

In 1812 the log house was razed and a stone structure took its place. The Sunday school was not organized until 1827, and the membership at once provided a library that was looked after by J. Watson McIlvain. When Alexander Campbell severed his relations with the Presbyterian church it affected these pious people, but not seriously.

In 1832 Dr. Blythe severed his relations to accept the Presidency of Hanover University, in Indiana. He was succeeded by Rev. Joseph Cunningham, who died early in his ministry, and in 1841 Dr. Price was called and he represented Pisgah in the General Assembly in Richmond, Va., in 1847, the round trip being made by stage coach, but before he reached his home he expired, and the Rev. S. M. Bayless was the successor.

January 8th, 1848, Pisgah elected her first trustees, William Allen, John Neet, John Martin and James Berry being selected. In 1853 Rev. W. C. McPheeters became the supply and took membership with the congregation, and it was not until this time that the record mentions deacons, although they may have had them from the first. On March 13, 1853, James Gay and John Valentine were chosen for that service. I neglected to say earlier in this sketch that the site of Pisgah church, two acres of ground, was donated by Samuel Stevenson and his wife, Jane. In 1851 their son Robert donated thirty acres near the church upon which to build a parsonage. The generosity of these Christian citizens was recognized by the congregation in the erection of a monument in the church yard in grateful remembrance. In November, 1853, Dr. Robt. W. Allen became pastor, the first to be domiciled in the new parsonage. He retired in 1857, and Dr. Rutherford Douglas succeeded him, beginning his long service, which was terminated by death in 1890.

In 1868 the church building was remodeled from the square style to the Gothic, the southern wall being removed to lengthen the building. In 1888 Dr. Robert C. James donated a set of stained windows in memory of his mother, and the oriel window above the pulpit was given by the congregation in memory of Dr. Douglas.

Dr. E. E. Erwin succeeded Dr. Douglas, and Rev. Coleman Graves succeeded Dr. Erwin in 1897. In 1903 Dr.

Graves resigned and the Rev. W. O. Shewmaker was called.

The early settlers in this community were nearly all Presbyterians and the names of the various families follow: Allen, Scott, Evans, Garrett, Rennick, Martin, Long, Ferguson, Berry, Black, Robb, Elliott, Watson, Campbell, Howe, Steele, Wardlow, Young, Stevenson, Gay, Dunlap, McIlvain, Wasson and Stewart.

The pastors who have recently served the congregation are: J. Cochran Hunt, 1912-14; and George M. Telford, 1915-20. The ruling elders who represented the several generations were: William Scott, Francis Allen, Alexander Dunlap, Isaac Stevenson, James Wardlow, Hugh Ferguson, Nathaniel Ferguson, James Martin, John Allen, John Stevenson, Sr., J. S. Berryman, William Allen, John Neet, John Martin, Dr. Louis Marshall, Chas. T. Cox, Almon Spencer, Dr. Robert S. Hart, J. Wilmore Garrett, Sr., William Allen Cox, Robt. H. Wason, and Dr. McFerran Crow. Deacons who have served the several generations were: Robert Allen, J. A. Elliott, William Burrier, John Valentine, James R. Gay, Chas. F. Cox, Elijah Watkins, Robt. Garrett, Charles Powell, Peter G. Powell, Robt. H. Wason, J. Horace Gay, James T. Cox, Joseph M. Garrett, Robt. H. Wason, Jr., Wilmore Garrett, Jr., J. Gay Hanna, Dr. Walter Cox, and D. W. Hart.

In 1795 a grammar school was inaugurated at Pisgah in a log house built for the purpose, and in this school the training was thorough, and some of the young men who passed through the curriculum at this institution have made their mark with both pen and tongue.

Although at times the teacher was a preacher, the rule was that no denominational instructions were to be tolerated, yet morality and piety were instilled into their minds and hearts, and I have no knowledge of any one who took a thorough course in this institution whose life was not above reproach.

In 1798 the Pisgah school was, in a sense, merged into Transylvania, but the community continued their interest in the community school, which is more than a century old. For a number of years Dr. Louis Marshall, of "Buck Pond," the scholarly son of Col. Thomas Marshall and Mary Randolph Keith, and grandfather of Louis Marshall, cashier of the Bank of Woodford, had charge of this school, and it flourished under his guidance. For a time he was an elder in the church at Pisgah. Later Prof. Almon Spencer conducted a successful school there, but with the advent of the interurban, with the frequency of its trips, has rendered the schools of Lexington accessible and lessened the attendance at Pisgah, so the school was closed a decade ago or more.

Some of the students who took a course in this school and have made their impress upon the affairs of the state and nation were: John J. and Henry Crittenden; John C., Robert, and William C. P. Breckinridge, Thomas F. and Edward C. Marshall, and Alexander Campbell.

The school building still stands and Woodford County should take great pride in this monument that stands for such achievement. The early settlers were nearly all Presbyterians, and many of them were buried in the community burial ground hard by.

Knowing that my good friend Willis W. Field, who was reared in the vicinity of the old Griers Creek church, was more likely to know the facts relating to that church than any one else living, I solicited his assistance and he gave me the following interesting facts in connection with its early history and the many changes that have characterized its existence from the beginning, more than a century ago. His brief statement follows:

"A deed acknowledged June 2, 1817, was made by Thomas Railey, Jr., to trustees of the 'Republican Meeting House,' viz.: Willis Field, Andrew Muldrow, Samuel Jesse, Joel M. Dupuy and Randolph Railey, Sr. This was the start of Griers Creek church, and it was avowedly a 'Republican Meeting House,' meaning one to be used by all denominations. Of these first trustees, Willis Field was committed to the Baptists, as was Joel Dupuy. Both the mother and father of Willis Field were Baptists. Randolph Railey, Sr., was a Presbyterian, but his wife, Patsy Pleasants, was an Episcopalian. I don't know the affiliations of the other trustees.

"In September, 1830, a deed was made by Charles Railey for another lot, adjoining the first, to trustees of the 'Republican Meeting House,' viz.: Willis Field, Joel M. Dupuy, Samuel Campbell, Randolph Railey, Sr., Charles Railey, Allen Rowland, and William D. Young. Of the new trustees Charles Railey and Allen Rowland were Methodists and William D. Young was a Baptist.

"I assume that the church building was erected some time in 1817 and that it was used by all denominations. Later on in the '40s and '50s the Presbyterians were the most numerous in the neighborhood. Nearly all of the Raileys, the Frazers, the Carrs, the Campbells, the Steeles, the Whites and Daniel Taylor were Presbyterians. Some time about 1856 the new school Presbyterians rather assumed ownership of the building, and had a regular pastor, the Rev. —— Gray. Afterwards the Rev. Ben Mills, of Frankfort, preached there.

"During the Civil War preaching in the church was rare, but all denominations were at liberty to use it. After the war a family moved into it and occupied it until about 1871. Not one of the trustees was then alive. After these people vacated, the various denominations renewed the services as of old. About 1874 the Rev. Keelon Route was instrumental in having needed repairs made on the building, and since then it has been used principally by the Presbyterians, and the Presbyterians of Versailles now call it Griers Creek Presbyterian chapel, but strictly speaking it is still a 'Republican meeting house.'

"Thomas Railey, Jr., who contributed the lot upon which this church was erected, was a son of Thomas Railey and Martha Woodson and a brother of your grandfather, P. I. Railey, Sr.

"The Rev. Cabell Harrison, of Lexington, who visited his kinspeople, the Raileys, was one of the first preachers to occupy the pulpit in this old church.

He was, I believe, a son, or a grandson of Carter Harrison and Susanna Randolph, of 'Clifton,' Va.''

This letter was written just before the death of ''Wis'' Field. Next to Col. Thomas Field, I presume Willis had a greater store of information on the early history of Woodford County than any other citizen, especially pertaining to that part of the county in which he was born and reared. I left Woodford County early in 1866, but I have a distinct recollection of attending the services at that old church before and during the Civil War, and I remember it as the shrine where worshipped my ancestors and kindred, and I recall sermons delivered by two of my kinsmen, the Rev. Thos. Railey Markham and the Rev. Samuel A. King from the pulpit of that church. The Rev. Joseph C. Styles and the Rev. John Newton Blackburn often preached there before my day. The latter was the grandfather of David L. Thornton, of Versailles. The contributions to the church building fund came from all of those living in the neighborhood. The church is still standing and is on the Tyrone or Shryock's Ferry pike, three and a half miles from Versailles, and the old* school house where I received my early training is hard by, and the lot contains about five acres of land. Rev. John Taylor, of the ''Ten Churches,'' calls it Grays Creek, but it is Griers Creek.

The old Clear Creek Baptist church in the early days had an enthusiastic membership, and many of the sermons delivered there were by able expounders of the gospel. Such men as the Rev. Joseph Craig, the Rev. Isaac Crutcher, the Rev. William Hickman, the Rev. John Dupuy, the Rev. John Taylor, author of the ''Ten Churches,'' and the Rev. ''Raccoon'' John Smith talked from the pulpit of this old church to a neighborhood of interested hearers on various and sundry occasions. I am not able to report any of the deacons who served this congregation during its existence. The church was approached from the Troy pike or Nicholasville road.

''The Ten Churches'' gives this information: ''As early as 1785 several preachers had moved into the Clear Creek neighborhood, among them John Dupuy, James Rucker, Richard Cave† and John Taylor, and during the year a church was organized with thirty members. Revivals were held, harmony prevailed and converts increased. Soon after, Great Crossings and Bryant's Station churches were organized and an association established, with Lewis Craig as moderator, and at that meeting John Taylor was chosen Clear Creek's first pastor, with a salary of $70.00 the first year, $100.00 the second year, but in two years only $40.00 of the $170.00 had been paid.

''Soon after discussion* arose, and John and James Dupuy, with other members, withdrew and organized a church on 'Buck Run,' near Griers Creek church, but it was short lived.''

In the history of the Kentucky Baptists I find the following: ''Among the early members of the Clear Creek

---

*Razed about 1931, and replaced by a more modern building.
*More properly dissensions.
†See pages 317, 391.

church were the representatives of many large families now scattered through the south and west. The Caves, Watkinses, Stuarts, Ruckers, Dupuys, Craigs, Graves, Wooldridges, Singletons, Mortons, Shaws and Youngs. They were, most of them, members of the old Spotsylvania church in Virginia, and followed the Craigs through the wilderness and formed the first church of any kind in Kentucky, the Baptist church of Gilberts Creek, and on the 18th of June, 1785, they were constituted into a church of Christ on Clear Creek by Lewis Craig, William Hickman, George Smith and James Garrard, Governor of Kentucky.''

Samuel Dedman was a ruling elder in the Clear Creek church.

Grassy Spring church was also one of the pioneer churches of the county, as it was dedicated early in the 19th century, more than one hundred years ago. The original building was erected and dedicated before the activities of the Rev. Isaac Crutcher and the Rev. Joseph Craig had ceased, and I am told under the consent and direction of the old Forks Baptist Association. The first building was of logs, the second a square brick building. About 1840 the Baptists sold the property to the Disciples of Christ, a denomination or sect that was supporting scriptural interpretations from the viewpoint of Alexander Campbell, who were very strong in that vicinity at that time. The present building at Grassy Spring, the third, was built by the purchasers just after the Civil War, I believe, and they continue to hold services there with a fair sized congregation despite automobiles and good roads that have in recent years placed country churches at a decided disadvantage.

The first pastor of Grassy Spring church, I am informed, was the Rev. Isaac Crutcher, a prominent Baptist minister, and he is buried in the graveyard within the shadow of the church walls. Afterwards such men as the Rev. Joseph Craig, the Rev. William Hickman, the Rev. Joseph Dupuy and other shining lights of the Baptist persuasion preached revival sermons from that pulpit. Since the church was transferred to the Disciples such able men as the Rev. Alexander Campbell, Walter Scott, "Raccoon" John Smith, Robert Rice, John I. Rogers, John T. Johnson, William Morton, Jacob Creath, Sr., Sam'l Rogers, Sandy Jones and Phillip S. Fall occupied the pulpit at various times. Since the Civil War they have had these pastors: Rev. Jacob Huguely, J. B. Jones, G. W. Yancey, Samuel Crutcher, William Stanley (father of the Governor), M. C. Kurfees, J. B. Grubbs, Thomas N. Arnold, and J. K. P. South. Besides the pastors named, I recall some very able evangelists who have held meetings there, such as Benjamin Franklin, J. W. McGarvey, Moses E. Lard and John S. Shouse.

When the property was transferred to the Christian denomination all of the children of the Rev. Isaac Crutcher that I knew united with them, and great grandchildren hold membership there now, one of them, Arthur Crutcher, being an officer, and each of the generations has furnished officers as well as members. For seventy years or more the church records there disclose the following elders: Richard Crutcher, Lewis Crutcher, George Rogers, William McDaniel, Robert McMillan, John R. Darnell, William Bailey, J. K. P. South, James R. Shaw and Virgil Gaines. The present elders are: Arthur G. Crutcher and Dr. Mathew Cotton Darnell. The deacons of the church who are yet remembered were: James Henry Gaines, William W. Jett, Washington Crutcher, Lafayette Crutcher, Sr., W. Samuel Fogg, Thomas Bedford, Lafayette Crutcher, Jr., Robert Crutcher, Hiram Jett and Redd Crutcher. The present deacons are Robert Duncan, J. D. Smith, J. E. Crutcher, and Polk South, Jr.

The late Mrs. J. K. P. South and Mrs. W. W. Jett were influential members and workers, and each organized societies in the church that have rendered, and are rendering great service in mission work.

Quite a number of those who dwelt in this community years agone were married in the church. They were: William Petty and Mamie Shaw; Thomas Edwards and Atlanta Darnell; Richard J. Fogg and Susan Hawkins; Oakley Thompson and Jennie Fogg; William H. Graddy and Mamie Field; John Lewis Utterback and Phena Morris; John Church and Fannie Fogg; Dudley Chase Chaffee and Spicie Belle South, and Dr. Mathew Cotton Darnell and Ermina Jett.

The two oldest members of this congregation, in both point of years and length of service, are Mrs. Anna Graves Crutcher and Mrs. Jennie Fogg Thompson.

This quotation is from a poem by Vachel Lindsey, "My Fathers were Born in Kentucky:"

"And the church at Grassy Spring,
Under the red bird's wing—
Sweet as dew and honeycomb."

Since writing the above narration the following clipping from the Woodford Sun, Aug., 1913, and extracts from letters written by Rev. John T. Johnson have been placed before me.

The Sun says: "Grassy Spring church, named from a beautiful spring of water nearby, is an offspring of the Forks of Elkhorn Baptist church, near Duckers. It was organized prior to 1800, and the Rev. Isaac Crutcher, we believe, was the first pastor . . . . The church went over to the Reformed faith in about 1830 (at least ten years later, I think) under the preaching of Rev. Alexander Campbell, with scarcely a dissenting voice. The original church was built of logs. The present brick building was erected about 1869 or 70, under the direction of a committee consisting of Washington Crutcher, Capt. Elijah Fogg and William McDaniel. . . . For many years Grassy Spring church had a membership of about 250, and was one of the most influential churches in this section."

I am sorry the extracts of the letters of Rev. John T. Johnson carry no dates. They are: "It is one of the most liberal churches in the state." And again: "At the request of brother Whittington I preached at the Glenns Creek Republican Meeting House (it is near Millville and in full view of the old home of Isham Keith Hawkins and is still standing. It was built of stone.) "We continued with brother Whittington until Lord's day and preached the last two days at Grassy Spring, and the brethren there were joined by those from the Forks of Elkhorn, acted a noble part and we gained, in all, 60 noble, choice spirits.''

When the Baptists sold their church property at Grassy Spring in 1840 they purchased the old Harmony church, on the Cole road, two miles below Spring Station. The Presbyterians built the Harmony church and worshipped there many years before they sold it. After they disposed of the Harmony property they merged with a portion of the membership of the old Woodford church, on the Alexander estate, and erected a building at Midway that was, in every particular, a duplicate of the Northern Presbyterian church at Frankfort. However, it was remodeled a few years ago, and the interior is much changed. The Midway congregation has always been an active band of Christian workers, and has done a great service in the mountains and in foreign lands. The remnant of the old Woodford church, I think, took membership with the congregation at Versailles before the Civil War. Judge Caleb Wallace was a presiding elder at the old Woodford church from the organization of the congregation until his death. Several of the county court meetings were held in this church in 1789. It was erected of stone and was in fairly good shape a few years ago. Some of the families who worshipped there in pioneer days were the Wallaces, Alexanders, Steeles, Shipps, Flemings, Colemans and many others.

The South Elkhorn Baptist Association was organized in 1785, soon after the first settlers came to the county—they being in the forts at Lexington and Harrodsburg until 1781-2, from whence they did not venture except for the sake of forage, until about 1783. Lewis Craig was the first moderator, and Col. Richard Young, one of the founders of Versailles in 1792, was the first clerk.

The last meeting of this association was held in Sept., 1920, the 136th that had been held, and John Stout, Jr., was the moderator. His father, John Stout, Sr., was moderator for a great number of years. All of the meetings have been held in the bluegrass belt of counties.

I regret very much indeed not to be able to give an account of the early history of the Mt. Vernon Baptist church, for it is one of the oldest in the county, and has accomplished so much good in the name of humanity and Christianity.

I wrote to several of the most influential men of the congregation, and talked with several of the earnest lady workers to no avail—each referred me to another—so I feel that I discharged my duty in an earnest and sincere effort to have a record of the sayings and doings of this bright star in Woodford's galaxy of working churches.*

The following names constitute a partial list of men of Woodford County who enlisted in Company F, commanded by Captain Thomas F. Marshall, in the Mexican War: Samuel F. Patterson, 1st Lieut.; John Brown, 2nd Lieut.; William L. Moseley, Walter L. Peters, Samuel H. Bradley, William C. Gilles-

*See page 385 for a record.

pie, James M. Kinkead, Boone Major, Henry C. Brady, John I. Ashmore, Thomas A. Booth, Andrew Brown, John S. Darnell, Benjamin E. Ellis, James W. Eddings, John M. Ellis, John Kemp Goodloe, Fleming G. Hearn, William Hale, Lucien Hensley, James Jeter, Nathaniel Johnson, John E. Miles, Joseph Morrison, Jefferson Petty, David Rogers, Hiram W. Skelton, Simeon Scearce, John Searcy, Andrew M. Stevenson, Patrick Sullivan, James Thornton, George Thornton, Archibald Wood, Samuel Wallace, Landon Elliston, Lafayette Haydon, Lewis Johnson, John Morton, Robert Brown, William A. Hawkins, Abner Hunter, Alvin Bates, John Frost, William A. Graves, Samuel Helm, William Strother Hawkins, Jr., Benjamine Dabney Hawkins (sons of William Strother Hawkins and Katherine Keith—see Strothers), John Crittenden Railey (see page 259), William H. Smith, Robert Taylor, James Toppass, William Woods, G. W. Wallace and John W. Watkins.‡

John Gregory was a private in the Revolution and came to Woodford County from Culpepper County, Va., at a date not thought to be later than 1800. His name appears on the census of 1810 and he then had a family consisting of ten members. Abraham Gregory lived in the county at the same time with a family of four, and slaves to the number of seventeen. From the best information I have been able to obtain none of the descendants of these people were in the county as late as the Civil War.

John Gregory's eldest daughter Anne

married Merriman Stevens, and they were living in Woodford County in 1810, and only left the county a short time prior to the Civil War, when they moved to Boone County, Mo. Merriman was a captain, and his son Mitchell Stevens was a lieutenant of a company of militia that did not participate in the active service during the Mexican War, but were regarded as a reserve force ready to be mustered into the regular service if the exigencies of the situation required it. In other words, I think they were home guards.

Polly Stevens, eldest daughter of Merriman Stevens and Anne Gregory, married Hiram Williams, of the county, and they were living in Woodford County in 1850, but soon thereafter moved to Pike County, Mo.

John Gregory died and was buried in Woodford County, but I do not know where. The D. A. R.'s will do well to locate and mark the spot. Merriman Stevens lived in the vicinity of Midway.

In the May, 1921, issue, page 236, I gave a brief account of the Scearce family, who were descended from the pioneer John Scearce, and I am here presenting additional names to supplement that account.

Henry Scearce, Sr., son of John, married first America Berry, in 1822, and they had Susan Ann, who married Dr. William L. Crutcher in 1841; Samuel B. Scearce, born in 1825, died in 1877, *married Lucy Vaughan in 1840; William H. Scearce, born in 1827, married Mary Johnson in 1849; John Scearce, born in 1832, married Martha Crutcher

‡See page 400 for others.
*See page 282 and supplement.

in 1854; James L. Scearce, born in 1834, married Ruhama Ellis, of New Castle, in 1854; Jefferson B. Scearce, born in 1837, died in 1911, married Louise Vimont, of Millersburg, in 1860; Amelia Scearce, married James Barnes.

Henry Scearce, Sr., married second Elizabeth Thompson in 1841 and had Henry L. Scearce, who died unmarried; America, who married James Gilkie in 1861; Alice M., born in 1846, married first Joseph Owen in 1861, second W. L. Gilkey, in 1895; Evern, born in 1843, married Gilson West in 1861, and Millard Scearce, who served in the Confederacy, never married, and is now an in-, mate of the Confederate Home at Pewee Valley.

The children of Henry Scearce, Sr., and America Berry, whose lines were not run out in the May Register, were William H. Scearce, who married Mary Johnson. They have a daughter, Amelia, who lives in Shelbyville.

John Scearce and Martha Crutcher moved to Liberty, Mo., where they died and left three daughters, Minnie, the eldest, married S. D. Peters and they have a son who married Ruth Watkins.

James L. Scearce and Ruhama Ellis had Volney, who is a resident of Texas; Henry, who has a widow and three children living, and James P. Scearce, who is a resident of Kansas.

Dr. Jefferson B. Scearce and Louise Vimont moved to Chillicothe, Ohio, where he was quite prominent in his profession. Their daughter, Elizabeth Welch, has an only son.

Of the children of the second marriage America Scearce and James Gilkie had five children, as follows:

William, Elizabeth and Eva, neither of whom ever married; Henry married Elizabeth Jackson, and Taylor married J. W. Lunsford and are residents of Lawrence, Indiana.

John Scearce, Jr., son of John Scearce, the pioneer, married Elizabeth Middleton in 1821, and they lived and died on the Shelby County estate, to which county he moved, an honored citizen. William Middleton Scearce, born in 1822, died in 1845; Adam Fulton Scearce married Susan White and they had John C., who married Anna Henton and had Evan Fulton Scearce, born in 1822, died in 1907; Fred Hale, who married —— ——, and Ralph, who married Rosa Dudley, daughter of Rev. R. M. Dudley and Mary Henton. They have a son, Dudley Henton Scearce, born in 1920. Ralph saw service in the World War. His sister, Fannie Scearce, is a resident of Shelbyville.*

Other descendants of John Scearce, Sr., are Lillie Dale, who married W. A. McGrath, of Shelbyville; James H. Dale, who lives with his family in Alabama, and Mary S. Dale, who married Professor C. C. Freeman, of Transylvania College.

————

Relative to the Blantons, who received mention in the January, 1921, issue, page 132, the data that I used came from several different sources, and on page 133 I stated that Thomas Blanton, Sr., deeded prior to his death in 1810 the property upon which the widow of Lafayette Crutcher now lives, to his son John. That data was evidently in error, as a sketch of the Thomson family in the September issue,

———

*See page 365 for correction. His aunt.

1921, page 274, clearly proves that this was a part of the estate of Anthony Thomson, Sr., that was inherited by his son Anthony Thomson, who lived there with his family until his death in 1827. John Blanton may have lived there for a time after that, but not before. They lived on the farm now owned by William E. Bradley, Jr. They had a son, Thompson Blanton, who married a niece of Anthony Thomson, Jr., and it is likely that it was he who lived on the Anthony Thomson farm instead of Willis, his brother. Willis Blanton married Rebecca Ware and they were living at a very early date, according to a record I have seen recently, on a farm that adjoined the estate of the Rev. Isaac Crutcher, on the summit of a hill that not only commands a view of the "Big Eddy" and its romantic surroundings, but also overlooks all of the hills that surround Frankfort. Willis Blanton sold his farm to Levi Crutcher before the Civil War, and I think the Crutchers are still in possession of it.

————

The Sept., 1920, issue of the Register, page 110, contained a brief account of Mann Butler, who arrived in Versailles from Maryland in 1806, where he established perhaps the first academy in Woodford County. At that time I instituted a vigorous search for descendants of his and Martha Dedman's to whom he was married in the county, but without avail. I gave what little I heard of him when a boy, and the recollections of others with whom I talked, but not until recently did I learn that he was the author of Butler's History of Kentucky. In our library (Kentucky Historical Society) is a small

volume, bound in calf, that bears the marks of age, and indistinctly on the back it bears this inscription: Butler's History of Kentucky. My curiosity led me to open it and read the preface, which, to my surprise, said that it was written by the man whose brief career in the county I had already noted. From a cursory perusal of its pages I found it a very interesting account of the state, and from the preface I take the following extracts to show that he used the best of means of that day to give an up to date account of Kentucky and its citizenship: "The author has been no inattentive observer of public events in Kentucky from his migration to the state in 1806; nor has he been destitute of intercourse with public characters. His curiosity—he may add his heart was early engaged in the story of Kentucky heroism, hardship and enterprise. Not during twenty-eight years' residence in the bosom of the state has he felt his interest lessen in the fame and fortunes of his adopted Commonwealth. Still the author places the claims of his history to the public attention on a basis higher than any personal intercourse he may have enjoyed at the late period of his removal to the west. It is on a body of private papers belonging to some of the principal actors in Kentucky history. These have come into his possession from the numerous sources in the most cheering and friendly manner. They constitute the papers of General George Rogers Clark, the interesting correspondence with Patrick Henry and Jefferson, and the McAfee papers. Also Col. Chas. S. Todd, John J. Crittenden and Nathaniel Hart have favored me with the Shelby,

Innis and Floyd papers. Messrs. Thomas and Edmund Rogers, Humphrey Marshall, Judges Rowan, Underwood and Pirtle; Henry Clay, James Guthrie, John and James Brown and Gov. Pope have all most freely and kindly contributed everything in their power. Gen. James Ray, of Mercer County, himself a living chronicle, and Captain Gaines, of Woodford County (Bernard Gaines. See Jan., 1921, issue Register, page 165) have contributed much that was interesting.''

It is a splendid little volume of four hundred pages. The Woodford County Historical Society, so recently organized, would do well to get this book, together with Marshall's and McClung's histories and read them closely for any facts concerning early Woodford.

Richard Shipp and Sallie McCracken, of Woodford County, were married in Franklin County, Dec. 23, 1802.

Samuel Montgomery settled in Woodford County about 1784. The maiden name of his wife is not known to any one with whom I have communicated, but it is known that he was the father of nine children, six sons and three daughters. His eldest son, Robert, served in the Revolution and received many wounds inflicted by both gun and sabre, at Guilford's Court House, but he survived them all and reared a large family of children, the late H. P. Montgomery, a lawyer of Georgetown, being a grandson.

Another son was John Montgomery, who moved to Franklin County and settled on "Big Benson" in 1794. His wife was —— Thomas, and they had a son Samuel. John Montgomery and his family removed to Hopkins County in 1810. He served in the Indian wars and was wounded on the Wabash. If I am correctly informed, they also had a son John, who married Linda Parker whose daughter Rosa Lee Montgomery married N. B. Hays, who was Attorney General during the incumbency of Gov. Beckham, and afterwards sought the Gubernatorial nomination.

Another son of pioneer Samuel Montgomery was James Montgomery, who accompanied the Lewis-Clark expedition across the continent to the Pacific coast in 1805.

Susanna Strother Hawkins, widow of Captain Moses Hawkins, whose descendants were mentioned in the sketch of the Strothers, page 142, Jan., 1921, Register, married a second time, and had two sets of children, but my notes relative to them were out of the state at that time, and as I have had inquiries about them I will mention them here. Susan Strother Hawkins married second †Thomas Coleman, of Culpeper County, in 1780. He was a corporal in the company commanded by Captain Moses Hawkins, of the 14th Virginia regiment, and a friend of long standing. They had these children: Nancy Coleman, who was born May the 2-, 1781, married Joseph George, brother of William George, who married Lucy Hawkins, half-sister of Nancy; Strother Coleman, who died unmarried; Susanna, who married in 1808 Lewis Sublett, Jr., son of Lewis Sublett and Mary

†See page 144.

Trabue (see Subletts for descendants, page 44) ; and John Coleman, who was killed in the Indian wars.

Many of the descendants of Thomas Coleman and Susanna Strother Hawkins were in affluent circumstances. The Logans and Huggins families, of St. Joseph, Mo., were wealthy descendants of Lewis Sublett, Jr., and Susanna Coleman.

John Smith was a Revolutionary soldier who resided in Culpeper County, Va., until 1790, when he migrated to Kentucky with his family and settled in Woodford County. He married in Virginia Mary Stephens, and they had several children, John, Jr., being one of them. He was born in Kentucky in 1800 and married Ellen Toppass in 1836. They had George, Nancy, John McCoun, Edwin, Mary Ellen, Benjamin, Newton and Logan R. Smith.

George is now a resident of Lancaster, Ky.; Logan R. is living in Chicago and Ellen Carter, a niece, is a resident of Shelbyville, Ky.

John Smith, Jr., and his wife, Ellen Toppass, lived at the old toll-gate house on the Shryock Ferry pike, opposite the Sam Nuckols place, for a lifetime. After his death his widow married Lewis Cheek. Many of the present generation will recall this party as being the cultivator of the juciest and best melons ever produced in Woodford, and also as a perennial candidate for the legislature at a time when that honor was so tempting to Col. James W. Brookie, who also ran quite frequently, the one a Republican and the other a

Democrat, neither caring to attain to the honor of an election, but both loved the game and loved to worry the other candidates, in which they succeeded admirably.

The data I followed in my short story of the Bullock and Redd families was in error in one point and led me to say that Mordecai Bullock, son of Thomas Bullock and Lucy Redd died without issue.* To my surprise I recently received a letter from his granddaughter, Agnes Redd, who resides at El Paso, Ill., advising me of her relationship and assuring me that he was the proud father of eight children and thirty-two descendants living. She further informs me that her grandfather married Sarah Saltonstall in 1830, a cousin, and stepsister of the Rev. John McGarvey, daughter of Dr. Gurdon Flower Saltonstall, and a descendant of Gurdon Saltonstall, Governor of Connecticut 1707 to 1724.

They moved to Illinois in 1834 where †Mordecai Bullock surveyed the lines of Woodford County in that state, gave the land upon which Versailles, Ill., was built, and jointly with his brother, Major Thomas Bullock, looked after the formation of the new county and the building of the new town of Versailles. (See page 119- 162.)

I was not able to trace the line of Peter Hurst and his brother, W. G. (Harry) Hurst, back to any of their ancestors at the time I wrote of the Hursts in the January, 1921, issue, page 122. Since that publication the

---

*See Bullocks, 120, Redds, 165 and 399.
†See pages 121, 165.

wife of LeRoy B. Cox, of Chicago, has furnished me with this additional data.

The father of Peter and W. G. (Harry) Hurst was James Hurst, of the 3rd generation in America, born in 1744, died in 1829. He married Mary Gunnell, daughter of Henry Gunnell, and granddaughter of William Gunnell.

James Hurst was a resident of Fairfax, later of Berkley County, Va., which is now, I believe, Jefferson County. The eldest son of James Hurst married Catharine Daniel and remained a resident of Jefferson County when Peter and his brother came to Kentucky.

James Hurst, of the 3rd generation, was a son of John Hurst, Jr., of the second generation in America and he married first Elizabeth Summers, daughter of John Summers, first in Fairfax; second Sybil Moxley, daughter of William Moxley. James was a son of the first marriage. John Hurst, Jr., died in 1789. He was a son of John Hurst, Sr., born in Northumberland County, Va., died in Fairfax County in 1747. He, accompanied by John Summers, Jr., George Harrison, William Gunnell and Thomas Moxley moved into Stafford County, between 1720 and 1730.

John Summers, Jr., was a brother of Elizabeth Hurst, and he had a son, William, who was in the Revolution, corporal in Company F, first continental artillery, which was officered by Col. Charles Harrison and Captain John Champe Carter. They experienced much suffering, and did much heroic work at Valley Forge and in the campaigns that followed.

After the Revolution Wm. Summers settled in Mason County, Ky., with his family. He was the great grandfather of Mrs. LeRoy B. Cox and she gathered the above data from his record. His great grandson, Richard Bean, was but recently elected President of a Louisville bank, of which Lieut.-Gov. Ballard is a moving spirit, his mother being Pauline Summers (daughter of Dr. Thomas Summers, of Sharpsburg, Ky.), who married Robert T. Bean, of Mt. Sterling. The paternal grandmother of Mrs. Cox was Elizabeth Stout, daughter of David and Sarah Parke Stout,* who came from Hopewell, N. J., to Mason County. David Stout was also a soldier of the Revolution. He was likely a relative of the Woodford County Stouts, who came to that county from Mason County immediately after the war of 1812.

———

Dr. John Sublett Logan was a son of Thomas Logan and Francis Sublett, the latter a daughter of Lewis Sublett and Lew Coleman, and she a daughter of Thomas Coleman and Susanna Strother Hawkins. (See Susanna Strother Hawkins, page 297). He married Emma Cotton (see Cottons, Sept., 1920, page 71), and moved to St. Joseph, Mo., before the Civil War and died there several years ago. He spent much time and money in research work, especially along the direct and collateral lines of the Subletts and Dupuys, from whom he was descended. He collected, compared very critically and compiled much data relating to these people which, either during the period of the Civil War or directly thereafter, he

*See page 30.

had printed in a small volume. I had the pleasure, fifty years ago or more of reading this little volume, and tried without success to procure a copy in order to post myself on the several lines of relationship when I undertook to write of them in the recent past. However, a friend has favored me with the following extracts copied from his manuscript many years ago, and as they are not only authentic, but also interesting, I will record them here in order that they may supplement the sketches of the Subletts, Cottons, Trabues and Dupuys, of whom I have written. The extracts follow: "Dupuy is a very ancient French name and means an abode in the mountains. In the first crusade, Hughes Dupuy, a French Knight, and his sons, Adolph, Romain and Raymond accompanied Godfrey de Bouillon to Palestine. About the year 1113 Raymond Dupuy founded, and was the first grand master of the Military order of the †Knights of St. John of Jerusalem," in Masonic parlance, termed the Knights of Malta.

"Count Bartholomew Dupuy, the immediate progenitor of the Virginia family, was an officer of the guards under the regime of Louis the XIV, which position aided him and his wife, who was Countess Susanne La Villion, and their relatives, the Fontains, the Subletts and the Trabues, to make their escape from France to Germany, where all remained for about fourteen years, then migrated to America, where they settled in Virginia, many of them for only a brief period, then pushed west-

ward over the vast empire that lay along, and even beyond the path blazed by Boone and his contemporaries."

"Abraham Soblett, or Sublette, and his wife, Susanna Dupuy, arrived in Virginia in 1700. Of their several children was one whose name was Pierre Louis Sublett, who married Marte Martain, and this couple had a son, Louis Sublette, who married Frances McGruder. Louis and Frances had six sons, all of whom consecrated their lives and all that they possessed to the cause of Liberty, bearing arms in the Revolution, and all of them witnessed the surrender at Yorktown."

The second of these sons by birth was Louis Sublett, whose first wife was Mary Trabue, a sister of Edward and Daniel Trabue, pioneers of the county of Woodford. She died in Woodford County in 1792. His second wife was Sarah Samuel, daughter of Anthony Samuel, to whom he was married about 1794. For children of the first marriage see May, 1920, issue, page 44. By the second marriage to Sarah Samuel were Araham Sublett who, I think, never married; Ann Maria, who was the first wife of William A. Cotton; Elizabeth, who was the second wife of William A. Cotton, and Samuel Sublett, born in 1800, married Fannie Aynes. Samuel inherited the old homestead and he and his wife died there about 1870. In the May, 1920, issue of Register, relative to Subletts, I said that Dunlap Cotton† was the last of the descendants to own this home, when I should have said Randolph Cotton. See notes on Harris and Cottons in this issue of the Register, page 45.

What appears here is to extend one of the lines of Harrison Harris, whose family was treated in the January, 1921, issue, page 134.

Mourning Harris, 6th of Harrison Harris and his wife, Martha, was the wife of William Adams. They had these children: John, Randolph, Cary, Elizabeth, who married —— Hubbard; Polly, who married —— Dedman; Sarah, who married Lewis Brassfield, and Susan Adams, who married John Cotton, a Revolutionary veteran who was living in the county of Woodford in 1810, had a family of seven at that time and owned two slaves.

John Cotton and Susan Adams had John, Jr., Randolph, Elizabeth, Polly, Susanna, Martha Ann, Catharine, Sophia, and William A. Cotton.

William A. Cotton was the youngest of the children, his birth in 1807. He married first Maria Sublett, second Elizabeth Sublett, both daughters of Lewis Sublett and Sarah Samuel, of the county. By the first marriage were Elizabeth Cotton, of whom I am unable to give an account; Susan Cotton,* who married John R. Darnell, and Martha Ann (Matt) Cotton, who married James Sublett. By the second marriage were John Lewis Cotton, who married Emma Moss; William Samuel Cotton, who married Mollie Stockton, a portege and kinswoman of popular Matt Haydon; Abraham Randolph Cotton, who married Henrietta Anderson, and Dunlap Cotton, who went to Colo-

rado with Milton and Wiles Craig about 1880, where he engaged in the banking business until his death more than a score of years ago.

My impression is that the above John Cotton was a kinsman of William Cotton, the father of George Taylor Cotton, Sr., and great grandfather of the widow of James Gay, who now resides at Versailles, but I have not been able to establish it thus far. Both John and William Cotton were in the Revolution.

The above William Cotton of the Revolution, was born in Virginia about 1745. His descendants received mention in Sept., 1920, page 71. Frances Taylor, his wife, daughter of George Taylor, one of the signers of the Declaration of Independence, came with him from Loudon County, Va., in 1787, to Kentucky, and both located in 1826 in Clark County, Ky.

Emma Frazer, second wife of George T. Cotton, Jr., was a daughter of George Frazer and Margaret Lewis, and Margaret Lewis was a daughter of Col. Thomas Lewis, of Virginia.

Elizabeth O'Bannon, the first wife of George T. Cotton, Sr., was a daughter of Major John O'Bannon, who was a comrade-in-arms and a personal friend of General Lafayette. and when that distinguished veteran visited in Kentucky in 1825, he was entertained at "Sugar Grove," the home of Elizabeth O'Bannon Cotton, in the suburbs of Versailles.

†Major John O'Bannon was a pioneer of the county of Woodford. In 1810 his children were all married, and only he and his second wife were living in

---

*See Darnells 94 and 210.
†See pages 41, 248, 276, 305, 362, 387.

the home. They had seventeen negroes. In 1805 he was sheriff of Woodford County, and George T. Cotton, his son-in-law, was his deputy. More of O'Bannons will be found on page 41.

Beginning on page 176, Jan., 1921, I gave a brief outline of the Marshall family. Since then I have received through the courtesy of Louis Marshall, of Versailles, great grandson of Col. Thomas Marshall, the following clipping from the Cincinnati Enquirer of Jan. 30, 1897, relating to "Buck Pond," the pioneer home of Col. Marshall, and also to several interesting incidents in connection with members of the Marshall family and other prominent men of that period. It includes a cut of the "Buck Pond" home, the exterior of which is today practically as it was when it was built, only a slight change in the front porch, and Louis Marshall, who is now cashier of the Woodford Bank & Trust Co., owns the old farm and occupies the old residence.

This clipping says that Col. Thos. Marshall married a niece of George Keith, Earl of Scotland.* She was a daughter of Rev. James Keith, and he a cousin of the Earl. Clipping follows:

*See page 179 for relationship.

BUCK POND,

Home of the Marshalls.

House Built Over One Hundred Years Ago,

From Material Bought From the Then Far East.

Occupied By the Ancestors of a Famous Family.

Pistol With Which Aaron Burr Killed Hamilton—Other Very Valuable Relics.

Special Dispatch to the Enquirer.

Versailles, Ky., January 30, 1897— Few places in Kentucky possess the historic interest which attaches to "Buck Pond," which has been the home of the famous Marshall family for more than a century. In all that time it has never been out of the family, and is the only estate in this county not held by deed, but by the revolutionary land grant received by Colonel Thomas Marshall, the great grandfather of the present owner.

This Colonel Marshall saved the American army at Brandywine, and was presented with a sword by the Continental Congress. He built the fine old house at "Buck Pond" in 1783, having emigrated from Virginia. He had all the nails and hinges used in its construction made by the blacksmiths of his native state, brought them down

"BUCK POND"

the Ohio river and hauled them for many miles overland on backs of mules.

The house is built of logs and weatherboarded, and shows no signs whatever of decay, in spite of its 113 years. It was a very handsome residence for those days, and its massive

*Colonial Interior Woodwork

would make lovers of that period wild with delight. The present owner, Louis Marshall, has altered the appearance of the front somewhat by adding a large porch, and was compelled to replaster a number of rooms, but otherwise the old house has suffered no alteration.

The cellars are tremendous, with ceilings nine or ten feet high. One is filled with thousands of hickory laths taken off the walls recently replastered. These laths are thicker in the center, and taper toward the ends. They are very large and heavy, and were every one of them hewn out by hand, all of the many thousand lath nails being fashioned in the same manner.

The huge oak girders are a curiosity, and there is enough hardwood in the building, if sawed up in modern thicknesses, to almost build a village.

The Marshall family is of Norman origin, and traces back easily to Gilbert Mareshal, Duke of Pembroke, in the thirteenth century. The Colonel Thomas Marshall first mentioned married a niece of George Keith, the last hereditary Earl of old Scotch Mareschals, who

Fled to Prussia

after the rebellion of 1715, and became famous in the service of Frederick the Great. So it will be seen that the Marshall blood is of the most cerulean hue, and is equally distinguished at both ends of the family tree.

Colonel Thomas Marshall's eldest son was the great Chief Justice of the United States—John Marshall, perhaps the most celebrated Judge who ever occupied that bench, and who is the hero of many stories, setting forth the great simplicity and kindness of his character. Everybody has heard the story of how the Chief Justice played marbles with the little boy. A younger brother was Dr. Louis Marshall, who received "Buck Pond" from his father, Colonel Marshall. Dr. Louis was the father of the famous Thomas F. Marshall, the noted Congressman, brilliant orator and humorist. The latter was reared at "Buck Pond" and died there.

The great orator was devotedly attached to the place, and spent much of his time there. His brother, Edward Colston Marshall, also noted for his brilliant oratory, made a celebrated race against Senator Joe Blackburn for Congress in 1874, which created more of a sensation than any race ever made in the political history of the Ashland District. He removed to California a number of years ago with his family, where he became Attorney-General of the state, acquired a large practice, and

---

*Buck Pond, sold to Major T. C. McDowell, Feb., 1934. Home of Marshalls 150 years.

Good-sized Fortune.

He died some years ago, and it is his son Louis who now lives at the old home. Louis Marshall went with his father to California, became prominent in business, and was for a long time President of the San Francisco Stock Exchange. From the time he left Kentucky, however, he cherished constantly the idea of returning to his old home, and when he had a sufficient quantity of California gold to bring back with him fulfilled his dreams. He is a charming man, and the very soul of hospitality.

The Marshalls, by the way, are close blood relatives of Mr. Edward Colston, of Cincinnati, the prominent lawyer and member of the firm of Hoadly, Harmon, Colston & Hoadly.

"Buck Pond House" contains a wealth of history of pioneer days in the west in the shape of rare old books, long since out of print, historic relics of Indian wars, etc. One of the most valued antiquities is a book printed in 1526, entitled "A Cornucopia of Ancient History," which was presented in 1863 to Dr. Louis Marshall by Dr. Davis, of Mississippi, the father of Jefferson Davis, and which contains the autograph inscription of the giver. The book is bound in vellum and printed in Latin. It is the size of Webster's Dictionary and weighs about 12 pounds.

Famous Duelling Pistols.

The present occupant of "Buck Pond" also became heir to a valuable collection of famous old duelling

pistols, including the weapon with which Aaron Burr killed Alexander Hamilton. The authenticity of the Burr pistol is unquestioned, and it has had a remarkable history. Judge Van Ness, who was the second of Aaron Burr, marked the fatal pistol and gave it to Colonel James Bowie, together with its mate, the Hamilton pistol. Colonel Bowie wore the pair as belt pistols, but lost the Hamilton weapon in swimming a bayou.*

Subsequently he gave the Burr pistol to Dr. Carr, the Superintendent of the United States Arsenal at Baltimore, who acted as second for Thomas F. Marshall in his duel with James Watson Webb, editor of the New York Courier and Enquirer, in which Webb was shot in the knee and crippled for life.

It was while Marshall was in Congress that an attack upon him appeared in the Courier and Enquirer. Marshall demanded a retraction, and when Webb refused he challenged him. After this duel Dr. Carr presented the Burr pistol to Captain Marshall, who afterward gave it to his brother, Edward C. Marshall. The latter carried it through the Mexican War, and at his death bequeathed it to its present owner, Louis Marshall. While in the possession of Captain Tom Marshall he had it altered from a flint to a percussion lock. It shoots very accurately, and carries a two-ounce ball. Its barrel is 12 inches long, and resembles a section of a shotgun.

His fight with Webb was only one of four duels fought by Thomas Marshall, and it was through no fault of his that

*On a hunting visit to Louisiana.

a fifth was not added to the list. He never struck a blow with his hand, but when insulted he promptly

Issued a Challenge

which was not always accepted. His first "affair" took place in Louisville in 1835. The story goes that he received an insult in the dining room of a hotel, which was followed up after dinner by the same individual, whose name is now forgotten, but the name of his second is one still remembered in the south as that of the most terrible duelist of that day—John Rowan.

They met and exchanged three shots without effect, and it was in consequence of this duel, particularly Rowan's unfair conduct on the field, as claimed by Marshall, that a second duel was fought between Rowan and Marshall in which the latter received a bullet in his hip, which he carried to his grave.

Marshall's fourth duel was fought with General James S. Jackson, during the Mexican War. He sought to fix a quarrel upon the desperately brave General Cassius M. Clay, and was only prevented from fighting by being arrested and threatened with court-martial.

After such an adventurous life, he sleeps quietly enough in his ancestral domain, his grave being within sight of the old house, now tenanted by the fourth and fifth generations of the family it has sheltered so long.

William Porter married Hannah Kennedy, at Covington, Ky., about 1800, and moved to Franklin County, where he reared a large family of children, three of whom were: Thomas Kennedy, who married Geraldine Horton; William, Jr., who married Sarah Ware, daughter of William Ware and Sarah Samuel, of Woodford County, and John Porter, who married Sarah Ann Blanton, daughter of Willis Blanton and Rebecca Ware, a sister of Sarah Ware. In writing a sketch of the Wares for January, 1921, issue, page 128, I was not in possession of the name of Sarah, consequently her name did not appear as one of the children of William Ware, nor was I in possession of the name of Sarah Ann Blanton, hence her name did not appear in the list of either the Wares or Blantons— both families written of in previous chapters, from whom she was descended. John Porter, to whom she was married, was a brother of William, who married her aunt Sarah.

These three Porter brothers were students at the academy of Keene O'Hara, at Frankfort. With their father and their respective families they moved to Henry County, Tenn., in 1822.

Thomas Kennedy Porter was born Feb. 19, 1801, studied medicine and was graduated from Transylvania University in 1822. He entered the practice of his profession at Paris, Tenn., in 1823. His wife, Geraldine Horton, to whom he was married in Feb., 1824, was the youngest daughter of Josiah Horton, who settled in Davidson County, Tenn., in 1795.

Thomas Kennedy Porter and Geraldine Horton had several children. The third born, James Davis Porter, was elected Governor of Tennessee in 1875 and served until 1879. He studied law in the office of Gen. John H. Dunlap, at Paris, Tenn., and began the practice in 1851; married Susan Dunlap (related to the Woodford County family of that name) daughter of his preceptor. He was a member of the legislature when the state seceded and was the author of the "Porter resolution," passed Jan., 1861, which pledged Tennessee's co-operation with the south in case of war. He was with Gen. Pillow as Adjutant General. Was with Gen. Cheatham as chief of staff, and after the war resumed the practice of law. Was in the constitutional convention of 1870; elected circuit judge of the 12th district in 1874 and elected Governor in 1875.

Gov. Porter and Susan Dunlap had Susan, who married Dr. W. T. Bibb, of Montgomery, Ala.; and Dudley Porter, Sr., who married Clintie Atkins, daughter of Hon. J. D. C. Atkins and Elizabeth Bacon Porter (daughter of William Porter, Jr., and Sarah Ware) and they have Dudley Porter, Jr., a lawyer of Paris, Tenn., who married Mary Randolph Bolling, who is related to the prominent family of Bolling in Virginia. They have a son, Dudley Porter, Jr., III.

The sixth child of Thomas Kennedy Porter and Geraldine Horton was Thomas Kennedy Porter, Jr., younger brother of the Governor. He served with distinction at Ft. Donaldson, at Hoovers Gap, and at Chicamauga with General Simon Bolivar Buckner.

Hon. J. D. C. Atkins, who married Elizabeth Bacon Porter, was Commissioner of Indian Affairs under President Cleveland; was a member of the Confederate Congress; member of the National House of Representatives, and

a colleague of Captain Joe Blackburn. In the National House he was chairman of the Committee on Appropriations when Samuel J. Randall presided over that body. As stated above they were the parents of Clintie Atkins, who married Dudley Porter, Sr.

Elizabeth Ware (sister of Sarah and Rebecca) and her husband, John Bacon, of Frankfort, were the grandparents of former U. S. Senator A. B. Fall (now a member of President Harding's cabinet), and of Mrs. Jouett Taylor Cannon, of the Historical Society.

The above Porter family were of good old English stock, who had pride enough to preserve the family record. The first of them of whom we have a record was John Porter, born in 1590, at Kenilworth, Warwickshire, Eng., in Waxhall Abbey, the ancient home of the family, where many of them are buried. He married Rose ——, and they, with their children, sailed from England in the ship Anna, arriving at Dorchester, Mass., May 30, 1627. They had nine children, who lived to rear families. Their eldest son, John, was born in 1618, and was just nine years old when the family came to America. He married Mary Stanley, daughter of Thomas Stanley, of Hartford, Conn.

John Porter and Mary Stanley had twelve children, and the fourth son, whose name was Samuel, was born Mar. 5, 1664. He settled in Chester County, Penn. Married —— —— and reared a large family. His son William was born in 1695, owned and lived on his father's estate, where he died Aug. 3, 1749, leaving several sons, the youngest of whom was William, Jr., born in 1729, emigrated to Adams County, Penn., and married Sarah Pierce, of Delaware. He died in 1802, his wife surviving him several years. They were buried at Toms Creek Presbyterian church, Emmettsburg, Maryland, and they were the parents of William Porter, who was introduced in the beginning of this sketch as migrating to Kentucky, where he married Hannah Kennedy at Covington in or about 1800.

I regret that I have not been able to write something relative to Lieutenant Gov. Thomas P. Porter and his brother, David Porter, and their antecedents.*

----

†Prudence Berry, who married George Blackburn, the pioneer, who settled at Spring Station, and her sister, Ann, who married Jonathan Taylor,– cousin of Captain Zach Taylor, of Woodford County, were daughters of Col. William Berry, of Gloucester and Caroline counties, Va. Col. William Berry married ‡Mary Pryor, daughter of Col. Samuel Pryor and Prudence Thornton, of Gloucester County, and I am informed that Samuel Pryor's Bible is extant. He was the ancestor of Judge William S. Pryor, of Henry County, so long a member of Kentucky's highest court, and at one time Chief Justice of the state.

Col. William Berry was the ancestor of the Campbell and Oldham County Berrys.

Prudence Thornton was of the same family as the two James Thorntons, who came early to Woodford County. Also as to Margaret Thornton, the

grandmother of William Strother, who was a pioneer of Woodford County.

The data used in sketches of Dunlaps, Gays, McIlvains, and Stevensons was largely contributed by Hon. Boutwell Dunlap, of San Francisco and Auburn, Cal. He has done a noble part in the effort to preserve the record of these pioneer families, and I trust that the descendants of these old families appreciate as fully as I do the work he has done for the present and unborn generations. I am certainly grateful and thankful for his generous contributions.

In 1810 James Gough was living at Midway, Ky., on the farm now owned by James W. Parrish. I am not able to state when he came to Kentucky, but as he was not born until 1789 it is likely he had not been in Woodford County many years prior to the taking of the census of 1810, at which time he was just twenty-one years of age, unless his father was also a pioneer of the county and brought his son at a tender age. If that was the case, the father was dead before 1810, as James Gough was the only person of the name in the county at that time.

He married Rebecca Davis, daughter of William Davis and Ann Worley. (See Patrick Davis, page 283.)

In 1810 James Gough was reported in the census as having only two members in his family, likely he and his wife, and three slaves. The farm upon which he lived was the farm now owned by James W. Parrish, and the frame house that he built was replaced by the splendid residence built by the present

----

*See page 355.
†See pages 33, 175.
‡See page 220.

owner. This is a very fine farm and is one of the prettiest sites in the vicinity of Midway, and adjoined the estate of his father-in-law, William Davis, and many members of the two families are buried in the private graveyard of the Davis family, which is in view of both premises.

James Gough died in 1837, in the prime of life, just forty-eight years of age. As in the case of other families that I have sketched, I am unable*to write anything concerning the antecedents of James Gough because of the fact that the family record has been lost for several generations. His grandson, G. G. Gough, of Russellville, who doubtless knows more of his relationship than any other descendants, informs me that his grandfather and Rebecca Davis had a large family, seven boys and two girls. The sons were William, John, Sylvester, Joe, Church, Frank and Ben. The girls were Sarah and Caroline. Sarah never married; Caroline married Ben Whitaker and moved to Russellville, where she died, leaving two sons in that vicinity.

William never married; John married a widow whose name is not recalled; Sylvester married —— Rogers; Joe and Church married sisters, —— and —— Gorin, of Russellville, Ky.; Frank married Rebecca Frazer, daughter of Joe Frazer; Ben married Eliza Sublett.

Sylvester has a son, G. G. Gough, who is now a resident of Logan County.

Frank Gough and Rebecca Frazer had William and Frankie. The latter died while yet in her teens, and William married Sarah Elizabeth Bird of Shelby

County. He was in business in Versailles in the '80's, afterwards at Georgetown, and they have a daughter, Patterson Gough, who is an employee in the State Agricultural Office at Frankfort. After the death of Frank Gough his widow became the second wife of P. I. Railey, Jr.

Ben Gough and Eliza Sublett had Bennie Gough, who married Grant Allin, of Harrodsburg, and they had a son who went west and married. After the death of Ben Gough, his widow married William Strother Hawkins, Jr. (See Subletts and Strothers.) Frank and Ben Gough were the youngest sons of James Gough and Rebecca Davis, and I think the only two of the children who remained in Woodford County. I think one of the Goughs lived for a time on the old Gillespie farm that adjoins the cemetery at Midway and followed the Spring Station pike to the Wallace Harper farm. The wreckage of this old home is perhaps a quarter of a mile from the pike. I think it was the father of Judge John Gillespie, or perhaps the grandfather, who once owned this tract of land.

———

I regret that I could get nothing definite as to these prominent families: Dedman, Hitt, Lindsey, Beard, Dale, Goodloe, George, Morrow, Moffit, Rowland, Rucker, Searcey, Shipp.

———

Hon. Boutwell Dunlap, of San Fran-* cisco, who furnished me data from which I wrote the sketches of the Dunlaps, Stevensons, McIlvains and Gays, of Pisgah, in the Jan., 1921, Register,

*See pages 149-156. I gave his manuscript, after extracting what I wanted, to the Kentucky Historical Society.

adds the following interesting details concerning the incident referred to by me in the May, 1921, Register, page 308, second paragraph, second column, relative to the activities of the Rev. John Mahan in aiding runaway slaves, and also extends what I have said about the above families:

"The Mahan incident illustrates how families were divided before the Civil War over the question of slavery, and how William Dunlap, educated at Pisgah, a son of Col. Alexander Dunlap, a pioneer of Woodford, was one of the figures in the anti-slavery agitation, he having moved to Ohio.

"Practically all of the Dunlaps and Gays of Virginia, Kentucky and Missouri stood for the principles of the Confederacy, while the Ohio Dunlaps and Kinkeads, formerly of Woodford, were as intense anti-slavery advocates, and as a result, much feeling existed between the two branches.

"The case of the Rev. John Mahan created much excitement in Ohio and was a powerful factor in the defeat of Gov. Vance, of that state, for re-election.

"John Mahan was a Methodist preacher of note in Ohio, Brown County, where the Dunlaps lived. While in the field plowing the Rev. Mahan furnished one of his horses to a runaway negro on which to accomplish his escape. He was arrested, Gov. Vance granting a requisition, but no offense against the laws of the state of Kentucky was proven, so he was dismissed. He was, however, re-arrested under an attachment for the value of the escaped slave. William Dunlap signed Mahan's bond in order to get him out of the Kentucky jurisdiction. (See life of James G. Birney.) William Dunlap married Mary Shepherd, daughter of John Shepherd, son of the founder of Shepherdstown, Va. She was a niece of Col. David Shepherd, Colonel of Ohio County, which extended from Pittsburg to the Ohio river on the west, commander in the siege of Fort Henry, and second in command in the Coshocton expedition against the Ohio Indians.

"The Shepherds, Dunlaps, Kinkeads and their connections were all Presbyterians, and they made Brown County, Ohio, a center of anti-slavery activities. William Kinkead, formerly of Woodford County, and his wife, Ann Dunlap, were the parents of Mary Kinkead, who married Rev. Adam B. Gilliland, son of Rev. James Gilliland, a native of North Carolina, and lifetime pastor of 'Red Oak' Presbyterian church, Brown County, Ohio. In 1797, at the Broadway church, Charleston, S. C., he preached a doctrine known as immediatism, which meant the immediate abolition of slavery, as distinguished from gradualism. He was so outspoken on slavery that his presbytery was appealed to, and while they did not act directly upon the appeal, they admonished him to leave unsaid his radical views. He resigned his Charleston charge and started immediately north through Kentucky, preaching en route.

"William Dunlap and Mary Shepherd had a daughter, Amanda Dunlap, who married Rev. Samuel Crothers, D. D. Born in Pennsylvania in 1782, he came with his parents in childhood to the vicinity of Lexington, about 1787. He was educated at Lexington Academy—afterward Transylvania University.

"In 1805, the year of its founding, he entered the Theological Seminary of the Reformed Presbyterian church, at New York, the first institution of its kind in the United States, under Dr. John M. Mason. After a year in Kentucky, likely some of the time in Woodford, he began his Ohio career. He returned to Winchester, Ky., but in 1820 he returned to the Presbyterian church and to Ohio.

"He was the author of two theological works, one in 1839, and the other in 1847, and numerous lectures and sermons. As early as 1831 he published fifteen letters in the Cincinnati Journal entitled, 'An Appeal to Patriots and Chieftains in Behalf of the Enslaved Africans.' In 1833 he organized the Abolition Society of Paint Valley, at Greenfield, Ohio. In 1834 he replied to the publication of Dr. Young, of Centre College—'Remarks on the Declaration and Resolutions of the Synod of Kentucky, in reference to slavery,' in which Dr. Young preached gradualism.

"Dr. Crothers' first wife was Mary McChord, sister of Rev. James Mc-Chord, pastor of the McChord or Second Presbyterian church, of Lexington, Ky., by whom he had a son, John Mason Crothers, member of the Illinois legislature, who married Amanda Dunlap Foster, granddaughter of William Dunlap; Dr. Crothers' second wife was Martha Alexander, sister of Rev. Samuel Rannels Alexander, who married a granddaughter of Col. Alexander Dunlap and William Scott, both of Woodford County. Dr. Crothers' third wife was Mary Jane Young, of

Kentucky, by whom he was the father of Rev. Samuel Dickey Crothers; and his fourth wife was Mrs. Amanda Dunlap McCague, a member of the Greenfield, Ohio, Presbyterian church, as was her brother, Dr. Milton Dunlap. She had been the wife of William Foster, and later of William McCague. (See life and writings of Rev. Samuel Crothers, D.D. Moore, Wilstach and Keys & Co., 1857. P. 234, frontis part.)

"William Dunlap and Mary Shepherd had a son, Rev. James Dunlap, born in 1804, a Presbyterian minister, who opposed slavery but was not so famous as the other members of the family I have mentioned. His granddaughter married Rev. Charles B. Newton, D.D., of the Presbyterian church, in the East Indies, a son of Rev. John Newton, D.D., a Princeton graduate who went to the Indies early in the nineteenth century.

"Dr. Milton Dunlap, third of William Dunlap and Mary Shepherd, married Frances Louisa Kinkead, daughter of Major David Kinkead and Narcissa Calhoun. Their daughter, Mary Narcissa Dunlap, married Rev. Samuel Dickey Crothers. The latter's daughter, Minnie Crothers, married Dr. Edwin Waddel, of Springfield, Ohio. Their son, Dr. George Dunlap Crothers, married Anna Chesboro, daughter of Rev. G. W. Chesboro, and they had a son, Rev. William Heber Crothers.

"In 'Who's Who in America,' there is credited to Dr. Otto Juettner a 'Biography of Dr. Alexander Dunlap.' He was the famous ovariatomist. There are accounts of him in Kelly and Burrage. 'American Medical Biographies,' (1920); Kelly 'Cyclopedia of American

Medical Biography' (1912); 'Transactions of American Associations of Obstetricians and Gynecologists' (1895); 'Album of American Gynaecological Society' (1918) with portrait of Dr. Dunlap.

"There has been erected at Richmond, Ohio, by the McDowell Society, a monument to Dr. John Lamert Richmond, to whom the society attributes the honor of having performed in 1822 the first Caesarian section in America.

"Dr. Otto Juettner in 'Beginnings of Medicine in the Middle West (Johns Hopkins Hospital Bulletin, Vol. xxvi, 1915),' with portrait of Dr. Dunlap, says:

" 'McDowell died in 1830. His operations fell into disrepute after his death and the fruits of his labors would have been lost if it had not been for the work done by Dr. Alexander Dunlap, of Springfield, Ohio, who, twelve years after his master's death, performed the classical ovariatomy of McDowell and precipitated an unparalleled avalanche of condemnation among the profession. Dunlap stuck to his post and convinced the profession, by hundreds of good results, that McDowell had really been a pathfinder in the interests of the human race. That McDowell's name and work were saved we owe to the heroism and matchless professional ability of Dunlap and of his distinguished eastern Collaborator, Washington Atlee, of Philadelphia, whose name is likewise linked to that of the great Danville surgeon for all time to come.'

"Some accounts state Dr. Dunlap did not know Dr. McDowell's ovariatomy.

"Dr. Charles W. Dunlap, of Spring-

field, Ohio, was a son of Dr. Alexander Dunlap, and his wife was Mary Elizabeth Bell. Dr. Charles W. Dunlap was the father of Dr. Robert Scott Dunlap, of Greenfield, Ohio. A niece of Dr. Alexander Dunlap was the wife of Dr. O. M. Marquat, of Springfield, Ohio."

In the data that Mr. Boutwell Dunlap furnished me for the January issue of the Register, 1921, he was misled by information in his possession he thought was correct, but proved in the end otherwise. He stated the wife of John Gay was a daughter of Captain James Lockridge,* but instead she was a daughter of his brother Robert.

The following corrections in the sketch of the Dunlaps in the January, 1921, Register have been called to my attention and I gladly make note of them here. I can't say where the fault lay, as I did not see the proof before publication, but I wrote the sketch from data furnished me and I assume all responsibility. Of course I regret that so many errors should have occurred in one sketch—four times as many in this one sketch as occurred in the other one hundred and fifty-seven I have written.

Page 65, 2, l. 37, for "Orange" read "Augusta."

Page 66, c. 1, l. 35, for "Dunlaps of Dunlap" read "Dunlop of Dunlop."

Page 66, c. 1, l. 37, for "Colan" read "Clan."

Page 66, c. 2, l. 17, for "Robert" read "Bert."

Page 67 c. 1, l. 7, for "John" read "William."

Page 67, c. 1, l. 23, for "James W. McMurtry" read "James G. McMurtry, dean of Colorado College.

*See page 160.

Page 67, c. 1, 1. 24, for "W." read "M."

Page 69, c. 2, 1. 30, for "Wasson" read "Wason."

Page 69, c. 2, 1. 35, for "Harney" read "Harvey."

Page 70, c. 2, 1. 19, for "McCogne" read "McCague."

Page 71, c. 1, 1. 4, after "and" and "whose brother."

P. 72, c. 1, 1. 11, for "Union" read "U. S."

Page 72, c. 1, 1. 19 for "George" read "John."

Page 74 c. 1, 1. 3, for "brother" read "father."

Page 75, c. 1, 1. 12, for "years" read "time."

Page 75, c. 1, 1. 14, for "James Brown" read "James Brown Ray."

Page 75, c. 1, 1. 28, after "of" add "Robert, brother of."

Page 75, c. 2, 1. 4, for "John Gay, 7th," read "James Gay, 5th."

Page 75, c. 2, 1. 8, for "the United States" read "Maryland."

Page 75, c. 2, 1. 16, for "Henry" read "Harvey."

Page 75, c. 2, 1. 25, for "Herbert" read "Harvey."

Page 75, c. 2, 1. 28, after "Brooks" add "He married second Hattie Pieatt."

Page 76, c. 1, 1. 17, after "Margaret" add "Tilford."

Page 76, c. 1, 1. 25, for "Redding" read "Reading."

Page 76, c. 1, 1. 39, for "C." read "W."

In writing these corrections and additions, and comparing them with the account I wrote into the January issue of the Register, I am satisfied that the major portion of them may be traced to the data I used. But as I said, I assume the responsibility. For instance, I could hardly write Orange when it was Augusta; or John when it was William, or W. when it was C. On the

other hand, I can see how the printer might mistake Dunlop for Dunlap, etc.

In May, 1921, on page 250, in referring to Sowel Woolfolk, who was one of the wealthy pioneer settlers in Woodford County, I was in error in stating that he was the father of Richard Woolfolk, who married Sarah Taylor, daughter of Captain Zachary Taylor, Jr., of the county, and his wife, Alice Chew. My authority was mistaken, as I am now in possession of positive proof that the above mentioned Richard Woolfolk was a son of Robert Woolfolk and Anne George, of Orange County, Va. He came to Kentucky and settled in Jefferson County, now Oldham County, prior to 1800. He married Sarah Taylor, of Woodford County, in Nov., 1792, and their home was located about fifteen miles above Louisville, on Harrods Creek, in the vicinity of Col. Richard Taylor, her uncle.

Sowel Woolfolk* was a neighbor of Capt. Zach Taylor in Woodford County, and Richard Woolfolk was a neighbor of Col. Richard Taylor, in Jefferson County, so the natural conclusion is that Richard Woolfolk and Sowel were cousins, but I am unable to state it as a fact. In 1810 Sowel Woolfolk was in Woodford County with a family of five, and owned twenty-two slaves, and this is the only Woolfolk name in the census of 1810. Yet I have received this memorandum that indicates there were other Woolfolks in the county at that time or at least that owned property there at that time. "Will of John H. Woolfolk, dated Sept. 12th, 1813, record Woodford County Court, de-

*See Woolfolks, page 396.

vises to Sam'l Cox, Pendleton County, Ky., brother Thomas Woolfolk; brother Sowel Woolfolk, Jr., brother Joseph Woolfolk, sister America Baker certain properties, &c.'' While this record doesn't say that John H. Woolfolk, or his several sisters and brothers were residents of the county, it is clear that he owned property in the county at that time, and it is more than likely that the Sowel Woolfolk, Jr., mentioned in this will is the one mentioned in the census of 1810. I have written many letters in an effort to get a line on the descendants of Sowel Woolfolk practically without result.

I am also in receipt of the following dates of the Woolfolks, taken from the Woodford County records: Polly Woolfolk married Benj. Garnett June, 1789; Mary Woolfork married Samuel Cox April, 1795; Patty Woolfolk married William Baker March, 1798; Mary Elizabeth Woolfolk married —— Harris in 1840.*

In Sept., 1920, on page 76, is a brief sketch of the Graves family of Woodford County. From a friend I have just received the following sketch of the late Judge Richard Cave Graves, taken from a newspaper at the time of his death in 1895, and as he was one of the most popular and upright citizens of the county during the entire period of his long and useful life, I reproduce it here:

''On the 16th day of Dec., 1895, at the home of his son, James M. Graves, on Rose Hill, Judge Richard Cave Graves passed away in the 93rd year of his age. He was born in Woodford County, five miles south of Versailles, on May 19, 1803, and was the fourth son of John and Hannah Page Graves.

''John Graves moved to Kentucky from Culpeper County, Va., and was one of the earliest settlers of Woodford County. His wife's father, Rev. Rich-‡ ard Cave, came to Kentucky with the 'Traveling Church,' led by Elder Lewis Craig, and settled at Craig's Station, near the present town of Lancaster, in 1781, but moved to Woodford in 1784 and was one of the charter members of Clear Creek Baptist church, organized in 1785. In the vicinity of this church, of which his father and mother were members, Judge Graves was born and lived the greater part of his life.

''On Oct. 10, 1824, he was united in marriage with Lucy Mitchum.† She died in 1849, and in Sept., 1851, he was married to Mrs. Helen M. Scott, of the county, who died recently.

''Two children are living, born of the first marriage—James M. Graves and Mrs. Laura Wasson, wife of B. W. Wasson, of Cincinnati. The four children born of the last marriage are Richard Cave, of Beattyville; Frank, of St. Louis, and Clifford and Alice, of the county of Woodford.

''In 1824, the year of his first marriage, Judge Graves united with the Christian church, and for seventy-one years was an earnest and active member, taking especial interest in its educational enterprises. He was one of the incorporators of Bacon College in 1837, and a warm friend of its successor, Kentucky University. In 1850 he was elected State Senator from the district of Woodford and Jessamine, and in 1854 was elected Judge of Woodford County Court, continuing in office four years. He afterwards served six years as police judge.

"Judge Graves was a man of commanding appearance and of remarkably pleasing address; was gentle and unassuming with a friendly greeting and a kindly smile for all. His county paper, the Woodford Sun, voiced the sentiments of all who knew him when in its issue of Nov. 21st, it said: 'Judge Graves was one of the most popular men in Woodford County, and deservedly. During all of his long life he enjoyed the fullest confidence and highest esteem of every one who knew him. He was the friend of each succeeding generation, and always staunch and true; as a husband, as a father, as a citizen, as a Christian gentleman, he was an example of all that was admirable. His was, indeed, a well spent life, and the grave had no terrors for him.''

Robert Catlett, of Frederick County, Va., was born in 1721, and married Mary Floyd. They had a son, George, born in 1770, who married Letitia Buck, daughter of Charles Buck and *Mary (or Anne) Richardson, a granddaughter of Marquis de La Calmes and his wife, Winifred Waller.†

George Catlett and his wife, Letitia Buck, a sister of Col. John, Rev. William and Charles Buck, who were early arrivals in Woodford County, were briefly written of in May, 1920,

page 34. My information is that George Catlett and Letitia Buck also came to Woodford County, but in 1816 removed to Morganfield, Ky. They had the following children: Fannie Madison, born in 1797, died in 1837, married Captain Calmes Catlett, her cousin; Mary married Dr. —— Sutton, who was a professor in Kentucky University; Henrietta married Joseph Major, of Hopkinsville (a descendant of the Woodford County Majors); Thomas Washington Catlett, born in 1796, married Isabella Field Helm, daughter of Thomas Helm and Elizabeth Buck, of "Helmsley," near Versailles, Ky. (see Jan., 1921, page 175), and I am told they have descendants in Lyon, Christian and Caldwell counties; Dr. Henry Catlett married Mary Buck, of Hickman, Ky., Rebecca married Armistead Ludwell Churchill.

Thomas Catlett and Isabella Helm had a grandson, Thomas Catlett Skinner, who married Belle Anderson, daughter of Gov. Anderson, of Ohio, and they had a daughter, —— Skinner, who married Lieut. —— Ferguson, of the Newport, Va., navy ship yards.

The Catletts descended from John Catte, of County Kent, family name and mansion of Hugh de Catte, in 1442.

The Claggett family was somewhat identified with early Woodford County. James Wilson Claggett was a son of Ninnian Claggett and Euphron Wilson, his wife, of Maryland, who came to Kentucky when a youth and located at

*See page 35 and 36.
†A discrepancy—see page 37; probably twice married.

Athens, Fayette County. He married Miriam McKee, of the Woodford and Garrard County families of that name. They moved to Elkton, Todd County, where they reared the following children: William, Ann Elizabeth, Zerelda Jane, John James, Mary Euphron, Lutitia McKee, David McKee, Sarah Ellen, Marion and Squire Henry.

The father, J. W. Claggett, died at "Hillside," the home of his son-in-law, Alexander McPheeters Hutchison, in Woodford County about three miles northwest of Troy, and within a half mile of "Elm Corner" Presbyterian church, and his remains were interred in the family burying ground immediately back of the residence. His wife, Miriam McKee, was a daughter of David McKee, who was an early settler in Woodford, coming with his brother, Robert, grandfather of the late Dr. John R. McKee. David McKee married Anne Dunlap, of Woodford County, and later moved to Jessamine County, near Union Mills. (See May, 1921, page 226.)

Wilson Claggett, son of J. W. and Miriam, married Mary Robinson near Greenville, Muhlenburg County, and died there during the Civil War. They have descendants in that vicinity; Ann Eliza, daughter of J. W. and Miriam, married Thomas H. White near Elkton, Todd County, and descendants reside there; Zerelda Jane Claggett married Alexander McPheeters Hutchison, of Woodford County, whose home, "Hillside," was mentioned above. They had these children: Emma America, Alice Bell, Andrew James, George Alexander Calvin, and Marion Lee.

Emma married Dr. John Gilbert Gordon and they have a son, Thomas Hutchison Gordon, who married Effie Lena Williams and reside near Harrodsburg, or did ten years ago; Alice Belle Hutchison married Angus Neal Gordon, of Lexington; Andrew James Hutchison married Katherine Hieatt, of Woodford County, and moved to Warrensburg, Mo.; George Alexander Hutchison married Eugenia Barkley and was a druggist at Nicholasville; Marion Lee Hutchison married Charles Matthew Holloway, of Keene, Jessamine County, but moved to Boyle County, near Danville. (See May, 1921, page 211). Kitty Claggett married James Gay,* of Woodford County, March 6, 1817.

On page 128, Jan., 1921, Dr. James Ware was mentioned as having married Catharine Todd, but no mention was made of children for the reason that I was not informed. Since then I have learned that their daughter, Lucy Ware, born Nov. 12, 1773, married Captain Isaac Webb, Dec. 23, 1790, and their son, Dr. James Webb, born May 17, 1795, was the father of Lucy Ware Webb, who married President Rutherford B. Hays.

On the same page of Jan., 1921, issue I failed to mention James Ware, born May 12, 1780, as one of the children of William Ware and Sarah Samuel.

I am reliably informed that the Rev. Gideon Blackburn, (referred to on page 172), deposited a manuscript sermon in the corner-stone of the old Presbyterian church that stood on Main street, be-

---

*Page 160 states that Kitty Claggett married John Gay, and I am sure that that is right.

tween the two railroads in Versailles, and when that old church was razed, more than a score of years ago, the sermon was removed and delivered to the wife of James A. Edwards, who was a great granddaughter of the Rev. Gideon Blackburn, and sister of David L. Thornton. The sermon is now in charge of her nephew, Ab Hunter George, of Meridian, Miss. (See page 187.)

When approached four years ago by Mrs. Jennie C. Morton with the suggestion that I undertake to make as complete a record of Woodford County's pioneer families, and the incidents associated with the life of each, as was possible at that late date to procure, I shrank from the undertaking, and did not consent until I was invited two years later to accept a position with the Historical Society.

Two reasons actuated me in declining the work. In the first place I felt that I was too old to undertake a work that would require a correspondence with descendants scattered over that vast empire west of us to the Pacific, bounded on the north by Canada, and on the south by the Gulf and Republic of Mexico. In the second place the last of the generation born prior to 1850 who knew so well the history of the past had either crossed the great divide, or old age had so impaired their memories that they could not recall the

past except in a desultory way that was very unsatisfactory. Since undertaking the work I have given a chapter in each of the six issues, beginning with January, 1920, and including this issue. If I have trespassed upon the patience of those who have been reading the Register, instead of offering apologies, I will say that I have done the best I could with the information obtainable. It is well enough to say, however, that this work was not begun with any expectation of remuneration for services rendered, or reimbursement for the outlay of nearly one hundred dollars that was necessary in prosecuting the work. If the descendants of the various families I have sketched care to have my work consolidated into a single volume I would be glad to have it done, if a sufficient number will subscribe to justify the undertaking, and that would enable me to get back at least a part of my outlay.

If, however, the work is not sufficiently appreciated to demand its publication into one volume, I will in no sense regret what I have done for this and future generations.

I wish to acknowledge indebtedness to correspondents in the states of Indiana, Illinois, Ohio, Missouri, Kansas, Oklahoma, Texas, Colorado, California, Tennessee, Louisiana, Mississippi and others for favors. I am especially indebted to Mr. Boutwell Dunlap, of San Francisco for much data.

INDEX OF "WOODFORD COUNTY*

In Register.

By W. E. Railey.

*These numbers represent the pages of the several issues of the Register that contained the sketches.

MARRIAGE RECORDS OF WOODFORD COUNTY, KENTUCKY.
1789-1799.

Compiled by Wm. E. Railey.

1789

Date		Minister
Dec. 9	..John Brooky (Brookie)	A. Dudley
	Mary Scott.	
Nov. 5	..William Cave........	Elijah Craig
	Peggy Threlkill (Threlkeld).	
July 26	..Robert Dale.........	James Dupuy
	Mary Johnson.	
July 29	..Jacob Deringer.......	John Taylor
	Elizabeth Hendricks (Hendrix).	
Dec. 15	..David Dryden....	Samuel Shannon
	Jean Stevenson.	
June —	Benjamine Garrett....	John Taylor
	Polly Woodfolk (or Woolfolk).	
Oct. 10	..Amos Harbour......	James Dupuy
	Juda Dale.	
July 29	..Henry Henricks (or Hendrix)	
	Catherine Deringer...	John Taylor
Nov. 24	..John Jack.......	Samuel Shannon
	Mary Mason.	
June 19	..John January...	Samuel Shannon
	Susanna McFarling (McFarland).	
Sept. 26	..James Kay	A. Dudley
	Betty Shipp.	
Dec. 1	..William Kinkead.	Samuel Shannon
	Ann Dunlap.	
July 15	..Charles Logan......	James Dupuy
	Polly Admiren.	
May 15	..John Major	John Taylor
	Judith Trabue.	
Aug. 13	..John Moffett.....	Samuel Shannon
	Martha Dickey.	
Sept. 3	..Charles More....	Samuel Shannon
	Elizabeth Kirkham.	
Nov. 9	..William Rogers......	Elijah Craig
	Sally Hill.	
Dec. 24	..Michael Sheeky..	Samuel Shannon
	Agnes Evans.	

Date		Minister
Aug. 26	..Coleby Shipp...........	A. Dudley
	Sally Ely.	
Dec. 31	..John Snell......	Samuel Shannon
	Polly Burton.	
June 3	..Jacob Stucker........	Elijah Craig
	Betsy Rogers.	
Nov. 3	..William Thompson,	Sam'l Shannon
	Peggy Hambleton.	
Dec. 27	..George Vahlandingham (Villandingham)	James Dupuy
	Jean Brumley.	

1790

Date		Minister
June 10	..Daniel Applegate,	William Hickman
	Rachael Lindsay.	
Dec. 19	..John Bailey.............	J. Taylor
	Rebeckah Shreeve.	
Sept. 22	..Alexander Black.	Samuel Shannon
	Nancy Kinkead.	
Dec. 2	..William Bond...........	J. Dupuy
	Sally Cranson.	
Nov. 1	..Daniel Branham..	Samuel Shannon
	Ann Bohannon.	
Dec. 25	..Thomas Bullock..	Samuel Shannon
	Lucy Redd.	
Jan. 24	..Henry Cave.........	Elijah Craig
	Peggy Hawkins.	
Sept. 4	..London Carrell.......	Elijah Craig
	Elizabeth Schell.	
July 29	..William Coleson..	Samuel Shannon
	Mildred Pulham.	
Sept. 21	..Elijah Davis.....	Samuel Shannon
	Sarah Christy.	
Oct. 14	.Silas Douthitt.........	J. Reading
	Peggy Castleman.	
Jan. 29	..Barnebery Donaly....	Elijah Craig
	Mary McCullock.	

Date	Minister
Nov 25..Benjamin Elliston........J. Taylor	
Sally Hiter.	
Feb. 15..James Farquhar..Samuel Shannon	
Besty Jack.	
Jan. 24..John Ficklin...........J. Reading	
Anna Herndon.	
Dec. 5..William Fisher........J. Reading	
Catherine Hurst.	
Sept. 17..Jesse Gardy ....W. Lee	
Violet Dale.	
Aug. 1..John Graves.............J. Taylor	
Hannah Cave.	
Dec. 23..Obed Hancock...........J. Dupuy	
Dicey Perry.	
Dec. 16..Jno. Hutcheson..........J. Dupuy	
Mary Young.	
Dec. 2..Sherwood Knight........J. Dupuy	
Alcey Walker.	
Sept. 2..Matthew Latta...Samuel Shannon	
Mary Williams.	
Aug. 4..Benjamin Locke.....James Dupuy	
Rachel Knox.	
June 16..Thomas Martin......Elijah Craig	
Elizabeth Vanzant.	
May 13..James McConnell.Samuel Shannon	
Steve Stevenson.	
Sept. 3..Wm. McConnell..Samuel Shannon	
Jenet Teague.	
Mar. 16..Charles McDaniel.Samuel Shannon	
Hannah Campbell.	
Sept. 16..Robert McLaughlin...Elijah Craig	
Mary Grayson.	
Aug. 13..James McMeane..Samuel Shannon	
Margaret Alexander.	
Dec. 7..Archibald McHallow	
Jean Culberson...Samuel Shannon	
Dec. 19..John O'Bannon.........J. Taylor	
Susanna Martin.	
Feb. 4..William O'Neal......W. Hickman	
Mary Craig.	
Dec. 31..James Renfro...........J. Dupuy	
Margaret Jackson.	
May 6..Dudley Roundtree....W. Hickman	
Martha Richardson.	
Nov. 11..Richard Rowland.....B. McHenry	
Lucy Dale.	
June — John Violett ....J. Rice	
Nancy Thomas.	
Dec. 19..Daniel White........Elijah Craig	
Polly Stucker.	

Date	Minister
1791	
Sept. 21..James Alliso (Allison).J. Reading	
Lettice Ray.	
June 2..John Baker.........James Dupuy	
Ann Jackson	
Dec. 14..John Baldwin...........J. Dupuy	
Elizabeth Rogers.	
June 2..Samuel Brown...Samuel Shannon	
Eleanor McConnell.	
Jan. 6..George Caldwell..Samuel Shannon	
Susanna Harris.	
Dec. 21..Josiah Collins....Samuel Shannon	
Jurette Bohanning (Bohannon?).	
May — Timothy Connelly.Gab'l Woodfield	
Mary Wolf.	
Dec. 20..George Coonrod.........J. Dupuy	
Rhody McHusen.	
July 14..Peter Fox.............J. Reading	
Fanny McHenry.	
July 14..John Davis............J. Reading	
Jeney Herndon.	
Dec. — John Dawson..........Jno. Taylor	
Hannah Valandingham (Vallan-	
dingham?).	
Nov. 8..Jonas Davenport.Samuel Shannon	
Alice Redd.	
June 11..James Donelson........J. Reading	
Lucy Robins.	
June 21..Andrew Downing.Samuel Shannon	
Cally York.	
Dec. — ——— Galloway.....Jno. Taylor	
Mary Isaacs.	
June 2..Ambrose Gordon...........J. Rice	
Sally Thomas.	
Aug. 5..George Groves.......Sam Shannon	
Catherine Dowden.	
July 2..Jacob Gudshall....Gab'l Woodfield	
Drusey Druskill.	
Oct. 6..George Hanks......James Dupuy	
Lucy Mitchell.	
July 4..George Hendricks....James Dupuy	
Catherine Boge.	
Dec. 10..Henry Jenkins...Samuel Shannon	
Polly Stapp.	
Jan. 11..Elizaphan Hume..Samuel Shannon	
Patsy Sleet.	
Jan. 11..Matthew Mount..Samuel Shannon	
Elizabeth Stevens.	
Dec. 22..Lewis Nall......Samuel Shannon	
Jean Nall.	

Date   Minister

Oct. 11..Joseph Rardin....Samuel Shannon
Nancy Searcy.

Aug. 11..Benjamin Sample.Samuel Shannon
Mary Gum.

Sept. 22..David Sample....Samuel Shannon
Mary Townsen.

Dec. 15..Weedon Sleet....Samuel Shannon
Betsy Green.

Sept. 1..Archibald Stewart, Samuel Shannon
Nancy Hutton.

Oct. 10..Robert Stubs...........J. Reading
Sarah Edwards.

Mar. 24..Jacob Stucker....Samuel Shannon
Sally Gudshall.

Mar. 3..Jesse Suiter....Samuel Shannon
Rebeckah Meek.

June 30..Elisha Thomson.......J. Reading
Polly Saunders.

Nov. 24..David Trobridge.....James Dupuy
Mary Scott.

Nov. 3..William Walker...Samuel Shannon
Nancy Green.

Aug. 5..Lucy Long......Samuel Shannon
William Whittington.

Nov. 10..Polly Marshall....Samuel Shannon
Joshua Whittington.

May 6..Thomas Whitaker.....Jno. Taylor
Elizabeth Connor.

Feb. 16..Obediah Williams....B. McHenry
Elizabeth Bell.

April 6..Thomas Wilson....Sam'l Shannon
Sarah McClure.

1792

June 11..James Anderson......Jas. Dupuy
Salley Kersey.

Mar. 29..Joseph Bealey...Samuel Shannon
Mary Bealey.

Jan. 31..James Bell........Sam Shannon
Easter Stevenson.

Feb. 15..Robert Berry.......Sam. Shannon
Margaret Lockridge.

June 28..Benjamin Branham.Sam. Shannon
Nelley Miller.

June — John Britton............J. Taylor
Mary Barr.

Dec. 4..Jesse Brown.......Sam. Shannon
Eliza Scrogin.

Sept. — Presley Bryant........Jas. Dupuy
Nancy Miskill.

Date   Minister

Jan. 5..Reuben Burton.....Sam. Shannon
Polly Head.

Jan. — John Bush...............L. Craig
Sally Craig.

Jan. — Richard Cave...........J. Reading
Sally Wood.

June — Rhody Coppage.........J. Reading
Nancy Collins.

Dec. 13..Edward Davidson...Sam. Shannon
Eliza Stevenson.

Mar. — David Egbert............J. Taylor
Betsy Walker.

May 3..Hugh Ferguson.....James Dupuy
Hetty Ellis.

Dec. 25..Solomon Givens.......Jas. Dupuy
Polly Reading.

June — James Grymes.........J. Reading
Jemima Neal.

Jan. 12..Andrew Gudshall...Sam. Shannon
Jean Mitchell.

July — Jesse Gum..............J. Reading
Nancy Simpson.

Mar. 4..Elijah Hanks............J. Dupuy
Winfrent Bryant.

Feb. 16..Johnathan Hedges..Sam. Shannon
Polly Caplinger.

Aug. 14..William Hicklin...Sam. Shannon
Margaret Thorn.

July — John Hill...............J. Reading
Grace Coppage.

Aug. 2..Joseph Hunter......Sam. Shannon
Sally Ellis.

Feb. — John Jackson............J. Taylor
Ailcy Young.

Mar. 11..William Jackson.......Jas. Dupuy
Betsy Bartlett.

Dec. 4..Archibald Kinkead..Sam. Shannon
Pricilla McBride.

April — William Lizinby.........J. Taylor
Sarah Tinder.

May 15..Charles McDaniel...Sam. Shannon
Eliza Thomasson.

April 5..Robert Mitchell....Sam. Shannon
Jenny McMeans.

Dec. 13..Robert Moseby........Jno. Taylor
Hannah Hancock.

June — John Moss...............J. Taylor
Elizabeth Wooldridge.

Oct. — Michael Odam.........Jas. Dupuy
Polly Gudshall.

Date		Minister
Jan.	— Aldet (Albert?) Pleogh.Jno. Taylor	
	Fanny Crawson.	
Oct.	— Thomas Righthouse....Jas. Dupuy	
	Peggy Stucker.	
Aug. 30.	.Berry Searcy.......Sam. Shannon	
	Frances Jack.	
July	— James Smith...........Jas. Dupuy	
	Rebecca Ray.	
May 29.	.John Stucker.......Sam. Shannon	
	Rebeckah Castus (Casteel?).	
July	— John Tanner ....J. Taylor	
	Sally Rucker.	
July	— Robert Terry...........J. Reading	
	Cloe Worley.	
Ja.	— John Walker...........Jno. Taylor	
	Betsey Stott.	
Jan. 10.	.John White.............J. Dupuy	
	Mary Davidson.	
Oct. 1.	.Samuel Wilson..........J. Dupuy	
	Winney Lee.	

1793

Date		Minister
May	— John Allen..............J. Taylor	
	Alice McCoy.	
April 1.	.Natus Dale...........John Taylor	
	———— Shepherd.	
May	— Henry Field.............J. Dupuy	
	Sally Watkins.	
July	— Edward George..........J. Taylor	
	Polly Thomas.	
Oct.	— Andrew Gudshall.Gabriel Woodfield	
	Betsey Payne.	
Feb. 12.	.Hudson Harmer.........J. Dupuy	
	Caty Lee.	
Aug. 23.	.Thomas Hickman......M. Bledsoe	
	Polly Bartlett.	
Feb. 23.	.Charles Holloway.Gab'l Woodfield	
	Hannah Bell.	
June	— John Inlow..............J. Dupuy	
	Mary Duley.	
April	— Thomas Major...........J. Dupuy	
	Susanna Trabue.	
May	— Anthony Maloy...........J. Dupuy	
	Prudence Jackson.	
Feb.	— Thomas Morton.......John Taylor	
	Sally Moore.	
Feb. 28.	.Daniel Ploegh...........J. Dupuy	
	Sally Driskill.	
June	— Jeremiah Ploegh.........J. Dupuy	
	Sally Roberts.	

Date		Minister
Sept. 9.	.John Price, Jr...........J. Dupuy	
	Betsy Major.	
Feb.	— Abner Rucker..........Jno. Taylor	
	Nancy Morton.	
Feb.	— Richard Thomas.........——— ———	
	Polly Dawson.	
Mar. 19.	.Poindexter Thompson...J. Dupuy	
	Sally Dupuy.	

1794

Date		Minister
Nov. 22.	.John Armstrong..........J. Dupuy	
	Betsy Mahan.	
Feb.	— John Bunton ....David Rice	
	Margaret Guinn.	
June 30.	.Benjamin Chadwick....Jas. Dupuy	
	Charlotte Peak	
Aug. 14.	.Joseph Covenhoven....Jas. Dupuy	
	Mary Yates.	
Nov. 14.	.Thomas Elley.......James Dupuy	
	Patsy Dupuy.	
Feb.	— Joseph Fields.........Jas. Reading	
	Jane Dupuy.	
Mar.	— Benjamin Frakes........J. Taylor	
	Winney Reading.	
Dec.	— Stephen Harman.........J. Taylor	
	Susanna Cogshill.	
Dec.	— Charles Hiter............J. Taylor	
	Betsy Oliver.	
Dec. 24.	.Ephram Huge (Hughes?)	
	Catey Shouse.........Jas. Dupuy	
July	— David Johnson...........J. Taylor	
	Salley Thurman.	
June 11.	.Garrett Lambert.......Jas. Dupuy	
	Darcus Yates.	
April 3.	.Joseph Martin......James Dupuy	
	————Salyers.	
June 28.	.Elijah Perry..........Jas. Dupuy	
	Nancy Snelling.	
Oct. 1.	.Hanley Roberts.....James Dupuy	
	Abbie Reading.	
Sept. 12.	.Rhodenham Rout....James Dupuy	
	Phebe Blanton.	
Aug. 5.	.Benjamin Veach.....James Dupuy	
	Sarah Powers.	
May 1.	.Achilles Wilhite.....James Dupuy	
	Polly Hall.	
April 17.	.Fenelon Wilson.....James Dupuy	
	Elizabeth Trabue.	
Oct. 6.	.David Wilson........James Dupuy	
	Milly Reaves.	

1795

Date		Minister
Mar. 11	George Bane	Jno. Taylor
	Betsy Blanton.	
Sept. 3	Herman Bowmar	Jas. Dupuy
	Frances Adams.	
April 28	Samuel Cox	Jas. Dupuy
	Nancy Woolfolk.	
Sept. 24	Andrew Deringer	Jas. Dupuy
	Dowry Stodghill.	
Aug. 15	Lewis Deweese	J. Rucker
	Ann Wilcoxin.	
Feb. 5	George Dockins	Jas. Dupuy
	Polly Searcy.	
Aug. 1	William Duly	Jas. Dupuy
	Mary Denbow.	
Nov. 12	John Harris	J. Rucker

———— ————.

Dec. 5	John Harris	J. Rucker
	Polly Black.	
Dec. 29	Samuel January	Jas. Dupuy
	Betsy Marshall.	
Jan. 15	Joshua Jackson	Jas. Dupuy
	Margaret Underwood.	
Feb. 19	Joseph Magness	Jas. Dupuy
	Betsy Stewart.	
Feb. 4	Jabish Osmond	Jas. Dupuy
	Rachel Wiggins (or Higgins).	
May 25	Alexander Phillips	J. Rucker
	Susanna Rentfro.	
Nov. 11	George Rearden	Jas. Dupuy
	Eliza Rearden.	
Feb. 3	Jeremiah Rucker	Jas. Dupuy
	Lucey Tanner.	
Dec. 24	William Samuel	Jas. Dupuy
	Judith Trabue.	
Feb. —	Charles Scott	Jno. Taylor
	Fanny Cook.	
Aug. 27	John Shepherd	Jas. Dupuy
	Mary Shipp.	
Mar. 1	Jacob Shouse	Jas. Dupuy
	Susanna Hoghy (or Hogby).	
April 15	John Virtue	Jas. Dupuy
	Elizabeth McNeal.	
June 12	John Watkins	Jas. Dupuy
	Sally Clay.	
Feb. 12	Littleton Whittington	Jas. Dupuy
	Salley Hearn.	

1796

Dec. 28	William Abbit	Jas. Rucker
	Margaret Campbell.	

Date		Minister
April —	William Barrow	Jas. Rucker
	Susanna Mitchell.	
April 4	James Brackenridge (or Breckenridge)	Jacob Larton
	Amy Driskill.	
Jan. 6	Here, or Harve) Brisco.	Jas. Dupuy
	Phebe Young.	
Sept. 8	Daniel Bromley	J. Dupuy
	Patty Wilcoxen.	
Nov. 10	Elijah Burbage (or Burbridge)	
	Bety Garnet	J. Dupuy
Aug. 24	Henry Coleman	J. Dupuy
	Ellen Stout.	
Oct. 27	Andrew Combs	J. Dupuy
	Ellenor Oliver.	
Oct. 27	Rawleigh Dale	J. Dupuy
	Sally Beasley.	
Sept. 13	Johnathan Ellis	J. Dupuy
	Betsy Shepherd.	
May 1	Thornton Farrow	J. Dupuy
	Kitty Searcy.	
Mar. 3	Henry Fin	J. Dupuy
	Chrosa Coleman.	
April 7	Spencer Gill	Jas. Rucker
	Rachel Powell.	
Dec. 22	William Hager	Jas. Rucker
	Rosanah Black.	
Oct. 3	William Jamison	J. Dupuy
	Nancy Kirkham.	
Mar. 11	Lawrence McGuire	Jacob Larton
	Peggy McCown.	
Sept. 6	James Mitchell	J. Dupuy
	Unes Harmer.	
May 22	Ambrose Pitman	J. Dupuy
	Susanna Warren.	
Aug. 7	Philip Powell	James Rucker
	Elizabeth Kelso.	

1796

April 10	Samuel Rouzee	Jas. Dupuy
	Betsy Dupuy.	
Dec. 28	John Scearce	Jas. Rucker
	Nancy Holman.	
July 31	Henry Searcy	J. Dupuy
	Elizabeth Haynes.	
Sept. 8	Edmund Searcy	J. Dupuy
	Hannah Miller.	
July 28	Leonard Seay	Jas. Rucker
	Parmelia Hensley.	
Oct. 20	William Shepherd	Jacob Larton
	Nancy Ellis.	

Date	Minister
April 11..Aquilla Sugg.......Jacob Larton Lucinda Ashby.	
Aug. 31..James Tinder........Jas. Rucker Tabatha Redding.	
Aug. 4..George Vanlandingham (Vallan- dingham?) ....Jas. Rucker Judy Haggar (Haggard).	
July 19..Randolph Walker.....Jas. Rucker Polly Hoblett (or Sublett).	
Feb. 16..Jeremiah Walts (or Watts). Sus'a Sano (or Gano) Jas. Rucker	

1797

Sept. 29..John Andrews........R. Marshall Eliza Calhoun.	
Oct. 20..William Hamilton....R. Marshall Jane McConnell.	
Jan. 1..Pitman Hanks........Jas. Rucker Eliz'a Mitchell.	
Aug. 12..William McFarland...R. Marshall Jean Trotter.	
Oct. 25..William Page.........Rich'd Cave Nancy Redding.	
Jan. 11..Abraham Redding.....Jas. Reding Martha Dupuy.	

1798

Nov. 8..Edwin Alexander.....Jas. Rucker
Phebe Mullican.
Nov. 31..John Adams..............R. Cave
Eliza Bledsoe.
Mar. — Will Baker........Carter Tarrents
Patty Woolfolk.
June 1..Martin Boggess...........R. Cave
Rebecca Hanes.
Sept. 10..John Bryant..........Jno. Tanner
Cloe Bowmar.
Nov. 18..Presley Colbert...........R. Cave
Isapena Johnston.
Nov. 3..James Craig.............R. Cave
Sally Mitchum.
July 11..Will Christopher..Carter Tarrents
Ellen Howard.
July 1..Robert Dale......Carter Tarrents
Eliza Cathurder.
Aug. 15..Reuben Dale......Carter Tarrents
Polly Mahan.
April 19..Stephen Furr....Carter Tarrents
Arlimacia Taylor.
Sept. 10..Joseph George........Jas. Rucker
Ann Coleman.
June 6..Henry H. Hazard..Carter Tarrents
Sally Holeman.

Date	Minister

Mar. 22..Samuel Hedden...........R. Cave
Hannah Harmon.
Mar. 22..Elias Hedden.............R. Cave
Abigal Harmon.
April 14..Hardy Holeman..Carter Tarrents
Eliz. Wilson.
Dec. 31..John Lewis...............R. Cave
Nancy Claxton.
May 28..Joseph Martin.....Carter Tarrents
Rachel Shouse.
Oct. 18..Thomas Mitchell.........R. Cave
Eliz'b Harmon.
April 22..Robert Montgomery, Wm. Hickman
Rachel Bohannon.
Feb. 10..John Mullican....Carter Tarrents
Jenney Lott.
Nov. 7..Reason Ricketts......John Tanner
Mary Rowland.
Feb. 7..A. Rucker............Jno Tanner
Nelly Rucker.
Mar. 21..Robert Scearce...Carter Tarrents
Caty Scearce.
Aug. 1..Henry Taylor.....Carter Tarrents
Fanny Dale.
Jan. 21..Nathan Watson...........R. Cave
Franky Tucker.
Mar. 21..Stephen Weekly...Carter Tarrents
Betsy Arnold.

1799

Feb. 16..Thomas Beasley..Carter Tarrents
Patty Winn.
May 25..John Clinton......Carter Tarrents
Eliz'a McDowgall.
Dec. 17..Martin Hardin........R. Marshall
Julia Calhoun.
June 26..Henry Harrison..Carter Tarrents
Eliz'a Dale.
Aug. 28..Isaac Howard.....Carter Tarrents
Lucy Willis.
Aug. 29..John McGinn......Carter Tarrents
Sally Gibbony.
July 21..John Moss............Jas. Rucker
Betsy Burton.
Oct. 20..Alex Stinson..........R. Marshall
Mary Pollock.
Mar. 18..Fleming Trigg....Carter Tarrents
Parmelia Sharp.

1800

Dec. 18..John Keith...........R. Marshall
Jennie Matthews.

Jan. 11..Fleming Trigg....Carter Tarrents
Maria ———.

1802

Nov. 3..William Strother Hawkins........
Rev. James Garrard
Katherine Keith.

1804

Oct. 4..William Maddox.......R. Marshall
Eliza Russell.
Aug. 4..Ezias Welch..........R. Marshall
Eliza Conley.

1806

June 16..Michael Goddard.....R. Marshall
Margaret Pignan.
Mar. 20..Ezekiel Kirtley.......R. Marshall
Anne Kyle.
Oct. 13..Samuel Kyle..........R. Marshall
Mary K. Bell.
May 15..William Scearce......R. Marshall
Nancy Walker.

1807

Dec. 12..David Foreman.....R. M. Thomas
Margaret Galloway.
July 15..Hiram Higgins.....R. M. Thomas
Millie Dean.
Oct. 19..Thomas Adams...Carter Tarrents
Docia Tippett.
Oct. 29..Richard B. Bohannon
Fannie Menzies......Jacob Creath

1808

Feb. 9..William Bohannon
Jane Wilcoxon....Carter Tarrents
June 20..John W. Brooking
Polly Long.......Carter Tarrents
Nov. 18..George T. Brown....Jacob Creath
Sally Perry.
Sept. 13..William Campbell, Carter Tarrents
Lucy Berry.
Mar. 17..Major Chetham...Carter Tarrents
Patsy Wooldridge.
Oct. 31..John Dale........Carter Tarrents
Ellen Vaughan.
Dec. 24..William Deckerman..John Creath
Harriet Price.
July 14..Daniel T. Elberson
Priscilla Hammon.Carter Tarrents
Mar. 29..William Endicott, Carter Tarrents
Patsey Scearce.

Mar. 6..William Florence..Carter Tarrents
Lettie Dale.
Dec. 24..George Fulzlin...Carter Terrants
Betsy Egbert, dau. of Delency E.
and Sally E.
July 4..Vincent Howard....R. M. Thomas
Fanny Hammond.
Dec. 25..William Johnson, Carter Tarrents
Peggy Shadreck.
Sept. 18..John McKinney..Carter Tarrents
Margaret Crittenden.
Dec. 20..John McMinnery..Carter Tarrents
Sally Smith.
Mar. 19..Edward Meredith, Carter Tarrents
Malinda McGurthy.
June 22..Solomon Mitchell, Carter Tarrents
Sally Bain.
Sept. 21..Joseph Redding..Carter Tarrents
Elizabeth Redding.
Mar. 25..Joseph Roper.....Carter Tarrents
Millie Shouse.
Jan. 5..John Smith.......Carter Tarrents
Rachel Berry.
June 18..Samuel Smith.....Carter Tarrents
Elizabeth Reece.
Aug. 27..William Truman...John Edwards
Emma Shipp.
Mar. 24..Handie Vance....Carter Tarrents
Lucy Collins.
Aug. 21..Abednego Walden, Carter Tarrents
Nancy Stanford.
Aug. 4..Travis Walker....Carter Tarrents
Elizabeth Bowdry.
Oct. 20..William White......Jacob Creath
Mildred Blackburn.
Oct. 4..John Williams...Carter Tarrents
Sally Dale.

1809

July 20..James Atwood.......Jacob Creath
Polly Pace.
Mar. 7..Andrew Hawkins, Edmond Waller
Malinda Shelton.
July 18..Robert Phillips......Jacob Creath
Sally Kenny.
Aug. 5..Joseph Sallee......J. Shackelford
Elizabeth Duvall.
Mar. 25..Samuel Shouse......Jacob Creath
Caty Perry.
May 18..Samuel Stevenson...Jacob Creath
Elizabeth Clark.

April 25..Lewis Sublett.....Edmond Waller
 Susan Coleman.

Mar. 16..James Patterson......R. Marshall
 Susan Smith.

July 3..James W. Brand.....Jacob Creath
 Mary Smith.

July 18..John Ford...........Jacob Creath
 Sally Berry.

Jan. 10..Elisha Jeter.........R. Marshall
 Polly Matthews.

Feb. 1..Vincent Ross............J. Creath
 Elizabeth Florence.

Oct. 6..George W. Rucker...Jacob Creath
 Maria Vawter.

1810

Dec. 20..Isham Browder...Edmond Waller
 Elizabeth Scearce.

Oct. 15..John Carpenter...Edmond Waller
 Fanny Norwood.

Nov. 29..Thomas Casey....Edmond Waller
 Polly Claxton.

Mar. 10..William H. Cosby, Edmond Waller
 Sallie Minter.

Dec. 24..George Dale......Edmond Waller
 Nancy Taylor.

July 26..William Dawson..Edmond Waller
 Priscilla Smith.

Feb. 5..William Duvall...Edmond Waller
 Eliza Ragan.

Oct. 11..Fielding Etherton, Edmond Waller
 Elizabeth Williams.

Feb. 28..John Gill.........Edmond Waller
 Elizabeth Wilson.

Oct. 28..John Hackley.....Edmond Waller
 Jane Hawkins.

Feb. 24..Thomas Hardesty, Edmond Waller
 Lucinda Dedshaw.

Sept. 6..James Hicklin....Edmond Waller
 Catharine Scearce.

Oct. 16..John Holman.....Edmond Waller
 Elizabeth Duvall.

Apr. 27..Joseph Lindsey...Edmond Waller
 Catharine Phillips.

Feb. 7..Thomas Long...........G. Smith
 Nancy Jackson.

Oct. — Samuel McKee......Jno. Edwards
 Sally Carlisle.

Dec. 23..Thomas Montague.......G. Smith
 Susan Ford.

Apr. 19..Thomas Moody....Edmond Waller
 Anna McDurgan.

Feb. 1..Frederick Norwood
 Patsy Torbit......Edmond Waller

May 17..John Preary......Edmond Waller
 Ellen Hazzard.

Sept. 6..Vincent Rush.....Edmond Waller
 Elizabeth Singleton.

Nov. 5..Garland Simms...Edmond Waller
 Elizabeth Forson.

Mar. 29..John Smithy......Edmond Waller
 Polly Taylor.

July 19..William Smithy...Edmond Waller
 Margaret Eaton.

Aug. — John Stucker.......Jno. Edwards
 Sally Mitchell.

Oct. 25..Samuel Underwood...J. Andrews
 Esther Rennick.

1811

June 28..William Bromley......J. Andrews
 Elizabeth Boze.

Sept. 2..Robert Clark.......Joseph Creath
 Sally Long.

Nov. 10..Reuben Cluff.......Jno. Edwards
 Catherine Henton.

Sept. 13..Matthew Cundy....Joseph Creath
 Jane C. Smith.

Dec. 24..Leroy Dale.........Jno. Edwards
 Nancy Taylor.

Feb. 10..Fortunatus Davenport
 Mary Williams.....Joseph Creath

June 26..Landon Lindsey....Joseph Creath
 Susan M. Hall.

Feb. 12..Samuel Mason......Joseph Creath
 Ann Walker.

Feb. 5..Philimon Stout.....Joseph Creath
 Penelope Anderson.

Feb. 27..William Douglas Young
 Maria Jackson.....Joseph Creath

Dec. 6..Richard Dallam..... —— Ruddell
 Maria Ann Hart.

May 2..Castalow Dawson...Jno. Edwards
 Winnie Hammon.

Oct. 3..Thomas G. Dickens....J. Andrews
 Sally Dunlap.

Apr. 14..Wiley Edwards.....Jno. Edwards
 Nancy Sullenger.

Feb. — Jno. Gernsey.......Jno. Edwards
 Fanny Garnett.

Oct. 16—John Holman........Jno. Edwards
 Elizabeth Duvall.

Nov. 30..Benjamin Johnson..Jno. Edwards
Martha Eaton.

Sept. 13..John Lawson.............S. Jesse
Sally Cutting.

Dec. 24..James McQuiddy..Edmond Waller
Jane Perry.

Oct.   1..Joseph Minter.......Jno. Edwards
Elizabeth Cosby.

Oct.   9..Robert Musik.......Jno. Edwards
Sally Roach.

Nov.   5..Thomas Mitchell..Edmond Waller
Nancy Hazard.

June 30..John Nicholson....Edmond Waller
Priscilla Furr.

Oct.   — James Patterson..... —— Ruddell
Nancy Fleming.

Aug. 11..James Scatson....Edmond Waller
Martha Leggett.

Dec.   — Richard Smither..Edmond Waller
Sarah Ashford.

Dec. 23..Henry Story........Jno. Edwards
Catharine Buckley.

Feb. —..Levi Stapp..........Jno. Edwards
Nancy Jones Carlisle.

Oct. 16..William M. Thomasson
Susan McQuiddy, Edmond Waller

June 15..Elijah Utterback....Jno. Edwards
Polly Garnett.

1812

July   8..Hawkins Adams..Edmond Waller
Elizabeth Raine.

July 20..Thompson Blanton..Jno. Edwards
Elizabeth Thomson.

June 28..Jesse Brown........Jno. Edwards
Lydia Bevis.

Mar. 26..William Campbell...Jno. Edwards
Polly Hudson.

June 13..Nathaniel Claypool..Jno. Edwards
Rebecca Gunn.

Dec. 24..Benjamin Cook....Wm. Patterson
Betsy Singleton.

Jan. 16..Thomas Dale.....Edmond Waller
Polly Arnold.

Dec. 12..Henry Davis.......Joseph Creath
Elizabeth Hicks.

May 28..William Fanning..Edmond Waller
Catharine Florence.

Apr. 15..James C. Fallis.........J. Suggett
Nancy Jenkins.

May   6..George Gaines......Jno. Edwards
Millie White.

Sept.   2..George Gayle......Joseph Creath
Sophia L. Bohannon.

Dec. 31..Benjamin Guthrie...Jno. Edwards
Catharine Ramsey.

Jan. 31..Francis Hawkins..Edmond Waller
Betsy Douthitt.

May 31..John Hawkins.....Edmond Waller
Catharine Elkin.

Apr. — James Harris.......Samuel Jesse
Bethenia Turner.

Jan. 10..James P. Henry...Edmond Waller
Mary Ann Johnson.

Jan. 16..James Henry.....Edmond Waller
Margaret Johnson.

Jan.   2..George Henton......Jno. Edwards
Elizabeth Buckley.

May 27..Robert Hudson....Edmond Waller
Nancy Lightfoot.

Jan.   9..James Hunter.......Jno. Edwards
Jane Davis.

Jan. 11..Gideon Howard......Samuel Jesse
Sally Johnson.

Nov. 12..Edmund Johnson.......J. Suggett
Betsy Peyton.

Nov. 12..Stephen Livingston..Jno. Edwards
Martha Jackson.

May   5..James Miller.......Jno. Edwards
Amy Anderson.

Mar. 23..Thomas Railey, Jr...Samuel Jesse
Sarah B. Railey.

Jan.   2..Thomas W. Sellers
Sarah Ashford....Edmond Waller

Mar. 12..Ezekiel Shepherd...Joseph Creath
Peggy Carlisle.

Jan.   2..Richard Smithy...Edmond Waller
Nancy Smith.

Apr. 24..Joseph Stipe........ —— Ruddell
Polly Stone.

May 13..George Stone ....————
Sally Catter.

Oct.   7..Samuel C. Steele...Joseph Creath
Elizabeth Mitchum.

Feb. 27..James Tellery...... —— Ruddell
Sarah Nash.

Feb.   6..John Thompson...Edmond Waller
Kitty McGuinn.

May 13..Gabriel Thomson.... —— Ruddell
Polly Lacey.

July 16..Charles Thomas..Edmond Waller
Cassandra Thomas.

Jan.   8..William Tomlinson.. —— Ruddell
Nancy Spillman.

June 16..Henry Utterback..Edmond Waller
Caty Martin.

June 14..David S. Vawter..Edmond Waller
Harriet Rucker.

June 18..Richard Y. Walker
Jane Shouse......Edmond Waller

Jan. 29..Joseph Walden...... —— Ruddle
Nancy Davenport.

Mar. 20..Achilles Webster......J. Suggett
Elizabeth Peckham.

Feb. 2..Joseph Wilson.........J. Suggett
Lucinda White.

May 14..Thomas Wilson...Edmond Waller
Polly Beasley.

Nov. 1..Lydall Wilkinson..J. P. Campbell
Elizabeth Lee.

Nov. 15..William Woods.....George Smith
Ann Blanton.

1813

May —..Robert H. Arnett...Samuel Jesse
Alice Heiatt.

Jan. 29..William Ashford..Edmond Waller
Judith Elgin.

Nov. 5..William Bond.........John Penny
Rebecca Marshall.

Feb. 3..Joseph Edwards...Edmond Waller
Susanna Duvall.

July 1..Lewis Endicott.....Samuel Jesse
Jane Cooper.

Jan. 25..James Etherington..Jno. Edwards
Dolly Dennis.

Jan. 19..Robert Hatcher.......J. Hoggins
Eliza Trabue.

Sept. 22..William M. Hawkins
Nancy Taylor.......Jno. Edwards

Aug. 31..Francis Hawkins..Edmond Waller
Parmelia Shelton.

Oct. 26..Allen Heiatt.....Edmond Waller
Hannah Moore.

July 31..Waller Kennedy....Jno. Edwards
Judith Ashmore.

June 7..Archibald Maxwell....R. Marshall
Rebecca Martin.

Oct. 30..John D. Mitchell...Jno. Edwards
Maria Abbett.

May 3..Joseph Moore........John Penny
Sarah Arbuckle.

Jan. 6..James Plough........John Penny
Lucy Rucker.

Nov. 21..Legrand F. Rucker
Caroline Wooldridge, Edm. Waller

May 27..Medley Shelton....Edmond Waller
Malinda Wilhoit.

Oct. 5..Edmond Shipp......Jno. Edwards
Polly Thompson.

Oct. 3..William Stucker.....Jno. Edwards
Rosanna Mitchell.

Feb. 16..Jeremiah Thornton, Edm. Waller
Sally Claxton.

Dec. 10..Benjamin Todd......Jno. Edwards
Elizabeth Green.

Dec. 25..Joshua Warren......Jno. Edwards
Elizabeth Summers.

1814

Aug. 23..John Armstrong.Thomas Clelland
Eliza Garrett.

Dec. 7..Rastin Barnes..........J. Rucker
Matilda Gill.

Nov. 19..Lewis Beasley..........J. Rucker
Rebecca Pullen.

June 8..Walter Bohon...........J. Rucker
Gemimah Reid.

Apr. 17..Jack Carter (colored)
Easter ....J. Rucker

Jan. 12..George Chrisman...Jno. Edwards
Celia McDowell.

Apr. 15..Thomas Collins.........J. Rucker
Polly Elam or Blaine.

Jan. 23..Jesse Dale..........Jno. Edwards
Ann Scott.

Nov. 17..James Dixon....Thomas Clelland
Nancy Morton.

Dec. 29..John Fink........Edmond Waller
Matilda Hammon.

Apr. 4..Charles Forston........J. Rucker
Rebecca George.

Mar. 27..James Gaines.......Jno. Edwards
Rebecca Adams.

Feb. 17..Henry Johnson.....Jno. Edwards
Elizabeth White.

Sept. 20..Robert Johnston....Samuel Jesse
Paulina Pleasants.

Dec. 27..Silas Johnson.....Edmond Waller
Nancy Poor.

Dec. 22..John McDaniel......Samuel Jesse
Mary Ann Walden.

Dec. 20..Hudson Martin.....Samuel Jesse
America Jackson.

Mar. 7..James Moore.....Edmond Waller
Hannah Sutterfield.

Dec. 22..Lemuel Moore.......Samuel Jesse
Millie Collins.

Oct. 6..Jesse Morse.........Samuel Jesse
Polly Stanford.

Dec. 27..William Pitman.....Samuel Jesse
Tabitha Minter.

Apr. 17..Nelson Pullen..........J. Rucker
Fanny Hanks.

Aug. 28..William Simpson..Edmond Waller
Lodacia ———.

June 18..Archibald Sparks.......J. Rucker
Elizabeth Carter.

Dec. 24..John Smith.............J. Rucker
Betsy Hall.

Mar. 22..William Suiter......Jno. Edwards
Elizabeth Mitchell.

July 24..Asa Vitch.........Edmond Waller
Mary Wilson.

Oct. 6..Abraham Wilhoit..Edmond Waller
Patsy Mosby.

Nov. 17..Isaac Williams........R. Marshall
Susan Hicks.

July 17..Phillip Woodson....Samuel Jesse
Mary Woodson Railey.

1815

Mar. 9..Wiatt Arnold.....Edmond Waller
Sally Rice.

Feb. 22..Isaiah Boone......Edmond Waller
Elizabeth Brown.

Aug. 24..Collice Brown......Jno. Edwards
Nancy Atkinson.

July 16..Joseph Carrell.....Samuel Jesse
Polly Dawson.

Apr. 7..John Carter.....Edmond Waller
Jenetta Hammon.

Oct. 25..Hosea Cook.......Jno. Edwards
Elizabeth Livingston.

May 17..Henry Davis.........R. Marshall
Millie Scroggin.

Sept. 1..Richard Dawson.....Samuel Jesse
Harriet Hammon.

Feb. 19..Price Edrington....Jno. Edwards
Ellen Livingston.

Sept. 7..Isaac Felix.........Jno. Edwards
Mary Edwards.

Oct. 17..John Frazer..........R. Marshall
Eliza Davis.

Dec. 5..John Gale...........Jno. Edwards
Sally Tutt.

Feb. 12..Reuben Garnett...Edmond Waller
Phoebe Claxton.

May 21..William Harper.....Jno. Edwards
Rebecca Wallace.

June 5..Joseph Henderson...Samuel Jesse
Susan Ratcliffe.

July 30..John Henton........Jno. Edwards
Polly Martin.

Oct. 22..Robert Guthrie......Jno. Edwards
Sally Long.

May 4..Benjamin Hiter...Edmond Waller
Elizabeth Combs.

Jan. 12..Marshall McClanahan
Melissa Bullock...Edmond Waller

Apr. 13..Carter T. McGee....Jno. Edwards
Polly White.

Aug. 20..Samuel B. Mills.....Samuel Jesse
Clarissa Longberry.

June 1..Benjamin Motherhead
Lucy Morton......Edmond Waller

Apr. 4..Francis Norval......Jno. Edwards
Nancy Revel.

Jan. 5..Jeremiah Nash....Edmond Waller
Elizabeth McQuiddy.

Feb. 26..Robert Scroggin.....Samuel Jesse
Sydney Terrill.

Nov. 30..Elijah Searcy.......Jno. Edwards
Sally Ramsey.

Sept. 10..George Smith.......Samuel Jesse
Fannie Walker.

Oct. 12..John Stone..........Jno. Edwards
Mary McKnight.

Nov. 9..James Tutt.........Jno. Edwards
Lucy Sargent.

July 12..Joseph Walden......Samuel Jesse
Nancy Rearden.

June 4..Benjamin Walker..Edmond Waller
Nancy Mitchell.

Aug. 10..Daniel T. Williams.. ——— Welch
Sally Hicks.

Sept. 10..John T. Wilson.....Samuel Jesse
Rebecca Walker.

Sept. 5..William Woods.....Jno. Edwards
Catharine Coleman.

July 12..Arthur G. Young...... ————
Evelina Kinkead.

1816

May 9..Daniel Baker......Edmond Waller
Elizabeth Lampkin.

June 4..James Barchor......Samuel Jesse
Nancy ———.

Mar. 4..John Buchannon..Edmond Waller
Elizabeth Cunningham.

Nov. 1..Levi Buchannon........J. Rucker
        Frankie Mitchell.
Jan. 7..Perry Carroll......Samuel Jesse
        Nancy Tindor.
Sept. 19..John Cave........Edmond Waller
        Mary Cave.
Dec. 17..John Cave........Edmond Waller
        Mary Harris.
July 30..George Clark......Edmond Waller
        Polly Padget.
Feb. 15..William Corbin.....Jno. Edwards
        Annie Burnett.
Nov. 10..George Chambers...Jno. Edwards
        Patsy New.
Nov. 26..Ancil Cox.........Edmond Waller
        Polly Buchannon.
Feb. 1..Leroy Dale..........Samuel Jesse
        Jemima Hudson.
Mar. 2..John Dorr..........Jno. Edwards
        Elizabeth Atkinson.
May 16..John Davis.........Jno. Edwards
        Minerva Guthrie.
Mar. 12..Samuel Elliott......Samuel Jesse
        Ann Ford.
Oct. 10..Lawson Jett........Jno. Edwards
        Elizabeth Mitchell.
June 16..Nathaniel Goodrich..Jno. Edwards
        Martha Pace.
Sept. 19..Sydnor D. Hanks..Edmond Waller
        Polly Graves.
Apr. 22..George Hill.........Jno. Edwards
        Jane Lee.
Sept. 26..John Hill...........Jno. Edwards
        Polly Reardin.
June 12..James Hutcheson.......J. Suggett
        Susanna Petty.
Nov. 14..William Hunter.....Samuel Jesse
        Catherine Canfield.
Dec. 24..William Jackson....Jno. Edwards
        Letitia Pace.
Aug. 5..Elijah Kennedy.....Joseph Creath
        Elizabeth Hoggard.
Dec. 20..Milton King........Joseph Creath
        Susan T. Wiles.
Aug. 6..William Long........ —— Elmore
        Susan Holeman.
Jan. 13..John Latta..........Jno. Edwards
        Margaret McKee.
Apr. 12..Daniel Mays............J. Rucker
        Cynthia A. Bowmar.
Apr. 2..Joseph McFarlan....Samuel Jesse
        Rebecca Edwards.

Sept. 17..James McCormick, Edmond Waller
        Polly Elgin.
Sept. 26..John McBride...........J. Rucker
        Elizabeth Snellen.
Apr. 18..Benjamin McQuiddy
        Dicie Shouse......Edmond Waller
Apr. 4..William Nash.....Edmond Waller
        Kitty Williams.
Dec. 3..Charles Norwood..Edmond Waller
        Virginia Thomas.
Dec. 3..Sanford Owens......Jno. Edwards
        Maria Sullinger.
June 12..James Phillips......Samuel Jesse
        Jeansea Carpenter.
Nov. 24..Anderson Shipp.....Jno. Edwards
        Elizabeth Blanton.
Nov. 12..James Smith......Edmond Waller
        Susan Hanks.
Nov. 14..John Stockton....Edmond Waller
        Lucinda Mitchell.
Jan. 18..John Steele, Jr......Samuel Jesse
        Catharine Swann Railey.
Apr. 16..J. W. Stone........Joseph Creath
        Nancy Goodloe.
Nov. 21..William Stone........R. Marshall
        Eliza Rankin.
Oct. 10..Bartlett G. Tutt....Jno. Edwards
        Henrietta Yancy.

1817

Apr. 8..Robert Adams......Jno. Edwards
        Nancy Thomson.
Apr. 23..Larkin N. Akin.....Jno. Edwards
        Sallie Harrison.
Jan. 22..Reuben B. Berry........J. Rucker
        Francis D. Bowmar.
July 3..George B. Bartlett..Joseph Creath
        Mary M. Jackson.
Sept. 18..Alvin Brooking.....Jno. Edwards
        Permelia Brooking.
Apr. 23..Anderson Brown....Jno. Edwards
        Priscilla Stevenson.
Oct. 16..Drew Brown........Samuel Jesse
        M. M. Kidd.
Feb. 27..Allen Claggett......Jno. Edwards
        Ann Summers.
Aug. 21..John Cochran......Jno. Edwards
        Peggy Sheets.
Mar. 9..Jeremiah Collins....Jno. Edwards
        Malinda Sullivan.
Dec. 18..Richard M. Cosby...Jno. Edwards
        Henrietta Duvall.

Sept. 17..David C. Creed....Edmond Waller
        Nancy Creed.

Apr. 18..Benjamin Dale.....Joseph Creath
        Nancy Barnes.

June 6..Edward Darnall....Joseph Creath
        Phoebe Dale.

Apr. 27..Benjamin Davis.....Jno. Edwards
        Catharine Walker.

Jan. 23..Squire Dean.........Jno. Edwards
        Caty Finn.

Nov. 4..Isaac Elliott........Samuel Jesse
        Avangeline Ford.

June 7..Henry Eden..............J. Price
        Caroline ————.

Nov. 20..John Florence......Samuel Jesse
        Hannah Ross.

Jan. 23..William Galloway...Samuel Jesse
        Elizabeth Tinder.

Mar. 6..James Gay.........Jno. Edwards
        Kitty Claggett.

Mar. 8..William Gilmore...Joseph Creath
        Jane Torbit.

Jan. 20..Randolph Givens....Jno. Edwards
        Elizabeth Collins.

May 8..Caleb Guthrie.......Jno. Edwards
        Betsy Smith.

Feb. 13..Joseph Highbarger......J. Rucker
        Nancy Hord.

Dec. 28..William Hill........Jno. Edwards
        Polly Vincent.

Sept. 25..Thomas Jelf......Edmond Waller
        Jane Spaulding.

June 16..James Kidd.........Samuel Jesse
        Dianna Fisher.

Oct. 23..Jonathon Karsner.....J. Fishback
        Janetta McCreath.

Apr. 26..Samuel Lewis......Joseph Creath
        Elizabeth Pearl.

Dec. 19..Pleasant Matthews..Samuel Jesse
        Sally Mosby.

May 1..Harris Mitchell...Edmond Waller
        Betsy Carpenter.

Aug. 28..Burgess S. Moody.....J. E. Welch
        Felicia Toles.

Sept. 11..Brinkley Morris.....Jno. Edwards
        Catharine Adams.

Apr. 24..James Mosby.......Jno. Edwards
        America Lewis.

Nov. 14..Christopher Newman
        Catharine Magee....Samuel Jesse

Oct. 23..Jesse Poor.......Edmond Waller
        Elizabeth Elgin.

Aug. 21..Peter I. Railey, Sr., Joseph Creath
        Judith Woodson Railey.

Mar. 18..Thomas Roberson...Samuel Jesse
        Ann Mangun.

May 15..David Rogers........Jno. Edwards
        Elizabeth Sargent.

June 18..John Sheets........Jno. Edwards
        Betty Reardin.

Dec. 6..Thomas Shouse.....Samuel Jesse
        Susanna Edwards.

Jan. 7..David Shouse.......Jno. Edwards
        Nelly Florence.

Apr. 29..Robert Slaughter...Jno. Edwards
        Lucy Reed.

Mar. 23..James Smith.....Edmond Waller
        Mariah Hanks.

June 10..Gabriel Smith.......Jno. Edwards
        Elizabeth Frawner.

Feb. 6..Edward Stevens.....Jno. Edwards
        Polly Ramsey.

July 24..James Stockton...Edmond Waller
        Peggy Torbit.

Oct. 23..Ralph Stuart.......John Edwards
        Agnes Kirkham.

Apr. 3..William Sullivan........J. Rucker
        Peggy Hartman.

Dec. 7..John Usher.........Jno. Edwards
        Martha Meredith.

Dec. 25..William Walker.....Jno. Edwards
        Sally Mitchell.

Dec. 19..Edward Walker.....Samuel Jesse
        Martha Torbit.

Aug. 4..William Walker.....Samuel Jesse
        Nancy Hudson.

Feb. 26—William C. Wallace...R. Marshall
        Racheal Carlyle.

1818

Dec. 17..Wesley Ashford...Edmond Waller
        Nancy Potter.

Jan. 4..John Baker.......Edmond Waller
        Delilah Redmon.

Mar. 26..Beverly Branham...Jno. Edwards
        Martha Brooking.

Dec. 1..Wrice Cave......Edmond Waller
        Susan Rice.

Dec. 3..Henry Casteel.......Jno. Edwards
        Lucinda Peters.

Sept. 16..Jonathon Conover..Joseph Creath
        Martha D. Burgin.

May 16..Henry Crow.........Jno. Edwards
        Polly Wimsby.

Jan. 28..William Dunnigan...Jno. Edwards
Catharine Collins.

Feb. 26..James H. Elliott...Edmond Waller
Sarah Johnson.

Nov. 5..Jacob Ebberly....Edmond Waller
Catharine Elgin.

Feb. 12..John Garrard..........J. Elmore
Eliza Allen.

Aug. 16..James Gibbany......Jno. Edwards
Parvis Harten.

Mar. 16..Richard Graves.........J. Suggett
Nancy Martin.

May 1..Milton Gray........Samuel Jesse
Betsy Mott or Moss.

Aug. 26..Hayden Hardin.....John Edwards
Betsy Sisk.

Dec. 22..David Harris.......Jno. Edwards
Margaret Peters.

Feb. 27..George Hufford.....Samuel Jesse
Polly Vest.

Dec. 17..John Johnson.......Jno. Edwards
Nancy Usselton.

Feb. 27..Milton W. Lockett...Samuel Jesse
Kitty Taylor.

May 21..James C. Lee.........R. Marshall
Eliza Christmas.

Mar. 5..John Long........Edmond Waller
Betsy Martin.

Mar. 19..John Markley......John Edwards
Frances Turpin.

Mar. 7..Ovid McCracken....Jno. Edwards
Susan Garnett.

July 2..Edward Mooney...Edmond Waller
Mary Nicholson.

Feb. 17..Joseph Morton......Samuel Jesse
Nancy Morton.

Oct. 7..Robert Norish...........J. Elliott
Eliza Stevenson.

Nov. 23..William H. Patterson....J. Elliott
Sarah S. Moffitt.

Nov. 17..David Paxton.......Jno. Edwards
Lucy Edwards.

Dec. 29..Joseph Petty...........A. Rucker
Susanna Arnett.

Oct. 1..James Smith...........J. Rucker
Nancy Rucker.

Feb. 1..Madison Sparks.......T. Boulware
Fanny Sparks.

Aug. 4..John Sullinger......Jno. Edwards
Elizabeth H. Pepper.

Oct. 18..Hiram Wilhoit.....Edmond Waller
Mary Mosby.

Dec. 22..John Williams......Jno. Edwards
Kitty Eddings.

Apr. 2..Cumberland Wilson..D. Robinson
Mary Parker.

1819

Aug. 12..Isaac Beaucham....Jno. Edwards
Elizabeth Moore.

Aug. 9..John Berryman..........S. Jesse
Jane Railey.

Oct. 21..Moses Boone......Edmond Waller
Elizabeth Cunningham.

Dec. 1..Jonathon C. Burgin..Jno. Edwards
Mary Ann Conover.

Nov. 20..Edmond Chapman...Jno. Edwards
Elizabeth Good.

Oct. 20..James Cox..........Jno. Edwards
Jane Stevenson.

Apr. 13..John W. Craig....Edmond Waller
Sidney R. Young.

Oct. 4..Michael Dearinger
Polly Sutton......Edmond Waller

Feb. 23..Robert Evans.......Jno. Edwards
Sarah Hawkins.

Oct. 22..Thomas Ford........Jno. Edwards
Alcy Graddy.

Aug. 31..William L. Graddy...R. Marshall
Patsy Carlyle.

Apr. 15..John Haydon.....Edmond Waller
Sally Thomas.

Feb. 25..Samuel Harper......Jno. Edwards
Mary Dickerson.

Jan. 5..John Hufford...........A. Rucker
Patsy Doan.

Sept. 9..James S. Hutcherson
Sarah S. Elkin....Edmond Waller

Mar. 18..Ephriam January..Edmond Waller
Lucy Meek.

Oct. 7..James Jelf.............A. Rucker
Susanna Davis.

Dec. 23..Sol G. Jesse........Jno. Edwards
Permelia Shouse.

Sept. 21..Thomas Keyburn...Jno. Edwards
Harriet Dennis.

June 15..James Lemmon.......R. Marshall
Mary McConnell.

Dec. 28..Andrew Lockridge..Jno. Edwards
Anna Wallace.

Aug. 17..Thomas Miles......Jno. Edwards
Polly Henderson.

June 8..Thomas Proctor..Edmond Waller
Lucinda H. Craig.

June 4..William Richards........J. Penny
Rebecca Boggess.

Feb. 18..William Smith......Jno. Edwards
Ann M. Tutt.

Nov. 7..Benjamin Smither..Jno. Edwards
Sally Whiting.

Jan. 7..Thomas Stanford......R. Marshall
Eliza M. Brown.

Apr. 6..Aaron Trabue......Jno. Edwards
Patsy Trabue.

Oct. 1..George C. Thompson..S. K. Nelson
Sarah S. Hart.

Sept. 6..Samuel Tillery...Edmond Waller
Phoebe Dowdry.

June 6..Daniel Watkins..........J. Rice
Maria Wood.

Jan. 9..John Walker........Jno. Edwards
Jane Johnson.

July 15..Thomas Whittington.....B. Lakin
Lucy Brittenham.

Nov. 4..Littleton Whittington
Frances Glenn......Jno. Edwards

Feb. 4..Daniel ————.........B. Lakin
Mahala Rowland.

1820

Apr. 6..Edward B. Atkins...Jno. Edwards
Elvina Wilson.

July 20..Reuben B. Berry....Jno. Edwards
Betsy Holloway.

Mar. 16..Samuel Burge......Jno. Edwards
Mary Burnett.

Nov. 16..James D. Carpenter
Nancy Combs.....Edmond Waller

Apr. 6..Nathaniel Clough...Jno. Edwards
Cynthia Stanford.

Dec. 28..Silas Eaton.......Edmond Waller
Elizabeth Clinton.

Oct. 29..John Guynn.........Jno. Edwards
Mary Smith.

Sept. 19..Ezekiel Haydon...Edmond Waller
Jane Dale.

Feb. 6..Robert Hicks........Jno. Edwards
Magdalin Hager.

Nov. 22..John Hoagland.....Jno. Edwards
Rebecca Conover.

Sept. 7..James Holeman.....Jno. Edwards
Mary E. Martin.

Aug. 6..John M. Hopkins.....Jno. Edwards
Dorothy Blanton.

Jan. 23..Samuel Jeter.....Edmond Waller
Sarah Santa.

Aug. 8..Thomas L. Lee.........J. Elliott
Mary Davidson.

Feb. 10..Daniel McCoy......James Rucker
Elizabeth Homar.

May 30..Aaron Mershon......Jno. Edwards
Patsy Darnell.

Oct. 12..Edmond Mitchell..Edmond Waller
Elizabeth Jillson.

May 25..William M. Morris, Edmond Waller
Parmelia Walker.

Jan. 20..John Nicholson.....Jno. Edwards
Susan Gregory.

Feb. 20..David Thornton....... ——— Flynt
Nancy Railey.

1821

Jan. 23..Samuel Ayres.......Jno. Edwards
Elsey Malone.

Nov. 1..Jacob Beard........Jno. Edwards
Elizabeth Brown.

Oct. 4..John Bell..........John Edwards
Polly Johnson.

Oct. 11..John Berry..........Jno. Edwards
Rebecca Morrison.

Nov. 13..James Bennett.....John Edwards
Susanna Harris.

Feb. 22..Thomas Bullock...Edmond Waller
Ellen Dale.

May 9..Waller L. Brightwell
Parmelia Mitchell...Jno. Edwards

Nov. 5..Clement Calloway, Edmond Waller
Christina Violet.

Sept. 27..Moses Clamper or Clampet
Lucy Rucker........J. Chenowith

Nov. 8..Joseph Davidson....Jno. Edwards
Susanna Abbott.

Aug. 9..Daniel Deringer..Edmond Waller
Franky Veath.

Dec. 13..Baldwin Frazer...Edmond Waller
Polly Kinney.

Sept. 30..Thomas G. Gardner
Eliza Prellis....S. H. Montgomery

Aug. 19..John Graves........Jno. Edwards
Susanna McCoy.

July 15..James Green......Edmond Waller
Frances Nickelson.

Oct. 25..Jesse Hamilton......Jno. Edwards
Mary Price.

Oct. 13..John Hawkins..........B. Larkin
Nancy Wilhoit.

Mar. 14..George Horn.......... ———
Susan Goodrich.

Nov 27..Isaac Jelf..............A. Rucker
Elizabeth Wilson.

Dec. 20..Robert Hutcheson......J. Rucker
Martha Hendrix.

Dec. 13..Matthew Kennedy
Ann Price........Edmond Waller

Sept. 13..Leonard Malcomb......A. Rucker
Rebecca Tinter.

Nov. 23..Allen McAlister........A. Rucker
Rachael Gill.

Sept. 13..Leonard Malcomb......A. Rucker
Rebecca Tinter.

Jan. 17..John McCown..........A. Rucker
Eliza Y. Hiter.

Jan. 4..John Kirtly.........Jno. Edwards
Priscilla Calmes.

May 16..Samuel P. Menzies.......B. Lakin
Hannah Hunt.

Mar. 4..John Milton.........Jno. Edwards
Polly Tutt.

Sept. 20..John Ruthe.........Jno. Edwards
Frances Gregory.

Mar. 23..Thomas Smythey....T. Cleveland
Juda Bella Garrett.

Dec. 18..Samuel Talbott........J. Stamper
Ruth Rowland.

Jan. 4..Ira E. Tilford.......Jno. Edwards
Mary Young.

Aug. 16..Henry Tomlin......Jno. Edwards
Eliza Lewis.

Mar. 18..Harisford Tutt......Jno. Edwards
Mourning Nall.

Dec. 25..David Varth......Edmond Waller
Elizabeth Varth.

May 25..Absalom Veath....Edmond Waller
Polly Bunton.

June 7..Jacob Veath......Edmond Waller
Jane Bunton.

Mar. 23..Isaac Varral........Jno. Edwards
Polly Pullum.

Aug. 15..Ambrose Wickersham...N. Harris
Catherine George.

Sept. 6..John Wilson......Edmond Waller
Phoebe Londsberry.

1822

Sept. 26..James Anderson..Edmond Waller
Isabella Mosby.

Apr. 10..James B. Bell..........B. Lakin
Malvina Hunter.

Dec. 18..John Booth.......Edmond Waller
Frances Dale.

Sept. 26..William Brisby.......J. Fishback
Eliza Hogan.

Jan. 15..Joseph Cleveland
Nancy Allen.....John Shackelford

May 15..William Davis.......Jno. Edwards
Henrietta Nall.

Oct. 17..Joseph A. Combs, Edmond Waller
Nancy Ramsdale.

Feb. 13..John Downing......Jno. Edwards
Nancy Haven.

Aug. 8..Elijah Eaton......Edmond Waller
Elizabeth Morris.

May 16..Fielding Edwards...Jno. Edwards
Jane Wright.

Nov. 19..James Egbert.....Edmond Waller
Jeanette Dale.

Feb. 27..John Foster........Jno. Edwards
Sarah Banklow.

May 27..Reuben Graves......Jno. Edwards
Elizabeth C. Cox.

Jan. 10..Edward Griger......Jno. Edwards
Malinda Mills.

June 6..Thomas Harper.....Jno. Edwards
Mariah Christopher.

Sept. 19..John Hendricks...Edmond Waller
Betsy Dearing.

Jan. 6..George Hughes.........J. Elmore
Eliza Belt.

Jan. 15..Benjamin Jones.........W. Adams
Esther Alexander.

Sept. 12..Frederick Junott....Jno. Edwards
Mildred Gregory.

Feb. 5..Allen Kendall.......Jno. Edwards
Elizabeth Graves.

July 23..John Lee...........Jno. Edwards
Nancy Lee.

July 30..Armstead Long..........B. Lakin
Paulina Peters.

Mar. 27..Elijah Martin.......Jno. Edwards
Louisa Haggard.

June 6..Robert Martin....Edmond Waller

_____ _____.

July 22..John K. Merritt....John Edwards
Isaphine Dearing.

Oct. 22..Leonard Mahone....Jno. Edwards
Martha Pemberton.

Nov. 21..Harrison Morris..Edmond Waller
Parmelia Phillips.

Dec. 31..Wade Mosby......Edmond Waller
Rebecca Shouse.

June 13..Frederick Moss...Edmond Wal' ;r
Diana Davis.

July 10..Reuben Pitcher...Edmond Waller
          Ann Pitcher.

Mar. 26..Thomas Hickman.......W. Adams
          Harriet Brooking.

Sept. 26..Thomas Ramsey..Edmond Waller
          Crealla Torbit.
          Randolph Railey....... —— Jesse
          Caroline Elizabeth Crittenden.

Sept. 26..Will Allen Prewitt, Jno. Edwards
          Sydny Fox.

Oct. 31..William Proctor..........F. Davis
          Nancy Nicholson.

Dec. 19..William Sargent....Jno. Edwards
          Christina Rogers.

Dec. 19..Henry Scearce.....John Edwards
          America Berry.

May 18..William Smith......Jno. Edwards
          Margaret Truman.

Apr. 16..Richard Taylor.....Jno. Edwards
          Mary W. Brooking.

Mar. 5..William Thompson....J. Fishback
          Eliza Peters.

June 3..David Thornton....... —— Flynt
          Charlotte Railey.

June 27..Simeon Twyman....Jno. Edwards
          Mary W. Young.

Apr. 11..Fontain Mosby....Edmond Waller
          Lucy Lewis.

Oct. 26..Henry M. Trabue........B. Lakin
          Elizabeth Watson.

Dec. 29..Reuben Searcy..........F. Davis
          Sally Leathers.

May 15..Abraham G. Watts...Jno. Edwards
          Judith Ayres.

Jan. 27..J. Wilhoit...........Jno. Edwards
          Jane Scearce.

Jan. 3..John Williams.......Jno. Edwards
          Martha McCracken.

July 23..William Woodhouse.... —— Flynt
          Margaret Smith.

July 11..David Williams....Edmond Waller
          Elizabeth V. Howard.

1823

Aug. 14..Robert Allen......Edmond Waller
          Martha Allen.

Oct. 19..John Black.......Edmond Waller
          Ann Black.

Mar. 20..John Ballard.....Edmond Waller
          Susan Mitchum.

Apr. 8..John Campbell....Edmond Waller
          Mary H. Torbit.

Aug. 7..William Cassell...Edmond Waller
          Martha Taylor.

Mar. 18..Jesse Dalton...... —— Fishback
          Catharine Ray.

Dec. 18..Thomas Eastman..... —— Eastin
          Miriam Calmes.

Feb. 18..Anson Evans........ —— Rucker
          Parthenia Evans.

June 19..John Holbert.....Edmond Waller
          Eliza Dale.

July 23..Thomas Holeman..... —— Osburn
          Jane B. Langdon.

June 26..Alexander Hufman... —— Rucker
          Emily Edins.

July 29..Cave Johnson.....Edmond Waller
          Miriam Sublett.

Mar. 11..Aaron Johnson, —— Shackelford
          Mary Stamper.

Apr. 20..William Jones........ —— Buck
          Elizabeth Field.

Feb. 6..Shelby Prewitt........P. Bledsoe
          Lucy Daniel.

June 26..Danl. McCoy....... —— Rucker
          Rachael Daugherty.

Dec. 16..Benjamin Simms...Wm. Hickman
          Mary Ann George.

Dec. 25..John W. Sullivan.... —— Rucker
          Nancy Phillips.

Dec. 28..Nelson Thomasson, —— Fishback
          Sally Thompson.

June 10..Lottie Tillery.......... —— Hall
          Charlotte Holcomb.

June 3..David Thornton........ ——
          Charlotte Railey.

Jan. 7..John P. Thomas...Edmond Waller
          Sally Christopher.

July 13..William Thurman, Edmond Waller
          Sidney Dehoney.

Jan. 21..Samuel Ware...........B. Lakin
          Elizabeth Bullock Redd.

July — Zachariah White....... —— Penny
          Agnes Steele.

Aug. 20..James Wilson........ —— Rucker
          Polly Leathers.

THE QUARLES FAMILY AND THEIR WOODFORD COUNTY CONNECTIONS

By Wm. Railey.

The following notes relate to Col. Tunstall Quarles of Woodford County, and his descendants, of whom I wrote briefly in the Register, January, 1921, page 194. For much of the data I use in this sketch I am indebted to Hon. Boutwell Dunlap of San Francisco.

Besides the Quarles family, this data mentions a branch of the Kinkeads that was omitted when I wrote a sketch of that family in September, 1920, page 68, for the reason that I lacked the facts. It also supplies interesting details of the Morancy family, who were intermarried with many of the old families of Woodford County.

Col. Tunstall Quarles married Susanna Edwards, daughter of Ambrose Edwards and Wealthean Butler his wife, of King William Co., Va. Ambrose Edwards was born in 1726, and died at his country seat, "Cherry Grove," Va., in 1810.

Col. Quarles and his wife Susanna came to Woodford County in 1789 and settled in the vicinity of Pisgah Church. As stated in the former sketch, he represented Woodford County in the lower branch of the Legislature in 1796.

The impression prevails among his descendants that he was a veteran of the Revolution, but the belief has not been verified by any records of that war that we have seen, but his neighbors in Woodford County, as well as his acquaintances throughout the State addressed him as Col. Quarles, or Col.

John Tunstall Quarles. The Virginia records name John Quarles as a Revolutionary soldier and as Col. Quarles' full name was John Tunstall Quarles, the relationship think that John Quarles of the Revolution was John Tunstall Quarles who lived in Woodford County.

Many of the descendants also believe that Col. Tunstall Quarles was a son of James Quarles, Paymaster-General in the Revolution, but they lack the proof of that too.

In the vicinity of Pisgah, if not on an adjoining farm to Col. Quarles, lived James Quarles, who, according to A. C. Quisenberry, served in the Revolution. He was a kinsman of (I am not able to state the relationship) Col. Quarles. Both of these men were in Woodford County in 1810, and tradition says that Col. Tunstall Quarles was in the war of 1812, but I can find no record of his service, and of course doubt it. I think that report grew out of the fact that his son, Tunstall Quarles, Jr., served in that war and was Captain of a company in the 2nd regiment of Ky. Militia. (See Roster of War 1812, by Genl. Sam E. Hill, page 62). Capt. Quarles moved to Pulaski County several years before the war of 1812 and represented that county in the Legislature in 1811-12 and again in 1828, being a member of the House of Representatives when he entered the war. In 1840 he was in the State Senate from that county.

Col. Tunstall Quarles and Susanna Edwards, his wife, had the following children: (a) William Edwards Quarles, who married Elizabeth Haggin and moved to Franklin County, where he was elected sheriff June 21, 1813; (b) Ambrose Quarles who married Elizabeth Manning and went with his brother to Franklin County about 1800; (c) *Annie (Nancy) Quarles, who married, first, Horatio Hall, second, Archibald Kinkead, a merchant of Versailles, Ky., and son of John Kinkead of Augusta County, Va., who was a near relative of William Kinkead the pioneer of Woodford County, who was sketched in Sept., 1920, page 68; (d) James Edward Quarles, who married Sallie Wooldridge of Versailles; (e) Tunstall Quarles, Jr., who married Parmelia Springer and moved to Somerset, Ky.

William Edwards Quarles and Elizabeth Haggin of Franklin County had (I) James Tunstall Quarles who married April 10, 1823, Mary O'Nan; (II) John Quarles who married Martha Brooks Wallace. He was a lawyer and practiced at Clarksburg, Tenn. They had an only daughter, Martha Quarles, who at one time resided in the home of Joseph E. Davis, brother of President Jefferson Davis. She married Horatio J. Harris, a lawyer of Bloomington, Ill., and one of her three children, Eliza Harris married Chas. M. Flanagan, a merchant of St. Louis; (III) William Quarles, born near Frankfort in 1805, moved to Indianapolis, Ind., during the year 1827, where he became a leading lawyer. His son, Walpole Quarles engaged in the practice of law at

Kansas City, Mo., for many years, and a daughter, Margaret Quarles, married John P. Dunn, who served as Auditor of the State of Indiana; (IV) Nancy Quarles married in 1824 Benjamin Arnold of Franklin County. He died in 1878 and left these children: (1st) Professor William E. Arnold of Cornell and Wesleyan Universities. He married Mary Clark of Falmouth, Ky.; (2nd) Egbert Quarles Arnold of Franklin County, who married Fannie Green; (3rd) John Arnold who married Sophronia Marker and moved to Spencer County, Ky. One of their daughters, Victoria Arnold, married Grant C. Smither of Franklin County, an uncle of Kelly Smither, the Circuit Clerk; (4th) Englantine Arnold who married William H. Sparks of Scott Co. They moved to Placer County, Calif., where he was interested in mining at Sunny South, where Hon. Boutwell Dunlap, who furnished much of the data that enters into this sketch, knew him; (V) Sarah (Sallie) Quarles married Joseph Smith, but left no issue; (VI) Caroline Quarles married Wm. G. Harvie, who descended from a Scotch-Irish family of that name in West Virginia, Monroe Co. He lived for a time in Kentucky but finally moved to Doniphan Co., Kansas, where he died in 1856; (VII) Doctor Archibald Tunstall Quarles, born in 1817, married in 1841 his cousin Mary F. Quarles and moved to Caseyville, Union County, but later returned to Franklin County and located at Forks of Elkhorn, where he practiced until his death. They had (1st) George W. Quarles who married Josephine

Thompson of Scott County. His was a creditable record in the Confederacy during the Civil War. He died at the home of the old Confederates at Pewee Valley during the year 1921; (2d) John Tunstall Quarles who was a resident of Jacksonville, Ill., but later moved his family to Nevada, Mo. He, too, served the Confederacy gallantly in the Civil War; (3rd) Mollie Quarles who married Thomas W. Thompson of Woodford County. They had Quarles Thompson who married Mary Franklin of Frankfort, Ella, Lilian, Russell, William, Ben, Carrie, and Henton Thompson who married Mervin Parrent, City Clerk of Frankfort; (4th) Ambrose Quarles who married his cousin Susan Quarles; (5th) Elizabeth Quarles who married James W. Hughes of Franklin County. Other children were Caroline, Annie and Laura Quarles, the latter two now residents of Madison, Ind. (VIII) Elizabeth Quarles who married John Bates and had (1st) Mason Bates; (2nd) John Bates; (3rd) Archibald Bates who married Mary Sullivan and moved to Hiawatha, Kansas; (4th) Zadie Bates who married F. F. Sullivan and moved to Falls City, Neb.; (5th) Anna Bates who married John Rowan Claxton of Pewee Valley; (6th) Ellen Bates who married George Flynn of Washington, and (7th) Susan Bates who married George W. Malone of Woodford County, a kinsman of the Macey family.

(b) Ambrose Quarles and Elizabeth Manning had (I) John Manning Quarles; (II) William Quarles, who married first —— Myers, of Missouri, by whom he had a daughter, Ellen, who married James W. Gallahue of Frank-

lin County. By the second marriage to Katherine Lucket of Frankfort were two children; (III) Susan Quarles who married Benjamin Knott. Their daughter —— Knott married Dr. T. C. Brunson of Arkansas, whose daughter —— Brunson married Thomas Buck of Pine Bluff, Ark. (IV) Mary F. Quarles who married her cousin Dr. Archibald Quarles; (V) Ambrose Quarles who married Ellen Settle of Franklin County and (VI) Annie Quarles who married, first, William Mooney of Arkansas, second, Benjamine Hughes of Lexington, Ky.

(V) Ambrose Quarles and Ellen Settle had (1st) Susan Quarles who married her cousin Ambrose Quarles, Jr., and had Archibald Quarles who represented Franklin County in the Legislature, session of 1922; (2nd) William Quarles of Frankfort, who married Laura Noel.

(c) Anne (Nancy) Quarles and Horatio Hall, her first husband had (I) —— Hall who married Sandy Lindsey of Clinton, Miss. They had a daughter, Nancy Lindsey, who married Dr. J. B. Nailor of Vicksburg. Another daughter, Elizabeth Lindsey, who married first Costesworth Pinkey Smith who served as a member of the Supreme Court of Mississippi and was Chief Justice of that court; second James D. Stewart, U. S. Register of Public Lands.

(c) Anne (Nancy) Quarles and Archibald Kinkead, her second husband, had (I) Anne Kinkead who married, first, James Noland, second, Dr. Thomas Anderson at Clinton, Miss., in 1835. Dr. Anderson's home was at Vicksburg. I have no further record of the Nolands; but Dr. Anderson and

Anne Kinkead Noland had a daughter, Agnes, who married Louis Molinery Morancy. (I have a sketch of the Morancys I hope to get in print.) She died in 1921 in her 85th year. They had Mary Elizabeth Morancy who married her cousin H. P. Morancy, of Versailles; Louis P. Morancy who died in 1905 unmarried, and Ann Victoire Morancy who married, first, William Gray of Bastrop, La., second, Irvin Railey of Woodford County; (II) America Kinkead who married Isaac G. Bibby, a lawyer-banker of New York; (III) Agnes Kinkead, born in 1812, married Dr. Emile Morancy, a Louisiana planter. Their daughter Anne Victoire Morancy married Joseph Noland. (See Morancy sketch.) (IV) James Butler Kinkead married Martha Sellers; (V) John Kinkead of whom I have no record.

(d) James Edward Quarles and Sallie Wooldridge had (I) James Edward Quarles, Jr.; (II) Adeline Susan Quarles, born in Woodford County before the war of 1812 and married John O'Nan of Huguenot descent; (III) Caroline Quarles who married John Allen of Woodford County. The above Adeline Susan Quarles (II) and John O'Nan had (1st) James Quarles O'Nan who married Sallie Singleton of Jessamine County. He moved to Union County, Ky., where he died and where his family remained; (2nd) Henry Clay O'Nan who married Mary Morrison of Lexington and moved to Union County; (3rd) Mildred O'Nan who married James H. Elgin of Fayette County.

The above Caroline Quarles (III) and John Allen had, (1st) Sarah H. Allen who married Lemuel S. Lincoln and moved to Liberty, Mo.; (2nd) James Trimble Allen who married, first, Dora Young of Fayette County, second, Jane McCampbell of Nicholasville. He moved with his family to Harrisonville, Mo.; (3rd) Jane Allen who married Joseph T. Hughes of Lexington; (4th) Susan Allen, born 1836 in Woodford Co., married Dr. Benjamine Myers of Anderson County; (5th) Cary Allen who never married.

(e) Tunstall Quarles, Jr., and Permelia Springer left Woodford County before the census of 1810 was taken and identified themselves with the people of Southeastern Kentucky by taking residence in Pulaski County. In addition to his service in the war of 1812 and in the legislature which I alluded to earlier in this sketch, he served that constituency in Congress and as Circuit Judge of the district that includes Pulaski County.

They had these children: (I) John Tunstall Quarles, Jr., who was in the legislature 1847-49 but later moved to Quincy, Ill., where he was a resident for a time, but later moved to the State of Kansas. He married Ellen Huline; (II) Major Archibald Butler Quarles, born in Woodford County in 1811. (The mother was likely visiting relatives in Woodford at that time while her husband was serving Pulaski County in the Legislature). He married Susan J. Porter of Somerset. Some of their descendants were at Barry, Ill., during the Civil War; (III) James Quarles married Mary C. Jackson of London, Ky. He was killed there in 1848 by William Evans; (IV) Brent C.

Quarles who died young; (V) Nannie Quarles who married William Woodcock, a banker at Somerset; (VI) Sophia Quarles who married James Evans; (VII) Polly Quarles who married Geo. Glass; (VIII) Maria Louise Quarles who married Jas. A. Randall of London, Ky. Robert C. Randall who practiced law at Pittsburg, Kentucky, some years ago was a son of this couple.

THE MORANCY FAMILY OF WOODFORD COUNTY AND THEIR FRENCH ANTECEDENTS

By Wm. E. Railey.

The Morancy family has for many years been identified with the citizenship of Woodford County, and intermarried with many of the old families. Many of the descendants are yet maintaining homes within the county limits and are citizens of sterling qualities.

The first of the family of whom we have any information was Jean Francois Mont-Morenci who was born in France, his people having rendered great service in making history in the time of the Bourbon Kings. He left France upon the approach of the Revolution, knowing that her soil would be drenched in the blood of her sons. He dropped the title of Mont and sailed for the French province of San Domingo where he married Honorine Molinery, daughter of Pierre Molinery and ——— Boulegny. Of this marriage were born three children, two boys and a girl, whose names were Honore Perigne, Victorie, and Emile. Madame Moranci died after the birth of these children, and within a short period after her death an insurrection, led by the mulattos, who were joined by the slaves on the island took place and nearly all of the whites, including the Morancis and Molineries were massacred. However, the three Moranci children named above were rescued by a trusty slave, put on board a U. S. ship and sent to the Carolinas. Victoire, the girl, who was 14 years old in 1806, was taken back to France by Madam Peltiere, and she married in France and lived and died there.

Honore Perigne and Emile landed at Charleston, S. C., where they were cared for. The former was educated at St. Mary's College, Emmetsburg, Md. At the age of 18 years he was professor in Latin, Greek, and French in an Academy in Natchez, Miss. February, 1818, he married at Natchez, Eliza Jane Lowry, who was born at Frankfort, Ky., in 1803, and moved with her family to Natchez in 1809. She was raised a Presbyterian but after her marriage adopted the faith of her husband and remained a devout Catholic until her death in the State of Louisiana in 1884. Her husband died there in 1881. Many Woodford County citizens now living will recall this dainty, lovable little woman who spent several, if not all of the years of the Civil War, with the family of Col. Zach White and his wife,

Agnes Steele, at or near Lock No. 5. She was the grandmother of Mrs. John R. McKee, of the county, and of Mrs. H. P. Morancy, and Mrs. Irvin Railey of Versailles. Her husband, Honore Perigne Morancy, who had changed the last letter in his name to y, was an early settler in Vicksburg and became quite a factor in the community, but he later moved to Louisiana where he engaged in cotton planting until he amassed a fortune.

The children of Honore Perigne Morancy and Eliza Jane Lowry were: 1st Dr. Frances Emile Morancy, who married Elizabeth White, daughter of Col. Zach White and Agnes Steele (see Steeles, May, 1920, page 41). Dr. Morancy and Betty White had [1]Agnes Morancy, who married Dr. John R. McKee; [2]Honore Perigne Morancy, who married his cousin, Mary Elizabeth Morancy; [3]Emelius, who never married and was a farmer in the county, and grain merchant of Versailles; and [4]Frank who studied law at Versailles and later practiced at Louisville.

The children of Dr. John R. McKee and [1]Agnes Morancy were: Bettie, who married Vernon Forman of Lexington. They had one child, Agnes Morancy Forman; Agnes McKee, who married Dr. John Gilbert, of Lawrenceburg; Frank McKee, who married Stella Glogauer; Dr. Emelius, of Lexington, and James, who resides with his mother on their Woodford County farm.

Vernon Forman and Betty McKee have Agnes Morancy Forman. Dr. John Gilbert and Agnes McKee have Ilene, Betty, Agnes, Madeline, and John Gilbert, Jr. Frank McKee and Stella Glogauer have Caroline, John Robert,

Elizabeth Ann and Frank Morancy McKee, Jr.

[2]H. P. and Mary Elizabeth Morancy have, Frank Emelius, Louis, Marie, Angela, and H. P. Morancy, Jr., all of whom reside at Versailles, except Angela who married Mark Godman, State Supervisor of High Schools.

2nd. Anne Morancy, who married Dr. Thomas Minor Jackson, of Virginia.

3rd. Louis Molinery Morancy, who married Agnes Anderson, daughter of Dr. Thomas Anderson and Anne (Nancy) Kinkead. They had Mary Elizabeth Morancy, who married her cousin, H. P. Morancy of Versailles. Their children were given above; Louis T. Morancy who died unmarried in 1905, and Ann Victorie Morancy who married, 1st, William Gray (son of Dr. John Gray, a Confederate Veteran) of Bastrop, La.; second, Irvin Railey, of Woodford County. By the first marriage was Evelyn May, who married Robert Forbes Perkins, of Boston, Mass., and they have two children, Elise Hopper Perkins, born in 1913, and Robert Forbes Perkins, Jr., born 1916. By the second marriage to Irvin Railey is a daughter, Agnes Morancy Railey, who resides with her mother in Versailles. Irvin Railey died in 1919.

4th. Caroline Morancy, who married Antoine Dumesnil Hawkins of Louisiana. He is living at the advanced age of 88 years.

5th. Honore Molinery Morancy married Mary Barr, of Versailles, Ky., a half sister of Judge Watson Barr of Louisville, who was a former citizen of Versailles. Mary Barr's mother was a Bowmar, of Versailles, the second wife of Judge Barr's father. Honore Molinery Morancy and Mary Barr had a daughter, Eliza Jane Morancy, who married William Hayne of New Orleans, and from this union came Frank Hayne, who married Ann Dulany, of Virginia, and Mary and Morancy Hayne. Honore Perigne Morancy, one of the founders of the family in America, was one of the boys who escaped from the Island of San Domingo during the uprising. His brother, Dr. Emile Morancy, upon reaching the United States was adopted by a Mrs. Harper, who was a daughter of Charles Carroll, of Carrollton, signer of the Declaration of Independence. After reaching years of maturity he moved to Louisiana where he purchased a plantation and married Agnes Kinkead, daughter of Archibald Kinkead and Ann (Nancy) Quarles (see Quarles Family, page 335). Of this marriage was a daughter, Anne Victoire Morancy, who married Joseph Noland. They had Agnes Noland, who married W. H. Harvey; Ida, Emile, Thomas, who married Susan Irwin.

Since the Morancy sketch was turned over to the printer the following bits of history relative to the family came to me through a letter from Mrs. Robert F. Perkins of Boston, to her mother, Mrs. Irvin Railey, of Versailles, Ky. Mrs. Perkins is in Europe for the year 1924 and wrote from France, the home of her ancestors.

"In the old town of Carcassonne, which is ten centuries old, still stands the Palace of Duke de Mont Morenci. The statue of Anne, Duke de Mont Morenci, the head of the family Morancy, is in the palace at Versailles, France. On the walls of the Hotel de la Ceti in Carcassonne may be seen the names of men who distinguished themselves by deeds of valor between the 11th and 16th centuries, with their coat-of-arms. Among them is the shield bearing the coat-of-arms of the Duke de Mont Morenci."

Winn.

On page 277 I briefly mentioned Hezekiah Winn and family. He was twice married; first to Matilda Huggins by whom was Dr. Charles, Fannie, Sallie, Hezekiah, Jr., Thomas and Matty. By the second marriage to Sarah Elizabeth Vaughan were John B., Lucy and Nellie.

Dr. Charles married the stepdaughter of President Andrew Jackson; Fannie married Prof. Zach Brown; Sallie married John Allen; Matt married Gertrude Hughes and had ———, and Leonora who married James Leslie Cleveland. Of this union are Gertrude Farris and Emily Cleveland.

THE EDRINGTONS, TAYLORS, HANCOCKS AND CRAIGS OF WOODFORD COUNTY AND DESCENDANTS

By Wm. E. Railey.

Joseph Edrington and his brother Benjamin came to Kentucky about 1785. Some of the descendants think their ancestors came directly from Virginia probably Stafford County, where is located an old Edrington County seat, while others are of the opinion that the Kentucky branch migrated to North Carolina before coming to this state. At any rate, these two brothers settled in Fayette County. Joseph's home falling into Woodford County when it was taken from Fayette in 1788. My impression is that Benjamin drifted to either Nelson or Shelby, as we find names of Edringtons in the early records of those counties.

Joseph was in Woodford County when the census of 1810 was taken and reported a family of ten persons and one slave. He married the widow of Jesse Cook, who was killed by the Indians at the Old Innis Fort, three miles from Frankfort on Elkhorn April 28, 1792. A thrilling account of the defense of their homes by the wives of Jesse and Hosea Cook is given in Richard Collins' History of Kentucky, vol. 2, page 250. Both men were mortally wounded in this raid on the fort by the Indians.

The maiden name of Mrs. Jesse Cook was Elizabeth Bohannon, and I have no doubt that she was related to the Wood-

ford County Bohannons, but I have not been able to discover the link, though I have looked over much data relating to that family both in Kentucky and Virginia.

In 1820, or about that time, Joseph Edrington and his large family moved to Hickman County, Kentucky, and located in that part that afterwards became Ballard County. In a conversation I had with Col. Thomas G. Poor, Clerk of the Kentucky House of Representatives during the period I was an officer of that body, 1875-84, he told me that his grandfather either went to Hickman County with the Edrington family, or through their influence moved there later. His grandfather was Capt. Thomas Poor, a Revolutionary veteran who was in Woodford County with his family in 1810. Robert Poor, a son, was in Woodford as late as 1821, being a charter member of Webb Chapter, Royal Arch Masons in that year.

Joseph Edrington purchased, improved and sold several tracts of land in Hickman County prior to his death July 25, 1826, in his 57th year. The Bible of his son, John Price Edrington, gives the date of his father's death, and remarks that he was assistant judge of the Hickman Circuit Court which implies a course in legal training that is nowhere else recorded. This old Bible, which is in possession of Mrs. Sallie Smith, of Fort Smith, Arkansas, a descendant, was purchased by John Price Edrington in 1818 before leaving Woodford County. It records many births and deaths, including the name of Wm. B. Cook, who died in 1835, June 15th. It is likely that he was a half brother of John Price Edrington, as Richard Collins, in his account of the massacre of the two Cooks, mentions children in the house with the two women who fought so bravely to save their home.

The children of Joseph Edrington and Elizabeth Bohannon Cook, his wife, were in part as follows: John Price Edrington, who married Sarah Beeler June 13, 1816, she a daughter of Captain Christopher Beeler and his wife Elizabeth ———; Joseph C. Edrington; Elbridge G.; Captain H. S.; Benjamin F., who married in Hickman County Ann E. Milburn; and Rebecca Edrington, who married John Eastin Taylor in Hickman County.

John Eastin Taylor and Rebecca Edrington were personally acquainted, if not sweethearts before they moved to Hickman County, the former from Franklin County the latter from Woodford. It is possible that the two families moved to southern Kentucky at the same time, but Richard Taylor, Jr., the father of John Eastin, was a magistrate in Franklin County in 1813, going to Hickman County a few years later where he engaged in surveying government lands, and it was at Columbus, Hickman County, that John Eastin Taylor and Rebecca Edrington were married. They reared several children in that vicinity, one of whom was Col.

E. H. Taylor, Jr., of Frankfort, who was born at Columbus, February 12, 1830. In his youth Col. Taylor lost his father and soon thereafter left Columbus for Frankfort, the year being 1840. When he arrived at manhood he accepted a position with the Branch Bank of Kentucky, of which his uncle, Edmund Haynes Taylor, Sr., was cashier.

In 1852 Col. Taylor accepted the position of cashier of the Commercial Bank at Versailles, of which David Thornton was President, and Col. Lewis Berry was a director. He remained with the institution until a short time before the Civil War was launched.

In the early stages of the Civil War he returned to Frankfort and engaged in cotton speculation; later was an agent of the government in purchasing supplies for the prosecution of the war. After the war he engaged extensively in the manufacture of whiskey, first in Franklin County, then on Glenn's Creek in Woodford County in the '80s. He also invested extensively about that time in farming lands in Woodford, purchasing the George T. Cotton farm and others in the vicinity of McKees cross roads. Upon these fertile farms he cultivated much of the grain that entered into the product of his distillery. Later he disposed of the farms and devoted his time and attention exclusively to his distillery interests.

However, about 1900, or a little later, Col. Taylor decided that the cattle interests of the United States were being neglected and immediately took advantage of the opportunity to promote a higher grade of cattle in Kentucky, so he purchased the splendid farm of Alex Wright that fronts on the Frankfort pike and from the Railey heirs the Dr. Theoph. Steele farm that adjoined it but faced the Glenn's Creek pike, and he established his celebrated Hereford Farm which is now attracting attention in Europe as well as America.

Woodford County is justly proud of this farm and its splendid herds, as well as of Col. Taylor, who has done so much to focus the eye of the world upon the county that gave birth to his mother, Rebecca Edrington. (Since the above was written, Col. Taylor has died and the splendid farm has been purchased by Mr. Richard Baker.)

Col. Taylor married Frances Miller Johnson, stepdaughter of the late Jacob Swigert, brother of Philip Swigert who as a young man settled in Woodford County and was a charter member of Webb Chapter, Royal Arch Masons, organized at Versailles December 4, 1821, as you will see by referring to May, 1920, page 24.

To Col. Taylor and Frances M. Johnson were born the following children: J. Swigert, who married Sarah Bacon Crittenden, whose grandfather was Governor John J. Crittenden, of Woodford County; Mary Belle, who married Dr. J. Lampton Price; Rebecca, who married Richard Kline; Kenner, who married Juliet Johnson; Margaret, who married P. Fall Taylor; Edmund Watson, and Frances, who married Phythian Saffell.

Benjamin F. Edrington and his wife, Ann E. Milburn, the former born in Woodford, the latter in Jefferson county, were married in Hickman County in 1849. He moved his family to Mississippi County, Mo., where he died during that year in his 44th year. They had

an only child, William Joseph Edrington, born January 4, 1831. After the death of her husband the widow and son returned to Ballard County where the son engaged in several enterprises successfully, but in 1857 he purchased a large tract of land near Arlington in that county and engaged in farming the remainder of his life. Early in the '70s he had one of the finest herds of Shorthorns in Kentucky, a select flock of Cotswold sheep and his stock of Chester White hogs was not equaled in high grade. From these sources he received handsome returns each year. In 1854 William Joseph Edrington married Mary E. Grundy, of Ballard County, daughter of —— Grundy. They had the following children: Annie, who married P. F. Stayten; Mary, who married T. N. Holt; Felix Grundy married Julia Cummins; Sue married Fon Robinson; Milburn married Loula LaRue; Rebecca married Frank Fox; Dora married Silas Reddick; Joseph married Lucy Liep; Josephine married Robert Murphy; Sarah married Roy A. Nelson, and Benjamin married Carrie Flegle.

William Joseph Edrington represented Ballard County in the Kentucky House of Representatives during the sessions of 1875-6, 1877-8, and 1881-2, and the writer, who was an officer of the House of Representatives from 1875-84, knew him as a popular and high-toned gentleman. He never violated a pledge or deceived a friend, and his word was never doubted.

In appearance he resembled his kinsman, Col. Taylor, but was not so striking a personality. His modesty was proverbal, and his courteous and pleasing manners were very noticeable and will pass to others, as it was in the blood.

His admiration of, and interest in fine stock was manifested by his frequent visits to Woodford County stock farms during the sessions of the legislature. The writer accompanied him on several of these drives.

John Price Edrington and his wife Sarah Beeler had a number of children whose descendants are in Kentucky and Tennessee, Arkansas, Texas and many other states. J. P. Edrington, Jr., and William Bard Edrington, prominent business men of Memphis, Tenn., are sons of James Hancock Edrington and his wife, Nancy Ann Bowen, and grandsons of John Price Edrington and Sarah Beeler of Ballard County.

The Edringtons of Virginia descend from John Catesbury Edrington, who left Wales about 1725 and settled in Farquier County, Virginia. He married ―――― Wickliffe and they had these children—perhaps others: Austin and John Catesbury the II, and several girls.

John Catesbury Edrington II married first Miss Tolson; second Sallie Porter Stone, widow of William Stone. No children reported by first marriage. Issue by second marriage were: John Catesbury III, who married Elizabeth Hawkins Stone, of Stafford County; James, who married ―――― Withers, and Angeline, who married Major Selden Brooke.

John Catesbury III and Elizabeth Hawkins Stone established their county seat in Stafford County, where they reared a large family, and descendants own the property now.

I am not able to link Hon. William Joseph Edrington and his people to the above John Catesbury Edrington, of Wales, but I remember distinctly that in a conversation with him in 1876 he told me that his grandfather, Joseph Edrington, was a citizen of Woodford County at an early period in its history. He also told me that he was related to the Wickliffe family through the marriage of one of his ancestors to a Wickliffe, and so far as I have been able to examine data relative to the Edringtons this is the only instance in which such a marriage took place.

I have been told that some of the Kentucky Edringtons came from North Carolina. If so, it is likely that they drifted to that state from Virginia and then to Kentucky, as did so many of the early settlers of this state.

―――――――

The Hancocks and Craigs.

William Hancock of Woodford County married Mary Ann Wiles of Burkesville, Kentucky, Oct. 4, 1815. She was a daughter of William Wiles and Nancy Grimes, born at Norfolk, Virginia, July 2, 1798. Her mother, after the death of William Wiles, married the Rev. Rice Haggard and they were residing at Burkesville at the time of the marriage of the daughter.

William Hancock and Mary Ann Wiles had the following children: Emily Carraway, born Aug. 4, 1816, married Henry Harrison Craig June 25, 1835, and died December 27, 1900; Mary Elizabeth, born Nov. 27, 1818, died Sept. 26, 1906, married Dr. Ridge-

ley Greathouse Nov. 12, 1837; William
Hancock, who never married, and
Susan Ann Virginia, born Aug. 25, 1832,
married Gov. Thomas Payne Porter
Mar. 16, 1848, and died Feb. 8, 1906.

Henry Harrison Craig and Emily
Carraway Hancock lived on a part of
the ancestral estate of the Craigs near
Clifton, where they were at home to a
wide circle of friends at "Glenwood"
for more than half a century, and it was
a most hospitable home where they
raised a most charming family of children. For the sake of romance (no parental objection existed) Henry Harrison Craig and Emily Carraway Hancock rode horseback to New Albany,
Indiana, where they were united in
marriage. This incident was given me
by a granddaughter, who is well versed
in family history. A descendant of another line, however, says that Dr.
Ridgeley Greathouse and Mary Elizabeth Hancock were the principals of
this romance. It certainly was an incident in the life of one of these sisters.

Henry Harrison Craig was born
March 22, 1813, in Woodford County
and died Oct. 27, 1891. Two months
before her death I talked with Mrs.
Craig in Kansas City and I little
thought she would be dead in sixty
days. They were blessed with eight
children, six of whom lived to man's
and woman's estate, and each so lived
and conducted him or herself in the
business, social and religious affairs of
life that the influence of each will be
felt by generations unborn. In short,
this was one of the most charming
and popular families reared in the
county, and we sustained a great loss

when they decided to cast their fortunes with the citizenship of the west
and southwest, where so many of our
early settlers had preceded them. The
names of their children follow: William H., born Oct. 13, 1836, joined
Gen'l John Hunt Morgan's command
in 1861, and was mortally wounded at
the battle of Cynthiana, July 17, 1862;
Milton Philip, born Oct. 30, 1838, married Margaret Elizabeth Buford, daughter of Col. William McDowell Buford,
of Woodford County, July 15, 1873,
and died in Corpus Christi, Texas, Dec.
5, 1914; Mary Elizabeth, born Dec. 18,
1840, married at New Orleans John W.
Hickman, of Lawrenceburg, Kentucky,
Dec. 14, 1865, and died at Portland,
Oregon, July 2, 1916; Louis Wiles, born
March 1, 1844, married Lucy Kate
Sherman, of Galveston, Texas, Feb. 24,
1886, and died at Houston, April 14,
1917: Henry Harrison, Jr., born Mar.
13, 1848, married Nellie Louise Morgan,
of Franklin County, Kentucky, Sept.
18, 1884, and died in Corpus Christi,
Texas, Oct. 4, 1914; Doddridge Helm
Craig, born Nov. 6, 1850, married
Laura S. Hallis at Lexington, Missouri,
Sept. 25, 1877, died at Salida, Colorado,
May 17, 1918. The other two children,
Sue and Susan E., died in childhood.

Milton Philip Craig entered the service of the Confederacy, General Morgan's Command, in 1861, at the time of
the enlistment of his brother William,
and served under that leader throughout the war. He was seriously wounded
in the battle at Cynthiana where his
brother lost his life, but rejoined his
regiment as soon as he was able to
mount his steed. His regiment escorted
President Davis and his Cabinet from

Charlotte, North Carolina, to Washington, Georgia, and he was one of a detail of sixty men who guarded the wagon train loaded with gold and silver from Richmond.

The Craigs, as men, were gentle and kind, but as soldiers they were brave and fearless, and Milton Philip was of that type—a courteous gentleman of the old school. In private life he was very popular and companionable and commanded the respect of all. He moved to Franklin County about 1880 and owned and cultivated the farm now known as the Hoge farm at the intersection of the Versailles pike with the L. & N. Railway. He moved to Colorado about 1900, from there to Kansas City several years later, from whence he removed to Corpus Christi, Texas, in 1907 where he established a real estate business that proved profitable to him. *His widow continues to reside at Corpus Christi. They had these children, Margaret Robertson who married Burton J. Hickman of Kansas City; Mary Katherine who resides with her mother, and William Buford Craig who married Sidbury Bingham, and they have an only child, Charlotte Buford Craig. They also have a residence at Corpus Christi.

Mary Elizabeth Craig and her husband, John W. Hickman, lived in St. Louis, where he was a prominent merchant. They afterward removed to Kansas City where he was engaged in business for a long period and enjoyed a wide circle of friends. They were ready and glad always to entertain their Kentucky friends. After the death of John W. Hickman his widow left Kansas City to be with children in Colorado. Many persons still residents of Woodford County can recall with pleasure this Craig family whose charms were unsurpassed. Mrs. Hickman was an unusually handsome woman, attractive in manner and queenly in her bearing. She was a great student and was a charming conversationalist. The names of their children were: Daphne, who married A. A. Smith; Agnes, who lives at Kansas City; Mary Greathouse, who married Frederick Glenn of Portland, Oregon. They have a son, Philip Glenn.

Louis Wiles Craig and Lucy Kate Sherman lived at Huston, Texas. In his youth he joined the Confederacy, was captured and imprisoned in St. Louis for a long time, where he was ill and his life despaired of. He was finally paroled and returned to his home in Woodford County, where he was practically an invalid for several years. After recuperating he returned to St. Louis and traveled out of that city for a wholesale drug company. Later he engaged in banking with his brother Dodd at Salida, Colorado. In that business they were assisted by Dunlap Cotton of Versailles, Kentucky, an experienced banker who was mentioned in the Cotton sketch in Sept., 1921, page 299. Louis Wiles later removed to Galveston, Texas, where he married and engaged in the real estate business, but finally transferred his business to Houston, Texas, and pursued it until his death. They have, first, Leonard Wiles Craig, who married Bessie Boyle of Houston, and they have Leonard Wiles, Jr., Bessie Louise, Lucy Sher-

---

*She and her children are now residents Frankfort, Ky., near the place of her birth.

man and William Reavis; second, Doddridge Henry; third, Emily Belle, and fourth, William Kendall.

Henry Harrison Craig, Jr., and Nellie Louise Morgan lived for a decade or more at Kansas City, where he was eminently successful in the practice of the law. He removed to Corpus Christi about 1908 and continued in the practice of his profession; also was interested in real estate with his brother Milton Philip. After graduating from school he studied law under the guidance and in the office of Gov. Thomas P. Porter at Versailles. Chief Justice Robertson of Lexington examined him and gave him his diploma. His death, October, 1914, so affected his brother, Milton P., that he died within sixty days.

Henry Harrison Craig, Jr., and Nellie Louise Morgan have these children, Henry Harrison, III, who married Kathryn Chastain of Corpus Christi, and Nellie Morgan Craig. Henry Harrison, III, and Kathryn Chastain have Henry Harrison, IV, and Louis Chastain.

Dodd Helm Craig and his wife, Laura S. Hollis, lived in Missouri for many years, he going to that state while yet a youth, but he finally removed to Salida, Colo., where he and his brother Louis Wiles engaged in business. The children of this couple are, first, Emily Wiles Craig, who married Guy Wayne Larimer, and they have a son Craig Wayne Larimer; second, Marie Rose Craig, who married Thomas A. Frazier, and they have two children, Thomas Vernon and Marie.

I recall this Woodford County family with the greatest pleasure and regret that the ties that were shaped during the trying days of the Civil War have been severed by death, but nothing but death can obliterate the memory of such friendships. They were staunch rebels, and in trying hours of the bitter strife, when others were seemingly disconsolate, they could always give forth a merry laugh that cheered their friends. Henry Harrison, Jr., and Doddridge Helm Craig had the military spirit and the parental eyes were constantly focussed on these two boys who so earnestly wished to go to the front and fight. I recall an incident in 1863 that often comes into my memory and causes a smile of pleasure mingled with sadness. I was in the room with my young friend Doddridge Craig when he conceived the idea of an elopement. He packed his haversack and requested me to toss it from an upstairs window. In a moment he was off for the yard fence, but before he could clear it he was a prisoner in his father's clutches. Of course he got what he deserved, and I got a scolding. Henry Craig was so thoroughly imbued with that spirit that he organized a crack military rifle team at Kansas City, of which he was captain, and it was so thoroughly and skillfully drilled that it became famous throughout the west. Its personnel was made up of the flower of the young manhood of Kansas City.

Mary Elizabeth Hancock and Dr.* Ridgley Greathouse lived many years in Versailles. He was born January 14, 1804, and died in Sacramento, California, September 16, 1852. They had two

*See the supplement of the Woodford County History for a most interesting sketch of the Ridgley family. Not obtainable for first edition.

children, Mary, born September 30, 1841, married in San Francisco, California, Alexander Keith Marshall, November 8, 1877, and died in that state, but her remains repose in the Versailles cemetery. She was an unusually gifted woman, possessing many charms of heart and head. Clarence Greathouse was born September 17, 1843. He was a great student and developed into a very great lawyer. He practiced in Versailles until about 1880, when he moved to California where he engaged in the practice of law. He was both eloquent and graceful, a man who would attract attention anywhere and in any company. He visited President Cleveland in Washington City soon after the advent of that administration, and that great student of human nature and judge of real men was so impressed with his personality that he tendered him the Consulship to Japan. It was accepted and his services were so eminently satisfactory to both countries that the administration under President Harrison retained him, and as he continued to grow in the esteem of the peoples of both countries he was not disturbed during the second administration of Cleveland. In the meantime many questions had arisen between Japan and Korea that were so delicate they had to be handled cautiously requiring a knowledge of international law and a well poised and diplomatic mind to handle and solve. The Emperor of Korea had watched young Greathouse and was convinced that he was the man of the hour demanded by Korea, so he tendered him a position

that would make him not only the legal adviser of the powers of that government, but also the confidant of that monarch. This honor carried with it greater power than the combined positions of Attorney General and Secretary of State in our government. He accepted and enjoyed the confidence and esteem of the Korean oligarchy, and the respect of all diplomats. His mother was with him until his death in Seoul, Korea, October 21, 1899, where he was buried with honors among the orientals. His Woodford County friends were always glad to note any achievement in the career of this brilliant son of her soil. He and his sister Mary were social favorites in Versailles and are well and pleasantly remembered by those remaining of their generation.*

Susan Ann Virginia Hancock, born August 25, 1832, died February 8, 1906. She and Gov. Thomas P. Porter were married in Versailles, Kentucky, March 16, 1848, and lived and died there. He was a leading lawyer at that bar for fifty years or more. He was elected to represent Woodford County in the lower house at the session of 1853-54, and was elected to represent that district in the state senate sessions 1858-59 and 1860-61. These were the days when the lowering clouds of the Civil War were casting their shadows before and it required courage and alertness. Gov. Porter was always equal to the hour. During the session of 1859 Lynn Boyd, the Lieut. Governor, was ill, and Gov. Porter was elected Speaker pro tem. of

*Miss Joe Carter and Mrs. Jo Bailey are the only two left. The former's passing occurred during the year 1937, 96 years old, a lovely woman, Mrs. Agnes McKee is also here, and youthful at about 88 years.

the senate. Boyd died during the session and the Speaker of the Senate succeeded to the Lieut. Governorship. He was born at Richmond, Kentucky, July 7, 1821, the son of Charles C. Porter of Virginia, who came to Kentucky at an early date. The father of Charles C. was one of three brothers who followed the fortunes of the house of Campbell in the Highlands of Scotland and came to the United States, one of them settling in Pennsylvania, another in Tennessee, and the third in Virginia. Gov. Porter's sympathies were strongly with the south during the Civil War and he was forced to leave the state for a time. They had an only child, Jessamine, born Dec. 27, 1857, who married Dr. John D. Neet, June 1, 1896, and they have an only son, Thos. Porter Neet, who married Roberta Bond. Dr. Neet and his wife reside in Versailles, and the son on a farm in the county, and they are the only descendants of William Hancock and Mary Ann Wiles in the county at this time. For other data relating to the Porters see Sept., 1921, page 304.

William Hancock, bachelor brother of the three sisters I have just sketched, lived with the family of Henry Harrison Craig. He was an aristocratic, soldierly bearing gentleman of the "old school," and his picture could be substituted for Bismarck's with but slight prospect of detection, but thoroughly democratic in dress and associations was he. He was a gentleman to the manor born. Later he lived with the family of Gov. Porter.

I have often heard the wife of Henry Harrison Craig (Emily Carroway Hancock), when visiting in our home speak of her Revolutionary forebears, and as

I recall it she said that her grandfather was William Hancock who married —— Wooldridge and came from Virginia to Kentucky to live as early as 1790. Now the census of 1810 for Woodford County gives the names of two Hancocks who were residents then, Obed and William Hancock, the former having a family of twelve and the owner of seven slaves; the latter had a family of five and owned eleven slaves and was a Revolutionary veteran (see page 19.) I have not been able to verify through correspondence the belief, but I am quite sure that the William Hancock whose name is disclosed in this census was the father of William Hancock who is the subject of this sketch and who married Mary Ann Wiles; and if the wife of this William was a Wooldridge there is no doubt about my belief. Edmond Wooldridge came to Kentucky during the second expedition of Daniel Boone and settled in Woodford County (see page 213) and the Hancocks, Wooldridges, and Craigs all settled in adjoining neighborhoods and were of either blood or marriage relationship. I often heard Mrs. Craig and her brother William Hancock (who never married) say that their Virginia ancestor was a close kinsman of John Hancock of the Constitutional Convention, but I can't say whether they said brother or cousin.

Mary Ann Wiles who married William Hancock was a daughter of William Wiles and Nancy Grimes of Norfolk, Virginia, and Nancy Grimes was a daughter of Major William Grimes of the "Continental Line" and Jane Pratt of Norfolk. Susan Wiles was a sister of Mary Ann and was a celebrated beauty.

She was married to Milton King of Kentucky, a son of General John Edwards King of Revolutionary fame, and they were the parents of General J. Q. A. King, a prominent politician of Southwestern Kentucky after the Civil war, a candidate for Governor in the latter 60's or early 70's. He married his cousin Lee Ann King, went west and I think became Governor of Colorado. I suspect he visited Woodford County before the Civil War. I recall the fact that he visited the Hancock relationship several times after the war.

Nancy Grimes, after the death of William Wiles, married the Rev. Rice Haggard and lived and died at Burksville, Kentucky, June, 1862. She was of the prominent Grimes family of Virginia.

Samuel Wiles was a brother of Mary Ann and Susan Wiles. He married Eliza Nash, daughter of General ——— Nash of Norfolk, Va. I don't know whether the Woodford County Nashes were related or not.

I attempted three years ago to write a brief sketch of these families but could get no one to give me dates and full names, so abandoned it until recently I got in touch with Miss Mary Katherine Craig of Corpus Christi, Tex., who has done much research work the last two years, and I am very much indebted to her for valuable assistance. Also to the wife of Dr. Neet of Versailles.

WOODFORD COUNTY NOTES

By Wm. E. Railey.

Bell-Thompson-Monroe-Berryman.

———

In the September, 1921, issue of the Register, page 274, Woodford notes, I gave an account of the family of Anthony Thomson, Sr., one of the early settlers of Woodford County. At that time I had failed to get in touch with any of his descendants who settled on his Ohio County estate prior to the War of 1812, going from Woodford County to that county. I also tried to get in touch with descendants of the Bell family who intermarried with the Thomson family and came to Kentucky with them, but later moved to Ohio County, but was unsuccessful in locating them. However, in the month of January, 1925, I met Anthony V. Thomson, a business man of Louisville, who told me he was a descendant of the Thomsons, Bells, Monroes, and Berrymans who came from Virginia to Woodford County the latter part of the eighteenth century. He said that his grandfather, Anthony Thomson, Jr., lived and died on the farm now owned and occupied by Mrs. Lafayette Crutcher, Sr., near Grassy Spring Church, a part of the Anthony Thomson, Sr., tract in Woodford County.

From data he furnished me I am able to write briefly of the Bells, Monroes, and Berrymans, and at the same time extend the Thomson family line.

Bells.

The Woodford County Bells descended from one of the three brothers, Thomas, Samuel, and James Bell, all born in Scotland, but emigrated to Ireland when quite young where they remained for some years before deciding to embark for America. When they reached our shores they concluded to settle at or near Canacadig, Pennsylvania, the year 1740, and each found himself a life companion within a short period of time.

Thomas and James Bell later removed to Virginia. James settled in Augusta County where many of his descendants still reside, but Thomas, who married Elizabeth Weir at Canacadig in 1742, settled in an adjacent county where he remained until 1786 when he and his family removed to Woodford County, Kentucky, with the Thomsons and others. He died there in 1792, and his will was probated in the Woodford County Court, April term, 1792, being of date, September 9, 1791, while the county was yet a part of Virginia.* His wife, Elizabeth, was executrix, and his son, Thomas, Jr., was executor. Witnesses were Chapman Taylor, Samuel Shannon, Lewis Snell, and William Coleman.

Thomas Bell, Sr., and Elizabeth Weir had the following children: Betsy, who married William Montgomery; John, who married Elizabeth Morrow; Mary, who married Samuel Carroll; James married Frances Burch; Thomas, Jr., born June 4, 1754, married Judith Thomson about 1777 in Louisa County, Va.; Samuel married Lucy Pope; Ann married Andrew Monroe, and William married Patsy Wood.

Many of the above children came to Kentucky with their parents, but some of them removed to Jefferson, Ohio, and Daviess counties, by or before 1830.

Thomas Bell, Jr., remained a citizen of Woodford County until his death in 1830. His son, Robert Thomson Bell, was appointed administrator of his estate, and also to complete the unfinished settlements of the estate of Thomas Bell, Sr. The court records show a complete settlement soon thereafter, with the names of Monroe, Hardin, Patrick and others equally as familiar in early Woodford County, participating in the settlements.

Thomas Bell, Sr., was a captain in the Revolution, and his son Thomas, Jr., was a sergeant, hence all of the descendants are entitled to membership in either of the patriotic societies—Sons or Daughters of the American Revolution, which can be verified by reference to file K. 2, in the war office or the file rooms of the Sons and Daughters of the

Revolution. My information also directs me in the statement that Thomas Bell, Sr., was a member of the Society of the Cincinnati, in confirmation of which you will only have to refer to the Year Book Kentucky Society of the Revolution, 1913, page 302.

Thomas Bell, Jr., and "Judy" Thomson, daughter of Anthony Thomson, Sr., and Ann Bibb, (September, 1921, page 274) had the following children: Thomson Bell, born October 18, 1778, died March 23, 1861, married Sarah Hewlett in Jefferson County, February, 1822; she was born January 16, 1800, died January 27, 1846; John, born about March, 1782, died St. Louis, Mo., 1850; Samuel, born July 14, 1786, died March 6, 1857, married Joanna Hewlett in Jefferson County; Thomas, III., born December 14, 1789, married Elizabeth Hewlett, April 6, 1812; Robert Thomson Bell born November 26, 1792, died August 7, 1876, married Mary Ann Monroe in the fall of 1814, she was born August 24, 1786, died July 8, 1870, daughter of John Monroe and Winifred Berryman; Jefferson Bell, born November 15, 1800, died about 1853, married Ruth T. Hord, January 20, 1820. In Southwest Kentucky these names of descendants of the Woodford County Bells, Thomsons, Monroes and Berrymans appear: Ashby, Atcherson, Atherton, Baker, Barnett, Barnard, Blair, Boggs, Brasher, Brooks, Bruce, Bristow, Davenport, Daniel, Davis, Demmett, Duncan, Dunn, Felix, Foss, Howard, Jett, Lewis, McDaniel, Montgomery, Parker, Poindexter, Riley, Rowan, Swearinger, Thornton, Underwood and Waller, many of

*Mistake; Woodford was established 1788.

them very familiar in Woodford County during the pioneer period.

Robert Thomson Bell was in War of 1812, enlisted in Captain Virgil Mc-Cracken's company, recruited in Woodford County. After settling up the estates of his father and grandfather in 1832, he moved to Ohio County where so many of his kindred had preceded him. While living in that county he enlisted for service in the Mexican War from which he emerged with the rank of colonel, and by that title he was ever afterward greeted by his kinsmen and neighbors. His wife, Mary Ann Monroe, was a granddaughter of William Berryman and Rebecca Vowels. They had these children: Eleanor, born September 15, 1815, married Berg B. Sullinger, October 16, 1836; Catherine, born December 29, 1821, died October 25, 1862, married January 11, 1844, her cousin Henry Thomson who was born in Woodford County on the farm before mentioned near Grassy Springs. This Henry Thomson does not appear in the Thomson sketch, page 274, for the reason that he left Woodford County about 1827 and located among his relatives in Ohio County, and for that reason had passed out of the memory of the party who furnished me the data from which that sketch was written. He died in Ohio County, July 31, 1877. His children were: Annie Josie, born January 25, 1860, married Richard Edmundson and had Emmet, Blanch, Henry and Anna; Anthony V. Thomson, born March 17, 1862, married Mary L. Daniel, she was born December 20, 1865. They have two sons, Captain Robert R., born February 13, 1889 and Major Daniel D. Thomson, born Oc-

tober 24, 1892. Both of these young men rendered valiant service in the World War and each has a record to be proud of. The former was highly complimented as a disciplinarian while preparing our boys for service in France. The latter won public praise from his superior officers for intrepid bravery on more than one field of carnage in France in the World War. I had the pleasure of meeting him recently and he is every inch a chevalier.

- - -

Monroe.

As the Monroes had a part in the early history of Woodford County I take pleasure in relating as much of it as the facts before me warrant.

John Monroe and his wife, Winifred Berryman, came to Woodford County very early in its settlement. He removed to Scott County about 1807, his wife having previously died, so as to be nearer his Monroe kin who were living in that county, but he returned to Woodford County in 1816 and remained there until 1832 when he accompanied his son-in-law Robert Thomson Bell to Ohio County. He died in that county May 25, 1838. He was born in Westmoreland County, Virginia, November 10, 1749, where he lived until he came to Kentucky. His wife, Winifred Berryman, to whom he was married December 17, 1778, was born September 16, 1757, and died January 24, 1798. They had these children: William, born September 16, 1779, died October 21, 1833; Rebecca Newton, born March 28, 1782, died August 12, 1805; Elizabeth, born January 28, 1784, died January, 1836; Mary Ann, born

August 24, 1786, died July 8, 1870, married Robert Thomson Bell, 1814; Winifred died young; Andrew Monroe, born November 25, 1794, died April, 1862.

John Monroe served in the Revolution and was attached to several different companies from 1775 to 1781 (see file 31267 War Department). Of course his descendants are entitled to membership in the Sons and Daughters of the Revolution.

Andrew Monroe, a kinsman of the above John Monroe, settled in Scott County in 1793, just after Scott was formed from Woodford County, and both were closely related to President Monroe. He married Ann Bell, daughter of Thomas Bell, Sr., and Elizabeth Weir an aunt of Colonel Robert Thomson Bell who married Ann Monroe, daughter of John Monroe and Winifred Berryman. They were the parents of Judge Ben Monroe who married Cynthia Montgomery, and of Judge Thomas Bell Monroe, born October 7, 1791, in Albemarle County, Va., who died in 1865. The latter served as U. S. Attorney in 1833-34, and Judge of the U. S. District Court from 1834 until his death. His wife was Eliza Adair, daughter of Governor John Adair. Their son John Adair Monroe died in Frankfort, 1873, and was as well known in Woodford as in Franklin County.

Berrymans.

Winifred Berryman, who became the wife of John Monroe, was the daughter of William Berryman and Rebecca Vowels, the granddaughter of Benja-

min Berryman and Elizabeth Newton, and the great granddaughter of John Berryman and Miss Tucker.

James Berryman, one of the uncles of Winifred, was born 1716, died January 25, 1772, married Sarah Dishman, 1752. They had a son, James Berryman, born March 28, 1764, died May 23, 1812, married Margaret Sthreshley, October 13, 1787. This couple had, among others a son, John Berryman, born August 9, 1792, died May 17, 1874, who married Jane Railey in Woodford County, August 9, 1819. For their descendants see Register May, 1921, or page 255. Clifford Berryman, a prominent newspaper man of Washington City is a grandson. He married Kate Geddis Durfee, July 5, 1893, and they have Mary Bell, Florence Seville and James Thomas Berryman.

William Berryman, father of Winifred, was born in 1713, died March 11, 1784, in Westmoreland County, Virginia, where he was born. His wife, Rebecca Vowels was born in Maryland in 1720, died in 1772.

William Berryman assisted in establishing American independence. He was appointed Committeeman for Westmoreland County, Va., Tuesday, January 31, 1775, and for this service his descendants are entitled to membership in the Sons and Daughters of the Revolution.*

Much of this information was taken from a manuscript the data of which was assembled by Mary Emma Dunn, clerk of the Federal Court at Owensboro, Kentucky. Her kinspeople will never realize how great a debt they owe this lady who has worked so faithfully

*See page 372.

in gathering and preserving the record of her ancestors. Her work is of great credit to her now, and will be more enduring than a marble shaft. Her lines of descent from these Woodford County ancestors follow: Thomas Bell, Sr., and Elizabeth Weir; Thomas Bell, Jr., and Judith Thomson; Robert Thomson Bell and Mary Ann Monroe; Mary Rebecca Bell and Sanford Ashby; Victoria Frances Ashby and William Bristow; Aminia Bristow and John William Dunn; Mary Emma Dunn and William Thomas Mastin.

General Lafayette's Visit to Versailles

On page 243 of my Woodford County history (Page 109 May, 1921, Register) I gave an account of the visit of General Lafayette to Versailles the latter part of May, 1825. I described the scene that took place at the home of the widow of George Taylor Cotton, whose maiden name was Elizabeth O'Bannon, see page 381. That story was given to me by the wife of James Gay, a granddaughter of George T. Cotton who is to-day a resident of Versailles. At the time I wrote that incident I wrote of another that was just as interesting but was crowded out for the lack of space in the Register, so I am inserting it here as a part of Woodford County history. It took place the same day and on the same occasion. After leaving the home of Mrs. Cotton, on Elm Street near the entrance to Versailles, the procession moved down Main Street to the Watkins Tavern, conducted by Henry Watkins (the stepfather of Henry Clay) for many years. The old hostelry stood

where Amsdens Bank now stands, and when he reached there he was met by his old friend and comrade in the Revolution, General Marquis Calmes.* When General Lafayette stepped from his carriage he discovered his old friend approaching with outstretched hands and they fell into each other's embrace and wept like children. I have often heard Judge Wm. E. Ashmore and Mrs. Betsy Young, both my relatives and both witnesses, relate this incident in our home before the Civil War. For Judge Ashmore, see page 204 (page *68, May, 1921, Register). (For Youngs see page 36, May, 1920 Register) or 69 Woodford County history. On page 181 (page 98, January, 1921, Register) you will find a picture of the old tavern, so long the property of Henry Watkins and his wife, who was the mother of Henry Clay. You will also find some interesting reading about the Clays and Watkins families from the pen of Mrs. Sam Wooldridge, and will also find on page 36 much of interest about General Calmes from the pen of Captain John Andrew Steele whose grandfather headed the procession from Frankfort to Versailles, an escort for General Lafayette (page 77, May, 1920 Register). General Calmes came to Kentucky with Colonel Thomas Marshall about 1785, and settled in Woodford County, and his claim for services in the Revolution was adjacent to that of Colonel Marshall's running to the Lexington road. Stories about Lafayette, Calmes and others of that period were quite frequently related about the fireside—by the elderly citizens who witnessed important events in

*See pages 36, 38 and 184.

early Woodford—as late as the Civil War. When General Calmes came to Woodford County there was no town and he assisted in the organization of Versailles and was sufficiently influential as to name the town for his loved town of that name in France. These old people were delighted to tell how pleased Lafayette was to greet so many old comrades, especially the Trabues, Subletts, Dupuys, Franciscos, Lafons, and others, all of French extraction, and how feelingly he spoke from the balcony of the old Watkins Tavern (see page 98½ Register, January, 1921), 181½ Woodford County history, and thanked the throng before him for the tribute of respect.

General Calmes was also a veteran of the War of 1812, as well as of the Revolution, enlisting as a private in the company of Captain John Christopher of Woodford County, regiment of Col. George Trotter, but before the end of the war, was promoted to the rank of a brigadier general. His rank in the Revolution was Lieutenant-Colonel. In Captain Steele's article (page 77, Register May, 1920) page 36, Woodford County history, he states that Sarah Calmes, daughter of the General, headed a committee of young ladies who cast flowers in the path of General Lafayette upon the occasion of his visit to Versailles and I am exceedingly sorry that I am not able to write here the names of that committee. General Calmes married Priscilla Hale of Woodford County. See page 224 (page 88, May, 1921, Register) and they are both buried in a mausoleum within three miles of Versailles on the farm that he earned in the Revolution. The

Daughters of Revolution did themselves proud in taking the name of General Calmes when they organized in Woodford County. It will be a part of their duty to look after the mausoleum, within the walls of which repose the remains of him and his wife.

Tradition says that Henry Watkins and his wife, widow of the Rev. John Clay and mother of Henry Clay, came to Woodford County in 1792, and ran the old Watkins Tavern until after Lafayette's visit, but Mrs. Sam Wooldridge said in her notes that Mrs. Clay gave up the tavern several years earlier and moved to her farm where she died in 1829 on the Mortonsville Pike, three miles out of Versailles.

On page 181 will be found an account of the settlement between Henry Clay and his stepfather, Henry Watkins, (pages 98-9, Register, January, 1921.)

CORRECTIONS OF WOODFORD COUNTY NOTES.

By Wm. E. Railey.

Terrell—

Mention was made of the Terrell family, in the September, 1921, issue, and on page 269 column 2, par. 3, I stated that Dr. William Henry Terrell, Jr., married Mrs. Virginia Bonney Cotton, "daughter of William Cotton," etc. Miss Bessie Todd, of Shelbyville, informs me that she was the widow of William Cotton, and daughter of Dr. C. D. Bonney, of Shelbyville.

Scott-Gist—

I stated in the September, 1921, issue, page 271, column 1, that "Governor Charles Scott married the widow Gist, of Lexington, soon after the expiration of his term as Governor, and that he died in 1820, on her farm, 'Canebrake,' in Fayette County." That statement was taken from a sketch of Gov. Scott, written by Miss Patty Burnley, of Frankfort (who was the great granddaughter of Gov. Scott by his first marriage to Miss Sweeney), and published in the Register, September, 1903.

Col. Thomas G. Stuart, of Winchester, has given us the following statement on the subject:

"I read with interest your articles on Woodford County, in the Register, but I find in the last issue that you are slightly in error as to Gov. Scott having lived in Fayette County. He married a very brilliant and noted lady, Mrs. Judith Gist, widow of Col. Nathaniel Gist, of Clark County, and lived at 'Canewood,' a magnificent old estate near our old home in northern Clark, where he lived and died, and was buried, but by a resolution of, and appropriation by the legislature, his remains were later (Nov. 8, 1854) moved to Frankfort, where they rest in the State lot.

"The daughters of Mrs. Gist by the former marriage were prominently married. Jesse Bledsoe married one of them. Another married a Blair, and she was the grandmother of Frank P. and Montgomery Blair. Another married a Brown, and she was the mother of B. Gratz Brown, and still another married a Gratz, and they were the ancestors of the beautiful Miss Gratz, of Philadelphia, who was the prototype of

'Rebecca,' in Sir Walter Scott's Ivanhoe.

"Col. Gist's grant of 6,000 acres in Clark County cornered with the 1,000 acre tract of my grandfather, James Stuart, a Revolutionary soldier from Culpeper County, Va.

"Col. Gist sold 3,000 of his 6,000 acre tract to Thomas Lewis, and it is one of the first deeds recorded in Clark County's first deed book.

"'Canewood' some time after the death of Gov. Scott and his wife, became the property of Matthew D. Hume, and is now owned in part by his descendants."

The daughter of Col. Nathaniel Gist referred to above, by Col. Stuart as having married Francis Preston Blair, Sr., was Elizabeth Violet Gist. Francis P. Blair, Sr., edited the Frankfort Argus, and afterwards the Daily Globe, at Washington City, both papers being ardent supporters of Andrew Jackson and his policies.

Col. Stuart is mistaken about the marriage of one of the daughters of Nathaniel Gist "to a Brown." His granddaughter, the daughter of Sarah Gist and Jesse Bledsoe, married Judge Mason Brown, of Frankfort.—Ed.

Francis Preston Blair, Sr., was a son of James Blair and Ann Preston, of Virginia. James Blair came to Kentucky with his family and practiced law at Frankfort.

B. Gratz Brown, who is mentioned by Col. Stuart as a son of one of Col. Gist's daughters, was the son of Judge Mason Brown, of Frankfort. He removed to St. Louis, Mo., and was elected Governor of that state in 1870, and was candidate for the Vice Presidency on the ticket with Horace Greely in 1872.

In the September, 1921, Register, page 295, Miss Fannie Scearce is mentioned as a sister of Ralph Scearce. She was his aunt, the sister of his father, John C. Scearce.

In the Hiter sketch which appeared in the issue of September, 1921, I stated on page 271, from notes in my possession, that Elizabeth Combs, who married Benjamin Hiter, was a sister of General Leslie Combs, but I was in error. She was a daughter of Col. Andrew Combs and a sister of John W. Combs, who was sheriff of Woodford County before the Civil War and Provost Marshal during the war. Col. Andrew Combs and General Leslie Combs were related.

Upon the same page I said that Porter Hiter and his wife died upon their estate near Clifton, but I am reminded that he died in Louisville, and his wife died in Missouri.

On page 69 I briefly stated that Douglas Young married 1st Maria Jackson, 2nd Elizabeth Randolph Pleasants in 1835. Of this last marriage I said there was an only child, Susan Railey Young who married Dr. T. K. Layton, but did not mention the children of the first marriage, because I did not learn who they married. I now give them as far as my information

directs. Logan Young was the oldest child and he moved to Nodaway, Missouri, at an early age where he died at the advanced age of 90 years; Ambrose Young, as popular in Woodford as he was in his adopted county of Jessamine. He married Lucy Carr. Helen Young, the eldest daughter married her cousin Richard B. Young of Fayette County; Phoebe Young remained a spinster and died in Versailles at an advanced age; Jane Young married W. R. Smith and they had Marie Elizabeth who married Dan'l M. Bowmar of the Woodford Sun (see Bowmar sketch, page 84). Other children were Millard and Meade who lived and died in Illinois.

These children were born to Richard B. and Helen Young, Ambrose, never married, William married Annie Prewitt and they have three children living at Liberty, Kentucky.

Upon the death of his first wife, Richard B. Young married Jane O'Neal, daughter of Frank O'Neal and Mary Ferguson, who was a sister of Henry and Joshua Ferguson, well known citizens of the county back in the 60's and 70's.

The children of Susan Railey Young and Dr. Layton were: Jennie who married Andrew Wallace; Elizabeth married John M. Garth; David W. married Maude Vance; Whitney married Ida Yeaman; D. Y. married Zada McCulloch; T. K., Jr., died 1902; Nannie married Chas. J. Crabb; Susan L. married Marshall Reid; Hugh and Ambrose Young Layton.

WOODFORD COUNTY NOTES

By Wm. E. Railey.

Ashbys and Peters Families.

These two families were very prominent in Virginia. The Ashbys crossed
the ocean to that state during the Crom-
wellian period and were representative
of the cause of Charles the 1st.

The first of the name to appear in
Virginia is revealed through the name
of Thomas, who located in what is now
Farquier County, between 1690 and
1700, and tradition says he was the
grandson of Edward Ashby, but fails
to enlighten us as to who were his parents. He died in that county in 1752,
leaving ten children, of whom John
(Captain Jack) was one. He was born
in 1707, died 1797, married, first Jane
Combs, May 11, 1731; second, Catherine Huffman, 1781. He was a captain
in the 2nd Virginia Rangers Oct. 21,
1755, and was with Washington during
Braddock's campaign, bringing dis-
patches containing news of Braddock's
defeat, from Winchester to Williamsburg, Virginia, and returned with Gov.
Dinwiddie's reply before the English
commander supposed he had started on
his journey.

A letter from Williamsburg June 2,
1774, that is still in files in Virginia,
says: "At the battle of Point Pleasant
the noted Captain Ashby, who in the
last war brought the first account of

Braddock's defeat to this city (Williamsburg) with amazing expedition,
was killed." This reported death of
Captain Ashby was a mistake. He was
in Kentucky at that time.

In October, 1774, Col. Ashby, accom-
panied by John W. Willis and William
Ballard, was in Kentucky, going by
way of the Ohio river, and when they
returned, the trip was by way of New
Orleans, Pensacola and Charleston, to
Virginia. In a little booklet by Judge
B. J. Peters, of Mt. Sterling, many
graphic and thrilling stories of the
three men and their experiences on the
Ohio and Mississippi are related. See
Western Journal, Vol. 12, page 116.
Also Collins' History, Vol. 1, page 18.

Col. Ashby held a commission in the
Colonial army and commanded Fort
Ashby, at the junction of Patterson
creek and the Potomac river, in West
Virginia, during the French and Indian War; was with Washington during his Indian campaign, and at Braddock's defeat.

In 1774, while Col. Ashby was in
Kentucky he located land in Jefferson
County, then came to Woodford Coun-*
ty and located and surveyed 2,000
acres in the very heart of the county.
This tract was adjacent to the tract

*Then Fayette County.

surveyed by Col. Thomas Marshall, and known as Buck Pond, and also close to the tract taken by Gen. Marquis Calmes. It included much of what has always been known as the "Big Sink" belt, lying between Versailles and Midway. This land was for services rendered in the French and Indian Wars, as per grant signed by Thomas Jefferson, Governor, in the fourth year of the Commonwealth. Col. Ashby went from Woodford (then Fayette, I believe) to Lewis County, and located another tract, then started on the trip to Virginia by way of New Orleans. Not many years elapsed before grandsons of Col. Ashby came to Kentucky to take charge of his grant, and fight off squatters.

Col. John Ashby and his wife, Jane Combs, had several children, but I will only mention his daughter, Elizabeth who, as I am informed, was the fourth born. Her birth occurred March 1, 1741, and she married Col. John Peters, of Farquier County, Va., and died in Woodford County, Ky., in 1830.

Col. John Peters was born 1738, and died in Farquier County in 1782. He was a Revolutionary soldier of the continental line, and was born on a 500 acre farm in Farquier County, the son of an Englishman who emigrated to Virginia at an early date. As above stated, he married Elizabeth Ashby, and they were blessed with five—likely six—sons, whose names were Nathaniel, John, James, Lewis and William. Another account that I have seen adds Nimrod to his list of children. I was told many years ago that all of these sons except Lewis and William came to Kentucky not later than 1790, and set-

tled on the grants in Jefferson and Woodford, and possibly Lewis counties. Papers I have seen recently belonging to Miss Fannie Lillard, of Versailles, Ky., confirm this report.

Judge B. J. Peters, before mentioned, a grandson of Col. John Peters, at the age of 86 years, arranged some notes on the experiences of Col. John Ashby that were printed, and I had the pleasure of looking over a copy belonging to Col. Lucien Beckner, of Winchester. In it he says: "After the death of Col. John Peters, Judge Peters' father, William, and his uncle, Lewis Peters, remained on the Farquier County farm with their mother, Elizabeth, until the fall of 1809, when all joined a caravan that consisted of several families, conveyed in many four-horse wagons that also transported their furniture, and about twenty slaves, who looked after and cared for the herds of live stock, and headed for Woodford County, Kentucky. When they reached their destination, 9th of December, 1809, they found that the brothers who had lived on the land in Woodford County for about twenty years, had prepared comfortable log houses for them. Although only five years old, Judge Peters had a vivid recollection of that eventful trip and his account of it is as interesting as his narrative of the experiences of Capt. Jack Ashby's trip to Kentucky thirty years earlier was thrilling.

Having known Judge Peters, his brother "Lon" and sister Virginia, and their cousin, Waller Peters, from my childhood, I started seaching for data five years ago of this family, but like other Woodford County family sketches I have worked on since 1919,

I found very few living descendants in whom I could arouse an interest in the work, so I have gotten the data I am using in such a broken and tardy manner that I have not been able to get it in shape until now, and even now I lack many dates that I would like to have.

Nathaniel Peters, the first of Col. John and Elizabeth Ashby Peters, as before stated, came to Kentucky about 1790 and settled on a part of "Big Sink" grant. I was not able to get the maiden name of his wife, but was informed that his daughter, whose name was either Mattie or Natille, married Seth Tuley, of Louisville, and a son(Rowan Boone Tuley, is, and has been for fifty years, a citizen of Washington City. He was private secretary to Senator Joe C. S. Blackburn during his more than thirty years' service in Congress. He collected some of the data that I have used in these sketches. The above Nathaniel Peters appeared upon the Woodford County census of 1810, representing a family of two, and the owner of ten slaves.

John Peters, the second son of Col. John and Elizabeth Ashby Peters, was born Dec. 28, 1762, and married Nancy Rousseau, whose birth was August 11, 1764. Their children were William, Jr., born March 25, 1786, married Elizabeth Bronaugh; Margaret, born Feb. 25, 1789, married Dan'l H. Harris, of Woodford County; Elizabeth, born May 18, 1792, married William Hope, Nov. 13, 1814; Nathaniel, Jr., born June 8, 1795, married Eliza Lane, of Templemore, Ireland; John Rousseau, born June 1, 1800, married Frances Giltner, of Woodford County; Nancy,

born February 9, 1804, married Edmond Coppage, Scott County, and Priscilla Mauzy, born May 30, 1812, married Johnson A. Young, of Bath County. The above John Peters is mentioned in the census of Woodford County in 1810, representing a family of nine and the possessor of seven slaves. He also came to the county as early as 1790.

James Peters was the third son of Col. John Peters and Elizabeth Ashby, and came very early to Woodford County and settled on a part of the "Big Sink" grant, and the census of 1810 gives him a family of nine and credits him with seven slaves. I was also unable to get the maiden name of his wife, but the names of his children follow: Carr, Mary, Emily, Matilda, Julia, Eliza, Ann and Bettie. Mary, married Johnson Young, of Bath County; Emily, married Toliver Young, of Bath County; Matilda, married James Cox, of Woodford County, and had two children, Alexander, who married Hettie Price, and moved to Illinois, and Charles, married Mollie Allen and they have Mary, William, James and Matilda, who are residing in the county. Julia, married ——— Combs, of Scott County; Eliza, married William Thompson, and they had a daughter Mary, born January 1, 1825, died Aug. 16, 1918, married May 23, 1848, Col. Robt. McConnell, born Oct. 18, 1797, died Feb. 19, 1869; and they had Eliza, married W. Hawkins Cleveland; William, married Nannie Carpenter; Robt., married ——— Glover; James, married Lizzie Hunter; Martha, married William Hunter Railey, and Elizabeth McConnell, who married John Ball. The above William Thompson was born Oct. 18, 1797, died Feb. 10, 1869, married March 5, 1823, Eliza Peters, born Oct. 6, 1802, died Feb. 6, 1852. Ann Peters, married ———— Terrell, and Betty, married William Dickey, of Virginia, and members of this family were just before, during and for a time after Civil War, in Woodford County, but my recollection is that they merely had a temporary residence, and later moved to Louisville, where several times I renewed acquaintanceship with one of them that I knew in my boyhood.

Lewis Peters, the fourth son of Col. John and Elizabeth Ashby Peters, married Francis Waller, of Virginia, and they had these children: Waller, Marcus, Charles, Pauline and Mary. Waller, married first ———— Stockton, of Fleming County, who was a cousin of Mollie Stockton, the wife of William Cotton, of the county; second, Helen Armstrong of Mercer County; Marcus, married Miranda Young, who was a daughter of Thomas Young, of Bath County, and a sister of Congressman John D. Young and Judge Van Young, of the Appellate Court, and they had Thomas, James, Charles, Jr., and Bettie Peters; Charles Peters, married *———— Porter, sister of Gov. Thos. P. Porter, of Versailles; Pauline, married first Armstead Long, of Woodford County, second, Frank Duvall, of Versailles; Mary, married Dr. Henry F. Lillard, who came to Versailles from Virginia when quite a young man and established himself in the medical profession and became one of the very popular physicians of the town.† In

1861 he heeded the clarion call to arms of the Confederacy. He became a prisoner in Camp Douglas, and after the war he returned to Versailles and resumed his practice. They had several sons and daughters with whom I had a pleasing childhood acquaintance. The daughters were Mary and Frances, or "Fanny," as she was popularly known during her four score and two years or more. The boys were Charlie and Frank, who have been dead many years, but the two girls still live in the old home on Lexington street, that sets back in a locust grove in the center of a full city block, and is one of the oldest residences in town. It was originally built for a seminary for young ladies, but by whom I can't say.

Their uncle Marcus was a pioneer merchant in Versailles and would go overland to Philadelphia and haul his merchandise to Versailles in wagons drawn by four horses. Since this was written Fannie Lillard passed into the unseen state October 16, 1925.

Frances Waller, who married Lewis Peters, was of the prominent Waller family of Virginia, and related to the Rev. John L. Waller, a distinguished minister who was a leader of the Baptists in Woodford County so long; in fact, was a leader of that denomination in Kentucky; a pioneer in that cause.

William Peters was the fifth of the sons of Col. John Peters and Elizabeth Ashby. He and his brother Lewis came to Woodford County and settled on two parts of the "Big Sink" grant that, I am persuaded, extended as far as Weisenberg's mill, near Midway. He

*The wife of Dr. Neet says this is a mistake; likely a relative.
†He was a druggist at Versailles also.

married Frances Woodruff in Virginia, about 1804 and the overland trip was in 1809. Their children were: 1st, Belvard January, 2nd Katherine, 3rd Ann, 4th Caroline, 5th Joe, 6th Albert, 7th Frances, 8th Leonidas, 9th Adaline, 10th Virginia, and 11th Henrietta. Numerals denote position of child as to birth.

Belvard January Peters, 1st born in Virginia, Nov. 3, 1805, and was about five years old when he reached Woodford County. His early training was in a log school house in Woodford County on the Peters estate, then he was for three years under the tutorship of Dr. Louis Marshall at the "Buck Pond Academy," the home of the late Louis Marshall, of Versailles · (see Register January, 1921, page 93, col. 1) or Woodford County History, page 177, col. 1. He then entered Transylvania University, from which he graduated in 1825. At the suggestion of his father he chose law as his profession and was admitted to the bar and established himself at Owingsville, Ky., in 1827. Was county attorney of that county from 1829-32, when he resigned to accept appointment to the same office in Montgomery County and served that county in that capacity until 1845, when he was elected to the Legislature. In 1848 he was appointed clerk of the circuit court of Montgomery County by Judge Farrow, and in 1860 was elected a member of the Court of Appeals, from which he retired in 1876. He married Elizabeth Farrow Sept. 1, 1831, but no children blessed the union. He was a kindly, popular gentleman of the old school, as I remember him in his declin-

ing years, and he died near the four score and ten marker.

In the class with Judge B. J. Peters at college were Robert J. Breckinridge, Thomas Francis Marshall, J. A. McClung and Lewis Green, all prominent in after life in the political arena and in the forum. In his "Notes" he expresses great love for Dr. Louis Marshall, of the Buck Pond Academy.

Katherine, the 2nd, married Rev. ───── Paine, and had these children: William, John, Jilson, Burk, Leonidas, Eliza; Katherine married ───── Botts, and Fannie I know nothing of descendants.

Ann Peters, 3rd, married Bickum Henry and had Bettie, who married ───── Farrow; Mollie, who married ───── Gracie; and Col. Al Henry, who was a sculptor, of Louisville, and designed the statue of President Lincoln that stands in one of the parks of that city.

Caroline Peters, 4th, married John Botts, of Shelby County, who had Ada, who married ───── VanPelt; Annie, who married ───── Marble; Rose, who married ───── Jones, and Lon, who married ───── Ritter. Have no record of their later descendants.

Joe Peters, 5th, married ───── Darneal, of Woodford County, and had Wilder and Marian, both of whom were adopted by Judge B. J. Peters and lost their lives in the Confederacy.

Albert, 6th, married Sarah Calk, of Mt. Sterling, and had Belvard, Jr., Albert, Jr., William and Elizabeth. The latter married Col. Thomas Johnson, of Mt. Sterling, who represented Montgomery County in the Kentucky Legislature during the session of 1883-4. I was an officer of the House of Representatives and remember that no member was more highly regarded than he, being a man of strict integrity. He was an old Confederate soldier who dared to do his duty regardless of consequences. I am told that Mrs. Sherman Goodpaster, of Frankfort, is his daughter.

Frances Peters, 7th, married ——— Keys, of Missouri, and had Julia and Mary.

Leonidas Peters, 8th, married Ermine Creel in Louisville in 1854. He died in 1887, and his wife died in 1884. They had Fannie, Charlie, Roger Hanson, Walker, Mattie and Margaret. The latter married ——— Bryant. Roger Hanson spent much of his time with his aunt, Virginia Hanson, and is now a minister in the Episcopal church, located at Anchorage. During the Civil War and for several years after Lon Peters was associated with the Versailles post office, and as I remember, was very popular with its patrons. He was a union man on the question of the Civil War, but like many Democrats of that period came back to his first love when the clouds rolled by. Some years later he moved to Mt. Sterling and was associated with one of the county offices there. He was a popular citizen always and everywhere.

Adaline Peters, 9th, married Coleman Chinn, of Bourbon County. They had no children.

Virginia Peters, 10th, married General Roger Hanson, of Winchester, in 1852. He was killed at Murfreesboro, Tenn., Jan. 2, 1863. Immediately after the war his widow returned to Versailles and purchased property and opened an up-to-date boarding house. It was at once filled with old Confederate soldiers, many of them bringing their families, among them Capt. Jo. C. Bailey and his wife Sallie Berry Bailey. In a letter from this lady recently about this household she says: "I love to live over those days, as it is one of the memories that sweeten my life. It has been truthfully said that there is in the brain of every normal man and woman a memory room, and I often wander in mine, where I find the faces of those dear friends. I am the only living member of that dear household of the long ago, and the only living member of my father's household sketched by you in September, 1920, Register, page 69." (Woodford County History, page 104.)*

Virginia Peters Hanson later gave up her boarding house and was elected State Librarian by the Kentucky Legislature in 1884, and as Sergeant-at-Arms of the House of Representatives, I was one of the first to congratulate her. She was re-elected in 1886, and again in 1888, but died in 1889.

Henrietta Peters, the 11th, married Isaiah Calk, of Mt. Sterling. They had no children.

In 1810 six members of the Peters family were living on the "Big Sink" property, which includes the five brothers written of above, and Nimrod, who is mentioned by one authority as a brother. That vicinity was generally known as "Petersburg" in 1810. In operation on this estate was a carding mill, a grist mill, a saw mill and a brick kiln, hence it was a busy locality. The

*She is living at 96 years of age July, 1937, so Mrs. Agnes McKee informs me.

grist mill supplied many adjacent neighborhoods with its output, hauling much of it as far as Frankfort.

In the concluding paragraph of the notes of Judge B. J. Peters, on the experiences of the Ashbys and Peters families in coming to Kentucky, and their experiences for a few years after he says: "In 1818 my hardest labor commenced. My father built a large brick house and I had to help carry the brick in the mould from the moulders' table to the yard and spread them in the sun to dry, and after they were burned, to carry them from the kiln to the wall for the bricklayers. This work made my hands very sore, the sand broke the skin and caused them to bleed."

I am indebted to the Rev. Roger Hanson Peters for one of these booklets and have placed it in our library.

My grandfather, P. I. Railey, was secretary of the company who owned the iron foundry at Owingsville, in Bath County, and many of the early settlers of Woodford owned stock in the company. I presume the Peters family were interested in the stock and that that was the inducement that led Judge B. J. Peters to locate there and practice law. I am told that the old books kept by my grandfather are in good shape and carefully stored there. This foundry was famous in its day.

I would like to know how many of the citizens of Woodford County know that the Peters family settled on 2,000 acres in the "Big Sink" about 1790 to 1809, and that the vicinity was known as "Petersburg" until after the Mexi-

can War. I knew of it as a boy, but it has taken five years to gather the data here used.

Berryman.

In September, 1925, page 355, I gave brief outline of the Berryman family, but didn't know at that time that the descendants of John Henry Berryman, who married Jane Railey in Woodford County in 1819, were entitled to membership in the Daughters or Sons of the Revolution, as John H. Berryman's grandfather, James Berryman, died in 1772, and his father, James Berryman, Jr., was too young, but the wife of Clifford Berryman, of Washington City, has recently called my attention to some papers she discovered in the state library at Richmond, Va., during a visit on research work. She mentions Tyler's Quarterly, 1923, Vol. 5, No. 1, which quotes from an old MSS. book the statement that "Sarah Dishman Berryman, widow of James Berryman, gave material aid to the Revolution by furnishing clothes, horses and money for the soldiers of King George County, Va., during the war," therefore all of the descendants of John Henry Berryman and Jane Railey are entitled to membership in either of the above orders. Many of them are still living in Woodford County. So any of them wishing to enter either of the above orders will use the following names and dates of ancestors back of the children of John H. Berryman and Jane Railey;* James Berryman, born Jan. 12, 1716, died Jan. 25, 1772, married Sarah

---

*Also on names of John Railey and Elizabeth Randolph; Ensign Thos. Railey and Martha Woodson; and Col. John Woodson and Dorothy Randolph. See pages 360-61, 377.

Dishman 1752, she born April 5, 1733, died April 19, 1812; their son James Berryman, Jr., born March 28, 1764, died May 23, 1812, married October 15, 1787, Margaret Sthreshley, born Sept. 23, 1768, died December 22, 1819; their son, John Henry Berryman, born Aug. 9, 1792, died May 17, 1874, marreid Aug. 9, 1819, Jane Railey; she born in 1794, died Nov. 28, 1865. You can consult the Register published by the Kentucky State Historical Society, Sept., 1920, and you will find the names and dates of all of the descendants of John Henry Berryman and Jane Railey, beginning at page 56, col. 2, then including all pages to page 60, col. 1.

This is the concluding chapter of the History of Woodford County, which has appeared from time to time in the "Register" of the Kentucky Historical Society since January, 1920. I have regretted the lack of co-operation upon the part of many, and whatever of error or lack of perfection exists is chargeable more to the indifference of other interested parties than to myself. While I have paid but little attention to diction, I have tried to assemble as many facts as possible without embellishment to serve future as well as present generations.

I love Woodford County because it was the adopted home of my great grandparents in all lines, and the birthplace of my grandparents and parents, as well as of this humble scribe. Their bodies are mouldering into dust beneath the county's green sward, but their names have been affectionately inscribed upon the pages of her history by this scion of honored antecedents. Peace to their ashes, and treasured be the memory of their deeds of benevolence and well spent lives. They are all good citizens.

Many of the citizens of Woodford County were urged to write a brief history of the county before I was approached. I reluctantly yielded to persuasion to undertake the work, but now that it is completed I am more than glad that I undertook it. I feel quite sure that it will not prove to be labor's love without an echo down the vista of time, as it has already proven a friend in time of need. The "Woodford Sun" gave through its columns ten knotty questions for the school children to answer in June, 1925, and many of them came here with their teachers and with a few minutes perusal of my Woodford County History had the answers to all of those questions.

After my body has returned to mother earth that gave it, if any one cares to use my work as a foundation upon which to build a more perfect superstructure, they will do so only through the consent of the Kentucky State Historical Society, as Woodford County, my birthplace, is very dear to me.

Five Railey brothers settled in the old Grier's Creek Church neighborhood about 1790 and furnished the land and most of the money that built the church. To them I dedicate this work. It is finished and will await a time when, it is hoped, the good citizens of the county will have it printed and distributed over the county.

Very truly,
Wm. E. Railey.

In writing a sketch of the Strother and Hawkins families on page 143, col. 2, par. 2, I said that Jeremiah Morton's wife was Judith Coleman, a sister of Thomas Coleman who married Susanna Strother Hawkins. I remembered that my maternal uncles and aunts always spoke of them as uncle and aunt Morton, when referring to them, and I asked Mrs. Annie Miles, a daughter of Isham Keith Hawkins, the maiden name of Mrs. Morton. She told me it was Judith Coleman, sister of Thomas Coleman, and, so I wrote it. But it is more than likely a mistake. Mrs. Wade Hampton George informs me that her name was Judith Moore, and as she is a descendant of Jerry Morton and his first wife, I am sure she is right.

January, 1920, Register.

Mr. William E. Railey, now Assistant Librarian of the Kentucky State Historical Society, has yielded to the solicitation of a number of prominent citizens that he write the history of their own county of Woodford. The first chapter appears in this issue of the Register. We hope the citizens will lend their assistance in gathering the data for the history of their county, long regarded as one of the wealthiest counties in Kentucky, and bearing the sobriquet, "The asparagus bed of the bluegrass." Its wealth and distinction will be written of, and where it is possible, the genealogy of its citizens will be given.

Mr. Railey as a writer is scholarly, direct, and most pleasing to readers of history. His genealogies have been sought throughout the United States, and enjoyed because they are correct and reliable, in their lines and dates, and the style is so simple and clear, one is not confused with elaboration and repetition, that so often tire the reader of genealogies. Mr. Railey desires that every good citizen of Woodford will assist him to make the history one of the best and most valued county histories in Kentucky.*

THE WITHERSPOON GOLDEN WEDDING.

Attended By 500 Guests—Notable Event In Woodford's Social Annals.

(Woodford Sun.)

The celebration of a golden wedding is, of course, a rare event, but it was not its rarity, but the profound esteem felt for the couple celebrating it, which brought nearly 500 people—many of them from a great distance—to Glenartney, the beautiful country home of Mr. and Mrs. Lister Witherspoon on Monday afternoon and evening.

No one who greeted this handsome pair—both of them representatives of distinguished families famous for their brave men and beautiful women—could fail to be impressed with the fact that they looked too young to have been married fifty years ago. The beautiful devotion of Mr. and Mrs. Witherspoon to each other has kept them young in face and heart, and the happy event spoke eloquently of the power of Love.

Glenartney's hospitable rooms were

---

*Mrs. Jennie C. Morton was the Editor of the Register, and Secretary-Treasurer of Kentucky Historical Society, and paid the author the above compliment.

adorned with Southern smilax, ropes of evergreen, and with yellow chrysanthemums. An orchestra furnished music.

Just across the road gleamed the lights of Stonewall, the historic Viley home (the residence of Col. Breckinridge Viley), where half a century ago the Rev. Cadwallader Lewis united Lister Witherspoon and Miss Nettie Viley in marriage. The officiating minister and all the attendants at that wedding have passed on except Mrs. Fannie Witherspoon (nee Gatewood), of Lawrenceburg, who would have been present Monday but for the recent death of her son.

Mr. and Mrs. Witherspoon stood under a wedding bell in receiving their guests: Receiving with them were their son, Warren V. Witherspoon and Mrs. Witherspoon, of Lexington; their two daughters, Mrs. M. A. Buffington, of Fall River, Mass., and Mrs. O. L. Alexander, of New York; Mr. Buffington, Mr. Alexander, Mrs. Ben F. Roach, of Harrodsburg; Col. and Mrs. Breckinridge Viley, Col. B. H. Cameron, of Raleigh, N. C., a kinsman of the family.

A delicious supper was served by Benedict, of Louisville. The ices and cakes were in gold and white and the cakes were marked in icing with the dates, "1869-1919."

The couple were remembered with many beautiful gifts.

The Lexington Herald says: Mr. and Mrs. Lister Witherspoon celebrated their fiftieth wedding anniversary on Monday with a reception in the afternoon and evening at Glenartney, their home in the country, near Versailles.

Glenartney is a wonderful, beautiful old place with spacious halls and rooms and wide verandas and situated in a woodland. It is just opposite the place where Mrs. Witherspoon, who was before her marriage, Miss Nettie Viley, was born and reared.

For the golden wedding the house was elaborately decorated in yellow, white and green, with Southern smilax, ropes of evergreen and festoons of yellow flowers over the doors and windows, on the stairway and chandeliers. Quantities of yellow chrysanthemums were placed all about and a wedding bell suspended under which the bride and bridegroom of fifty years ago, a very unusually handsome couple, stood to receive their guests. They were assisted in receiving and entertaining by their children and grandson, Mr. and Mrs. Warren Witherspoon and Lister Witherspoon II, of Lexington; Mr. and Mrs. Alton Buffington of Fall River, Mass.; Mr. and Mrs. Oakley L. Alexander, of New York, and by Mrs. Witherspoon's brother and wife, Mr. and Mrs. Breckinridge Viley.

The hostess wore a gown of white lace and satin and carried a bouquet of bride's roses and yellow chrysanthemums. The other ladies of the receiving line were all beautifully gowned.

A delicious supper was served, the ices, cakes and bonbons being all in the gold and white and marked with the dates 1869-1919.

The host and hostess received a large number of handsome gifts and good wishes from friends far and near.

Hundreds of guests were present for the afternoon and evening from Versailles, Woodford County and the surrounding places and a few from distant states.

The Register takes pleasure in reproducing from the Woodford Sun and Lexington Herald the above accounts of the golden wedding of Mr. and Mrs. Lister Witherspoon, of Versailles. Mrs. Witherspoon is one of the vice presidents of the State Historical Society, and has for many years been one of the Society's valued friends.

We extend our congratulations and wishes for many more years of happiness and usefulness to this distinguished couple.

—Editor.

On page 60 you will find a sketch of the Fleming family. That family descended from Col. William Fleming, a Scotchman who settled in Virginia, at an early date. The Governor, of Virginia, appointed him Land Commissioner of the District of Kentucky, soon after the Revolution. In the course of his duties as Commissioner he met one William Butler of Kentucky who was a land-owner. Butler was a fugutive from Virginia at the age of 16 years for having killed his rival, Wm. Veach. His real name was Simon Kenton. After a short diplomatic talk with Col. Fleming about Virginia people and affairs, he learned that his rival Wm. Veach had recovered and was hale and hearty, so he unbosomed himself to Col. Fleming and had him to see that the title of his land was transferred from William Butler to Simon Kenton. See Collins, vol. 1, p. 17. Also Biographical Encyclopedia of Kentucky,

page 781, and Register of the Kentucky State Historical Society, 1923, page 64.

Henry L. Martin Young at Eighty.*

When Robert Browning wrote of the last of life as being the best, he must have had in mind such lives as that of Henry L. Martin, Sr., of this county, who celebrated his eightieth birthday on Tuesday of last week.

Having led a long life of usefulness and of happiness, Senator Martin continues to lead such a life after fourscore years. No stranger could imagine that he is eighty, and we don't believe he realizes it himself. Surrounded by everything which can promote human happiness, he possesses within himself those qualities without which all other blessings are vain.

We think Mr. Martin is one of the most fortunate men we have ever known. He has had a very full and rich life, and has been blessed with the intellectual qualities, the vitality and the intense interest in life which double every pleasure, and which enable one to go triumphantly over the rough places. He has been a brave Confederate soldier, a banker, a politician, a business man and a farmer. He has farmed the rolling acres surrounding his beautiful old home, "Calumet," near Midway and he has been a sugar planter in Louisiana. He has been engaged in large business enterprises in cities far apart as Louisville and New Orleans. He served as a member of the Kentucky Senate in most stirring and exciting times, and was also as familiar with politics in the national capital as

*See page 67.

MISS FLORENCE S. BERRYMAN

with politics at Frankfort. The writer will never forget how as a young man he sat spell-bound, listening to Senator Martin tell to a few friends the story of his fight at Washington for the sugar planters of Louisiana.

While serving in the state Senate, Senator Martin was within almost a hair's-breadth of being sent to the United States Senate, although not a candidate. Afterwards, in 1898, he was the nominee of the gold standard Democrats for U. S. Senator. It was perhaps the most fortunate event of his life, so far as its felicity is concerned, that he did not go to Washington. Had he entered national politics, he might have been even more useful, but could not possibly have been so happy.

May he celebrate many more birthdays in the fine old home which forms such an admirable setting for the dignity and substantial worth of its owner, enjoying the companionship of his charming wife, the devotion of his children and that high respect from his fellow men which has always been his.

—Woodford Sun.

The Little Lady of the Decorations. 1920.

Register Kentucky Historical Society.

By W. E. Railey.

There lives in the city of Washington a young lady who has not yet reached her 19th birthday, who, doubtless, is a member of more patriotic societies than any other young lady in America, and is heir to several others as soon as she reaches her 21st birthday, that age being the only requisite to eligibility, as

her mother is now a member of those societies and her rights descend to the daughter. This young lady is Miss Florence Seville Berryman, who enjoys the unique distinction of having already established an unusual number of ancestral lines entitling her to membership in the various societies organized to commemorate the chivalry, valour and heroic deeds and incidents pertaining to the Revolutionary and Colonial periods.

She has twelve lines for Revolutionary service already established and they are represented by twelve gold bars attached to the insignia she wears on stated occasions of the Daughters of the American Revolution, and the names of those twelve loyal patriots who were her forebears are as follows: Robert Church, Kentucky and Virginia; Col. John Woodson, Virginia; Col. John Dickinson, Virginia; Capt. William Sthreshley, Virginia; Capt. Samuel Steele, Virginia; John H. Oliver, Kentucky and Virginia; James Thacker, Virginia; Rev. Jeremiah Moore, Virginia; Capt. Samuel MacPherson, Maryland; Joseph Fearson, Maryland; Attovix Fearson, Maryland, and William Shaw, Maryland.

She also has pending for confirmation, papers almost completed showing services rendered in behalf of the revolution by John Upshur, Virginia; Col. John Railey, Virginia; James Dishman, Virginia; James McClung, Virginia; John McClung, Virginia; Francis Renneau, Virginia; William Moore, Virginia, and George Newman, Maryland. These papers only lack a few dates and a little clarifying as to the character of service rendered before confirmation by the proper D. A. R. authorities.

She was a member of the junior order of the D. A. R.'s for several years but transferred her membership to the D. A. R.'s, October, 1917, and in the spring of 1918, when the National Congress of the Daughters assembled in Washington she was delegated one of the pages. She was again appointed one of the pages upon the convening of the Congress in the spring of 1919, and at both sessions she attracted much attention on account of her youthful appearance and the number of insignias she wore, the delegates dubbing her "The Little Lady of the Decorations," and other terms as expressive, which compliments she received with characteristic modesty and that sense of dignity that left her unspoiled.

Besides being a very youthful D. A. R. she is perhaps the youngest member of the Colonial Dames in any of the states, being a member of the Virginia Society of the Colonial Dames of America, entering that society through Col. William Randolph's name, associated with the names of Henry Isham, Richard Kennon, Capt. Joseph Royall, Dr. John Woodson, Col. John Woodson, and Col. Isham Randolph of the Colonial period—all Virginians.

She is also a member of the Colonial Dames of the 17th century through the names of Dr. John Woodson, Adam Dickinson and Col. Robert Woodson, and is a member of the Colonial Daughters through John Newton, who arrived in America prior to 1671, and is a

member of the United States Daughters of 1812, through Capt. William Church, Capt. Thomas Railey, James Thacker and Capt. Samuel Steele, and her papers for membership in the order of the Golden Horseshoe have been filed and accepted, but she cannot be initiated until she is 21, when she will become a full-fledged member through John Berryman, who arrived at the Tide Water section in 1654 and held numerous offices.

Miss Berryman and her mother, Mrs. C. K. Berryman, have been very successful in historical research and have secured much rich lore in the way of genealogical nuggets. Mrs. Berryman is a member of the Huguenot Society of N. Y.; the Daughters of the Order of the Cincinnati of N. Y.; the Order of the White Crane, and the Order of Lafayette, to all of which the daughter is heir when she reaches the required age.

Miss Berryman is the daughter of Mr. C. K. Berryman, the popular newspaper man and cartoonist of Washington City, who enjoys not only the acquaintance, but the friendship of many of our noted men. He was born and reared in Woodford County, Kentucky, where he has many friends and relatives who take great pride in his success. Although he has maintained a residence in Washington for a decade or more, where his duties claim all of his attention, he is still a Kentuckian, "for a' that," and he and his interesting family take great pride in the affairs of the State and the welfare of its citizens.

Soldiers of Woodford County War of 1812.

The names of these soldiers of the War of 1812 were taken from General Sam Hill's roster in possession of the Kentucky State Historical Society at Frankfort. They were taken from the following pages of that book: 30, 31, 117, 120, 122, 126, 203, 204, 212, 214, 216, 232, 250, 251, 262, 263, 270, also a book containing commissioned officers, pages 137, 147, 227 pertaining to services of Moses Hawkins, Jr., who was an officer.

Capt. Virgil McCracken, Lieut. Thos Brooks, Ensign Henry Stone, 1st Sergeant Geo. W. McClary, 2nd Sergeant James H. Bowman, 3rd Sergeant Saml. Steele, 4th Sergeant Nathaniel Mitchell, 1st Corp. James Brooks, 2nd Corp. Edward B. Merideth, 3rd Corp. George Pugh, 4th Corp. William Brown, Bugler Wm. Reardin, privates Robt. Atwood, Wm. Bevis, Augustus Bryan, Thos. B. Bell, A. Buchannon, John Brown, Anderson Brown, Alexander Brooks, Robt. Bell, Collins Bartlett, John Christopher, Seth Cook, James Caldwell, Thos. Daugherty, Wm. Dickey, Reubin Ford, George Henton, Francis Hawkins, Alexander Latta, Ellis Lee, Solomon Mitchell, Samuel McGuire, James McKnight, Orvid McCracken, Garrett Morgan, Archibald Mitchell, John Mosley, Wm. H. Nall, Wm. Peacock, Lewis Palmer, Joseph Pace, Asa Pitman, Joel Pace, William Railey, Jr., George W. Railey,* Abraham Resler, Henry L. Rowland, Silas Raney, John Read, William Rooney, Nehemiah Reddin, Robt. Stevenson,

John Stone, James Slocum, Thos. G. Summers, Calmer Spencer, Robt. Scroggins, George Smith, John Scroggins, John Steele, Leonard Searcy, George Stucker, Thos. Stansberry, Merrett Searcy, Wyatt Stapp, Lewis S. Todd, Lewis Y. Tutt, Dan'l Vasvill, Wm. Williams, John Williams, Robt. Wooldridge, James Willmin, Merritt Young, Richd. M. Young. Page 30 Roster War of 1812.

Another Woodford County company was that of Capt. John Christopher, Lieut. Solomon Dunnegan, Ensign Thos. W. Sellers, 1st Sergt. Francis W. Cook, 2nd Sergt. John F. Cook, 3rd Sergt. Silas Johnson, 4th Sergt. Willis Long, 5th Sergt. Arthur Gregory Young, 1st Corp. Merritt Young, 2nd Corp. Wm. Wooldridge, 3rd Corp. James L. Russell, 4th Corp. John Hawkins, privates Fielding Arnold, Levy Ashford, Thos. Ashford, James Baker, Benj. Berry, Jr., John M. Bingley, Saml. P. Bowdry, Wm. Brittenham, Saml. Brooking, Joseph Brown, Marquis Calmes, Perry Carroll, Strother Coleman, Wm. Conover, James Cox, Wm. Dawson, John Donnald, Alexander Dunlap, Jr., Acre Dunegan, Obediah Easley, Thos. P. Elgin, McClanihan Elkin, Strother Elkin, Robert Elliott, Isaac Felix, Wm. Florence, John Frazer, Richd. Gaines, Reubin Garnett, John Garrett, Wm. D. Gay, James Gibbony, Isaac Gray, Cornelius Coleman, John Kirby, Robt. Lankford, Fielding Lewis, James B. Long, Zachary Long, Benj. McQuaddy, Carter McGhee, John McGuire, Richd. Manning, James Morris, Nicholas Moseby, Danl.

O'Brien, John Parker, James Paul, Jess Poore, Randolph Railey, Jr., Lyvand F. Rucker, Joseph Sellers, George Smith, Allen Smith, James Smith, Jno. W. Smith, Dick Son, James Spaulding, James Spillman, Wm. Stephenson, David Stanford, John Stone, Vivion Terrell, Latte Tilberry, John Walker, Wm. Walker, Nathaniel W. Walker, Saml. Watkins, Saml. Wharton—Page 120 Roster War 1812.

In Capt. Mason Singleton's company of Jessamine County, were the following privates from Woodford County: Saml. Holloway, Jesse Roper.

Joel Henry of Woodford County was captain of a company organized Mar. 29, 1813, which was a part of Col. Wm. Dudley's regiment, but afterwards transferred to the regiment of Col. John Francisco, of Midway, Ky. July 12, 1813, Capt. Joel Henry was promoted and his brother Zachary was elected his successor with Isaac Howard, Lieut.; Benj. Hiter, Ensign; Lemuel Ford, Sergt.; Geo. W. New, Sergt.; Thaddeus Wilson, Sergt.; Joseph George, Sergt.; Anthony Samuel, Corp.; John Gill, Corp.; John Latta, Corp.; Wm. Bardin, Fifer. Privates—James Armstrong, John Allen, Isaac Baylor, Thos. Benson, Joseph Clark, John Coleman, John Craig, Jesse Dale, Elijah Dale, John Dale, Walker Garrett, Richd. Graves, Thos. Hudson, Rody Hudson, Saml. Hunter, Wm. Johnson, Wm. Lafon, James Malone, Gilbert Mastin, Joel D. McDaniel, Alfred Metcalf, Waid Mosby, Thos. Mosby, Benj. Oliver, Robt. Poore, Seth Porter, James Scott, James Searcy,

Henry Sheats, Benj Smither, John Stevenson, Saml. Stevenson, Wm. Steele, Danl. M. Stout, Arthur Sublett, Littleberry Sublett, Acy Veach, Chas. Weathers, Wm. Wilson, Thos. Wilson, Bledso Watts, Henry Ward, Burket G. Yancey, Geo. Yancey—page 103 and 4 Roster 1812.

On Sept. 18, 1812, Capt. Zechonia Singleton commanded a company of troops and the following Woodford countians were under his command: Solomon Donegan, Sergt.; Thos. W. Sellers, Sergt. Privates—Wyatt Arnold, John Armstrong, Thos. Blanton, James Cunningham, John Cave, John Dale, Absalom Graves, John Hackney, Robt. Poor, Henry Shouse, Lewis Sublett, William Sublett, James Sublett, John Sublett. Littleberry Sublett, James Stevenson, Wm. Shouse, Wm. Stevenson, Saml. Torbett, Edward Turner, Vivian Terrell, Wm. Utterback, James Walker, Zachariah White,* Wm. Walker, Wm. Wilson, Philip White. Between September and October, 1814, Col. John Francisco was absent from his regiment, the 11th, and Major Zechonias Singleton, who had been promoted to Major was acting Colonel of the 11th regiment, and on September 1, 1815, Colonel in command of the 11th regiment. John and David Calahan fought in the War of 1812 under Capt. Joseph Straughan and came to Woodford and kept bachelors' hall until about 1866, when both died on what was afterward known as the McClellan farm near Griers Creek Church. Thos. Edrington and Moses Hawkins of Woodford County served in the

*As a boy I knew personally Col. Zach and Capt. Phil White, John and David Callahan, J. C. Frazier, and Capt. Peter Dudley; also Col. Kemp Goodloe.

company of Capt. Lyddall Bacon of Franklin County. Andrew Muldrough served in the company of Wm. Croutch. He was a kinsman of Joel C. Frazer who fought under Col. Andrew Porter.

On page 109 appears the name of Col. Kemp Goodloe, on page 214 Larkin M. Samuel and Chapman Coleman are in the company of Capt. Peter Dudley of Frankfort. Col. John Francisco of Midway appears on page 262 with the name of Geo. W. Reed. James and Wiley Brassfield can be located on page 126 under Capt. Isaac Cunningham.

Wiley Brassfield also appears on pages 113 and 125.

Joseph H. Woolfolk was a lieutenant in Capt. Micah Taul's Company (page 74), and an Ensign in Capt. Abraham Miller's company (page 151) and also in our book of commissioned officers (page 163) as a captain. Sowyel (Sowel) Woolfolk, Jr., appears among commissioned officers as a lieutenant on page 145. John Woolfolk was with General Winchester as aid and was killed at "River Raisin."

The Kentucky Historical Society has a roster that recorded only the commissioned officers of the state militia. Col. John Francisco of Midway, Ky., (see page 168) is quite frequently mentioned in this roster as you can see by referring to pages 24, 58, 61, 99, 108, 121 and 140, when he commanded the 11th regiment in War of 1812.

Richard Cave served in the company of Capt. Leaman, and later in the company of Capt. Sebree as you will see on pages 208 and 212, General Hill's roster. The Woodford County soldiers were frequently transferred from one company to another, presumably to be with congenial associates.‡

On page 160 I stated that Jere Morton's wife was *Judith Coleman, but later I learned that it was a mistake which I corrected on page 360. I am in receipt of additional history of the Mortons that will show that I was in error. The wife of Wade Hampton George sent me this additional history and I am giving it here.

At the time I wrote the sketch of the Mortons I was not able to go back of Jeremiah Morton who settled at Mortonsville, but the above lady has put me in position to run the family back another generation in Kentucky.

The first of the name to come to Kentucky from Virginia and settle in Woodford County was John Morton, and he arrived about 1790 and settled near the present site of Mortonsville, and he lived there until his death in 1810. His will probated that year mentions his wife, Sarah, his sons, James, Jeremiah, John Benjamin, William and Thomas, and his daughters, Frances Watts, Ann Rucker and Lucy Haden. It is presumed these children were born in Virginia and came to this state with their parents as their names appear on the court records soon thereafter.

William, the fifth son of John the pioneer, died during the year 1826, and his will mentions his wife, Elizabeth Moore, and his children, Reuben, Simeon, Sally, Ann Eliza, James Hawkins, Elijah, Joseph, Jeremiah, Jr., and Lucy White. The above William Morton was

‡See page 400, Jo Railey also served.
*Judith Moore.

a Revolutionary soldier who was drawing a pension in 1810. Many of his descendants live in Anderson County, the Rev. Dudley Moore, the popular Baptist minister, being one of them.

Jeremiah Morton, son of John, and brother of the above William, was the founder of Mortonsville as stated in my former sketch, page 160. His first wife was—Rowzee, who was mentioned in deeds as late as 1812. As a result of this marriage two daughters were born. Nancy married Abner Rucker, and Lucy married Isaac Wilson.† Jerry Morton's second wife was Judith Moore, to whom he was married in 1819, but there were no children by this marriage. Three of Judith Moore's sisters lived in the vicinity of Mortonsville. Hannah married Allen Hieatt (see page 57) in 1813; Elizabeth married William Morton, and Sally married Thomas Morton in 1793, the same day that his niece, Nancy Morton, married Abner Rucker.

Judith Moore Morton died in 1829. Allen Hieatt and Reuben Morton were the executors of her estate. In her will she made bequests to her three sisters mentioned above. Noah Haden, son of John Haden, and Lucy Morton witnessed the will of his uncle, Jerry Morton, Sr.

Knowing that the Ruckers were among the early settlers of Woodford County, and that they were quite numerous and popular, I made an earnest effort to include them in my sketches but failed at that time to get sufficient data to write a saisfactory account of them. Later I found that Mrs. Wade

Hampton George was a descendant, and as she delights in research, I persuaded her to interest herself in gathering data pertaining to this family. This sketch is the result of her efforts and it is a very creditable result. It follows:

The Ruckers are of early Teutonic origin. Members of the family proudly display today the coat-of-arms of Johann Von Rucker in 1096. He was an Austrian who was the founder of the family and a member of the First Crusade.

Descendants of his may be found in all countries of Europe, and there are fourteen Rucker Coat-of-Arms, all showing their descent from one granted to the head of the family in 1096.

The first of the name in America was Peter Rucker, but whether he belonged to the English or French branch remains to be proven. He was naturalized by the Virginia Burgess in 1704 and married Elizabeth Terrill in Orange County, Va. He died in that county in 1743. Many of his descendants came to Kentucky with the first settlers.

Captain Anthony Rucker, son of Peter the emigrant, received land in Kentucky for services in the Revolution, yet he never came to the state but died in Amhurst County, Va. However, his son Abner Rucker came and in 1793 married Nancy Morton, one of the two daughters of Jerry Morton in the vicinity of Mortonsville. They had seven children, namely, Betsy, Agatha, Anthony, Jeremiah, Jr., Jefferson, Julius and Jonathan. His wife, Nancy Morton, died and Abner Rucker married Nancy ——, by whom there were two children, Rebecca and Dolly. Rebecca was named for her grandmother, Rebecca Burgess, the wife of Captain Anthony Rucker.

It was the custom in those days for relatives to marry and the Ruckers observed that rule as you will notice. Agatha Rucker married her cousin, Isaac Rucker, son of John Rucker and Sally Plunkett. This John Rucker and the Rev. James Rucker, the Baptist minister mentioned in the history of the "Ten Churches," were brothers, and their line of descent from Peter Rucker was Peter Rucker and Elizabeth Terrill of the first generation; then John Rucker and Susanna Phillips of the second (this John Rucker being a captain who received 5,850 acres of land in Virginia from the King of England for services in the Indian war); then John Rucker and Eleanor Warren 3rd (this John Rucker was killed in battle during the Revolution and was a brother of Captain Anthony Rucker).

The children of John Rucker and Eleanor Warren were: 1st, Rev. James Rucker who married in 1749 Nancy Morton (not the daughter of Jerry Morton); 2nd, John Rucker who married Sally Plunkett; 3rd, Sally Rucker who married William Pendleton in 1769; 4th, Susanna Rucker married Reuben Cowherd; 5th, George Rucker who married Martha Tucker; 6th, William Rucker who married Sally North in 1782; 7th, Elizabeth Rucker who married Dan'l North; 8th, Isaac Rucker who married Minty Ogden; 9th, Nellie Rucker who married John Morton in 1786. These children represent the fourth generation from Peter the Emigrant.

John Rucker and Sally Plunkett had nine sons and two daughters, all reared in Woodford County. They follow: Rachel, born 1774, died 1805, married John Rucker; Ahmed, born 1775, died 1840 in Jessamine County, married Nellie Rucker Barnett; William, born 1780, died 1854, married Sallie Morton; John, born 1772, married Eliza Burton; James, born 1784, died 1845, married first Sallie McDaniel, second, Polly McDaniel; Joshua, born 1786, died 1858, married first Elizabeth Chambers, second, Margaret Yost (a kinswoman of Elizabeth, the wife of Col. Thomas F. Marshall); Isaac, born 1788, died 1856, married Agatha Rucker; Benjamin, born 1790, died 1859, married first, Melinda Rucker, second, Eliza Walker; Mildred, born 1792, married James Rucker; Lewis, born 1794, died 1869, married, first, Margaret Goddard, second, Amelia Bracamp.

John Rucker, the father of these children, is listed as a Revolutionary soldier living in Woodford County in 1810, but at the time of his death in 1814 he was living in Fayette County.

Isaac Rucker and his wife, Agatha Rucker, had four children, Nancy Jane, Martha, Edwin and Susan. Nancy Jane never married. Martha married Charles Ware of Shelby County; Edwin married ――― Daniels and moved west, since when nothing is known of them; Susan M. Rucker married James Hudson of Fayette County in 1861. This couple had an only son, William Henry Hudson, who lived in the old Rucker home at Mortonsville, the home of his ancestors for four generations. He sold it in 1920 and moved to Franklin County where he now resides. He married Emma Bond, daughter of the Rev. Preston Bond and Melinda Arthur of Anderson County. They have three children, Leva Ware who married Wade Hampton George; James Bond who married Caroline Vincent Noel of Frankfort, and Susan Belinda Hudson who married Fred Ward of Indianapolis, Ind. Wade Hampton George and James Bond Hudson are both now residents of Woodford County.

The Morton and Rucker names were familiar in Woodford County as late as the Mexican war period, but are now only a memory, the only living descendants known to me are the two families named above.

The Ruckers are remembered as intensely religious—stern and puritanical in their piety.

The Rev. Ahmed Rucker was the first local Methodist preacher at Mortonsville. He built his church that stood where the graded school now stands, built of logs, and for many years it was known as Ahmed Rucker's Church. In the log part of the residence of Isaac Rucker, on the McCoun's ferry pike, recently sold by W. H. Hudson, near Mortonsville, Bishop Kavanaugh held meetings when he was a young circuit rider.

The descendants of the Woodford County Ruckers are living in many states, and a number of them have been eminently successful. One branch emigrated to Chicago when it was but a town and have attained distinction.

Cecele Noel Hudson of Woodford County and Nannie Louise Ward of Indianapolis, are of the ninth generation from Peter the Immigrant.

————

Isaac Wilson, Jr., who married Lucy Morton, daughter of Jeremiah Morton, Sr., was a son of Isaac Wilson and Eliza Cook, who were married in Culpeper County, Virginia, in 1793. (See Culpeper, Va., page 74, paragraph 2). He, Isaac Wilson, Sr., served in the Revolution as a Corporal for three years, and he and his wife came to Kentucky by way of the "Wilderness Road" and received 200 acres of land in Rockcastle County, bringing their young son, Isaac, with them, the child being strapped to a pack-horse. This son grew to man's estate and migrated to Woodford County, where he met and married Lucy Morton, sister of Nancy Morton, who married Abner Rucker. (See Morton sketch.) They remained in the vicinity of Mortonsville for many years, but finally moved to Franklin County and settled near the Forks of Elkhorn, where they lived the remainder of their lives. Isaac Wilson, Jr., served as a corporal in Captain Edmund Bacon's company in the war of 1812, being promoted to the rank of Captain March 26, 1814. They had the following children: Benjamin Franklin, born December 15, 1816; died February 11, 1900; Isaac III, born ——, and John Wilson, born ——. Benjamin F. married Martha Wilson and had Frank, who married Elizabeth Taylor, a popular young lady of Midway, where he was in business for many years; Lucian Wilson, who married Bessie Rankin, of North Carolina, and they spend their winters in Florida and their summers in Kentucky; Dr. J. W.

Wilson, who married Mamie Erdman, lives in Frankfort, where he is a specialist in the treatment of the eye, nose and ear. They have a widowed daughter, Carroline, who lives with her parents; Mary Miller Wilson, who married Preston L. Gibson.

Isaac Wilson, III, moved to Texas and fought in both the Mexican and Civil War. His descendants live at Lockport, Texas, where they are prominent. John Wilson, the youngest of the three brothers spent much of his life in and about Lexington.

Through the efforts of Claude S. Williams, of the Mt. Vernon Church, I am able to preserve for future generations much that is worth while from the minutes of the old church referred to on page 293. In 1820 a small band of Baptists gathered on a small tract of land in Woodford County and held services in a house built for the purpose. The interior was whitewashed and a balcony constructed of plank. The church was organized with only eight subscribers and was styled the Baptist Church of Christ. Those who subscribed to the articles of covenant were, Randolph Harris, Henry Cassell, Joseph Eddings, Mary Cassell, Nancy Eddings, Mary Moffett, Mary Conover, and Milly Eddings. This organization became effective June 1, 1822. It was at this time that Tavner Branham and David Harris made deeds to the land, each giving a half acre, and both tracts deeded to D. J. Williams, Alexander Dunlap, John Glanton, David Harris, and Robert Adams, Trustees, and they solicited money for the construction of the house of worship which cost

$1,350.00, and they superintended the construction.

James Fishback was the first pastor at a salary of $100.00, payable semi-annually. He served the congregation until November, 1838, giving the congregation one Sunday each month for several years, then two Sundays, but finally gave all of his time.

Randolph Harris was an early deacon, Henry Wallace, Clerk, and David Harris was treasurer. Henry Wallace resigned in 1829, and J. F. H. Crockett was elected. David Harris died in 1830, and Henry Wallace succeeded him.

In the early '30s this congregation joined the Elkhorn Baptist Association although solicited to join with the First Baptist Church at Lexington. Later they found that many of the members of the Elkhorn Association were deeply impressed with the views of Alexander Campbell and they retired from that Association, and united with the First Church at Lexington, but in 1840 reunited with Elkhorn. For several years the Mt. Vernon congregation was undecided as to whether it should have elders, finally deciding they would not.

During the early period of the church they observed the ceremony of communion quarterly, then every two months, but later decided to participate once a month, and that is the custom of today.

In 1824 Robt. Adams was elected a deacon, and during 1830 Branham and Bennett were added to the board. In 1834 —— Branham was elected clerk, Christian succeeding him on the board of deacons. The same year Henry

Wallace, James Bennett, and Robt. Hicks were appointed trustees. One year later James Craig and Jonathan Hager were added to the board. In 1837 M. F. Rice was elected treasurer, and in 1838 Robert Hicks was made a deacon.

The Rev. James Fishback resigned the pastorate after 17 years of faithful and successful work. He was succeeded by the Rev. James Frost in 1839, and during that year William H. Harris was elected clerk and Jonathan Hager was installed as one of the deacons.

The first Sunday School was organized in 1828, and the Woman's Missionary Society was organized the year before, as was the Indian Mission by the men of the church, and they did a great work in that field.

The Rev. Lyman W. Seeley was called to preach for the congregation March 1842. He accepted the call and was ordained in July of that year and preached every fourth Sunday in each month, the pulpit to be occupied by visiting ministers the other Sabbaths, including Broadus, Dillard, Hewitt and Frost. In 1844 Bennett and Davis superintended the Sunday School.

The Elkhorn Association met with Mt. Vernon in 1845, and William Duvall was made a deacon. In 1846 J. M. Davis was elected to succeed Jonathan Hager as church clerk. The same year Spencer Anderson donated a plot of ground for burial purposes, making William Price, L. Praul and William S. Harris trustees. John Stout and John Branberger were added to the Board of Deacons. William S. Harris was also added to the board in 1847. J. W.

Goodman agreed to occupy the pulpit that year, but not as a regular pastor.

In 1852 Rev. Pratt and Rev. Combs were called and agreed to preach one Sunday each during every month. In 1853 John Stout and J. M. Davis were elected trustees to fill vacancies occasioned by death of Robert Hicks and resignation of Willis Price.

In 1854 the Rev. D. B. Campbell was called and he accepted, with the understanding that his services were not to begin until 1855. During that year James Blackburn was dismissed for fighting a duel. B. W. D. Seeley was elected a deacon, and Asa Payne succeeded J. M. Davis as one of the trustees. Newton Alexander, Thomas S. Williams, and Willis Price were elected deacons to fill vacancies.

In 1856 G. W. Williams resigned as clerk, and Robert Risk succeeded him. During that year Elkhorn Association met in the woodland of Thomas Steele. In 1857 Newton Alexander resigned as trustee and Thomas S. Williams succeeded him. In 1859 license was granted James A. Orr to preach.

In 1860 Rev. C. R. Campbell resigned the pastorate, and the Rev. J. W. Crawford accepted a six months call. That year the church decided to select its deacons annually, and chose John Stout, J. M. Shipp, Robt. Risk, W. Price and B. W. D. Seeley. At a later date Robt. Risk resigned and H. G. Williams succeeded him.

In 1862 the Rev. William M. Pratt was called and accepted the pastorship. In 1863 William S. Harris resigned as deacon, and H. G. Williams gave up the clerkship. S. M. Shipp was elected as deacon, and B. W. D. Seeley accepted the clerkship. The next year Messrs. Stout and Drake were chosen to act jointly as superintendent of the Sunday School.

Rev. William M. Pratt resigned as pastor in 1865, and the Rev. L. B. Woolfolk supplied for the remainder of the year. In 1866 he was unanimously called to serve the church as pastor, but in 1869 the congregation called the Rev. Cadwallader Lewis. During that year the Rev. Amos Stout was granted license to preach.

In 1872 Robert Stout was cited to appear before the board for engaging in a fight in Midway, and the result was a settlement that was satisfactory to both parties. During the year Robt. Stout, Hammond and wife, Lacey and wife, sisters Peper and Kertcheval were granted letters to assist in the organization of a church at Midway to which the Mt. Vernon congregation subscribed $150.00 for building purposes.

In 1874 the Mt. Vernon church subscribed $1,440 in bonds to locate and build a Theological Seminary in Louisville. During the year 1877 Mrs. Julia Thomson gave to the church a beautiful communion service of silver for which thanks were duly expressed and noted on the minutes. (I think she afterwards was Mrs. W. Viley.)

In April of that year the Elkhorn Sunday School Convention was held at Mt. Vernon, and the Union, Pisgah and Bethel schools united in the exercises.

In 1884 Mt. Vernon Church was remodeled, and in 1891 a splendid parsonage was built. In 1893 the weakened condition of the old church was discovered and immediately two committees were appointed, one on building composed of C. S. Williams, Colvin B. Patterson, F. P. Drake, and another on finance composed of W. D. Drake, Warren Wheeler, C. B. Patterson, and C. S. Williams. The personnel of these committees was a guarantee of success, so by 1895 the old landmark disappeared and the splendid new building that supplanted the old, which is a monument to the memory of the above committees, was dedicated April 30, 1895, and the dedicatory service was preached by the Rev. C. O. Dawson.

The following distinguished men, once citizens of Woodford County were later of the citizenship of Logan County, Kentucky. Their names appear on the records of that county between the years 1797 and 1820. William B. Blackburn (see pages 33, 61 and 172) was in Logan County as early as 1797; John J. Crittenden (see page 49) in 1804; Presley O'Bannon in 1807. The latter lived only a short period in Woodford County with his brother, Major John O'Bannon, prior to his Tripoli experience (see pages 41, 72, 244, 272, 301, 356). The two latter were in Woodford through youth and young manhood, Blackburn nearly his entire life.

Presley O'Bannon represented Logan County in House of Representatives in 1812, 1817, 1820, and 1821, and in the State Senate in 1824 and in 1826. He married a granddaughter of General Daniel Morgan and was at one time in affluent circumstances, but his social nature and prodigal spirit robbed him of his fortune and left him almost penniless. However, his bravery at Tripoli wrote his name high on the scroll of fame where it will be read by unborn generations.

William B. Blackburn migrated to Logan County as early as 1797 and engaged in the practice of law. He remained in that county only a few years when he returned to Woodford. The record shows that he represented the latter county in the Legislature in 1804 and was in either one or the other branch of the Legislature until 1838. (See pages 22 and 23.) A very good account is given of him on pages 172 and 173.

John J. Crittenden studied law under, and practiced that profession with Judge George M. Bibb in his law office at Russellville about 1804. In 1811 he represented Logan County in the Legislature, and the next year entered the army as an officer in the War of 1812. At the conclusion of the war he returned to Logan County and again represented that county in the Legislature for six consecutive terms, elected Speaker of the House in 1815 and 1816. In 1817 he was elected to the United States Senate, but resigned in 1819 and removed to Frankfort where he spent the remainder of his active years. He was again Speaker of the Kentucky House in 1829 to 1832, after which he was again elected to the United States Senate where he remained many years, from which he was once drafted for the Governorship, and several times by the Presidents to serve as a Cabinet officer.

He died at the home of his daughter, Mrs. Chapman Coleman, of Louisville, in 1863, well advanced in years and full of honors.

Todd.

Judge Thomas Todd was born in King and Queen County, Virginia, January 23, 1765. He was one of the sons of Richard and Elizabeth Richards Todd, both of English ancestry.

The Biographical Encyclopedia of "Old Kentucky Families" says briefly that he, upon his arrival in Kentucky was engaged by his old friend, Judge Innes, to teach his children in the home in Frankfort, he to remain as one of the family in that home. While instructing the children, he was himself receiving instructions in law from that eminent jurist who had employed him to look after the education of the children.

Judge Todd was appointed clerk of the Federal Court of the District of Kentucky, which position he held until 1792, when he was appointed clerk of the Court of Appeals. This position he held until 1801. He was later appointed one of the judges of the Court of Appeals, where he remained until he succeeded to the position of Chief Justice. In 1807 he was appointed Associate Justice of the United States Court, where he remained until his death, February 7, 1826.

During the period that I was devoting all of my spare time and energies to sketching the pioneer families in 1920 and 1921 who settled in Woodford County, I was aware of the fact that Todds were associated with the early history of the County, but was not in touch with any one who knew any facts in connection with their residence in the county—only heard of them in a casual way, so I made no mention of them in the earlier sketches. Recently, however, I had a talk with Admiral Chap C. Todd, a retired officer of the Navy, who is sojourning in his native town of Frankfort, where he is renewing the friendship of other days.

Incidentally I asked him if his father, Captain Harry I. Todd, was born in Woodford County. He said: No, I think not; but my grandfather, John Harris Todd, son of Judge Thomas Todd, was. He was born on the farm seven miles out of Frankfort on the Versailles road near Grassy Spring Church, which Judge Thomas Todd owned as early as 1795, perhaps earlier. The farm he said had gone under several names since his great grandfather sold it about 1808, first as the Lafon home, then as the Jackson place, and for more than a half century known as the Elijah Fogg farm. The splendid old residence which stood there for nearly a century was built of brick that were pressed on the premises. When the building was razed thirty years ago or more, marks on the rafters bore date of 1795, and he likely lived in a temporary frame building while the brick house was in the course of construction. This farm joined the old Railey farm that is now the home of Arthur Crutcher.

Judge Thomas Todd married Elizabeth Harris in 1788 and lived on the Woodford County estate until about 1808, when the health of his wife became so impaired by the demands of farm life that he sold the estate to Captain Nicholas Lafon, of Frankfort, (see page 36) and bought property in Frankfort to which he moved his

family. His wife died there in 1811, and he married the following year Lucy Payne Washington, widow of George Steptoe Washington, nephew of the President, she a sister of the wife of President Madison.

Judge Todd had by the first marriage these children: Charles Stewart, born 1791, married Letitia Shelby, daughter of Gov. Isaac Shelby in 1816; John Harris, who married Maria K. Innes; Ann married Edmund Starling, and Elizabeth, who married John H. Hanna. By the second marriage were: James Madison Todd, who married Allisonia Rennick, and Johnson Todd, who married Mary Willis Rennick.

Descendants of Charles Stewart Todd are now living on the farm in Shelby County given his wife by Gov. Shelby.

John Harris Todd and his wife, Maria K. Innes, had these children: Harry Innes, Elizabeth Ann, Catharine Lucy, and Thomas Todd.

Harry Innes Todd married Harriet Davidson. He was a prominent business man of Frankfort for many years and represented that county in the Legislature during the '70s, and was warden of the State Prison for several terms, during which time he was in close touch with the farmers of Woodford from whom he purchased the entire hemp crop of the county. They had these children: Harriet, who married J. W. Pugh; Ann Innes, who never married; John H., who married, first, Bonnie Brodhead, sister of Lucas Brodhead of Woodford, second, Annie Bennefellet; Chapman C., who married, first, Ann Mary Thornton, second, Elizabeth James; Harry I., Jr., who never married; Julia Maria, who re-

mained single; George D., who married
Laura Durkee; Mary Hanna, who married J. L. Watson; Kitty Thomas, who
married Dr. Samuel Holmes, and R.
Crittenden Todd, who married Willie
Cotton. Of the above children of Capt.
Harry I. Todd, Chapman C. served in
the Navy for forty years, and is today
enjoying the leisure of a retired Admiral. He will spend much of that
time in Frankfort, where he was born,
and where he can refresh the memories
of his childhood and silently stroll
through the city of the dead on the
beautiful hill, where so many of his
friends and kindred will sleep until the
resurrection morn. His son, Chapman
Todd, Jr., is now an active officer of the
Navy.

George D. Todd, fourth son of Capt.
Harry I. Todd, located in Louisville
about forty years ago and was very successful in business. He was elected
Mayor some years ago. Recently he
came to Frankfort, and while here
made a trip to the old home in Woodford County where, in the old burying
ground he located the graves of many
of his relatives whose remains he had
disinterred and removed to the family
lot in the Frankfort cemetery during
the year 1927. The family used the
Woodford County burial ground for
several generations.

On December 7, 1927, some months
after the above was written, Admiral
Todd came into the rooms of the Kentucky State Historical Society to see if
we had any history relating to Judge
George Muter, of Woodford County. I
gave him my Woodford County History to see what I had briefly written

about Col. Muter. He was referred to
on pages 8 and 58. After reading my
sketch of that soldier and jurist, he said
that he had just returned from the old
Todd home near Grassy Spring, and
while looking over the old burial lot,
he discovered other graves of his relatives, and stumbled upon a headstone
bearing the name of Judge George
Muter, who was a close friend of Judge
Thomas Todd, both having served on
the Appellate Court, and said he would
also have his remains removed to the
Frankfort lot at the time he had his
relatives removed. Said further, that
Judge Muter was not only a welcome
guest in both the Frankfort and Woodford County homes, but spent much
time during his declining years with
the Todd family. He confirmed my
surmise in the sketch I had written
where I said it was likely that Judge
Muter was a bachelor, as I could find
no trace of wife or children. I am inclined to think that the Muter home
was in the vicinity of Judge Todd's
home, likely near Ducker.

---

*The Rev. Richard Cave was a Bap-
tist minister who arrived in what is now
Garrard County about 1781 and settled near the town of Lancaster, but
removed to Woodford County about
1784 and settled in the Clear Creek
vicinity. He and his family came with
the "Traveling Church" to Kentucky.
He was one of the charter members of
the Clear Creek Baptist Church in
1785. (See pages 290 and 312.)

As early as 1785 some very able
preachers had addressed that congregation, such men as James Rucker, John

Dupuy, John Taylor (he of the "Ten Churches") and Richard Cave. (See page 290.) This church was near Troy and is one of the oldest in the county.

The Rev. Richard Cave married Elizabeth Craig, daughter of the first Toliver Craig and Mary Hawkins, both of whom were in the besieged fort at Bryan's Station. (See pages 124 and 127). They had five children in 1810, and owned sixteen slaves, but one of his children I am not able to account for.

Richard Cave died early in 1816, and his will was probated in November of that year. It only mentions three of his children, John, Mary and Richard, but says that others had been provided for. It is well known that Hannah Paige Cave, who married John Graves in 1790, was a daughter of Richard Cave and Elizabeth Craig. Richard, Jr., married Sally Woods, but no record of John having married at all. I have seen no record of the fifth child at all. There was a Henry Cave, who married Peggy Hawkins in 1790, and a William Cave, who married Peggy Threlkeld in 1789, but they may have been sons of Reuben Cave, who came with Rev. Richard to the county.

John Graves and Hannah Cave had in 1810 nine children, and owned nine slaves. (See pages 76 and 312). He was born in Culpeper County, Virginia, in 1768, and died in Woodford County in 1824. (See the Graves family.)

In 1791, while Kentucky was yet a part of Virginia, the Legislature of that State passed the following act: Be it enacted by the General Assembly that an inspection of tobacco shall be, and same is hereby established on the lands of James Wilkerson at Frankfort in the County of Woodford, to be called and known as the Frankfort Warehouse, the proprietor whereof shall build the same at his own expense.

At a little earlier period an act passed the Virginia Legislature providing that one hundred acres of land, the property of James Wilkerson, which have been laid off into lots and streets, shall be vested in Caleb Wallace, Thomas Marshall, Joseph Crockett, John Fowler, Jr., John Craig, Robert Johnson, and Benjamin Roberts, gentlemen trustees, and shall be established a town by the name of Frankfort.

By the above act the citizens of Woodford County of today will understand that the tobacco industry was a factor in the business interests of the county during infancy, so to speak, as well as at this time, and Frankfort was then in Woodford County.

———

When the first Circuit Court was established in Woodford, the Commonwealth's Attorney, Humphrey Marshall, had a rude log house built in 1789 that cost the modest sum of $22.50, and it was used until a stone building supplanted it two years later. The third building erected was to accommodate both the district and county courts, and was built of brick, so say the Draper papers.

———

John Hudson came to Woodford County with the very earliest of the settlers with his wife, bringing with them a small son whose name was Thomas. The pioneer raised a family of children in the county. When

Thomas reached his majority year he married Jennie Cavender, and they had eight children, of whom Robuck was the second, born Oct. 2, 1817. In 1826 the family moved to Boone County, Mo., when Robuck was just nine years old. Thomas Hudson died there in 1844, and his wife died in 1856. Robuck moved to Howard County, Mo., in 1850. He married Mar. 17, 1842, Mary Washington Preston, of Clark County, Ky. Of this union seven children were born, four of whom are now living. They are, Mary C. Cassandra, Joella and Ida Lee Hudson.

The above notes were sent to me by Mrs. Paul Klayder, of Neodesha, Kansas. (See page 56), who copied it from a history of Boone and Howard counties, Mo. She has written a history of the Buford, Twyman and Kindred families

---

Captain Jack Jouett, born in Albemarle County, Virginia, December 7, 1754, died in Bath County, Kentucky, Mar. 1, 1822, was an officer in the Revolution, and for his bravery and famous all-night ride, in which he thwarted the British officer, General Tarleton, in his effort to capture Gov. Thomas Jefferson and the Virginia Legislature.* Tarleton left "Old Cuckoo Tavern" in Louisa County, Virginia, on one route to Monticello, and Captain Jack Jouett, a little later, took another route and beat the doughty General Tarleton to Monticello, in time to get Thomas Jefferson and nearly all of the Legislators to safety.*

Captain Jack Jouett came to Mercer County, Kentucky, in 1782, and married Sallie Robards in 1784. He represented that county in the Legislature in 1792, but soon thereafter moved to Woodford County, where he took an active interest in business and politics. He represented Woodford in the Legislature during the sessions of 1795-96, and 1797. (See page 23.)

His son, Matthew Jouett, second of twelve children, was born in Mercer County, April 22, 1788, and of course was a mere boy when he came to Woodford County. He developed into a lawyer of fair ability but devoted the greater part of his time in developing face and form on canvas, and of course developed into an artist of the first magnitude.

Capt. Jack Jouett, it is said, was noted for his fine physique, being six foot four, and also for his well poised mind.†

It is not known to this scribe when he left Woodford County and returned to Mercer, but likely before the census of 1810, as his name does not appear in that census. He later moved to Bath County, where he died.

Matthew Jouett, Sr., and his wife, Susanna Moore, were the grand parents of Capt. Jack Jouett, and it was from their "Old Tavern Cuckoo" that the famous ride was made to Monticello. Captain Jack Jouett was the son of Capt. John Jouett, who served in the Continental Army, and his mother was Mourning Harris.

The "Old Tavern Cuckoo," of the

---

*For which he was given a gold sword by the Virginia Legislature.
*The first of this sketch is taken from a little booklet by Mrs. Wm. B. Ardery, of Paris, Ky.
†Dan'l M. Bowmer located his farm between Griers Creek and Kentucky river near Mortonsville.

elder Matthew Jouett, was so named because of the fact that the first cuckoo clock brought to Virginia hung on its walls.

The ancestors of the Jouett's were French Huguenots, who bore the name de Jouett, of Touraine, France.

Capt. Jack Jouett's mother, Mourning Harris, was the daughter of Robert Harris, who was descended from Sir. Wm. Harris, one of the incorporators of the third Virginia charter, who was knighted at White Hall in the year 1603, and whose son, Thomas Harris, came to this country as early as 1611. On his mother's side, he was the grandson of Col. William Claiborne, first secretary of the Virginia colony.

You will note that the mother of Captain Jack Jouett was Mourning Harris. If you will turn to page 135 you will see that the sixth child of Harrison Harris, a Revolutionary soldier of Virginia, who settled in Woodford County about 1786, bore the name Mourning Harris. So it is my judgment, and is reasonable, that these two Harris families had a common source not far back, but no mention was made of it when the Harrison Harris line sent me the data that entered into the sketch, beginning on page 134, notwithstanding the fact that the two families came to Woodford County about the same time.

John Gilbert Mastin, whose descendants have long been prominent in the affairs of Woodford County, where their homes have been noted for generosity and hospitality, and whose sons have volunteered their services in every war of the Nation, was born in Kent County, Delaware, Oct. 27, 1793. He was the son of John and Priscilla Hopkins Mastin.

Orphaned in early childhood he was brought by his uncle William (?) Hopkins to Woodford County where he lived until his death about Dec., 1867. His family and descendants have lived for three generations in the old homestead on the McCracken's pike in the vicinity of Glenn's Creek Baptist Church, with which congregation they always been identified as members.

In the War of 1812 John Gilbert Mastin served in the company of Captain Joel Henry, regiment of Col. William Dudley. He took part in the engagements at the River Raisin, Dudley's defeat and others, and witnessed the massacre of his comrade William Hutton, whose sister he later married, at the Rapids of the Ohio. Many Kentuckians were brutally killed at both of those battles. William Hutton was buried at Ft. Meigs.

Himself a prisoner of the Indians, Gilbert Mastin was compelled not only to run the gauntlet, but to sit by the campfire and listen to their tiresome jargon. During one of the campfire experiences the Indians imbibed too freely of an intoxicating fluid, which so stupefied them that they did not observe young Mastin when he slipped out of the camp, but they soon discovered his absence and sent out a pursuing party which made the trail so warm that Mastin was compelled to plunge into a stream, which he crossed in safety, and was soon in a friendly camp where he was protected.

He returned to his home with several wounds that crippled him for life, but his spirit of perseverance was undaunted, even in his declining years as this scribe well remembers.

He was twice married, first to Sarah Hutton, daughter of Henry Hutton, a Revolutionary soldier, and wife Hannah Woods, the heroine mentioned by Collins and other historians. She was one of the pioneer mothers of the Commonwealth, and of the "Wilderness Road." The family annals relate an incident in her life at her home near Crab Orchard where Indians sought the life of a child. Coming to the rescue with an axe she felled the leader and put the others to flight as she sounded the alarm.

After the death of his first wife, Sarah Hutton, in 1883, John Gilbert Mastin married Jane Miller, a niece of his first wife. She died in 1894 surviving her husband many years.

By the first marriage were these children: James Hutton Mastin, who had no children; John W., who married, first Martha Morris, second, Eliza Jane Cammack, and Bettie, who married John Rearden.

By the second marriage were Sarah Jane Mastin, who married William Boyette; William Henry, who married Thomson Ann Hawkins; Ann Mary, who married Davis W. Edwards; Robt. G., who married Mattie Hammon, (see page 114, and George Hutton Mastin, who married Bettie Veach, of Shelby County.

John W. Mastin and Eliza Jane Cammack had John C., who married Cecile Henderson, to whom was born a daughter, Marie, who died when quite young; Gilbert Mastin, who married Daisy Mason and had Charlotte and Gilbert,

Jr. The latter is a bachelor; Charlotte married Guy Vanzant and they have three boys, Gilbert, Guy, and Mason. Lucien Mastin, son of John W. and Eliza Jane Mastin never married, and his sister, Bettie Mastin, married Harvey Bain.

Bettie H. Mastin and John Rearden had Kate, Martha, Lizzie, Price, Sally, William, Robert, Dennis, and James.

The children of John Gilbert Mastin and Jane Miller, his second wife, had the following descendants: Sarah Jane and William Boyett were childless; William Henry and Thomson Ann Mastin had William H., Jr., who married Flora Williams and had Stuart and Shirley; Fannie B., spinster; Ruth S., who married Irvin Mantle and had Murry S.; George R., who married Grace Murray and had Lemar; Pink married J. H. Laval and had Henry and Charles L.; Theoph S. married Lillian Taylor and had Theoph, Jr., Henry and Evaline; Ethel married Thos. E. Henton.

Ann Mary Mastin and Davis W. Edwards had John G., who married Margaret Wooldridge, and had Gilbert and Margaret; William H. married Elizabeth Cotton and had Harvey, Florence and Sarah Puryear; James Y. married Saraware Branham and had Mary, Fielding. Peyton, Francis, Rebecca, Pearl, and Virginia; Alex Edwards married Nellie Henton; Boyette married Edna Wilson and had Bertha and Boyette; Jane and Davis Edwards, who have not married.

Robert Y. Mastin and Mattie Hammon had Robert, who married Katherine Pierpont and had Geraldine and Francis; Jennie, who married Capt.

Fred Wilson and had Emmie, Scott, and Martha; Howard married Marcia Parker; Vernon married Mary Belle Edwards and had Wilyou Macey, and Howard.

George Hutton Mastin and Betty Veach had Leroy and Russell.

John Gilbert Mastin was an intense partisan in the cause of the South during the Civil War, and on account of his active support his home was raided by Federal soldiers and his crops and horses confiscated, yet notwithstanding that incident, he and his family continued to give aid to the Confederacy. His two younger sons, Robert G. and George Hutton served in Morgan's command. Campbell's company, until they were captured during the Ohio raid. They were both sent to a Chicago prison. George Hutton made his escape, but his brother, Robt. G., remained a prisoner.

The family name was represented again in the World War by Henry Stuart, and Shirley Williams Mastin, sons of William H., Jr., and Dr. Flora Williams Mastin. Each of these boys, after a creditable service, returned to their homes in Frankfort.

Lemar Mastin, daughter of George R. and Grace Murray Mastin, married Ensign Gilbert L. Parker, of New London, Conn. He was decoding officer under Admiral Oman, of Newport, Rhode Island, during the World War.

Capt. Fred Wilson, who married Jennie Mastin, served in the Spanish-American War in the command of Col. Gaither, Company D. From a Lieu-

tenant by promotions he attained to the rank of Major.

_____

Joseph Minary was born in Ireland in 1810, and came to Chester County, Penn., where he married Mary Sloan, also born in Ireland. They reared in that state these children: John Sloan Minary, Ellen, Thomas and Mary.

John Sloan Minary was born Feb. 20, 1820, died Dec. 30, 1899. He came from Harrisburg, Penn., to Versailles in 1847, where he met and married George Ann Stone in 1849. They raised in Woodford County children as follows: *Thomas Jay Minary, born 1850, went to Louisville in 1872, where he identified himself with the City Railway Company. His efficiency caused his promotion, and in 1902 he was elevated to the Presidency, which he held until about 1923 when his resignation was accepted, but he was immediately drafted as Chairman of the Board of Directors. He married Amelia Stephens, July, 1876; Charles Kearns Minary, who married Margaret Bowmer in 1901; Joseph Sebastian Minary married Lizzie L. Jett, of Frankfort, in 1890. She died in 1914, and he married, second, Isabel McLeash; Mary E. Minary, who resides in Versailles; †George B., who married Lula M. Graves, October 27, 1904, and William Sloan Minary, who remains a bachelor.

Thomas J. Minary is a resident of Louisville; Charles K. is now, and has been for twenty years, President of the Benton Harbor and St. Joseph Ry. and Light Company; is also President of a

_____

*Died August 2, 1935.
†Died 1934.

bank at that place; Joseph Sebastian Minary is also located at Benton Harbor, Mich., where he is associated with his brother in business; George B. is established in business in Versailles where he is universally popular, and William Sloan Minary is in business in Dowagiac, Mich. All of these boys have developed into splendid business men, each of whom is a credit to the county of their birth.

George Ann Minary was a daughter of George Stone, a prominent farmer of Woodford County and his wife, Sallie Cotter, and a granddaughter of Sebastian Stone, and his wife, ———— Reeves, who came from Virginia to to Woodford with the pioneers, and he was the owner of a large tract of land on the Versailles and Midway road.

———————

A branch of the Woolfolk family of Virginia came to Woodford County just after the Revolution, and the head of that family was Sowel Woolfolk (the Census of 1810, on page 9, has it Loyel) who married Mary Harris in Virginia. They settled on a large estate, said to be 2,000 acres at Elm Corner. The census above mentioned gives him a family of five, and twenty-two slaves.

They had these children: Joseph Harris Woolfolk who served in the war of 1812 and married Martha Mitchum; John, who also fought in the war of 1812 on the staff of Gen'l Winchester and was killed at the River Raisin, in which battle he was highly complimented by that officer for bravery; Sowel Woolfolk, Jr., served in the war of 1812 and married Sallie Bowman, and they were residents of

Fayette County, living on Harrodsburg pike; William never married, and a daughter married ———— Givens of Boyle County.

The "Oak Hill" farm upon which Col. Joseph Harris Woolfolk lived after his marriage in 1816 was a part of the original tract of his father, Sowel Woolfolk, whose country seat was, after his death, owned by Clough Harris who married his daughter Martha M. Woolfolk. This farm remained in possession of descendants until 1914, when it passed out of family ownership.

Col. Joseph Harris Woolfolk was born 1788, married Martha Mitchum in 1816, and died in 1860. Their children were: John Harris Woolfolk who married 1st Florida Ricks, 2nd Sallie V. Marshall; Dudley Mitchum Woolfolk, who married Sallie B. Woolfolk, daughter of Sowel Woolfolk, Jr.; Susan married David Barrow; Bettie married Albert Harris; Martha married Clough Harris; Sarah married Greene Cowles Meade; Joseph Sowel Woolfolk married Lucy Dupuy Craig; Margaret never married, and Elizabeth died at sixteen years.

Martha M. Woolfolk and Clough Adams Harris had seven children. Their names were Mary Elizabeth who married Paschal Thomas of Louisville. They had two children, Joseph W. and Madeline; Flora Harris who has never married and resides in Lexington; John W. Harris who died at Arcadia, Florida; Martha M. Harris who married Joseph Minter Gregory of Memphis, Tenn.; Margaret Woolfolk Harris married William F. Davis of Lowell, Mass. They have Carl S. and Walter Harris

Davis; Susanna Barrow Harris married Archibald M. Robinson of Louisville. They have a daughter Edith G. who married in 1916 William M. Wood, Jr., of Boston, Mass., and they have Ann Dorris Worthington and William M. Wood, Jr., III. Mrs. William M. Wood, Jr., married 2nd Harry Boon Porter and is now a resident of Louisville.

Sarah Woolfolk and Greene Cowles Meade had a daughter, Adah M. Meade, who married Daniel Saffarans and resides in Chicago. They have a daughter, Adah Saffarans.

Descendants of Sowel Woolfolk and Mary Harris, like most of the descendants of the early settlers, are now widely scattered and may be found in Illinois, Missouri, Tennessee, New Mexico, West Virginia and many other of the states.

An interesting story in connection with "Oak Hill," the country home of Col. Joseph H. Woolfolk, near Elm Corner, appeared in the Woodford Sun, May 10, 1928, and I am using it here by consent. It follows:

VENERABLE LANDMARK PASSES.

Oak Hill Stone Dwelling, Over 130 Years Old, Long the Home of Woolfolk Family.

May 10, 1928.

Oak Hill, the old Woolfolk home, near Elm Corner, a noted two-story stone dwelling, the main part of it believed to be more than 130 years old, has been dismantled by its owner, W. B. Boston, who will rebuild on the site a two-story home of modern arrangement, also constructed of stone. Much of the material from the old house will be used. The foundation has been partly completed by Stephen Sallee, of Wilmore.

Oak Hill was a remarkable relic of the sound construction of and the substantial materials used in building houses in the pioneer days. It was built of white stone, cut by hand, taken from what is now the Gosser farm, originally a part of the Woolfolk estate. The walls were about 18 inches thick, with deep embrasured windows. All joists and rafters were hand-hewn. Pegs were used and hand-wrought nails. The timbers were massive. A timber in the comb (or ridge) of the roof was 42 feet long, 13x12 inches, a solid piece. The window casings were of cedar, the door casings black walnut, the stairway hand-carved poplar, the floors ash and oak.

Although so solidly built, and fitted, it would seem, to endure for centuries, a portion of the house had begun to give way, as even the solidest structures sometimes will, and Mr. Boston, therefore, decided to tear it down and start over.

From Mrs. Ada M. Saffarans, now living in Chicago, (who spent her childhood at Oak Hill) we learn that her grandfather, Joseph Harris Woolfolk, a young officer in the war of 1812, bought the Oak Hill estate in 1815; that he was married in 1816 to Martha Mitchum, daughter of Dudley Mitchum, prominent and wealthy land owner of Woodford County, and brought his bride of 17 to his home. (Dudley Mitchum was the maternal great grandfather of John, Dudley M. and How-

*ard Ball). Joseph H. Woolfolk had several brothers, one of them, Sowel Woolfolk, the owner of an immense estate. Joseph H. and Martha M. Woolfolk had nine children: (1) John Harris; (2) Dudley Mitchum; (3) Susan Barrow, who married David Barrow of Louisiana; (4) Betty, wife of Albert Harris, of Virginia; (5) Martha, wife of Clough Harris of Virginia; (6) Sara, wife of Green Meade, of Mississippi; (7) Joseph Sowel; (8) Margaret, never married; (9) Eliza, died at 16. Joseph H. Woolfolk died in the early '60s. His widow remained on the farm until 1871, when she went to Lexington to live in a handsome home that her son, Joseph S. Woolfolk, built for her. She died in 1888 at the age of 91.

Joseph S. Woolfolk in 1877 bought the interests of the other heirs in Oak Hill estate, which at that time comprised 934 acres. He sold the place in 1889 to R. Harvey Risk, of Scott County. The late R. B. Boston bought Oak Hill in 1901 and made his home there until his death, in March, 1919. The late Beverly P. White bought the property from Mr. Boston's executors. W. B. Boston, son of R. B. Boston, has owned the place since 1923.

Mrs. Saffarans a few years ago wrote the following poem to the old home of her people:

The Old Stone House.

Way down mid the rocks and the crannies
Is a house that was built long ago;
And deep in the heart of its shelter
Are figures and faces I know.

The old house stands in the woodlands.
Remote from the strife of the town,
Far back from the roadway it stands,
A silhouette picture in brown.

In the halls and in chambers they gather,
These dear ones so loved by me,
No sound, not a step whatsoever,
They only are ghosts that I see.

I hear in the twilight their laughter,
Their swift feet flit to and fro,
But only a hush follows after,
A whisper that creeps soft and low.

My old stone Castle of Dreams,
And legends I see through a blur,
Embalmed in their mystical beams,
''Are my tears of Cassia and Myrrh.''

A. M. SAFFARANS.

Dudley Mitchum was born July 2, 1759, and married Susan Allen Feb. 10, 1779. They came to Kentucky and settled on a farm near Elm Corner, in Woodford County, and the farm is now in possession of his great grandsons, the Ball brothers, whose names appear on page 32 under Maple Hill.

Dudley Mitchum and Susan Allen were blessed with the following children: Sallie, born Mar. 28, 1780; married James Craig; James, born Dec. 24, 1784, married Polly Craig; William, born June 12, 1787, never married; John, born Jan. 31, 1789, married Peggy ———; Nancy, born Aug. 12, 1792, married Noah Hayden; Elizabeth, born June 25, 1795, married Samuel Steele; Patsy, born Aug. 20, 1797, married Joseph H. Woolfolk; Polly, born June 2, 1800, married John Bowman; Susan, born Feb. 15, 1804, married 1st John Ball, 2nd Dr. Hall.

Sallie Mitchum and James Craig had Eliza, Luanda, Susan, Jemima, Sallie and Elijah Craig.

James Mitchum and Polly Craig had Lucy, Susan and Sallie. Lucy married Judge R. C. Graves (see page 312). They had James who married Katherine Chrisman; Laura who married B. W. Wasson; Flora and John Graves. James Graves and his wife Katherine Chrisman had Lula, who married George B. Minary; Lena who is not married; John T. who married Pattie Elmore; Charlton, who is not married, and Belle who married Joseph Burk.

Laura Graves and B. W. Wasson had Lucy, Mary, Joe, Florence, James, Laura and Bessie.

John Mitchum and Peggy ——— had Willie, Claude and two daughters who married Dudley and John Steele.

Nancy Mitchum and Noah Hayden had Mary, Anne, Bettie and Dudley Hayden. Anne married Will Stone whose son, William G. Stone, married Belle Railey, daughter of Logan Railey and Harriet Rowland. Their children were Hadley, William, Charles Logan, and Cornelia Stone.

‡And House of Representatives.

Elizabeth Mitchum and Samuel Steele had Dudley, John and Sue Steele.

Patsy Mitchum and Joseph H. Woolfolk had Sue, Dudley, John, Mattie, Bettie, Sallie, Maggie and Joe. Sallie married Daniel Saffarans of Chicago, and had Ada Saffarans; Joe married Lucy Craig. See Woolfolks for other descendants of this line.

Polly Mitchum and John Bowman had John Dudley, Hite and Josephine, the latter adopted.

Susan Mitchum and John Ball had Dudley (page 32), Will, Maria and Sue. Maria married Robert Gray and had Ben, Dudley, Bob and John Gray.

Susan Mitchum and Dr. Hall had Bettie, Alice, Ben and Jemima.

———

Thomas Francis Marshall and Jo. C. S. Blackburn represented the Ashland District in Congress, the former before the Civil War, and the latter after the ‡war. Senator Jo. C. S. Blackburn also served for about 18 years in the United States Senate. J. N. Camden was also in the United States Senate during the term of Gov. James B. McCreary. Jo. C. S. Blackburn was Governor of Panama during the Roosevelt Administration.

———

The following story as to Woodford County, Ill., was taken from a newspaper, and inasmuch as that county was named by Woodford County, Kentucky pioneers, and inasmuch as Abraham Lincoln was born in Kentucky, I will ask you to turn to page 297 and read of Bullocks.

Old Metamora, Ill., Courthouse Last Where Lincoln Practiced.

*Metamora, Ill., July 12 (By A. P.)— Sentinel-like in the middle of a business block, facing a shady square in a peaceful village, stands the "house of giants," old Woodford County courthouse, known as the last existing hall of justice where Abraham Lincoln practiced law.

It is the only courthouse of pioneer days remaining in the old eighth judicial circuit of Illinois, covered by Lincoln in his days as a circuit riding lawyer in the forties and fifties.

Its appellation was acquired from the frequent visits there of such figures as Stephen A. Douglas, Robert G. Ingersoll and Lincoln.

Many are the tales told by pioneers of the tall, magnetic young lawyer who tried cases often in the courtroom and achieved considerable local fame as a story-teller in the old Metamora tavern after court hours.

The courthouse was constructed when Metamora won a fight for the county seat. Later the town lost the distinction and the old structure was deeded to the state of Illinois. Now it is a Lincoln shrine.

Native forests furnished the timbers used in the structure. The roof is of hand-split walnut shingles. The timbers are sawed oak and walnut logs. Finished for use in 1845, it was the pride of the community and the envy of other towns.

Within the massive brick walls the voice of Lincoln was heard at almost every term of court from 1845 to 1857, the old docket shows.

Ingersoll enjoyed a large practice before the bar in the old courthouse. Judge Samuel H. Treat was the first jurist to hold court in the newly organized county. He afterward became a Federal judge. See pages 119, 297.

In the sketch of the Hawkins family† I only included two of the children of Benjamin Dabney Hawkins and Jane Watts for the reason that I was not able to get in touch with descendants (see Strothers, page 145). Recently I met a great granddaughter who gave me this information and I am sure it is correct. (Mollie) Mary Jane Hawkins married her cousin, William Watts. They had four children, one of whom was Elizabeth Lee Watts. She married A. J. Crutchfield, and their daughter, Stella Watts Crutchfield, married Nody Starkey. They reside at Pikeville and are in comfortable circumstances. She has done much research work and is well posted as to all of her lines.

These are additional names of Woodford Countians in War of 1812: David Alexander, James Hervie Bowmar, Charles Bradley, Gen'l Jacob Castleman, James Gay, John Garrett, Guy Henton, John Hurst, Harry Hurst, Capt. James Meade, Thomas Sellers, Edmund Shipp, Thomas Shouse, John Steele, Samuel Steele, Col. John Steele, Sam'l Stevenson, Joseph F. Taylor.

*See pages 121, 302.
†See page 147.

MEXICAN WAR.

Abraham Buford and Col. Ezekiel Field.

When I announced on page 354 that my efforts on a Woodford County History were at an end, I did so of course with a mental reservation. At that very time I was working on the lines of several old families and one old church that I was anxious to include, but with varying prospects of success that were not encouraging, but during the last year several opportunities to extend my knowledge of those people enabled me to extend my work about thirty pages, which I am very glad to do even at the increased cost of printing.

I wish to say to the descendants of these old families that it is my sincerest hope that my work may inspire in them a compelling impulse to take up their individual lines and extend them on paper you can paste in the back of my book. By this means you will enable someone in the future to write a more complete work.

As I said before, if any one in the future wishes to use my work as a foundation for a bigger and better history of the county, they must get the consent of the Kentucky State Historical Society to whom I delegate such right.

Very truly,
Wm. E. Railey.

Let me here direct the attention of the boys and girls, and the young men and young women of the county to a few men who were born and reared in the several neighborhoods who have won high places in the business and professional world. They are Henry L. Martin, Sr., John P. and Isaac Starks, Dr. A. J. A. Alexander, Thomas Minary and his several deserving brothers, Cliff K. Berrymen, Judge Davis W. Edwards, Leslie Morris, Alexander Henry, R. Ward Macey, Sr., Claude S. Williams, Dr. Alford Blackburn, and last but not least, the Bowmar brothers. May it please those who have charge of the educational interests of the county to study the life of each of those men and point the students to the accomplishments of each in their several lines of pursuit.

The students could render no better service than by studying the life of each of them, then write an essay setting forth the merits of each to be published in the Woodford Sun. Each of these men ordered by return mail from one to three of my books, and I wish you could read their encouraging letters. They have accomplished wonders and I am delighted that each was born and raised in Woodford County.

Their lives are not only worth studying, but their conduct worth emulating. My greatest regret is that I have not done so much as they for humanity and Christianity.

The people of Woodford County should feel a great pride in the fact that the county has been so signally honored by the election of so many native born and adopted sons to the Governorship. On page 109 of this book, I gave an account of Governor Scott, a native of Virginia, who came to Woodford County at the conclusion of the Revolution and was elected Governor in 1808. On page 382 you will see that John J. Crittenden, though elected to the Governorship from Franklin County in 1851, was born and reared in Woodford County, and owned the ancestral home when elected to that office. On page 33 you will see that Dr. Luke P. Blackburn, though elected Governor from Jefferson County in 1879, was not only born and reared at Spring Station but practiced his profession at Versailles for many years. And, the latest citizen to receive this honor is Albert Benjamin Chandler who, though born and reared in Henderson County, was elected Governor from the County of Woodford in 1935.

So Kentucky has had two Governors who were natives of Woodford, and two Woodford Sons by adoption. Can any other county produce such a record?

Albert Benjamin Chandler was born in Henderson County, July 14, 1898. Here he received his elementary and high school education, paying his expenses by selling newspapers, and by other various jobs in the community. Even at this early age he showed the "singing spirit" which later found expression in the well-known name "Happy Chandler."

The determination to go to college readily pushed aside difficulties which to others seemed insurmountable. The well-known "five dollar bill, a red sweater and a smile" being his stock in store when he knocked at the door of Transylvania College. Here he received his A.B. degree having worked his way, achieving outstanding success in athletics, and displaying many qualities of leadership. Three years later he received his Bachelor of Law degree at the University of Kentucky, having studied one year at Harvard and two at Kentucky.

His law practice began at Versailles where he supplemented his income by coaching athletics in several schools in Woodford County, and later at Center College. He soon had a liberal clientage because his ability was readily recognized, and with meteoric speed he traveled the road to success.

He was elected to the State Senate in 1929, and as Lieutenant-Governor in 1931. His observation and study of state government during these years in office led to the formation of the high ideals of statecraft, and to the policies on which he drafted his platform in his whirlwind campaign for Governor.

Having been elected to the State's highest office with tremendous majority, he has begun his administration by rapidly fulfilling his campaign pledges. His statesmanship is evidenced in his reorganization of state planning along business lines, so that the budget is now balanced for the first time in over thirty years and the state debt is being reduced rapidly.

Realizing his need of expert advice and desiring the best of his people, he has surrounded himself with splendid co-workers who are laboring harmoniously with their Governor to make Kentucky a greater state.

Among the outstanding accomplishments of his administration thus far are:

1. The Repeal of the Sales Tax.
2. The Reorganization Bill.
3. Balanced State Budget.
4. Reduction of the State Debt.
5. Increased Appropriation for Schools.
6. Penal and Eleemosynary Reform.

For more than a quarter of a century the people of Kentucky have realized the deplorable conditions existing in their prisons and asylums for the insane. With the breaking of the ground in Oldham County on June 15, there began a program which will place Kentucky among the first states of the Union in the humanitarian care and aid of its wards both in penal and eleemosynary institutions.

As a leader, as an executive and as a man, Albert Benjamin Chandler deserves the ranking of a statesman. Kentucky will do well to carry on the noble work that he, in his short term of office, has time only to begin.

Because of the remarkable achievements of this splendid young man his two Alma Maters, Transylvania and the University of Kentucky, have recently conferred on him the honorary degree of Doctor of Law.

There is always the note of home life in the Mansion, where Happy Chandler resides with his charming wife, formerly Mildred Watkins, of Keysville, Virginia, and their four lovely children.

There has perhaps never been a more hospitable Governor and First Lady. There is a constant stream of visitors and no meal is served without some guest. Often a score or more are entertained for luncheon or dinner and each is made to feel that the party was arranged largely in his honor. The Governor and Mrs. Chandler entertain extensively and handsomely.

WOODFORD NOTES CONCLUDED.

The January number of the Register of the Kentucky State Historical Society contains the concluding chapter of Woodford County historical notes written by William E. Railey, which have appeared from time to time in the Register since January, 1920; also, an excellent full-page likeness of the author. Mr. Railey's very interesting notes are exceedingly valuable for reference and form the only extensive record in existence of the families that have made Woodford County. It is to be regretted that the demand has not been great enough to justify Mr. Railey —after his years of unrecompensed labor—in putting his sketches together and publishing them in a single bound volume.

In his final instalment Mr. Railey gives interesting accounts of the distinguished Ahby and Peters families, from Virginia. Captain "Jack" (John) Ashby was conspicuous in the French and Indian wars and was with Washington in Braddock's campaign. He located, in 1774, a 2,000-acre tract in what is now Woodford county, northeast of Versailles, and a large tract in Jefferson County. Mr. Mr. Railey mentions only one daughter of Capt. Ashby and wife, Jane Combs—Elizabeth Ashby, who married Col. John Peters, of Fauquier County, Va. The descendants of Col. John Peters and Elizabeth Ashby, some of whom are in Woodford now, have been prominent here and elsewhere in Kentucky. Judge Belvard J. Peters, Judge of the Court of Appeals 1860-1876, was their grandson.

Jane Ashby, another daughter of Captain Jack Ashby and Jane Combs, married Joseph Darneal, grandfather of the late Swift Darneal, of Versailles. They came into possession of part of the Ashby lands, including the present "Bosque Bonita" farm (owned by John H. Morris). This farm was their home and afterward the home of their son, Edward Darneal, until 1854, when it was bought by Col. "Abe" Buford.

SUPPLEMENT

OF THE

WOODFORD COUNTY HISTORY

Mrs. Theodore Harris (nee Mamie Buford Steele) paid the author of the Woodford County History this compliment soon after the book came from the press in 1929.

BRYAN STATION CHAPTER MEETS AT PISGAH

The Bryan Station Chapter, D. A. R., held its last meeting before the summer adjournment at Pisgah church, in this county, last Thursday afternoon.

Mrs. Theodore Harris, Mrs. Anna Douglas, Mrs. S. M. Stedman, Mrs. Horace Gay and Mrs. Chas. M. Harris were transferred to membership at large to enable them to become members of the new chapter in Woodford County.

Mrs. Theodore Harris delivered her very fine paper, "Memories of Old Homes in Woodford County."

Mrs. Harris, in making a special tribute to William E. Railey, said: "Before I come directly to the subject in hand I would like to say that it is not only my duty but my privilege to say a word of praise and gratitude to Mr. William E. Railey for his great work, 'The History of Woodford County,' 'a labor of love' as he calls it.

"Captain John Andrew Steele and his cousin, Mrs. Jennie C. Morton induced Mr. Railey to give it his time. Captain Steele said he knew of no one better fitted for the purpose. Truly it has proved a work of inestimable benefit, conscientiously undertaken and without remuneration. Nothwithstanding enfeebled health, Mr. Railey loved Woodford County and the people so well that he has with strong will and forceful purpose written this splendid memorial, and future generations will also deeply appreciate his book."

"In Frankfort he may be found at work in the historical rooms of the Old Capitol building, unvaryingly courteous, investing articles of vertu with that halo of the past which crowns them.

"His subject is always presented in a way that those who come to this shrine take away a lasting memory of him and his noble sentiments. May he be spared for years as an inspiration to noble work and endeavor."

Mrs. Harris of course was not aware of the hours, usually devoted to pleasure, that I sacrificed for ten years in an effort to produce a fairly good account of the privations, courage, and sacrifices endured by the pioneers in establishing a suitable government for their descendants.

If you will visit the Old Capitol at Frankfort you will find that the

"Register," magazine of the Historical Society, carried a chapter three times each year for ten years of the Woodford County History.

SUPPLEMENT

During the ten years devoted to the Woodford County History, I did my utmost to get in touch with descendants of many of the early settlers whose names appear on the Census of 1810, and many of whose descendants were in the county as late as the Civil War, but without success. I have, however, recently gotten in touch with a few of them, and will give brief sketches of each under the head of Supplement, the Vaughans appearing first.

Edmond Vaughan, Sr., was born in Virginia, Dec. 16, 1760, the son of Cornelius Vaughan who was born April 18, 1729, died Feb. 12, 1785. There were several sisters, but Edmond was an only son. He came to Kentucky at an early age, about 1780, and settled in that part of Fayette County, that became Woodford County in 1788. His farm was in the neighborhood of the Major, Blanton, Crutcher, Thomson, Samuel and Blackwell families, all of whom were sketched in my Woodford County History, and are quite extensively written of in Mrs. M. C. Darnell's sketches of "The Jett Neighborhood."

Edmond Vaughan's farm was selected soon after his arrival in Kentucky, but his residence was not erected until the establishment of Woodford County in 1788. The site is on a prominent point to your right as you travel from Frankfort to Versailles—three miles out, and it is in fair condition today.

Edmond Vaughan, Sr., was first married to Sarah Samuel about 1784, who died April 30, 1797. His second marriage was to Susanna Thomson in 1801. (See page 279.)

The children of Edmond Vaughan and Sarah Samuel were: William, John, Edmond, Jr., who married Sythy Blanton; Walker, who married Fanny Blackwell; Thomas, who married Mary Hughes, and Elizabeth, who married Samuel Tinsley. By the second marriage to Susanna Thomson were James, who married Charlotte Ashmore Hawkins, aunt of this deponent (see pages 146-7 and 280, also "Raileys and Kindred Families," page 124); and Mary Ann, who married Dandridge Crockett, Sr., whose father, Anthony Crockett, rode with General Lafayette in 1825, from Frankfort to Versailles, on a memorable occasion see page 362). Edmond Vaughan, Sr., died Sept. 24, 1823. Of the above children, John was a bachelor and lived with his brother Walker in his home until he was quite an old man. Edmond, Jr., and Sythy Blanton, his wife, had several children. One of them, Lucy, married Samuel B. Scearce (see pages 240 and 298). Mr. Scearce and his family moved to Missouri about 1870, after he sold his fine Woodford County farm. Another daughter, Sarah, married Hezekiah Winn of Woodford County, and they were the parents of popular John Winn who lost his life in an automobile accident, between Lexington and Versailles during the summer of 1932. Mrs. Winn was born Sept. 8, 1833, and died Sept. 22, 1917. (See page 282.)

"Uncle Walker and Aunt Fanny Vaughan," as I knew them in my boyhood at the close of the Civil War, were two of the most delightful old people I ever knew. Many a Sunday in my boyhood was spent in their home, listening to their interesting stories of early days in Woodford and Franklin counties. Her niece, Mary Blackwell, married Tarlton Railey, brother of Logan Railey, Aug. 15, 1839. (See Raileys and Kindred Families, page 65.)

Walker Vaughan had several children, some of whom I remember very well—John went to Louisville, where he married and was clerk of the city for many years after the Civil War. Dr. Robert also went to Louisville, where he married Miss Culver and practiced medicine after the Civil War, but finally returned to Woodford County and practiced at Grassy Spring for a time, then went to Versailles, where he practiced many years; eventually returned to Louisville in the 80's and practiced until his death. Mollie Vaughan was a very handsome woman; she married Daniel Hitt of Woodford County, but they moved to Louisville—where they died in the 90's. Ed Vaughan was the youngest; he served through the Civil War as a Union soldier, remained with his father and mother until they died in the 90's of old age, when he sold his interests in Franklin County and went to Missouri, to be with relatives, who were long-time residents of that state. He was a most lovable gentleman, and this scribe accompanied him on many coon and possum hunts in his boyhood—building fires under trees in which our game had taken refuge, until

daylight gave us the opportunity to bag our meat.

James Vaughan and Charlotte Ashmore had two sons, Edmond, who lost his life in the Nicaraguan expedition—at the time when young Crittenden refused to turn his back to the enemy, or bend the knee to any but God. His brother William married the widow of his cousin Dandridge Crockett and died without issue.

Mary Ann Vaughan and Dandridge Crockett, Sr., had several children: Dandridge, Jr., and Professor W. O. Crockett. Dandridge, Jr., had a son, Hiter, who practiced law in Frankfort for many years. Prof. W. O. (Dale) Crockett taught a male school at Frankfort for many years, where this deponent was a student, but when Captain Will Henry gave up his popular school at Versailles in the 70s Professor Crockett succeeded him, and many of the citizens of Woodford County today bear evidence of his mental, moral and physical training.

The Blackwells, I am reliably informed, lived at the intersection of the Frankfort, Versailles, and Grassy Spring roads, adjoining the Henton farm and were neighbors of the Blanton and Thomson families. The Samuel farm was on the road to Duckers and bordered on the Versailles road.

Mrs. Vaughan's neice, Mary W. Blackwell, married Tarleton Railey of Woodford County, and their daughter, Kittie Steele Railey, died at Sweet Springs, Missouri, some years ago, 80 years old. Her brother, Judge Robert Tarleton Railey, of the Supreme Court of Missouri, died some years ago at St. Louis. (See page 265.)

Daniel M. Bowmar, of the Woodford Sun, had correspondence with Mr. Henry Houston Crittenden, of Kansas City, Missouri, during 1931, with reference to converting the old Major John Crittenden home into a shrine. He is one of the sons of Governor Thomas T. Crittenden, and a grandson of Henry Crittenden of Shelby County, who was a son of Major John Crittenden of Woodford County.

In one of his letters to Mr. Bowmar he said: "I was born in Woodford County on the John M. Nuckols farm near Versailles. My mother, formerly Caroline Wheeler Jackson, was the sister of Mrs. John M. Nuckols, both being daughters of Samuel Grant Jackson." He also said that, "in order to complete your record of Major John Crittenden's family, his children were: John J., b. 1787, d. 1863, he was three times married; Thos. T., b. 1788, d. 1832, (m) Mary Parker; Henry, b. 1792, d. 1834, (m) Ann Maria Allen; Robert, b. 1796, d. 1831 (m) Ann Morris; Lucy, b. 1800, d. 1855 (m) Judge Harry Innis Thornton; Harriett, b. 1786, (m) Judge John Smith; Margarette, b. 1790, (m) John McKinney; Caroline, b. 1794, (m) Randolph Railey."

At the time of this correspondence Mr. Crittenden was associated with his two brothers, Thos. T., Jr., and William J. in the Crittenden Investment Company of which he was Vice-President. He was also a democratic candidate for Congressman at large from Missouri.

He expressed much pleasure over the effort to make a shrine of the old Crittenden Home on the Lexington road.

This is a picture of the old Crittenden home which should be an inspiration to young men to know that so many of our great men saw the light of day under such conditions and surroundings. You will find quite a sketch of the Crittendens on pages 50 and 388.

On page 36 is a sketch of the Calmes family, and on other pages are complimentary passages of General Marquis Calmes, as citizen, gentleman and soldier.

I am giving here a picture of the home in which Genl. Calmes and his family lived, and also a picture of the Mausoleum not far from the residence; both built under his supervision by his slaves, and both standing today in fair condition, between the Lexington and Big Sink roads, over a century and a half old, and within a couple of miles of Versailles. The remains of the General and his wife rest within its walls, and the Mausoleum is now cared for by the Marquis Calmes Chapter of the D. A. R., which is a guarantee that it will receive generous attention.

It is wonderful how well preserved they are after so long a period of the ravaging effects of weather.

In remarks pertaining to the Pepper family, on page 41 and again on page 113, I briefly mention William Crow, (should be James Crow) an educated Scotchman who came to this country at an early day, and to Woodford County soon thereafter, where he and his wife and daughter lived and died, and whose remains repose in the Versailles Cemetery.

This man made the Peppers rich, and himself famous by his method of distilling whiskey. Two of his brands were "Old Pepper" and "Old Crow," two brands that became very famous, tickling the palates, and pleasing the tastes of even foreign nations.

As he left no heirs, and as all of those who knew him personally were dead when the Woodford County History was written, I was not able to get in touch with any one who could give me a satisfactory account of the man, only recalling my recollections of him, as a famous distiller, so my mention was brief. However, Danl. M. Bowmar gave an interesting account of him in a Louisville paper recently, and I am here giving a few extracts from that letter: "James C. Crow, the man who gave value and renown to Kentucky whiskey. He is credited with having originated the scientific process of distilling that made Kentucky whiskey famous. A plain, small marble slab marks his burial place in the Versailles Cemetery. He died in 1861; his wife in 1862.

"James Crow was a native of Scotland, born in the city of Edinburg in 1789. He came to this country soon after completing his education. For a time he engaged unsuccessfully in mercantile business in New York City, after which he came to Frankfort, Ky., in 1825, and from there came almost immediately to Woodford County. He first tested his theories how whiskey should be made at both the distilleries of Col. Willis Field (see page 112) and Capt. Zachary

Henry (see page 170) before accepting a position at Oscar Pepper's distillery, where his experiments reached their fruition, and according to tradition, whiskey made by him was regularly shipped to Philadelphia, New York and Boston, as well as England, Scotland and other foreign countries, the demand always exceeding the output. Henry Clay, a personal friend, and admirer of Crow always had a cask of his liquor with him in Washington, and Daniel Webster was a patron."

News Clip

"James Crow was a man of culture and literary attainments. Besides an expensive chemical apparatus, he possessed a large library. Like all Scotchman, he was passionately fond of Burns, many of whose poems he readily recited from memory. He read or recited 'The Cotter's Saturday Night' with such depth of feeling as to move his hearers to tears."

The Fleming family was sketched on page 62. Judge William Bowyer Fleming, Jr., was born and reared on a farm near Midway, Kentucky, in Woodford County. During his service as a representative from Louisville in the Kentucky Legislature during the 80s, he was my good friend and placed my name in nomination for a legislative office to which I was elected. He gave me much of the data I used in writing a history of the Fleming family. From that sketch you will understand that he held many prominent positions of trust, both state and national, before his death in 1918. He gave me the interesting bit of history of Simon Kenton that you will find on page 376, but I cut out the latter part of the story as I thought it lacked interest for Woodford countians. But I have decided to use it in the supplement as it is an interesting sequel to a bit of history associated with the Fleming family traditions that will excite the emotions of the average reader, if it does sound like fiction.

A few years after the incident referred to on page 376 of Kenton getting his affairs in shape in Kentucky, he decided to return to his old home in Virginia on a visit. Soon after reaching the vicinity he learned that William Veach had married the girl who was the innocent cause of the tragic encounter of the two young men, many years before, and that they were domiciled not far away, and were the proud parents of several children. With these facts before him, Kenton lost no time in conveying to Veach and his wife the fact that he was in the community. An exchange of regrets for indiscretions of youth, and expressions of good wishes for the future ensued, followed by an invitation to a turkey dinner at the home of Veach, which was accepted. Soon thereafter Kenton returned to his home in Kentucky where he remained until old age and poverty caused him to go to Urbana, Ohio, where he died.

———

The Greathouse family was another of the prominent families who established a home at an early date in Woodford County, and they became a popular part of the social structure.

Major Isaac Greathouse, of the Revolution, was the head of this family, and his wife was Elizabeth Ridgeley. They had the following children, born in Woodford County: Isaac, Jr., William, Samuel, Ridgeley, Nancy, Sarah, Elizabeth and America (names not arranged chronologically).

Before 1810 this family, to the regret of a wide circle of friends in the county, decided to join other Woodford countians who had adopted Shelby County as a home, and their children were partly raised in Shelby. Isaac, Jr., became a doctor and married Mary Logan Johnston, Sept. 14, 1824; Samuel married Sarah Ann Reynolds, Nov. 13, 1837; Nancy married Clark McAfee Nov. 22, 1808; Sarah married Samuel Tevis, Dec. 23, 1817; Elizabeth married Thomas P. Wilson, Nov. 25, 1819; America married James W. Buchanan, Oct. 16, 1829; William married ——— ———; and Ridgeley, who also became a doctor, returned to Woodford County, a double purpose in view, ostensibly to practice medicine, but more especially to be in social touch with one of Woodford's fairest daughters—"The girl I left behind," so on November 12, 1837, he led to the marriage altar Mary Elizabeth Hancock who doubtless was responsible for the motive that brought him back to Woodford County.

On pages 351 to 354 is a brief account of the Hancock family, and on page 355 you will see that Clarence Greathouse, a son of Dr. Ridgeley Greathouse and Mary Elizabeth Hancock, wrote his name upon the scroll of fame, and his life work reflects great lustre upon his county and state as well as on the family escutcheon. Samuel Tevis, who married Sarah Greathouse was the father of Lloyd Tevis who was a deputy in the circuit clerks office of Woodford County some years before the Civil War. He afterward migrated to California and developed into a multi-millionaire, and I presume, that was the temptation that lured so many of the relationship to the golden west from Woodford and Shelby counties.

Another son of Major Isaac Greathouse and Elizabeth Ridgeley was William Greathouse who married —— ——. He moved to Washington, Mason County, many years ago where he owned a splendid estate. He had a son Ridgeley, Jr. In an issue of the "Shelby Record" of August 8, 1902, appeared a most interesting and thrilling story of this gentleman. During the war between the states he was a most daring and dashing officer of the Confederacy, and the scope of his activities was wide, and his many captures were as thrilling as his escapes were miraculous. I wish I had room for its insertion here, but will reserve it for future publication where it can be preserved. It said, however, that he was the son of William Greathouse, who was one of the sons of Major Isaac Greathouse and his wife, Elizabeth, and was born in Shelbyville, Kentucky.

Major Isaac Greathouse and his wife Elizabeth Ridgeley, are buried in the old graveyard at Shelbyville.

Ridgeley Greathouse, Jr., became a citizen of Texas and died in that state in 1902. On page 246 you will see that his father, William, was employed as a lawyer in a case of "run-away-slaves" during the ante-bellum era.

In writing a sketch of the Francisco family for my Woodford County History in 1921, I was guided by recollec-tions of conversations with Andrew Francisco and his brother who were merchants at Rich Hill, Mo., during the early 1880s when I visited that city. I also met their sister, Priscilla, and as their grandfather was an early citizen of Woodford County, the occasional meetings were very pleasant as we exchanged recollections of early times in the county as they had received it from their kin, and as I recalled them from hearsay as a boy.

At that time I had no thought of ever writing a county history, yet the happy exchanges. left an impression, and I would frequently recall them in quiet moments, but not until 1919 when I consented to write sketches of the Pioneers of Woodford County for the Register, a magazine published by the Kentucky State Historical Society, did I tax my memory seriously to recall substantially what the Missourians had said about their Woodford County ancestors, and their experience in "traveling through the wild west to Missouri back in the 30s." However, my appeals to memory produced a fair sketch, which included a statement by Capt. John Andrew Steele, that Col. John Francisco of Midway, had married Priscilla Steele, his kinswoman, and moved west before the Mexican War, emphasizing the statement that he was the head of the Woodford County Franciscos. So I arranged my notes thinking that I had a perfect story. I made a trip to Lawton, Oklahoma, soon thereafter to visit a relative, which resulted in a pleasing surprise, a meeting with Miss Priscilla Francisco, whom I had met nearly forty years earlier in Missouri.

As luck would have it I had my Francisco paper with me. I asked her to look it over and give me her opinion.

After carefully looking the paper over she said: "I recall that the Franciscos and Steeles were intermarried, and as Col. John Francisco married Priscilla Steele, a daughter of Capt. Andrew Steele, and as my name is Priscilla, and I have one brother, Andrew, and another John Steele Francisco, I feel sure your paper is right." But it wasn't. There was just one defect. I used Col. John Francisco as the head of the line I brought down, instead of George Francisco his father. You will find the Francisco sketch on page 170.

Recently I received a letter from Mrs. Mary Harrison Moore of Independence, Missouri, a niece of the Rich Hill, Missouri, Franciscoes in which she said I was mistaken about Col. John Francisco being the head of her line. And to prove it, she sent me a copy of her D. A. R. papers showing complete dates of birth, marriage and death of each generation of her line, which I am using for the supplement to the Woodford County History. It follows: George Francisco, b. 1739, d. at "Cowpastures" in 1809; m. Mary Murray, 1761; she b. 1741, d. 1802. He was a soldier of the Revolution; his son, George, b. 1773, d. 1839, m. Elizabeth Mays, 1812, she b. 1792, d. 1844, and their son, Andrew, b. in Woodford County, Jan. 3, 1814, d. Feb. 2, 1868, m. Joan Christy, Sept. 3, 1835, she b. March 2, 1817, d. Sept. 30, 1895; whose children were: Andrew Francisco, b. in Fayette County, Kentucky, Mar. 26, 1837; Charles, b. in

Fayette County, Kentucky, Dec. 2, 1838; Elizabeth, b. Saline County, Missouri, Mar. 1, 1843; Joseph b. in Missouri, Mar. 10, 1845; Priscilla, b. in Missouri Nov. 29, 1847; William, b. in Missouri, Jan. 2, 1850; Mary Adelia, b. in Missouri, Jan. 11, 1852; John Steele, b. Missouri Aug. 7, 1854; Simeon Payne, b. June 14, 1856; and Albert B., b. May 13, 1861. Mrs. Moore who sent me the above D. A. R. paper is the daughter of the above Elizabeth Francisco who married Alfred Bell Harrison, April 1, 1862. I am very thankful for the correction. She knew nothing of the other lines, but I have gathered additional information and am giving it to those who may be interested.

The above George Francisco, Sr., soldier of the Revolution, came to Woodford County, Kentucky, in 1795, and purchased of Charles and Andrew Lewis 145 acres of land that today is on the boundary lines of Midway. He built his residence, that is now standing, in the suburbs, nearly a century and a half old. He lived there until his wife died in 1802. Before 1810 he left for Virginia and died there in 1809. That accounts for the absence of his name from the census of 1810. Col. John and Andrew, two of his sons, were the only male members of his family of four sons in the county in 1810. George, Jr., was living in Fayette County at that time and two of his children were born there, before he migrated to Missouri. By referring to page 11, you will see that Col. John is listed with a family of three, and credited with two slaves; while Andrew listed a family of six, and is credited with six slaves. At that time Andrew was living in the ancestral home, and Col. John was living on a small farm recently owned by Dr. Theoph Steele, but more recently by his son, Capt. John Andrew Steele, on the Georgetown road in the outskirts of Midway.

I recall that when I called at the home of Capt. John Andrew Steele to inquire about the Francisco family, he took me out and showed me the ruins of the old John Francisco home, and said that his father knew Col. Francisco personally, and told him that he had visited him when a young man.

However, I am sure that Col. John Francisco later owned the ancestral home, as George Francisco, Jr., had moved to Fayette County where several of his children were born before he went west, and Andrew, who owned it in 1810, sold it and went west.

I am giving here a picture of this old pioneer home built by George Francisco, Sr.

Col. John Francisco owned all of the Francisco land in Woodford County in 1831. When the Lexington and Ohio railroad (now the L. and N.), the first built in Kentucky, or this side of the Allegheny mountains, passed through his farm, and within one hundred feet of the residence, Col. Francisco was so incensed at the building of the big fill across the ravine, which obscured a beautiful view of nature's artistic touch, that he sold his possessions and left the State too. The old home is in full view of the Orphan School which was built upon a part of the Francisco farm.

I copied the names of the children of George Francisco, Sr., from his will dated March 9, 1805, of record in the office of the county clerk at Versailles. They were: Andrew, John, George and Charles. His daughters were: Nancy, Sally Frazer, and Polly Frazer, and his son-in-law, George Frazer. Also grandchildren, Nancy, George and Peggy O'Bannon, who were likely children of Nancy, who probably was a widow.

I am also giving here a magazine article taken from the Woodford Sun within the last year. It is most interesting and bears out much of what I have written of the Franciscos.

THE KENTUCKY F. O. SCHOOL

(Woodford Sun, April 30, 1931.)

Following extracts from an article on the Kentucky Female Orphan School at Midway, by Edgar C. Riley, business director of the school, in the April number of the L. & N. Employes Magazine, reference to which was made in The Sun week before last:

"In the year 1795, George Francisco purchased from Charles and Andrew Lewis, 145 acres of land for 115 pounds sterling. This land was located in Woodford County, Ky. In 1835, Col. John Francisco sold to the Lexington and Ohio Railroad Company his farm of 216 acres for $30.00 an acre. On this farm is now located the city of Midway. On part of this land, with the balance adjacent to it, is the beautiful 55-acre campus of the Kentucky Female Orphan School.

"This school was opened in 1849. Nine years later the building was destroyed by fire, and on the ashes of that fire was erected, in 1859, Pinkerton Hall, named in honor of Dr. L. L. Pinkerton, at whose suggestion the orphan school was founded.

"For almost forty years this was the only brick building on the campus, but in 1895 Parrish Hall was built, and named in honor of the co-founder, James Ware Parrish, and in 1905, the Patterson Heating Plant, named in honor of another early trustee, Wm. H. Patterson, was erected.

"In 1925, through the inspiration of John P. Starks, of Louisville, Starks Hall and Alumnae Hall, two fire-proof buildings were added. Starks Hall, an academic building and Alumnae Hall, a fire-proof dormitory, were erected in 1925, under the dynamic leadership of John P. Starks, Zach C. Offutt, Henry N. Johnson and Max Barker, of Louisville, and the many trustees in Central Kentucky co-operated. This institution is fast becoming one of the big schools in Kentucky. Hundreds of worthy orphan girls need this institution, but lack of funds and buildings prevent it from multiplying its work."

The Sun is indebted to Editor Thomas E. Owen of the L. & N. Employes Magazine for use of the cut of the more-than-a-century-old Francisco log house (weatherboarded) still standing at Midway, near the Starks walk to the orphan school. This was the home of Col. John Francisco, who left the state in disgust, when the first railroad to be built west of the Allegheny mountains came through his farm.

The Woodford Sun, in its issue of December 21, 1934, gave the following notes with reference to Capt. Jack

Jouett, Jr., of whom I gave a fairly good account on pages 282 and 392. It said that Jack Jouett, Jr., was a member of the fourth convention at Danville upon the question of Kentucky becoming an independent state, and was one of the candidates named by the Legislature of 1792 from which the five commissioners were chosen by lot to fix on a permanent seat of Government for the new state of Kentucky.

The Moores, Allens and Johnsons were quite numerous in Woodford County about the year 1800, but I was never able to find a source that would unfold enough about them to make a creditable showing upon Woodford's map.

I was with the Kentucky Historical Society for fifteen years before old age and deafness caused my resignation, November, 1934. During that time I entertained many thousands of visitors each year, of Kentuckians, Americans and foreigners. During that time I was paid many compliments, but it was left to the Register, the magazine published by the Society to pay me a tribute that stands out, and above all others. My highest ambition, even in childhood, has been to be a "Kentucky Gentleman"—as—they were.

Here is what the Register said: "We take this occasion to express for the Register and the entire staff of the Society our deep appreciation of the faithful, efficient and always courteous service rendered by Mr. Wm. E. Railey through the years. He is a Kentucky gentleman, both of the old and the new school, for he has kept step with the progress of the times. He has been a valued member of the Society, both in his official position and as a contributor to the Register."

If I had been consulted about it could I have asked more? That man (the Kentucky gentleman) has caught the eye of the poet, the artist, the musician, the scribe and the sculptor. It will serve as my epitaph.

It is not generally known in the county that a woman who became nationally known during the last half of the 19th century, spent her girlhood in Woodford, and received her educational training at Midway, where she devoted much of her time to church and Sunday-school work, and was very popular with the society folk. Her name was Carrie Moore, daughter of George F. Moore.

She was born in Garrard County, lived in Boyle in childhood, and came to Woodford County with her father and family in 1854, a young girl, and they located at Midway.

After a residence in Midway during her entire girlhood, the family moved to Missouri where they remained for a short period of time, then moved to Kansas, where her name is still, not only readily recalled, but deeply revered, and where the people but recently refused to repeal the prohibition law.

In the course of time she met what she thought was an ideal man. After a brief courtship she was married to a lawyer by the name of Nation to whom she was devoted. Unfortunately he developed an appetite for whiskey, and became an addict of the drink habit, over which she was so grieved

that she finally swore vengeance against the whiskey demon.

As a result of that determination, manifestations of her methods begun to take shape away back in the 70s and 80s, when it was not unusual to pick up your morning paper, and have your eyes attracted by such heavy headlines as this—"Carry Nation, with hatchet in hand, enters a bar-room and smashes furniture and fixtures, and spills all liquor in sight, creating consternation among the patrons."

About the year 1900, upon the invitation of some of her friends of long standing, who were then living, she returned to Midway and delivered a most interesting and impressive lecture on temperance. As a listener, I easily discerned that it was earnestness, rather than eloquence, that gave her the power she possessed over audiences, although she was blessed with both.

In the course of a few years other Carrie Nations will develop to meet the demands when suffering humanity cries out. She was truly a great woman.

The above mention of Carrie Nation was written in April, 1935. In looking over a June Magazine I found the following news item: "Mother smashes booze joint," in the town of Medicine Lodge, Kansas, where Carrie Nation opened her saloon-smashing crusade, and people are wondering tonight (May 13th) whether Mrs. J. D. Montgomery, sixty years old, has launched a similar campaign." She and her daughter-in-law marched to the Depot Cafe last night with a hammer. When she left, not a bottle or other glassware remained intact. She said: "I stood it as long as I could." The barkeeper who had been selling her boys whiskey, backed up against the wall, as she said: "That's that!"

I was very anxious for a sketch of the Goodloe family for my Woodford County History, first, for the reason that I, a boy, had a speaking acquaintance with Col. Kemp Goodloe, who was to my mind a high-class gentleman, and secondly that the Goodloe family intermarried with some of the leading families of the county; but was unable to do so, although I had a promise of data from a kinswoman at Louisville, and even now I am unable to say who was his father or grandfather, but think that Kemp Goodloe, the son of the Rev. Henry Goodloe and Frances Kemp, whose names will appear later, were his grandparents.

The Rev. Henry Goodloe was born in Caroline County, Virginia, in 1730, and married Frances D. Kemp. They were the proud parents of seventeen children, whose names follow: Annie, b. 1752; Thomas, b. 1754; Garrett, b. 1755; Kemp, b. 1757; Mary, b. 1758; Vivion, b. 1760, d. 1819; Phoebe, b. 1762; Frances Diana, b. 1764; George, b. 1766; Jane, b. 1767; Isabel and Robert (twins), b. 1769; Henry, b. 1771; Elizabeth, b. 1772; Ann, b. 1774; Katherine, b. 1777, and Sarah, b. 1781.

The above, and the immediate following data came to me from Mrs. W. G. Wiglesworth of Cynthiana, whose husband was a grandson of Vivion Goodloe and Dorothy Tompkins, whose son, Henry Goodloe, married Frances Eliza Monet; Mary Frances Goodloe married William Tompkins Wigles-

worth, and W. G. Wiglesworth married Annabel Hazelwood.

The Rev. Henry Goodloe was for many years the pastor of Piney Branch Baptist Church, Spottsylvania County, Virginia. He enlisted in the Revolution, Sept., 1775, in Capt. William Talliferro's Co., Col. John Woodford's Regiment for twelve months, and was honorably discharged at Williamsburg, Va., pension was granted Dec. 31, 1831.

Vivion Goodloe, b. 1760, d. 1819, fourth son of Rev. Henry and Frances D. Goodloe, left a will dated April 20, 1819, in which he left his estate to the management of his wife until his youngest son, Joseph T. Goodloe, reached his legal age. A record of the will may be found in the Woodford County Court. His wife was Dorothy Tompkins, b. 1768, in Virginia; d. in Woodford County in 1832. The remains of both are buried in the private cemetery at the old log house on the Paynes Mill road opposite the old Goodloe house, still standing, with a few additions, and it is now occupied by Henry Karle.

In Deed Book M, page 400 in the Court House at Versailles a deed to Henry Goodloe dated October 20, 1830, gives the names of the children of Vivion Goodloe, as follows: Henry Goodloe, Frances D. Goodloe, Ann Stout, Mary D., Caroline, Louisa, and Joseph T. Goodloe. The Minute Book of Mt. Vernon Church, page 130, says that "Louisa Jesse was formerly Louisa Goodloe, 1836."

Henry Goodloe, b. 1800, d. 1868, the son of Vivion, and grandson of the Rev. Henry Goodloe, is frequently mentioned in the old records of Mt. Vernon Church. His wife, Frances Eliza Monet,

b. 1810, d. 1892, was the daughter of the Rev. Dr. Samuel Monet (1778-1823) and Mary Wayland of old Chillecothe, Ohio, as recorded in the old Huguenot Bible.

Dr. Monet was a member of the first Legislature of Ohio, and Frances Eliza was their only daughter, but there were five sons in the family, all of whom adopted the medical profession, and one of them, Dr. Wesley Monet, was a graduate of Transylvania College, and the author of "The History of the Mississippi Valley," and his home "Sweet Auburn," a charming plantation in Mississippi. Two vols. of his history autographed, were given to his mother, Mrs. Mary Wayland Monet by the author, and they are now in possession of her grandson, William Goodloe Wiglesworth, Sr., of Cynthiana. Mrs. Mary Monet spent her declining years in Woodford County and sleeps today in the old Goodloe cemetery. Her estate passed to her son-in-law, Henry Goodloe, which is of record in Will Book O, page 506, Versailles, Ky., 1851.

Henry and Frances Eliza Monet Goodloe, had four children: James William, 1835-94, married Jennie Payne and had four children; Mary Frances, 1838-1905, married William Thompson Wiglesworth and had eight children; Ann Cornelia, married Frank Collier; and Dorothy, 1844-1901, married Capt. Gabe Davie and had three children.

William Thompson Wiglesworth, 1822-1893, was the son of John (1781-1848), and Jane Bush Wiglesworth (1791-1832) ; and Jane Bush was a daughter of Philip Bush (1737-1819), and his wife, Frankie Vivion (1761-1842) pioneers of Clark County, Ky.

William Thompson Wiglesworth and Mary Frances Goodloe had eight children, as follows: Lillie, 1859, m. Kemp Woods; Harry Rodes, 1860-1907, m. Allie Van Deren; Robert Lee, 1863-1911; Thomas Garnett, 1866-1912, m. Nora Ming; William Goodloe, 1869, m. Anabel Hazelwood and they have William Goodloe, Jr., and Winifred Frances; Ann Cornelia, 1872-1924, m. John B. Woods; James Monett, 1874. 1929, m. Jessie Staley and Frances Louisa, 1879, m. Simeon Elliott Drake.

William Thompson Wiglesworth brought his bride, Mary Frances Goodloe, back to the land in Harrison County, Ky., that his grandfather, Lieut. James Wiglesworth, Jr., a Revolutionary soldier, of Spotsylvania County, Va., had purchased in 1797.

Lieut. James Wiglesworth, Jr., married Mary Thomson in 1779. She was a daughter of William Thomson and Ann Rodes, Louisa County, Va., and her father deeded to James Wiglesworth, Jr., property, according to Louisa County Record.

James Wiglesworth, Sr., was a member of the Committee of Safety, and his wife was Mary Durrett, daughter of John Durrett and Katherine Goodloe (1720-1751).

The Wiglesworths and Goodloes intermarried in Virginia as they did in Kentucky.

In Yorkshire, England, is the ancestral home of the Wiglesworth family, and the estate was in possession of a descendant as late as 1934. It contains 4,181 acres, and was known as "Wiglesworth Hall." It, and the village of Wiglesworth, are in possession of the family of William Goodloe Wiglesworth. If you will turn to page 98 you will see that Frances Diana Goodloe married George Carter, of Spottsylvania, Virginia, and their son, Goodloe Carter, came to Woodford County as a citizen prior to 1810; and on page 57, you will see that Margaret Carter, daughter of Goodloe Carter and Mary Crenshaw, married Dr. T. W. Twyman, and her sister, Ellen Virginia, married Joel W. Twyman. On page 97 you will see that Dr. Joe Coleman Carter, son of Goodloe Carter, married Margaret Carlyle; and on page 98 you will see that Sarah Carter, daughter of Goodloe Carter married Thomas Graddy.

The line of Mr. W. G. Wiglesworth, of Cynthiana, as I understand, runs thus—Rev. Henry Goodloe and Frances Kemp; Vivion Goodloe and Dorothy Tompkins; Henry Goodloe and Frances Eliza Monet; Mary Frances Goodloe and William Thomson Wiglesworth; William Goodloe Wiglesworth and Anabel Hazelwood.

I was not able to get in touch with any of the descendants of the Guthries who came early to Woodford County, and whose names appear in the county records in 1810, hence, when I was gathering notes for my Woodford County History I only gave a brief mention of them at that time. However, I was fortunate enough recently to open a correspondence with Mr. Joseph A. Guthrie, a lawyer of Kansas City, who was born and partially reared at Midway and Versailles.

He volunteered to give me an account of his branch of the family, and it is so well prepared I am giving it just as he arranged it.

"I appreciate very much indeed that you have taken the time to write me as fully as you did in your recent letter concerning the Guthrie family."

"James Guthrie, of Louisville, is not connected with my own line of ancestry. The following, bearing on my own genealogy, I have definitely established."

"Thomas Guthrie, of King William County, Virginia, removed to Cumberland County, Virginia, in the year 1750, where he spent the remainder of his life, and died at a ripe old age in the year 1800."

"Thomas Guthrie had eight children and, among others, a son Alexander, Sr., who also came to Cumberland County, Virginia, at about the time his father did, and lived there until he died in the year 1817."

"He was one of the 'Minute Men' under the Cumberland County, Virginia Committee of Safety, of which Edward Carrington, I think, was Chairman, and he was also a captain of militia during the Revolution."

"Alexander Guthrie, Sr., had, among others, a son Alexander, Jr., who came to Woodford County, Kentucky, some time prior to 1802. (This fact is established by a deed that his father made to him in that year to certain lands in Hardin County, Kentucky, and in this deed, Alexander Guthrie, Sr., refers to his son, Alexander, Jr., as being a resident at that time of Woodford County, Kentucky.)"

"Just when Alexander, Jr., removed from Woodford County, I do not know, but I do know that in 1812 he was living in Owen County, Kentucky, for one of his sons was born there in that year."

"Alexander Guthrie, Jr., died about

the year 1832, leaving the following children: A son, Livingston S. Guthrie, who married Hannah Davis; Alexander Iverson Guthrie; Elizabeth Guthrie, who married Ennis Hardin, and Amanda Guthrie, who married John Brewer.''

"Livingston S. Guthrie, above named, was my grandfather. His wife, Hannah Davis, was a daughter of Jesse Davis, of Cumberland County, Virginia, whom he married on the 10th of April, 1819, and several years after his marriage, he removed to Henry County, Kentucky, where my father was born in the year 1836, whose name was the same as my own, Joseph A. Guthrie.''

"Livingston S. Guthrie's family removed from Henry County to Carroll County in the year 1850, and after remaining there a few years, settled in Louisville, where he died on the 19th of August, 1874, and he and his wife and several of their children, including my father are buried in Cave Hill Cemetery.''

"Alexander Iverson Guthrie, brother of Livingston S., was a member of the old firm of Chilton, Guthrie & Company at Louisville, in the wholesale trunk business.''

"My father, Joseph A. Guthrie, you may recall, married Margaret Elizabeth Harris, daughter of Major Arnold Harris. He only lived a few years after his marriage, leaving two children, Joseph A., Jr. (myself), and my sister, Susan A., who married Charles E. Beach and is now a widow living in Bronxville, New York.''

"Several years after my father's death, my mother married Judge John W. Gillespie, and the family resided at Versailles until the spring of 1887 when we moved to Kansas City, Missouri. After completing my course in law at the University of Virginia I returned to Kansas City where I have since practiced law, except for five years from 1911 I was one of the judges of the circuit court of this county. I was married to Corinna Shreve of Louisville, Kentucky, June 27, 1900. We have only one child, Grace, who is the wife of John W. Carroll, of New York City.''

"I have always taken, and continue to cherish a likely interest in the people of Woodford County, of whom I shall always bear an affectionate remembrance.''

Many citizens of Versailles and Midway will recall this popular family. In connection with this statement of Mr. Guthrie as to his family history, several incidents run parallel with incidents in my own line, that makes his sketch most interesting to me, and they might be said to be contemporaneous. For instance, he says that his ancestor, Thomas Guthrie, left King William County, Virginia, in 1750, and settled in Cumberland County, that state, where his son, Alexander Guthrie, Sr., entered the service of the Revolution under the command of Capt. Carrington of the "Minute Men," and that Alexander Guthrie, Jr., son of the above Alexander Guthrie, Sr., came to Woodford County and settled on inherited land prior to 1802.

In my "Raileys' and Kindred Families" I say that Capt. John Railey married Elizabeth Randolph in 1750, and lived in Goochland County until 1754, where his sons, John and Thomas, were born, then moved to Cumberland

County, Virginia, where nine of his twelve children were born before he moved to Chesterfield County in 1769 where his twelfth, Randolph Railey, was born. John and Thomas born in Goochland County, were in the Revolution. John was killed at the battle of Norfolk, and Thomas was an ensign in Capt. Carrington's "Minute Men." About 1790 Thomas came to Woodford County and purchased a farm that he called "Clifton Heights" immediately overlooking the village of Clifton. There certainly must have been an acquaintanceship between Alexander Guthrie, Jr., and Thomas Railey, as both were raised in Cumberland County, and both were members of Carrington's "Minute Men," and both came to Woodford County about, if not at the same time.

This generation of Woodford County's citizenry know but little of early villages and neighborhoods except those that are fortunate enough to have, to an unusual degree, the same strains of the early settlers, like Pisgah, Mt. Vernon and others who have kept in view, so to speak, the history of the past. Hence but little is known of "Petersburg," "Coles Tavern," and "Leesburg," all early day settlements.

For Petersburg, see page 371. For "Coles Tavern" turn to page 64. I did not refer to Leesburg as I was under the impression at that time that it was over the line in Fayette County. It is an old village, but still extant, or was twenty years ago when I last passed enroute to Lexington, at which time I think the population was almost, if not entirely colored. It is several miles beyond the

Weisenberg Mill and very close to the Fayette line.

In April, 1932, Dr. W. R. Jillson, of Frankfort, had gotten hold of an old account book that was used by a merchant of Leesburg, and it was a very interesting old relic as many of the customers' names are yet very familiar in the Pisgah and adjacent neighborhoods. Dr. Jillson was preparing an article for the Register of the Kentucky Historical Society, and asked me to locate Leesburg for him. I told him it was over the line in Fayette County, but he afterward learned that it was near the line, but in Woodford, so he prepared a very interesting story for the magazine showing that it was a thriving village in early days. However, the Woodford Sun in its issue of June the 16th, 1935, says that Leesburg was originally at Offutts Crossroads, and had the first Tavern established between Lexington and Frankfort on the stage route. It was the property of Horatio Offutt, but leased to Kenneday and Dailey for a term of years. Lees branch passes by it and on through Midway, so I have an idea that Major John Lee who was one of the founders of Versailles, and a kinsman of the immortal Robert E. Lee, owned property in that vicinity at one time. This property was known for many years before and after the Civil War, as Offutts Crossroads, but I think is now called Nugents Crossroads. It is located in the center of some of the finest land in Kentucky.

———

John J. Crittenden and Joseph C. S. Blackburn have already been mentioned as U. S. Senators. I will here note the fact that J. N. Camden was appointed U. S. Senator by Gov. James B. Mc-Creary to fill an unexpired term.

This spirit has always characterized our county.

Woodford Sun, May 16, 1937:

CRIMELESS COUNTY TROUBLES JUDGE.

Circuit Judge William B. Ardery, Paris, whose district includes Woodford County, has his troubles. He admitted that while addressing the Woodford County grand jury this week at Versailles: "It is a difficult matter to charge a grand jury in a county like Woodford," he declared, "where there is almost no crime to talk about. The county jail is empty and only two cases were referred to the grand jury, by the lower courts. Some Kentucky counties, Judge Ardery said, have more indictments returned at one term of court than Woodford County grand juries have returned in five years."

In mid June, 1919, I was asked to take a position with the Kentucky Historical Society, at Frankfort, which I accepted and held until November, 1934, when, at 82 years of age, I resigned. I had hardly acquainted myself with the duties incident, when the head of the society informed me "that she had urged other parties to write a history of the early pioneers of Woodford County, and such interesting incidents as actuated their lives and movements, in the early days, but all had declined with the suggestion that you

were best fitted for the duty. Now I want you to begin the work without offering an excuse." Which I did.

Understanding that all of the hours of the day would be occupied entertaining visitors, the register showing an average of 100 visitors per day, I was confined to the hours of 7:30 p. m. to midnight to produce a Woodford County History, so I sat in the Library, every night from the summer of 1919 to 1929, ten years, working on this book. In doing so, I denied myself all social and recreational pleasures, even losing sight of relatives and old friends during that time, except those who dropped in to see me now and then. It was a great sacrifice, but I endured it, and, it grieves me now to learn that a few citizens of the county have criticised the work.

If they had known that most of the information between its covers was obtained from sources outside of Woodford County, and very much of it was from sources outside of Kentucky that necessitated a lengthy correspondence with people whose parents had gone west, northwest or southwest and south of us many years ago, they would have been more charitable. As an instance, take the sketch of the Blackburn family. Some of that information was obtained from the late David L. Thornton, some from Mrs. Prue Hunt Rodman, of Frankfort, but the greater portion came from the descendants of the Rev. Gideon Blackburn, for many years resident in Illinois. So it was with descendants in other parts of Kentucky, in Indiana, Missouri, Kansas, Texas, Colorado, California and Ohio. Most of the data relating to the Dunlaps came from far away California.

One criticism that came to me was that I "used much space in glorifying my kin." That was an unfair viewpoint. Five Railey brothers and three sisters came to Woodford County during the latter part of the 18th century and built homes. All of them like their progenitor, Capt. John Railey, of Virginia, loved a spirited horse, but many of them, like myself, didn't lose sight of the "Family Tree." That is my reason for giving fair space for a record of my kin. It is well remembered that I urged personally and through the Woodford Sun that scions of other families give me a full record of their ancestral lines. If I failed to produce a worthwhile book, ask yourself the question. What did I do in the way of co-operation, knowing that the book was in course of construction?

The first letter I wrote for help was to a boyhood friend. I said: Dear John, tell me all you can about your grandfather and mother, and your great grandfather and mother. This was his reply: "Dear Will, I am in receipt of yours of ——— date, and your very name brings back memories of the long ago. But Will, I didn't know that I ever had a granddaddy or mammy until your letter brought it to mind," etc. Now, this was not literally true, but he was well versed in the pedigree of his animals. That was why I had to go out in the State, and out of the State, to get most of the data sought.

———

In tracing family history I find that results will sometimes reach the surface that were not in the remotest way

contemplated, yet they parallel other lines so closely that you have either written, or read of other authors, that you wonder at the analogy.

Having traced many family lines, including my own, back from one to two centuries, I decide to trace back as far as possible some of the lines of Douglass Wheeler King of San Antonio, Texas, who married Jennie Farris Railey, of Woodford County. In doing so I discovered that one of his lines was very similar in names and dates to the Wallace family sketch that you will find on page 59 of this book, that I had written into it nearly a decade ago.

The three times great grandfather of Douglas Wheeler King on his maternal side, was Capt. Benjamin Wallace who rendered distinguished service in the revolution, and who was a son of Adam Wallace of Lancaster County, Pennsylvania, and that Adam Wallace was one of the four sons of Peter Wallace and his wife, Elizabeth Woods, of Ulster, Ireland.

Peter Wallace, though a Scotch Highlander, died and was buried in Ulster, Ireland, but his widow, with her four sons, Peter, Jr., Andrew, William and Adam, in the company of her kinsman, Michael Woods and family, sailed for America during the early years of the 18th century and settled in Lancaster County, Pennsylvania, where they all worshipped at "Old Donegal Church" that has withstood the ravages of time and is sheltering religious sects of this generation.

The first three of the above sons, Peter, Jr., Andrew and William, married three of the daughters of Michael Woods. About 1734 Peter Wallace, Jr., and his wife, Martha Woods, moved to Rockbridge County, Virginia, and Andrew and William Wallace with their wives, moved to Albemarle County, Virginia, but Adam and his wife —— —— remained in Lancaster County, Pennsylvania.

Peter Wallace, Jr., and his wife, Martha Woods, were blessed with a son they named Samuel Wallace, who married —— —— and had a son they named Caleb Wallace, who, after reaching years of maturity, came to Kentucky where he became a leading lawyer and a prominent member of the judiciary.

Andrew and William have descendants in Albemarle and other counties in Virginia. Adam Wallace and his wife —— —— remained in Pennsylvania, where many descendants now reside, and it was his son, Benjamin Wallace, who won honors as a captain in the Revolution. Benjamin's son, Dr. John Culbertson Wallace, of Erie, Pennsylvania, had a daughter, Jane Foster Wallace, who married Captain Otis Wheeler; and they had a daughter, Clara Wheeler, who married Archibald McKee, Jr. Their daughter, Lillie McKee, married Ed. E. King, and they were the parents of Douglass Wheeler King, of San Antonio, Texas, who as aforesaid, married Jennie Farris Railey.

Dr. John Culbertson Wallace, mentioned above, was a surgeon in the regular army and Lieut. Col. in the War of 1812. He had a son, Major Ben Wallace, who served in the Mexican War, and was killed with Fannin's men at Galiad, not far from San Antonio, Texas.

The Kings and McKees were Harrison County, Kentucky, people who moved to Missouri some years after the War of 1812, and on to Texas after the Mexican War.

The above Archibald McKee, Jr., was a son of Archibald McKee, born at Cynthiana, Kentucky in 1800, the son of David McKee, born 1767, and his wife, Jane Wallace, the latter a descendant of either Andrew or William Wallace.

The Wheelers were New Hampshire people, and the above Capt. Otis Wheeler, was a captain in the United States Army, who laid out the town of Fort Smith, Arkansas.

The above is in compliment to one of the finest girls in Texas, but raised in Woodford County, Kentucky.

———

Through the Woodford Sun I urged all descendants of pioneer families to give me sketches of their ancestral lines for the Woodford County History, when I was gathering the facts 1919 to 1929, but it either escaped the attention of many, or was overlooked. But my supplement will carry several additional families. Miss Jennie Scearce, of Versailles, has furnished the following data of the pioneer family of Scearce, and it affords me pleasure to include it in the supplement.

Among the early pioneers who came to Woodford County after the Revolution was that of the family of Scearce. They came from England and settled in Prince George County, Maryland, later to Virginia, and then to Kentucky.

James Scearce and his wife, Henrietta, and their children, in company with David Scearce and his wife, Cassandra, settled near Craigs Fort, about three miles from Versailles. The above James Scearce and his son, William, were among the early surveyors of that section.

The children of James and Henrietta Scearce were: William, b. in Virginia in 1771, m. Anna Thompson, daughter of David Thompson, a Baptist minister from Louisa County, Va.; Nathan, b. 1773, and Henry, b. 1775. They married sisters, Letitia and Rebecca Weakley, and moved to Shelby County; Robert Scearce married his cousin, Katherine Scearce; Elizabeth married John T. Minter, and Sallie Scearce.

The children of William Scearce and Anna Thompson were: James, married Maria Cluke; Henry, married 1st America Berry, 2nd Elizabeth Thompson; John, married Elizabeth Middleton, and moved to Shelby County; Laban, married Jane Ashurst; Patsy, married Caleb Baker, and moved to Missouri.

Laban Scearce and Jane Ashurst, who was a descendant of Robert Ashurst and Jane Frances Flournoy, a daughter of Jacob Flournoy, a Hugenot settler of Manakintown, Va., had the following children: William, moved to Missouri and died unmarried; Lucinda, married 1st ——— Graves, 2nd Joseph Craig, and moved to Missouri; Martha, married James Watkins, and moved to Missouri; Robert moved to Missouri and married Miss Atkins; Laban went to California and married Josephine Thompson; Jane, married Lewis Pence and moved to Missouri; Simeon, married Susan Katherine Dwyer and remained in Woodford County on the homestead until his death; Mary, married Robert Todd of

Fayette County, but later moved to Missouri.

The children of Simeon Scearce and Susan Katherine Dwyer are the only members of the name now residents of Woodford County, and Susan married John Y. Rout whose children are Katherine who married Evan McChord and are residents of Dallas, Texas; Mary died young.

Annabel Scearce married Ulysis Turner, and they have Susan Jane Turner; Jennie Scearce, and Allen Scearce, who went west where he died unmarried.

John Y. Rout and wife and Ulysis Turner and wife and Miss Jennie Scearce are still residents of Woodford County.

———

Mrs. Matthew Cotton Darnell suggests these additions and corrections in the sketches of the Colemans on page 96, and Blantons on pages 134 and 299. As she is a great granddaughter of Edward Spillsbee Coleman and Margaret Blanton, she is well equipped to have additional information, and I am quoting her here:

"Richard Blanton, the sheriff who arrested the Rev. Joseph Craig, was a son of the first Richard Blanton and his wife, Elizabeth, and a brother of Thomas who married Jane. Richard, the sheriff, married Nancy Sneed, who was an aunt of Achilles Sneed, and their children were: John, Charles, Richard, who married a Combs and was the father of Harrison Blanton, of Frankfort; Carter, born 1765, married Susanna Sneed in Caroline County, Va., in 1787, whose daughter, Margaret, married Edward Spillsbee Coleman (see

Coleman sketch); William; James; Mrs. Vaughan; Mrs. Daniel; Nancy; who married Rev. Isaac Crutcher in Caroline County, Va., in 1790.

"Maria Sneed was the daughter of Achilles Sneed. She married Richard Blanton, son of John and Nancy, and grandson of Thomas and Jane, in 1819. Other children of Thomas and Jane Blanton, besides those previously mentioned, were: Thomas, Jr., and Nancy, who married Benjamin Berry. Mary Blanton, who married Richard Fox, is thought to have been another daughter of Thomas and Jane."

The Woodford Sun in a recent issue contained this mention of the Clifton driveway. "Some of the most beautiful scenery in America can be viewed on the drive between Versailles and Clifton. One can travel a thousand miles without finding anything in nature that, for scenic beauty excels the winding drive alongside the Canyon of Clifton Creek."

Ensign Thomas Railey of the Revolution, one of the five brothers who came early to Kentucky and settled in Woodford County, bought and settled on his farm on the heights above Clifton Creek, named him home "Clifton" in compliment to his uncle, Carter Harrison, in Virginia whose home was called "Clifton" (see page 258). Some years later the village of Clifton in the Valley below was organized and named in compliment to the farm above. The creek that skirted the farm on another side also assumed that name, and the Berrymans, who were grandsons of Thomas Railey, carried on an extensive business at Clifton during the latter half of the 19th century. From Clifton Heights,

and the Trabue farm upstream several miles you can see the beautiful landscapes in Anderson County, across the river, and along Clifton creek, as the Woodford Sun says, you get a beautiful picture of miniature cascades that are beautiful during the spring and fall freshets.

———

The five Railey brothers who came to Woodford County about 1790, and settled in the Griers Creek section, built their several abodes, and a church on a corner of my great grandfather's estate that they called "Griers Creek Church," a creek that was in sight. They lived and died in these old homes. The church they built was under their supervision, but the money that built it was largely contributed by their generous neighbors, whose names appear on the old church roster of that period, the larger number of whom were Presbyterians, but many of them were Baptists and Methodists, a few of them were of the Episcopalian faith; yet, as stipulated in the deed, it was a republican or union church to be used by any denomination upon arrangement for a date.

In January, 1923, Mrs. Wade Hampton George copied some of the early minutes of the old church and kindly sent them to me for use in the Woodford County History, but so much of interest to the readers of the Historical Society Magazine, in which my History was being printed was sidetracked in 1920-21 and 22 in favor of my work, that I was denied space for the year 1923, so I laid them aside for future use, but when I was in position to use them I was not able to locate them, but found them and used them in my "Raileys and Kindred Families" in 1929, which can be found in the Helm Library at Versailles, on page 80. I am now inserting them in the supplement to the Woodford County History.

The old records follow:

"Griers Creek Church was organized in 1818 by (1st) the Rev. Eli Smith, with elders Samuel Campbell and Alexander McClure. Brother Smith labored faithfully in the vineyard for many years, and in the providence of God was removed to Paris; (2nd) the Rev. Gideon Blackburn succeeded him and served the church from 1829 to 32; (3rd) the Rev. John N. Blackburn commenced his ministerial labors among this people from 1832 to 36; (4th) the Rev. Jo. C. Styles (for whom Capt. Jo. C. S. Blackburn was named) accepted and preached as a stated supply until 1840; (5th) the Rev. A. W. Campbell supplied the pulpit with great acceptance from 1840 to 43; (6th) the Rev. John Black supplied the pulpit from 1844 to 48.

"The pulpit has since been supplied by order of the Harmony Presbytery to April 1, 1849, all constitutional— Amen." Harmony Presbyterian church is near Spring Station and was sold to the Baptists as you will see on page 208, column 2; (8th) "The Rev. J. R. Gray commenced his labors as stated supply January, 1851. A Missionary Society was organized in 1844." Here appears a solemn protest against the unconstitutional measures of the General Assembly of 1837-38. Many whereases characterize the resolutions of protest against the General Assembly for deposing a neighbor minister of a

neighboring church without due process of law. The resolutions cover four pages of legal cap paper, and the spirit that characterized the members then, everafter has characterized their descendants, even defying an ecclesiastical court if they conscientiously believed it was actuated by a spirit of injustice.

I only wish I could afford the space that the above mentioned resolutions require that you might know the spirit of the membership of this congregation. You might, so to speak, lead them to water, but you couldn't force them to drink, if it was tainted. That is the reason why Woodford Countians have always displayed an upright hand in politics as well as business, as each neighborhood was affected with the same spirit.

The resolutions were signed by the following members: "Martha Railey, Caroline W. Frazer, Jane Carr, Judith Woodson Railey, Elizabeth Frazer, Susan C. Frazer, Jane Shryock, Olivia Shryock, Martha A. Shryock, Martha W. Railey, George C. Gough, Pauline Pleasants, Elizabeth Epler, Sarah Ann Epler, Sarah McLain, Jane Wilson, Agnes White."

While a boy I knew personally most of the above persons who grew up under the wholesome training of the two Blackburn preachers, father and son, who taught school in that community and impressed upon their pupils the spirit of morality, religion and intellectuality.

The above resolutions were adopted and signed December 16, 1840, and bear the names of my grandmother, Judith Woodson Railey, daughter of

William Railey and Judith Woodson; other relatives were Caroline Woodson Frazer, who was a daughter of Isham Railey and Susanna Woodson, and wife of Captain Joseph Frazer of the War of 1812; Pauline Pleasants was a daughter of Matthew Pleasants and Anna Railey, and neice of Gov. James Pleasants of Virginia; Jane Wilson and Agnes White were daughters of Col. William Steele and Sarah Bullock. Mrs. White was the wife of Col. Zach White, and the grandmother of Mrs. Agnes Morancy McKee, widow of Dr. John R. McKee of the Frankfort and Versailles road. The Eplers and Shryocks I knew in my childhood. They were splendid people and good neighbors.

I have a complete roster of the old church, but haven't the space for it here. It can be seen in the copy of "Raileys and Kindred Families" in the Helm Library in Versailles, on pages 80-81. I will say, however, that they were a liberty-loving, God-fearing class, noted for their generosity, fidelity, and courage, and those characteristics were general over the county, and that explains the statements of jurists from the bench in the Versailles court house as to the light criminal dockets at the opening of many courts. Even the colored population seems to have absorbed the spirit of the whites in good citizenship. See page 7.

In a letter from Mr. W. G. Stanard, the venerable historian and librarian of Richmond, Virginia, some ten years ago, in response to one that I had written him concerning the old "Stonehenge" home of Captain John Railey in Chesterfield County, Virginia, he reported that the house was passing into a dilapidated state, and that the estate had passed to Martin Railey, a son (and brother of the Raileys who settled in Woodford County), when the father died in 1783, and later to Lilburn Rogers Railey, a grandson, who sold it early in the 19th century to the Wooldridge family of Virginia, who developed and operated the coal pits to exhaustion, then moved to Kentucky where they became extensive holders of coal lands in this state and Tennessee.

The Wooldridges who came to Woodford County at an early period were of the above family. They were related to the families of Trabue, Major and Dupuy, who settled in the Griers Creek section. They purchased the home of Samuel Railey who moved to Missouri about 1830, and Will, John and Andrew Wooldridge lived there until the close of the Civil War when John R. Darnell, father of Dr. Matthew C. Darnell, of Frankfort, leased it for a term of years. This farm adjoined the farm of Col. Ed. Trabue that overlooks Tyrone and a beautiful landscape in Anderson County. The brick house on the Wooldridge farm is in good condition and was built by Bartholomew Dupuy (son of John James Dupuy, of Virginia), who was the owner of the farm about 1784. He married Mary Mottley in Virginia and died on his farm about 1790. John James Dupuy was the father of other children who migrated to Woodford County and built homes. The Rev. John and the Rev. James Dupuy were brothers of Bartholomew, and Olympia, the mother of Col. Ed Trabue, was a sister. She lived to be 93 years old and is buried on his farm whose residence of brick, over a century old, is in good condition today. During the Civil War Christopher Neal owned it, but it has been the home of Willis Field, Jr., for a number of years.

Bartholomew Dupuy had a son, Joel, who married Lucy Craig of Craigs Station. He built a wonderful house, "Stony Lonesome," on the road from Shryocks Ferry to Munday's Landing road, just over the hill from the noted Muldrow home, which has so frequently been written up, and in easy reach of Craig's Fort. The stone used in its construction was quarried from the surrounding hills and bears no evidence of age today except in style, the thickness of its walls, and the unique design of its closets and cupboards. The house is now owned by Mr. and Mrs. Gordon Wilder, of Lexington.

All of these old houses are attractive in design, and they are within a radius from Clifton to Munday's Landing—river line—with the old Griers Creek Church as a pivot. Joel Dupuy later sold his lovely and picturesque home and built another on a farm that adjoins "Hartland Farm" in the direction of Frankfort. It was also built of stone, and charming in style, and the thickness of its walls, through which both heat and cold travel slowly. I think it was for many years the home of Claiborne Nuckols.

I have pictures of several of these old houses in the supplement, and would have had others if the owners had felt the interest of linking the sacred and charming past to the interesting present, and the unseen but hopeful future.

Woodford Countains who have so much to be thankful for, should not lose sight of these charming spots, where nature, and artisans of the past combined to give a wealth of beauty and attractiveness to comfort generations of the past, and charm those of the present, who should preserve it in type and brush for unborn generations. We should not only visit, but should linger amidst the beautiful and picturesque country that smiles from Clifton, by way of the Narrows, to Munday's Landing. The old buildings prove that Woodford County in the early days had within her borders builders of artistic skill as well as poetic touch, and I regret that I am unable to recall their names here. Several homes at Jett, built by the Majors, were by the same builders, and in good condition today.

———

On page 242 I said that the first paper established in the county was the "Woodford Pennant," in 1859, but the Pioneer Press, on its 71st page names the "Kentucky Farmer" as published at Versailles in 1824, and the "Constitutionalist" as published there in 1825.

———

Woodford County has been signally honored by the voters of Kentucky. Two of her native born sons, and two of her sons by adoption have been elected to the governorship. On page 110 of this book General Scott is mentioned as having come to the county soon after the Revolution and built his home, that is still standing (see page 244) on the Kentucky river at Scott's Landing. He was elected Governor in 1808, while a citizen of the county.

On page 388 you will learn that John

Jordan Crittenden, though elected from Franklin County, as Governor in 1851, was born and reared in a Woodford County home that is still standing (see supplement) and was in his possession when he was elected Governor.

On page 33 you will see that Dr. Luke P. Blackburn, though elected Governor from Louisville, was not only born and reared in a home near Spring Station, but practiced his profession at Versailles for many years before going to Louisville, and the home in which he was born is still in the family name.

Somewhere about 1920 a young man named Albert Benjamin Chandler, who was of a happy disposition and much enthusiasm came to Woodford from Henderson County, where he was born July 14, 1898, and reared. Like Lincoln, he was self-made, and had hope in the future, and faith in his star.

His all-around ability was soon recognized, and, with meteoric speed he is traveling the route to inevitable success. He was elected to the State Senate in 1929, where he became painfully aware of the state's financial plight, and decided to enlist as the friend of a long suffering people. So, with dynamic force he entered the political arena to the confusion of the Buccaneers, and in 1935 was promoted to the Governorship of the State. The debt will be wiped out during his administration—so will the Buccaneers, many of whom are still infesting the New Capitol.

TIES THAT CROSS OCEAN.

See page 18.

"Binding two cities to be made stronger by local legionnaires.

"Ties of friendship between the city of Versailles, France, and its namesake, our Versailles, will be further strengthened when local Legionnaires and Legion Auxiliary members who sailed from New York the latter part of last week, visit the French city, next week, and are received by its mayor, Senator Henri Haye.

"District Highway Engineer, W. W. Pardon and Mrs. Pardon, Mr. and Mrs. William P. Haydon, and Mrs. S. A. Blackburn, American Vice President of Fidac Auxiliary, are members of groups to be guests of the French government in celebration of the 20th anniversary of America's participation in the World War.

"Mr. Pardon, when he left Versailles, Thursday, accompanied by Mrs. Pardon, carried an official letter from Mayor W. C. McCauley to Mayor Haye.

"Readers of the Sun will recall the exchange of friendly correspondence in 1935 and 1936 between Mayor Haye and Mayor McCauley, and General Marquis Calmes Chapter, D. A. R.; the presentation to our city of a bronze urn by the French mother city, and the D. A. R. Chapter's reciprocal gift of a walnut gavel to Mayor Haye.

"The gavel, made from wood taken from the old home in the county of Gen. Marquis Calmes, son of a Frenchman, who named our city for Versailles in France, was personally delivered to Mayor Haye by Miss Harriet McCauley, who made a trip to France last year and represented the local D. A. R. The gavel is being used regularly, it is said, to call council meetings to order in the Hotel de Ville of the old 'vairsi,' across the sea.''

Two of my great grandfathers were brothers, Ensign Thomas Railey of the Revolution, and William, a younger brother. They and their wives lived and died in Woodford County where they are buried. William and his wife in the Versailles Cemetery and Thomas and his wife in a plot walled in on their farm on "Clifton Heights." Destructive moss had obliterated the marks on the headstone of William and his wife, and miscreants had removed the markers of Thomas and his wife. It gave me the greatest pleasure of my life during the year 1937 to remove the remains of Thomas and his wife from Clifton to the Railey lot in Versailles and place new marble markers at the head of each of the four.

Each of the five Railey brothers who came to Woodford about 1790 had a walled in burial ground on the farms they owned, but the ravages of time are showing. My maternal three times grandfather, "Wm. Strother of Orange," is buried on his farm, at Mortonsville. He was the father-in-law of three Revolutionary soldiers, Col. Richard Taylor, father of President Zach; Capt. Moses Hawkins, my great grandfather, and Thomas Coleman, are also buried at Mortonsville, and all were Revolutionary soldiers.

Daniel Bowmar, in an issue of the Woodford Sun, gives this bit of history of the author of "Tempest and Sunshine:"

The following extracts were taken from the Woodford Sun, September 30, 1937. As they relate to subjects that I had mentioned briefly I am, with consent, using them here to be preserved in the county's annals. See my remarks upon the Singletons on page 92, 257 and 344. The Dorsey Tavern receives mention on pages 240 and 253. Versailles, Kentucky, and Versailles, France, are mentioned on page 356.

Woodford Sun, September 30, 1937:

THEY REST IN UNMARKED GRAVES

The Heroines of "Tempest and Sunshine," Famous Novel of Three Generations Back, Having Its Locale in Woodford County.

"A report in circulation that a scenario is being written for a motion picture production of "Tempest and Sunshine" has revived local interest in this "best seller" of the years following the War Between the States, and in the prototypes of the novel's chief characters."

"'Tempest and Sunshine'' was dramatized and for many years the play was presented successfully upon the stage. Several years ago (probably up to the present) it was being portrayed by repertoire companies."

"Woodford County and Versailles are the locale of this famous novel by Mary Jane Holmes, a young Yankee 'school marm,' who with her husband, Daniel Holmes, lived and taught here for two years in the early 1850s. Upon their return to New York state, Mrs.

Holmes wrote "Tempest and Sunshine" and other novels in which she introduced characters and customs with which she had become familiar in Woodford County."

(See page 344.)

"It was generally understood here that Susan Singleton, of this county, was the "Sunshine" of Mrs. Holmes' most celebrated novel; that the character of quick-tempered, impetuous "Tempest" was drawn from Bettie Singleton, sister of Susan, and that John Singleton, a Woodford County farmer, father of the two girls, was the model for Mr. Middleton."

"Sunshine and Tempest" both are buried, in unmarked graves. "Tempest" (married several times, the wife of a Mr. Robertson when she died) passed away in 1898. "Sunshine," who survived by a number of years her husband, Nathaniel Porter, conducting a boarding house at Midway during her latter years in the large dwelling on Winter street now owned by Miss Margaret Martin—a bright, well-educated, lovable woman, remembered by many persons now living in the county. Mrs. Porter died at Midway, following a stroke of paralysis, January 23, 1902, in her 73d year."

"Daniel Holmes and his wife, Mary Jane Hawes Holmes, came to Versailles shortly after their marriage and for almost a year taught in a private school, or seminary, in the town. Then they went to the country, to the vicinity of the Old Glen's Creek Church, where they lived for a year in the home of the late Dr. Theophilus Steele, and taught a school in the neighborhood.

It has been some time since the writer has seen a copy of "Tempest and Sunshine," but it is his recollection that the title page shows the book was dedicated to Mrs. Steele. The old Steele home in which the Holmes boarded, is still standing, though considerably changed."

(See pages 240-253.)

The "Eagle Hotel in Versailles," mentioned by Mrs. Holmes in the introductory paragraph of "Tempest and Sunshine," was the Shelton Tavern, that stood at the corner of Main and Lexington streets, the present site of the Miller building.

The "Dorsey Tavern" building (afterwards Perham's), on the Frankfort pike three-quarters of a mile beyond McKee's cross-roads, is the last landmark remaining in the neighborhood that knew the Holmes. The old graveyard of the first Glen's Creek Baptist Church, on the "Hezekiah H. Winn farm" (now part of the Hereford farms), on a road extending east from the Steele's pike, is entirely obliterated, not a tombstone remaining. In a novel entitled "Glen's Creek," Mrs. Holmes wrote: "Not far from the old brick church are numerous timestained gravestones * * * a little farther down the hill stands a low white building, the school house of Glen's Creek."

"A year or so ago, a Florida author, Hermon Pitcher, who is writing a book devoted to the life and work of Mrs. Mary J. Holmes, spent several weeks in Woodford County collecting facts concerning her residence in this county, and visiting scenes mentioned in her novels. His book will probably be published within the next few months. Mr. Pitcher lived in Brockport, N. Y., where the Holmes resided for some time and was well acquainted with Daniel Holmes, who survived his wife by some ten or twelve years and died in 1919. Mrs. Holmes, it is said, often gave lectures at the Brockport Normal School on her travels, and frequently told the students of her experiences in Kentucky "before the war."

She wrote many novels. After 70 years, her "Tempest and Sunshine" is still a popular book, called for in libraries."

Through the kindly offices of Mrs. M. C. Darnell and Miss Nina Visscher, the latter of the Kentucky Historical Society, I am able to reproduce my Woodford County History with a supplement. But for the kindness of these two ladies, and the skill of Dr. M. C. Darnell I would have cancelled the contract the last week in August, that I entered into early in June, 1937. The ladies volunteered to read the proof, and the doctor built up a physique exhausted by the summer's heat and old age.

I am truly grateful to these ladies and the doctor for rendering the reproduction of the history, as it is the last act in life's drama for this scribe—a life that has always applauded manliness and progressiveness, and felt a contempt for the pusillanimous, and I take off my hat to Gov. A. B. Chandler with heart-felt thanks for making it possible to earn the money that paid the bills.

The author had no thought of profiting by the reproduction of the Woodford County History, only yielding after earnest solicitation upon the part of friends who earnestly wanted copies.

Of the four hundred copies issued all but thirty-five will be given to parties interested in Woodford County.

INDEX